THE

BARONETAGE

OF

ENGLAND,

OR THE

HISTORY

OF THE

ENGLISH BARONETS,

AND SUCH

BARONETS OF SCOTLAND

AS ARE OF ENGLISH FAMILIES;

WITH

GENEALOGICAL TABLES,

AND ENGRAVINGS OF THEIR

ARMORIAL BEARINGS.

COLLECTED FROM THE PRESENT BARONETAGES—APPROVED HISTORIANS—PUBLIC RECORDS—AUTHENTIC MANUSCRIPTS—WELL-ATTESTED PEDIGREES—AND PERSONAL INFORMATION.

BY THE REV. WILLIAM BETHAM,

EDITOR OF THE GENEALOGICAL TABLES OF THE SOVEREIGNS OF THE WORLD.

It is hardly necessary to observe, that Genealogy is so intimately connected with Historical Knowledge, that it is impossible to arrive at any proficiency in the one, without being minutely versed in the other.

RICHARDSON, on the Languages, &c. of the Eastern Nations.

VOL. III.

LONDON:

PRINTED BY W. S. BETHAM, FURNIVAL'S-INN-COURT, HOLBORN,

FOR E. LLOYD, HARLEY STREET.

1803.

TO THE RIGHT HONOURABLE

SIR WILBRAHAM TOLLEMACHE, BARONET,

LORD HUNTINGTOWER,

AND

EARL OF DYSART,

THIS THIRD VOLUME

OF THE

BARONETAGE OF ENGLAND,

IS

MOST RESPECTFULLY INSCRIBED

BY

HIS LORDSHIP'S

MOST FAITHFUL

AND

OBLIGED HUMBLE SERVANT,

WILLIAM BETHAM.

Stonham,
June 7, 1803.

BARONETS

CREATED BY

KING CHARLES II.

CONTINUED.

194. DYKE, of HOREHAM, Sussex.

Created Baronet, March 3, 1676.

THE family of Dyke, or Dikes*, were seated at Dykesfield, in Cumberland, before the Norman conquest, but removed their seat to Wardale, or Wardhole, in the parish of Plumland, in that county, being the place were watch and ward used to be kept in former times, when the Scots made their inroads into Cumberland, from whence the watchmen gave warning to them who attended at the beacon, on Morthay, to fire the same. It is a small manor but hath large demesnes, and belonged formerly to the abbey of Caldre, and is now the property of the family of Dykes, who came from Dykesfield, in Burgh barony, from whence they took their name†.

A branch of this family very early removed into Sussex, where they have ever since been seated, at Henfield, and other places; of whom, Henry Dyke, of that county, Esq. married Eleanor, daughter of John Pagenham, of Sussex,

* Ex inf. Dom. Tho. Dyke, Bar. 1741.

† Burn's Cumberland, Vol. II. P. 117.

Esq. by Margaret, daughter of John Bramchett, Esq. son of Sir John Bramchett, of Sussex, Knt. and Catharine his wife, daughter of Sir John Pelham, Knt. of the present Duke of Newcastle's family; we find also that this family, for several generations, lived at Cranbrook, in Kent, of which was Reginald de Dike, high sheriff of that county, 29 Edw. III.* who married Lora, widow of Sampson Attleeze, and much improved his estate, and purchased lands † in Shepey, Shelvich, and Rutlandshire, and lies buried in an obscure chapel, on the north side of Shelvich church; and also that Thomas Dyke, of Cranbrook, in Kent, Esq. married Joan, daughter and heiress of Thomas Walsh, of Horeham, in the parish of Waldron, in Sussex, Gent. by the daughter and heiress of Horeham, of Horeham, aforesaid, by which match that seat came into this family; he died in April, 1632 ‡. They had three sons, Abraham, Herbert, and Thomas, hereafter mentioned; and four daughters, Margery, Judith, wife of Robert Edwards, of Wrexham, in Denbighshire, Esq.§ who died 1673, aged seventy-eight, and was buried in St. Giles's in the Fields, Elizabeth, and Sarah. Of the sons, Abraham, died Oct. 15, 1632, as appears by another inscription on the top of the last-mentioned gravestone ||.

Thomas, was knighted, and married Catharine, daughter of Sir John Bramston, of Skreens, in Essex, Knt. some time lord chief justice of the king's

* Philpot's Kent, p. 23.

† Ibid.

‡ He lies buried under a grave stone in Waldron church, with the following inscription on a brass plate fixed thereon, viz.

Heere under lieth, (expecting the comming
of his Saviour,) the Body of Thomas Dyke, Esq.
who left behind him 3 Sons, viz. Abraham, Herbert,
&Thomas, and 4 Daughters, Margery, Judith, Elizabeth,
& Sara: all which, he begatt uppon the Body of Mrs.
Joane Walsh, Daughter of Thomas Walsh, Gen. late
of Horeham, deceased; Having with her in Mariage,
the Inheritance of Horeham, she died 6to Aprilis,
1632. Anno Ætatis suæ 69o.

His wife died before him, and lies buried under another stone in the same church, with this inscription in brass over her, viz.

Heere under lieth, (expecting the comming
of her Saviour,) the Body of Joane Dyke,
late Wife of Thomas Dyke, of Horeham,
Esq. who died primo Januarii, 1632.
Anno Ætatis suæ 46°.

§ Stow's Survey, Vol. II. B. iv. P. 81.

|| Heere at her Peete lieth the
Body of Abraham Dyke, Esq. who
Died 15° Die Octobr. 1632.
Anno Ætatis suæ 24.

bench, who, together with his wife, lies buried in the said church*, by whom he had three sons, 1, John, who died young; 2, William, died 1675 †, and was buried in the Temple church; 3, Sir Thomas, of whom hereafter, and nine daughters, 1, Mary, was wife of William Quatermaine, Esq.; 2, Catharine; 3, Elizabeth, of Thomas Master, Esq. son of Sir William Master, of Cirencester abbey, in Glocestershire, Knt.; 4, Bridget, lies buried in Waldron church ‡; 5, Sarah; 6, Dorothy; 7, Bridget; 8, Martha; 9, Lucy. Sir Thomas died Dec. 13, 1669, aged fifty-one, and his lady, May 28, 1695, aged seventy-six.

I. THOMAS DYKE, of Horeham, Esq. the second son, was advanced to the dignity of a Baronet, of this realm, 29 Car. II. He was knight of the shire for Sussex, 1685, and member of parliament for East Grinsted, in Sussex, in 1688, 1690, and 1695; but, for many years before he died, he declined the honour of serving his country in parliament. He married Philadelphia, the eldest daughter and coheiress of Sir Thomas Nutt, of Mays, in the parish of Selmiston, in Sussex, Knt. by Catharine daughter of Sir Thomas Parker, of Ratton, in Sussex, Knt. ancestor to Sir Walter Parker, of the same place, Bart. by whom he had two sons and three daughters, Thomas and Catharine died young; Philadelphia was wife of Lewis Stephens, D. D. rector of Droxford, in Hamp-

* To whose memories is the following inscription on marble there, viz.

In this Alley lye
the Bodys of Sir Thomas Dyke,
of Horeham, in this Parish, and
of Dame Katharine, his
Wife, (one of the Daughters
of Sir John Bramston
of Skreens, in Essex, Lord Chief Justice
of the King's Bench, in the reign of King
Charles the First,) by whom he had twelve
Children, viz. three sons, John, Thomas,
William; and nine daughters, Mary,
Katharine, Elizabeth, Bridget, Sarah,
Dorothy, Bridget, Martha, Lucy.
He died 13° Dec. Anno Domini,
1669, Anno Ætatis 51.
She died 28° May, 1695.
Anno Ætatis 76.

† Stow's Survey, Vol. I. b. 3. p. 274.

‡ Over whom is the following inscription, viz.

Near this place lies interr'd
the body of Mrs. Bridget Dyke,
Daughter of Sir Thomas Dyke
of Horeham in this parish;
She was born the 19th of June,
in the year of our Lord, 1654
And died on the 7th of November
in the year 1728.
Mrs. Dorothy Dyke, her Sister, and sole
Executrix, of her last Will and
Testament, caused this Monument
to be erected in memory of her;
And designs herself to be
buried near her.

shire, archdeacon of Barnstable, archdeacon of Exeter, and canon-residentiary, and prebendary of York and Southwell; Elizabeth, who died Sept. 1739, of John Cockman, of Kent, doctor of physick, brother to Dr. Cockman, master of University college, Oxford, and left one daughter, the wife of Nicholas Toke, Esq. barrister-at-law; and Thomas. He died, Oct. 1706 *, and was succeeded by his only surviving son,

II. Sir THOMAS DYKE, Bart. who married, May, 1728, Anne, relict of John Bluet, of Holcomb Regis, in Devonshire, and heiress of Percival Hart, of Lullingston, in Kent, Esq. (son of Sir Percival Hart, Knt. and grandson of Sir Henry Hart, K. B. at the coronation of Charles I. two of whose ancestors were knights of the body to Henry VIII.) by whom he had three sons; John, who died in his father's lifetime; Sir John-Dixon, the present Baronet; and Percival, who died July, 1740; and one daughter, Philadelphia, wife of William Lee, of Tokeridge, in Hertfordshire, Esq. son of the late lord chief justice. Sir Thomas died 1756, and his lady in 1763 †, and was succeeded by his only surviving son,

* In Waldron church, on a monument, is the following inscription:—

Near this Place lies the
Body of Sir Thomas Dyke,
of Horeham, in this parish, Bart. who
marryed Philadelphia, the eldest Daughter
and Coheir of Sir Thomas Nutt,
of Mays, in this County, Knight, by whom
he had issue, viz. Thomas and Catherine
who died young. Philadelphia,
Elizabeth, and Thomas, who still survive; to whose Memory,
Dame Philadelphia, his
Relict, erected this monument,
Designing herself to be
buryed near it.
Obiit 31 Oct. { Anno 1706.
{ Ætatis 57.

† On the north side of the chancel of Lullington church, Kent, is a very elegant mural monument, with her head in relievo, encircled with a palm branch, and supported by two cherubims on a pyramid of dove colour: on each side are two fine urns of brown marble, and beneath is the following inscription:—

Sacred to the memory of Dame Anne Dyke, who died November 24, 1763, aged 71. A lady of exemplary piety and virtue, in religion most sound and sincere; in her love and friendship steady and constant; only child of Percival Hart, of this place, Esq. She was twice married, first to John Bluet, of Holcomb-Court, in the County of Devon, Esq. and afterwards to Sir Thomas Dyke, of Horeham, in the county of Sussex, Bart. to whose Memories she, by her will, ordered this monument to be erected. Mr. Bluet was a worthy descendant of a very ancient family, a man of great endowments and sound learning, which he manifested to the world by some excellent writings. He departed this life, December the 17th 1728, aged 29, and was buried in this place. Sir Thomas Dyke was a truly honest Englishman; in his domestic con-

III. Sir JOHN-DIXON DYKE, the present Baronet, who married Philadelphia, daughter of George Home, of East-Grinstead, in Sussex, Esq. by whom he had 1, Philadelphia; 2, Anne, one of which was wife of Colonel Hotham,.

TABLE 1.

Sir JOHN BRAMCHETT ═ CATH. PELHAM

John Bramchett

Margaret ═ John Pagenham

Eleanor ═ Henry Dyke

Reginald de Dyke ═ Lora Attaleeze

Thomas Dyke, 1632 ═ Joan Walsh, 1632

Abraham, Herbert — Sir Thomas, 1669 / E. Bramston, 1695 — Margery — Judith / R. Edward, 1673 — Elizabeth — Sarah

John, d y. — I. Sir Thomas, 1706 / Philadelphia Nutt — William, 1675 — Mary / W. Quatermaine — Elizabeth / T. Master — Bridget, Sarah — Dorothy, Bridget — Martha, Lucy

II. Sir Thomas, 1756 ═ A. Hart, 1763 — Catharine — Philadelphia ═ L. Stephens — Elizabeth ═ J. Cockman

John-Hart — III. Sir John Dixon, Bart. / Philadelphia Home — Percival, 1740 — Philadelphia / William Lee — —— / Nicholas Toke

Philadelphia — Anne / Col. Hotham — Thomas — Percival-Hart / —— Jenner — Harriot / Ch. Milne

cerns discreet and frugal; in all acts of hospitality magnificent and noble; ever zealous to maintain and defend the true principles of religion, liberty, and loyalty. He departed this life the 18th of August 1756, in the 58th year of his age, and lyes buried in this chancel.

On the upper part of the pyramid are these arms, in a lozenge, viz. In the center, HART, party per chevron, azure and gules, three harts trippant, or. On the right, BLUET, Or, a chevron, argent, between three eagles displayed sable. On the left DYKE, Or, three cinquefoils, sable, with the arms of Ulster.

N. B.—Sir Thomas Dyke erected, at his own expence, the window on the south side of the body of Lullington church, in the year 1754, it is of coloured glass, in the first pannel is the figure of St. Botolph, to whom the church is dedicated, beneath is the arms of DYKE, the arms of Ulster, and an escutcheon of pretence of HART, impaling forty-two quarterings. In the middle pannel is the ascension. In the third pannel is the figure of St. Luke; and under the arms as before. The other windows have likewise the arms of Dyke, &c.

in 1790; 3, Thomas; 4, Percival-Hart, who, July 26, 1798, married ———, daughter of Robert Jenner, of Chislehurst, Esq.; 5, Harriot, wife of Charles Milne, of Preston Hall, in Kent, Esq.

ARMS—Or, three cinquefoils, sable.
CREST—A cubit arm, in armour, proper, garnished, or and sable, holding a cinquefoil, slipped, as in the arms.
SEAT—At Lullington Castle, in Kent.

---

195. COTTON, of CUMBERMERE, Cheshire.

Created Baronet, March 29, 1677.

THIS ancient family is descended from the Cottons, near Hodnet, in Shropshire, seated there before the Conquest*.

1, Sir Hugh Cotton, Knt. temp. King John, married Elizabeth, daughter of Hammond Titley, of Titley, in the county of Chester, Esq. and after several descents in a direct line, was †,

2, William Cotton, Esq. seated there temp. Hen. VI. married Agnes, daughter of William Young, of Cainton, in the said county, Esq.; by whom he had,

3, John Cotton, Esq. who married ———, daughter of ——— Mainwaring ‡, of Ightfield, in Shropshire, by whom he had six sons, 1, William, who left no issue male; 2, Sir George, of whom hereafter; 3, Sir Richard Cotton, Knt. of Bedhampton, in Hants, and Warblington, in Sussex, who married Jane, daughter of John Onley, Esq. cousin to Sir George's lady, and had a daughter, Susan, wife of Charles, Earl of Kent. This Sir Richard was a courtier, temp. Ed. VI. but outlived that King §, and was ancestor to Richard Cotton, Esq. who married Elizabeth, sister to Richard, the first Earl of Scarborough; 4, Ralph, of London; 5, Thomas; 6, Robert, buried at Richmond, in Surry.

4, Sir George Cotton, Knt. who was the first of that name, (temp. Hen. VIII.) that seated himself at Cumbermere ||, in Cheshire, (an abbey of Benedictine monks, founded by Hugh Malbanc, Baron of Nantwich, A. D. 1133), was esquire of the body to King Henry VIII.¶ He was likewise sheriff of Denbighshire; steward of Bromfield, Yale, Chirk, and Chirkland; keeper of the castles of Holt, and Chirk, with the park of Holt, and the black park at Chirk, with all fees thereto belonging; also vice chamberlain of the household of Prince Edward, son of King Henry VIII.

* Ex inf. Dom. Rob. Sal. Cotton, Bar. 1727. † Ibid. ‡ Le Neve's MSS. Vol. III. p. 212. § Ibid. || Ex inf. Dom. Rob. Sal. Cotton, Bar. 1727. ¶ Ibid.

and of the privy council to that king. He married * Mary, daughter of John Onley, of Catesby, in Northamptonshire, Esq. and by her had, Richard, his only son and four daughters; Mary, wife, first, of Edw. Stanley, Earl of Derby, afterwards, of Henry Grey, Earl of Kent, but had no issue by either; 2, Elizabeth, of William Francis, of Tickill, in Derbyshire; 3, Dorothy, of Edward Torback, of Torback, in Lancashire; and 4, Winifred, of Thomas Deering, of Hampshire, Esqrs.

5, Richard Cotton, Esq. only son of Sir George, married † Mary, daughter of Sir Arthur Mainwaring, of Ightfield, sen. by whom he had George Cotton, who succeeded him, Arthur, and Andrew, who lived to a good old age, and never married; also a daughter, Mary, wife of Ralph Bulkeley, of Over, in Shropshire, Esq. He married secondly, —— Silliard, thirdly, ——, widow of John Dormer, in Bucks, Esq. and by all had a numerous issue ‡, of which, Philip was a captain, and killed in the service of King Charles I. (passing a river,) against the Scots; and a daughter, wife of Richard Cave, in Northamptonshire, Esq.

6, George Cotton, Esq. son and heir of Richard, married § Mary, daughter of Sir George Bromley, chief-justice of Chester, and by her had Thomas Cotton, and many daughters.

7, Thomas Cotton, Esq. son and heir, married || first, Frances, daughter of Robert Lord Viscount Kilmurry, and one son, George Cotton, Esq. who married Mary, daughter of Sir Thomas Smyth, of Haugh, in Cheshire, Knt. and had only one daughter, who died young, before her father; secondly, Elizabeth, daughter of Sir George Calveley, of Lea, in the county of Chester, Knt. by whom he had Sir Robert, Knt. and Bart. Charles, colonel of the cold-stream regiment of guards, in the reigns of King James II. and King William III. who married a daughter of —— Ady, of Kent, and had issue; and Lettice, who died unmarried.

I. Sir ROBERT COTTON was knighted at the restoration of King Charles II. and afterwards created Baronet by that Prince. He served in parliament for the county palatine of Chester thirty-six years ¶, and married Hester, daughter of Sir Thomas Salusbury, of Llewenny, in Denbighshire, Bart. (sister and heiress of John Salusbury), by whom he had five sons; 1, John, died unmarried; 2, Hugh-Calveley, married Mary, the only daughter and heiress of Sir William Russel, of Langherne, in Carmarthenshire, Bart. by whom he had a daughter Catharine, wife of Thomas Lewis, of St. Pier, in Monmouthshire, Esq. and died without issue. Mrs. Cotton surviving her husband, became the wife of Arthur, second surviving son of Henry, Duke of Beaufort; 3, Robert, died young; 4, Sir Thomas, succeeded his father; 5, George, died unmarried. Sir Robert had also eleven daughters: 1, Hester, wife of John Lacon, of West-Coppice, in Shropshire, Esq.; 2, Mary, of Sir William Fowler, of Harnage-Grange, in the same county; 3, Elizabeth, of Sir William Glegg, of Gayton, in Cheshire, Knt.; 4, Charlotte, died unmarried, and was buried at Esher, in Surry; 5, Anne, was wife of Sir Thomas Taylor, of Kelles, in the county of Meath, in

* Ex inf. Dom. Rob. Sal. Cotton, Bar. 1727. † Ibid. ‡ Ibid. § Ibid.
|| Le Neve, ibid. ¶ Ex inf. Dom. Rob. Sal. Cotton, Bar. 1727.

Ireland, Bart. of that kingdom: she died in 1758, aged ninety; 6, Arabella, was wife of Sir Henry Tichborne, of Beaulieu, in Ireland, Bart. afterwards Lord Farrand; 7, Jane, died young: 8, Sidney, wife of Nathaniel Lees, of Darnel, in Cheshire, Esq.; 9, Penelope; 10, Jane; 11, Catharine, died an infant. Sir Robert died Dec. 18, 1712, having survived his lady about two years, and was succeeded by his only surviving son,

II. Sir THOMAS COTTON, Bart. who married Philadelphia, daughter and heiress of Sir Thomas Lynch, of Esher, in Surry, Knt. who died 1709, and was buried at Esher (by his wife Vere*, daughter of Sir George Herbert, sister to the judge and admiral of that name, afterwards Earl of Torrington), who was thrice governor and captain-general of Jamaica. Sir Thomas had by her nine sons and six daughters, of which, Sir Robert-Salusbury, his successor; John-Salusbury; and Sir Lynch-Salusbury, successor to his brother. Of the daughters, Philadelphia, the wife of Thomas Boycott, of Henton, in Shropshire, Esq.; Sophia; Hester; Sidney; and Vere. Sir Thomas died June 2, 1715, and was buried at Esher, and was succeeded by his eldest son,

III. Sir ROBERT-SALUSBURY COTTON, Bt. who represented the county of Chester, in the first parliament of George II. He married Elizabeth Tollemache eldest daughter of Lyonel, Earl of Dysart, by his wife Grace, daughter and coheiress of Sir Thomas Wilbraham, of Wodney, in Cheshire, Bart. Sir Robert-Salusbury dying August 27, 1748, without issue, was succeeded in title and estate by his only brother,

IV. Sir LYNCH-SALUSBURY COTTON, Bart. who married Elizabeth, daughter of Rowland Cotton, of Bellaport, in the county of Shropshire, Esq. by his wife Mary, daughter of Sir Samuel Sleigh, of Etwall, in Derbyshire, Knt. who died 1777, by whom he had nine sons, 1, Robert-Salusbury, the present Baronet; 2, Rowland, an admiral, who died in 1795, and left by his wife Elizabeth, daughter of Sir Willoughby Aston, Bart. one son Willoughby, now in the guards, and one daughter Sidney-Arabella, wife of Richard Moore, of Kentwell-Hall, in Suffolk, Esq.; 3, Lynch, who died S. P. in the East-India service; 4, George, dean of Chester, who married ——, daughter of —— Tomlinson, of Nantwich, by whom he has six or seven children; 5, Thomas, a clerk in the treasury, who married, Oct. 8, 1779, ———, eldest daughter of —— Attwick, of Portman-square, Esq. by whom he has one son William; 6, William, a colonel in the army, unmarried; 7, Richard, killed at the battle of Camden, in America; 8, John, died young; 9, Henry-Calveley, who married ——, only daughter of —— Lockwood, of Sunbury, in Middlesex, by whom he has several children. Sir Lynch had also five daughters, 1, Elizabeth, wife of Colonel Davenant, of Drayton, Shropshire; 2, Philadelphia, of Henry Shelley, Esq.; 3, Mary, of the Rev. John Tench, of Middlewich, Cheshire, by whom she has three sons, and one daughter; 4, Salusbury, unmarried; 5, Hester-Salusbury, wife of Sir Thomas Corbet, son of Colonel Davenant, of Adderley-Hall. Sir Lynch died 1775, and was succeeded in honour and estates by his eldest son,

V. Sir ROBERT-SALUSBURY COTTON, Bart. who married Frances, daughter of James Russel Stapleton, Esq. by whom he has had four sons, 1,

* She died 1680; and, in commemoration of her, there is an annual sermon preached at Esher on September 30.

TABLE 2.

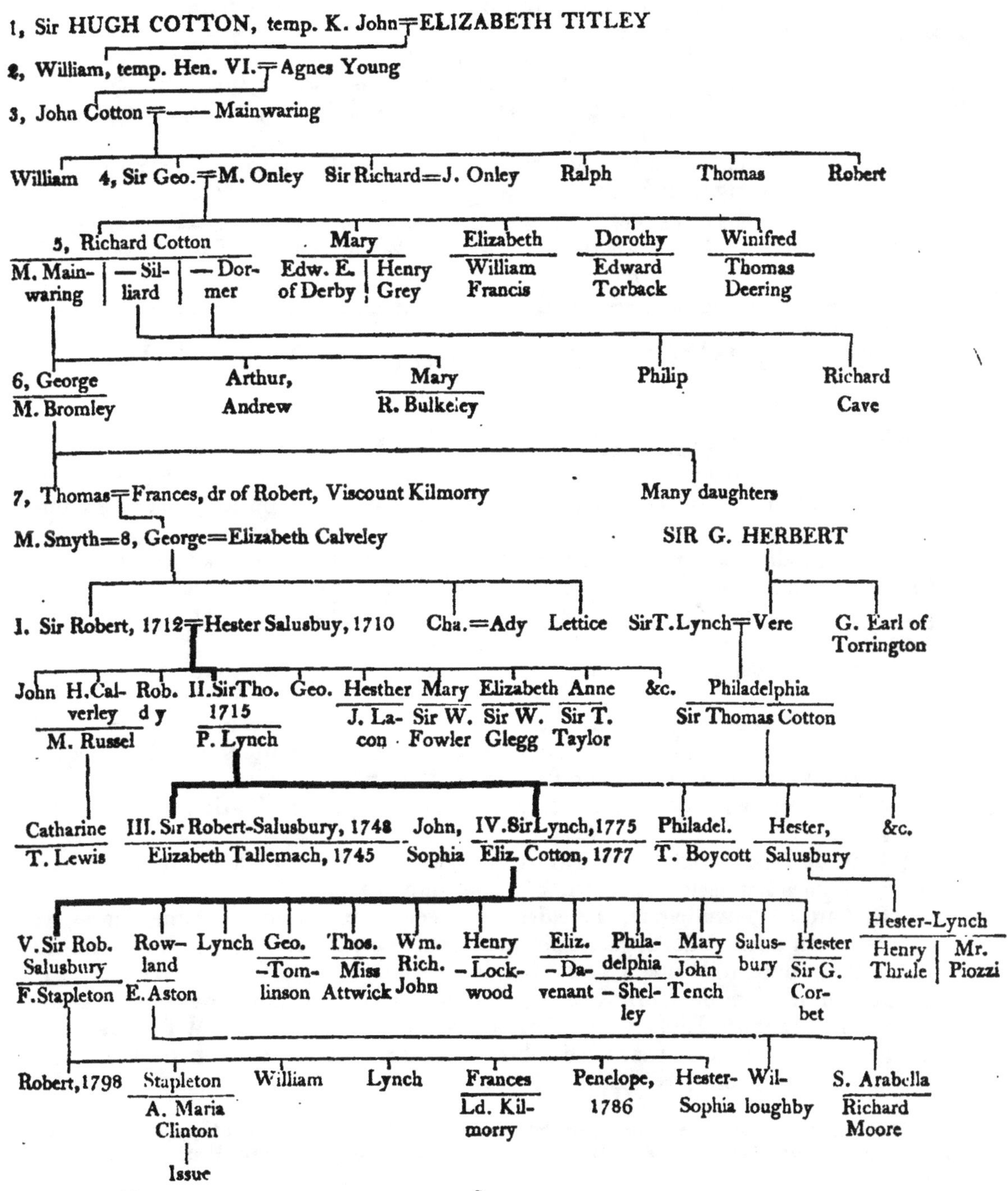
1, Sir HUGH COTTON, temp. K. John=ELIZABETH TITLEY
2, William, temp. Hen. VI.=Agnes Young
3, John Cotton=—— Mainwaring
William
4, Sir Geo.=M. Onley
Sir Richard=J. Onley
Ralph
Thomas
Robert
5, Richard Cotton
M. Mainwaring
— Silliard
— Dormer
Mary
Edw. E. of Derby
Henry Grey
Elizabeth
William Francis
Dorothy
Edward Torback
Winifred
Thomas Deering
6, George
M. Bromley
Arthur, Andrew
Mary
R. Bulkeley
Philip
Richard Cave
7, Thomas=Frances, dr of Robert, Viscount Kilmorry
Many daughters
M. Smyth=8, George=Elizabeth Calveley
SIR G. HERBERT
I. Sir Robert, 1712=Hester Salusbuy, 1710
Cha.=Ady
Lettice
SirT. Lynch=Vere
G. Earl of Torrington
John
H. Calverley
M. Russel
Rob. d y
II. SirTho. 1715
P. Lynch
Geo.
Hesther
J. Lacon
Mary
Sir W. Fowler
Elizabeth
Sir W. Glegg
Anne
Sir T. Taylor
&c.
Philadelphia
Sir Thomas Cotton
Catharine
T. Lewis
III. Sir Robert-Salusbury, 1748
Elizabeth Tallemach, 1745
John, Sophia
IV. Sir Lynch, 1775
Eliz. Cotton, 1777
Philadel.
T. Boycott
Hester,
Salusbury
&c.
Hester-Lynch
Henry Thrale
Mr. Piozzi
V. Sir Rob. Salusbury
F. Stapleton
Rowland
E. Aston
Lynch
Geo.
-Tomlinson
Thos.
Miss Attwick
Wm. Rich. John
Henry
- Lockwood
Eliz.
- Davenant
Philadelphia
- Shelley
Mary
John Tench
Salusbury
Hester
Sir G. Corbet
Robert, 1798
Stapleton
A. Maria Clinton
Issue
William
Lynch
Frances
Ld. Kilmorry
Penelope, 1786
Hester-Sophia
Willoughby
S. Arabella
Richard Moore

Robert Salusbury, who died about 1798; 2, Stapleton, a colonel in the army, who married Anna Maria, daughter of the Duke of Newcastle, by whom he has issue; 3, William, now at Cambridge; 4, Lynch, in the army: and three daughters, 1, Frances, wife of Lord Kilmorry; 2, Penelope, who died December, 1786, she went to bed in apparent good health, and was found dead in the morning; and 3, Hester-Sophia.

ARMS—Azure, a chevron between three cotton-hanks, argent.

CREST—On a wreath, a falcon, close, proper, with bells, jessant, or, sustaining with his dexer talons, a garter.

SEATS—At Cumbermere, Lea, and Newhall, in Cheshire; Llewenny, Cotton-hall, and Beraign, in Denbighshire.

Hester Salusbury, third daughter of Sir Thomas, the second baronet, was wife of —— Salusbury, Esq. governor of Nova Scotia, by whom he had one daughter, Hester-Lynch, wife, first, of Henry Thrale, Esq. secondly, of Mr. Piozzi.

196. NEWIGATE, of Arbury, Warwickshire.

Created Baronet, July 24. 1677.

THIS family, from time immemorial until the beginning of the reign of King Charles the First, possessed the manors and lands of Newdegate, in the county of Surry; and, from many records of very high antiquity, it appears, that the name was written variously, Niwudegate, Niwodegate, Newedigate, Niudegate, Neudegate, originally, perhaps, from Saxony, and of the city of Nieuweide, upon the Rhine; and the name of the manor and parish being in all those records uniformly spelt, as the name of the owner, seems to justify a conjecture, that they took the name from the family.

The intermarriages of this family, before that with Malmains, are set forth in an ancient MS. * with the arms imblazoned, thus: Newdegate and Warren, Newdegate and Pugeys, Newdegate and Monfitchet, Newdegate and Roan, Newdegate and Sudeley, Newdegate and Ashburnham, Newdegate and Wintershull, Newdegate and Clare, Newdegate and Chenduit, Newdegate and Malmains.

The first, from whom a regular descent for twenty-two generations commences, is,

1, John de Niwudegate, who was living in the 14th year of King John, and by his wife Agnes had issue, Richard, William, and Robert.

2, Richard de Niwudegate, the eldest, succeeded, to whom William Yonge, as appears by an ancient deed, grants for homage half a yard of land; and, by another deed without date, of William Testardus, he held other lands. He married Alicia, daughter of William de Horley, as appears by a deed of William de Longsponte, whereby he grants to Richard de Niwudegate, all that land which Walter de Horleia, gave to the said Richard, with his daughter Alicia, in free marriage. He had issue by her, John, William, and Peter.

* From an illuminated pedigree, first taken by Henry Lillie, Rouge Croix, in 1610, and by Sir William Dugdale, Garter King at Arms, 1684, and lastly, by Gregory King, Lancaster Herald, 1691.

3, John de Nywdegate, his heir, by deed, grants to Galfred de la Wytecrofte, the land which Norman de la Bere, and Mabilia, his wife, gave to the said Galfred in Nywodegate; also Richard, son of Roger le Balch, gives the said John, twenty acres in Newdegate, called Lamputtes-Feldes; and by another deed, Norman de la Bere, gives him two fields in Newdegate, called Suthleze and Northleze. He lived in the reign of Henry III. and, by his wife Agnes, had issue William, and Richard.

4, William de Nywedegate, the eldest son, succeeded, to whom Thomas de la Lynde, by a deed of 17th Edw. I. grants his woods in Lynde, and Henry Kymer, gives to William de Nyudegate, and Alicia his wife, lands in Nyudegate; and William Eglaff, and Gilbert Wytecroft, by other deeds, grant lands in Nyudegate, and Chorlewode. He left issue,

5, Sir Henry de Newdegate, Knt. living in the reign of Edward the First, married Catherine, daughter and coheiress of Sir Nicholas Malmains, Knt. (whose sisters were Beatrix, married to Otho de Grandison, brother to Lord Grandison; Petronilla, to Sir Thomas de Sancto-Moro; Elizabeth, and Johanna), by her he had issue, John and William.

6, John, the eldest, died without issue, and was succeeded by William de Niewdegate, his brother, who, by a deed of Reginald de Wytecroft, 7th Edw. II. obtained a croft in Nyudegate, called Edward's Croft. He had to wife the daughter and heiress of John Echingham, by whom he had four sons, John, Richard, Robert, and William.

7, John de Nywedegate, the eldest, about the third of Edw. III. married Agnes, by whom he had three sons; William, who succeeded his father in the manor and lands of Neudegate; John, of whom hereafter; Thomas, to whom his father, by a deed of the seventh of Edw. III. gave his tenements, called Hullond, for his life, remainder to his brother John for his life, with remainder to William and his heirs.

8, William de Neudegate, the eldest, was sheriff of Surry and Sussex *, twenty-fifth of Edw. III. and in thirty-fourth Edw. III. with Nicholas Farran, was returned Knt. of the shire for the county of Surry; and was returned again for the same, on the thirty-seventh, forty-fifth, and fiftieth of Edw. III. by a deed dated thirty-third Edw. III. Simon Rolff, son of Adam Rolff, gives to William de Neudegate, and Amycia, his wife, and son John, four fields in the parish of Cherlwoods and Neudegate; and, by other deeds of the same reign, he obtained of John de Montford, woods in Berland, and of John Egelaff, and others, lands in Neudegate. He died about first Rich. II.

9, John de Neudegate, his son, succeeded to his estates in Neudegate, &c. in whose male line this elder branch of the family continued in the possession of the same, till about the sixth year of King Charles I. when it terminated in two daughters of Thomas de Neudegate; Mary de Neudegate, who married William Steper, and by the death of her sister Anna, the wife of William Smythman, became sole heiress of the manor of Neudegate, and lands in Horby Cherlwood, &c. in Surry and Sussex.

10, Sir John Newdegate, of Herefield, in the county of Middlesex, Knt. was

* See Prynne's Brev. Parliament, part I. p. 88, and p. 4.

second son of John and Agnes, and brother of William de Neudegate, last mentioned; he served in the wars with France, under Edward the Third, obtained the honour of Knighthood, and a Fleur-de-lis argent for his crest. He married Joanna, daughter of William de Swanlond, by Joanna, heiress of Richard de Bacheworth, in Hertfordshire, who, by the death of William de Swanlond, her eldest and other brothers, without issue, became possessed of the manor and estates of Herefield, in the county of Middlesex.

11, John Newdegate, Knt. married Elizabeth, daughter * of Walter Knoll, of Crawley, Esq. and Margaret his wife, to whom, by deed of intail, dated seventh of Hen. V. of Sydeney and others, the manor of Downe, in the hundred of Godalming, in Surry, is demised for her life, with remainder to Elizabeth, her daughter, for her life, remainder to William Newdegate, son of the said Elizabeth, and his heirs. By her he had issue, William, and Thomas; by his second wife, Catharina, daughter and heiress of Roger Chambers, he had a daughter, Margaret, wife of —— Castlemain.

12, William Newdegate, his son, succeeded to the manor of Herefield, &c. married Editha Bowett, daughter of John Bowett, of ———, in Surry, Esq. by whom he had one son, John. †

He married, secondly, Leticia, daughter and heiress of ———, who, after his death, became the wife of George Danijel, Esq.

William died thirty-sixth of Hen. VI. and was succeeded by,

13, John Newdegate, his son, and heir to the manor of Harefield, and was also possessed of that of Crawley, in the county of Surry, his wife was Elizabeth, daughter of Thomas Yong, Esq. one of the justices of the common pleas, 5 Edw. IV. and sister and heiress of Thomas Yong, of Bristol: she died fourth of Hen. VII. and left a son,

14, John Newdegate, Esq. Lord of the manor of Harefield, studied the law at Lincoln's-Inn, ‡ and was advanced to the dignity of the coif, 18th of Nov. second Hen. VIII. and in the fifth of the same, he impleaded John, Earl of Oxon, for the manor of Bachesworth, in Herts, as heir to the Swanlands, who descended from the heiress of Penger de Bacheworth. In the twelfth of Hen. VIII. he had the honour to be appointed king's serjeant. He married Amphelicia, daughter and heiress of John Nevill, of Sulton, in the county of Lincoln, Esq. by whom he had issue, John, who was his heir; and Silvester, and Duncan, Knights-Hospitallers of St. John's, in Jerusalem; and Sebastian, who, upon his wife's death, became a Carthusian monk, and twenty-seventh Hen. VIII. suffered for opposing the king's supremacy. His daughters were Barbara, wife of John Crugg, of Exon, and with her husband, was interred in Brackenbury chapel, under a flat marble gravestone, with their portraitures in long robes in brass; Jane, the wife of Sir Robert Dormer, of Wenge, in the county of Bucks, from whom descended the Earls of Caernarvon, and Barons Dormer, of Wenge; and, by a sister of the first Baron, the Dukes of

* Walter Knoll and Margerie, in an old deed, 15 Rich. II. still remaining.

† She was buried at Herefield, in Brakenbury chapel, where is a flat marble with this inscription:—

Hic jacet Editha, quondam Ux. Willi. Neudigate,
Quæ obiit XI° die Septembr. Anno D[ni] M°CCCCXLIIII.
Cujus anime propitietur Deus, Amen.

‡ Dugdale's Orig.

Feria, in Spain; Mary, a nun at Sion, in Middlesex; Dorothy, wife of Leonard Chamberlayn, of Shireborne, Oxfordshire, Esq.; and Sybil, a nun at Holywell, Midddlesex*.

15, John Newdegate, of Harefild, Esq. born sixth Hen. VII. suceedeed. He married Anne, daughter and heiress of Nicholas Hylton, of Cambridge, Esq. in the thirty-fourth of Hen. VIII. by deed of R. Tyrwhitt, he obtained the manor of Moor-Hall, in Harefield, with the rectory and peculiar Jurisdiction, which by the gift of his ancestors belonged to the Knights-Hospitallers of St. John's, in Jerusalem, and on the dissolution of monasteries, by Hen. VIII. was in the same year, granted by the king to the said R. Tyrwitt. He died in 37 Hen. VIII. leaving issue by the said Anne, 1, John, born fifth Hen. VIII.; 2, George, who was a monk at Chertsey; 3, Anthony, of Hawnes, in Bedfordshire, born eight Hen. VIII. and died 1568, as appears by his monument in the church of Hawnes; 4, Francis, of Hanworth, in Middlesex, born eleventh Hen. VIII. who was one of the gentlemen of the household to the Duke of Somerset, protector of the realm, and uncle to Edw. VI. who being taken off by the arts of a faction, Francis married his dowager, Dutchess of Somerset, who was daughter of Sir Edward Stanhope, of Shelford, Knt.; 5, Thomas; and 6, Nicholas, of London, born twelve Hen. VIII.; and 7, Robert, born twentieth Hen. VIII. The daughters were, Amphilicia and Johanna, who died young, Amphelicia, and Anne, who was the wife of William Gardiner, of Grove, and Rosa †.

16, John Newdegate, his eldest son, succeeded to the manor of Harefield and Moor-Hall, in Harefield, now united, and with his brother Francis Newdegate, in 1571, thirteen Elizabeth, was chosen knight of the shire for the county of Middlesex. In 1573, and again in 1574, John was chosen to represent the said county. He married, first, Mary, daughter of Sir Robert Cheney, of Chesham-Boys, Bucks, Knt. thirty-four of Hen. VIII. by whom he had one son, John; his second wife was Elizabeth, daughter of Thomas Lovett, of Astwell, Northamptonshire, relict of Anthony Cave, of Chichley, Bucks. He died seventh of Elizabeth 1565.

17, John Newdegate, his son, succceeded to the manors of Harefild and Moor-Hall, and his other possessions of Hanworth, in Middlesex, Ashted, &c. in Surry,

* In the aforesaid chapel is a plain altar tomb of grey marble with the figure, in brass, of him in his serjeant's robes, and his wife, ten sons, and 7 daughters; out of his mouth a scroll *Sancta Trinita un' Deus*, out of hers, *Miserere nobis miseris*, with this inscription:—

> Hic jacent humata corpa. Johannis Newdegate, fuien ad Legem, et Amphilicie Uxor ejus, Filie et Hæred. Johannis Nevill, Armigeri, qui quidem Johes. Newdigate, obiit XVI° die Augusti, An° D[ni] M°V,°XXVIII, et prædicta Amphilitia XV Julii, An° Dni. M°V°XLIII. Quor. Anmbs. ppiciet[r] de[s].

† In the wall of the chancel of Harfield, is an altar tomb of grey marble, with a canopy of the same, and beneath is his effigy in brass kneeling, with eight sons kneeling behind him, and of his wife, also kneeling, with five daughters, with this inscription underneath:—

> Off yo[r] charitie, pray for the soules of John Newdigate, Esquyer, and Anne, his Wyff, y[e] whiche John decessyd the XIXth day of June, in the year of our Lorde God, a thousand, fyve hundred, fourtye, and fyve, and the said Anne decessyd the day of in the yere of our Lorde God, a thousand, fyve hundred
>
> On whose soules and all Christen soules Jhu have mercy. Amen.

Lathbury, &c. in Bucks, &c, to which he added by marriage with Martha Cave, daughter and heiress of Anthony Cave, of Chichely, in Bucks: by her he had seven sons, 1, John; 2, Francis; 3, Henry; 4, Robert; 5, Charles; 6, Carew; 7, Robert; and three daughters, 1, Elizabeth; 2, Griselda; and 3, Mary. Upon her decease, he married Mary, the daughter of —— Smith, by whom he had issue Henry, to whom he gave the manor of little Ashted, in Surry *. He had a third wife, Winifred, daughter of —— Wells, of ——, in Staffordshire, who survived him; and lived in her jointure-house, called Brackenbury, a capital messuage in Harefield, with about four hundred acres annexed, which at her death descended to his son, Sir John Newdegate, Knt. not being included in the exchange; which in the † twenty-eighth of Eliz. Nov. 20, 1586, was made between Sir Edmond Anderson, Knt. chief-justice of the common-pleas, and John Newdegate, who conveyed his manors and lands in Harefield, (with the ancient seat of the family, a large quadrangular edifice, situated where is now the garden of the house, called Harefield-Place, and which was then only two lodges; with the iron gates leading into the court, but since, joined by a hall built by the last Sir Richard Newdegate, Bart.) to the said Sir Edmond, who conveyed to him in exchange, the fair quadranguler edifice of stone, which he had just completed, upon the site of the dissolved priory of Erdbury, in Warwickshire, which he had obtained of the heirs of the Duke of Suffolk; who upon their dissolution had the grant of this, and many other religious houses by the favour of King Henry VIII ‡. John Newdigate died 1592.

18, Sir John Newdegate, of Arbury, in Warwickshire, and of Brackenbury, in Harefield, Knt. succeeded; he was born in 1570, and married Anne, eldest daughter of Sir Edward Fitton, of Gawsworth, Cheshire, Knt. by whom he had two sons, John, and Richard; and two daughters, Maria-Lettitia, wife of —— Bolton; and Anne, wife of Sir Richard Skeffington, of Fisherwich, Staffordshire, and mother of John Skeffington, Viscount Mazareen, of the kingdom of Ireland: she survived her husband, and died 1618 §.

* He resided at Hampton, in Middlesex, of which, as appears by the following inscription on his tomb, in the church of Hampton, he had the manor:—

M. S.
Henrici Newdigate, Arm. quondam hujus Mancoii, Dom: Filii secundo geniti
Johannis Newdigate de Arbury, in com. Warw. Militis.
Qui quidem Henricus magnam hospitalitatem tenuit. Improlis ob. An. Ætatis suæ 48, A. D. 1629.

† Sir Wm. Dugdale's Warwickshire.

‡ It is observed, by the historians of his time, that the civil wars of York and Lancaster being at an end, and peace firmly established, the nobility of the kingdom were no longer satisfied with the wooden mounted mansions of their ancestors, but procuring architects, from Italy, and other parts, they erected, in every part of the realm, many fair and solid quadrangular buildings of stone and brick.—*Camden Annal. Elizab. An.* 1574.

Uná conviviorum luxuria insepit et ædificorum splendor. Plures enim et nobilium et privatorum villa elegatiâ, laxitate, et cultu conspicuæ, jam passim in Anglia surgere cœperunt, quam alio quovis seculo; magno sane regni ornamento, verum hospitalis gloriæ detrimento.

§ In Brakenbury chapel, fixed to the south wall is a monument of white and purple marble with columns, at the top of which are the arms of Newdigate, with quarterings underneath, he is represented in white armour kneeling, and his lady opposite to him in the same posture, with a desk with books between them, over

19, John Newdigate, his eldest son, born in 1600, succeeded to his father's estates in Warwickshire and Middlesex, and married Susanna, daughter of Arnold Luls. In first of Charles the First, he was sheriff of the county of Warwick. He died in 1642, and was buried at Harefield *. He was the first of the family who wrote the the name with an i, probably to distinguish it from the elder branch still remaining in possession of Newdegate, in Surry, but in this he was not followed by his brother and heir.

them a death's head with wings, and this inscription on black marble:

Sir John Newdegate, Knyght, was
buried the 12th of April, 1610.

Underneath him are two young men in cloaks kneeling, and three young women underneath her, and this inscription in gold on black marble:

In funeribus Joannis Newdigate Militis,
Cui in connubio stabili, juncta fuit Anna
Edwardi Fitton Militis filia promegenita
Non mirum si sorte loqui didicere sepulcra
Conditur hoc tumulo Religionis Honos,
Si taceant lapides et non tibi carmina cantent,
Hoc potius mirum non didicisse loqui,
Non tamen hoc loquitur flebit tua funora tantum,
Marmor guttatim flebile flumen erit.
Servi mœstissimi
Lessus lacrymabilis.

Here Wisdom's jewel, Knighthood's flower,
Cropt off in prime and youthfull hower;
Religion, meekness, faithful love,
Which any Hart might inly moove.
These ever lived in this Knight's brest,
Dead in his death with him doth rest;
So that the marble self doth weepe,
To think on that which it doth keepe.
Weep then whoe'er this stone doth see,
Unless more hard than stone thou be.

* On his monument is this inscription: M. S.
Clarissimi Viri Joannis Newdigate filii et
Hæredis Joannis Newdegate Equitis aurati
Ex antiquâ Newdegatorum gente oriundi
Qui licet immaturè parentibus orbatus,
Parentum vota superavit et splendorem ab
Eis acceptum amplissimo cum fænore rependit
Homo structuræ non vulgaris
Acuti Ingenij, solidi Judicii
Animi sublimioris,
Altioris Disciplinæ Investigator.
Politioris Cultor
Poeta adeptus
Maritus amantissimus.
Ac tamen
Frater amicissimus.
Rigidus Pietatis et Virtutis Custos,
Explicatæ erga omnes Humanitatis
Amicis Amicus immortalis
SISTE VIATOR
Hæc accipe non temerè dicta sed *ab eo*
Qui et verè novit et sanctè asseverat
Mortalitatem senivit ætà 42. Sal. Hum. 1642.
Prolem suscepit superstitem non reliquit,
Prohibuit natura tantum Homínem
Viâ tam tritâ
Famæ et posteritati litare
Suum sibi ipsi monumentum ære perennius.

I. RICHARD NEWDEGATE, of Arbury and Harefield, Esq. and the first Baronet of the family, who had made the law his study, and and was at his brothers death in high practice at the bar, which he continued with much reputation for his learning and integrity, and was advanced to the dignity of Sergeant at law. In * 1653, Cromwell having beaten down all opposition, and arrived at the summit of power, on the twelfth of December, by proclamation, the government by a Lord Protector, and trienniel parliaments was established on the twenty-first, by another proclamation, the Lord Protector, "Lest the settled and ordinary course of justice in the commonwealth might receive interruption, ordains that all persons possesed of judicature shall proceed in the performance and execution thereof" †. Thus having with consummate policy, determined to re-establish the courts of justice, summoned the most eminent and respectable professors of law, who attended with the worthy and learned Sir Mathew Hale, at their head. He told them that his purpose was to rule according to the laws of the land, and had sent for them to make them judges; they all with one consent, begged to be excused; and being pressed, declared, that they could not act under his commission. Highly offended, he turned away in a rage, crying out, if you, gentlemen, of the red robe, will not execute the laws, my red coats shall. Upon this Mr. Hale, and his companions all exclamed: "Make us Judges! we will be Judges!"

On the twenty-fifth of January, 165¾, ‡ Mr. Hale, was by writ made Serjeant at law, and soon after one of the justices of the common bench.

On the second of June, 1654 §. Three new Judges were made, Serjeant Pepys, Serjeant Newdegate, and Serjeant Windham.

Nor was the new Judge, unworthy his situation, for on the question of the sale of the crown-lands; being put to the Judges, he hesitated not to declare that no title could be made to them, and upon the north circuit at the assizes at York, where many of the cavaliers where arraigned for high-treason, the Earls of Bellasis and Dumfries, Colonel Halsey, and others; he acquitted them all, declaring from the bench, that there was no law that made it high-treason, to levy war against a Lord-Protector, by this he drew upon himself Cromwell's indignation, and in May, 1655 ||, Baron Thorpe, and Judge Newdegate, were put out of their places, for not observing the protector's pleasure in all his commands. After the death of Cromwell, and his son Richard's degradation; Serjeant Newdegate, was again called to the bench, and on the seventeenth of January, 1659, chief-justice of the upper bench, soon after, his health being much impaired he retired from business.

In 1677, at the instance of the Duke of Ormond, Lord Grandison, Colonel Halsey, one of those whose lives he had saved, and others, Serjeant Newdegate, was commanded to attend his Majesty, who received him very graciously, and thanked him for his kindness to his friends in the worst of times, and gave orders for a warrant to be issued for a grant of the dignity of Baronet, "which said dig-

* Whitlock's Memorial. † Ibid. ‡ Ibid. § From information of the Right Hon. Arthur Onslow, speaker of the House of Commons.

|| Whitlock's Memorial.

nity we are pleased to confer upon him, in consideration of several good services performed to us, and our faithful subjects in the time of usurpation." In this warrant, the king remits the services or sums usually paid in exchange, for them on granting the patent.

In 1631, he married Juliana, daughter of Sir Francis Leigh, of Newnham-Regis, in the county of Warwick, K. B. and sister to Francis, Earl of Chichester. His surviving children were Sir Richard, his successor; Robert, of Hillingdon, who had two wives, Frances, daughter of Thomas Harrison Esq. and Juliana, daughter of Robert Beals, Esq. his third son was Thomas of Lewes, in Sussex, and Hawton, Nottinghamshire, who by his wife Charitie, daughter and heiress of Stephen French, of Lewes, had two sons, Richard Newdegate, of the Inner-Temple, who was his heir, born 1680, died 1745; and John, of the Six Clerks Office, who died in 1740. Two daughters only survived the serjeant: Anne, wife of German Pole, of Radborn, in the county of Derby, Esq.; and Mary, wife of Sir George Parker, of Willington, in Sussex, Baronet. Sir Edmond Anderson, had conveyed the manors of Harefield and Moor-Hall, to Alicia, Countess Dowager of Derby, who resided at the Place-House, in great splendour, where she was honoured with a visit, by Queen Elizabeth, and received her with the pomp and pageantry of her times. The large ancient seat of the family, of which the present Place-House, was then only two lodges since joined by a hall, where the iron gates of the court stood, was burned to the ground, whilst in possession of her heirs; she died and lies under a sumptuous monument in the chancel. Of her heirs, Sir Richard Newdegate, the serjeant, repurchased this ancient estate of his ancestors in 1674. He also added to his estates the castle and manor of Astley, and the manor of St. John's, in Jerusalem, both in Warwickshire. He died 1678 *.

* Upon his monument, in Brakenbury Chapel, is this inscription:

M. S.
RICHARDI NEWDEGATE
SERVIENTIS' AD LEGEM
ET BARONETTI.
Filii natu minimi IOHANNIS NEWDEGATE, in agro
Warwicensi Militis. Natus est 17° die 7^{bris}. A° D^{ni}. MDC.II.
Et post tyrocinium in academiâ Oxon. fæliciter inchoatum juris
Municipalis studio, in Graiorum Hospitio reliquum temporis impendit.
Vitam degit animi fortitudine et mirâ æquitate spectabilem: summo
Candore et morum suavitate ornatus erat, nec minore probitate, et
Prudentiâ: deplorandis illis inter Carolum I. Regem et ordines Regni
Controversiis non omnino se immiscuit, nec adduci potuit ut prædiorum
Regis, vel illorum qui ab ejus parte steterunt, emptione rem suam
Contaminaret, sed nobiliore quamvis minus expedito ad divitias contendebat itinere indefesso, nempe studio et labore, summâq. in arduis forti
Negotiis peritiâ et fide: quibus ita claruit, ut reempto hujus loci manerio
Antiquæ suæ familiæ pæne collapsæ atque in veteri NEWDIGATORUM,
In Surriâ prosapiâ oriundæ sedi, plurima adjecit latifundia, quæ nullæ
Viduarum lachrymæ, nec diri Orphanorum gemitus, infausto omine
Polluerunt. Uxorem duxit lectissimam Fæminam Julianam Francisci
LEIGH, de Newnham Regis, in Agro Warwici, Militis Balnei filiam,

II Sir RICHARD NEWDIGATE, of Harefield and Arbury, Baronet, succeeded; he married Mary, daughter of Sir Edward Bagot, of Blithfield, in the county of Stafford, Baronet, by whom he had, Richard, born 1668, and seven other sons, John; Francis; Walter; John; Charles; Gilbert, who all died infants or unmarried, except Francis, the eighth, born 1684, who settled at Nottingham, and married Millisent, daughter of German Pole, of Radburne, in the county of Derby, Esq. by whom he had one son, Francis, who married Elizabeth, daughter of General Pole, and died 17—, leaving no issue; and one daughter Millisent, wife of William Parker, of Salford, in the county of Warwick, Esq. by whom he had three sons, Robert; Francis, of Kirkhallam, in Derbyshire, who, by his uncle's will, took the name of Newdigate, and married Frances, daughter of Ralph Sneyd, of Keal, in Staffordshire, Esq. and had one son, Francis Newdigate. His third son was Charles Parker, of Harefield-Lodge, in Middlesex, who died April, 24, 1795, leaving by his wife, daughter of Sir John Ansmither, of Ansmither, in the county of Fife, Bart. one son, Charles Newdigate-Parker, and four daughters, infants. Sir Richard, had seven daughters, 1, Amphelis died unmarried; 2, Mary, wife of William Stephens, of Barton, in the Isle of Wight, Esq.; 3, Frances, of Sir Charles Sedley, of Chartley, in Kent, Bart. 4, Anne, of John Venables, of Woodcote, in Hampshire, Esq.; 5, Jane, of Samuel Boys, of Hawkhurst, in Kent, Esq.; 6, Juliana, of Robert Glegg, of Gayton, in Cheshire, Esq.; 7, Elizabeth, of Abraham Meur. Mary, Lady Newdigate, died Sept. 14, 1692*. He represented the county of Warwick, in parliament in the years 1681, and 1685. His second

Eandemq. illustrissimi Comitis Cicestrensis Sororem, ex qua sobolem
Suscepit amplam, sex filios, et filias quinque quorum Ricardus,
Robertus, Thomas, Anna, et Maria, jam supersunt.
Tandem re familiari optimè dispositâ, liberisq. omnibus amplissimè dotatis, nepotes suos usq. ad quartam generationem
Complexus, sine ullis delirantis animi paroxismis
Omni sollicitudine et sordidâ cura immunis,
Cœlum tantum et Deum spirans, annis plenus,
Bonisq. operibus coopertus,
Obiit 14 Oct. A. D.
MDCLXXVIII. Ætatis suæ 76.

Upon a prostrate black marble under the said monument:

Hic jacet Sepultus RICVS. NEWDEGATE, &c. qui duxit in
Uxorem IVLIANAM LEIGH tertiam Filiam Francisci Leigh, &c.
Hic jacet Sepulta Juliana uxor.
P̄DICT. RICI fidelis et carissima quæ obiit ———
Ætatis Suæ.
She was married 1630, and died at Harfield 1685.

* She was buried at Harefield, where is a costly monument of white marble, with her effigy at full length upon a base, with a canopy supported by Corinthian pillars, with two cherub's heads upon each, and a curtain drawn back: above the entablature is a dome, crowned with a vase inflamed with a torst and trumpet. On the base is this inscription:—

lady was Henrietta, daughter of —— Wiggington, Esq. who survived him and married Sir Francis Windham, of Trent, in Somersetshire, Bart. by whom he had no issue.

III. Sir **RICHARD NEWDIGATE**, of Harefield, and Arbury, Bart. succeeded; he married Sarah, daughter of Sir Cecil Bishopp, of Parham, in Sussex, Baronet, who died in a short time after, in her 27th year*. His second lady was Elizabeth, daughter of Sir Roger Twisden, of Bradburne, in Kent, Baronet, by whom he had seven sons of which, 1, Richard, 2, John, 3, Thomas, and 4, Charles, died very young, 5, Sir Edward, his successor; 6, Richard, who died of the small-pox at Westminster-school, 1733. The seventh and youngest son, Sir Roger Newdigate, Bart. is

Juxta hic situs jacet
D^nus^ Ricardus Newdigate,
2^dus^ ejus Nominis Bar^tus^. Filius 3^tius^.
D^ni^. Ricardi Newdigate,
Servientis at Legam et Bar.
Nat. 4 Maii, 1644.
Ob. 4. Jan. 1709-10. An. Ætat. 66.

And underneath is written:
To the Memory of the fair and vertuous lady, Mary Lady Newdigate, wife of Sir Richard Newdigate, of Arbury, in com. Warw. Bart. & daughter of Sir Edward Bagot, of Blithfield, in com. Staff. Bart. a lady who, besides the great antiquity of her family, and nobleness of her extraction, (as being descended from the same paternal stock with the Barons of Stafford, sometime Dukes of Buckingham, was most eminent for the excellent endowments of her mind, and all conjugal virtues, She was mother of many children, whereof ——

* She was buried at Harefield, where is her monument, an urn inflamed, supported by two angels weeping on a base of white marble, with this inscription:

Hoc juxta Marmur
Conduntur Cineres Dominæ illustrissimæ
Saræ Newdigate,
Ricardi Newdigate, armigeri, filii primogeniti D^ni^. Ricardi
Newdigate, de Arbury, in comitatu
Warwicensi, Baronetti, uxoris: & domini Cecilii Bishopp,
de Parham, in comitatu Sussexiæ, Baronetii, filiæ natu
Maximæ, omnibus et animi et corporis dotibus ornatissimæ; quæ toto
Vitæ, heu nimium brevis!
Curriculo, omnium quibus nota esset deliciæ: Sexus sui
Ornamentum, parentum cura, et Mariti decus.
Parentes Pietate, Maritum amore et obsequio conjugali,
Amicos, et familiares morum suavitate, sibi
devinciens, quæ cum prolem daturam se spem haud
vanam, dedisset, partus doloribus diu quassata,
Præmatura morte surrepta est, Anno Ætatis 27° v^to^.
Octobris 1695, postquam annum et menses circiter
tres nupta esset. Magnum sui desiderium
relinquens: omnibus jure flebilis, at nulli, quam
Marito, quem unice dilexit, flebilior, qui in
Memoriam ejus perennem tumulum hunc
erigi curavit.

now living *. Sir Richard had also by his second lady three daughters, of whom, Elizabeth was wife of the Honourable John Chichester, only brother to the Earl of Donnegal, in the kingdom of Ireland, and mother of the Marquis of Donnegal; Mary, of Charles Palmer, of Ladbrooke, in the county of Warwick, Esq. mother of Charles Palmer, Esq. now living, who, by his wife, Anne Goodwyn, has two sons and one daughter; and Juliana, of John Ludford, of Ansley-Hall, in the same county, mother of John Ludford, Esq. who by his wife Elizabeth Boswell, had three daughters, and is now living. Sir Richard Newdigate died at Arbury, 1727, in his 59th year, and was buried in the family vault at Harefield †. Lady Newdigate guardian to her son Sir Roger Newdigate, continued at Arbury till he

* In memory of Sir Edward and her other sons, and their sister Jane, who also died young: Lady Newdigate their mother, erected a monument with a profile of Sir Edward Newdigate, in white marble with this inscription.

S. I.
Edvardus Newdigate,
De Arbury, in com. Warwicencsi, Baronettus,
Ob religionis cultum,
Ingenii accumen,
Facilemq. morum elegantiam
Nuper omnium deliciæ.
Avitiis et levitate juvenili alienus
Innocuæ lætitiæ amans
Honesti et Decori non immemor,
Hisce primordiis dum teneros annos consecraret,
Lentâ tabe consumptus spem suorum fefellit.
16 Ætatis suæ, anno Apr. 4th 1734
Ad latus fratris dilectissimi obdormiscunt

Ricardus	Newdigate	Ob. Apr. 16th 1732, æt. 16.
Carolus		Ob. Mar. 27th 1724, æt. 5.
Jana		Ob. Apr. 1st 1724, æt. 11.

† Where is a monument with his bust in white marble, and in a compartment underneath are the arms of Newdigate, and on the sinister side the arms of Bishopp, and on the dexter the arms of Twisden, with this inscription.

M. S.
Dni. Ricardi Newdigate,
De Arbury, in com. Warwic, Baronetti,
Vir erat sine fuco pius
Sine obsequio amicus,
Sine Fastu liberalis et beneficus,
Denique sine partium studio
Communi tam ecclesiæ quam reipublicæ
Utilitati addictus;
Munificus cleri patronus
Pater et conjux amantissimus.
Obiit 20, Julii, anno dom. 1727,
Ætat. 59.

Uxores duxit duas;
Primum Sarah
Filiam Dni. Cecilii Bishopp,
De Parham in com. Sussexiæ, Bart.
Cujus virtutes
Memorat marmor vicinum;
Secundam Elizabetham,
Filiam Dni. Rogeri Twisden,
De Bradburn, in commitatu Cantii, Bart.
Quæ domino suo superstes
Hoc monumentum,
Vidui amoris pignus
Poni curavit.

married and afterwards resided at Harefield-Place and at Astley Castle, where she died, 14th of Sept. 1765, and was buried at Harefield *.

IV Sir EDWARD NEWDIGATE, Bart. succeeded his father in title and estate: from Westminster School, he was entered at University College, Oxford, lived only to his eighteenth year, and died 1734.

V. Sir ROGER NEWDIGATE, of Harefield and Arbury, Bart. succeeded a minor, and, at his brother's death, a Kings scholar at Westminster School, where, by his own choice, he continued three years, and became a member of University College, Oxford, and made the tour of France and Italy. Soon after his return, he had the honour to be unanimously elected Knight of the shire for the county of Middlesex, upon a vacancy by the creation of the Right Honourable William Pulteney, Earl of Bath, in 1742, and in 1743, he married Sophia, daughter of Edward Conyers, of Copth-Hall, in Essex, Esq.; who, after a long continued state of ill health, died in 1774, and was buried at Harefield †. In 1749, Sir Roger Newdigate was admitted to the degree of LL. D. at Oxford, and on the 31st of January, 1750, upon a vacancy made by Lord Cornbury's being called to the house of peers, he had the high honour to be returned the first upon the poll, for

* Where is her monument; a vase of white marble with three figures in basso relievo, representing Faith Hope, and Charity, and above, on the top, a small statue of religion, as a matron, supports a cross. Upon the plinth is written,

ΤΩΝ. ΑΓΑΘΩΝ. Η. ΜΝΗΜΗ. ΑΕΙΘΑΛΗΣ

Upon a tablet of white marble below
IN Memory
Of that truly pious and good lady
Elizabeth,
Daughter of Sir Roger Twisden, of Bradbourne, in Kent, Bart.
Widow of Sir Richard Newdigate,
Of Arbury and Harefield, Baronet
Born May 31st 1681, died September 14th 1765,
Sir Roger Newdigate, Bart her son
erected this monument.
Can faith unshaken, hope's still springing bloom,
Heart-feeling charity sink in the tomb!
No! see they mount above th' empyreal sky,
On seraphs wings to never fading joy.

† Where is her monument, a white marble vase with a female figure, in basso relievo recumbent, on the top an angel leaning on an extinguished torch: on the plinth, are these lines from Petrarch.

Per me non pianger piu ch' miei di sersi
Morendo eterni e nel' eterno lume
Qando mostrai chiuder gl' occhi gli apersi!
On a tablet underneath
In memory
Of his most truly amiable, much and long loved wife
Sophia, Lady Newdigate,
Daughter of Edward Conyers, of Copped-Hall, Essex, Esquire,
By Matilda, daughter of William-Baron Lempster,
Born Dec. 20th 1718, married May 31st 1743,
Died July 9th 1774.
Sir Roger Newdigate, Baronet, with many tears,
Erected this monument.

TABLE 3.

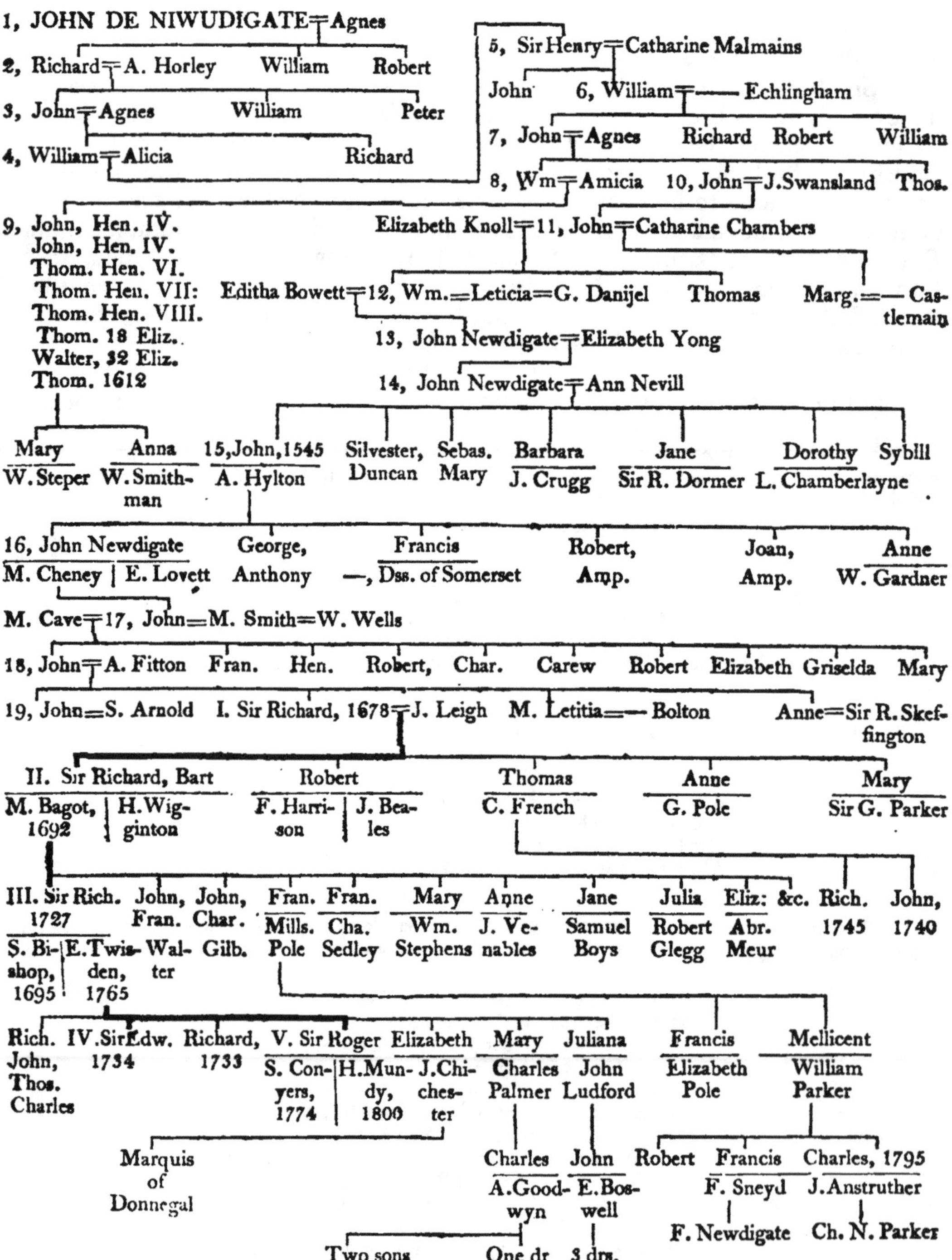
1, JOHN DE NIWUDIGATE Agnes
5, Sir Henry Catharine Malmains
2, Richard A. Horley William Robert
John 6, William —— Echlingham
3, John Agnes William Peter
7, John Agnes Richard Robert William
4, William Alicia Richard
8, Wm Amicia 10, John J.Swansland Thos.
9, John, Hen. IV.
John, Hen. IV.
Thom. Hen. VI.
Thom. Hen. VII.
Thom. Hen. VIII.
Thom. 18 Eliz.
Walter, 32 Eliz.
Thom. 1612
Elizabeth Knoll 11, John Catharine Chambers
Editha Bowett 12, Wm.=Leticia=G. Danijel Thomas Marg.=— Castlemain
13, John Newdigate Elizabeth Yong
14, John Newdigate Ann Nevill
Mary W. Steper
Anna W. Smithman
15, John, 1545 A. Hylton
Silvester, Duncan
Sebas. Mary
Barbara J. Crugg
Jane Sir R. Dormer
Dorothy L. Chamberlayne
Sybill
16, John Newdigate M. Cheney | E. Lovett
George, Anthony
Francis —, Dss. of Somerset
Robert, Amp.
Joan, Amp.
Anne W. Gardner
M. Cave 17, John=M. Smith=W. Wells
18, John A. Fitton Fran. Hen. Robert, Char. Carew Robert Elizabeth Griselda Mary
19, John=S. Arnold I. Sir Richard, 1678 J. Leigh M. Letitia=— Bolton Anne=Sir R. Skeffington
II. Sir Richard, Bart M. Bagot, 1692 | H. Wiginton
Robert F. Harrison | J. Beales
Thomas C. French
Anne G. Pole
Mary Sir G. Parker
III. Sir Rich. 1727 S. Bishop, 1695 | E. Twisden, 1765
John, Fran. Walter
John, Char. Gilb.
Fran. Mills. Pole
Fran. Cha. Sedley
Mary Wm. Stephens
Anne J. Venables
Jane Samuel Boys
Julia Robert Glegg
Eliz. Abr. Meur
&c.
Rich. 1745
John, 1740
Rich. John, Thos. Charles
IV. Sir Edw. 1734
Richard, 1733
V. Sir Roger S. Conyers, 1774 | H. Mundy, 1800
Elizabeth J. Chichester
Mary Charles Palmer
Juliana John Ludford
Francis Elizabeth Pole
Mellicent William Parker
Marquis of Donnegal
Charles A. Goodwyn
John E. Boswell
Robert
Francis F. Sneyd
Charles, 1795 J. Anstruther
Two sons One dr
3 drs.
F. Newdigate
Ch. N. Parker

a burgess for the University of Oxford. Such is the noble example of independence and untainted purity in elections, set to all electors, by that most learned and most respectable body, that to declare, to canvass, to treat, or even to be seen within the limits of the University, during a vacancy, would be, in any candidate, a forfeiture of all favour, and an uttter exclusion. By this distinguished conduct, invariably pursued, by the honour they confer on the object of their choice, they reflect the highest honour upon themselves. Thus honoured was Sir Roger Newdigate, not knowing that he was proposed, supported, and elected, till he received a letter from the vice-chancellor by one of his beadles, and in the same manner, without application or expence whatsoever, he was re-elected in 1754, and again in 1761, and in 1768: and, for the fifth time in 1774, being then absent in Italy, which he had revisited that summer. Upon the dissolution of that parliament in 1780, after 35 years service in parliament, advanced in years, and his health affected by a town life, much ill health in his family, and wishing for repose, he solicited his dismission, and retired from public life.

In 1776, he married his second lady, Hester, daughter of Edward Mundy, of Shipley, in Derbyshire, Esq. and sister to Edward Miller-Mundy, Esq. Knt. of the shire for that county, who died Sept. 30, 1800. In 1786 he built a villa, in a beautiful situation which overlooks the valley of the river Colney, with in a mile of Uxbridge.

ARMS—Three lions gambs, erased, argent, on a field, gules.
CREST—Fleur de lis, argent, swan, and horse,
MOTTO—*Confide rectè agens*, and *foyall loyall.*
SEATS—Harefield Lodge, Middlesex, Arbury and Astley Castle, Warwickshire.

---

197. POOLE, of Poole, Cheshire.

Created Baronet, Oct. 25, 1677.

THIS family is very ancient, and the stem of many eminent branches; as, the Poles, of Devonshire, and others. They are denominated, according to the custom of early times, from the lordship of Poole, in Wirrall hundred, in Cheshire; where, as Mr. Camden observes, they had lived honourably, and in a flourishing condition, many years.

1, Robert Pull *, alias Poole, alias De la Poole, lord of Barretspoole, 8 Ed. I. by Elizabeth, daughter of Hugh Raby, was father of,

2, Reginald, who was the father of,

3, James, who died, 1 Ed. II. leaving,

* Ex inf. Dom. Fra. Poole, Bar. 1726-7.

4, Robert de Pull, his son and heir, who married, 2 Rich. II. ———, the daughter and heiress of Thomas de Capenhurst.

5, Sir John de Pull, Knt. his son, lived 8 Hen. IV. and 3 Hen. V. and was father of,

6, Sir John Poole, of Poole, in Wirrall, living about 19 Rich. II. who, by ———, daughter of —— Mainwaring, of Peover, had issue, 1, Sir Thomas Poole, of Poole, Knt. lord of Poole, and Capenhurst, 35 Hen. VI.; 2, Robert Poole, who left posterity; 3, Sir Richard Poole, Knt. who had progeny; and, 4, James Poole, grandfather to John Poole, of Stratford, in Essex.

7, Sir Thomas Poole, eldest son, married Elizabeth *, daughter of Sir William Stanley, of Hooton, in Cheshire, Knt. by whom he had,

8, Thomas, who married ———, daughter of Sir Edward Fitton, of Gawsworth, in Cheshire, Knt. by whom he was father of, 1, Sir Thomas; 2, John, who died without issue; 3, Randle, a priest; 4, Sir William Poole, of Poole, Knt.; also several daughters, Elizabeth, wife of John Minshull, of Minshull, Esq.; Margaret, of Thomas Scarbridge; Elizabeth, of —— Hurliston; Blanch, of —— Bunbury, of Staney; another, of —— Billington, of Chester; another, of —— Standish; and another, of —— Whitmore, Esqrs.

9, Sir Thomas Poole, of Poole, Knt. before-mentioned, intailed all his lands on his heirs male †, and married, 11 Hen. VII. Mary, daughter of Sir John Mainwaring, of Peover.

10, Thomas, his son, living temp. Hen. VII. married ———, daughter and heiress of Thomas Dedwood, of Chester.

11, Sir Thomas, his son, married Maud, daughter of Randle Mainwaring, of Peover, by whom he had,

12, Sir William, who was sheriff of Cheshire *(durante bene placito)* 16 Hen. VIII. He married Margaret, daughter of Thomas Hough, of Leighton, by whom he had, Thomas, and a daughter, Matilda, first the wife of Sir Thomas Grosvenor, Knt. and afterwards of Robert Fletcher.

13, Thomas Poole, of Poole, Esq. married Mary, daughter of Sir John Talbot, of Grafton, Knt. by whom he had four sons, 1, John; 2, Randle, or Ranulph, who married Eleanor, daughter of Sir Henry Delves, Knt. but left no issue; 3, Thomas, who married Elizabeth, daughter of Lawrence Rope, of Stapeley; and 4, Barnabas; also three daughters, 1, Margaret, wife of George Vernon, of Richmond; 2, Elizabeth, of John Butler, of Dunstable; and 3, Frances.

15, John Poole, of Poole, Esq. eldest son, living 1566, married, first, Susan, daughter of Sir John Fitton, of Gawsworth, in Cheshire, Knt. but by her had no issue; secondly, Catharine, daughter of John Minshull, of Minshull, Esq. by whom he had four sons, 1, John; 2, William; 3, Rowland; and 4, Reginald, who married Cecily, daughter of Matthew Wood, vicar of Wibbenbury, and had issue; also four daughters, 1, Margaret, wife of Richard Skrymshire, of Norbury manor, in Staffordshire, Esq.; 2, Maude; 3, Anne, wife of John

* Ex inf. Dom. Fra. Poole, Bar. 1726-7. † Ibid.

Culchith, in Lancashire Esq.; and 4, Bridget, wife of Sir Thomas Steward, of Ely, Knt. He died Dec. 5, 1618.

15, John Poole, Esq. eldest son, married, temp. Eliz. Mary, daughter of Sir Rowland Stanley, of Hooton, Knt. sister to Margaret, wife of Sir John Egerton, of Egerton, Knt. and dying in his father's life-time, left issue, John Poole, heir to his grandfather, living 1613, Francis, who married Elizabeth, daughter of Thomas Frogge, of Minshull; and Henry; also two daughters, Mary, wife of Ralph Peshall, of Oulton, in Staffordshire, Esq. third son of Sir John Peshall, of Horseley, Bart.; and Eleanor, of John Bowes.

16, John Poole, Esq. successor to his grandfather, as before-mentioned, married Dorothy, daughter of Thomas Tildesley, of Morleys, in Lancashire, Esq. by whom he had, James, Thomas, and Margaret. He died, May, 1641.

James, son and heir, aged ten, 1613, married, first, Catharine, daughter of Sir John Talbot, of Grafton, in Worcestershire, Knt.; secondly, Catharine, daughter of Sir John Peshall, of Horsley, in Staffordshire, Bart. by whom he had a daughter, Margaret, who died unmarried. He died of his wounds, received at the siege of Chester, about 1645, and was buried at Namptwich, in Cheshire.

17, Thomas Poole, Esq. second son, and heir to his brother, James, married, first, Dorothy, daughter of John ap Meredith Vychan, of Merionethshire, Esq. by whom he had, James: he married, secondly, Ellen, daughter of Francis Draycott, of Staffordshire, Esq. by whom he had no issue. She, surviving him, was remarried to Sir Edward Mostyn, of Talacre, in Flintshire, Bart. and was buried at St. Giles's in the Fields, Middlesex.

18, James Poole, of Poole, Esq. married Mary, daughter of John, and sister of Sir Edward Mostyn, of Talacre, in Flintshire, Bart. who, surviving him, remarried with Sir William Gerard, of Garswood, in Lancashire, Bart.: by her he had issue, James, and William, who married Mrs. Hesketh. daughter of —— Hesketh, in Yorkshire, Esq.* and had issue.

I. JAMES, his eldest son, was created a Baronet by King Charles II. which title was, on failure of issue-male of his body, further limited to his brother, William, and the heirs-male of his body. He married, first †, Anne, daughter of Thomas Eyre, of Hassop, in Derbyshire, Esq. by whom he had three sons, and a daughter; John, died young; James, married Meliora, daughter of —— Gumbleton, of Kent, but had no issue; and Sir Francis, of whom hereafter; Anne, his daughter, was wife of Robert Molineux, of Mosborough, in Lancashire, Esq. His second lady was, Anne, daughter of —— Kirkham, of Devonshire, Esq. relict of Sir Thomas Escourt, of Pinkney, in Wiltshire, Knt.

* Quære, if this William was not of Birchley, in Lancashire, and married Mary, daughter of Sir Thomas Estcourt, of Cherston-Pinkney, in Wiltshire, Knt. and had issue, William, about eight years old, 1704, and other children.—*Le Neve's MSS. Vol. III. p.* 219. This William, son and heir of William, (I take it) was treasurer of the Stamp-office, and married the sister of Thomas Pelham, of Stanmer Place, in Sussex, Esq. member of parliament for Lewes, and had a brother, Edward Poole, M. D.

† Ex inf. Dom. Fra. Poole, Bar. 1726-7.

master in chancery, (she died, March, 1698, and was buried at Easton, in Cheshire); by her he had three sons, William, and Thomas, who died young, and Rowland, who married Bridget, daughter of Richard Hudleston, of Milom Castle, in Cumberland, Esq. and had issue three daughters, Bridget, Anne, and Elizabeth.

Sir James, married to his third wife, Frances, one of the daughters and coheiresses of Major-general Randolph Egerton, of Betley, in Staffordshire, (relict of Sir John Corbet, of Stoke, and Adderley, in Shropshire, Bart.) but by her had no issue. He was succeeded by his only surviving son,

II. Sir FRANCIS POOLE, Bart. who married Frances, daughter of Henry Pelham, of Lewes, in Sussex, Esq. brother to the late Lord Pelham, by whom he had two sons, Henry, and Ferdinando, successively Baronets; and one daughter, Frances, wife, Oct. 6, 1767, of Henry Temple, Lord Viscount Palmerston, who died at his lordship's house, in the Admiralty, June 1, 1769, without issue *. Sir Francis † was elected representative in parliament for Lewes, in Sussex, in 1743; and died, Feb. 16, 1763, and was succeeded by his eldest son,

III. Sir HENRY POOLE, Bart. who was appointed one of the commissioners of the Excise, in 1763, and, by a new commission, in 1765. He died, July 8, 1767, and was succeeded by his only brother,

IV. Sir FERDINANDO POOLE, Bart. who married. in 1772, ———, daughter of —— White, of Horsham, in Sussex. He was sheriff of Sussex, in 1789.

* Epitaph in Ramsey Church, Hants.

In the vault beneath are deposited the remains of Frances,
Viscountess Palmerston,
Daughter of Sir Francis Poole, Bart.
She was married to Henry, Viscount Palmerston, Oct. 6,
1767, and died in childbed, June 1, 1769.
With the nobler virtues that elevate our nature,
she possessed the softer talents that adorn it.
Pious, humble, benevolent, candid, and sincere,
she followed the dictates of humanity. And her heart
was warm with all its best affections.
Her sense was strong, her judgement accurate, her
wit engaging, and her taste refined.
While the elegance of her form, the graces of her manners,
and the natural propriety that ever accompanied
her words and actions, made her virtues doubly attracting,
and taught her equally to command respect and love.
Such she lived, and such she died, calm, and resigned to
the dispensation of heaven, leaving friends
to deplore her loss, and cherish the dear remembrance of
that worth they honoured living, and lament in death.
To the memory of the best of wives,
the best of friends,
He, for whom she joined those tender names,
dedicates this marble.

† Lodge, Vol. V. p. 244.

TABLE 4.

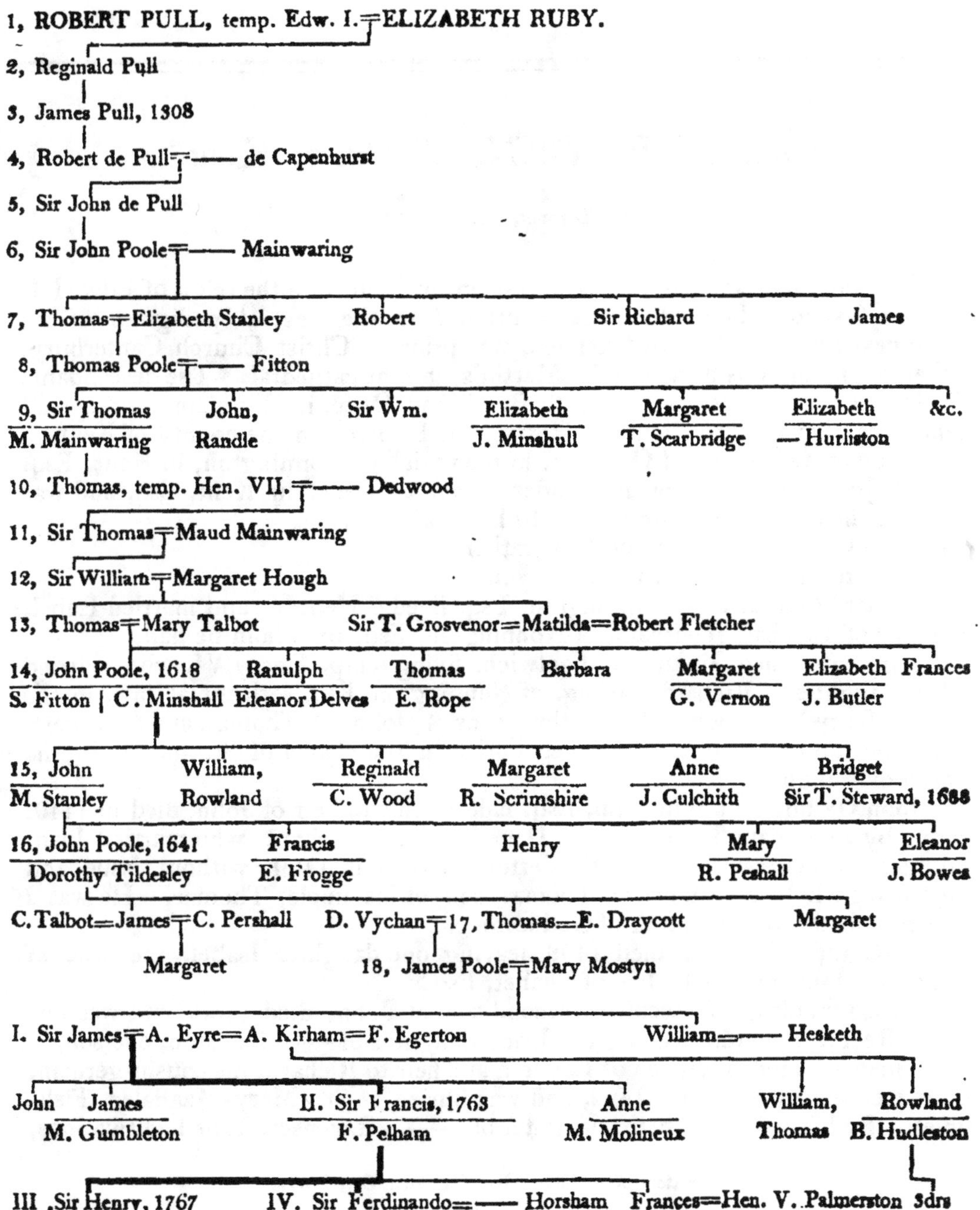
1, ROBERT PULL, temp. Edw. I.=ELIZABETH RUBY.
2, Reginald Pull
3, James Pull, 1308
4, Robert de Pull=—— de Capenhurst
5, Sir John de Pull
6, Sir John Poole=—— Mainwaring
7, Thomas=Elizabeth Stanley
Robert
Sir Richard
James
8, Thomas Poole=—— Fitton
9, Sir Thomas
M. Mainwaring
John,
Randle
Sir Wm.
Elizabeth
J. Minshull
Margaret
T. Scarbridge
Elizabeth
— Hurliston
&c.
10, Thomas, temp. Hen. VII.=—— Dedwood
11, Sir Thomas=Maud Mainwaring
12, Sir William=Margaret Hough
13, Thomas=Mary Talbot
Sir T. Grosvenor=Matilda=Robert Fletcher
14, John Poole, 1618
S. Fitton | C. Minshall
Ranulph
Eleanor Delves
Thomas
E. Rope
Barbara
Margaret
G. Vernon
Elizabeth
J. Butler
Frances
15, John
M. Stanley
William,
Rowland
Reginald
C. Wood
Margaret
R. Scrimshire
Anne
J. Culchith
Bridget
Sir T. Steward, 1688
16, John Poole, 1641
Dorothy Tildesley
Francis
E. Frogge
Henry
Mary
R. Peshall
Eleanor
J. Bowes
C. Talbot=James=C. Pershall
Margaret
D. Vychan=17, Thomas=E. Draycott
Margaret
18, James Poole=Mary Mostyn
I. Sir James=A. Eyre=A. Kirham=F. Egerton
William=—— Hesketh
John
James
M. Gumbleton
II. Sir Francis, 1763
F. Pelham
Anne
M. Molineux
William,
Thomas
Rowland
B. Hudleston
III. Sir Henry, 1767
IV. Sir Ferdinando=—— Horsham
Frances=Hen. V. Palmerston
3drs

ARMS—Azure, semée of fleurs-de-lis, or, a lion rampant, argent.
CREST—In a ducal coronet, or, a griffin's head, argent.
SEATS—At Poole, in Wirrall, Cheshire; and at the Friery, in Lewes, Sussex.

---

198. OXENDEN, of Dene, Kent.

Created Baronet, May 8, 1678.

THE family of Oxenden have been resident in Kent from the reign of Edw. III. Solomon Oxenden being the first mentioned in the several pedigrees of it; whose near relation, Richard Oxenden, was prior of Christ Church Canterbury, in that reign, and was buried in St. Martin's, in that cathedral. The descendants of Solomon became possessed of both Brook and Dene, in Wingham, and spread themselves likewise into Riculver, Herne, and Burham, in the county of Kent.

1, Solomon Oxinden*, of Oxinden, in the parish of Nonnington, in Kent, Esq. married Joyce, daughter of Alexander Dene, of Dene, in Kent, Esq, and was buried in the church of Nonnington, 40 Edw. III. leaving,

2, Alan Oxinden, his son and heir, father of

3, Richard living 10 Ric. II. whose son,

4, Richard Oxinden, of Nonnington, Esq. lived 6 Hen. V. and married Isabel, daughter of Theobald Twitham, of Nonnington, Esq, by whom he had,

5, John, surnamed Ginkin, of Woolwich, living temp. Henry VI. who married Isabel, daughter of Richard Ratling, of Nonnington, Esq. serjeant at law, in the reign of Henry VI. by whom he had three sons, 1, John; 2, Thomas, and 3, Robert. John, the father of these sons, lies buried in the chapel of St. John's, in the church of Wingham.

6, John Oxinden, of Wingham, Esq. eldest son and heir of John, died in 1440, leaving by Jane, daughter of——— Dene, one son, Richard, who married Joan, daughter and heiress of——— Wenderton, he died in 1469, without issue and and left his whole inheritance to Thomas, son of his uncle, Thomas. He was a good benefactor to the church of Godnestone.

Robert, the third son, died 1498, leaving one daughter Isabel, the wife of Nicholas Sprackling, of the Isle of Thahet, Esq.

Thomas Oxinden, of Recolver, second son of John, died 1450, and was buried in Reculver church, leaving by Joan, daughter of——— Urleston, one son,

8, Thomas Oxinden, citizen of London, and heir to Richard, his cousin-german, before mentioned, who died 1492, and was buried at St. Mary-Magdalen, Fish-Street. By his wife, Elizabeth, daughter of——— Ravenscroft, he had two sons,

* Ex stem penes Dom. Geo. Oxenden, Bar. 1741.

1, Edward Oxinden, of Broke, of whom hereafter; 2, William, who married Anne, daughter of ———, and relict of ——— Macket, of Hode; but died without issue, leaving his whole inheritance to his nephew, Henry Oxinden, of Broke, Esq.

9, Edward Oxinden, of Broke, in Wingham, lived in the reigns of King Henry VIII. Edward VI. Queen Mary, and Queen Elizabeth. He married Alice, daughter of ——— Barton, by whom he had one daughter, Mary, wife of Thomas Hardres, of Hardres, in Kent, Esq. and two sons, 1, William Oxinden, of Broke, his eldest son and heir, who married Elizabeth, daughter of ——— Hill, but died 1576, without issue.

10, Henry Oxinden, of Dene, Esq. second son of Edward, married two wives; by his second, Thomasine, daughter of Vincent Sea, he had no issue; but by his first wife, Elizabeth, daughter of ——— Young, relict of ——— Herne, who died 1588, he had five sons; 1, Edward, who was heir to his uncle, William, of Broke, who married Alice, daughter of Edmund Fowler, of Islington, in Middlesex, Esq. sister to Sir Thomas Fowler, Knt. by whom he had a numerous issue, the male branch whereof is now extinct, but the female descendants are now remaining at Broke; 2, Sir Henry Oxinden, Knt. of whom hereafter, 3, Thomas; 4, Christopher; and 5, William, who married Mary, daughter of Bartholomew Saunders, of Minster, in Thanet; which three last died without issue.

11, Sir Henry Oxinden, of Dene in Wingham, second son of Henry, before mentioned, was knighted Feb. 17, 1606. He married two wives; by the second, Mary, daughter of ——— Theobald, he left no issue; but by his first, Elizabeth, daughter and heiress of James Broker, of Maydekin, in Barham, in Kent, Esq. who died Sept. 2, 1588, he had two sons, 1, Sir James; 2, Richard Oxinden, of Maydekin, who died May 20, 1629, leaving, by Catharine, daughter of Sir Adam Sprackling, of Canterbury, Knt. a numerous progeny, whose male issue are now extinct.

12, Sir James Oxinden, of Dene, eldest son and heir of Sir Henry, was knighted at Whitehall, Nov. 17, 1608, and died Sept. 1657, leaving by Margaret, daughter of Thomas Nevinson, of Estry, in Kent, Esq. five sons, 1, Sir Henry; 2, James, who died unmarried, 1638; 3, Sir George Oxinden, Knt. Governor of the Island and fort of Bombay, and president of the honourable East-India Company in India, Persia, and Arabia. He lies buried at Surat, where there is a stately monument erected to his memory by the East-India Company*; 4, William, who died young; 5, Christopher, who was a merchant, and died at the East-Indies in 1659, and lies buried at Surat. Sir James had also five daughters, 1, Anne, wife of Richard Master, of East-Langdon, in Kent, Esq. 2, Mary; 3, Elizabeth; 4, Margaret; and, 5, Jane, wife of Sir Thomas Pierce, of Stonepit, in Kent, Bart. of N.S.

I. Sir HENRY OXINDEN, of Dene, the eldest son and heir, was knighted July 11, 1660, and advanced to the dignity of a Baronet 30 Car. II. He was elected to parliament for Sandwich, in the first parliament of Char. II. and married first, Mary, daughter and heiress of Robert Baker, of St. Martin's in the Fields, Esq. by whom he had only one daughter that died young; secondly, Elizabeth,

* In 1660, he gave the velvet cushion and pulpit cloth at the church of Wingham. He also gave, in 1682, five hundred pounds for the repairing and beautifying the said church and the Dene chancel.—*Hist. of Kent*, Vol. III. P. 696.

daughter of Sir William Meredith, of Leeds-abbey, in Kent, Bart. who died 1659, by whom he had several sons, and six daughters; 1, Sir James, his successor, 2, Sir Henry, successor to his brother; 3, George Oxenden, L.L. D. who was first, fellow of Trinity College, where after he had taken the degree of doctor of laws, admitted an advocate of the arches court, afterwards regius professor of law in the same university. Upon the death of Sir Thomas Exton, he was made official of the arches, dean of the peculiars, and vicar-general to the archbishop of Canterbury, he likewise succeeded him in the mastership of Trinity-hall; and and was elected to parliament for Cambridge university, temp. King William III. He married Elizabeth, daughter of Sir Basil Dixwell, of Broome, Bart. by whom he had three sons, Sir Henry, of whom hereafter; James, who died an infant; and Sir George, who was successor to his brother; Dr. Oxenden, died Feb. 21, 1702, at Doctors-Commons, and his relict at Bath, Sept. 1704; 4, Richard, of Gray's-Inn, who married Elizabeth, daughter and coheiress of Henry Oxinden, of Broke, Esq.; by whom he had only one daughter, Elizabeth, the wife of Strensham Masters, Esq. brother to the countess of Torrington, who was a commander of several of his majesty's ships of war, by whom she had no issue *; 5, William, 6, William who died infants; and 7, Christopher, who died in the East-Indies. Of the daughters, 1, Susan, wife of Sir Robert Booth, Knt. chief-justice of Ireland; 2, Elizabeth; 3, Margaret, who both died unmarried; 4, Jane, wife of William Penrice, of London; 5, Anne, of Thomas Belk, D. D. prebendary of Canterbury; and 6, Mary, of Dr. John Battley, archdeacon of Canterbury. The third lady of Sir Henry, was Elizabeth, daughter and coheir of Mathew Read, of Folkston, in Kent, Esq. relict of Mark Dixwell, of Broomehouse, Esq. by whom he had no issue. Sir Henry was succeeded in title and estate by his eldest son.

II. Sir JAMES OXENDEN, knighted March 22, 1671, married first, Elizabeth, daughter, and, at length, heiress of Edward Chute, of Bethersden, in Kent, Esq.; secondly, Arabella Watson, sister of Lewis, Earl of Rockingham; but leaving no issue by either of them, was succeeded in title and estate, Sept. 1708, § by his next brother,

III. Sir HENRY OXENDEN, Bart. who was a deputy-governor of the honourable East-India company in the island, castle, and port of Bombay; but dying Feb. 1708-9, without issue, was succeeded in title and estate by his nephew,

IV. Sir HENRY OXENDEN, Bart. eldest son of Dr. George Oxenden before mentioned, who was a member of parliament for Sandwich at his death 1720. He married Anne, daughter of John Halloway, Esq. and grand-daughter of judge

* He gave an annuity of four pounds a year for ever to the minister of this parish for the reading of divine service, and preaching a sermon in the church at Wingham, on every Wednesday in Lent, and Good Friday; and he at the same time gave twenty shillings yearly for ever, to be distributed by the minister with the consent of the heirs of the Brook estate, to eight poor people, who should be at divine service on Easter Day, to be paid out of the lands of Brook, now vested in Sir Henry Oxenden, Bart.

Mrs. Sybilla Oxenden, of Brook, spinster, gave a large silver patten for the holy communion.—*Hist. of Kent*, Vol. III.

§ He founded and endowed a school in the parish of Dene with 16l. a year for ever, for teaching twenty poor children reading and writing, now in the patronage of Sir Henry Oxenden, Bart.—*Hist. of Kent*, Vol. III.

Halloway, by whom he had no issue; she surviving him, was remarried to the Right Honourable Richard Coote, Earl of Bellamont, in Ireland, whereupon the dignity and estate devolved upon his only brother,

V. Sir GEORGE OXENDEN, Bart. who was born Oct. 26, 1694, and married 1729, Elizabeth, eldest daughter and coheiress of Edmund Dunch, of Little S. Wittenham, Berkshire, Esq. then master of the household to King George I. she died in Feb. 1779, by whom he had issue, three sons and two daughters, who died infants or unmarried, except Henry his successor; George, the youngest son, was made heir to the estate of Sir Basil Dixwell, of Broome, in Berham, in Kent, Bart. by his last will; and changed his name to that of Dixwell; but dying Oct. 20, 1753, demised his mansion-seat at Broome, and his lands to his father, Sir George who gave them to his son the present Bart. Sir George was elected member of parliament for Sandwich, in 1720, in the room of his brother, Sir Henry deceased, and continued to sit for that place till the year 1734. He was made one of the admirality by King George I. 1725, and upon the demise of the said king, 1727, was by George II. promoted to the treasury, at which honourable board, he sat for the space of ten years and upwards: Sir George died Feb. 20, 1775, aged 81, and was succeeded by his son,

VI. Sir HARRY OXENDEN, Bart. who married in July 1755, Margaret, younger daughter and coheiress of Sir George Chudleigh, of Halden, near Exeter, Bart. by whom he has one son Henry who married June 20, 1795, Mary, daughter of Colonel Graham, of St. Laurence, near Canterbury.

ARMS—Argent, a cheveron, gules, between three oxen, sable; which arms were confirmed to this family by Guyan, King at arms, Feb. 1, 24 Hen. VI.

CREST—Out of a ducal coronet, gules, a lion's head or.

SEAT—At Wingham, in Kent.

In Wingham church, the south chancel is called the Dene chancel, under which is a vault, in which the family of Oxenden, owners of it, are deposited. In the middle, on the pavement, is a very costly pyramidical monument, having at each corner four large black oxen's heads, in allusion to their arms: it was erected in 1682. On the four tablets on the base is an account of the family of Oxenden, beginning with Henry, who built Dene-house, and ending with Dr. Oxenden, dean of the arches, who died in 1702.

The north chancel is called Brook chancel, in which is a small tablet at the east end, for Sir James Oxenden, Knt. obiit, 1657; Elizabeth, wife of Sir Henry Oxenden, Knt. and Bart. obiit 1659; William, their son, obiit 1661; Susanna, their daughter, wife of Sir Robert Booth, obiit 1669; and Margaret, relict of Sir James Oxendeh, obiit 1671; Elizabeth, daughter of Sir James Oxenden; and Elizabeth, his wife, 1675.

Henry Oxenden, who built Dene, obiit 1597.—*Hist. of Kent*, Vol. III. p. 702.

TABLE 5.

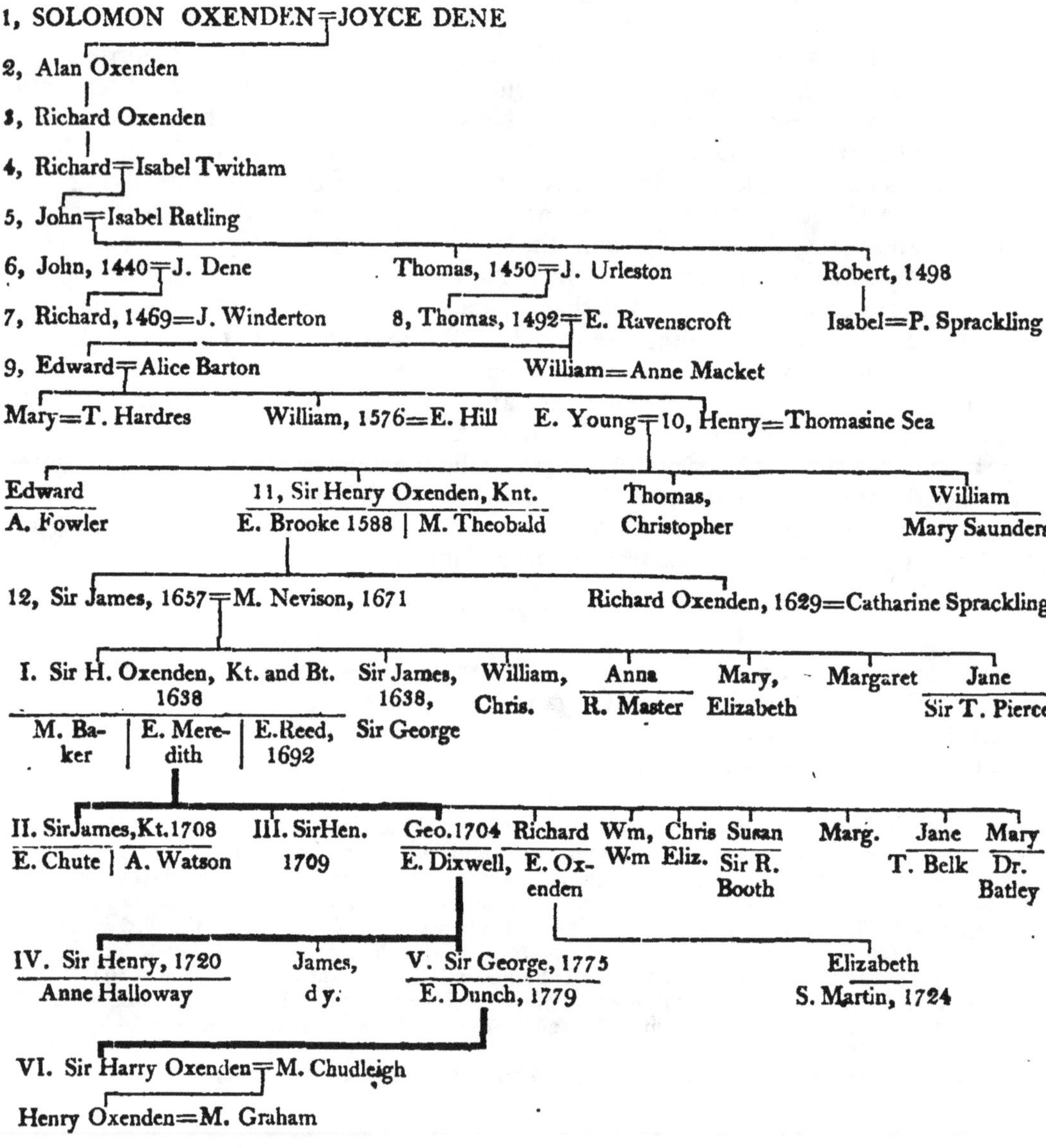

1, SOLOMON OXENDEN = JOYCE DENE
2, Alan Oxenden
3, Richard Oxenden
4, Richard = Isabel Twitham
5, John = Isabel Ratling
6, John, 1440 = J. Dene — Thomas, 1450 = J. Urleston — Robert, 1498
7, Richard, 1469 = J. Winderton — 8, Thomas, 1492 = E. Ravenscroft — Isabel = P. Sprackling
9, Edward = Alice Barton — William = Anne Macket
Mary = T. Hardres — William, 1576 = E. Hill — E. Young = 10, Henry = Thomasine Sea
Edward = A. Fowler — 11, Sir Henry Oxenden, Knt. = E. Brooke 1588 | M. Theobald — Thomas, Christopher — William = Mary Saunders
12, Sir James, 1657 = M. Nevison, 1671 — Richard Oxenden, 1629 = Catharine Sprackling
I. Sir H. Oxenden, Kt. and Bt. 1638 = M. Baker | E. Meredith | E. Reed, 1692 — Sir James, 1638, Sir George — William, Chris. — Anna = R. Master — Mary, Elizabeth — Margaret — Jane = Sir T. Pierce
II. Sir James, Kt. 1708 = E. Chute | A. Watson — III. Sir Hen. 1709 — Geo. 1704 = E. Dixwell, — Richard = E. Oxenden — Wm, Wm — Chris Eliz. — Susan = Sir R. Booth — Marg. — Jane = T. Belk — Mary = Dr. Batley
IV. Sir Henry, 1720 = Anne Halloway — James, d y. — V. Sir George, 1775 = E. Dunch, 1779 — Elizabeth = S. Martin, 1724
VI. Sir Harry Oxenden = M. Chudleigh
Henry Oxenden = M. Graham

199. DYER, of Tottenham, Middlesex.

Created Baronet, July 6, 1678.

I. WILLIAM DYER, Esq. was a younger brother of a family of this name at Heytesbury, in Wiltshire*. He was bred to the law, and was of the Inner-Temple, London; though he had a good paternal estate, which he increased by his industry. But the greatest accession to his fortune, was his marrying Thomasine †, sole daughter and heiress of Thomas Swinnerton, of Stanwey-hall, in Essex, Esq. third son and heir of the famous Sir John Swinnerton, Knt. Lord-mayor of the city of London, a younger branch of the ancient and noble family of the Swinnertons, of Shropshire, formerly peers of this realm; this match brought above 30,000l. into the family. He was advanced to the dignity of a Baronet, 30 Car. II. and died Jan. 27, 1680, leaving behind him the character of a learned and religious gentleman; and was interred at Newnham, in Hertfordshire, where he had a seat. He had four sons, and three daughters; of which only four survived him, two sons, Sir John Swinnerton, and William, and two daughters, Joanna, wife of Thomas Griffith, of Denbighshire, Esq. and Sarah, of John Hooke, of Gaunt's-house, in Dorsetshire, Esq. barrister at law. His lady, who survived, was afterwards, Aug. 8, 1683, the wife of John Hopwood, of Stanwey-hall, Esq, (descended from the ancient family of Hopwood, of Hopwood, in Lancashire). She was a very religious and charitable lady, and died Aug. 13, 1697, being, according to her desire, buried at Newnham church, near to the body of her first husband; where are monuments erected for them both ‡.

* Ex inf. Wil. Holman, de Halstead, com. Essex, Gen. 1741.

† Ibid.

‡ Chauncy's Hertf, p. 521.

Here lieth the Body of Sir William Dyer, Bart.
Who departed this Life the 27th of January, 1680, he
married the Grand-daughter and sole Heiress to Sir
John Swinnerton, once Lord-Mayor of the City of
London, had issue by her, four sons and three
Daughters, whereof four is now living, viz. two
Sons and two Daughters: he was a true Christian,
An upright Liver, a faithful Husband, a tender Father,
and Lord of this Manor of Newnham.

Here under lies, now buried, in this Dust,
The Man, whose Life was sober, pure, and just.

Against the chancel's south wall, is a monument for

The Lady Thomasine Dyer, Relict of Sir
William Dyer, of Tottenham High-Cross, in Middlesex,
Bart. Grand-daughter of Sir John Swinnerton. She died
April 13, 1697. 73 Years of Age.

William Dyer, Esq. second son of Sir William aforesaid, had the estate at Newnham, in Hertfordshire, left him by his father, where he built a noble seat, and was high-sheriff of that county the latter end of the reign of King William. He * married, first, Mary, daughter of —— Howard, Esq. with whom he had a considerable fortune, but by her had only one child, which not long survived her: he married to his second wife, Anne †, youngest daughter of Sir Thomas Hooke, of Tangier-Park-House, in Hants, Bart. and one of the three coheiresses to her brother, Sir Hele Hooke; by her he had three sons, and two daughters. But to return to,

II. Sir JOHN-SWINNERTON DYER, Bart. eldest son and heir of Sir William, before-mentioned, who succeeded his father, lived at Newton-hall, and married Elizabeth, daughter of Rowland Johnson, of Gray's-Inn, Esq. by whom he had five sons, 1, John-Swinnerton, who died unmarried; 2, Sir Swinnerton; 3, Sir John-Swinnerton; 4, William; 5, Thomas; and four daughters, 1, Elizabeth; 2, Joanna; 3, Anne; and 4, Mary. He died May 17, 1701, aged 44, and lies buried in the church of Great Dunmow, under a marble monument.

III. Sir SWINNERTON DYER, Bart. (his elder brother, John, dying before his father, unmarried), succeeded to the title and estate. He was a gentleman-commoner of Bennett college, in Cambridge, and married Anne, fourth daughter of Edward Belitha, of Kingston-upon-Thames, in Surry, Esq. by whom he had only one daughter, Anne, wife of Paul Whitehead, Gent. His lady died, Aug. 21, 1714, aged thirty-three, and lies buried on the south side of the chancel of Dunmow church ‡.

Sir Swinnerton married, secondly, Dec. 1727, a sister and heiress of John Kempe, of Spain's-hall, in Finchinfield, in Essex, Esq. by whom he had no issue. She died at Bath, Oct. 1730; and Sir Swinnerton, at Kensington, in March 4, 1735-6, and was succeeded by his next brother,

IV. Sir JOHN-SWINNERTON DYER, Bart. married Elizabeth, daughter of Major Jones, by whom he had two sons, Sir John-Swinnerton, the late Baronet; and Thomas, a clerk in the Treasury, who married ———, daughter of —— Grant, by whom he had three children, and died in 1800; and one daughter, Elizabeth. Sir John-Swinnerton Dyer died Sept. 1780, and was succeeded by his eldest son,

* Ex inf. Wil. Holman, de Halstead, com. Essex, Gen. 1741, † Ibid.

‡ Le Neve's Mon. Ang. vol. IV. p. 277.

Under this Stone lies deposited the Body of
Anne, late Lady of Sir Swinnerton Dyer, Bart.
of Newton-hall, in the County of Essex, and
4th Daughter of Edward Belitha, of Kingston
upon Thames, in the County of Surry, Esq.
As she always shewed herself dutiful to her Parents,
So the Duties of Love and Obedience, Fidelity, Modesty, and
Chastity, Comfort, and Help, friendly and kind Society and
Conversation, she prudently paid to her Husband.
She died Aug. 21, 1714, Aged 33 Years; leaving her
disconsolate Husband only one Child, a Daughter,
named Anne.

V. Sir JOHN-SWINNERTON DYER, Bart. who was colonel in the army, captain of a company in the guards, and groom of the bed-chamber to his Royal Highness George, Prince of Wales. He married ——, daughter of —— Vicary, by whom he had one son, Thomas-Richard-Swinnerton, his successor, and one daughter, Eleanor. June 1801, Sir John-Swinnerton Dyer was succeeded by his only son *,

VI. Sir THOMAS-RICHARD-SWINNERTON DYER, the present Baronet.

ARMS—Or, a chief indented, gules.

CREST—Out of a ducal coronet, or, a goat's head, sable, armed of the first.

SEAT—At Spain's-hall, in Finchinfield, in Essex.

TABLE.

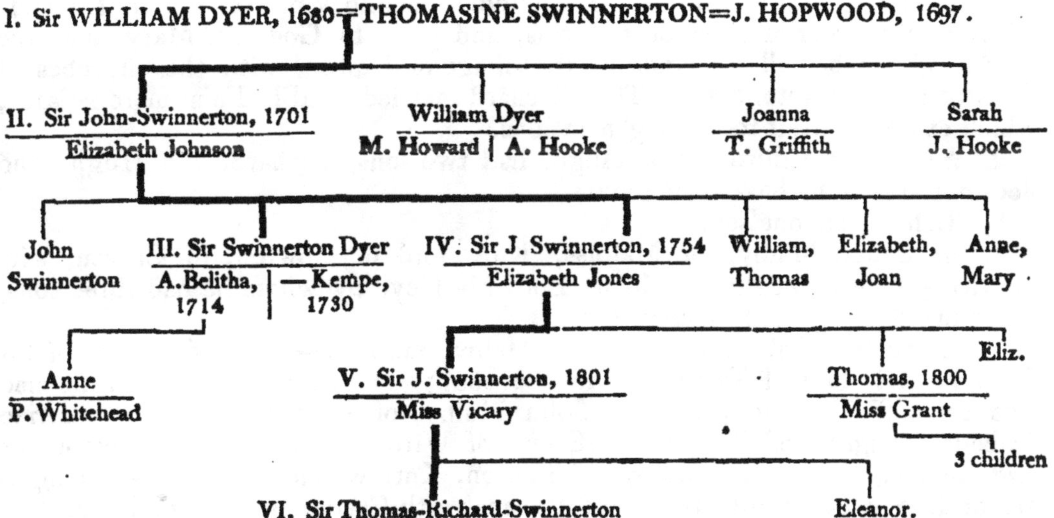

* Sir John, in a fit of insanity, shot himself with a pistol. He had become melancholy, since the death of his only brother, about a year before, whom he affectionately loved. His melancholy increased by the absence of his son, who went out aid-de-camp to Sir Ralph Abercromby, in the expedition to Egypt. He was disappointed of letters, which he had, for some time, impatiently expected, and which did not arrive till two days after this unfortunate event. Sir John was formerly a colonel in the Guards. His character, as a master, a father, a brother, and a friend, was truly excellent and exemplary.

Mont. Mag. Jan. 1, 1801.

200. BECKWITH, of Aldbrough, Yorkshire.

Created Baronet, April 15, 1681.

1, HUGO DE MALEBISSE *, *frater Ricardi, testis anno* 3 *Stephani*, 1138, married, first, Emma, daughter and coheiress of William de Percy, and of Adalid de Tonbridge: he married, secondly, Maud, daughter of —— Knyveton, of Knyveton, by whom he had no issue; but by his first wife he had three sons, 1, Hugo de Malebisse, 3 Ric. I. 1 John, *Justiciarius ad assisas*; 1 Hen. III. 1216, he paid twenty marks composition for the plea of the forest; he married two wives, but died without issue; 2, Richard, the second son of Hugo, was *Justiciarius ad assisas*, 4 John, 1203; 2 Ric. I. he paid twenty pounds to be forester, as he had been in the time of King Henry. 1 John, he paid five pounds for the farm of Gultres. He founded the abbey of Newbo, in Lincolnshire, of the order of Præmonstratensis, and gave to God, St. Mary, and the canons of Newbo, all his lands in the village of Newbo, with the churches of Acastor and Knyveton, &c. This Richard married, and had a numerous issue, which extended itself to many generations.

2, William, the third son of Hugo, had two sons, Richard, and Hugh, who does not appear to have issue; but,

3, Richard left one son,

4, Sir Simon Malby, or Malbiss, Knt. lord of Cowton, in Craven, who married ———, daughter of John, Lord Methley, by whom he had three sons, 1, John; 2, Roger; 3, Hercules †.

5, Hercules, third son of Sir Simon Malby, married ———, daughter of Sir John Ferrers, lord of Tamworth, in the county of Stafford, by whom he had two sons, Sir Hercules, and Sir John Malby, of Stanton, Knt. who married Isabella, daughter of Sir. William Evers, of Witton Castle, Knt. by whom he had one son, Sir William Malby, of Stanton, Knt. who married ———, daughter of Henry Bacon Fitz-Hugh, of Ravensworth Castle, but had no issue.

* The account of this family is chiefly taken from the original pedigree, done on vellum, and finely illuminated, which is now in the possession of Sir Roger Beckwith, Bart. and was entered in the visitation of Yorkshire, April 9, 1666, at Doncaster, by Sir William Dugdale, Norroy King of Arms.

† John, the eldest, married ———, daughter of Sir Allen Zouch, Knt. by whom he had Sir John Malbie, lord of Cowton, who married ———, the daughter of Sir John Audbrow, of Audbrow, by whom he had John Lord Malbie, who married ———, daughter of Sir Edmund Walstrope, by whom he had three daughters; from the eldest, Margaret, 7 Edw. II. 1314, descended Thomas Fairfax, of Walton, Esq. 2, Roger, second son of Sir Symon, married ———, daughter of Sir Hugh Haigh, by whom he had Ambrose, who married Timothea, daughter of Sir John Pensax, Knt. by whom he had Edward Malbie, who married ——, daughter of Sir Hugh Copley, Knt. and died without issue.

6, Sir Hercules, eldest son of Hercules before-mentioned, married Dame Beckwith Bruce, daughter of Sir William Bruce, lord of Uglebarnby; when Sir Hercules was obliged, by marriage covenants, dated 10 Hen. III. to change his name to Beckwith. He left one son,

7, Nicholas, who married ——, daughter of Sir John Chaworth, Knt. by whom he had one son,

8, Hamond, who was obliged to take the name of Beckwith, by virtue of the marriage contract between his grandfather, Sir Hercules, and Dame Beckwith Bruce, his wife, when it was agreed, he should either do that, or else his coat of armour; but he chose to retain the latter *.

This Hamon Beckwith, Esq. was seised of the lordship of Clint, bounding of the north side of Nid, juxta Hampesthwait, and of Uglebarnby, in Whitby-Strand, certain lands in Pickering and Roxbie, with the manor of Beckwith and Beckwithshaw, 13 Edw. III. 1339. He married ——, daughter of Sir Philip Tilney, Knt. by whom he had three sons, 1, William Beckwith, of Beckwith, Esq. of whom hereafter; 2, Thomas; 3, John, from whom descended the Beckwiths, of Scough, now extinct: also four daughters, 1, ——, wife of Sir John Filiot, Knt.; 2, ——, of Sir William Cathorp, Knt.; 3, Anne, of Williom Trevile, Esq.; 4, ——, first, of William Constable, and secondly, of William Banvile, Esqrs.

9, William Beckwith, of Beckwith, Esq. son and heir, married ——, daughter of Si. Gerard Ufflet, of Wighill, in Yorkshire, Knt. by whom he had three sons, 1, Thomas; 2, Hercules, who married ——, daughter of William Waldgrave, Esq.; 3, John, who married ——, daughter of Sir John Ratcliffe, of Cresall, Knt. This William was seised of the manor of Beckwith and Beckwithshaw, 38 Edw. III. 1364, and was succeeded by his son,

10, Thomas Beckwith, who married ——, daughter of John Sawley, of

* "Be it known to all nobles where this present writing shall come, be seen, or heard: Whereas Hammon Beckwith, Esq. son and heir of Nicholas Beckwith, was warned by the earl-marshal of England, by process, that was dated from the aforesaid earl-marshal's manor of Ryseing Castle, in the county of Norfolk, Jan. 18, in the 13th year of the reign of our sovereign lord the king, in the year of Our Lord 1339, that the said Hammon Beckwith should usurp, and take unto him, a coat of arms, which was appertaining unto John, Lord Malbie; for which better use, by virtue of this process, we charge you, that you will appear at the now mansion-house, and manor of Saymor, before us, and bring with you all such evidence and records of arms, that we may allow, grant, and set our hands to your teste and posterity for ever. And also, that your appearance shall be the 14th day of October next coming, in the aforesaid year above written.

"And the said orator did appear at the said day appointed, and did bring with him such evidence; whereof one piece, bearing date from the 10th year of Hen. III. which was in the year of Our Lord 1226, from one Hercules Malbie, the third son of Sir Symon Malbie, Knt. which married the Lady Dame Beckwith Bruce, one of the daughters of Sir William Bruce, Lord of Uglebarnby, and certain lands in Pickering, that the said Hercules should change his name, or else his coat, and his posterity for ever; and so it was that the said Hercules changed his name from Malbie to Beckwith, and did hold his coat: whereof I, the said earl-marshal, Peter Mawlam, Lord of de Luke, lord-chamberlain to our sovereign lord King Edward III. and Henry, Lord Percy, Sir Robert Boynton, Knt. and Sir William Acton, did see and allow of it in due proof, and the aforesaid coat to be his own, lineally descended, whereof we have set our hands and seals to the aforesaid teste, the day and year above written, in the presence of many."

Saxton, in Yorkshire, by whom he had two sons, 1, William; 2, John, who married Amye, daughter of Arthur Chambers, Esq. by whom he had one daughter, Amye, wife of John Padslew, Esq. living 3 Hen. VI. 1424; and three daughters, 1, Margaret, wife of Richard Hulse, Esq.; 2, Anne, of John Chancy, Esq.; and 3, Amye, of Thomas Santon, Esq.

11, Sir William Beckwith, of Clint, Knt. son and heir, seised also of the manor of Beckwith and Beckwithshaw, married ——, daughter of Sir John Baskervile, Knt. by whom he had one son,

12, Thomas, his son and heir, who married ——, daughter of Sir William Haslerton, Knt. in whose right he was lord of the third part of the moiety of Fylemaston and Thorp, by whom he had five sons, 1, Thomas; 2, William; 3, John; 4, Adam; 5, Robert; and two daughters, Ellen, wife of John Vavasor, of Weston, Esq. who made his will, 1461; and Joan, of Thomas Althere, Esq. Thomas, the eldest son, married ——, daughter of William Ingleby, of Ripley, in Yorkshire, and died without issue, 1478. Sir William, second son, and heir to his brother, married, first, ——, daughter of Sir William Plumpton, of Plumpton, Knt. living 1456, by whom he had one son, William-Gascoigne, who died, 16 Edw. IV. 1476, leaving no issue by his wife, Janetta, daughter of William Beckwith, of Clint, Esq.: he married, secondly, ——, daughter of Sir John Ratcliff, K. G. by whom he had no issue. This Sir William was made knight-banneret in Scotland, by the Duke of Gloucester. 20 Edw. IV. 1480. John Beckwith, third son of Thomas, of whom hereafter, Adam, fourth son, married Amy, daughter of William Redman, of Harwood Castle, Esq. and died without issue; Robert, the fifth son, married Barbara, daughter of John Leventhorp, Esq. by whom he had John and Mary: which John was ancestor to Sir Leonard Beckwith, high-sheriff of Yorkshire, 4 Edw. VI. and to Ambrose Beckwith, of Stillingfleet, near York, which Sir Leonard served Hen. VIII. in the French wars, and afterwards was servant to Edw. VI. and had the scite of the abbey of Selby granted him, 4 Edw. VI. He married Elizabeth, daughter and coheiress of Sir Roger Cholmley, Knt. by whom he had two sons, Roger and Rancy, who died without issue: and two daughters, Elizabeth, wife of William Vavasor, of Weston, in Yorkshire, Esq.; and Frances, wife of Geo. Harvey, of Marks, in Essex, by whom they had issue Ellen.

13, John Beckwith, the third son of Thomas, married ——, daughter of Thomas Ratcliffe, of Mulgrave, by whom he had two sons, Thomas, heir to his uncle Sir William; he married Maud, daughter of Henry Pudsey, of Berford, in Richmondshire, Esq. from whom descended the Beckwiths, of Clint, who continued there till 1655, when Huntingdon Beckwith, Esq. the last of that branch, died.

14, Robert Beckwith, Esq. (son of the last-mentioned John), of Boxholm, near Ripley, in Yorkshire, confirmed to John, his son, all his lands in the town of Thorpe, near Ripon, which he had with John, his father, of the gift and feoffment of John Beckwith, son of John Beckwith, of Tolleston, 8 Edw. IV. 1468, He was succeeded by his son,

15, John Beckwith, who left one son,

16, Robert Beckwith, of Dacre, near Ripley, who made his will Oct. 6, 1536, and left two sons, Robert, who is supposed to have died unmarried, and

17, Marmaduke, of Dacre, who sold lands in Clint, and purchased Acton, or Ackton, and the manor of Featherston, near Pontefract. He married, first, Anne, daughter of Robert Dynely, of Bramhope, near Otley, in Yorkshire, Esq. secondly, Ellen, relict of William Style, of Hadockson, in the same county, Esq. by whom he had no issue, but by his first wife, he had four sons and seven daughters, 1, Thomas, of Acton, Esq. living 1612, married Frances, daughter and heiress of William Frost, of Aicton, from whom descended the Beckwiths, of Aicton, now extinct; 2, William, of Dacre-Pasture, from whom descended the Beckwiths, of Kirby-Milzard, and those of Bueerly, of which last family was John Beckwith, a major in the king of Prussia's service, in 1771. From this William are also descended the Beckwiths, of Lamb-Hall, High-Burton, and Masham; 3, Roger Beckwith, sold his lands in Clint, and purchased Aldbrough, and died Jan. 19, 1634, but of him more hereafter; 4, Simon; of the daughters, 1, Jane, wife of John Thorp, of Danthorpe, in Yorkshire, captain of a troop of horse, 1665; 2, Barbara, of Matthew Lockwood, of Sowerby, near Thirsk, Esq.; 3, Dorothy; 4, Grace, of John Nesfield, of Hasby-in-Craven, Yorkshire; 5, Catharine, of Henry Pudsey, of Arnsforth, in the same county; 6, Anne; 7, Alice, wife of, in 1650, of James Smith, of Rippon, Esq.

18, Roger Beckwith, Esq. third son of Marmaduke, beforementioned, sold his lands in Clint, and purchased Alborough. He married, first, ——, daughter of Mr. Currier, of Leeds, by whom he had a son, Thomas Beckwith, of Beverley, who suffered greatly for his loyalty to Charles I. and had his estate sequestered, and two daughters, Catharine, wife of Thomas Norton, of Elveston, and Anne, of John Robinson, of Bolton-upon-Swale, in Yorkshire. His second wife, was Susanna, daughter of Mr. Brakenbury, of Sellaby and Dinton, in Durham, by whom he had three sons, and three daughters; 1, Arthur, his successor; 2, Matthew, of Tanfield, in Yorkshire, who was a justice of the peace, and a captain in the parliament army. He was ancestor to the Beckwiths, of Thurcroft, and married Elizabeth, daughter of Sir John Buck, of Filey, in Yorkshire, Knt.; 3, William, of Thurcroft, in Yorkshire, who married Margaret, daughter of Bernard Ellis, Esq. recorder of York; the daughters were, 1, Susan, wife of John Alnaby, of Alnaby, in Yorkshire, Esq. (grandmother to Arthur Onslow, Esq. speaker of the house of commons); 2, Judith, of William Parker, M. D. in Kent; and 3, Hester, living 1630, wife of Thomas Odingfells, of Eperston, in Nottinghamshire, Esq. This Roger lies buried at Masham, in the north riding of Yorkshire*.

* Where, on a monument in the choir of that church, is this inscription:

In Memory of Roger Beckwith, of Aldbrough, Esq.
who dyed on Monday, the 19th Day of Janaary, in
the Year 1634, and was buried near this Place. He

19, Arthur Beckwith, of Aldbrough, Esq. son and heir, married Mary, eldest daughter of Sir Marmaduke Wyvill, of Constable-Burton, Yorkshire, Bart. by whom he had two sons, Marmaduke, who died unmarried, and Roger, his successor; also three daughters, Mary, Isabel, and Susan, who all died unmarried, he died in 1642*.

I. ROGER BECKWITH, of Aldbrough, Esq. son and heir, was created a Baronet, 33 Car. II. he married first, Elizabeth, daughter of Sir Christopher Clapham, of Beamsley, Knt. by whom he had one son, Arthur, who died 1700, beyond sea; his second lady was, Elizabeth, daughter of Sir Edmund Jennings, of Ripon, Knt. by whom he had four sons and two daughters, 1, Sir Roger, his successor; 2, Marmaduke, successor to his brother; 3, Edmund; 4, Marmaduke; 5, Margaret; 6, Elizabeth; the four last died young. Sir Roger died December 6, 1700, and lies buried in Ripon church †.

married Susanna, the Daughter of Mr. Brakenbury, of Sellaby, in the County Palatine of Durham, by whom he had Arthur, his Successor, and seven other Children, four Sons, and three Daughters. She departed this Life the 28th Day of October, Anno Domini 1670, and lyes buried in the Parish Church of Skelbrough. He was the Son of Marmaduke Beckwith, of Acton, by Ann, Daughter to Mr. Dynley, of Bramhope, which Marmaduke was the next in Descent to Huntington Beckwith, of Clint, where the Family had continued from the tenth Year of King Henry the Third, Anno Domini 1226, until the Year 1597, when the aforesaid Roger Beckwith sold his Lands in Clint, and purdhased Aldbrough.

* He lies buried also at Mosham, with this inscription:

To the Memory of Arthur Beckwith, of Aldbrough, Esq. who died in the Service of his Country, Anno 1642.

He married Mary, eldest Daughter of Sir Marmaduke Wyvill, Knt. and Bart. by whom he left two Sons, and three Daughters. She died in the Year 1646, and was buried in the Church of St. Clement Danes, London.

Roger, his Successor, married two Wives, first, Elizabeth, daughter of Sir Christopher Clapham, of Beamsley, Knt. who departed this Life the first Day of December, in the year 1673, and was buried near this Place: secondly, Elizabeth, Daughter of Sir Edmund Jenings, with whom he lyes buried, in the Collegiate Church at Ripon.

† In the south isle of the choir, at the east end, is an atchievement of Sir Roger Beckwith, Bart. who bore baron and femme, *argent, a cheveron between three hinds' heads, erased, gules; on a canton in the middle, argent, a sinister hand, gules; with argent, a cheveron, gules, between three plummets, sable; being the arms of his lady, daughter to Sir Edmund Jennings, Knt. his crest, an antelope, with a green branch in its mouth*; and, upon a blue marble stone on the ground, is this inscription *(b)*:

Here lieth the Body of Sir Roger Beckwith, Bart. late of Aldbrough, who died at Rippon Dec. 6, 1700.

(b) Hist. of Rippon, p. 122.

TABLE 2.

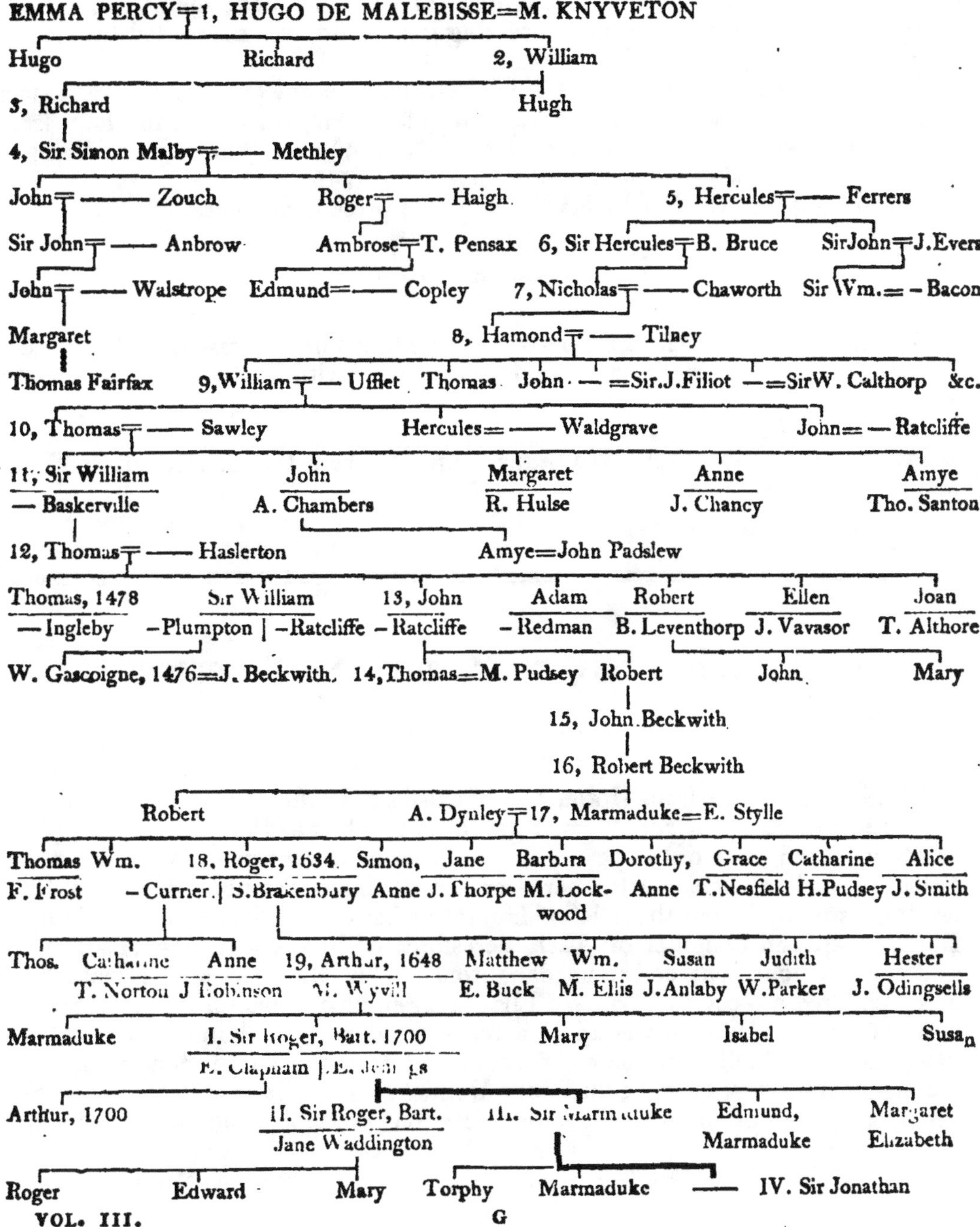
EMMA PERCY=1, HUGO DE MALEBISSE=M. KNYVETON
Hugo
Richard
2, William
3, Richard
Hugh
4, Sir Simon Malby=—— Methley
John=—— Zouch
Roger=—— Haigh
5, Hercules=—— Ferrers
Sir John=—— Anbrow
Ambrose=T. Pensax
6, Sir Hercules=B. Bruce
SirJohn=J.Evers
John=—— Walstrope
Edmund=—— Copley
7, Nicholas=—— Chaworth
Sir Wm.=—Bacon
Margaret
8, Hamond=—— Tilney
Thomas Fairfax
9, William=— Ufflet
Thomas
John
—=Sir.J.Filiot
—=SirW. Calthorp
&c.
10, Thomas=—— Sawley
Hercules=—— Waldgrave
John=— Ratcliffe
11, Sir William
— Baskerville
John
A. Chambers
Margaret
R. Hulse
Anne
J. Chancy
Amye
Tho. Santon
12, Thomas=—— Haslerton
Amye=John Padslew
Thomas, 1478
— Ingleby
Sir William
—Plumpton | —Ratcliffe
13, John
—Ratcliffe
Adam
—Redman
Robert
B. Leventhorp
Ellen
J. Vavasor
Joan
T. Althore
W. Gascoigne, 1476=J. Beckwith.
14, Thomas=M. Pudsey
Robert
John
Mary
15, John Beckwith
16, Robert Beckwith
Robert
A. Dynley=17, Marmaduke=E. Stylle
Thomas
F. Frost
Wm.
—Curner.
18, Roger, 1634
S.Brakenbury
Simon,
Anne
Jane
J. Thorpe
Barbara
M. Lock-wood
Dorothy,
Anne
Grace
T.Nesfield
Catharine
H.Pudsey
Alice
J. Smith
Thos.
Catharine
T. Norton
Anne
J Robinson
19, Arthur, 1648
M. Wyvill
Matthew
E. Buck
Wm.
M. Ellis
Susan
J.Anlaby
Judith
W.Parker
Hester
J. Odingsells
Marmaduke
I. Sir Roger, Bart. 1700
E. Clapham | E. Jennings
Mary
Isabel
Susan
Arthur, 1700
II. Sir Roger, Bart.
Jane Waddington
III. Sir Marmaduke
Edmund,
Marmaduke
Margaret
Elizabeth
Roger
Edward
Mary
Torphy
Marmaduke
—— IV. Sir Jonathan

II. Sir ROGER BECKWITH, eldest son and successor to his father in dignity and estate, who was born June 13, 1682, was high sheriff of the county of York, 1706, and married Jane, daughter and sole heiress of Benjamin Waddington, Esq. of Allerton-Gleadhow, in Yorkshire, by whom he had two sons, Roger and Edmund, and one daughter, Mary, who died young. Sir Roger died in May 1743, without any surviving issue, and was succeeded by his only surviving brother,

III. Sir MARMADUKE BECKWITH, Bart. born Jan. 1687, was a merchant and clerk of the peace in Virginia. He married and had issue, 1, Torpley, who died in England, Dec. 27, 1748; 2, Marmaduke, living in Virginia, 1771; 3, ——, a daughter, living in 1748.

IV. Sir JONATHAN BECKWITH, is the present Baronet.

ARMS—Argent, a chevron, between three hinds heads erased, gules.

CREST—On a wreath, an Antelope, proper, with a branch in its mouth, vert.

MOTTO—*Joir en bien.*

SEATS—At Alborough, Walburne, and Allerton-Gleadhow, all in Yorkshire.

201. PARKYNS, of Bunny, Northamptonshire.

Created Baronet, May 18, 1681.

THIS family came from Upton and Mattisfield, in the county of Berks.

1, Richard Parkyns, Esq.* great grandson to Thomas Parkyns, of the places aforesaid, was justice of the peace, and recorder of the towns of Nottingham and Leicester, and an ancient utter barrister of the Inner Temple. He died 1603, leaving issue, by Elizabeth, relict of Humphry Barlow, of Stoke, in the county of Derby, Esq. and daughter of Aden Beresford, of Fenney-Bentley, Esq. in the said county, four sons and four daughters. This Richard, and Elizabeth his wife, suffered a recovery, Trin. 16 Eliz. †, of eight messuages, six cottages, six hundred acres of land, two hundred acres of meadow, three hundred acres of pasture, half a windmill, sixty acres of wood, and free warren in Boney, parcel of the manor of Boney; he was called John Dethick, Esq. The said Richard, 18 Eliz. suffered another, of one messuage, one toft, one dovecote, one garden, one hun-

* Ex inf. Dom. Tho. Parkyns, Bar. 1741. † Thoroton's Nott. p. 46.

dred acres of land, &c. in Boney and Bradmere, and called to warranty John Smith.

This Richard Parkyns, Esq. an apprentice of the law, of the Inner Temple, and a reverend man in his time for his learning and judgment, purchased * the entire manor of Boney, and with his posterity it still continues. This Richard lies buried in Bunny church †.

2, Sir George Parkyns, Knt. eldest son and heir, died 1626, leaving issue by Mary, daughter and heiress of Edward Isham, of Walmer-Castle, in Kent, Esq. seven children ‡.

Isham Parkyns, his eldest son and heir, married Catharine, daughter of Henry Cave, of Barrow, in Leicestershire, Esq. and died in 1671, leaving two sons; Theophilus, who married Jane, daughter and coheiress of George Cotton, of Sussex, Esq. but died without issue; and,

I. Sir THOMAS, who was advanced to the dignity of a Baronet, 32 Car. II. for his father, Colonel Isham Parkyns's, faithful services in the Civil Wars ‖, who, being governor of the garrison called The Place, in Ashby-de-la-Zouch, Leicestershire, held it out to the last for the King against Oliver Cromwell, and spent a good estate in his service. He married Anne, daughter and heiress of Thomas Cressey, of Berkyn, in Yorkshire, Esq. whose ancestors came in with William the Conqueror, (and Elizabeth, his wife, sole daughter of Sir Henry Glemham, of Glemham-hall, in Suffolk, by whom he had five children; 1, Cressey, who died without issue; 2, Sir Thomas, his successor; 3, Beaumont, who left eight children, all dead without issue; 4, Catharine; and 5, Anne, who died unmarried, and left land, to the value of two hundred pounds, for put-

* Thoroton's Nott. p. 46.

† Where, on a handsome monument in the chancel north wall, is this inscription (a):

> Here lieth Richard Parkins, Esq. justice of the Peace and quorum, in the County of Nott. and Recorder of the Towns of Leicester and Nott. and an ancient Utter Barrester in the Inner-Temple, who married and took to wife Elizabeth Barlowe, then a Widow, late Wife of one Humfrey Barlowe, of Stoke, in the said county of Dar. Esq. deceased, being the eldest Daughter of Aden Beresford, of Fenne Bentlye, in the county of Darby, Esq. deceased, by whom the said Richard had 8 Children, viz. 4 Sons, and 4 Daughters, that is to say, Sir George Parkins, Knt. his Son and Heir; Adrian Parkins; John Parkins; Aden Parkins; Fraunces, Anne, Elizab. Margaret, and died the third day of July, 1603. Upon whose Soul, &c.

‡ Sir George Parkyns, Knt. married, about the latter end of Eliz. to Mary, daughter and heiress of Edward Isham, of Walmer, in Kent, Esq. and had a daughter Mary, married to Sir Richard Minshull, of Cheshire, created Baron of Minshull 1642, descended from that eminent soldier, Michael de Minshull, who for his glorious services performed in the quarrel of Richrrd I. at the siege of Acon, had the assignment for ever of the crescent and star, for the coat-armour of this family.—*Philpot's Kent*, p. 351.

‖ Ex inf. Dom. Tho. Parkyns, Bar. 1741.

(a) Thoroton's Nott. p. 47, 48.

ting forth apprentices out of the towns of Bunny, Bradmore, and Cortlingstock. Sir Thomas died July 15, 1684, and his lady Jan. 1725-6, aged 96, and was succeeded by his son,

II. Sir THOMAS PARKYNS, Bart. who married Elizabeth *, granddaughter and heiress of John Sampson, of Hewby, in Yorkshire, Esq. alderman of London, and daughter and heiress of John Sampson, of Breason, in Derbyshire, Esq. Sir Thomas was educated at Westminster School, under Dr. Busby and Dr. Knypes †, was two years and a half of Trinity College, Cambridge, and afterwards of the inns of court, and constantly performed his mootings, as a student, for eight years. He had the perpetual advowsons of the rectories of Cortlingstock and Keyworth, and the vicarage of Bunny, he being impropriator of the latter. The first thing he did after his father's death (being then come of age), willing to begin with God's house ‡, he new roofed the chancel at Bunny, which is a very large one, being fifty-eight feet in length, and twenty-four feet within the walls. He built the free-school and four alms-houses, which cost four hundred pounds, and which his mother endowed with sixteen pounds per annum, he also built the vicarage-house §, and gave the two treble bells to the church, with this motto on them, *Cantate domino novum canticum*, which make the peal six; and, jointly with his mother, advanced two hundred pounds, to obtain as much more of the late Queen's bounty for augmenting the vicarage of Bunny, as is recorded on monuments erected by himself, to the memories of himself and mother in the said chancel, at the east end of which he hath built a large vault for himself and family ‖. He also gave five pounds four shillings per annum to the poor widows, and widowers of Bunny, and Bradmore, to be distributed in bread, every Sunday, in Bunny church, to such only that constantly frequent the same, as long as able. He also erected the manor-houses, in Bunny, and East Leak ¶; and a very large house, called, Highfield-Grange, in the parish of Cortlingstock. He built a park-wall of brick, three miles in compass, in three years, in the liberty of Bunny **, all on arches, being the first that was built in England, after that method; and since followed by most eminent builders of houses, and park-walls; but especially gardiners, for the advantage of trees, shooting, and spreading their roots under the said arches, and yielding the bigger head for the benefit of the fruit; for it is observable the head is bigger, proportionable to the root. He built all the farm houses, &c. in Bunny and Bradmore. He was the first that brought that noble science of Wrestling into a method ††, as appears by a book he wrote on that subject. He also compiled a concise grammar, for the use of his two sons by his second lady. Likewise, for the good and benefit of his country, he wrote his queries and reasons, why the county hall, for the county of Nottingham, should be built on the county ground, which he purchased of Julius Hutchinson, Esq. for that purpose ‡‡, and not in the market place in the town, and county of the town of Nottingham, and out of the county at large, and thereby prevented their spoiling the fine prospect of that large and spacious market place. He studied physic for the good and benefit of his neighbours; and had, not only

* Ex inf. Dom. Tho. Parkyns, Bar. 1741. † Ibid. ‡ Ibid. § Ibid. ‖ Ibid. ¶ Ibid. ** Ibid. †† Ibid. ‡‡ Ibid.

a competent, but a perfect and complete knowledge of all parts of the mathematics, of which he was a great lover, especially of architecture and hydraulics, contriving and drawing all his plans without an architect. He acted as justice of the peace * in King Charles II.'s reign, and ever since, till his death, for the counties of Nottingham and Leicester, being never out of commission, but one month in King James II.'s reign.

He had issue by his first lady, Elizabeth, two sons, Sampson and Thomas †; Sampson married Alice, daughter and heiress of —— Middlemore, of Lusby, in Lincolnshire, Esq. by whom he had four children, 1, Thomas, who died an infant; 2, Thomas, who died June 1, 1735, aged twenty-five years: he left one daughter Jane, the first wife of the present Sir Thomas Parkyns, Bart.; Anne, dead; and Harriot, the wife of Richard, the eldest son of the most judicious Dr. Farrer ‡, of Market-Harborough, in the county of Leicester; Sampson died in his father's life-time, and was buried April 1713, aged twenty-seven years; Thomas, his youngest son, died a bachelor, and was buried Sept. 21, 1706, aged nineteen years.

Sir Thomas married, secondly, 1727 §, Jane, daughter of George Barnat, alderman and citizen of York, by whom he had two sons, Sir Thomas, his successor, and George, an officer in Gen. Elliot's light horse, and one daughter, Anne, wife of Colonel Miles. Lady Parkyns died August 1740; and Sir Thomas, in March 1740-1, and was buried under a handsome monument in Bunny church, which he had erected many years ago, whereon is his own statue, in a wrestling posture, with Time ‖. He was succeeded in title and estate by his eldest son,

* Ex inf. Dom Tho. Parkyns, Bar. 1741. † Ibid. ‡ Ibid. § Ibid. ‖ Sir Thomas, some years before his death, sent some English verses to Dr. Friend, master of Westminster School, from which model the doctor wrote the epigram hereafter mentioned. On the top of the monument, between two flaming urns, are his arms, and those of Cressy, his mother, quartered, with the crest of a pine-apple, and motto, *Honeste audax*.

The monument is divided into two compartments: in the first of which stands Sir Thomas, in a wresting posture, in his waistcoat and cap, and this motto at the top of it, round his head, *Artificis status ipse fuit*; n the second compartment, at the bottom of it, is represented Time, with his scythe, wings, &c. and at his eet Sir Thomas, stretched along, in the same habit, in the posture of a man thrown on his back, and on the upper part of it these Latin lines:

Quem modo stravisti longo in certamine tempus,
Hic recubat Britonum clarus in orbe pugil:
Jam primum stratus, præter te vicerat omnes;
De te etiam victor, quando resurget, erit.
Per R. Friend, pr. ludimagist. schol. Westmonast.

Thus translated:

Here, thrown by Time, Old Parkyn's laid,
The first fair fall he ever had;
Nor Time, without the aid of *Death*,
Could e'er have put him out of breath;
All else he threw, and will those twain,
As soon as he gets up again.

His Faith. Καιρὸς ὁ Πανδαμάτωρ. Tempus edax rerum.

III. Sir THOMAS PARKYNS, Bart. born Dec. 8, 1728, he married April 7, 1747, Jane, daughter and heiress of Thomas Parkyns, son of Sampson, and grandson of Sir Thomas, the second Baronet of this family, by whom he had one son and two daughters, 1, Thomas-Boothby, born Jan. 24, 1755, created Lord Rancliffe, in Ireland, in 1795, F. R. S. and Vice-president of the Society for encouraging arts and manufactures, representative, in the two last parliaments for the borough of Leicester. He married, Dec. 16, 1788, Elizabeth-Anne, daughter and heiress of Sir William James, of Park-Farm-place, in Eltham, Kent, Bart. so created July 25, 1778, by his third lady, Miss Goddard, cousin to the late General Goddard. She died Jan. 18, 1797, leaving one son George, and five daughters, 1, Eliza; 2, Salina; 3, Harriott; 4, Anne; 5, Maria. Jane, the eldest daughter of Sir Thomas, born Nov. 11, 1752, was wife of Clement Winstanley, Esq. of Branston House, Leicestershire, by whom she has four sons, 1, Clement; 2, James; 3, Thomas; 4, George; and two daughters, Anne and Mary. Elizabeth, the second daughter, born Jan. 3, 1757, wife of ——— Charlesworth, Esq. of Thringston, in Leicestershire. Sir Thomas' first lady dying in Dec. 1760, he married secondly, Sarah, daughter of Daniel Smith, of Bunny, Esq. born July 3, 1746, by whom he has had four sons and six daughters, 1, Frederick-Cressey, born Aug. 26, 1767; 2, Sampson, born Dec. 25, 1769. He was rector of Costock and Keyworth, in Nottinghamshire, and LL.B. and died at Burlington-Quay, Yorkshire, aged 32, Sept. 5, 1801; 3, Richard, born June 24, 1771; 4, Anne, born May 9, 1774, died young; 5, Charlotte, born Oct. 6, 1775; 6, Sarah, born Dec. 18, 1776; 7, Francis, born Feb. 20, 1779, died 1787; 8, Penelope, born Oct. 5, 1780; 9, Catharine, born Nov. 26, 1781; 10, Sophia, born Aug. 3, 1783, died April 7, 1791. Lady Sarah died Mar. 22, 1796, aged 50. Sir Thomas married, thirdly, ———, daughter of ——— Boultbie, by whom he has ———, a daughter, born 1799.

ARMS—Argent, an eagle displayed, sable, on a canton, or, a fess, dancette, sable, between seven billets, ermines*.

CREST—In a ducal coronet, or, a pine, proper, leaved vert.

MOTTO—*Honestè audax.*

SEATS—Bunny, East-Leake, and Highfield-Grange, Nottinghamshire.

At the bottom of the monument, on a broad square, is this inscription:

> Here lies the Body of Sir Thomas Parkyns, of Bunny, Baronet, one of his Majesties Justices of the Peace, (& Quorum,) and Deputy-Lieutenant for the Counties of Nottingham and Leicester; second Son of Sir Thomas Parkyns, of Bunny, Baronet, and Anne, the sole Daughter and Heiress of Thomas Cressy, of Berkin, in the County of York, Esq. whose Ancestors came in with William the Norman.

* He bears quarterly, first, as above; second, argent, a bear sejant, sable, chained, or; third, argent, a lion rampant, double queed; fourth, gules, three piles, issuing from a fess-way, argent.

SUPPORTERS.—Two pegasus's, argent, and winged, argent, spotted with billets ermines, the same as in the coat of arms, each gorged with a ducal coronet, or, fastened each with a chain to the coronet, or, cross the body and loins.

TABLE 9:

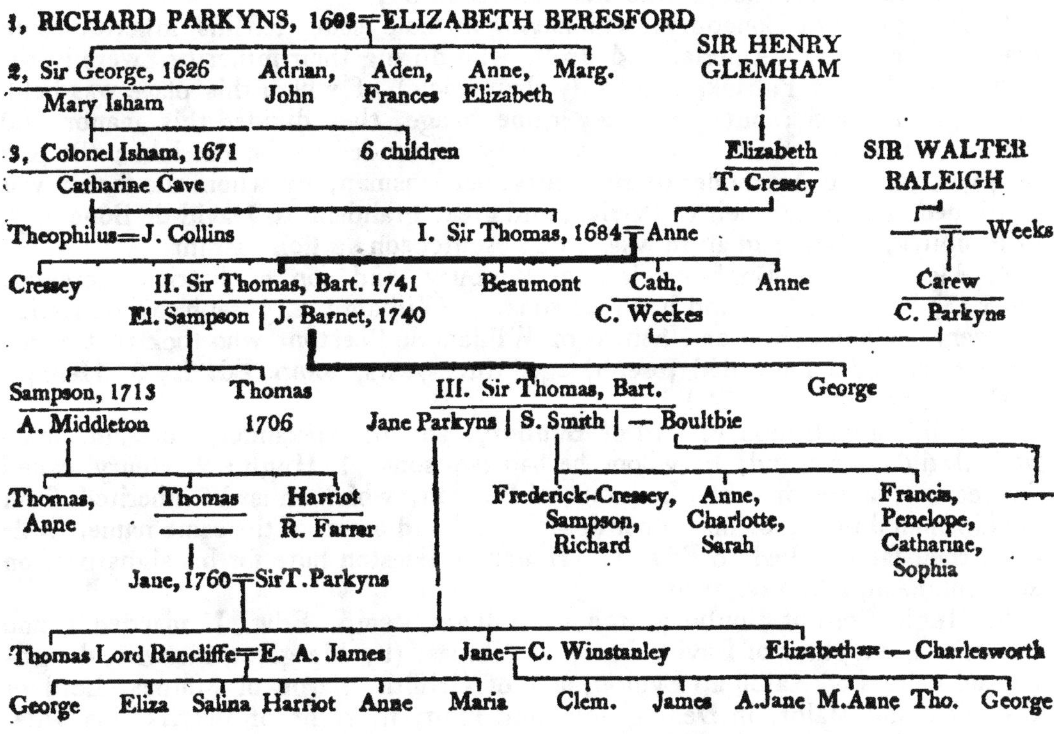

202. BUNBURY, of BUNBURY, Cheshire.

Created Baronet, June 29, 1681.

THE family of Bunbury, originally called St. Pierre, a Norman commander *, came over at the time of the conquest, and shared the fortune of Hugh Lupus, first Norman Earl of Chester, and was by him rewarded, for his merit and valour, with divers goodly lands and possessions, and amongst them the manor or lordship of Bonebury (a contraction of Boniface Bury, to which saint the church of

* Ex inf. Dom. Hen. Bunbury, Bar. 1727.

that place was dedicated), and from thence this family have since taken their denomation. The first of which was *,

1, Henry de Bonebury, temp. K. Stephen, whose signature was a fleur de lis; he had a brother, called David, and was succeeded by his son,

2, William de Bonebury, who was succeeded by,

3, Humphrey de Bonebury, who having no male issue, left his inheritance to his two daughters, Ameria, and Joan, who during their minority, were in the custody of Robert Patrick, (probably their uncle) of whom this place was held, by knight's service; but when they came to age, they divided this manor and patronage between them. Ameria's moiety descended to the Patricks; the part of Joan, came to Alexander de Bonebury, her kinsman, by whom the family was continued, as son and heir to Patrick, and great grandson to David de Bonebury, or Bunbury, whose signature was, on an escutcheon, a lion passant.

4, Alexander de Bunbury, lord of Bunbury, and son of Patrick aforesaid, lived 15, K. Hen. III. and had four sons, 1, William; 2, Joseph, who married Margery, sole daughter and heiress of William de Beeston, who took that name, and by her had a son called Joseph, aged three years, temp. Ed. I.; 3, Henry; 4, Robert de Bunbury, 27 Ed. I.

5, William de Bunbury, lord of Bunbury, son of Alexander, aforesaid, married Matilda, or Maud, by whom he had two sons, 1, Hugh; 2, Henry, called de Beeston, ancestor to the Beestons, of Beeston, which must be inherited from his kinsman Joseph, or his father Joseph, and had a son of the same name. William, their father, died 16 Edw. I. Henry de Beeston bore for his signature, on an escutcheon, a lion rampant.

6, Hugh, Lord of Bunbury, son of William, temp. Edw. I. married Dame Christiana, daughter of David, Baron of Malpas, (by Margaret, his wife, daughter and heiress of Ralph ap Eynion, son of Griffith, Baron of Malpas, Lord of Bromfield and Malor, in Denbighshire and Flint, in right of Beatrix, his wife, legitimate daughter of Randle, third Earl of Chester.) This David de Malpas, commonly called Dan David, was secretary to the then Earl of Chester, and in right of his wife, had a moiety of the barony of Malpas. Hugh had issue, by Dame Christiana, 1, Richard; 2, Adam de Bunbury, clerk, chaplain to Rood-chapple, in Tarpoley, temp. 29 Edw. I; 3, David; 4, Mabell; 5, Robert.

7, Richard de Bunbury, Lord of Bunbury, temp. Edw. II. had two sons, David and Richard, and one daughter, Matilda.

8, David de Bunbury, Lord of Bunbury and Stannich, in right of his wife, the sole daughter and heiress of David de Stannich, or Stanny, (which fair lordship, near the city of Chester, is now in the possession of the family), by whom he had William, and David, prior of Bunbury, 4 Edw. II. as was afterwards this David's son, David.

9, William de Bunbury, of Stanny, in Wirral, had two sons, Roger and Henry.

10, Roger de Bunbury, of Stanny, living 36 Edw. III. was the first, who, for his signature, gave the present coat of arms of his family, given him (as by tra-

* Ex inf. Dom. Hen. Bunbury, Bar. 1727.

-dition) for his great skill in martialing the troops of that warlike and victorious prinae, Edw. III. He died without issue, and was succeeded by his brother, Henry de Bunbury, of Stanny, who had one son,

11, Richard de Bunbury, Lord of Bunbury and Stanny, 6 Hen. V. He married Alice †, daughter of Edward Dutton, by whom he had one son (1 Edw. IV.) John, and died 37 Hen. VI.

12, John Bunbury, of Stanny, Lord of Bunbury, living 24 Hen. VI. He married Catharine †, daughter of John Hooks, of Flint, (the Welch call her daughter of Jenkin Hollis ap Flint), by whom he had one son, John, his successor. He died 9 Edw. IV.

13, John Bunbury, of Stanny, Esq. his son and heir, lived 17 Hen. VII. He married (5 Edw. IV.) Agnes, daughter of William Norris, of Speake, Esq. and settled the manor of Bunbury for her jointure; he died 21 Hen. VII. and was succeeded by his son,

14, Richard Bunbury, of Stanny, Esq. living 12 Hen. VII. who married Blanch, daughter of Sir Thomas Poole, of Poole, in Cheshire, Knt. and sister of William Poole, Esq.; he died 32 Hen. VIII. and left one son,

15, Henry Bunbury, of Stanny, Esq. Lord of Bunbury, who married Margaret ‡, daughter and heiress of Hugh Aldersey, of Chester, merchant, thrice mayor of the said city, 1528, 1541, 1546, (younger son of Henry Aldersey, of Aldersey and Spurstoe), by whom he had two sons and one daughter, Thomas, Edmund, and Elizabeth, wife of Henry Birkenhead, of Huxly, Esq.; he died 38 Hen. VIII. aged 31.

16, Thomas, the eldest, married Bridget ‖, daughter of John Aston, of Aston, in Cheshire, Esq.; he died May 5, 1601, and left issue his only son,

17, Sir Henry Bunbury, of Stanny, knighted by Queen Elizabeth. He married, first, Anne, daughter of Jeffery Shackerley, of Shackerley, in Lancashire, and Holme, in Cheshire, Esq. by whom he had a son Henry. His second wife was Martha, daughter of Sir William Norris, of Speake, Knt. by whom he had a son Thomas, who married Elianor, daughter of Henry Birkenhead, of Backford, Esq. in Cheshire, by whom he had Diana, Dulcibella, Benjamin, and Joseph, who all settled in Ireland.

18, Henry Bunbury, of Stanny, Esq. son and heir of Sir Henry aforesaid, married Ursula §, daughter of John Bayley, of Hoddesdon, in Hertfordshire, Esq. by whom he had six sons and three daughters, 1, Sir Thomas, of whom hereafter; 2, John, who died unmarried; 3, Henry; 4, William; 5, Joseph; and 6, Richard, for whom he made a handsome provision, notwithstanding the many hardships put upon him for his unshaken loyalty to King Charles I. and all the royal family.

Henry, the third son, married Elianor Birch, relict of ——— Holcroft, of Holcroft, in Lancashire, Esq. but left no issue; William, the fourth, married Mary, daughter to Sir Richard Skevington, of Fisherwick, in Staffordshire, Esq. (whose heir is now Lord Viscount Mazarine, in Ireland), by whom he

* Ex inf. ibid. † Ibid. ‡ Ibid. § Ibid. ‖ Ibid.

had Charles, who died unmarried; and William, late fellow of Brazennose-College, Oxford, and rector of Great Catworth, in Huntingdonshire, who married Anne, daughter of Sir Villiers Chernock, of Hulcot, in Bedfordshire, Bart. (and by whom he had three sons and three daughters). Joseph, the fifth son, married Letitia, daughter of Sir William Neal, of Ireland, Bart. (by his wife, sister to major-general Randolph Egerton, of Betley, in Staffordshire), and by her had issue one son, Joseph, and two daughters, Helena, and Anne; Richard, the youngest, it is supposed, died unmarried. The three daughters of Henry were, Susan, wife, first, of William Davys, of Ashton, and secondly, of William Cowley, of Dodleston, in Cheshire; Elizabeth, and Ursula.

I. Sir THOMAS BUNBURY, son and heir of Henry, was created Baronet 33 Car. II. 1681, and Lord of Stanny and Bunbury: he married Sarah*, daughter of John Chetwood, of Oakley, in Staffordshire, Esq. by whom he had several children, of which only Sir Henry survived, and Ursula, the wife of Edward Green, of Pulton cum Spittle, in Cheshire, Esq. Sir Thomas married secondly †, Mary, daughter of Humphrey Kelsall, of Bradshaw, Esq. by whom he had two daughters, Priscilla and Lucy.

II. Sir HENRY BUNBURY, of Stanny, Bart. his successor, married Mary‡, daughter of Sir Kendrick Eyton, or Eyton, Knt. in Denbighshire, and judge of North Wales: he died Dec. 20, 1687, and had seven sons, and one daughter, of whom only Sir Henry, his successor, and William, survived.

William Bunbury, Esq. was his late Majesty's attorney-general for the county palatine of Chester, and married Sarah, daughter of Sir James Eyton, by whom he had six daughters, three of which, Mary, Isabella, and Susanna, died young and unmarried; Sarah, the eldest, was wife of Edward Mainwaring, of Whitmore, in Staffordshire, Esq.; Elizabeth was wife of Edward Fleming, of the Inner Temple, Esq. barrister at law: she died in childbed, Nov. 12, 1735, aged twenty-five, and was buried at Mortlake, in Surry); and Eleanor, the youngest of George Wilson, of the Inner-Temple, Gent.

III. Sir HENRY BUNBURY, Bart. son and heir to Sir Henry, was Lord of Stanny and Bunbury, and married Susanna §, the only surviving daughter of William Hanmer, Esq, and sister to Sir Thomas Hanmer, of Hanmer and Bettisfield, in Flintshire, and Milden-hall, in Suffolk, Bart. who died Sept. 30, 1744, by whom he had four sons and five daughters; 1, Thomas, who died an infant; 2, Henry, who died in the 19th year of his age, at Catherine-hall, Cambridge, April 29, 1722, and lies buried at Milden-hall, Suffolk; 3, Sir Charles, his successor; and 4, Sir Wm. Sir Henry's daughters were, 1, Susanna, wife of Colonel William Handasyd, third son of General Handasyd, of Gaines, in Huntingdonshire; 2, Isabella, of Col. John Lee, of Darnell, in Cheshire; 3, Mary; 4, Frances; and 5, Elizabeth. Sir Henry was chosen one of the representatives in parliament for the city of Chester in Jan. 1700, and continued to represent the said city in parliament till his death; and in the year 1711, was, by her late Majesty Queen

* Ex inf. ibid. † Ibid. ‡ Ibid. § Ibid.

TABLE.

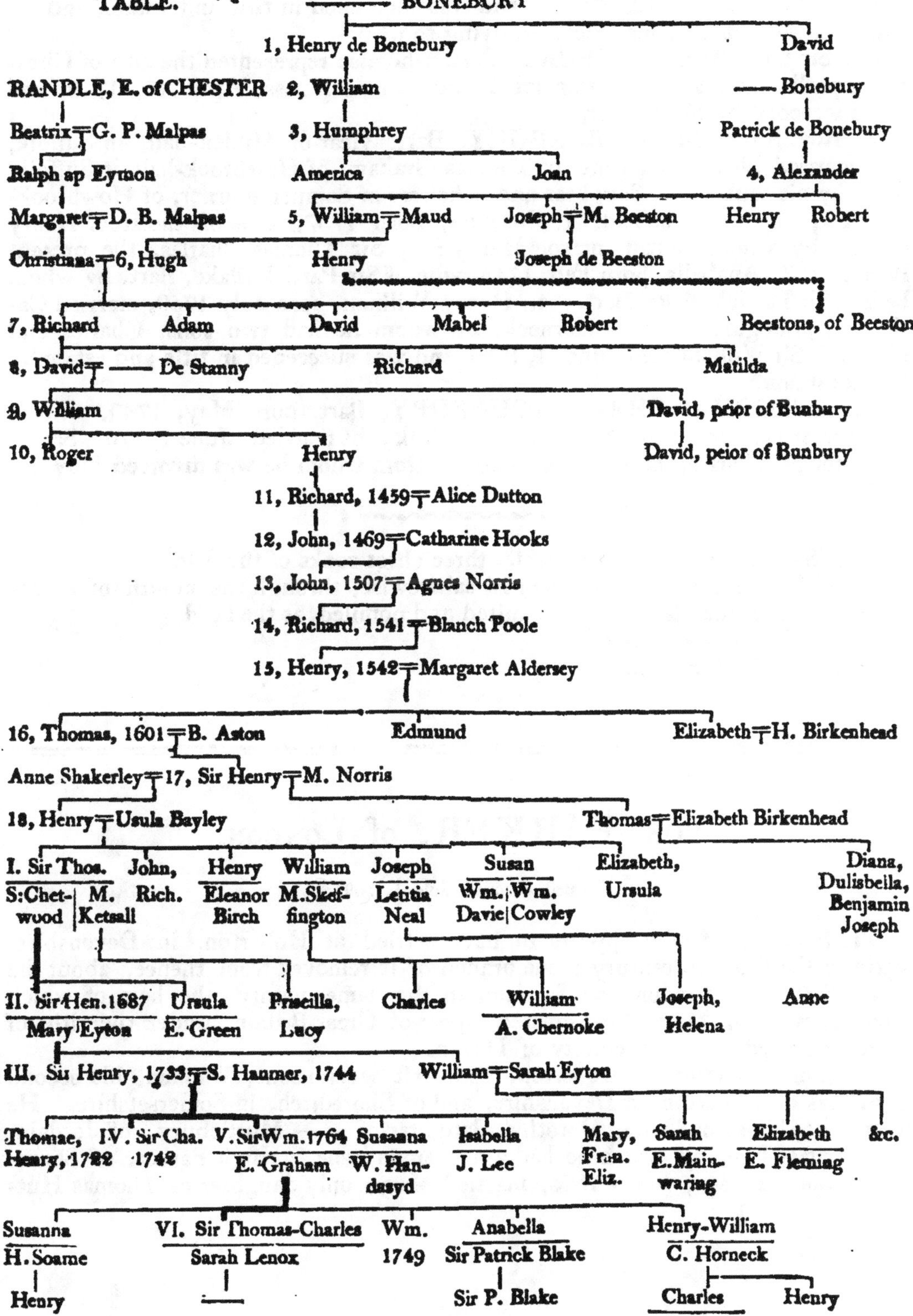

—— BONEBURY
1, Henry de Bonebury
David
RANDLE, E. of CHESTER
2, William
—— Bonebury
Beatrix=G. P. Malpas
3, Humphrey
Patrick de Bonebury
Ralph ap Eymon
America
Joan
4, Alexander
Margaret=D. B. Malpas
5, William=Maud
Joseph=M. Beeston
Henry
Robert
Christiana=6, Hugh
Henry
Joseph de Beeston
7, Richard
Adam
David
Mabel
Robert
Beestons, of Beeston
8, David= —— De Stanny
Richard
Matilda
9, William
David, prior of Bunbury
10, Roger
Henry
David, peior of Bunbury
11, Richard, 1459=Alice Dutton
12, John, 1469=Catharine Hooks
13, John, 1507=Agnes Norris
14, Richard, 1541=Blanch Poole
15, Henry, 1542=Margaret Aldersey
16, Thomas, 1601=B. Aston
Edmund
Elizabeth=H. Birkenhead
Anne Shakerley=17, Sir Henry=M. Norris
18, Henry=Usula Bayley
Thomas=Elizabeth Birkenhead
I. Sir Thos. S:Chetwood
M. Ketsall
John, Rich.
Henry Eleanor Birch
William M.Skeffington
Joseph Letitia Neal
Susan Wm. Davie Wm. Cowley
Elizabeth, Ursula
Diana, Dulisbella, Benjamin Joseph
II. Sir Hen. 1687 Mary Eyton
Ursula E. Green
Priscilla, Lucy
Charles
William A. Chernoke
Joseph, Helena
Anne
III. Sir Henry, 1733=S. Hanmer, 1744
William=Sarah Eyton
Thomae, Henry, 1782
IV. Sir Cha. 1742
V. Sir Wm. 1764 E. Graham
Susanna W. Handasyd
Isabella J. Lee
Mary, Fran. Eliz.
Sarah E. Mainwaring
Elizabeth E. Fleming
&c.
Susanna H. Soame
VI. Sir Thomas-Charles Sarah Lenox
Wm. 1749
Anabella Sir Patrick Blake
Henry-William C. Horneck
Henry
Sir P. Blake
Charles
Henry

Anne, appointed one of the commissioners of the revenue in the kingdom of Ireland: he died Feb. 12, 1732-3, and was succeeded in title and estate, and his seat in parliament, by his eldest surviving son,

IV. Sir CHARLES BUNBURY, Bart. who also represented the city of Chester in parliament, and died unmarried, after a long illness, April 10, 1742, and was succeeded by his brother,

V. Rev. Sir WILLIAM BUNBURY, Bart. vicar of Milden-hall, in Suffolk, who married Eleanor, daughter of Thomas Graham, of Howbrook-hall, in Suffolk, Esq. by his wife ——, daughter and coheiress of Samuel Warner, of Howbrook-hall, Esq. by whom he had, 1, Susanna, born 1737, wife of the Rev. Henry Soame, by whom he had one son Henry; 2, Sir Thomas-Charles, the present Baronet; 3, Anabella, born Feb. 1745, wife of Sir Patrick Blake, Bart. by whom he had Sir Patrick Blake, Bart.; 4, Henry-William, born July 1750, married Catharine, , daughter of —— Horneck, by whom he had two sons, Charles and Henry. Sir William died June 11, 1764, and was succeeded in title and estate by his eldest son,

VI. Sir THOMAS-CHARLES BUNBURY, Bart. born May, 1740, who is member of parliament for the county of Suffolk: he married, June 2, 1762, Sarah, daughter of Charles, Duke of Richmond, from whom he was divorced May 14, 1776.

ARMS—Argent, on a bend, sable, three chess rooks of the field.

CREST—On a wreath, two swords, saltirewise, through the mouth of a leopard's face, or, the blades, proper, hilted and pomiled, as the head.

MOTTO—*Firmum in vitâ nihil.*

SEAT——Barton, Suffolk.

---

203. PARKER, of LONDON.

Created Baronet, July 1, 1681.

THIS ancient family appears to have settled at Hoberton, in Devonshire, early in the fifteenth century; one branch of it removed from thence, about the year 1600, to Borrindon and Saltram, in the same county, the heir of which branch, was, in May 1784, created a peer of Great Britain, under the title of Baron Boringdon, in the county of Devon.

1, Thomas Parker, of Hoberton, Esq. left several sons, William, his second son, was of Hoberton, in Devonshire, and of Shoreditch, in Somersetshire. He married to his second wife, Dorothy, daughter of —— Muttlebury, of Jordain, in Somersetshire, by whom he had a numerous issue. Hugh Parker, of Shoreditch, his sixth son, living 1623, married Mary, only daughter of Thomas Hutchins, alias Lawrence, of Holway, in Somersetshire, by whom he left several children.

I. Hugh, his third son, his two elder brothers dying) heir to his father*, was an alderman of the city of London, and paid his fine for sheriff of the said city. He was advanced to the title of Baronet, 32, Car. II. and had the patent limited to himself, and the heirs male of his body, with remainder to his nephew, Henry Parker, of Hunnington, Esq. He married Rachel †, daughter of——— Brown, of Louth, in Lincolnshire, by whom he had no issue; and dying March 5, 1696-7, aged eighty-nine, was buried in the chancel, at St. Bride's church, in Fleet-street, London; and was succeeded in the title, and part of the estate by his said nephew, Sir Henry, son of his brother Henry, (who died 1670) by Margaret, daughter of John White, of London.

II. Sir HENRY PAKKER, Bart. who married Margaret ‡, daughter of Dr. Alexander Hyde, bishop of Salisbury, son of Sir Lawrance Hyde, of Dynton, in Wiltshire, Knt. by whom he had three sons and three daughters; 1, Hugh, whom hereafter; 2, Harry, who married ——, daughter of Dr. Harrison, master of St. Cross, at Winchester, by whom he had no issue; 3, Hyde, who was rector of Tredington, in Worcestershire, and married ———, daughter of ——— Reeves, and died may 21, 1726, leaving four children, Henry, Hyde, Anne, and Beata. Of the daughters, 1, Frances, wife of Sir John Pakington, of Westwood, in Worcestershire, Bart.; 2, Margaret, of John Banks, of Kingston-hall, in Dorsetshire, Esq.; and 3, Beata, of Sir Thomas Cookes Winford, of Glashampton, in Worcestershire, Bart. This Sir Henry, built a handsome seat, at Honington, and rebuilt, in a very neat manner, the church there, and died Oct. 25, 1713, aged 74§.

* Ex. inf. Dom J. Packington, Bar. 1727. † Ex inf. Dna. Marg. Parker ‡ Ex inf. Dom. 1727, J. Parkington, Bar.

§ He lies buried at the west end of Honington church, where there is erected a fine large monument of marble for him and his eldest son, with their statues standing upright, in full proportion, with this inscription in four celumns under them:

H. S. E.
Henricus Parker, Baronettus,
Nullo certe egens, qui sibi tot struxit Monimenta.
Elegantiam nempe in suis,
Pietatem in Dei Ædibus ædificandis,
Nullus non lapis confitetur.
Juventutem Legibus & Negotiis,
Ætatem adultam Senatui & Patriæ,
Senectutem Deo & Otio totus devovit.
Erat ei Animus largus & munificens,
Justitiæ fidus Minister,
Viciniæ indefessus Patronus.
Uxorem duxit Margarettam Hyde,
Episcopi Sarisburiensis Filiam,
Regia in causa Nomen satis notum,
Ideoq; ei nunquam satis carum.
Cum hac optima Conjuge per Annos 48 vixit
Summa Fide, mutuoq; Amore,
Numerosa prole ditatus.

Margaret, lady Parker, his relict, survived him, and died Jan. 6, 1728-9. Hugh Parker Esq. eldest son of Sir Henry, died in his father's lifetime, aged

Second Column.

Franciscam Filiam natu maximam,
Johanni Pakington, de Agro Wigorn. Baronetto,
In Matrimonium dedit;
Eam & Sposi & Humani generis delicias
Flebilis amisit.
Margarettam forma, Moribus spectatissimam
Johanni Bankes, in Com. Dorset, Armigero,
Auspicatum in Conjugium tradidit.
Beatam natu minimam, non minus caram,
Omni Elegantia, omni Virtute ornatam
Thomæ Cookes Winford, de Agro Wigorn. Baronetto
Conjugio ligavit.
Filios pariter tres ætate provectos vidit,
Hugonem, Harricum, Hyde,
Omnes sui munificentia pulchre dotatos.
Rebus domesticis ita feliciter stabilitis,
Conjugi, Liberis, Amicis, Servis carus,
Sui deciderium omnibus reliquit.
Obiit 25 Octob. An. Æt. suæ 74. a Christo.
1713.

Third Column.

Siste paululum, Spectator,
Et optimi Juvenis Vitam & Mores cognosce;
Effigiem vides Hugonis Parker, Armigeri,
Filii Henrici Parker, Baronetti, natu maximi.
Quem sive in Vita, seu in Morte contemplaris,
Miranda undiq; assurgit Scena.
Pueriles Ludos etiam Infans contemnens,
Vel incunabulis præluait Viro
Erat ultra ætatem sapiens,
Ultra fortunam literatus;
Conterebat Græcos Scriptores,
Callebat Romanos.
Erat Modestiæ singularis,
Pudicitiæ vix credibilis,
Pietatis vere antiquæ
Nec quisquam semel aut vidit Ebrium,
Aut audivit jurantem.

Fomrth Column.

Vel publice, vel inter Amicos loquendi parcus,
Judicandi ubiq; acutissimus.
In Senatu Legem studiosus, Ecclesiæ devotus;
Sui commodo nunquam consulruit.
Patriæ nunquam deseruit
Uxorem habuit Annam, Filiam Johannis Smyth *,
In Com. Middlesex, Armigeri;

* Ex prosapia Smithorum Lincolniensium oriund, &c. tumul. apud Abbathiam Westonasteriensem.—*Dugd. Warw. p.* 606.

39, Feb. 2. 1712. He married Anne, daughter of John Smith, of Beauford buildings, Esq. commissioner of the excise; (surviving him, she afterwards became the wife of Michael, Earl of Clanricard*, by whom she had four sons, and three daughters, 1, Sir Henry-John, successor to his grandfather; 2, Hugh; 3, John-Smith, who both died without issue; and 4, Hyde: of the daughters, 1, Margaret†, wife of Thomas Nugent, Esq. count de Valdesoto, (only son of Henry Nugent, Esq. of the house of Colambar, in the county of West Meath, who was created Count de Valdesoto, in the kingdom of Spain, by the Emperor, K. Cha II. of that kingdom; and was major-general in his service, and his allies, and was killed, deputy-gov. of Gibraltar; by whom he has one son, Edw. H. Nugent, Count de Valdesoto, was brought up in Germany, in the Roman Catholic religion, and was made a priest; 2, Anne, wife of Austin-Park Goddard, of Brompton, in Kent, Esq. who was educated at the court of the Grand Duke of Tuscany, and was honoured with the cross of the military order of St. Stephen; he had one daughter, Sophia, the wife of William-Mervyn Dillon, Esq. (third son of Francis Dillon, Esq. of Proudston, in the county of Meath, Ireland, by Mary, his wife, only daughter of Sir Mervyn Wingfield, Bart. (and has one son John-Joseph Dillon, of Lincoln's Inn, and a daughter Sophia; 3, Sophia, wife of Edward Cole, of Enston, in Oxfordshire, Esq.

Ex qua septem progenuit Liberos
Immaturum optimi Patris obitum
Perpetuo dolituros, nunquam satis.
Pthisi correptus, & lento tabescens Morbo,
Mira Animi Constantia occurebat Morti,
Eo indies crescente,
Summum Diem optans magis quam metuens,
Obiit 2do Feb. An. Ætat. suæ 39, a Christo
1712.

* Anne, countess of Clanrickard, mother of Sir Henry-John, &c. died Jan. 1, 1732-3, and lies buried under a very handsome monument in Westminster-Abbey, with this inscription:

Here lies the Right Hon. Anne, Countess Dowager of Clanrickard, eldest Daughter of John Smith, Esq, who is interred near this place: She married first, Hugh Parker, Esq. eldest Son of Sir Henry Parker, of Honnington, in the County of Warwick, Baronet, by whom she had Sir Henry-John Parker, Baronet; Three other Sons, and three Daughters. By her second Husband, Michael, Earl of Clanrickard, of the Kingdom of Ireland, the Head of the ancient and noble family of the Burke's, she had Smith, now Earl of Clanrickard, and two Daughters, Lady Anne, and Lady Mary. She died the first of January, 1732, in the forty-ninth Year of her Age.

† On a grave stone in Plumsted Church, in Kent, is this inscription:
Here lieth the body of Margaret Nugent, wife of Thomas Nugent, Esq. and daughter of Hugh Parker, Esq. eldest son of Sir Henry Parker, Bart. of Honington, in Warwickshire. She departed this life Oct. 12, 1748.

III. Sir HENRY-JOHN PARKER, eldest son of Hugh, and successor to his grandfather, Sir Henry, in dignity and estate, married on the 23d of October 1728, Anne, daughter and heiress of Simon Barwell, of Leicester, Esq. who died, at the age of nineteen, in 1733, leaving two daughters, Margaret, died single, and Anne. Sir Henry afterwards married Catharine, daughter of John Page, Esq. of Wandsworth, in Surry, by whom he had one son and two daughters. John, the son, died in 1767, in the life-time of his father, unmarried; Catharine, the eldest daughter, wife of Chichester-Fortescue Garstin, Esq. by whom she had one son, John, who died a captain in the 43d regiment, at Montreal, in 1779; Margaret-Sophia, the youngest daughter, was the wife of John Strode, Esq. of South Hill, in the county of Somerset, by whom she has no issue. Sir Henry-John Parker died in 1771, and was succeeded in his title by

IV. Sir HENRY PARKER, D. D. rector of Rotherfield Greys, in Oxfordshire, eldest son of Hyde, rector of Treddington, who died in 1726. Sir Henry dying unmarried, in 1781, was succeeded by his brother,

V. Sir HYDE PARKER, Bart. (second son of Hyde, rector of Treddington) vice admiral of the blue squadron of his Majesty's fleet, who upon many occasions distinguished himself in the service of his country, particularly on the fifth of March 1780, when he commanded at St. Lucia, and in the ever memorable action with the Dutch, on the Dogger Bank, on the 5th of August 1781. The impression made on the public mind from this hard fought battle, was such, as to induce the King, attended by the Prince of Wales, to pay the admiral the singular and distinguished honor of a visit at the Nore, when his Majesty was pleased to express the high sense he had of his merit and services. In the following year the vice-admiral was appointed commander in chief of his Majesty's fleet in the East Indies, and left England, in the Cato, in the month of September, aod having wooded and watered at Rio Janeiro, sailed from thence on the 12th of December, from which period no information whatever hath been received of him, so that it is presumed he perished by fire. In 1734, he married Sarah, daughter of Hugh Smithson, of London, Esq. by whom he left two sons, Harry, born 1735, and Hyde, born in 1739. He was knighted for his gallant services, as captain of his Majesty's ship the Phœnix, in the American War, and is now admiral of the Blue squadron of his majesty's fleet. He married Anne, daughter of John Palmer Boteler, Esq. of Henley, by whom he has three sons, Hyde. John, and Harry. Sir Hyde was succeeded in his title by his eldest son,

VI. Sir HARRY PARKER, of Melford Hall, in the county of Suffolk, who, in 1675, married Bridget, daughter of William Cresswell, Esq. of Cresswell, in Northumberland, by whom he has William, born in 1770; Louisa, born in 1777, wife of George-Robert Eyres, Esq.; Edmund, born in 1779; Hyde, born in 1785, and Sophia, born in 1787.

ARMS—Sable, a buck's head caboshed, between two flanches argent.

CREST—On a wreath, a dexter hand and arm, in a slashed sleve, gules, with a little cuff, argent, with the shirt seen through the slashes, proper, holding a buck's horn, erect, (or piece of coral) gules.

SEAT—Melford Hall, Suffolk.

TABLE.

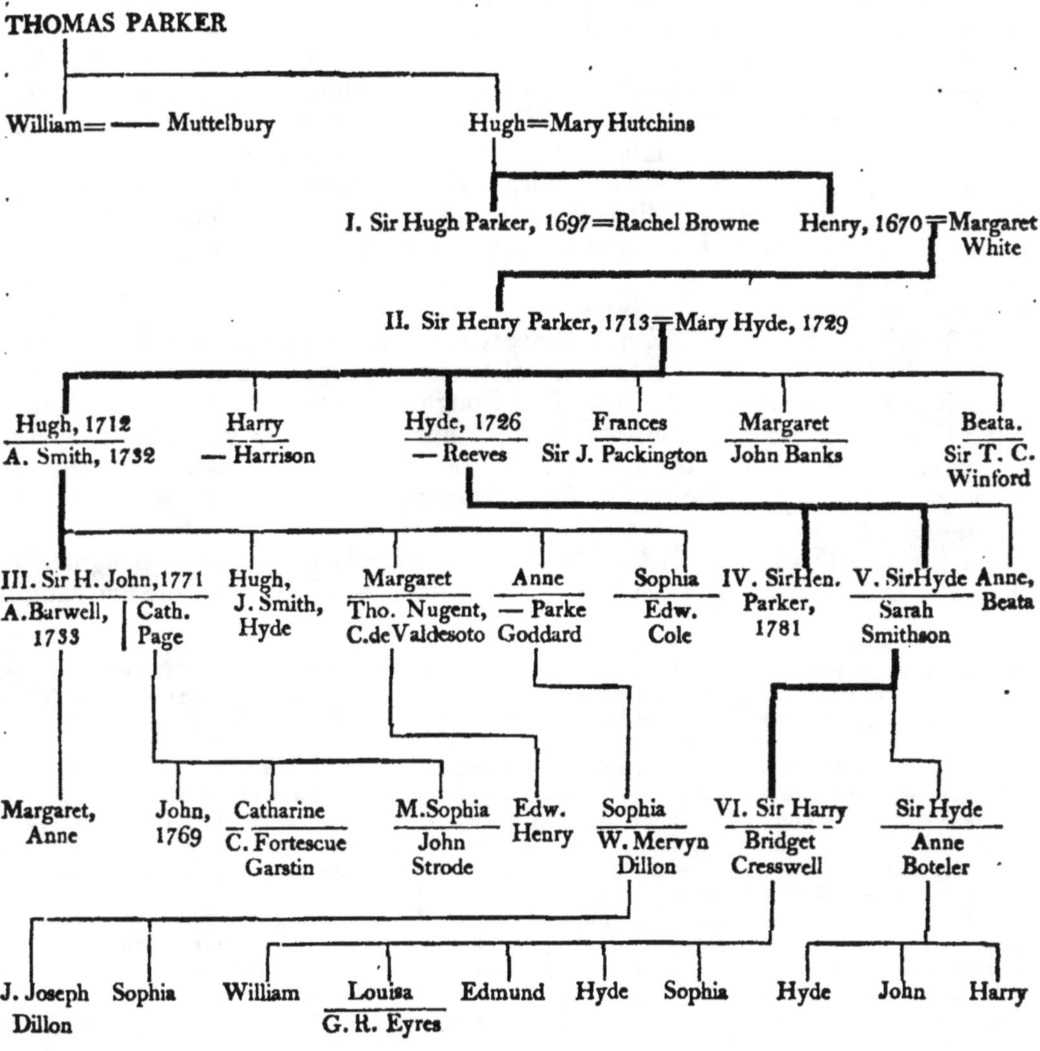
THOMAS PARKER
William=—— Muttelbury
Hugh=Mary Hutchins
I. Sir Hugh Parker, 1697=Rachel Browne
Henry, 1670=Margaret White
II. Sir Henry Parker, 1713=Mary Hyde, 1729
Hugh, 1712
A. Smith, 1732
Harry
— Harrison
Hyde, 1726
— Reeves
Frances
Sir J. Packington
Margaret
John Banks
Beata.
Sir T. C. Winford
III. Sir H. John, 1771
A. Barwell, 1733
Cath. Page
Hugh, J. Smith, Hyde
Margaret
Tho. Nugent, C. de Valdesoto
Anne
— Parke Goddard
Sophia
Edw. Cole
IV. Sir Hen. Parker, 1781
V. Sir Hyde
Sarah Smithson
Anne, Beata
Margaret, Anne
John, 1769
Catharine
C. Fortescue Garstin
M. Sophia
John Strode
Edw. Henry
Sophia
W. Mervyn Dillon
VI. Sir Harry
Bridget Cresswell
Sir Hyde
Anne Boteler
J. Joseph Dillon
Sophia
William
Louisa
G. R. Eyres
Edmund
Hyde
Sophia
Hyde
John
Harry

204. DAVERS, of Rougham, Suffolk.

Created Baronet, May 12, 1682.

THIS family is supposed to descend from John Davers, of Worming Hall, in Buckinghamshire, Esq. who married the daughter and heiress of —— Popham, by whom he had issue, John Davers, of the same place, Esq. who married Isabel, daughter of Sir John Wriothesley, Garter king at arms, (from whom descended Wriothesley, Earl of Southampton). By her he had issue, 1, Rowland, his son and heir; 2; John, slain at Bulloigne, temp. Hen. VIII.; 3, Luke, slain at New-haven; and, 4, Mark, who was of Cleare Hall, in Suffolk, and twice married, first, to Jane, daughter of Richard Beale, of Cleare Hall, in Suffolk, by whom he had issue, William, his son and heir, Wriothesley, Dorothy, wife of John Aylmer, Joan, Barbara, Bridget, and Elizabeth. His second wife was Joan, daughter of John de la Hoo, by whom he had issue, Richard.

I. ROBERT DAVERS, Esq. a descendant from these, (as is presumed) was born in England, but went to Barbadoes, where he acquired a large fortune, and came into England again, and purchased Rougham, in Suffolk, and other estates, and in consideration of his father's, and his own loyalty to Kings Charles I. and II. having been great sufferers, both in their persons and estates; in the civil wars, was advanced to the dignity of a Baronet, 34 Car. II. and was succeeded in dignity and estate by his son.

II. Sir ROBERT DAVERS, Bart. who married Mary, eldest daughter of Thomas, Lord Jermyn, of Rushbrook *, by whom he had five sons and five daugh-

* 1, This ancient and respectable family is descended from Scotland, of Rishbrooke, an odd christian name, but which seems to imply, that he or his ancestors were from North Britain. There are no dates to ascertain when he lived, but as his grand-daughter's husband was a justice of oyer in 1199, the first of King John, and allowing thirty years for a generation, this Scotland, of Rishbrooke, would be living in 1139. He was succeeded by his son,

2, Michael, of Rishbrooke, who married first, Beatrix, by whom he had two sons, 1, William; 2, Thomas, who both died without issue; and three daughters, 1, Agnes, wife of Sir Thomas Jermyn, of whom hereafter; 2, Isabel, of William Large, Esq. by whom he had a son William; and 3, Alice, died unmarried. Michael married secondly, ———, by whom he had a son Henry; but his half-sisters, on the death of their own last surviving brother, succeeded to the whole estate, to the total exclusion of Henry, a strange custom still existing.

3, Sir Thomas Jermyn, who married Agnes, daughter of Michael, was grandson of John Jermyn, by Emma his wife, and son of Hugh, which Hugh is called, of *Rishbrooke*, and which is confirmed by a note at the side of the pedigree, now in the possession of Mrs. Davers, of Bury St. Edmunds; but this, I apprehend, must be a mistake, and that the first Hugh, *surnamed of Rishbrooke*, was the great grandson of this Hugh, whose father's name also was John, as it is not probable that the Jermyns resided at Rishbrooke till that estate came to them by the marriage of Agnes with Sir Thomas Jermyn, who was justice of oyer: he left two sons, Sir William, and John: Sir William married Joan ——, but left no issue; they were living 1293.

4, John, the second son, bought the purpart of his mother's inheritance of William Large, his cousin, by which means the whole estate came to his son.

5, Hugh Jermyn, by Maud, his wife, had three sons, and two daughters; Agnes, and Alice, who both

ters, 1, Sir Robert, his successor; 2, Sir Jermyn, successor to his brother; 3, Thomas, an admiral, who married Catharine, daughter and heiress of William

died unmarried; 1, John, married Joan ——, and was living 1349, and died without issue; 2, Edmund, died without issue.

6, Hugh, the third son of Hugh, married, and left three sons.

7, Sir Thomas, who married Margaret, daughter of William Hord, of Boxted, who was living in 1380, by whom he had two daughters; 1, Eleanor, wife of William Raynham, or Ranum; 2, Anne, of Valentine Bayliffe, Esq. The second son of Hugh is in the pedigree called *Thomas*, but that must surely be a mistake: he lived at West Stow, and died 1418, which is another reason to suppose this Thomas was a grandson, and not a son of Hugh Jermyn. The third son was William. By a note at the side, containing his monumental inscription, he was of Barking, in Essex: he died 1432, and by Christian, his wife, who died in 1434, he left one son,

8, John Jermyn, of Rishbrooke, which he inherited from his uncle Sir Thomas, it being probably entailed on male issue. John was living in 1441, and was succeeded by his only son,

9, Thomas Jermyn, of Rishbrooke, Esq. living in 1479: he married Margaret, daughter of William Layman, of Ickworth, Esq. by whom he had,

10, Thomas Jermyn, who married Catharine, daughter of —— Barnard, of Akenham, in Suffolk, by whom he had four sons, and three daughters; 1, Sir Thomas; 2, Francis, who married ——, daughter and coheiress of —— Darrell, of Essex, and died S. P.; 3, Robert, who married ——, another daughter of ——— Darrell, and died S. P.; 4, Ambrose, of Annestey, or Ansty, near Barkaway, Herts, who married, and left three sons; William, of Annesty, who died S. P.; Robert, who gave his estate to his youngest brother, and died S. P.; Ralph married Jane, daughter of William Smith, of Mundein, or Mundon, near Puckeridge, Herts, by whom she had one son Ralph, of Annesty, who by Isabel, daughter of —— Bird, of the same place, had four sons, and five daughters; 1, Ralph, died young; 2, Thomas, living in 1646; 3, Charles, who married two wives: by the former, he had a son Charles, who died an infant; 4, John, of Barley, Herts, and of London, attorney in the King's Bench, living in 1646: he married Anne, third daughter of Robert King, of Barley, by whom he had a son Ralph, who died an infant. The daughters of Ralph were, 1, Margaret, died an infant; 2, Anne, wife of Walter Smith, of Lincolnshire, and of Gray's-Inn, London, by whom she had three daughters; 1, Elline, 2, Priscilla, both died young; 3, Millicent, born 1624, and living unmarried 1646. She had a second husband, John Ingham, of Charlton, in Kent, Gent. nephew to Sir Edward Ingham, by whom she had Henry and Mary, who died young; Elizabeth and Anne, living in 1646; 3, Margaret, wife of John Beaucock, of Annersty, living in 1647, by whom she had eight children; 1, John; 2, Charles; 3, Margaret; 4, Anne; 5, Elizabeth; 6, Mary; 7, Mercie; 8, ———, all living in 1646. Mercie, the fourth daughter of Ralph, was the wife of Edward Archibald, of the Chancery Office, by whom she had Elizabeth, and Anne. Dorothy, the fifth daughter of Ralph, was wife of Richard Langley, of Great Marlow, Bucks, by whom she had three sons; 1, Praise, 2, John, who died young; 3, Richard: and two daughters, Elizabeth, and Sarah *.

11, Sir Thomas Jermyn, the eldest brother of Ambrose, married, first, Anne, daughter of Thomas Spring, of Lavenham, in Suffolk, of whom hereafter; secondly, Anne, daughter of Sir Robert Drury, of Hawsted, Knt. and widow of George Waldgrave, Esq. Her great-grandfather was Nicholas Drury, of Saphara (In Sir John Cullum's Hawsted, it is wrote Saxham), in Thurston, being the second son of the family, by whom he had two sons; Henry, who married Elizabeth, daughter of George Eaton, Esq. (Sir John Cullum says, Henry was of Hires and Ickworth: his daughter Jane brought Ickworth to the Herveys); 2, Roger Drury married first, Jane Boys; secondly, Phillis, or Felice, daughter and heiress of John Denston, or Denson, of Besthorp, in Norfolk, Esq. by whom he had three sons; 1, John, died young; 2, Sir Robert, of whom hereafter; 3, William Drury, of Besthorp, who married Margaret, daughter and heiress of William Bridges, of Quidnam, Norfolk: they had many descendants. He married, thirdly, Anne ———, and died 1500.

Sir Robert Drury, of Hawsted, the second son, Sir John Cullum says, was a privy-counsellor to Henry VII. and was buried in St. Mary's Church, in Bury, 1535. He married, first, Anne, eldest daughter of Sir William Calthorpe, Bart.; and secondly, Anne, Lady Grey; by the former he had two sons, and four daughters; 1, Sir William Drury, of Hawsted, Knt. privy-counsellor to Queen Mary: he died 1557; he married Elizabeth, daughter of Henry Sothell, attorney-general to Hen. VII. His descendants continued at Hawsted till his great-grandson, Sir Robert Drury, left it to his three sisters; 2, Sir Robert Drury, of

* By the sons having the christian name of *Praise*, they were probably Puritans.

Smythson, M. D. by whom he had three children, 1, Catharine-Smythson, who died S. P.; 2, Thomas-Smythson, died S. P.; 3, Mary-Smythson.

Egerley, in Bucks, married Elizabeth, daughter and heiress of Edmund Brudenell, Esq. and died 1575, from him are descended the Drurys, of Linsted, Baronets. The daughters of Sir Robert Drury were, 1, Elizabeth, wife of Sir Philip Bottiler, Knt.; 2, Bridget, of Sir John Jerningham, of Cossey, in Norfolk, 3, Ursula, of Sir Giles Allington; 4, Anne, of George Waldgrave, of Smalbridge (q. Waldegrave); secondly, of Thomas Jermyn, of Rishbrooke, by whom she had two sons; 1, John; and 2, Thomas, who died S. P. John was of Depden, in Suffolk, and married Mary, daughter of Lyonel Talmash, of Helmingham, in Suffolk, Esq. by whom he had Thomas, and Anne, wife of Thomas Burlez, of Debden, Gent. I suspect that John Jermyn, or his son, had a much more numerous issue, which are confounded with those of Edmund, the fourth son of Sir Ambrose Jermyn, of the eldest branch of the Jermyns, of Rishbrooke, but of this hereafter. We now return to Anne, the first wife of Thomas Jermyn, by whom he had five sons, and eleven daughters; 1, Sir Ambrose; 2, Thomas; 3, John; 4, Edward; and 5, Robert, the four last died S. P. Of the daughters, 1, Mary, wife of Thomas Lucas, of Saxham, Esq.; 2, Anne, of Francis Nonne, of Martlesham, in Suffolk, Esq.; 3, Margaret, of William Clopton, of Kentwell-Hall, in Suffolk, Esq.; 4, Anne, of Robert Ashfield, of Stowlangtoft, Suffolk, (It is a little extraordinary, there should be two Annes, and both live to be married; 5, Elizabeth, of Thomas Playters, of Sotterley, Suffolk; 6, Bridget, of Robert Crane, of Chilton, in Suffolk, Esq.; 7, Ursula, of Thomas Coppinger, of Buxhall, in Suffolk, Esq.; 8, Barbara, of Thomas Bacon, of Hedgsett, in Suffolk, Esq.; 9, Martha, of Thomas Higham, of Higham, in Suffolk, Esq.; 10, Dorothy, of Lionel Gooderick, of Lincolnshire, Esq.; 11, Agnes, of Roger Martyn, of Long Melford, Suffolk.

12, Sir Ambrose Jermyn, the eldest son of Sir Thomas, married, first, Anne, daughter and coheiress of George Havingham, Esq. son of Sir John Hevingham, Knight Banneret; secondly, Dorothy, daughter of William Baddley, by whom he had no issue; but by his first wife he had eight sons and six daughters; 1, John, who married Margaret Stanley, daughter of Edward, Earl of Derby, (who was afterwards the wife of Sir Nicholas Poyntz, in Gloucestershire, Knt.) and died S. P.; 2, Sir Robert, of whom hereafter; 3, Ambrose, of Stanton, Esq. who married Anne, daughter and coheiress of John Paston, of Huntingfield, in Suffolk, Esq. by whom he had Edmund, of Stanton, who married Lettice, daughter of Henry Goldingham, of Essex, Esq. and Bridget, wife of Walter, son of Sir Thomas Mildmay; 4, Edmund, of Struston, in Norfolk, who married Dorothy, daughter of Sir William Spring, of Packenham, in Suffolk, Knt. by whom, *according to the pedigree*, he had sixteen sons, and five daughters; 1, John; 2, Thomas; 3, Talmash; 4, Clement; 5, William, died S. P.; 6, George, died S. P.; (these names are all on one ring in the pedigree; 7, Edward, died S. P. 8, Ambrose, died S. P.; 9, Edmund, died S. P.; 1, daughter Susan, died S. P.; 2, daughter Sarah, died S. P..; (these last five are in the next ring) 10, Sir John, called the second son: 11, Robert, called the third son; 12, Ambrose, called the fourth son:- the eighth is also called Ambrose. and the first and tenth sons called John; 13, Anthony, called the fifth son; 14, William, called the sixth son; (these last five in the next ring) 15, Thomas, called the seventh son; 16, Edward, called the eighth son; 3, daughter Susan; (this was the name of the first daughter) 4, Anne, wife of —— Phillips (these last four in one ring); 5, Elizabeth, wife of Sir Robert Wynde, of South Wotton, in Norfolk, Knt. *(a)* 5, Thomas, the fifth son of Sir Ambrose; 6, William; 7, Francis, died S. P.; 8, George, died S. P. His daughters were, 1, Anne, wife of Sir Thomas Tyndall, Knt; 2, Susanna, of Lyonel Talmash, Esq; and secondly, of Sir William Spring, Knt; 3, Dorothy, of Edward Duke, of Shenfield, Esq.; 4, Margaret, of Thomas Dighton, of Stanton, Lincolnshire, Esq.; 5, Hester, of Ambrose Blage, of Horniger, Esq.; 6, Frances, died S. P.

13, Sir Robert Jermyn, eldest surviving son of Sir Ambrose, married Judith, daughter of Sir George Blage, by whom he had two sons and five daughters; 1, Sir Thomas; 2, Robert, who married Dorothy, daughter of Sir Henry Warner, of Milden-Hall, in Suffolk, Knt; 1, Judith, wife of Sir Wm. Waldegrave, of Smallbridge, in Suffolk, Knt.; 2, Elizabeth *(b)*, or Susan, the wife of Sir Wm Hervey, of Ickworth, Knt.

(a) The pedigree thus contradicting itself in numbering the sons, it is clear there must be some mistake; and from the third son in the first ring being called Talmash, I apprehend the two first rings, containing together eleven children, must have belonged to the Jermyns, of Debden, and these being thus disposed of, it still leaves Edward and Dorothy Jermyn ten children.

(b) The Rev. A. Jacob, in his Peerage, Vol. II. p. 67, calls her Susan, which seems to be right; and this is the same Susan whom Mrs. Davers supposed to be the daughter of Sir Thomas Jermyn, by Mary Barber, whereas she was his aunt, the daughter of his grandfather, Sir Robert, and the dates of his marriage and death confirm this fact.

4, Henry, . died S. P.; 5, Charles, died S. P. Of the daughters of Sir Robert, 1, Mary, was the wife of Clemence Corrance, Esq. M. P. for Orford,

in 1613; 3, Anne, of Sir William Pooley, of Boxstead, in Suffolk, Knt.; 4, Frances, of Sir William Wodehouse, of Waxtonholme, in Norfolk, Knt.; 5, Dorothy, of Ralph Shelton, of Shelton, in Norfolk, Knt.

14, Sir Thomas Jermyn, eldest son of Sir Robert, married Catharine, daughter of Sir William Killigrew, Knt. groom of the privy-chamber to Queen Elizabeth, by whom he had a son,

15, Sir Thomas Jermyn, born in 1572, and died in 1644. He was privy-counsellor and comptroller of the household to Charles I. and married Mary Barber, by whom he had two sons, 1, Sir Thomas; 2, Henry, created Lord Jermyn, of St. Edmundsbury, Sept. 8, 1644, and at Breda, in Brabant, April 27, 1660, was, by King Charles II. created Earl of St. Albans; and, in 1672, K. G. he married Henrietta-Maria, widow of King Charles I. and daughter of Henry IV. of France, to whom he was master of horse, and chamberlain. According to Adam's Index Villaris, printed in 1680, he was possessed of the following houses, viz. St. Alban's-House, St. James's-square, London; Rushbrook-Hall, in Suffolk; (this must be a mistake, as that house then belonged to his nephew, Sir Thomas Jermyn) Pyfleet, Surry; and Thaffs, Norfolk. Count Hamilton, in his Memoirs of his sister's husband, Count Grammont, represents the Earl of St. Albans "as a man of very considerable fortune, raised by himself; that he lost money at play, and kept a great table, not only after the Restoration, but before that event in France and Flanders, where he eclipsed all the rest of King Charles's courtiers, except the Duke of Buckingham; and that he adopted the youngest of his nephews as his heir." But before we proceed further, it is necessary to return to the eldest brother,

16, Sir Thomas Jermyn, of Rishbrooke, who married Rebecca ——, (who, after his death, was the wife of Viscount Branker), by whom he had two sons, 1, Thomas; 2, Henry, who was created Baron Dover. Count Hamilton gives a lively account of him when he was a young fellow; but it must of all be remarked, that it was not one of the least evils attending the Civil Wars, that Charles II. and his brother, by living abroad, had acquired such a taste for French manners, as almost infected the whole court; and no young fellow would be regarded as *fashionable* that was not a man of gallantry. Henry, at the Restoration, was twenty-four years old: the account of Count Hamilton commences just before it took place. "Jermyn (says he) supported by his uncle's, the Earl of St. Albans, wealth, found it no difficult matter to make a considerable figure upon his arrival at the Princess of Orange's court (sister of Charles II.) The poor courtiers belonging to the king, her brother, could by no means contend with him in point of equipage and magnificence, which two articles often go further in love than real merit. There needs no other instance; for though Jermyn was brave, and by birth a gentleman, he had not the advantage of being distinguished by military exploits. As for his person, he was little, had a large head, and thin legs, but his features were agreeable enough. The Princess Royal (quære, did this mean the Princess of Orange, or Princess Henrietta?) first admired him, and Lady Anne Hyde followed her mistress. By this, his reputation was established in England before his arrival; and the Countess of Castlemain, afterwards Duchess of Cleveland, the king's mistress, was so much in love with him, that she was very near falling out with the king upon it. Jermyn gave up Miss Hyde to please her, but Lady Castlemain had so many intrigues, even down to Jacob Hill, a rope dancer, as gave little Jermyn leisure for other pursuits. He next made love to another abandoned peeress, the famous Countess of Shrewsbury. This lady was Anna-Maria, daughter of Robert Brudenell, Earl of Cardigan, and wife of Francis Talbot, the eleventh Earl of Shrewsbury, who afterwards, March 16, 1667, was on her account killed in a duel by George Villars, Duke of Buckingham. She married, secondly, Mr. Bridges, and died April 1702." Count Hamilton proceeds: "Jermyn was displeased that she had made no advances to him, but his scheme of taking her from the rest of her lovers, was highly imprudent. Howard, brother of the Earl of Carlisle, was one of them: there was not a braver or a more accomplished gentleman in England; and though he was of a modest air, and appeared gentle in his behaviour, no one had a greater spirit, or was more passionate.

"Lady Shrewsbury returning the glances of the invincible Jermyn, this was far from being agreeable to Mr. Howard; however, to keep fair with him, she agreed to accept a collation which he had often proposed, and Spring Gardens, (near Charing Cross, the Vauxhall of the time) was the place fixed on for the entertainment, of which Jermyn was immediately informed. Howard had a company in the guards, and as one of the soldiers played pretty well on the bagpipe, he had him to play to them. At the time appointed, Jermyn repaired to Spring Garden, as if by chance: he no sooner appeared in the walks, than Lady Shrewsbury shewed herself on the balcony. Howard was not well pleased at seeing him, but this

from 1740 to 1722, by whom she had 1; Clemence, who married, first, —— Brampton, secondly, —— Chester, by one of which he had a daughter, who

did not hinder him from coming up at the first sign the countess made to him; and he was not content with acting the petty tyrant, but having attracted the fair one's kind looks, he ridiculed both the repast and the music. Howard was master of little raillery, and still less patience, so that the banquet was three times on the point of being stained with blood; but he as often suppressed his natural impetuosity, that he might shew his resentment elsewhere with greater freedom. Jermyn, without taking the least notice of his ill-humour, pursued his point, continued to talk to Lady Shrewsbury, and did not leave her till the feast was over. The next morning he was waked with a challenge: he took G. Rawlings for his second, a man of intrigue, and one that played high. Howard had Dillon, who was dextrous, brave, much of a gentleman, and unfortunately an intimate friend to Rawlings. In this duel poor Rawlings was left stone dead, and Jermyn, having received three great wounds, was carried to his uncle's, the Earl of St. Albans, with very little signs of life." He however recovered, and, as was before observed, lived above forty years after this duel. Lord Dover was a roman catholic*, which so recommended him to K. James II. that in 1685, he created him Baron Dover, or, acccording to Beatson, Baron of Dover, in Kent; and that king added a fourth troop to the horse-guards, of which he made Lord Dover the captain and colonel. He was in great favour at cour, and by his recommendation, Dr. Watson was made Bishop of St. Davids; but he was unfortunate in this recommendation, that bishop being afterwards deprived for simony, and other crimes. At the revolution, he followed K. James into France, and thence into Ireland. After the battle of the Boyne in 1690, he tendered his submission to King William, who accepted it; after which, he retired to his estate at Cheveley, in Cambridgeshire, where he became a great manager. He married Judith Pooley, probably of Boxted. April 1, 1703, he succeeded to the title of Baron Jermyn, of St. Edmundsbury, on the death of his brother without male heirs: and in April 1708, he died at Cheveley, aged seventy-two, and was buried at the church of the Carmalites at Bruges: he left the bulk of h s estates to his nephew, Jermyn Davers, afterwards Sir Jermyn Davers; and the same year the title of the Duke of Dover was given to the Duke of Queensbury.

We now return to his elder brother,

17, Thomas Jermyn, who succeeded to the tittle of Baron Jermyn, on the death of his uncle, the Earl of St. Albans, which, according to Mrs. Davers's pedigree, and Bolton's extinct Peerage, took place in 1688, but according to Beatson, in 1683, which last seems the more probable, as Charles II. created his son Duke of St. Albans, Jan. 10, 1683–4. He married Mary Merry, by whom he had one son Thomas, born 1677, killed by a mast of a ship falling on him in 1692, and was buried at Rishbrooke: and five daughters, 1, Mary, wife of Sir Robert Davers, Bart. of whom hereafter; 2, Declariviere. of Sir Symond D'Ewes, of Stow-Hall, in Suffolk†, by whom, who died in 1702, she had four sons and four daughters, 1, Sir Willoughby D'Ewes, Bart. who died S. P.; 2, Simond, died S. P.; 3, Thomas, died S. P.; 4, Jermyn, died S. P.; 1 daughter Delariviere, wife of Thomas, eldest son of Sir Thomas Gage, Bart.; 2, Mary, of George Tasborough, of Bodney, in Norfolk. Esq. by whom she had one son George, who, in March 1755, married Theresa, daughter of Thomas Viscount Gage, she died S. P. 1773. He married, secondly, Barbara Fitzherbert‡; 3, Harriot, wife of —— Havers, by whom she had three sons and one daughter, 1, Thomas Havers, married —— Dewtree, by whom he had four sons, Eward, William, John, Thomas and five daughters, 1, Catharine, wife of —— Bedingfeld; 2, Mary, of —— Norris. 3, Lucretia, of Thomas Wright, Esq. banker, in Henrietta-street, Covent-Garden; 4, Frances; and 5, Harriot. The second son of —— Havers and Harriot D'Ewes, was William, who married —— Wike, by whom he had one son William, in the first battalion of the west-riding York millitia, and died 179–, and two daughters, Mary died S. P.; and Harriot, wife of —— Paston, Esq. captain in the West Suffolk militia.

The third son of —— Havers and Harriot D'Ewes, was Edward, who died S. P.

The fourth daughter of Sir Symond D'Ewes and Delariviere Jermyn, was Mesalina, wife of Richard Elwes, probably the third son of Sir Gervase Elwes, of Stoke College, in Suffolk, Bart.

* His brother and his uncle were Protestants.—*Complete History of Europe*, 1768, p. 398, 399.

† This is properly Stowlangtoft, to distinguish it from other Stows. Sir Symonds, or Symonds, for so it is spelt in the celebrated book he published of the Journals of Queen Elizabeth's Parliaments, and in Kimber, was created a baronet July 15, 1641.

‡ This Barbara, if I am not mistaken, after the death of Mr. Tasborough, from whom she had a large jointure, in 178– was the wife of Philip Saltmarsh, of York, Esq. Her brother was the husband of the celebrated Mrs. Fitzherbert.

died S. P.; 2, Robert Corrance, died S. P. 1, Mary, wife of Captain Castle, by whom he had one son, William Castle, who married Catharine Frome, by whom he had one daughter, Catharine, wife of —— Bouverie, Esq. The daughter of Captain Castle and Mary Corrance, was Mary, wife of —— Clavel. The second daughter of Clemence Corrance and Mary Davers, was Elizabeth, the wife of Israel Long, by whom she had Elizabeth Long, who died S. P. The third daughter Henrietta Corrance, died S. P. The second daughter of Sir Robert Davers, was Isabella, wife of Brigadier General ——— Moyle, by whom five sons and one daughter, 1, Jermyn, died S P.; 2, Robert, died S. P.; 3, John, married ——; 4, Thomas, married Sarah Coppenger, by whom he had one son and two daughters, Thomas, died S. P. Isabella and Mary. 5, Henry, married Mary Parker, by whom he had one son and six daughters, Robert, died S. P. 1, Elizabeth, wife of Edward Johns; 2, Mariana, of Robert Man, a captain in the navy; 4, Harriot, of W. S. Cooper, of the Victualling Office; 5, Isabella; 6, Charlotte.

The daughter of General Moyle and Isabella Davers, was Isabella, wife of Samuel Horsey, Esq. of Bury, he had been in the army, and was afterwards Bath, King at Arms, and died Nov. 2, 1771, by whom he had Caroline, the wife of George Waddington, Esq. brother to Mrs. Leheup, by whom she had two sons, Henry-Spencer, born Dec. 1781, and John Horsey. She was, secondly, the wife of the Rev. Samuel Kilderbee, of Campsey-Ash, by whom she has three children.

The third daughter of Thomas Lord Jermyn and Mary Merry, was Henrietta-Maria, who died 1698; she was wife of Thomas Bond, by whom she had two sons, 1, Thomas, died S. P.; 2, Henry, married Jenny Godfrey, by whom she had Charles Bond, who died S. P. and two daughters, 1, Charlotte, a nun; 2, Judith, died S. P.

Penelope, the fourth daughter of Thomas Lord Jermyn, was wife of Grey-James Grove, of Pool-Hall, in Shropshire, by whom he had three children.

Merilina, the fifth daughter, was wife of Sir Thomas Spring, of Packenham, Bart. descended from Thomas Spring, the rich clothier of Lavenham, who died 1510*. (She was afterwards the wife of Sir William Gage, by whom she had no issue), by whom she had three sons, 1, Thomas, died S. P.; 2, Jermyn, died S. P.; 3, Sir William Spring, Bart. died S. P.; and six daughters, 1, Merelina, died S. P.; 2, Merelina, wife of Thomas Disciplence, by whom she had Merelina, the wife of Michael Leheup, Esp. by whom she had Michael Leheup, Esq. who married Mary, sister of George Waddington, of Bury. Esq. by whom he had Michael, Mary, and Merelina, Delariviere Discipline, the second daughter, was wife of John Godbold, Esq.

The second daughter of Sir Thomas Spring and Merelina Jermyn, was Mary, wife of the Rev. John Symonds, rector of Horringeth, by whom she had two sons and two daughters, 1, John Symonds, Esq. L.L.D. recorder of Bury, and in 1771, appointed Professor of Modern History at Cambridge; living, in 1802, at his elegant villa called St. Edmund's Hill, an estate that came by his maternal grandmother, Merelina Jermyn; 2, Thomas Symonds, captain of a man of war: he died 1792. He married first, Mary Noble, secondly, Elizabeth Mallet, by whom he had three sons, 1, Jermyn; 2, Thomas, died young; 3, Thomas: and two daughters, 1, Mariana, the wife of John Benjafield, Esq by whom she had one son, Frederick; 2, Elizabeth, of the Rev ——— Higham, by whom she has two sons.

The daughters of the Rev; John Symondes, and Mary Sprig were, 1, Delariviere, wife of the Rev. —— Casburn, by whom he had, 1, Spring-Casburn; 2, Delariviere. The second daughter, Anna Maria Symonds, died S. P. The third daughter of Sir Thomas Spring and Merelina Jermyn, was Henrietta, who died S. P. The fourth daughter was Delariviere, who died S. P.

* Kirby's Suffolk Traveller, p. 261.

The third daughter of Sir Robert Davers, was Harriot, wife of Roger Pratt, Esq. by whom she had two sons and two daughters, and a fifth child died S.P. 1, Edward, married Blanch Astley, by whom he had one son, Edward, and two daughters, Sarah, wife of Charles Collyer, and Lucy. The second son of Roger Pratt and Harriot Davers, was Jermyn, who married Anne Stamford. The first daughter was Mary, the wife of —— Stafford. The second, Harriot, of —— Stafford.

The fourth daughter of Sir Robert Davers, was Penelope, wife of Dr. —— Pake. *Kimber puts Mrs. Pake before Mrs. Pratt.*

Elizabeth, the fifth daughter, was wife of John King, of Norfolk, Esq. Sir Robert Davers was M. P. for the county of Suffolk, from 1705, till his death, Oct. 1, 1722. He was succeeded in dignity and estate by his eldest son,

III. Sir ROBERT DAVERS, Bart. who in 1712, had been auditor of the excise, he died S. P. in 1723, and was succeeded in title and estate by his brother.

IV. Sir JERMYN DAVERS Bart. of Rishbrooke, now usually spelt Rushbrooke, he married Margaritta (Kimber calls her Margarilla) eldest daughter and coheiress of the Rev. Mr. Green, by whom she had four sons and two daughters, 1, Robert, who died S. P.; 2, Henry, died S. P.; 3, Sir Charles, the present Baronet; 4, Thomas, died S. P.. 1, Mary, the compiler of this pedigree; 2, Elizabeth, late wife of the Rev. Frederick Hervey, Earl of Bristol, and Bishop of Derry. He was, in his father's lifetime, M. P. for St. Edmundsbury, in Suffolk, and in 1727, he was chosen knight of the shire for Suffolk, and represented that county till his death, in Feb. 1743, he was succeeded by his only surviving son,

V. Sir CHARLES DAVERS, Bart. M. P. for St. Edmundsbury.

ARMS—Argent, on a bend gules, three martlets, or.

CREST—A jay, proper, in his bill an amulet, or; but since the marriage with the Jermyns, they give a talbot, passant, argent.

SEAT—At Rushbrook, near St. Edmundsbury, Suffolk.

TABLE.

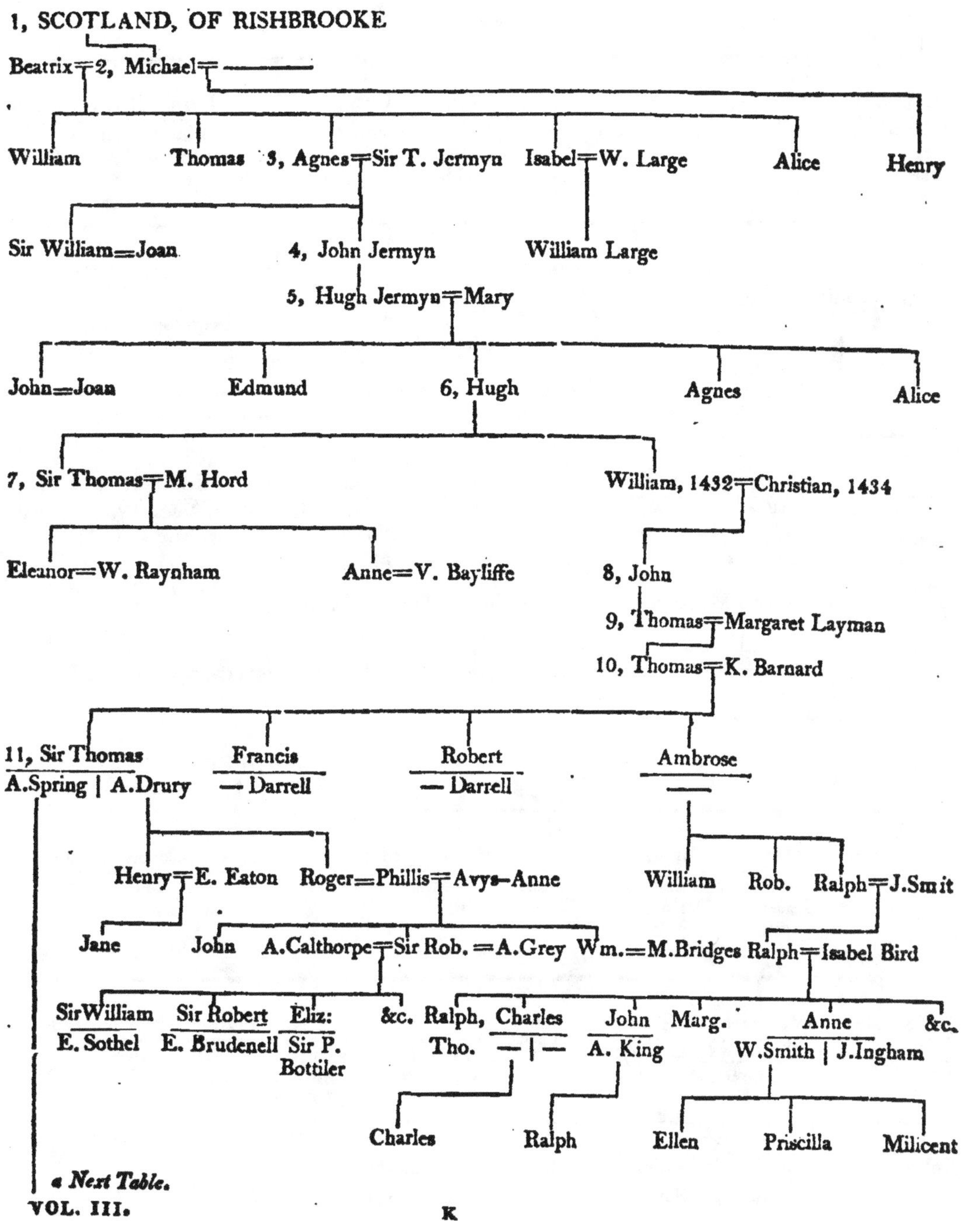

a Next Table.

TABLE OF DAVERS *continued.*

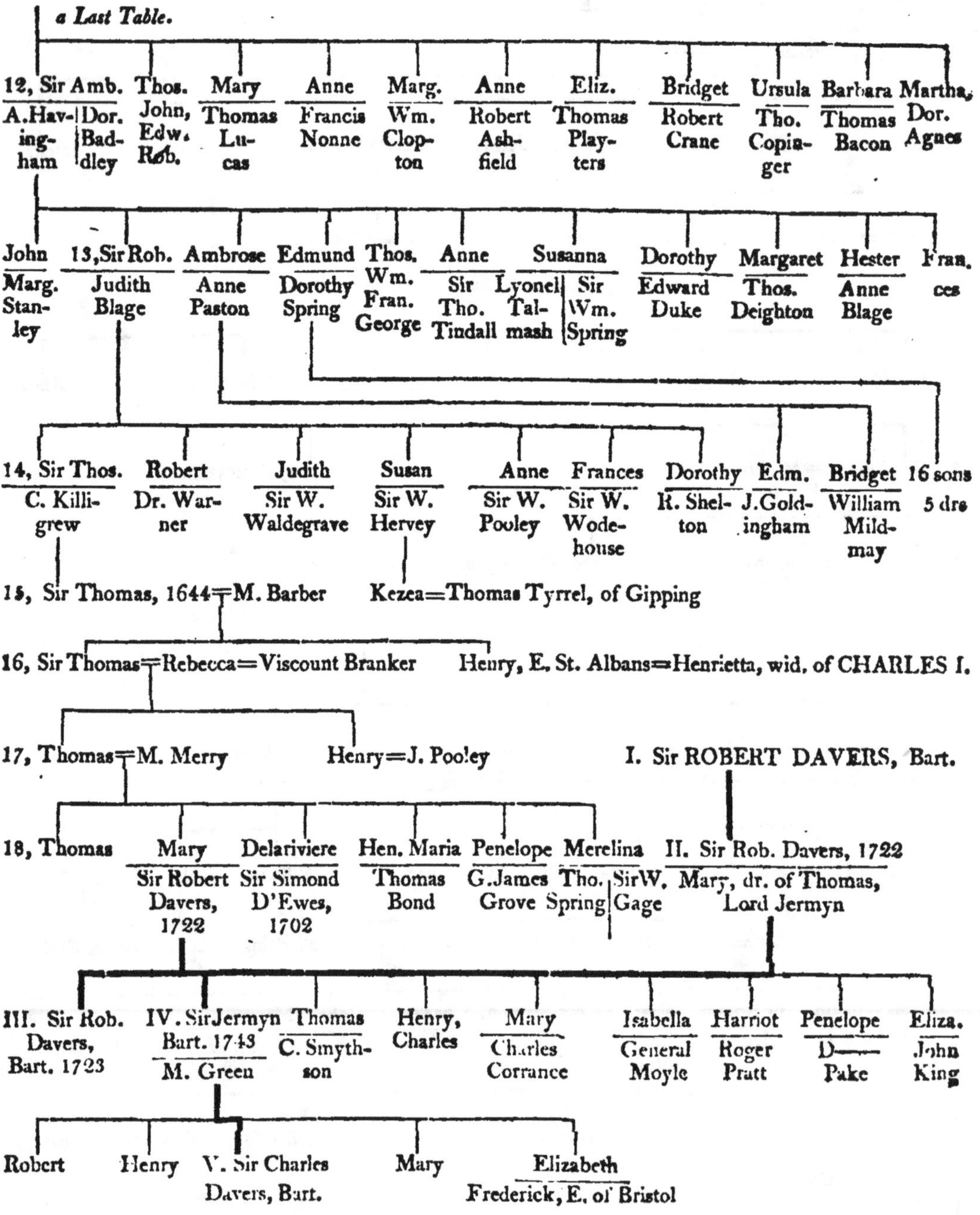

205. RICHARDS, of BRAMLETY-HOUSE, SUSSEX.

Created Baronet, Feb. 22, 1683-4.

JOHN RICHARDS, Esq. came into England with the Queen mother of Charles II. from Thoulouse, in France. He had a numerous issue.

I. JAMES, his youngest son, was knighted by his Majesty, King Charles II, for saving several men of war, and by the said King advanced to the dignity of a Baronet, the thirty-fifth of his reign. He married, first, Mrs. Anne Popely, of Redhouse, in Bristol, by whom he had two sons, Sir John, his successor, and Arthur, who died S. P. also one daughter, Elizabeth; secondly, Beatrice Herara, by whom he left four sons, 1, Sir Joseph, successor to his half brother; 2, Sir Philip, successor to his brother; 3, James; and 4, Lewis; also one daughter, Clara. Sir James settled in Spain, where he died, being succeeded by his eldest son, by his first lady,

II. Sir JOHN RICHARDS, Bart. who was colonel of a regiment of foot in the Spanish service, before he was twenty-one, which he afterwards quitted, and took to merchandize, and carried on a considerable trade at Cadiz; but dying unmarried, was succeeded by his half brother,

III. Sir JOSEPH RICHARDS, Bart. eldest son by the second lady, who died unmarried also, June 2, 1738, and lies buried in St. Pancras church-yard, in Middlesex*.

IV. Sir PHILIP RICHARDS, Bart. succeeded his brother, Sir Joseph, in dignity and estate, and married ——, the eldest daughter of the duke de Montemar†, who was general, and commander in chief of the Spanish forces sent into Italy,

* Where, on a black marble, raised on Portland stone, about two feet high, is this inscription:

Here lieth interred the Body of
Sir Joseph Richards, Bart.
who departed this Life
June 2, 1738, aged 53.
Requiescat in Pace.
†

† On his marriage with this lady, a demur was made, concerning the nature of the title claimed by Don Philipe Ricardo, who said he was an English Baronet, and the difficulty was about giving him rank; finally, it was decided, he should have the same precedency as the Spanish *Titulos de Castilla*. These are *Marquisses* and *Counts*, created by the King of Spain, by patent, enjoying certain privileges, but far inferior to the grandees of the kingdom. But this is only given on report, without any documental authority; however, it seems probable that marquisses and counts, as above, are in the eyes of an Englishman, as well as Spaniard, pretty much on a similar establishment of public opinion.

1735. The family having been settled in Spain, for about sixty years, we cannot take upon us, with any certainty, to say who is the present Baronet.

ARMS—Argent, a cheveron, and in base, a lion rampant, azure.
CREST—On a wreath, a lion rampant azure.
MOTTO—*Honore et amore.*
RESIDENCE—In Spain.

TABLE.

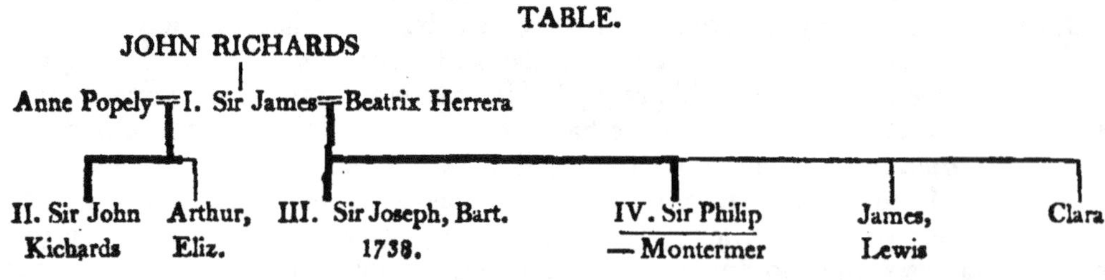

206. DASHWOOD, of NORTHBROOKE, Oxfordshire.

Created Baronet, May 16, 1684.

THIS family is descended from the second marriage of a worthy family in Dorsetshire*, and from thence transplanted into Somersetshire.

George Dashwood, Esq. a younger son of the said family, 21 Car. II.†, undertook, (with other persons,) the farming the whole revenue of the kingdom of Ireland, and afterwards was one of those who farmed the whole revenues of excise, and hearth-money in England, so long as those revenues were continued in a farm, and was, (whilst managed by commission,) continued one of the commissioners, till his death, 1682. He married Margaret, daughter of —— Perry, of Thorpe, in Surry, Esq. sister to Col. Perry, by whom he had three sons and two daughters, 1, Robert, of whom hereafter; 2, Richard, who married Mary, daughter of —— Garrat, of London, Esq.; 3, George, lieutenant-colonel of a regiment of foot, and died at Torbay 1706, married Angelina, daughter of Sir Algernoon Peyton, of Doddington, in the Isle of Ely, Bart.; Elizabeth, wife of Sir Thomas Hare, of Stow-Bardolph, in Norfolk, Bart.; and Anne, of Sir Sewster Peyton, of Doddington, in the Isle of Ely, Bart.

* Ex inf. Dom. Rob. Dashwood, Bar. 1727. † Ibid.

I. ROBERT DASHWOOD, Esq. the eldest son, was advanced to the dignity of a Bart. 36 Car. II.* with remainder (in case of failure of issue male) to the issue male of Geo. Dashwood, Esq. the father, which favour was granted to the family, as likewise, the precedence of a Baronet's widow, to Margaret, widow and relict of the aforesaid George Dashwood, Esq. in consideration that the said George Dashwood, Esq. had a warrant for a Baronet's patent, for some time lying by him, which he did not take out, as fully expressed in the patent.

Sir Robert, served in several parliaments, in the reign of King William, for Banbury, in Oxfordshire, and married Penelope, daughter and coheiress of Sir Thomas Chamberlayne, of Wickham, in Oxfordshire, Bart. by whom he had five sons, and four daughters; 1, Chamberlayne, who died a batchelor; 2, George, and 3, Charles, who died infants; 4, Robert, married Dorothea, daughter and coheiress of Sir James Read, of Brocket-hall, in Hertfordshire, Bt. by whom he had three sons, 1, Robert; 2, Sir James, successor to his grandfather; 3, George, and one daughter Love, who all died under age except Sir James. This Robert Dashwood, Esq. died at Paris, Sept. or Oct. 1728, and was brought over, and interred in Oxfordshire, as was George, his son. Richard, the fifth son, married Elizabeth, daughter of Thomas Lewis, of Stanford, in Nottinghamshire, Esq. and died April 1737, leaving two sons, Robert, and Chamberlayne. The four daughters of Sir Robert were, Margaret, who died an infant; Penelope, wife of Sir John Stonhouse, of Radley, in Berks, Bart.; Catharine, of Sir Robert-Banks Jenkinson, of Walcot, in Oxfordshire, Bart.; and Anne, of Anthony Cope, Esq. brother to Sir Jonathan Cope, of Brewern, in Oxfordshire, Bart.† Sir Robert died July, 1734, at Northbrooke, and was succeeded in dignity and estate by his grandson,

II. Sir JAMES DASHWOOD, who married Feb. 1738-9, Elizabeth, daughter and coheiress of Edward Spencer, of Rendlesham, in Suffolk, Esq. (the other daughter and coheiress was married to James, Duke of Hamilton,) by whom he had three sons and three daughters, 1, James, died an infant; 2, Sir Henry-Watkin, his successor; 3, Thomas; 1, Elizabeth, wife of George, Duke of Manchester; 2, Anne, of John, Earl of Galloway; 3, Catharine, of Lucy Knightly, of Fawsley, in Northamptonshire, Esq. Sir James was L.L.D. high-steward of the university of Oxford, which county he represented in several parliaments. Sir James died Nov. 10, 1779, aged 64, and was succeeded by his eldest surviving son,

III. Sir HENRY-WATKIN DASHWOOD, Bart. who married, July 17, 1780, Mary-Ellen, eldest daughter of ——— Graham, formerly a member of the council in Bengal, and niece to the late William, Lord Newhaven, governess to the Princess Charlotte, by whom he has four sons and two daughters, 1, Henry-George-Magne, born June 26, 1782; 2, Anna-Maria, born Feb. 16, 1785; 3, George, page of honour to his Majesty, born Sept. 17, 1786; 4, Charles, born Dec. 9, 1787; 5, Augustus, born Feb. 25, 1795; 6, Georgiana-Carolina, born Mar. 16, 1796.

* Ex Inf. Dom. Rob. Dashwood, Bar. 1727.

† Sir Robert was seised, in fee simple, of divers messuages, farms, lands, tenements, and hereditaments, situate, lying, and being in Kirtleton, Bletchingdon, Bigneil, Banbury, Baynton, Dunstew, North Aston, Bicester, Wiggington, and Tackley, in Oxfordshire; and also of divers fee-farm rents, tenths, and pensions, arising, or payable in the counties of Oxford, Nottingham, and other counties in England.

ARMS—Argent, on a fess, double cottised, gules, three griffin's heads erased, per fess, erminois, and gules.

CREST—On a wreath, a griffin's head erased, per fess, erminois, and gules.

SEAT—Kirtlington Park, near Woodstock, Oxfordshire.

TABLE.

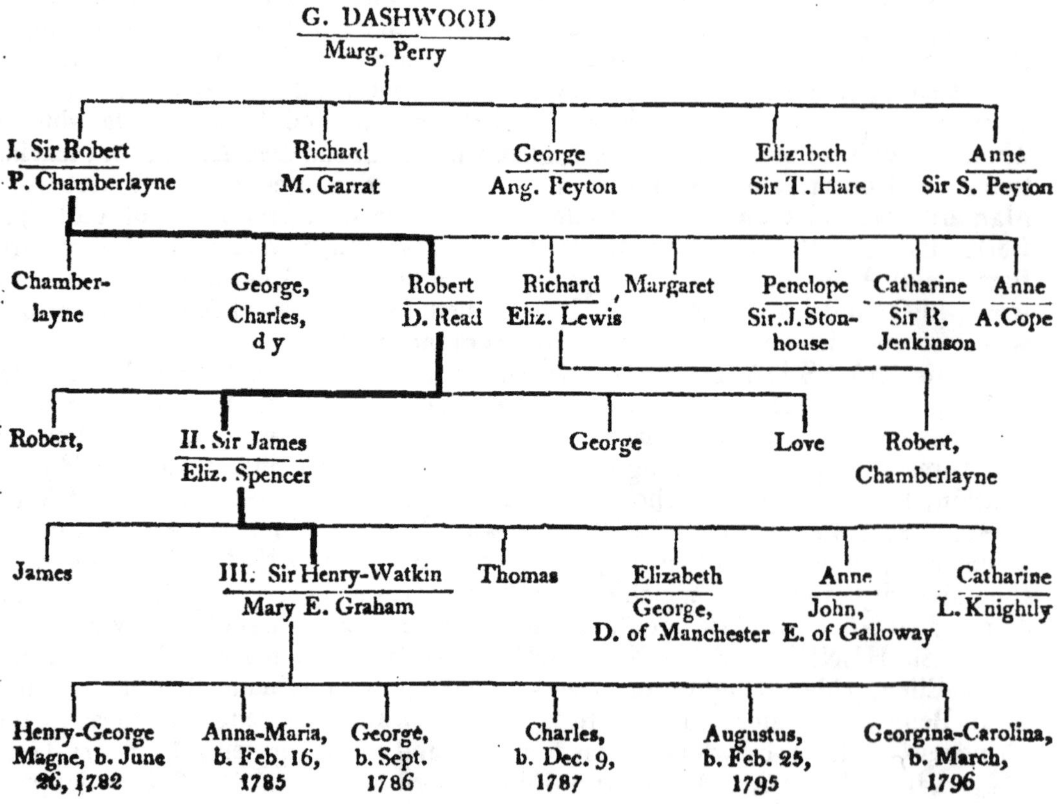

207. CHILD, of SURAT, in the East Indies.

Created Baronet, Feb. 4, 1684.

JOHN CHILD, of London, Gent. is the first of this family we have any account of: he married Frances, daughter of Francis Goodyer, of Hereford, by whom he had one son John, and two daughters; ——, wife of —— Ward, of Bombay, in the East Indies, merchant; and Dorcas, of Thomas Mitchel, of Bombay, merchant, descended from those in Sussex.

I. JOHN CHILD, Esq. only son and heir, was general of all the English forces by sea and land, in the northern parts of India, and president of the East India Company's council at Surat, at the time he was created a Baronet, as the patent mentions. He continued in India till the time of his death, at Bombay, where he was buried about 1690. He married, in India, Mary, daughter of John Shackstone, Esq. deputy-governor of Bombay, and had two sons, Sir Cæsar, his successor, and John, who died of the small-pox, unmarried, 1718.

II. Sir CÆSAR CHILD, Bart. successor to the title and estate in 1698, married Hester, daughter of John Evance, of London, Knt. and goldsmith, by whom he had four sons, 1, Sir Cæsar, his successor; 2, John, who died an infant; 3, Stephen; 4, John, who both died unmarried: and five daughters; 1, Hester, the wife of John Tyssen, Esq. and died 1723; 2, Susanna, of William Cleland, Esq.; 3, Anne, of James Collet, Esq. and died in childbed 1725; 4, Elizabeth, of William Cleland, of Tapley-Hall, in Devonshire, Esq. by whom she had three sons and three daughters; 5, Frances, of Nicholas Corselis, of Wivenhoe, in Essex, Esq. Sir Cæsar died of the small-pox March 7, 1724, and was succeeded in dignity and estate by his eldest son,

III. Sir CÆSAR CHILD, Bart.

ARMS—Vert, two bars engrailed, between three leopard's faces, or.
CREST—A leopard's face, or, between two laurel branches, vert.
MOTTO—*Spes alit.*
SEAT—Dervil, Essex.

TABLE.

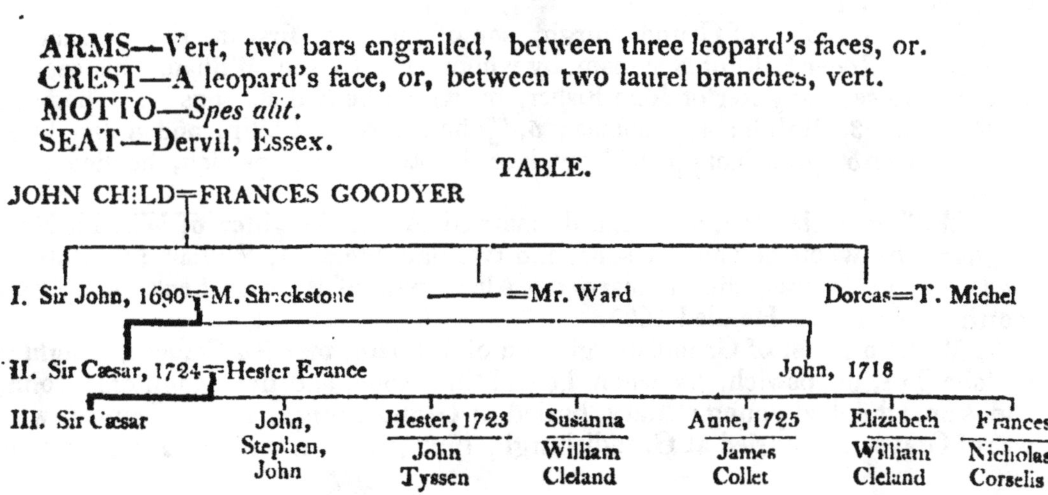

BARONETS

CREATED BY

KING JAMES II.

208. BLOIS, of GRUNDISBURGH-HALL, Suffolk.

Created Baronet, April 15, 1686.

THIS ancient family derives its name from Blois, a city in France, and came into England at the conquest. The seat was at Norton, in Suffolk, till the reign of King Henry VII. when it was removed to Grundisburgh-Hall, now in possession of the present Baronet.

1, Thomas Blois, living at Norton, 1470, was father of,

2, Thomas Blois, of the same place, whose son,

3, Thomas Blois, married Margery, the daughter of William Styles, of Ipswich, he died 1528.

4, Richard Blois, of Grundisburgh, son of Thomas, first married Elizabeth, daughter of Roger Hill, of Needham, by whom he had a son, William; his second wife was Rose, daughter of John Fisher, by whom he had six sons: 1, Thomas; 2, Richard; 3, Ralph; 4, Thomas; 5, John; and 6, Philip, and a daughter, Martha, wife of John Knapp, of Newplace, in Stoke, near Ipswich, he died anno 1559.

5, William Blois, son of Richard, married Alice, daughter of William Nottingham, by whom he had two sons, and two daughters; 1, William; 2, Robert, died young; Dorcas, died unmarried; Alice, wife of William Peck, of Spikesworth in Norfolk. He died 1607.

6, William Blois, of Grundisburgh, son of William, married Frances, daughter of John Tye, of Ipswich, by whom he had three sons, and five daughters: John, and Ann, who died young; Mary, buried at Grundisburgh, 1631; Francis, who was of Grays-Inn, buried at Grundisburgh, 1623; Dorcas, wife of George Downing, of Sandcroff; William, who succeeded his father; Alice, wife of John Acton, of Bramford, Esq. and Abigail, of John Hodges, of Ipswich, Esq. He died 1621, and was succeeded by his son,

7, William Blois, who married Cicely, daughter of Sir Thomas Wingfield, Knt. by whom he had five sons, and three daughters: Thomas, who died 1657; Cicely, buried at Grundisburgh, 1628; Abigail, buried there, 1652; Annah, Robert, Anthony, who died 1655; William, and Francis; he was one of the ten members of parliament, elected for the county of Suffolk, in 1654 and 1656, and died 1673.

8, Sir William Blois, Knt. eldest surviving son of William, married first, Martha, daughter of Sir Robert Brooke, of Cockfield-Hall, in Yoxford, Suffolk, by whom he had five sons, and three daughters; William, Robert, John, and Thomas, who all died young; Charles, Elizabeth, and Martha, who died S. P.; Mary, wife first, of Sir Nevill Catelyn; secondly, of Sir Charles Turner, Bart. His second wife was Jane, daughter of Sir Nathaniel Barnardiston, of Ketton, in Suffolk, Knt. relict of John Brooke, Esq. eldest son of Sir Robert Brooke, by whom he had a daughter, Jane, wife of Sir St. Andrew St. John, of Woodford, in Northamptonshire, Bart. and was grandmother to Lord St. John, of Bletshoe. He died 1675.

I. CHARLES BLOIS, Esq. youngest and only surviving son of Sir William Blois, was created a Baronet, 2 James II. He served in parliament for Ipswich, in 1690, and for Dunwich in 1701, first married, Mary, daughter of Sir Robert Kemp, of Gissing, in Norfolk, Bt. by whom he had three sons and one daughter: Robert, William, Charles, and Mary. Robert married Amy, only daughter of John Burrough, of Ipswich, Esq. and died in 1728, without issue. William, married Jane, the third daughter of Sir Robert Kemp, of Ubbeston, in Suffolk, Bart. and died in 1734, leaving issue an only son, Charles, who enjoyed the estate and title, after the decease of his grandfather, Sir Charles, and died unmarried, 1760, and a daughter, Mary, who died unmarried, in 1766. Mary, died unmarried in 1730. The second wife of Sir Charles was Ann, daughter of Ralph Hawtrey, of Riselip, in Middlesex, Esq. by whom he had two sons and one daughter, John, of Grays-Inn, Esq. who died a batchelor, Feb. 9, 1745-6, aged 47; Ralph, married and had issue, as hereafter set forth. Ann, wife of Samuel Thompson, of Ufford, in Suffolk, Esq. Sir Charles removed from Grundisburgh-Hall to Cockfield-Hall, in 1693, upon the death of Mary Brooke, his mother's sister, the only surviving child of Sir Robert Brooke, and died, April 9th 1738.

II. Sir CHARLES BLOIS, Bart. son of William Blois, Esq. second son of the first Sir Charles, dying, 1760, unmarried.

III. Sir CHARLES BLOIS, Bart. third son of the first Sir Charles, succeeded to the dignity, and died without issue, in 1761.

IV. Sir RALPH BLOIS, Bart. youngest son of the first Sir Charles, succeeded to the estate and dignity, upon the death of the last named Sir Charles, his brother. He married Elizabeth, eldest daughter of Reginald Rabett, of Bramfield, in Suffolk, Esq. lineally descended from William Rabett, who served, for Dunwich, the 12th parliament, at Westminster, in the reign of Edward IV. by whom he had three sons; John, and Ralph, who

TABLE.

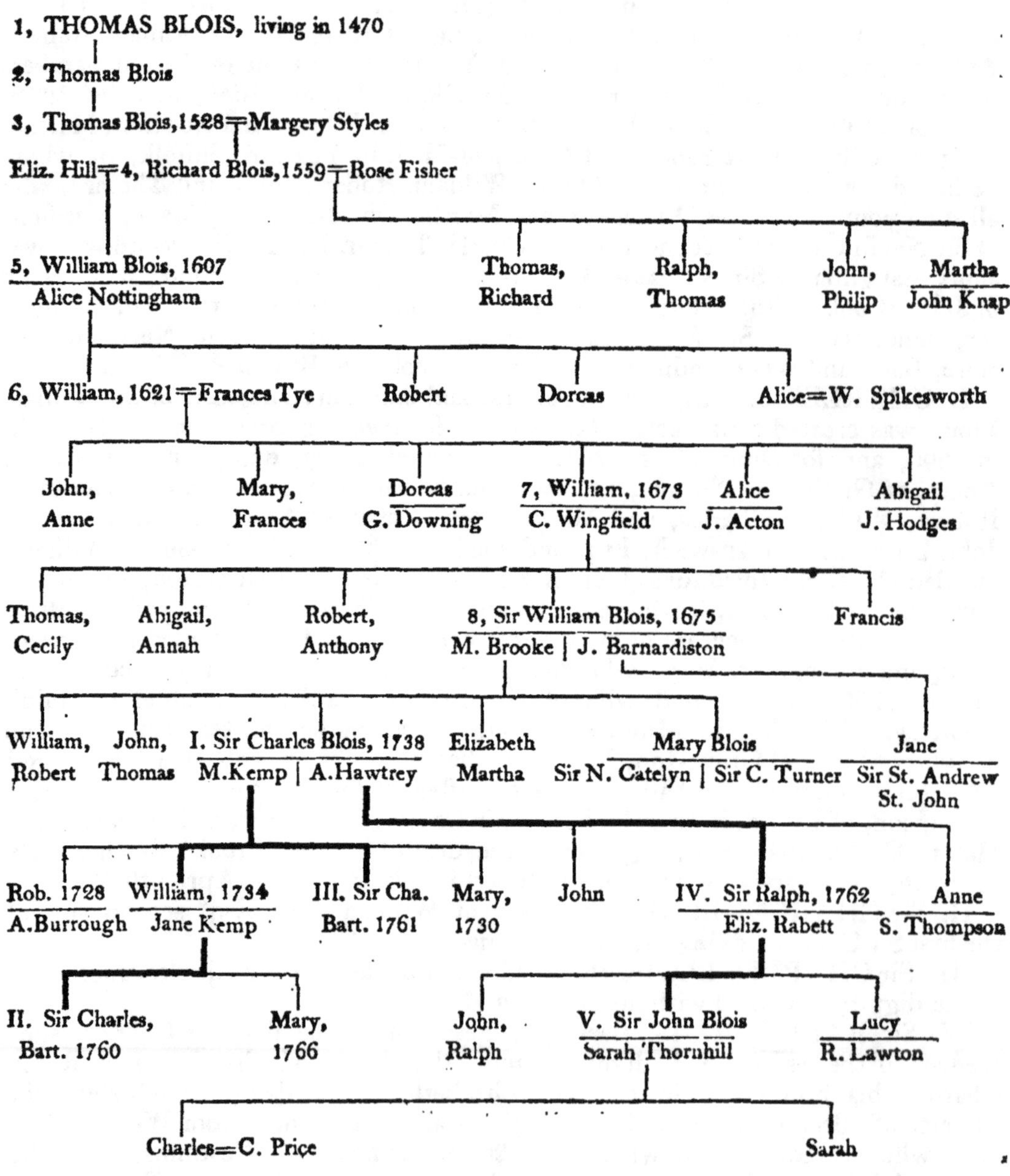
1, THOMAS BLOIS, living in 1470
2, Thomas Blois
3, Thomas Blois, 1528 = Margery Styles
Eliz. Hill = 4, Richard Blois, 1559 = Rose Fisher
5, William Blois, 1607
Alice Nottingham
Thomas, Richard
Ralph, Thomas
John, Philip
Martha
John Knap
6, William, 1621 = Frances Tye
Robert
Dorcas
Alice = W. Spikesworth
John, Anne
Mary, Frances
Dorcas
G. Downing
7, William, 1673
C. Wingfield
Alice
J. Acton
Abigail
J. Hodges
Thomas, Cecily
Abigail, Annah
Robert, Anthony
8, Sir William Blois, 1675
M. Brooke | J. Barnardiston
Francis
William, Robert
John, Thomas
I. Sir Charles Blois, 1738
M.Kemp | A.Hawtrey
Elizabeth
Martha
Mary Blois
Sir N. Catelyn | Sir C. Turner
Jane
Sir St. Andrew St. John
Rob. 1728
A.Burrough
William, 1734
Jane Kemp
III. Sir Cha. Bart. 1761
Mary, 1730
John
IV. Sir Ralph, 1762
Eliz. Rabett
Anne
S. Thompson
II. Sir Charles, Bart. 1760
Mary, 1766
John, Ralph
V. Sir John Blois
Sarah Thornhill
Lucy
R. Lawton
Charles = C. Price
Sarah

died infants,; John, the present possessor of the dignity and estate; and a daughter, Lucy, wife of Robert Lawton, of Ipswich, Esq. Sir Ralph died 1762, and she died, Jan. 1780.

V. Sir JOHN BLOIS, the present Bart. only surviving son of Sir Ralph, came to the possession of the dignity and estate upon the death of his father, married Sarah, youngest daughter of George Thornhill, of Diddington, in the county of Huntington, Esq. and sister to Thomas Thornhill, of Fixby, in the county of York, Esq. by whom he has one son, Charles, who married, Jan. 19th 1789, Clara, daughter of Joscelyn Price, Esq. of Camblesforth, Yorkshire, and a daughter Sarah.

ARMS—A bend vaire between two fleurs de lis argent.
CREST—A gauntlet proper, holding a fleur de lis argent.
MOTTO—*Je me fie en Dieu.*
SEATS—At Grundsburgh, and Cockfield-Hall, in Suffolk.

209. LAWSON, of ISELL, Cumberland.

Created Baronet, March 31, 1688.

THIS family is very ancient in the north of England, and the present Sir Wilfrid Lawson, Bart. is the twentyfourth generation in a lineal descent from

1, John Lawson,* Lord of Fawlesgrave, in Yorkshire, who lived, 1 Hen. III. and was father of,

2, John, living, 13 Hen. III. who, by Julian, daughter of ——— Covell, had one son,

3, Thomas, living, 2 Edw. I, who, by the daughter of ——— Chancie, had one son,

4, Robert, living, 6 Edw. II. whose wife was a daughter of ——— Harbet; his son,

5, Richard, living, 8 Edw. III. married Anne, daughter of ——— Conyers, by whom he had one son,

6, Thomas, living, 24 Edw. III. who, by Jane, daughter of Sir William Boynton, Knt. was father of,

7, Roger, living, 9 Hen. IV, who married Anne, daughter of ——— Etton, by whom he had one son,

* Thoresby's Leeds, p. 250. from whence this whole Pedigree is taken to Sir Wilfrid Lawson, the first Baronet.

8, John Lawson, who lived, 4 Hen. VI. and married Jacquina, daughter of —— Northrop, and was father of,

9, Thomas, who was living, 22 Hen. VI. who married ——, daughter of —— Threlkeld;

10, John, his son and heir, living 15 Edw. IV. married ——, daughter of —— Hilton, by whom he had two sons, William, and George, who died S. P.

11, William succeeded his father, and married ——, daughter of George Hedworth, Esq. by whom he had five sons, and four daughters: 1, Thomas; 2, Robert, who married Margaret, daughter of Ralph Swinnow, by whom he had William, Reginald, and Lionel; 3, William, who married Catherine, daughter of Rowland Bednell, by whom he had three sons, and three daughters, Ranalph, who married Jona Perkinson; John, Francis, Dorothy, wife of John Presich, Margaret, and Elizabeth; 4, George, who married Catherine, daughter of Robert Smerte, of London; 5, Rowland; 1, Alicia; 2, Anna; 3, Catherine; 4, Anna, wife of Richard Harbottle de Chester.

12, Thomas, the eldest son, living 27 Hen. VIII, married ———, daughter of Sir —— Dorrell, or Durnell, Knt. had three sons, and five daughters: 1, George Lawson, of Little Usworth, in Durham, who married Mabella, daughter and coheiress of Sir Reginald Carnaby, Knt. by whom he had four sons, and three daughters: 1, Thomas, who sold Little Usworth, to Sir Wilfrid Lawson, and died unmarried; 2, Edward, who married Mary, daughter of John Copley, by whom he had three sons, Wilfrid, who married Mary, daughter of John Watkinson, by whom he had one daughter, Elizabeth, wife of Richard Wilton; John, the second son, was a merchant; Godfrey, the third son, mayor of Leeds, 1699, he married Elizabeth, daughter of John Watkinson, and died 1709; 3, Robert, third son of George, married ——, and died S. P.; 4, Ralph,. The three daughters were Dorothea, Elizabeth, and Mabella. 2, Sir Wilfrid, the second son of Thomas, married Maud, daughter of —— Redmade,* or Redman, and died S. P. and left his estate to his nephew, William, son of Galfrid;† 3, Galfrid, of whom hereafter, 1, Barbara, wife of Thomas Whitehead; 4, Elizabeth, of William Lee; 5, Ursula.

13, Galfrid Lawson, living 9 Elizabeth, married ———, daughter of ——— Seamer, by whom he had

* Quære, if he had not two wives; Thoresby marries him to Redman; and Le Neve says, he married a daughter of Leigh, of Isel, and relict of Thomas Leigh, of Isel. He was buried in Isel church, where is the following monumental inscription:

Hic jacet ille cinis, qui modo Lawson erat.

Even such is time which takes in trust
Our youth, and joys, and all we have,
And pays us but with age and dust;
Within the dark and silent grave:
When we have wandred all our ways.
Shuts up the story of our days:
And from which earth, and grave and dust,
The Lord will raise me up I trust.

Wilfridus Lawson miles obiit 16 die Apr. anno etatis suæ 87. Annoque salutis 1632.

† Le Neve's MSS. vol. III. p. 274.

14, William Lawson, living 40 Eliz. who married Judith, daughter of —— Bewley,* by whom he had,

I. WILFRID LAWSON, Esq. living 6 Car. I. who was advanced to the dignity of a Baronet, by King James II. He married Jane, daughter of Sir Edward Musgrave, of Hayton-Castle, in Cumberland, Bart. of N.S. by whom he had five sons, and eight daughters; † 1, William, of whom hereafter; 2, Wilfrid, of Brayton, in Cumberland, who, by Sarah, daughter and coheiress of —— James, of Washington, in Durham, Esq. was father of Gilfrid Lawson, Esq. who was Knight of the shire for Cumberland, in several parliaments, in the reign of Queen Anne, King George I, and II. and other children; 3, Edward, who married Mary, daughter of —— Briscoe, of Grenhoe, in Cumberland, by whom he had no issue, 1694; 4, George, who died S. P.; 5, Henry, who married Mary, daughter of —— Taylor, by whom he had Wilfrid, æt. 16, 1694; Jane, wife of William Benson, of Broughton, in Cumberland; and Mary. Of Sir Wilfrid's eight daughters, Elizabeth, was wife of John Stapleton, of Wartre, in Yorkshire. Judith, of Miles Pennington, of Seaton, in Cumberland; Katherine, of Andrew Hudleston, of Hutton-John, in Cumberland; Jane, of Robert Constable, of Catfess, in Yorkshire; Frances, of Henry Tolson, of Woodhall, in Cumberland, Esqrs; Mary, the wife of Christopher Richmond, of Caterlane; Isabel, of D'Arcy Curwen, of Sells-Park, and Winifrid, of John Swinburne, of Hewthwaite, all in the county of Cumberland, Esqrs. Sir Wilfrid, represented the county of Cumberland in parliament at the Restoration, and the year following served for Cockermouth, in that county, and died 1689. William Lawson, Esq. eldest son and heir, died in his father's life-time; he married Milcha, daughter of Sir William Strickland, of Boynton, in Yorkshire, Bart. by whom he had, William, who died young; Sir Wilfrid, was successor to his grandfather; Jane, and Frances, unmarried, 1694.

II. Sir WILFRID LAWSON, eldest surviving son of William, succeeded his grandfather in dignity and estate; he represented the borough of Cockermouth, in parliament 2 William and Mary; he married Elizabeth, only daughter and heiress of George Preston, of Holker, in Lancashire, Esq. by Mary, only sister to John, Lord Viscount Lonsdale, by whom he had three sons, and three daughters: 1, Sir Wilfrid, his successor, ætat. 16, 1712; 2, William, who died unmarried; 3, John, who was an officer in the army on the Irish establishment, and lost his life at a review at Dublin, by a ball aimed at another officer, he stood near, out of some resentment, and died S. P. Elizabeth, the eldest daughter, lost her life by a fall from her horse, as she was riding in Castle-Howard Park, in Yorkshire, (the seat of the Lord Carlisle,) owing to an over excess of modesty; for, as her servant came to disentangle her petticoats from the saddle, she shrieked out, which so frightned the horse, that he flung out, and at one blow killed her on the spot; she, as well as her sisters Jane, and Mary, died unmarried. Sir Wil-

* Thoresby's Leeds, though Mr. Le Neve, in his MSS. vol. III. p. 274. makes it Beanley, of Hesketh, Cumberland.

† From hence downwards, to Sir Wilfrid Lawson, the second Baronet of that Name, is chiefly from Le Neve's MSS. vol. III. p. 274.

frid, died 1704, leaving behind him an excellent character,* and was succeeded in dignity and estate by his eldest son,

III. Sir WILFRID LAWSON, Bart. who was one of the grooms of the bedchamber to King George I. † and served in parliament for Cockermouth, in Cumberland, 2 George I. also, in the first and second parliament of King George II. till his death. He married ‡ Elizabeth-Lucy, daughter of Harry Mordaunt, Esq. brother to the Earl of Peterborough; by whom he left two sons, Sir Wilfrid, his successor, and Sir Mordaunt; and two daughters, Elizabeth, and Charlotte, Sir Wilfrid, died July, 1737, and was suceeeded in dignity and estate by his eldest son,

IV. Sir WILFRID LAWSON, Bart. who died at Kensington, in Middlesex, May, 1739, aged about seven years, and was succeeded in title and estate, by his only brother,

V. Sir MORDAUNT LAWSON, Bart. who also died a minor, Aug. 1743, and was succeeded in title by his cousin,

VI. Sir GILFRID LAWSON, Bart. son of Wilfrid, second son of the first Baronet. He died in August 1749, and was succeeded by his brother,

VII. Sir ALFRID LAWSON, Bart. who died in Feb. 1752, and was succeeded by his eldest son,

VIII. Sir WILFRID LAWSON, Bart. who served the office of high-sheriff of Cumberland, in 1756, and was elected Knight of the shire in 1761, and died in Deeember 1762, and was succeeded by his brother,

IX. Sir GILFRID LAWSON, Bart. who married Emilia, daughter of John Lovitt, Esq. who died, May 29 1769, by whom he had one son, Wilfrid, and one daughter, Emilia, who died single, 1798. Sir Gilfrid died at Brayton-Hall, about June 1794, and was succeeded by his son,

X. Sir WILFRID LAWSON, Bart. who married 1787, Anne, daughter of John Hartley, Esq.

ARMS—Per pale, argent, and sable, a cheveron, counterchanged.

CREST—Two arms embowed, issuing from the clouds, all proper, vested ermine, supporting in the hands a sun in splendor.

MOTTO—*Quod Honestum Utile.*

SEATS—At Isell, and Brayton-Hall, Cumberland, and Usworth, Durham.

* This Sir Wilfrid Lawson, Bart. was one of those, who, from a niceness of conscience, not often to be met with, thought himself obliged to give up the impropriate tithes of Isell, to the living for ever; which he did with so much exactness, that with the profits he had received himself to that time, he bought a piece of land, which he settled likewise on the living: He did the same for his estate to the government, which being, as he found, undertaxed, he calculated the difference, and left 600l. to be paid to make up the deficiency; which sum Queen Anne generously gave back to the family.—These particulars I have heard from gentlemen of credit in the country, and as they redound so much to his honour, have here inserted them.—*Wotton*, 1741.

† Ex inf. Dom. Wilf. Lawson, Bart. 1727.

‡ Ibid.

TABLE.

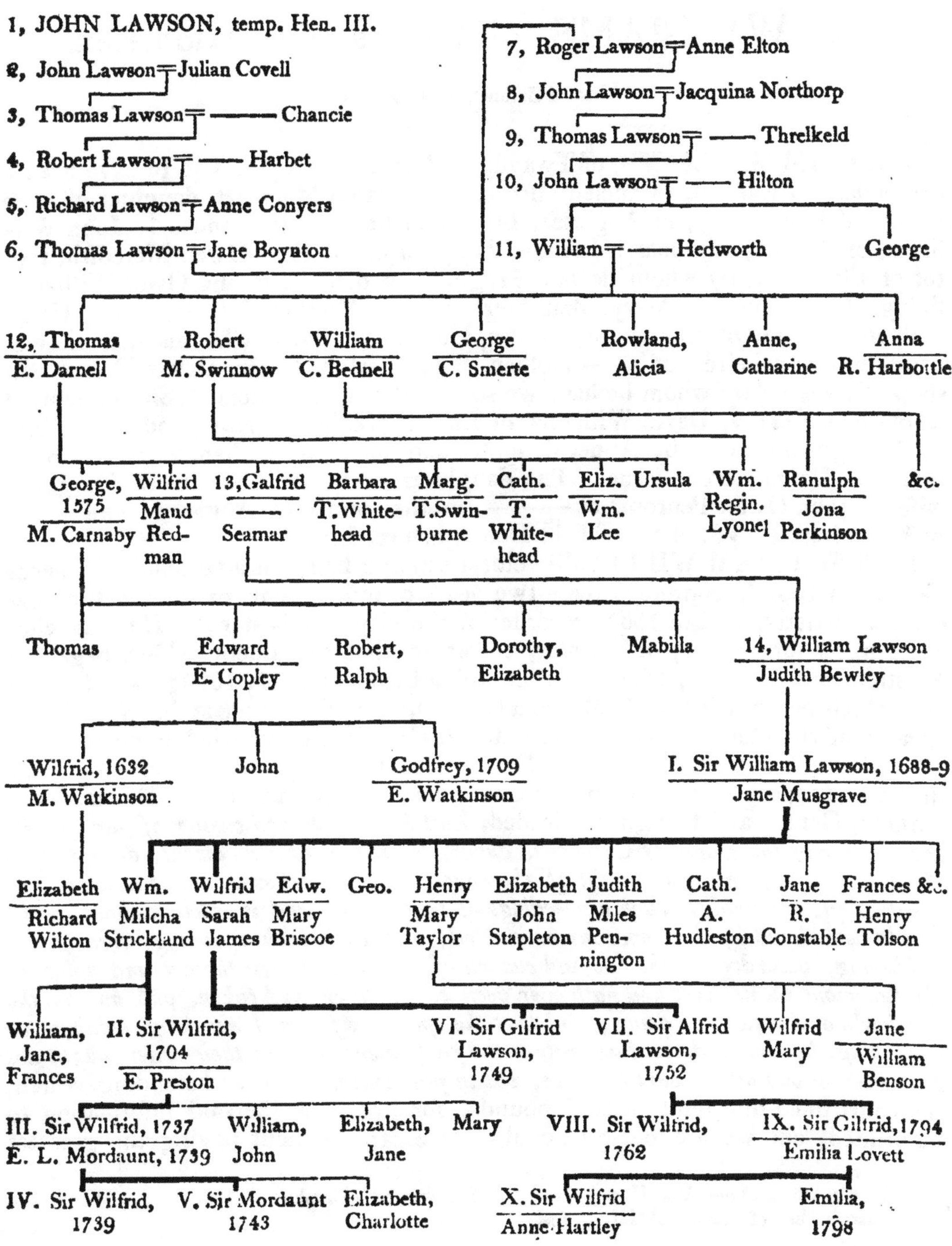
1, JOHN LAWSON, temp. Hen. III.
2, John Lawson = Julian Covell
3, Thomas Lawson = —— Chancie
4, Robert Lawson = —— Harbet
5, Richard Lawson = Anne Conyers
6, Thomas Lawson = Jane Boynton
7, Roger Lawson = Anne Elton
8, John Lawson = Jacquina Northorp
9, Thomas Lawson = —— Threlkeld
10, John Lawson = —— Hilton
11, William = —— Hedworth
George
12, Thomas
E. Darnell
Robert
M. Swinnow
William
C. Bednell
George
C. Smerte
Rowland, Alicia
Anne, Catharine
Anna
R. Harbottle
George, 1575
M. Carnaby
Wilfrid
Maud Redman
13, Galfrid
Seamar
Barbara
T. Whitehead
Marg.
T. Swinburne
Cath.
T. Whitehead
Eliz.
Wm. Lee
Ursula
Wm. Regin. Lyonel
Ranulph
Jona Perkinson
&c.
Thomas
Edward
E. Copley
Robert, Ralph
Dorothy, Elizabeth
Mabilla
14, William Lawson
Judith Bewley
Wilfrid, 1632
M. Watkinson
John
Godfrey, 1709
E. Watkinson
I. Sir William Lawson, 1688-9
Jane Musgrave
Elizabeth
Richard Wilton
Wm.
Milcha Strickland
Wilfrid
Sarah James
Edw.
Mary Briscoe
Geo.
Henry
Mary Taylor
Elizabeth
John Stapleton
Judith
Miles Pennington
Cath.
A. Hudleston
Jane
R. Constable
Frances &c.
Henry Tolson
William, Jane, Frances
II. Sir Wilfrid, 1704
E. Preston
VI. Sir Gilfrid Lawson, 1749
VII. Sir Alfrid Lawson, 1752
Wilfrid
Mary
Jane
William Benson
III. Sir Wilfrid, 1737
E. L. Mordaunt, 1739
William, John
Elizabeth, Jane
Mary
VIII. Sir Wilfrid, 1762
IX. Sir Gilfrid, 1794
Emilia Lovett
IV. Sir Wilfrid, 1739
V. Sir Mordaunt 1743
Elizabeth, Charlotte
X. Sir Wilfrid
Anne Hartley
Emilia, 1798

210. WILLIAMS, of Gray's-Inn, Middlesex.

Created Baronet, July 6, 1688.

WILLIAM WILLIAMS, of Twayll, in Anglesea, Esq. is said to have been a descendant of Kadrod, an ancient Briton: he married Margaret, daughter of John Owen, of Llanfrythly, in Anglesea, by whom he had two sons, 1, John Williams, of Twayll, who married Anne, daughter of the Rev. Owen Meredith, rector of Llanestyn, by whom he had Hugh, who died S. P. and Owen Williams, living 1695, who, by Mary, daughter of —— Hughes, left issue; 2, Hugh Williams, D. D. of Cantrisant, in the Isle of Anglesea, who married Emma, daughter and coheiress of —— Dolben, Esq. brother to Dr. David Dolben bishop of Bangor, by whom he had two sons and two daughters, 1, Sir William, of whom hereafter; 2, David Williams, of Llanallowe, in Anglesea, and Llansylian, in Denbighshire, who, by Anne, daughter and heiress of William Morris, of Kenbrant, had a numerous issue. The daughters of Dr. Williams were, Margaret, wife of John Owen Penrose, of ——, in the county of Anglesea; and ——, wife of Hugh Lloyd, of Segreid, in Denbighshire, Esqrs.

I. Sir WILLIAM WILLIAMS, eldest son and heir, became scholar of Jesus College in 1652*, continued there two years or more, went to Gray's-Inn, became a barrister, and in 1667, recorder of the city of Chester†. He was chosen burgess for the city of Chester, to sit in that parliament which began at Westminster, March 6, 1678, for that which began Oct. 17, 1679‡, and for that also which began at Oxford, March 21, 1680, in which two last he was chosen speaker of the House of Commons. In 36 Car. II. he was tried on an information, brought against him in the King's Bench, for a libel, in causing to be printed (as speaker of the House of Commons) the information of Thomas Dangerfield, Gent.; and though he pleaded, *that by the law and custom of parliament, the speaker of the House of Commons, during the sitting of parliament, according to the duty of his office, as a servant of the house, ought, and ever was accustomed, to speak, sign, and publish, such proceedings of that house, and in such manner as he should be ordered by the Commons assembled; and that such speaking, signing, or publishing, according to the law and custom of parliament, are the act and doing of the Commons themselves, and hath ever been so accepted and taken, and not as the speaker's own actions or doing; and that the speaker, for such speaking, signing, or publishing, by him made or done, sitting the parliament, and by their order, ought not to answer in any other court or place, but in parliament.* Notwithstanding which, the court fined him ten thousand pounds, for licensing the said information to be printed, and we are told § he could not escape without paying the greatest

* Wood's Athen. Oxon. Vol. II. p. 1192. † Leycester's Cheshire, p. 188. ‡ Wood, ibid.
§ Echard's Hist. of Engl. Vol. III. p. 742.

part of it. He was one of the most eminent lawyers of his time, and when King James II. came to the crown, he was in great favour *, and by him made solicitor-general, in the place of Sir Thomas Powis, promoted to be attorney-general in the beginning of December, 1687; on the 11th of which month he received the honour of knighthood at Whitehall, and acted as solicitor-general at the trial of the seven bishops. He was knight of the shire for the county of Carnarvon, in 1688, 1690, and 1695, and advanced to the dignity of a Baronet, 4 James II. He married Mary, daughter and coheiress of Watkyn Kyffin, of Glascoed, in Denbighshire, Esq. and died at his chambers in Grays-Inn, July 11, 1700, leaving two sons and one daughter, Sir William, his successor, and John Williams, of Chester, Esq. barrister at law, who married Catharine, eldest daughter of Sir Hugh Owen, of Orielton, in Pembrokeshire, Bart. (sister to Sir Arthur), by whom he left five sons and one daughter, 1, Hugh, who was member for the county of Anglesea, in the last parliament of King George I. and the first of King George II. who married first, Ursula, daughter of Sir John Bridgman, of Castle Bromwich, in Warwickshire, Bart.; secondly, ——, daughter of Edw. Norris, Esq. M. D. formerly M. P. for Liverpool; 3, John, a Welch judge, who married ——, daughter of Alderman Bennet, of Chester, and had one son; 4, Arthur Williams, archdeacon of St. David's, and rector of St. Mary's, Chester, who died August, 1737, unmarried; 5, Edward, who married, in May, 1739, ——, relict of Richard, Lord Viscount Bulkeley, and daughter and heiress of Lewis Owen, of Peniarth, in Merionethshire, Esq. (by a daughter of Sir William Williams, Bart.); Elizabeth, only daughter of John, was wife of William Owen, Esq. eldest son of Sir Arthur Owen, Bart.; Emma, the only daughter of Sir William, was wife of Sir Arthur Owen, of Orielton, Bart.

II. Sir WILLIAM WILLIAMS, Bart. eldest son and successor in the dignity and estate, represented the town of Denbigh, in the parliament summoned to meet July 1708. He married first, ——, daughter and heiress of Edward Thelwall, of Place y ward, in Denbighshire, Esq. (by Sydney, his wife, daughter and heiress of William Wynn, Esq. prothonotary of North Wales, sixth son of Sir John Wynn, of Gwidder, in Carnarvonshire, Bart. by Sydney, his wife, daughter of Sir William Gerard, Knt. lord-chancellor of Ireland), by whom he left three sons, 1, Sir Watkin, his successor; 2, Robert, knight of the shire for the county of Montgomery the latter end of the parliament of 2 Geo. II. who married Catharine, daughter of Roderick Floyd, of Essex-street, in Middlesex, Esq. (she died S. P.); and 3, Richard, married Charlotte, daughter and coheiress of Richard, third son of Sir Roger Mostyn, of Mostyn, in Flintshire, (by his second lady, Mary, daughter of Thomas, Lord Viscount Bulkeley), and had one son. Sir William had also several daughters, of which one was wife of Lewis Owen, of Peniarth, in Merionethshire, Esq. (whose daughter and heiress married first, Richard, late Lord Viscount Bulkeley; and secondly, Edward Williams, Esq. before-mentioned); another married —— Wynn, of Melly, in Denbighshire, Esq.

* Wood's Athen. Oxon: Vol. II. p. 1192.

Sir William married secondly, Catharine, daughter to Mutton Davies, of Gozanna, in Denbighshire, Esq. by whom he had no issue, and died at Llanvorda, in Shropshire, Oct. 20, 1740, aged near 80, and was succeeded in dignity and estate by his eldest son,

III. Sir WATKIN WILLIAMS WYNN, of Wynnstay, in Denbighshire, Bart. (which seat and great estate was given him by the late Sir John Wynn, Bart.) who, in the first parliament of King George I. was chosen knight of the shire for the county of Denbigh, in the room of Sir Richard Middleton, of Chirk Castle, for which county he served in parliament till his seat was vacated in Nov. 1740*. Soon after, he was again unanimously elected for the county of Denbigh.

Sir Watkin married Anne, daughter and coheiress of Edward Vaughan, of Llwydiart, and Llangedwyne, Montgomeryshire, Esq. by whom he had several children, who all died young. He married, secondly, Frances, daughter of George Shakerley, of Gwersett, Esq. by whom he left two sons: 1, Sir Watkin Williams Wynn, his successor; 2, William Watkin, who died April 12, 1759, unmarried. Sir Watkin died Sept. 26, 1749, aged 57†, and was succeeded by his son,

* "The House of Commons being informed, that Sir Watkin Williams Wynn, Bart. a member of this house, hath accepted the office of steward of his Majesty's lordships and manors of Bromfield and Yale, in the county of Denbighshire, now come to him on the death of his father, Sir William Williams, Bart. by virtue of a grant from Queen Anne; and that the said Sir Watkins Williams Wynn desired the opinion of the house, whether his seat in this house was thereby vacated:

"And the house being informed, that Mr. Thomas Gilbert attended at the door, with a copy of the said grant, he was called in, and at the bar produced the same.

"And then he withdrew.

"And the copy of the said grant, dated the 6th day of April, in the third year of her said Majesty's reign, was read; whereby the Queen (reciting a grant of the said office, by King Charles II. to Henry Wynn, Esq. for his life, and after his decease, to his son, John Wynn, Esq. for his life; and also reciting the death of the said Henry Wynn), granted the said office to Sir William Williams, Bart. deceased, for his life, to have the said office immediately after the decease of the said John Wynn: and also to his son, now Sir Watkin Williams Wynn, for his life, for him the said Watkin Williams Wynn to have, enjoy, and exercise the said office immediately after the decease of the said Sir William Williams, with an annual salary of twenty pounds, and with all profits to the said office belonging.

"And the 26th section of an act made in the sixth year of the reign of Queen Anne, intitled, An Act for the Security of her Majesty's Person and Government, and of the Succession to the Crown of Great Britain in the Protestant Line, whereby the election of any person, who, being chosen a member of the House of Commons, shall accept of any office of profit from the crown, is declared to be void, was also read.

"Ordered,

"That Mr. Speaker do issue his warrant to the clerk of the crown, to make out a new writ for the electing of a knight of the shire to serve in this present parliament for the county of Denbigh, in the room of Sir Watkin Williams Wynn, Bart. who, since his election for the said county, hath accepted the office of his Majesty's lordships and manors of Bromfield and Yale, in the said county of Denbigh *(a)*.

† In the church of Rhuabon, in Denbighshire, is an elegant marble monument, erected for Sir Watkin, in the front of which is the figure of Sir Watkin sitting, and looking at a shield supported by a weeping genius, who points to the figure of justice, represented on the shield; on the cornice is this inscription:

ADSESTOR LIBERTATIS PUBLICÆ.
Near this place is buried SIR WATKIN WILLIAMS WYNN, Bart.

(a) Votes of the House of Commons, No. 7, Nov. 25, 1740.

IV. Sir WATKIN WILLIAMS WYNN, Bart. who, April 6, 1769, married Henrietta, fifth daughter, of Charles Duke of Somerset, who died the 24th of July

(son of SIR WILLIAM WILLIAMS, of Llanvorda, Bart. and grandson of SIR WILLIAM WILLIAMS, Bart. twice speaker of the house of commons, and solicitor-general to King James II.) SIR WATKIN WILLIAMS, by his first wife, ANNE, daughter and heiress of EDWARD VAUGHAN, of Llangedwin, Esq. had several children who all died young. By his second wife, FRANCES, daughter of GEORGE SHAKERLEY, of Gwerselt, Esq. he left two sons, SIR WATKIN, and William-Watkin.

On the base is this inscription.

H. S. E.

WATKIN WILLIAMS WYNN, BARONETTUS.

Qui at illustri Britannorum veterum stirpe oriundus majoribus suis se dignissimum semper præbuit, & non modo nomine, sed virtute & fide hominem verè Britannum: Admodum juvenis in Senatum electus confistem cunctis innotuit gravitàtè & judicio; postquam vero & ipse de republicâ cœpit disputare, & libertatis patrocinium ac defensionem suscipere, incredibilem animi magnitudinem atq. ejus constantiam omnes ita suspexerunt, ut, cum Senatus princeps tum patriæ pater merito haberetur. Tam rectis studijs & ea singulari bonitate fuit præditus, ut non posset fieri, quin maximam sibi gratiam & venerationem compararet vir innocentissimus maritus, benignissimus hospes, optimus literarum patronus, & assiduus Dei & Christianæ veritatis cultor. Ad hæc quam suavis & jucundus fuit in convictu! Quanta fides ejus sermonibus! Qualis in ore probitas et decor! Quæ mensæ reverentia! quæ in cultu moderatis! Quæ in omni vitâ modestia, & elegantia, comitas liberalitas. Talis tantique viri immaturo interitu quam grave damnum fecit, Britannia, quum cuncti, qui ejus virtutes cognoverint (cognovit penitus, qui hæc mœrens scripsit,) coerepto, miserorum omnium perfugium, bonorum omnium delicias, doctorum omnium præsiduum, Walliæ suæ decus et ornamentum, et clarissimum reipublicæ lumen ereptum et extinctum esse fateantur.

Obijt 26to, die Septembris, 1749, Ætatis 57.

Vidua moerens posuit. M. RYSBRACK, sculpsit, 1754.

On one side of the monument are the arms for Sir Watkin and his first lady.

1 and 4, Wynn, vert, three eagles displayed in fess, or; 2 and 3, Williams, argent, two foxes, &c. as printed in this book. In pretence, 1 and 4 vert, a chevron ermine between three griffin's heads erased, argent; 2 and 3, sable, a goat passant, argent.

On the other side, Sir Watkin's arms empaled with his second lady's, argent, a chevron between three hills, and reeds growing on them, vert, for Shackerley.

Translation of the Latin inscription:

Here lieth interred SIR WATKIN WILLIAMS WYNNE, BART. who descended from an illustrious family of ancient Britons, was himself most worthy of his ancestors, not only in name, but in virtue and integrity truly a Briton. Though elected in a very early period of his youth into parliament, yet the dignity of his behaviour and maturity of his judgement was immediately distinguished by all. When afterwards he engaged in debates of national concern, and undertook himself the patronage and defence of liberty, all beheld the amazing greatness and constancy of his soul with so much reverence, that he was most deservedly both chief in the senate, and father of his country. With such upright principles, and such peculiar goodness was he endowed, as could not but excite in all the profoundest veneration and most intimate regard for that personage, whose innocency, if life, was so distinguished, whose œconomy

following. Sir Watkin married, secondly, Dec. 21, 1771, Charlotte, daughter of George Grenville, Esq. and sister to the Marquis of Buckingham, by whom he had eight children, Sir Watkin Williams Wynn, his successor;* 2, ——— a son born Dec. 28, 1773; 3, ———, a son born Oct. 9, 1775; 4, ——— a son born April 24, 1777; 5, ———, a daughter born 1779; 6, ———, a daughter born 1780; 7, ———, a son born Mar. 16, 1783; 8, ———, a son born Feb. 6, 1786. Sir Watkin fell from his horse, on his return from hunting, and broke his neck, in the 41 year of his age, on the 29th of July, 1789; he was M. P. for Denbighshire, lieutenant and custos rotulorum of Merionethshire, and a vice-president of the Westminster General Dispensary †. He was succeeded in title and estate by his eldest son,

V. Sir WATKIN WILLIAMS WYNN, Bart. born 1772.

ARMS—Quarterly, first and fourth, vert, three eagles displayed in fess, or, for Wynne; second and third, argent, two foxes, counter-saliant, in saltire, gules, the dexter, surmounted of the sinister, for Williams.

CREST—An eagle displayed, or.

SEATS—Nantantog, in the isle of Anglesea; Place y ward, and Wynnstay, com. Denbigh, and Llonvorda, com. Salop.

was most prudent, whose faith to the marriage bed most inviolable, whose hospitality most liberal; the best patron of learning; most constant in his devotions to the deity, and a warm professor of Christian truth. Yet more, how engaging was he, and how chearful in society, what sincerity in his conversation! What an open and becoming honesty in his countenance! What decency at his table! What moderation in his dress! What modesty, elegance, affability, generosity in his whole character! How heavy was the loss to Britain, the untimely death of so good, so great a man, when all, who knew his virtues, (well did the weeping author of this inscription know them), must confess, that when he was torn from us, the refuge of the distressed, the delight of all good, the patron of all learned men, the ornament and honour of his native Wales was lost in him, and utterly extinguished.

* On account of the birth of this son, Sir Watkin made a present of a neat marble font to the church of Rhuabon, on the outside of which is the following inscription:

For of such is the kingdom of God.
The Gift of Sir Watkin Williams Wynn, Bart. to the church of Rhuabon
on the Baptism of his son, Dec. 16, 1772.
The said font was made by Mr. Hinchliffe, mason, in Longacre, London,
where I took the inscription. B. Longmate.

† To the late worthy Baronet, more than to any other private individual, the Welsh charity-school, is indebted for its present celebrity, and he and lady Williams founded two schools in the parish of Rhuabon; and nearly 300 families were constantly supported in comfortable industry by his bounty. Of the elegant hospitalities of Wynnstay it is needless to speak. He substituted there, in the room of the barbarous games that were common in that part of the kingdom; by which he contributed to refine their manners and taste.

His patriotic character is equally known. He was a whig from pure conviction; and he supported the patriotic party with hearty zeal. The loss which Wales has sustained by his death will be long felt; but they have the consolation of seeing in his son the heir of his virtues, as well as of his estate.

His death, though considered for sometime past as an event, as far as human foresight could reach, inevitable, has not failed, when the period of so valuable a life arrived, of being most severely felt by those who were happy in his acquaintance—much more in habits of friendship with him. At the head of a great and commanding fortune, he did not enter into the vices and follies of his age, but spent it in a rational and noble manner.

In his public and private capacity, his disinterested integrity was unimpeachable; in the former, even those whose political sentiments did not perhaps always coincide with his own, from a thorough conviction of the uprightness of his intentions, never refused him their suffrages, the highest compliment any man receives from his constituents. In the latter few ever shone with greater splendor, as a son, a husband, a parent, a friend, and a master. He was adorned in each walk of life. The unfeigned tribute of tears shed for him, in these relations, are the best vouchers for the truth of the assertion. Oppression was an idea unknown to him; and the meanest dependant or neighbour never felt the weight of his rank or fortune, unless when exerted, as it often was, to assist even those whose conduct to him little deserved it. His mind was superior to considerations that too often actuate human nature; of such an habitual sense of honour and integrity, it required reiterated proofs of dishonesty and duplicity to render any one suspected of the want of those virtues.

Hence he was frequently made a prey of by the artful and the designing. He was early and happily impressed with a due sense of religion; uniform and regular in the discharge of the highest duties of it. Light and profane conversation ever gave him offense, though embellished by wit, or enlivened by ridicule. On a most peculiar manner it belonged to Sir Watkin to be the more beloved the better he was known, the surest indication of real worth.

Gent. Mag. 1789, p. 765.

TABLE.

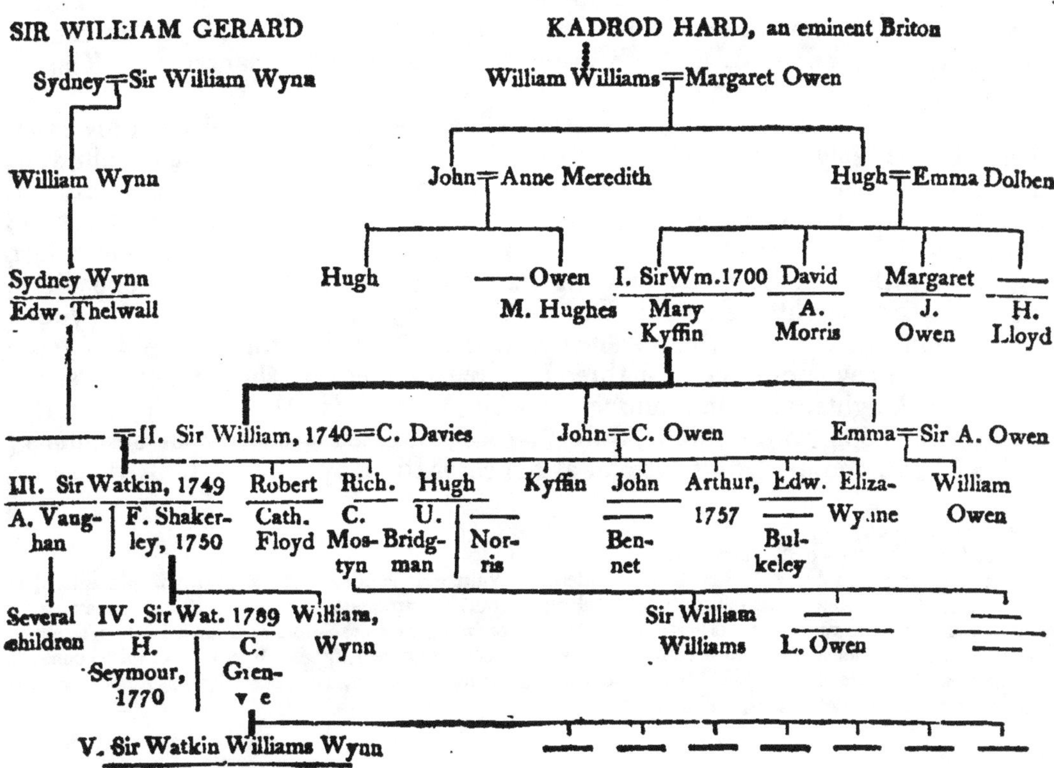

BARONETS

CREATED BY

KING WILLIAM III.

210. MOLESWORTH, of Pencarrow, Cornwall.

Created Baronet, June 32, 1688.

THE family of Molesworth anciently had their residence in the counties of Northampton and Bedford, where they flourished for many ages, and particularly in the reigns of Edward I. and II. in the person of Sir Walter de Moldesworth, or Molesworth; contemporary with whom was John de Molesworth, who, 12 Edw. I. was presented to the rectory of North Luffenham, in the county of Rutland, by Edmund, Earl of Cornwall, son of Richard Plantagenet, King of the Romans, youngest son of King John*.

1, The aforesaid Sir Walter de Molesworth attended K. Edward I. in his expedition to the Holy Land against the infidels (to which his coat armour alludes), and 26th of that reign, was constituted sheriff of the counties of Bedford and Bucks for the space of ten years †, an office in those early times of great trust and authority. In 1306, when the king, on a grand Whitsuntide festival, to adorn his court with great splendor, and augment the glory of his intended expedition into Scotland, knighted Edward, Earl of Carnarvon, his eldest son; the young prince, immediately after that ceremeny, at the altar in Westminster Abbey, conferred the same honour on near three hundred gentlemen, the sons of earls, barons, and knights, of which number was Sir Walter de Molesworth; and that prince succeeding to the throne, July 7, 1307, directed a charter of summons ‡ to Sir Walter and his lady to attend at his coronation, appointing him, that year,

* Lodge. Vol. V. p. 127.

† Fuller's Worthies of Bedfordshire.

‡ The charter runs thus: "Rex dilecto & fideli suo Waltero de Mollesworth, & consorti, salutem. Quia hac instanti die Dominica post festum Sancti Valentini, apud Westmonasterium proponimus coronari, vobis mandamus, quatenus vos & consors vestra hujusmodi coronationis nostræ solemniis, dictis die & loco celebrandis ad cometivam nobis & carissime consorti nostræ Isabeilæ, Reginæ Angliæ, ob nostris et ipsius consortis nostræ honorem faciendum personaliter, modis omnibus intersitis, et hoc, sicut nos diligeris, nullatinus omittis. Teste 8 Febii. Rot. Claus, 1 Ed. II. m. 12.

with Gilbert de Holme, sheriff of the aforesaid counties, and in 1313, sole sheriff of the same *. He was returned knight for the county of Bedford to the first parliament of that king, which met at Westminster the fifth of his reign, and (as was then the custom) had, with Gerard de Braybroke, his colleague, writs of their expences issued for their attendance and service; and three years after, he represented that county again; but not long surviving, was succeeded by his son,

2, Hugh, who was the same year, with Henry de Tilly, knight of the county of Huntingdon, in the parliament held at York, having the like writ for defraying his expences. He was succeeded by

3, Sir Walter de Molesworth, Knt. his son and heir, who was father of

4, Richard de Molesworth, mentioned in the pipe-rolls of Northamptonshire, 13 Edw. III. 1339 †, in relation to a fine of twenty pounds for a pardon granted to Sir Simon Drayton, Knt. John, his son, William, son of Thomas Seymour, and Simon Squire, of Drayton, and to the said Richard de Molesworth, at the king's suit for the peace, belonging to the royal cognizance, on the death of John de Sutton Lungeville. He married Eleanor, daughter and heiress of Sir Thomas Mortimer, of the county of Lincoln (a descendant of the noble house of Mortimer, Barons of England in the reigns of Henry III. and Edward I. whose coat-armour Lord Molesworth bears in the second quarter), and by her was ancestor to,

5, Sir Roger Molesworth, of the county of Huntingdon, Knt. whose son,

6, John, of the same county, became also seated at Helpeston, in Northamptonshire, served the office of escheator for the county of Rutland, and died May 14, 1542, leaving,

7, John, his heir, then twenty-six years of age, who married Margaret, daughter and heiress of William Westcot, of Hansacre, in Staffordshire, &c. by whom he had five sons, 1, Anthony, his heir, ancestor to the Viscount Molesworth; 2, Robert; 3, Bevil; 4, John; and 5, Wingfield.

Anthony, the eldest son of John Molesworth and Margaret Westcot, by his marriage with Cecily, daughter and heiress of Thomas Hurland, of Fotheringay, in the county of Northampton, Esq. became possessed of that inheritance, and made it his principal place of residence; but being a man of great generosity and hospitality, and profusely entertaining Queen Elizabeth, at *that* his seat, several days, at different times, he so far involved himself in debt, that (to shew he was just as he was generous), he sold the best part of his estate, and disposed of Helpeston to an ancestor of Earl Fitz-William. He left two sons, William, and Nathaniel, who accompanied Sir Walter Raleigh in his voyage to Guinea, and after his return perished by shipwreck on his passage to Ireland.

10, William Molesworth, Esq. the elder son, took share with the Duke of Buckingham in his unfortunate expedition to the Isle of Rhe, in aid of the Rochellers, and by his son-in-law, Gervais Holles, Esq. (a worthy and authentic

* Fuller's Worthies of Bedfordshire.

† Rot. Pip. resid. North. A°. 13 Edw. III.

antiquary), is stiled, *Protribunus Militum sub Regimine Peregrini Bertie Militis.* He married Mary, daughter of Sir Francis Palmer, of Ashwell, in the county of Rutland, by whom he had three sons, 1, Guy; 2, Edward; 3, Robert, who all bore arms in the service of Cha. I.; and ——, the wife of Gervais Holles, &c. Guy, the eldest, going early into foreign parts, served under Bernard, Duke of Saxe Weimar many years, and returned home by leave of that Duke in 1639; soon after which, the civil war breaking out, he engaged in behalf of his sovereign; was captain-lieutenant of the general's company, the Earl of Northumberland; and in 1642, lieutenant-colonel in Prince Maurice's regiment of horse, to the command of which he afterwards succeeded *. Edward, the second son, was captain-lieutenant to Sir Charles Vavasor, 1640; captain, in 1642, of a foot company in Ireland; afterwards colonel of foot and major-general. He married ——, daughter of —— Hatbean, and by her, who was buried in St. John's Church, Dublin, April 11, 1654, had three daughters, Mary, Jane, and Frances †. Robert, the third son, was engaged in the royal cause throughout the civil war, and served under his brother Guy. He married Judith, eldest of the two daughters and coheirs (that of survived of twenty-one children) of John Bysse, Esq. chief-baron of the exchequer in Ireland (afterwards wife of Sir William Tichborne, Knt.), by whom he had,

I. ROBERT MOLESWORTH, of Brackens-Town, in the county of Dublin, and of Edlington, in Yorkshire, Esq. who, at the Revolution, distinguished himself by an early and zealous appearance in the defence of the rights and liberties of his country, and enjoyed no small share in the esteem of King William, by whom he was sent envoy extraordinary to the court of Denmark, 1692, and during his residence therein, made those useful remarks on tyrannical governments which, on his return, he published in an account of that kingdom. He was afterwards elected fellow of the Royal Society, sworn of the most honourable privy council of the kingdom of Ireland, and made one of the commissioners of trade, 1 Geo. I. and created Lord Viscount Molesworth, of Swords, in the county of Dublin, in Ireland. By Lettice, his wife, third daughter of Richard Coot, Baron of Coloony, in Ireland, he had seven sons and three daughters; 1, Margaret, baptized Feb. 1, 1677, died July 19, 1759; 2, Mary, wife of George Monck, of Stephen's-Green, Esq. and died 1715; 3, Charlotta-Amelia, wife, in 1712, of Capt. William Tichburne, only surviving son of Henry Lord Ferrand; 4, Letitia, of Edward Bolton, of Brazeel, in the county of Dublin, Esq. M. P. for Swords; 1, John; 2, Richard, of whom hereafter; 3, William, surveyor of the lands in Ireland, and member of parliament for Philip's town, in that kingdom; 4, Edward; 5, Walter, both officers in the army; 6, Coote, of the Temple, and F. R. S.; and 7, Bisse.

II. JOHN, his eldest son, succeeded his father as Lord Viscount Molesworth, was sent envoy to the Grand Duke of Tuscany, 1710, and made a

* He is said by some, to die without issue; but it appears, from an inscription on a small marble monument in the church of Swords, that a daughter of Colonel Guy Molesworth, of London, was the first wife of Henry Scardevile, dean of Cloyne, archdeacon of Ross, and prebendary and vicar of Swords, who died Feb. 3, 1703, and was buried under the said monument. She died in childbirth, and left no issue.—*Lodge.*

† St. John's Registry and Dr. Dudley Loftus's MSS. in St. Sepulchre's Lib.

commissioner of the stamp-office; and 2 George I. was made one of the commissioners of trade and plantations, in the room of his father; and by his majesty King George, was sent to the courts of Sardinia, Florence, Venice, and Switzerland; and married one of the daughters and coheiresses of Thomas Middleton, of Stansted Mount Fitchet, in Essex, Esq.; (by Elizabeth, his wife, daughter of Richard, Lord Onslow,) by whom he had only a daughter, and died Feb. 17, 1726.

III. Richard, second son of Robert, Lord Viscount Molesworth, commanded a regiment in the army, and greatly distinguished himself in Flanders. He mounted on his own horse, the Duke of Marlborough, at the battle of Ramelies, by which means, he rescued that great general from being taken prisoner, at the manifest hazard of his own life. In 1714, he was made a lieutenant-general of the ordnance, in Ireland, and was a colonel of dragoons at the battle of Preston, being also member of parliament for Swords; and in the March, 1724-5, succeeded general Whetham, in his regiment of foot, and succeeded to the title and estate, on the death of his brother. He married first Jane, daughter of Mr. Lucas, of Dublin; by her, who died April 1, 1742, and was buried at Swords, he had one son who died an infant, and three daughters, Mary, wife of (in 1736,) Robert, created Earl of Belvidere; Letitia, of (in 1753,) lieutenant-colonel, James Molesworth, and died June 16, 1787; and Amelia, who died unmarried Jan. 30, 1758. He married, secondly, Mary, daughter of the Rev. William Usher, archdeacon of Clonfort, who died May 6, 1763,* by whom he had one son Richard Nassau, and seven daughters.

IV. Richard-Nassau, the fourth Viscount Molesworth was born Nov. 4, 1748.

Having thus traced the elder line, I shall now return to John, fourth son of John Molesworth, of Helpston, father of Anthony Molesworth, before treated of. John, brother of Anthony, settled at Pencarrow, in the county Cornwall, and made a good addition to his fortune, by marriage with two wives; by the latter,

* *Extract of a Letter, dated 7 May,* 1763. — "It is with the utmost horror that I relate to you the dismal catastrophe which befel poor Lady Molesworth, and her family: Yesterday morning about 5 o'clock, when a fire suddently broke forth in her house, by the carelessness of a servant in the nursery, in which she herself, two of her daughters, her brother, who was captain of a man of war, the children's-governess, and two other maid-servants perished. The other three daughters are indeed not consumed, but scarce in a condition preferable: the eldest jumping out of a second floor window, was caught upon the iron palisades, which tore her thigh so miserably, that the surgeons were obliged to cut it off directly, four inches above the knee; another has the thigh-bone broke, close to the hip; a third, bruised from head to foot, and both much scorched.—The Hon. Coote Molesworth, and his wife, who, unluckily for them, happened to be her guests, have escaped. He had the presence of mind to throw his bedding out of the back-windows, upon which his wife, and two children fell, otherwise they must have been dashed to pieces, for the children came from the garret down to the back area, no less than four stories high. Mr. Molesworth hung by an iron on the outside of the two pair of stairs windows, till a neighbouring carpenter brought him a ladder.—List of saved; Lord Molesworth, fortunately at school; Miss Harriet's thigh cut off, and the other leg much torn with spikes; Miss Louisa, thigh broke, near the hip, but set, and hopes of cure without amputation; head cut, but not fractured; Mr. and Mrs. Molesworth, Miss Betty, much bruised and scorched.—Perished: Lady Molesworth; Miss Melesina, Miss Molly; capt. Usher, Mrs. Moselle, governess to the children; Mrs. Patterson, Lady Molesworth's woman; the young ladies maid; capt. Usher's man, who got out, but perished by returning to save his master; and two black footmen."——*From Faulkner's Dublin Journal.*

Phillippa, daughter of Henry Rolle, of Heanton, in Devonshire, Esq.; he had only two daughters; but by the former, Catherine, eldest daughter and coheiress of J. Hender, of Botreaux-castle, in Cornwall, Esq.; he had two sons, and two daughters; Jane wife of William Risden, of Vileston, in Devonshire, Esq. and Elizabeth, of John Tredenham, of Philly, in the county of Cornwall, Esq. mother of Sir Joseph Tredenham, Knt. who married Elizabeth, daughter of Sir Edward Seymour, Bart. Of the two sons, John, the youngest, embarking with the Duke of Buckingham, in the expedition on the Isle of Rhe, was unhappily killed there; and,

9, Hender, the eldest, born 1597, married Mary, eldest daughter of John Spark, of the Fryery, in Plymouth, Esq. by whom he had three sons, John, Hender, and Richard, who died young.

I. Sir HENDER, of Spring-Garden, the second son, was bred a merchant, and settling in Jamaica, was president of the council of that island, in the reign of King Charles II. and upon the death of Sir Thomas Lynch, chosen to act as governor, by the constitution of the island, till a commission should arrive from England, appointing a successor; in which station he continued, until King James II. Sep. 15, 1687, conferred the government on Christopher, Duke of Albemarle;* upon whose death, there, in the beginning of 1689,† he succeeded by commission from the King, and favouring the revolution, was created a Baronet, 19 July, 1689, by King William, the first advanced to that dignity, with limitation of the honour to his elder brother, and his heirs male. He married first ———, daughter of Mr. Mangey, goldsmith, of London, widow of Thomas Tottle, a merchant, in Jamaica; and secondly, ‡ Mary, daughter of Thomas Temple, of Frankton, in Warwickshire, Esq. and widow of the aforesaid Sir Thomas Lynch, Knt. but by neither of them had any issue. Whereupon, according to the limitation in the patent, his eldest brother.

II. Sir JOHN MOLESWORTH, of Pencarrow, Knt. succeeded to the title; he was member of parliament for Bossiney, in Cornwall, 13 King William, and for Lestwithiel, 1 Queen Anne. He received the honour of knighthood from King Charles II, and by that King was constituted vice-admiral of the north parts of Cornwall, and was continued, by their Majesties King James II. William III. and Anne. He married § first, Margery, eldest daughter of Thomas Wise, of Sydenham, in Devonshire, Esq. son of Sir Thomas Wise, Knight of the Bath, temp. Jac. I. and sister to Sir Edward Wise, of Sydenham, Knight of the Bath, by whom he had three sons; Sir John, Hender, and Spark; and three daughters, Mary, Margery, and Prudence. He married secondly Margaret, eldest daughter to Sir Nicholas Slaning, of Moristow, in Devonshire, Knt. (who was a commander of great distinction and character, in the civil wars, and lost his life at the siege at Bristol, in the service of King Charles I.) but by her had no issue.

III. Sir JOHN MOLESWORTH, eldest son and successor to his father, married ———, daughter of John Arscott, of Tetcott, in Devonshire, Esq. and by

* Gazette, 1687. † Heylin's Cat. of Baronets. ‡ Le Neve's MSS. vol. III. p. 280. § Ibid.

TABLE.

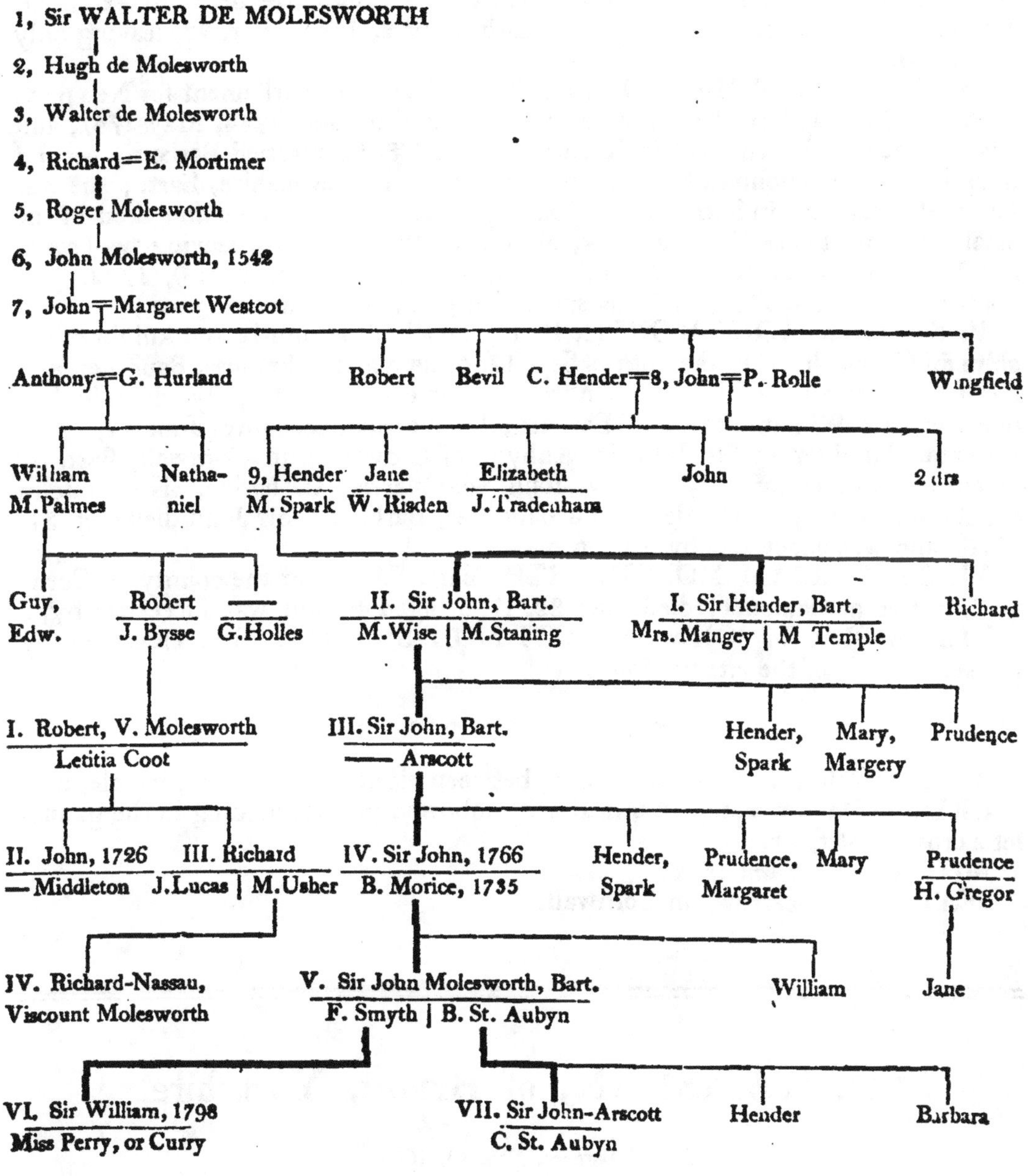
1, Sir WALTER DE MOLESWORTH
2, Hugh de Molesworth
3, Walter de Molesworth
4, Richard=E. Mortimer
5, Roger Molesworth
6, John Molesworth, 1542
7, John=Margaret Westcot
Anthony=G. Hurland
Robert
Bevil
C. Hender=8, John=P. Rolle
Wingfield
William
M. Palmes
Natha-
niel
9, Hender
M. Spark
Jane
W. Risden
Elizabeth
J. Tradenham
John
2 drs
Guy,
Edw.
Robert
J. Bysse
G. Holles
II. Sir John, Bart.
M. Wise | M. Staning
I. Sir Hender, Bart.
Mrs. Mangey | M Temple
Richard
I. Robert, V. Molesworth
Letitia Coot
III. Sir John, Bart.
— Arscott
Hender,
Spark
Mary,
Margery
Prudence
II. John, 1726
— Middleton
III. Richard
J. Lucas | M. Usher
IV. Sir John, 1766
B. Morice, 1735
Hender,
Spark
Prudence,
Margaret
Mary
Prudence
H. Gregor
IV. Richard-Nassau,
Viscount Molesworth
V. Sir John Molesworth, Bart.
F. Smyth | B. St. Aubyn
William
Jane
VI. Sir William, 1798
Miss Perry, or Curry
VII. Sir John-Arscott
C. St. Aubyn
Hender
Barbara

her, who died of the small pox, at Blandford, in Dorsetshire, had three sons, and four daughters: Sir John, his successor in dignity and estate; Hender, who died Feb. 6, 1732-3, unmarried; Spark, educated at Trinity-Hall, Cambridge, being a fellow commoner, and died at Naples, June 9, 1739; Prudence, Margaret, Mary, all died unmarried; and Prudence, wife of Hugh Gregor, of Essex-street, London, Esq. died of the small-pox at Bath, May 2, 1741, ætat. 23, leaving only one daughter, Jane.

IV. Sir JOHN MOLESWORTH, Bart. chosen to parliament for Newport, in April 1734, and in the parliaments which met in Dec. 1744, May 1747, and May 1754, for the county of Cornwall. In 1728, he married Barbara, second daughter of Sir Nicholas Morice, of Werrington, in Devonshire, Bart.; she was taken ill at Egham, in Surry, in her journey down to Pencarrow, and died of the small-pox, at Staines, in Middlesex, May 17, 1735, aged 24, leaving two sons, Sir John, his successor, and William, who died at Bath, Feb. 9, 1762. Sir John died, April 4, 1766, and was succeeded by his only surviving son,

V. Sir JOHN MOLESWORTH, Bart. colonel of the militia and knight of the shire for Cornwall. On the 28th of Sep. 1755, he married Frances, daughter and coheiress of James Smyth, of St. Andries, in Somersetshire, Esq. by whom he had one son, Sir William, the late Baronet; he married, secondly, June 22, 1762, Barbara, daughter of Sir John St. Aubyn, of Clowance, in Cornwall, Bart. by whom he had two sons; 1, the Rev. John, who married Catherine, sister of John St. Aubyn, Bart.; 2, Hender, and a daughter, Barbara. Sir John died Oct. 31, 1776, and was succeeded by his son,

VI. Sir WILLIAM MOLESWORTH, Bart. M. P. for the county of Cornwall, in two parliaments; died Mar. 22, 1798, aged 40, and was succeeded by,

VII. The Rev. Sir JOHN ARSCOTT MOLESWORTH, Bart. eldest son by the second lady of the late Sir John.

ARMS—Gules, an escutcheon vaire, between eight cross croslets, in orle, or.

CREST—On a wreath, an armed arm embowed proper, holding in the gauntlet a cross croslet, or.

MOTTO—*Sic fidem teneo.*

SEAT—At Pencarrow, in Cornwall.

---

211. RAMSDEN, of Byrom, Yorkshire.

Created Baronet, Nov. 30, 1689.

1, ROBERT RAMSDEN, of Langley, near Hothersfield, in Yorkshire, had one son, John, and one daughter, ———, wife of Henry Savile, Esq

2, John, son of Robert, living 1612, married ——, daughter of ——, by whom he had two sons, William, his successor, and John of Lascells-Hall, who married Eleanor, daughter of Richard Lewis, of Marr, in Yorkshire, Esq. by whom he had, William Ramsden, of Lascells-Hall, who married Mary, daughter of Thomas Waterton, of Walton, and had issue, but they all died young; so that his estate came to be divided amongst his sisters and coheirs; Mary, wife, first of Henry Grice, of Sandall, Esq.; secondly, of Sir Thomas Smith, of Nottinghamshire, Knt.; Ellen, first, of Tirringham; and secondly, of Henry Portington; Anne, of Marmaduke Wilson; Jane, first, of Leonard Wray, of Cusworth; secondly, of Roger Portington, of Barnby Dun; Elizabeth, of Thomas Wray; and, Grace, of Robert Portington. John, beforementioned, (the father of William, living 1612,) had also two daughters, Elizabeth, wife of Edward Beaumont, of Whitly-Hall, Esq. and Anne, of Samuel Saltonstall.

3, William Ramsden, Esq. eldest son and heir, married Rosamund, daughter of Thomas Pilkington, of Bradley, in Yorkshire, Esq. by whom he had two sons and three daughters: Sir John, William, Catherine, wife of William Pudsey, of Bolton, in Craven; Rosamund, of Richard Holland, of Heaton, near Manchester, in Lancashire, Esq.; and ——, of Sir Christopher Wandesford, Bart.

4, Sir John Ramsden, of Byrom, and Longley, in Yorkshire, Knt. eldest son and heir, was colonel of a regiment, temp. Car. I. and sheriff of Yorkshire, 13 Car. I. and married, first, Margaret, daughter of Sir Peter Frecheville, of Stavely, in Derbyshire, Knt. (afterwards Lord Frechville,) by whom he left two sons: William, and John, who died unmarried; his second wife was, Anne, daughter and heiress of Lawrence Overton, of London, relict of George Chamberlaine, of London, and of alderman Poole, of London, by whom he had no issue. This Sir John, died in Newark castle in the service of King Charles I.

5, William, the eldest son of Sir John, married ——, daughter of George Palmes, of Lindley, in Yorkshire, Esq. by whom he had three sons, John, Frechville, and Peter; and five daughters: 1, Brown, first, wife of Sir George Dalston, of Heath, in Yorkshire, Bart. secondly, of Edward Andrews, of Westminster, Esq. and after his death, of Sir Richard Fisher, of Islington, in Middlesex, Bart. (she died March 15, 1739-40;) 2, Margaret, of Sir John Dalston, of Heath, Bart.; 3, Frances, the wife of Charles, Duke of Bolton, by whom he had Charles and Harry, successively Dukes of Bolton; 4, Mary, of Thomas Wilkinson, of Kirkbridge, in Yorkshire, Esq.; 5, Elizabeth, of John Anderson, Esq. Frechville, and Peter, both died unmarried.

I. Sir JOHN RAMSDEN, his only surviving son, was created a Baronet by King William; he married Sarah, only daughter and heiress of Charles Butler, of Coates, in the county of Lincoln, Esq. by whom he had eight sons: Sir William, his successor; James, commissioner of the wine-licence office, who died Oct. 1770; William died at York, Nov. 16, 1770, the others died unmarried, except,

II. Sir WILLIAM RAMSDEN, Bart. who married Elizabeth, the second daughter of John, Viscount Lonsdale, who died his widow, in 1775, by whom he had six sons, and five daughters; of which, Catherine, the eldest, was wife of Sir

TABLE.

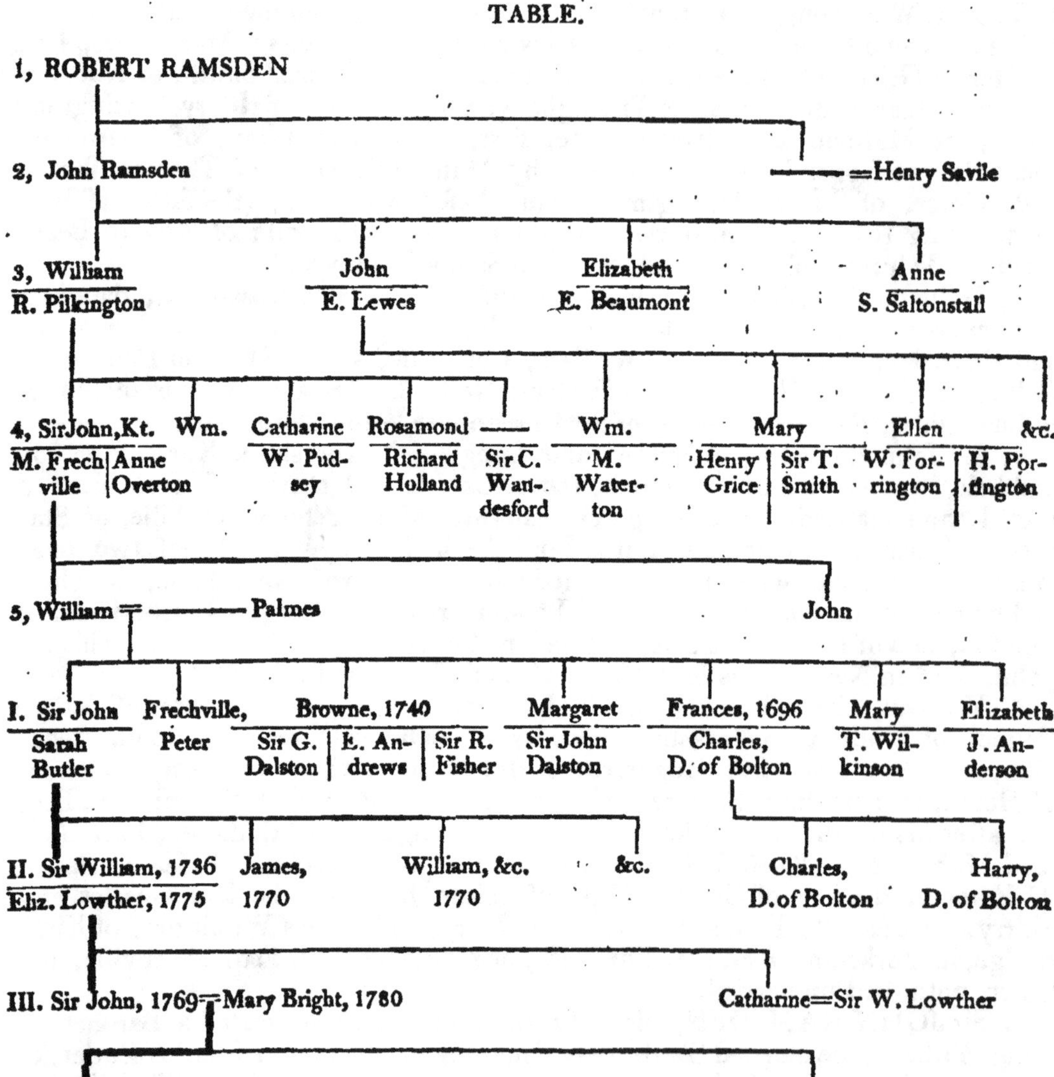
1, ROBERT RAMSDEN
2, John Ramsden
—— =Henry Savile
3, William
R. Pilkington
John
E. Lewes
Elizabeth
E. Beaumont
Anne
S. Saltonstall
4, SirJohn,Kt.
M. Frechville
Anne Overton
Wm.
Catharine
W. Pudsey
Rosamond
Richard Holland
——
Sir C. Wandesford
Wm.
M. Waterton
Mary
Henry Grice
Sir T. Smith
Ellen
W. Torrington
&c.
H. Porington
5, William = —— Palmes
John
I. Sir John
Sarah Butler
Frechville,
Peter
Browne, 1740
Sir G. Dalston
E. Andrews
Sir R. Fisher
Margaret
Sir John Dalston
Frances, 1696
Charles, D. of Bolton
Mary
T. Wilkinson
Elizabeth
J. Anderson
II. Sir William, 1736
Eliz. Lowther, 1775
James, 1770
William, &c. 1770
&c.
Charles, D. of Bolton
Harry, D. of Bolton
III. Sir John, 1769=Mary Bright, 1780
Catharine=Sir W. Lowther
IV. Sir John=L. S. Shepherd
——=Tho. L. Ducie, 1785

William Lowther, of Swillington, in Yorkshire, Bart. Sir William, dying June, 1736, was succeeded in dignity and estate, by his eldest son,

III. Sir JOHN RAMSDEN, Bart. who represented the borough of Appleby, in Westmoreland; he married Mary, only daughter of Thomas Liddel Bright, of Badsworth, in Yorkshire, Esq. and widow of Charles, Marquis of Rockingham, by whom, who died 1780, he had one son, Sir John, the present Baronet, and a daughter, ———, wife, Feb. 11, 1774, of Thomas Reynold, Lord Ducie. Sir John died 1769, and was succeeded by his son,

IV. Sir JOHN RAMSDEN, the present Bart.

ARMS—Argent, on a cheveron, between three fleur de lis, sable, three rams heads, erased, of the first.

CREST—On a wreath, an armed arm, couped at the elbow, and erect, proper, holding in the gauntlet a fleur de lis, sable.

SEAT—At Byrom, in Yorkshire.

212. LEIGHTON, of WATLESBOROUGH, Shropshire.

Created Baronet, March 2, 1692.

THIS family was in England long before the Norman conquest, and of noble extraction, as appears by Doomsday-book, wherein it is found, Anschitel, *tenuit humum Comite de Leton, &c.* (one of the old ways of spelling this name) which,* without doubt, was the reason why Camden stiles them, *Nobilem, & Equestrem Familiam*; in his Britannia.

Sir Titus de Leighton, Knight of the sepulchre, son and heir of Cuthbert, and grandson and heir of Totilus de Leighton, was one of those who went to the wars in the Holy Land, and at his return was a co-founder of the abbey of Buldewas, Shropshire, of which mention is made in some old manuscripts, wrote by Roger and John Challingworth.

William Fitz-Allan, soon after the conquest, re-conveyed the manor of Leighton, to Sir Richard de Leighton, Knt. † son and heir of Sir Titus, in as full and ample manner, as the said Sir Richard's ancestors had before conveyed it to the ancestors of the said Fitz-Allan; and out of this his manor, which is situate very near the abbey of Buldewas, Sir Richard gave lands to that abbey, as appears by his grant without date, inserted in Dugdale's *Monasticon Anglicanum*, prior to that, in which King Stephen confirmed the said abbey.

* Ex Inf. Dom. Ed. Leighton, Bar. 1741. † Ibid.

Sir Titus, Sir William,* and Sir Richard de Leighton, severally succeeded; the two last of which are mentioned as witnesses to some donations of land to the abbey of Hagmond; and this Sir Richard, levied a fine of lands in Cheshire to the abbot of Cumbermere, in which he acknowledges them to be the right of the said abbot. Some of the heirs and successors of these knights, highly advanced the reputation, interest, and fortune of their family, by their civil and military employments, in the service of their kings and country; of which John Leighton, in the reign of King Edward III. is a particular instance,† who had several pensions granted to him by that King, for the good and faithful services he had done for him, and the prince his son, as they, and others did by ther marriages, both with the daughters of the noble families of Le Brun, Butler, L'Estrange, Devereux, Sutton, and Gerard,‡ and with the daughters and heirs, or coheirs, of the ancient families of Warren, Cambray,§ Drake, Cornwall, and Stapleton, a family descended from the Earls of Chester, and Kings of France and Arragon, from whom they had divers manors and estates of great value, not only in Shropshire, where they lived, but also in the several counties of Cornwall, Gloucester, Wilts, and Somerset: with which they flourished for some ages, being persons of great distinction. They also intermarried with the families of Lacy, Pilhard, Standford, Pygot, Darrell, Deverreux, of Castle-Bromwich, and Stephens.

The castles and manors of Watlesborough and Alberbury, now in possession of the family, came to them, among other estates, upon the marriage of John Leighton, of Stretton, (who was thrice high-sheriff in Shropshire, in the reign of Edward IV.) with Anchoret, daughter and coheiress of Sir John Burgh,‖ Jane, his wife, daughter and heiress of Sir William Clopton, of Gloucestershire; he was son and heir of Sir Hugh Burgh, treasurer of England, who was descended from Hubert de Burgh, the famous politician, in the reign of Henry III. who married a daughter of William, King of Scotland. Sir Hugh Burgh, married ——, daughter and heiress of John, Lord Mouthwy, who married Elizabeth, daughter and heiress of Sir Foulk Corbet, of Morton Corbet, in Shropshire, and was son

* Many of the ancestors of this family were interred in the abbey of Buldewas, upon the demolishing of which abbey, two ancient monuments, or tomb-stones, were removed, for their preservation, into Leighton church; one is in memory of Sir William Leighton, and his wife; and the other, in memory of Sir Titus: the portraiture of the last is in armour, with his sword by his side, and his coat of arms on his left arm, in a shield, with a lion couchant at his feet. Ex inf. Dom. Edw. Leighton, Bar. 1741. † Ibid. ‡ Ibid.

§ Upon the marriage of John Leighton, with the coheiress of Cambray, in the reign of King Edward III. he took up his residence at Church-Stretton, in which church several generations of this family lie interred in a chancel there, called Leighton's chancel to this day; there are several inscriptions wrote on marble stones, in memory of several of them; but being wrote in an old Saxon character, and much wore, none of them are perfectly legible. Ex inf. Dom. Edw. Leighton, Bar.

‖ Upon the marriage of John Leighton, with the daughter and coheiress of Sir John Burgh, in the reign of Hen. VI. this family again changed their seat, and came to Watlesborough, where Sir Edward Leighton, the first Baronet, departed this life, and was interred in a chapel of his own, in the parish church of Alberbury, among nine generations of his ancestors; but there are no monuments erected to the memory of any of them; there is only one monument erected by himself, on his first lady, the daughter of Sir Job Charlton. Ex inf. ibid. 1741.

and heir of William, Lord Mouthwy, who was lineally descended, in the male line, from Blethyn ap Convyn, King of Powys, and, in the female line, from Gruffith ap Conan, King of North-Wales, Owen ap Edwin, Prince of Tegengle; the Princes of South-Wales, the Princes of Lower Powys, the Lords of Arustly, and the Lords of Dyffryn Cluyd. Which Lord Mouthwy married ——, daughter and coheiress of Thomas ap Llewelyn, who married ——, daughter and heiress of Philip ap Ivor, Lord of Iscoed, who married ——, daughter and sole heiress of Llewelyn ap Gruffith, the last Prince of Wales: she (the wife of William, Lord Mouthwy) was lineally descended, in the male line, from Rees ap Theodore, King of South Wales, who married —, daughter and heiress of Riwallon ap Convyn, Prince of Powys; and in the female line, from the Lords of Brecknock, the Lords of Cedewen, Llewelyn ap Jorwerth, Prince of Wales, Reynold, King of Man, Simon Mountford, Earl of Leicester, who married Eleonora, daughter of K. John, and Henry, Earl of Barr, who married Eleonora, daughter of K. Edw I.; so that this family, by the coheiress of Burgh, derive their descent from a great number of British and English nobility; by two marriages, from the royal family of England, by one, from the royal family of Scotland, and by several, from Roderic the Great, King of Wales, the original of whose genealogy is from those ancient British Kings and Princes who first possessed this island. And by this marriage, it is thought the heir of this family may claim a right to some baronies that lie dormant between him and the Earl of Bradford and Richard Mytton, of Hulston, in Shropshire, Esq. whose ancestors married the other coheiress.

This John Leighton, Esq. had two brothers, Sir Cuthbert Leighton, Knight of the order of St. John, of Jerusalem, who had a particular pension allowed him by act of parliament, at the dissolution of the monasteries, temp. Hen. VIII.; and Edward, who married the daughter of Thomas Hopton, from whom the Leightons, of Coats, in Shropshire, a very numerous family, were descended.

2, Sir Thomas Leighton, son and heir of John, and Anchoret, among others, was attainted, temp. Richard III. for espousing the interest of the Earl of Richmond, to whom he was collaterally allied, by the marriage of one of the Earl's ancestors, with the other coheiress of Tho. ap Llewelyn above mentioned*, upon whose accession to the crown the attainder was taken off, and a pardon granted to him: he was knight of the body to that king, and one of the chief commanders in the army sent over to France in the beginning of that reign, along with the Lord Brooke, in aid of the Duke of Britain, against the French king. He was again in the wars of France, with King Henry VIII. where he had the honour of being made knight-banneret under the King's own banner, displayed in the royal army, his majesty being present, for his conduct and bravery at the battle of Spurs, and taking of Tournay, and had estates granted in several counties for his life, in consideration of the services he had performed, both for King Henry VII. and King Henry VIII. in both which reigns he served in parliament as knight of the shire for the county of Salop, as divers of his ancestors had done in other reigns, for which, see the Parliament Rolls. He married Elizabeth, daughter of Walter, Lord Ferrers, of Chart-

* Ex inf. Dom. Ed. Leighton, Bar. 1741.

ley *, relict of Sir Richard Corbet, Knt. and died about 10 Hen. VIII. His brother, Sir William Leighton, was chief justice of North-Wales †, from whom the Leightons, of Plash ‡, in Shropshire, were descended, a family now extinct, but of great esteem in their time.

3, John Leighton, Esq. son and heir of Sir Thomas, being squire of the body to King Henry VIII. was, towards the end of that reign, particularly when the parliament was held at Blackfriars §, knight of the shire for the county of Salop, at which time he raised a considerable number of men, and attended the Duke of Suffolk to Calais, at his own expence, and died soon after his return. He had three brothers, who were by another wife, from one of which, the Leighton's, of Rodenhurst, were descended, now extinct.

4, Sir Edward Leighton, son and heir of John, was custos rotulorum, and knight of the shire for the county of Salop ||, in the reign of Queen Elizabeth, was one of that Queen's privy council, and much esteemed by her, as also was his brother, Sir Thomas Leighton, of Feckenham, in the county of Wilts, who was governor of the Isles of Guernsey and Jersey, and constable of the Tower of London. This is that Sir Thomas Leighton, who was knighted in 1579, and appointed to attend Robert Devereux, Earl of Essex, (his near relation) upon his expedition into France, to join the French King at the siege of Rouen; and being a person of great experience ¶, was to advise the said Earl in matters of moment, where conduct and council were required; he was also given as a hostage, together with Pelham and Horsham, or Horsey, at the siege of Cadiz, (see Camden's Eliz.) he married ——, daughter of Sir Francis Knowles **, who was maid of honour to Queen Elizabeth, by whom he had issue, Thomas Leighton ††, who married Mary, daughter and coheiress of Edward Lord Zouch, of Harringsworth, by whom he had two daughters, who were his coheiresses, Elizabeth, wife of Sherrington Talbot, Esq. ancestor to Earl Talbot; and Anne, of Sir John St. John, ancestor to the Viscount St. John. Sir Edward died 1594, and was succeeded by his son,

5, Thomas ‡‡, who married Elizabeth, daughter of Sir William Gerard, Knt. lord-chancellor of Ireland; he died in 1600, and was succeeded by his son,

6, Robert, then a minor, who died the 1st of K. Cha. I. and left, by Anne §§, his wife, second daughter of Sir Edward Devereux, of Castle Bromwich, in Warwickshire, Bart.

* In the parish church of Burford, in Shropshire, there is a monument erected to the memory of Dame Elizabeth Leighton, wife of Sir Thomas Leighton, and daughter to the Right Hon. Walter Devereux, Lord Ferrers, of Chartley. Ex inf. Dom. Edw. Leighton, Bar. 1741.

† Ibid.

‡ In the church of Eardington, there is a monument erected to the memory of Sir William Leighton, of Plash, and his lady, who was the daughter of Judge Corbet. Ex inf. ibid.

§ Ex inf. Dom. Edw. Leighton, Bar. 1741.

|| Ibid.

¶ Ibid.

** Quære, if not Elizabeth, daughter of Sir Robert Knollys, K. B. as in Segar's MSS. Baronetage.

†† Ex inf. Dom. Edw. Leighton, Bar. 1741.

‡‡ At Maerwale, in the county of Denbigh, is a monument erected to the memory of Richard Leighton, Esq. who was second son of Sir Edward Leighton, of Watlesborough; and to the memory of Catharine, his wife, who was the daughter of Sir —— Mostyn. Ex inf. ibid.

§§ Le Neve's MSS. Vol. III. p. 286.

7, Edward, his son and heir, then under age, who married first, Abigail, daughter and heiress of Wm Stephens, of Shrewsbury, Esq.; secondly, Martha, daughter of Thomas Owen, of Shrewsbury, Esq.; this last wife lies buried in the parish church of St. Chad, in Shrewsbury, where a monument is erected to her memory. During the time of these minorities, the family was deprived of several branches of their estate, and had great devastations committed on other parts thereof*, by the ill management and base practices of those persons to whom they unfortunately fell in ward, who prevailed upon Edward (being still a minor) to marry a second wife out of their own family, without any portion at all, and afterwards, when he came of age, to disinherit his only son by his first wife, with whom he had a very considerable fortune, and give his estate, or the bulk thereof, to the son by the second venter, notwithstanding their contract, and his promises before the first marriage, with his wife's father, and relations, to the contrary; by which means this family had been totally ruined, had not providence interfered, by taking off Thomas, son by the second wife, before he came of full age †; upon whose death,

8, Robert, the son of the first, came into the whole estate, as remainder in the entail; who was found, by the inquisition, taken upon the death of his father, 11 Car. I. ‡, to be about six years old, who, notwithstanding he was a minor, yet firmly adhered to the royal party in the time of the rebellion. He was burgess of the corporation of the town of Shrewsbury at the restoration of King Charles II. and served in parliament almost eighteen years; but though he continued all his life well affected to the government, yet refused the honour of being made a Baronet, both from King Charles II. and King James II. He married Gertrude, daughter of Edward Baldwin, of Diddlebury, in Shropshire, Esq. descended from the Baldwins, Kings of Jerusalem, and Earls of Flanders, and leaving a numerous issue by her, died in the year 1689.

I. EDWARD LEIGHTON, of Watlesborough, in Shropshire, Esq. son and heir (being the 23d generation of this family, from Totilus de Leighton) was created a Baronet the 4th year of King William and Queen Mary. He was knight of the shire for Shropshire, in the reign of King William, and burgess for the corporation of the town of Shrewsbury, in the reign of Queen Anne; he was zealous for the support of the Protestant interest at the time of the Revolution, and afterwards for the settlement of the crown in the House of Hanover. He married first §, Dorothy, daughter of Sir Job Charlton, of Ludford, in the county of Hereford, Knt. and Bart.; and secondly, Jane, daughter of Daniel Nicholl, of the city of London, Esq. By his first wife, he had issue, Robert, who died young; Sir Edward; Job, who died before he was of age; Lettice, who died unmarried Dec. 9, 1753; Dorothy, Jane, and Dorothy, who all died young; and by his second wife, he had Daniel Leighton, Esq. who died in Jan. 1765, lieutenant-colonel of general Evan's regiment of horse. He married Jane, daughter of Nathaniel Thorold, of the city of Lincoln, Esq. This lady died in London, being bedchamber woman to the Princess of Wales, and left

* Ex inf. Dom. Edw. Leighton, Bar. † Ibid. ‡ Ibid. § Ibid.

two sons and two daughters; 1, Herbert, page to the Princess Dowager of Wales; 2, Edward, a lieutenant of a man of war, and died in London unmarried, of a wound he received in the battle off Toulon; 3, Jane, who married first, Captain Cathcart; secondly, Jonathan, eldest son of Sir Jonathan Cope, Bart. by whom he had a son and two daughters; 4, ——, another daughter, whose first husband was Captain Sabine. The other children of Sir Edward were, Francis, lieutenant-general and colonel of the thirty-second regiment of foot; Gerard, captain in the army, deceased; Jane, who was first married to Thomas Jones, of the town of Shrewsbury, Esq. and since remarried to Sir Charles Lloyd, of Garth, in the county of Montgomery, Bt. by whom she had one son, who died young; and Victoria, wife of Edward Kynaston, of Hardwick, Esq.; Frances, Anne, and Elizabeth, who died young. Sir Edward died at Watlesborough, in the year 1711, and was interred at Alberbury, with his first lady, and was succeeded both in title and estate by

II. Sir EDWARD LEIGHTON, Bart his only surviving son by his first lady, who married first, Rachel, daughter of Sir William Forester, of Watling-street, in the county of Salop, by Lady Mary, his wife, daughter of James Cecil, Earl of Salisbury, by whom he had nine children, 1, Rachel, wife of Thomas Jenkins, of Shrewsbury, Esq.; 2, Mary, died 1776; 3, Forester, captain in Lord Powy's regiment, raised in the rebellion 1745, and died unmarried at Bath; 4, Sir Charlton, his successor; 5, Baldwyn, married Anne, daughter of Captain Smith, by whom he had six sons and five daughters, all living in 1771; 6, Burgh; and 7, Cambray, died unmarried; 8, Dorothy; and 9, Emma, died young. Sir Edward's first lady dying in 1720, he married secondly, Judith, daughter of John Ellick, of Mile End, in Middlesex, Esq. sister of Governor Ellick, and relict of Captain Thwaites, who was in the East-India company's service. By this lady, who died at Bath in 1764, he had no issue. Sir Edward died May 6, 1756, aged 74, and was interred in the family vault in the church of Alberbury, and was succeeded by his eldest surviving son,

III. Sir CHARLTON LEIGHTON, Bart. who married first, Anna-Maria, daughter of Richard Mytton, Esq. by Letitia, sister and heiress of Thomas Owen, of Condover, Esq. who died in Aug. 1750, leaving one son, Charlton, captain in the militia for the county of Salop; and three daughters, Anna-Maria, who, by the will of her grandmother, was heiress of Condover, wife of Nicholas Smith, Esq.; Honor, who died young; and Anna-Bella. Sir Charlton married secondly, Oct. 1752, Emma, daughter of Sir T. Maude, of the kingdom of Ireland, by whom he had Robert; Emma, wife of John Corbet, of Sundorn, Esq.; Louisa, Charlotte, Harriot, Richard, and Mary, which two last died young, Sir Charlton served in the army as an ensign in Ireland, till Dec. 10, 1739, when he was appointed captain in Colonel Moreton's regiment of marines, in which he served at Carthagena; and, in 1741, did duty in the Burford man of war, as captain of marines, with the admirals Matthews and Lestock, against the combined fleet off Toulon. On his return in May, 1745, he was appointed major of the same regiment, under the command of colonel John Cotterel. On the reduction of that regiment, he was appointed, in 1755, major of the marines at Plymouth, under the direction of the lord high admiral; and, soon after, having his Majesty's leave to retire on

TABLE.

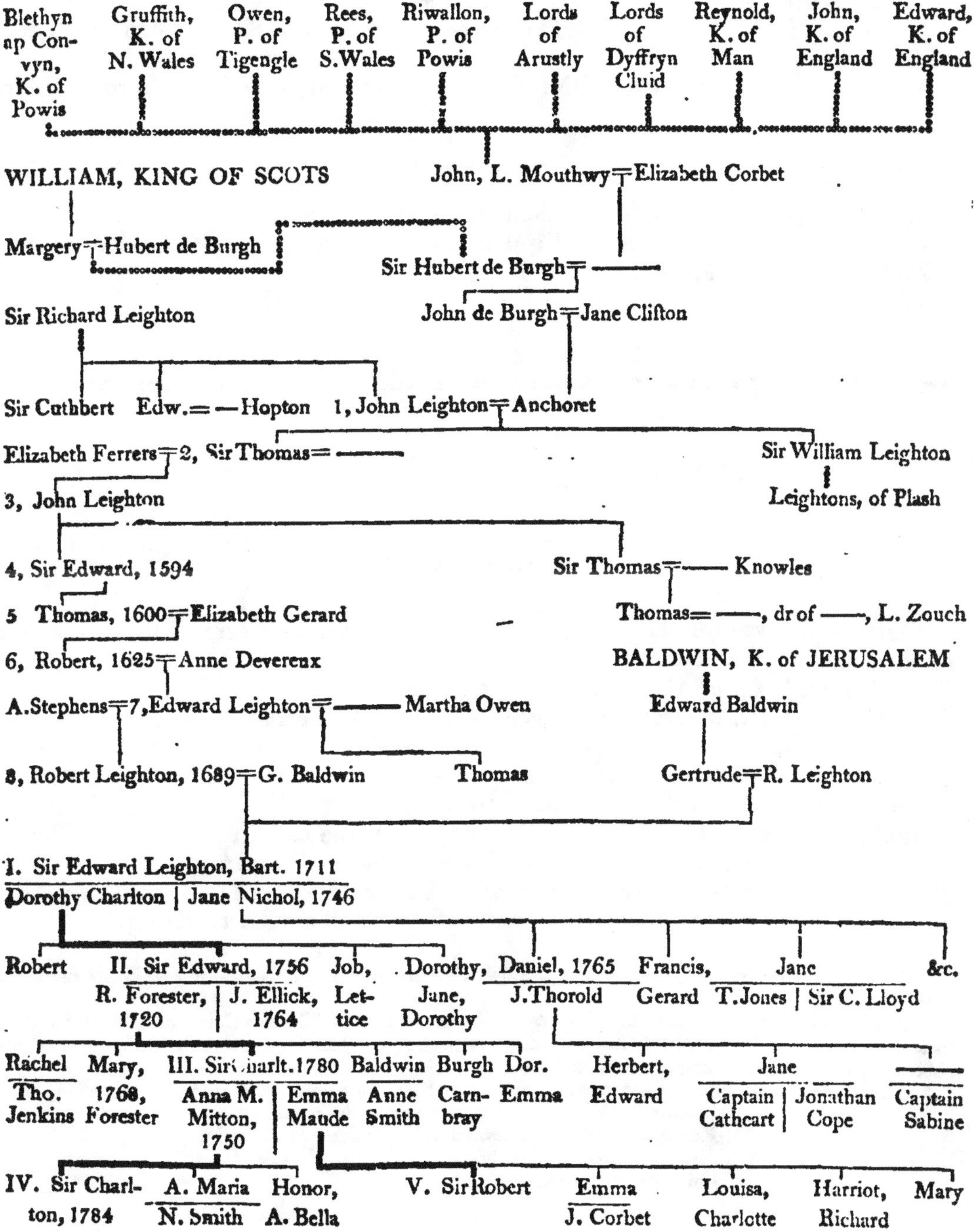
Blethyn ap Convyn, K. of Powis
Gruffith, K. of N. Wales
Owen, P. of Tigengle
Rees, P. of S.Wales
Riwallon, P. of Powis
Lords of Arustly
Lords of Dyffryn Cluid
Reynold, K. of Man
John, K. of England
Edward, K. of England
WILLIAM, KING OF SCOTS
John, L. Mouthwy
Elizabeth Corbet
Margery
Hubert de Burgh
Sir Hubert de Burgh
Sir Richard Leighton
John de Burgh
Jane Clifton
Sir Cuthbert
Edw.
—Hopton
1, John Leighton
Anchoret
Elizabeth Ferrers
2, Sir Thomas
Sir William Leighton
3, John Leighton
Leightons, of Plash
4, Sir Edward, 1594
Sir Thomas
Knowles
5 Thomas, 1600
Elizabeth Gerard
Thomas
——, dr of ——, L. Zouch
6, Robert, 1625
Anne Devereux
BALDWIN, K. of JERUSALEM
A.Stephens
7, Edward Leighton
Martha Owen
Edward Baldwin
8, Robert Leighton, 1689
G. Baldwin
Thomas
Gertrude
R. Leighton
I. Sir Edward Leighton, Bart. 1711
Dorothy Charlton | Jane Nichol, 1746
Robert
II. Sir Edward, 1756
R. Forester, 1720 | J. Ellick, 1764
Job, Lettice
Dorothy, Jane, Dorothy
Daniel, 1765
J.Thorold
Francis, Gerard
Jane
T.Jones | Sir C. Lloyd
&c.
Rachel
Tho. Jenkins
Mary, 1768, Forester
III. Sir Charlt.1780
Anna M. Mitton, 1750 | Emma Maude
Baldwin
Anne Smith
Burgh
Carnbray
Dor.
Emma
Herbert, Edward
Jane
Captain Cathcart | Jonathan Cope
Captain Sabine
IV. Sir Charlton, 1784
A. Maria
N. Smith
Honor, A. Bella
V. Sir Robert
Emma
J. Corbet
Louisa, Charlotte
Harriot, Richard
Mary

half pay, in 1765, he was made one of his Majesty's deputy-lieutenants of the county of Salop. Feb. 18, the same year, he was constituted colonel of the militia for the county of Salop, served the office of high-sheriff of Shropshire in 1748, and died May 5, 1780, and was succeeded by his son,

IV. Sir CHARLTON LEIGHTON, who died Dec. 1784, and was succeeded by his brother,

V. Sir ROBERT LEIGHTON, Bart. who was high-sheriff of Shropshire in 1786.

ARMS—Quarterly, per fess, indented, or, and gules.
CREST—On a wreath, or, and gules, a wivern, with wings expanded, sable.
MOTTO—*Dread Shame.*
SEATS—At Watlesborough and Loton, both in Shropshire.

213. COLT, of WESTMINSTER.

Created Baronet, March 2, 1692.

THIS family was formerly possessed of very considerable estates in Suffolk and Essex. They are descended from,

1, Thomas Colt, of Carlisle, who was father of,

2, Thomas Colt, of Greys, in Cavendish, Suffolk, Peches Newhall, in Essex, and Chelworth, in Cavendish, and Boxted, Suffolk*, who had also the manor of Aketon, in Suffolk, granted to him and his heirs male†; he was chancellor of the exchequer, and of the privy council to King Edward IV‡. He married Jane ||, daughter and heiress of John Trusbut, and one of the coheiresses of ——, Baron Trusbut, (*the other daughter and coheiress of Baron Trusbut, was wife of Lord Roos, ancestor to the Duke of Rutland. Quære)* and had two sons, and two daughters. She was afterwards the wife of Sir William Parr, Knt §.

* Vide Esch. 15 Edw. IV. † Pat. 1 Edw. IV. m. 14. ‡ Le Neve's MSS. of Baronets, Vol. III. P. 287.

|| In the antiquities of Essex, p. 21. she is called Joane, widow of Thomas Colt, and wife of Sir William Parr, Knt. and said to die 15 Ed. IV. and that she held the manor of Clayhill, in Barking, of the abbess, by the service one knight's fee, and 15s. 3d.

§ This Thomas lies buried at Cavendish, in Suffolk, where, on a great stone, was this inscription :

Nobilis ille Viri Tho. Colt, Armiger, hic requiescit
Edwardi Regis IIII. Consilarius honorificus prudens
discretus fortis tam Consiliis quam Armis, Vir talem
quis reperire potest.

3, John, Colt, of Newhall, in Essex, Esq. son and heir, had a special livery of his lands *. He married first †, Mary, daughter of Sir John Alne, Knt. by whom he left no issue; but by Elizabeth, daughter of Sir John Eldrington, Knt. he left two sons and five daughters, 1, George; 2, Thomas, who married Magdalen, daughter of —— Middleton, by whom he had two daughters, his coheiresses, Catharine, wife of —— Cave, of Bargrave, in Leicestershire, Esq. by whom he had Sir Alexander Cave, Knt. and Jane; the other daughter and coheiress was wife of Nicholas Brooke, servant to Queen Elizabeth. Jane, the eldest daughter of John, was wife of Sir Thomas More, Knt. lord chancellor of England ‡; Alice, of Edmund Buggs, Esq.; Mary of William Kemp, of Finchinfield, Esq. (whose great grand daughter and sole heiress, Jane, was wife of Sir John Burgoyne, of Sutton, in Bedfordshire, Bart.); Bridget, of Lawrence Forster, Esq.; and ——, wife of —— Copledike ‖.

4, George Colt. Esq. of Long Melford, in Suffolk, eldest son and heir, thirty years old § at his father's death; married Elizabeth, daughter of Henry Mac-Williams, of Stainborne, in Essex, Esq. by whom (who died Sep. 15, 1569) he had, 1, Henry Colt, of Essex, Esq.; 2, Thomas, who married, first, Elizabeth, daughter of John Conisby, of North-Mims, in Hertfordshire, Esq. by whom he had three sons, and one daughter: secondly, Elizabeth, daughter of Thomas Stopham, of London, by whom he had two daughters; the daughters of George, were Elizabeth, wife of Henry Smith, of Shouldam, in Essex; and Anne, of Henry Bretton, of Layer-Bretton, in Essex. He died 1758 ¶.

* Pat. 1 Hen. VII.

† The chief of this account is from Sir John-Dutton Colt's pedigree, 1741.

‡ In Mr. Roper's Life of Sir Thomas More, p. 28, he says, Mr. More went to the house of John Colt, Esq. of New Hall, in Essex; and Mr. Colt, who was extremely delighted with his company, proferred him the choice of any of his daughters, who were young gentlewomen of very good carriage, and agreeable persons. Mr. More, inclined to the second, whom he thought the handsomest, but considering that it would be a grief, and some reflection on the eldest, to see her preferred to her, he, out of a kind of compassion, settled his fancy upon the eldest, and soon after married her; she lived but about six years with him, and brought him every year a child.

‖ This John lies also buried at Cavendish. with the following inscription over him (*a*):

> Hic jacet strenuus Vir, Johannes Colt, Armiger,
> Filius Thome Colt, Ar. Elizabetha, Filia Johannis
> Eldrington, Milit. et Maria, Filia Johannis Alne,
> Militis, Uxores ejus.
>
> Children 15 { ix by the one.
> vi by the other

§ Antiquities of Essex, p. 21.

¶ This George was also buried at Cavendish, with this inscription over him:

> Hic jacet Georgius Colt, Armiger (*b*), qui obiit A. D. 1578,
> Et Eliz. Uxor ejus, quæ obiit 15 Sept. 1569.

(*a*) John Colt was eleven years old at his father's death, and died Oct. 22, 14 Hen. VIII.—Antiquities of Essex, p. 21. But p. 76, says, he lies buried at Roydon, in Essex, with the above inscription.

(*b*) Antiquities of Essex, says, Sir George Colt died March 21, 21 Eliz. and held the manor of Clay-Hall of the Queen, as of her manor of Barking, and that George was his son and heir, aged 38 years, and died 14 Jac. 1. and held the manor of Clay-Hall of the King, and that Henry was his son and heir, thirty years old. But in the pedigree, and in Le Neve's MSS. it is George, father of Henry, father of Sir George, father of Sir Henry, &c.

5, Henry Colt, Esq. eldest son, married first, Elizabeth, daughter of John Conisby, of North-Mims, in Hertfordshire, Esq. by whom he had, 1, Sir George Colt; 2, John; 3, Everard; 4, Francis; and 5, Henry, who died young, as did Anne, Mary, Catharine, and Frances; 5, Jane, wife of John Le Hunt, of Bradley, in Suffolk, Esq.; and 6, Elizabeth, wife first, of ——— Burdis, and secondly, of Robert Lovell; secondly, Margaret, daughter of John Heath, of Netherall, in Essex, Esq. by whom he had no issue; he died at Netherall, and was interred at Cavendish.

6, Sir George Colt, Knt. eldest son, was of Greys, in Cavendish, in Suffolk; he married Mary, daughter of William Pooley, of Boxted, in Suffolk, Esq. by whom he had Sir Henry, and other sons, that died without issue; also four daughters, Mary, wife of Sir Thomas Hogan, of Dunham, in Norfolk, Knt.; Martha, of ——— Sherborne; Jane, of ——— Fenwick; and Alice, of ——— Miller. This Sir George was buried with his ancestors at Cavendish.

7, Sir Henry Colt, of Greys, married Bridget, daughter of Sir William Kingsmill, of Sidmanton, in Hampshire, Knt. by whom he had four sons, 1, George Colt, Esq.; 2, Henry Colt, who was governor of Radcot-House, for King Charles I. and slain there; 3, John; 4, Thomas, which three last died unmarried; and three daughters, Judith, wife of — Slade, of Barkham, in Berks; Bridget, and Constance, died unmarried. This Sir Henry died beyond sea: he was seised* of the manor of Greys, alias Colts-Hall, in Cavendish, and Poslingford, in Suffolk, before Feb. 3, 11 Car. I. 1635.

8, Geo. Colt, of Colt-hall, in Suffolk, Clay-hall, and Parendon-hall, in Essex, Esq. the eldest son, married Elizabeth, eldest daughter and coheiress of John Dutton, of Sherborne, in Gloucestershire, Esq. by whom he had nine sons, and one daughter; 1, John-Dutton Colt, Esq. of whom hereafter; 2, George-Dutton Colt, who died unmarried; 3, Sir William-Dutton Colt, Knt. who was resident at the Elector of Hanover's court, being sent thither by King William, as envoy, in 1692. He was the first discoverer of Grandvall's design to assassinate King William as he was riding about, in his ordinary way, visiting the posts of his army in Flanders, which he discovered from some practices and discourses of one Dumont †, who had retired this winter to Zell, as one that had forsaken the French service; whereupon Grandvall was seized, tried, condemned, executed, and confessed the fact. Sir William married first, Lucy, daughter of Thomas Webb, of Kent ‡, by whom he had a son, Harry-Dutton, who by Elizabeth, his wife, daughter and coheiress of John Llewellin, of Herefordshire, had several children, but left issue only one son, George-Dutton, an officer in the army, and two daughters, Sophia, and Anne, wife of Mr. Elton, and Mr. Sopham; Eliz. relict of Harry-Dutton, was afterwards remarried to brigadier-gen. Groves. Sir Wm. by his first wife, had two daughters, Elizabeth, who died young; and Lucy, wife of Paul Burrard, Esq. member of parliament for Lymington, in Hants. Sir William married secondly, Dorothy, daughter and heiress of Henry Sanderson, of Hedley-hope, in Durham, Esq. § by

* Le Neve's MSS. of the family of Colt, Vol. III. P. 287. † Bishop Burnet's History of his own Times, Vol. II. P. 95. ‡ See Thorpe's Registrum Roffense, p. 930, for her monumental inscription. § See Bridge's Northamptonshire, P. 57, for ditto.

whom he had only one son William-Dutton, who died young; his third wife was Mary, daughter of John Garneys, of Moringthorpe, in Norfolk, Esq. by whom he had, William, who died unmarried; John who died unmarried; and a daughter, Sophia, (born at Hanover, and the princess Sophia, her godmother), wife, first, of Edmund Dummer, Esq. and had issue, a daughter, wife of Valentine Knightley, of Fawsley, in Northamtonshire, Esq. and secondly, of Dennis Bond, Esq. member of parliament for Corfe-castle, in Dorsetshire. Sir William died at the Elector of Hanover's court in 1693; 4, the fourth son of George and Elizabeth Dutton was, Sir Harry-Dutton Colt, created Baronet, of whom hereafter; 5, Charles, who died unmarried; 6 Edward-Dutton, who was colonel of a regiment, and killed in a duel in Hyde-Park; 7, Thomas; 8, James; and 9, George, who all died unmarried. Elizabeth, the only daughter of George, was wife of the Rev. Mr. Sidney. This George Colt, Esq. and his family* taking the part of King Charles I. and the Duttons, that of the parliament, John Dutton, Esq. his father in-law, would have had him left the royal cause, and come over to the parliament, and then he would have settled his estate upon him and his heirs: but he would not hear of it; upon which, Mr. Dutton cut off the entail of his estate; and by will, left it to his nephew; William Dutton, and the heirs male of his body, and for default of issue, to Ralph Dutton, and the heirs male of his body, (both sons of his younger brother, Sir Ralph,) and for default of such issue, to his own right heirs for ever.

This George Colt, Esq. was almost cut to pieces at Worcester fight, and after the battle of Worcester †, fled abroad with several of his children, and lived in Holland and Flanders. King Charles II. sent him to Spain, (but little was done for him there); afterwards, he was ordered to go to Ireland, to take possession of it, from Corn. Jones, for the King would not trust any other person with it. The night before he went, he called his children to him, and blessed them, and charged them never to have their fortunes told, for he had his, and was told, that if he lived to pass his forty-fifth year, he should live to be a great man; the next day, he went aboard a Dutch skipper, with forty gentlemen; the skipper was drunk, and the weather very bad, by which means they were all drowned within sight of land, Jan. 20, 1658. He was taken up the next day, and there was found in his pocket, a warrant for being an Earl. He was buried at Girtringdunbark. The other daughter and coheiress of John Dutton, Esq. was wife of Thomas Pope, Earl of Downe, who had only one daughter, Elzabeth, wife, first, of Sir Francis-Henry Lee, of Ditchley, in Oxfordshire, Bart. (father, by her of Sir Edward-Henry Lee, Earl of Litchfield,) and afterwards, of Robert, Earl of Lindsey ‖.

* From Mrs. Mary-Dutton Colt, taken from her father's account in MSS. 1741.

† John Dutton Colt was, when a little boy, at Worcester, with his father, when the battle was fought there, and was carried off by a servant (*a*). He was but sixteen years old at his father's decease, and on the

(*a*) From Mrs. Mary-Dutton Colt, who took it from her father's MSS.

9, John-Dutton Colt, Esq. eldest son and heir, married first, Mary, daughter and heiress of John Booth, of Letton, in Herefordshire, Esq. (she died Feb. 15,

news of the misfortune attending his father the king sent for him, and cried over him, and said, he would have him and his two brothers go back to England, and if ever he returned, he would take care of them, but never did any thing for them after his Restoration; and though his mother was left a widow, with so many children, her father Dutton would never see her to his dying day; and his father, George Colt, Esq. spent his fortune in the service of King Charles I. and II. He sold Colt-Hall, in Suffolk, and several other good estates, though his right so to do was afterwards disputed. The reward this John met with, for his and his family's sufferings, was, that he was thrown into prison the year before King Charles II. died: the reason was, he was then a member of parliament for Leominster, in Herefordshire, and voted for the bill of exclusion, and was zealous for preserving the charter of Leominster. Upon this, King Charles sent for him, and expressed a great concern that he had not done any thing for him or the family since the Restoration; but told him, that he knew he had the keeping of the charter of Leominster, and if he would deliver it up, he would give him a bill upon alderman Backwell for ten thousand pounds. He told him, he could not do it. The king bid him go home, and consider of it, and come to him the next morning, which he did, when the king sent for him into his closet, and shewed him two bills of ten thousand pounds each, one on alderman Backwell, the other on Sir Charles Duncombe, (both being the king's bankers. The king told him, that if he would deliver up the charter to him, he would give him the two bills, and do more for him and his family. Mr. John-Dutton Colt replied, it was not in his power, for that he had sworn to maintain the charter when he was bailiff of the town, and could not break his oath; and he verily believed, that his Majesty could not have any faith in him or any other person who did. Upon which, the king flew into a great passion, and shook Mr. Colt by the shoulder, and said, that he would ruin him and his posterity. Mr. Colt being moved by the usage, told the king, that it was in his Majesty's power to ruin him and his in this world, but not in the next, for he would never forswear himself. The king swore, God's fish, he would ruin him. Mr. Colt went home to Leominster, and soon after, they trumped up a bill of *scandalum magnatum* against him, for words he spoke against the Duke of York (*a*); upon which, Mr. Colt secreted himself for some time, and his friends would have had him gone abroad, but he told them, that he would not, as his country was in distress; and accordingly he stood trial before Lord Chief-Justice Jeffreys, when false witnesses were procured against him, who swore through stitch; but he owned, that at Mr. Coningsby's, at Hampton-court, in Herefordshire, he did say, when they drank the Duke of York's health, that he would not drink any popish duke's health in England. This trial was a little before King Charles died, and Mr. Colt was cast in one hundred thousand pounds damages, and was committed to the King's Bench Prison, Southwark, where he was confined almost three years. At last King James released him, by the interest of Lord Preston. When Mr. Colt kissed the king's hand, to return him thanks,

(*a*) His Royal Highness the Duke of York, in Michaelmas Term, 35 Car. II. brought his action upon the statute of *scandalum magnatum*, against John-Dutton Colt, Esq. some time bailiff of Leominster, in the county of Hereford, and burgess for that borough in the three last parliaments, for these words following, which were, no doubt, aggravated beyond the real expression of them. *The Duke of York is a papist, and before any such papist dog shall be successor to the crown of England, I will be hanged at my own door, and I will venture my life and fortune to prevent the same.—If the king had no worse bailiffs nor mayors in all his corporations in England, and no worse parliament-men than myself, we would soon rout the Duke of York, Lord Marquis of Worcester, and Lord Peterborough, and all such popish dogs, out of the kingdom, for I am sure they are damned ones.—If any of the members of parliament come to any accident or untimely end, it shall presently be laid on the papists, and from that time I will begin to cut the throat of the first papist I meet, if it be the Duke of York himself.—If the king follows the advice of that damned popish dog, his brother, Lord Marquis of Worcester, and such like evil counsellors, as I believe he does, in so often dissolving the parliament, it will in the end be worse for him.—I will be hanged at my own door before such a damned popish rascal as the Duke of York shall ever inherit the crown of England; and, to prevent that, we will first take off that damned rogue, our popish lord-lieutenant, Lord Peterborough, Lord Hallifax, Sir Lionel Jenkins, and several others, who, I am sure, are the imps and promoters of the interest of that damned popish dog, York.* In a trial at the King's-Bench, on May 3, 1684, the jury brought in their verdict for his Royal Highness, and assessed for damages 100,000l.—*Kennet's History of England,* Vol. III. P. 413, 414.

1702), by whom he had five sons and four daughters*; 1, John-Dutton Colt, Esq. of whom hereafter; 2, George-Dutton Colt, born in 1674, and died unmarried in Flanders, in 1708; 3, William-Dutton Colt, who died in the West-Indies, 1692, under age and unmarried; 4, Harry-Dutton Colt, Esq. who married first, Anne, third daughter of John Arnold, of Llanvihangell-Crucorney, in Monmouthshire, Esq. by whom he had no issue; and secondly, Lucy-Felia Jones, of the family on one side, of the Jones's, of Lee North, and of the other, of the Milborne's, both of Monmouthshire; and 5, Robert-Dutton Colt, who was an officer in the army, and died at Tinmouth castle, unmarried. The daughters were, 1, Mary †; 2, Lucy, married, 1697, to Major Anthony Stoughton, who died March 30, 1729, and his wife in July, 1729, leaving issue, John-Colt Stoughton, William-Colt Stoughton, and a daughter Anne, that died unmarried; 3, Anne-Dutton Colt, who died unmarried; and 4, Elizabeth, wife of the Rev. Mr. Rowland Parry, of Letton, in Herefordshire, by whom he had a son and a daughter, Robert and Mary.

John-Dutton Colt, Esq. married secondly, Margaret, relict of John Arnold ‡, of Llanvihangell-Crucorney, in Monmouthshire, Esq. (who represented the town of Monmouth, and the borough of Southwark, in several parliaments, in the reigns of King Charles II. King James II. and King William,) by whom he had no issue, and died April 29, 1722.

10, John-Dutton Colt, Esq. eldest son and heir, married Mary §, youngest daughter of John Arnold, Esq. before-mentioned, and died Feb. 2, 1729, leaving one son,

the king observed that he was turned gray, and said to him, that he was surprised at it, for that he was some years older than him. Mr. Colt answered, that trouble altered men. The king bid him go home, and live peaceably in the country. He answered, it was his design, and that he might do so, *he had a favour to beg of his Majesty*. The king stepped back, put his hand upon his breast, and said, *What would you have, Mr. Colt?* He replied, *I beseech your Majesty that you will never put me into any public employment, and then I shall never be envied, and be at rest.* The king smiled, and gave him his word, *that he never would*; and said, *it was the only favour of that kind that ever was asked him.* It is here proper to observe, that one Samuel Seward, of Leominster, who was one of the witnesses against Mr. Colt, owned, before he died, that he had forsworn himself at his trial, and that he was put upon it by major H———, who hired all the witnesses, and that they were promised one hundred pounds a man, but never received but five guineas, and all expences borne. This he confessed before several gentlemen, and Mr. Colt forgave him, upon his declaring that his conscience troubled him, and could not rest until he had obtained his pardon. When King William was settled on the throne, Mr Colt produced the old charter, and threw out the new one, and brought in all the old members. King William heard of it, sent for Mr. Colt, and asked him, *by what law he did it*; he answered, *By the same law that your Majesty wears the crown.* He served many years afterwards in parliament for Leominster, till an ungrateful family threw him out, by a petition, in Queen Anne's time, though he had a considerable majority.

* From the family, 1741.

† The lady to whom I am greatly obliged for the many curious particulars, which she sent me, of her father's MSS. 1741.—Wotton.

‡ This Mr. Arnold was the person who was cut and desperately wounded by John Giles, in Bell-Yard, Temple-Bar, April 15, 1680, for which Giles was tried, convicted, and fined 500l. and to stand in the pillory in Lincoln's-Inn-Fields, at Gray's-Inn, and at the May-Pole, in the Strand, and to find sureties for his good behaviour during life. Mr. Arnold being a justice of peace for Monmouthshire, and active for putting the laws in execution against papists, and particularly in prosecuting and convicting one Evans, a popish priest, was way-laid and wounded by this Giles and others.—See Giles's trial, in State Trials, fo. Vol. III.

§ From the family, 1741.

Sir John-Dutton Colt, Bart. born about 1725, of whom hereafter; and two daughters, Maria-Sophia, and Anne, who died unmarried. But to return.

I. HARRY-DUTTON COLT, Esq. fourth son of George Colt, Esq. and Elizabeth-Dutton, his wife, was advanced to the dignity of a Baronet, 4 William and Mary, for his services at the Revolution, by the name of Harry-Dutton Colt, senior, of St. James's, Westminster, Esq. and the heirs male of his body, and in case of failure of his issue male, to John-Dutton Colt, of Letton, in Herefordshire, Esq. and after his decease, to John-Dutton Colt, his eldest son, and the heirs male of his body; and in case of failure of his issue male, to William-Dutton Colt, another son of John's, and his heirs male, and in case of failure of his issue male, to Harry-Dutton Colt, another son, and his heirs male, and in case of failure of his issue male, to Robert-Dutton Colt, the youngest son, and the heirs male of his body, and in case of failure of his issue male, to the heirs male of Sir William-Dutton Colt, Knt. lawfully begotten.

This Sir Harry-Dutton Colt, Bart. represented the city of Westminster, in parment, in the reigns of K. Willam, and Q. Anne, and married Cecilia, daughter of Francis Brewster, of Suffolk, Esq. relict of Sir Thomas Hatton, of Thames-Ditton, in Surry, Knt. by whom he left no issue: she died Oct. 1712, and Sir Harry-Dutton, April 25, 1731, when the title and estate descended, according to the remainder in the patent, to his great nephew,

II. Sir JOHN-DUTTON COLT, Bart. only son of John-Dutton Colt, Esq. who was the eldest son of John-Dutton Colt, Esq. elder brother to Sir Harry, who married, in 1747, ——, daughter of —— Powel.

ARMS—Argent*, a fess between three colts, in full speed, sable.
CREST—On a wreath, a colt in full speed, as in the Arms.
MOTTO—*Vincit qui patitur.*
PLACE OF RESIDENCE—At Leominster, in Herefordshire.

* This coat was confirmed or assigned by William Camden, June 30, 1615, to —— Colt, of Canterbury, in Kent.—*Vide Visit. of Essex, and of Herefordshire.*

See a merry frolic of Sir Henry Colt's, of Nether-Hall, in Essex, related in Turner's History of Waltham-Abbey, P. 77, &c.

Near the east end of the north side of the chancel of New Windsor Church, in Berkshire, is a monument set in the wall with this inscription:

> The body of Mary Sandes, daughter of Robert Colt, of Woodwick, Esq. and Elizabeth, his wife, daughter and heir of Margaret Lady Roche; which Mary was wife, first, of John Johnson, Esq. citizen and goldsmith of London; and secondly, of Miles Sandes, of Latimer, Esq. who leading a lyfe of wisdom, godlyness, righteousness, sobriety, compassion, and much mercy to the needy and afflicted, in favour of God and man, and in faith and much assurance, joyfully triumphing over death, yielded her spirit into the hands of God, through Christ Jesus, the seventh of October, about the 74th yeare of her age.
>
> Her brother, Roger Colte, of Woodwicke, Esq. left issue John Colte, who left issue by Frances, daughter of Ralph Woodwick aforesaid, John Rowland and Mary Colte—*Ashmole's Berkshire,* Vol. III. P. 64.

TABLE.

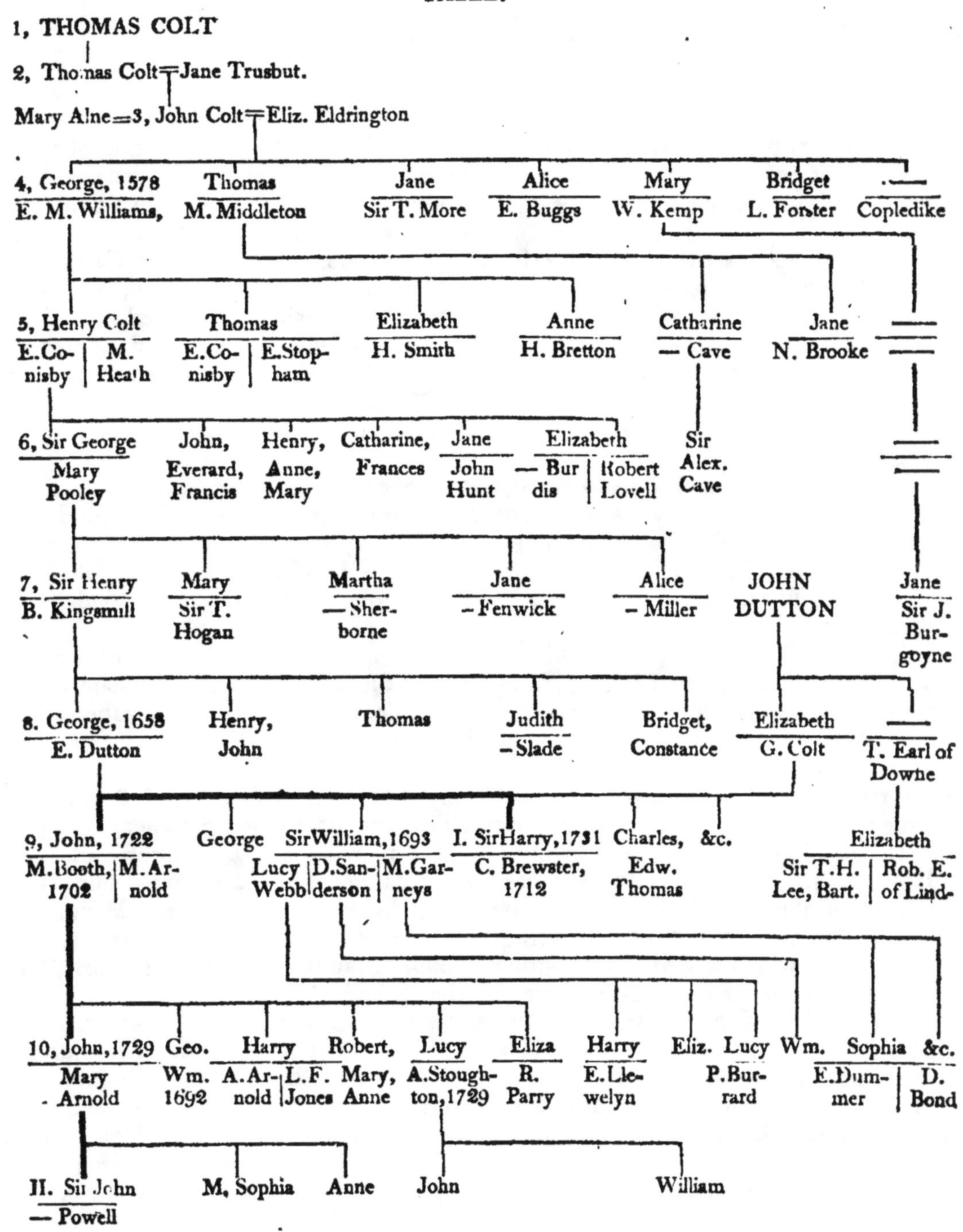
1, THOMAS COLT
2, Thomas Colt=Jane Trusbut.
Mary Alne=3, John Colt=Eliz. Eldrington
4, George, 1578
E. M. Williams,
Thomas
M. Middleton
Jane
Sir T. More
Alice
E. Buggs
Mary
W. Kemp
Bridget
L. Forster
Copledike
5, Henry Colt
E. Conisby
M. Heath
Thomas
E. Conisby
E. Stopham
Elizabeth
H. Smith
Anne
H. Bretton
Catharine
— Cave
Jane
N. Brooke
6, Sir George
Mary Pooley
John, Everard, Francis
Henry, Anne, Mary
Catharine, Frances
Jane
John Hunt
Elizabeth
— Burdis
Robert Lovell
Sir Alex. Cave
7, Sir Henry
B. Kingsmill
Mary
Sir T. Hogan
Martha
— Sherborne
Jane
– Fenwick
Alice
– Miller
JOHN DUTTON
Jane
Sir J. Burgoyne
8. George, 1658
E. Dutton
Henry, John
Thomas
Judith
– Slade
Bridget, Constance
Elizabeth
G. Colt
T. Earl of Downe
9, John, 1722
M. Booth, 1702
M. Arnold
George
Sir William, 1693
Lucy Webb
D. Sanderson
M. Garneys
I. Sir Harry, 1731
C. Brewster, 1712
Charles, Edw. Thomas
&c.
Elizabeth
Sir T. H. Lee, Bart.
Rob. E. of Lind-
10, John, 1729
Mary Arnold
Geo.
Wm. 1692
Harry
A. Arnold
L. F. Jones
Robert, Mary, Anne
Lucy
A. Stoughton, 1729
Eliza
R. Parry
Harry
E. Llewelyn
Eliz.
Lucy
P. Burrard
Wm.
Sophia
E. Dummer
&c.
D. Bond
11. Sir John
— Powell
M. Sophia
Anne
John
William

214. THOMAS, of WENVOE, Glamorganshire.

Created Baronet, Decr 4, 1694.

THIS family, originally named Harpwaye, have matched with the ancient houses of Croft, Wigmor, Monington, Bodenham, Baskerfield, Whitney, Talbott, Harley, Delabeere, Pennbridge, Baldwyn, Scydmore, Lyngin, Langley, and Kemeys.

1, Jevan ap Harpwaye, of Tresimont, in Herefordshire, married Catharine, daughter and sole heiress of Thomas ap Thomas, of Wenvoe castle, and took the name of Thomas, which his descendants have ever since continued.

2, Edmund Thomas, his son, by his second wife, Frances, daughter of George Catchmay, of Brixwere, had two sons, 1, William, who married —— daughter of Sir John Stradling, of St. Donat's castle, Bart. whose heir general conveyed the estates of Wenvoe castle and Ruperra, by marriage to General Ludlow.

3, James Thomas, Esq. second son, had one son

4, William, who, by ———, daughter and sole heiress of William Hopkins, of Court-y-Bettiws, had one son,

5, William Thomas, Esq. who married Sarah, daughter and heiress of John Powell, of Flemingston, by whom he had three sons, John, Edmond, and William.

I. JOHN THOMAS, Esq. eldest son and heir, was advanced to the dignity of a Baronet, the sixth of King William and Queen Mary, with remainder in his patent, to his brothers, Edmond and William. He married Elizabeth, relict of General Ludlow, who was grandfather to William Thomas, Esq. (by Jane, daughter of Sir John Stradling, Bart.) by which marriage, the estates before-mentioned, returned into the family; he died 17 Jan. 1702-3, without issue; whereupon the dignity and estate devolved on his next brother,

II. Sir EDMOND THOMAS, Bart. who married Mary, daughter of John How, Esq. paymaster of the forces, privy-councellor, vice-chamberlain, and knight of the shire for Gloucestershire, temp. King William, Queen Mary, and Queen Aune. He died 1723, leaving two sons, Sir Edmond, his successor, and and John, who married Lady Sophia Keppel, daughter of Arnold Joost Van Keppel, the first Earl of Albemarle, of that family.

III. Sir EDMOND THOMAS, Bart. the eldest son and heir, married, May, 1740, Abigail, daughter of Sir Thomas Webster, of Battle-Abby, in Sussex, Bart. and relict of William Northey, of Compton-Bassset, in Wiltshire, son and heir of Sir Edward Northey, Knt, attorney general, by whom he had three sons, 1, Sir Edmund, his successor; 2, Frederick, an ensign in the foot guards; 3, John. He was member of parliament for Chippenham, in Wiltshire; May 7, 1763, he was made surveyor-general of his Majesty's woods, in the several parks, forests, and chaces, and in the lands of the ancient inheritance of the crown, on the north and south of the river Trent. Sir Edmond died in 1767, and was succeeded by his eldest son,

IV. Sir EDMOND THOMAS, Bart. who was succeeded by

V. Sir JOHN THOMAS, Bart. who married ——, daughter of —— Owen, of Penthurst. He was succeeded by his son,

VI. Sir OWEN THOMAS, Bart. who married the Hon. Elizabeth ——, who, in 1787, became the wife of Sir Joseph *Noro*, (quære) late of Pennsylvania. He was succeeded by

VII. Sir JOHN THOMAS, the present Bart.

ARMS—Sable, a cheveron and canton, ermine.

CREST—On a wreath, a demi unicorn, ermine, armed, crined, and unguled, or, supporting a shield sable.

MOTTO—*Virtus invicta gloriosa.*

SEAT—At Wenvoe castle, Glamorganshire.

TABLE.

1, JEVAN AP HARPWAYE=CATHARINE THOMAS

2, Edmund Thomas=Frances Catchmay

William=Jane Stradling

3, James Thomas

4, William=—— Hopkins

5, William=Sarah Powell

Gen. Ludlow=Elizabeth=I. Sir John, 1703 II. Sir Edmund, 1723=M.Howe, 1744 Wm.

III. Sir Edmund, 1767=A. Webster John=Sophia Keppel

IV. Sir Edmund Frederick John

V. Sir John=—— Owen

VI. Sir Owen=Elizabeth=Sir Joseph

VII. Sir John

215. WHEATE, of GLYMPTON, Oxfordshire.

Created Baronet, May 6, 1696.

1, THOMAS WHEATE, of Walsal, in Staffordshire, Esq. had one son,

2, William Wheate, Esq. of Coventry, in Warwickshire, who married Anne, daughter of Abraham Quiney, of Stratford-upon-Avon, in Warwickshire, relict of Richard Bailey, of Litchfield, by whom he had,

3, William Wheate, of Glympton, in Oxfordshire, living 1634, who married Elizabeth †, eldest daughter of Thomas Stone, of London, by whom he had two sons, Thomas and William, and William, who died an infant, and two daughters, Anne, wife of Charles Thorold, of Harmston, in Lincolnshire, Esq. and of London, merchant, who fined for alderman, and Elizabeth, who died an infant.

4, Thomas Wheate, Esq. only surviving son and heir, married Frances, daughter of Sir Robert Jenkinson, of Walcot, in Oxfordshire, Knt. by whom he had one son,

I. THOMAS WHEATE, Esq. the first Baronet of this family, so created 1 Will. III. He married Anne, daughter and coheiress of George Sawbridge, of London, Esq. who fined for aldermen, who died Jan. 13, 1719, and was buried at Glympton, by whom he had three sons, William, who died young; Sir Thomas, his successor; and Sir George Wheate, who succeeded his brother; also two daughters, Frances, wife of Sir Francis Page, Knt. one of the justices of the court of King's bench, she died Nov. 1730, and Anne. Sir Thomas represented the borough of Woodstock, in Oxfordshire, in the three last parliaments of Queen Anne, and the first of King George I. and died keeper of the stores and ordnance, Aug. 25 1721.

II. Sir THOMAS WHEATE, Bart. his eldest son, and successor in dignity and estate, represented the borough of Woodstock in the second parliament of George I. and married ——, daughter and coheiress of Thomas Gould, of Iver, in Buckinghamshire, Esq. who died 1746. He died May, 1746, without issue, and was succeeded by his brother,

III. Sir GEORGE WHEATE, Bart. a barrister at law, and recorder of Banbury. He married, May 1742, Avice, daughter of Sir Jacob Ackworth, Knt. surveyor of the navy, by whom he had three sons, 1, Sir George, his successor; 2, Sir Jacob, successor to his brother; 3, Sir John Thomas, the present Baronet; and two daughters, Esther-Henrietta, unmarried, in 1784, and Anne, wife of Benjamin Barnet, of London, banker, living 1784. Sir George died June 4, 1752, and was succeeded by his eldest son,

IV. Sir GEORGE WHEATE, Bart. who was lieutenant in the Royal Artillery. who died 1760, unmarried, and was succeeded by his brother,

V. Sir JACOB WHTATE, Bart. who was commander of his Majesty's ship

Cerberus, and married Maria, daughter of —— Shaw, of New York, who after his death, 1788, became the wife of Alexander Cochrane, brother to the Earl of Dundonald. He died in 1783, and was succeeded by his brother,

VI. The Rev. Sir JOHN THOMAS WHEATE, Bart. A. M. vicar of Leachlade, born at London, Sept. 15, 1750, unmarried, 1784.

ARMS—Vert, a fess dauncette or, three garbs in chief of the last.

CREST—On a wreath, a buck's head, couped, or, in his mouth, three ears of wheat, proper.

SEAT—At Leachlade, Gloucestershire.

TABLE.

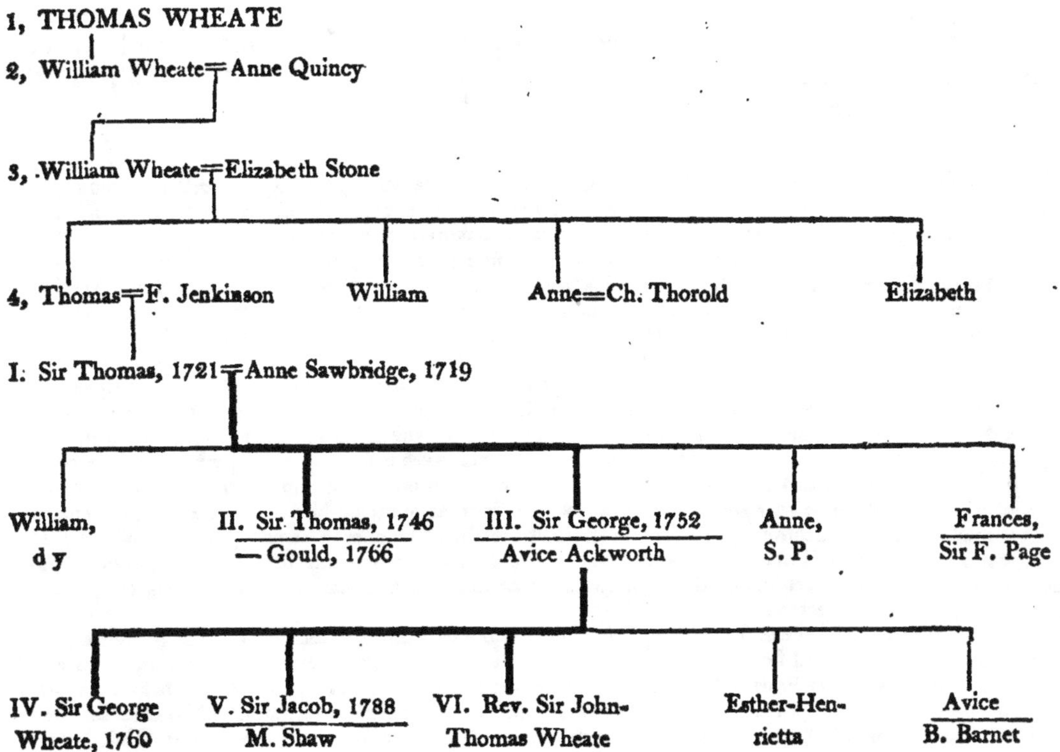

216. BUCKWORTH, of Sheen, near Richmond, Surry.

Created Baronet, April 1, 1697.

1, Richard Buckworth, of Wisbeach, in the Isle of Ely, who married Rose, daughter and coheiress of —— Skegnes, of Skegnes, in Lincolnshire, Esq. by whom he had,

2, Everard Buckworth, of Wisbeach, Esq. living 1619, who married Emme, daughter of Thomas Oxburgh, of Lenne, in Norfolk. and died 1641, aged 70, by whom he had, Everard Buckworth, of Wisbeach, Esq. and other children.

3, Sir John Buckworth, Knt. and alderman of London, was a younger brother of Everard before-mentioned; he married ——, and had one son, Sir John, and three daughters, Margaret, wife of Sir Peter Vandeput, Knt. sheriff of London, 1684; Elizabeth, of Thomas Hartopp, Esq. alderman of London; and Mary, wife of Sir William Hussey, Knt. who went ambassador from King William to the Ottoman Porte. Sir John died Dec. 1687 *.

* Dr. Scott, who knew him well, gives him the following character (a): "This excellent person, Sir John Buckworth, was as eminently known as ever any merchant that trod the exchange of London; and indeed, considering the great share he had of intellectual endowments, he was a gentleman that seemed to have been marked out by providence to make a considerable figure among men. For first, nature had enriched him with a clear bright mind, with a quick apprehension, a prompt memory, a steady and piercing judgment, together with a natural presence of mind, and fluency and readiness of speech, which enabled him, upon all occasions, easily to express his own conceptions of things, in very clear and apt language. All which natural endowments he had vastly improved and cultivated, by a long and curious observation and experience; for as nature had fitted him for an active life, so providence soon introduced him upon the stage of action; for, as he was born a gentleman, so he was educated a merchant, which, perhaps, is one of the most advantageous academies in the world to instruct the mind in the knowledge of men, and the management of human affairs. His education furnished him with a fair opportunity of seeing the world, as well abroad as at home, and of prying into the intrigues of commerce, and into the manners and interests of men, whence he drew so many wise and useful observations, as rendered him a prince among merchants and an oracle of trade; insomuch, that he was thought worthy to be chosen deputy-governor of that wise and great company of the Turkey merchants; and was, perhaps, as much consulted by his superiors about the interest of the English trade, and the mysteries of commerce, as any one merchant of this city or nation. Thus for his intellectuals.

"As for his morals, I believe that all that knew him, will allow him this character; that he was a gentleman of great integrity and fidelity to his trust; of exact justice and righteousness in his commerce and dealings: that he was a studious and successful peacemaker; and great part of his time, before he was called up by his prince into a more busy and active station, being spent in arbitrating differences between man and man; in which he was so expert, so impartial and prosperous, that I am apt to think he ce-

(a) Dr. Scott was rector of St. Peter-le-Poor, London, and preached his funeral sermon there, Dec. 29, 1687.

I. Sir JOHN BUCKWORTH, of Sheen, Knt. his only son and heir, the first Baronet of this family, was a person of extraordinary parts, and spoke Latin as fluently as he did English, (though few spoke English better) and having been well grounded in classical learning, travelled into Turkey, and other places, where he improved his natural and acquired abilities; was universally esteemed by all that knew him. He died at his seat at Sheen, June, 1709, in the flower of his age, and was buried with his father. He left by his wife, Elizabeth, daughter of Mr. Hall, a merchant, two sons, Sir John, his successor, and Everard Buckworth, Esq.; also one daughter, Elizabeth, who died unmarried. His wife surviving him, married Mr. Hiccocks, one of the masters in chancery. Lady Buckworth died at Sheen, in Surry, May 20, 1737.

II. Sir JOHN BUCKWORTH, Bart. his eldest son and successor, was member of parliament for Weobley, in Herefordshire; he married Mary-Jane, daughter of ———, who died June 26, 1775. Sir John died Dec. 1758, and was succeeded by his brother,

mented as many broken friendships, reconciled as many quarrels, and adjusted as many differences, (which otherwise might have flamed out into destructive breaches) as most of those blessed peacemakers that are gone before him.

" Consider him in his respective relations, and there all that knew him, I am sure, will allow him to have been a faithful, a loyal, and useful subject to his prince, a kind and obliging husband to his lady, a tender and a wise father to his children, a prudent, careful, and benevolent master to his servants; and, in a word, a wise counsellor, a faithful friend, and a just and diligent correspondent.

" As for his religion, he was a hearty Protestant of the Church of England, which, upon mature judgment, and upon thorough information, he preferred for the loyalty of its principles, the simplicity of its doctrines, and the primitive purity of its worship and discipline, before all the churches in the world; and what his judgment was of our church, he visibly expressed by his constant attendance upon the public offices of our religion, upon the Lord's day, from which he never absented, but when he was either detained by sickness, or some very urgent and unavoidable occasion, and in which he always demeaned him with all the profound reverence and devotion that outwardly expresses a mind inspired with a pious sense of its duty, and of the awful presence of the great majesty of heaven.

" Thus he lived; and, as for his death, though it was accompanied with all the circumstances that could render a man fond of life, though he had a plentiful estate, a loving and beloved wife, dutiful and hopeful children, and these all of them happily disposed of, and settled in the world, to his own heart's content—to leave all which at once, seems a very hard chapter to a mind not well resolved; yet all these together had no such effect upon him. Indeed, not long before his death, though then in perfect health, he seemed to have a boding of his approaching fate; for having, to his heart's desire, disposed of his only son in marriage (who was the last of his children undisposed), he hath been often heard to say, that now he thanked God his business in this world was all finished, and that it was high time for him to think of his departure into the other; and when, soon after, he was seized with his last sickness, he bore it with an invincible courage and constancy; and though the last part of it was extremely painful to him, he underwent it without complaint or murmuring, with a mind that seemed entirely resigned to the sovereign disposer of all events. And when he pereeived the approaches of death, and found that he was going off this stage of mortals, he never shewed the least sign of regret or reluctancy, but took a solemn leave of his friends, and which was much harder, of his dearest relatives, who stood lamenting and weeping about him; and this with a mind very serious indeed, but in all appearance very calm and composed. And finally, he gave up the ghost like a brave man and a good christian, with a firm and undaunted mind, and as one that had placed his main hope on the other side the grave, and did expect to exchange an uneasy mortal life for an immortal one of pleasure. And therefore, though I make no doubt after all, but that as a man, he had his faults, (and he that hath none, let him cast the first stone), yet I am sure he had his virtues, and those very eminent ones too; and therefore it will highly become us who survive, in charity to cast a veil over the one, and in piety imitate and transcribe the other."

III. Sir EVERARD BUCKWORTH, Bart. who was assistant gentleman-usher to his Majesty, and married Mary, daughter of William Dipple, of the county of Worcester, Esq. who died in Nov. 1767, by whom he had one daughter Charlotte, who died Dec. 5, 1773, as she was entering the drawing-room of Dr. Baker, in Jermyn-street; he died Feb. 10, 1779, and was succeeded by his son,

IV. Sir EVERARD BUCKWORTH, Bart.

ARMS—Sable, a cheveron, between three crosslets, fitchy, argent.

CREST—On a wreath, a man's head, full-faced, armed with an helmet, the beaver open, all proper.

SEAT—At Sheen, near Richmond, in Surry.

TABLE.

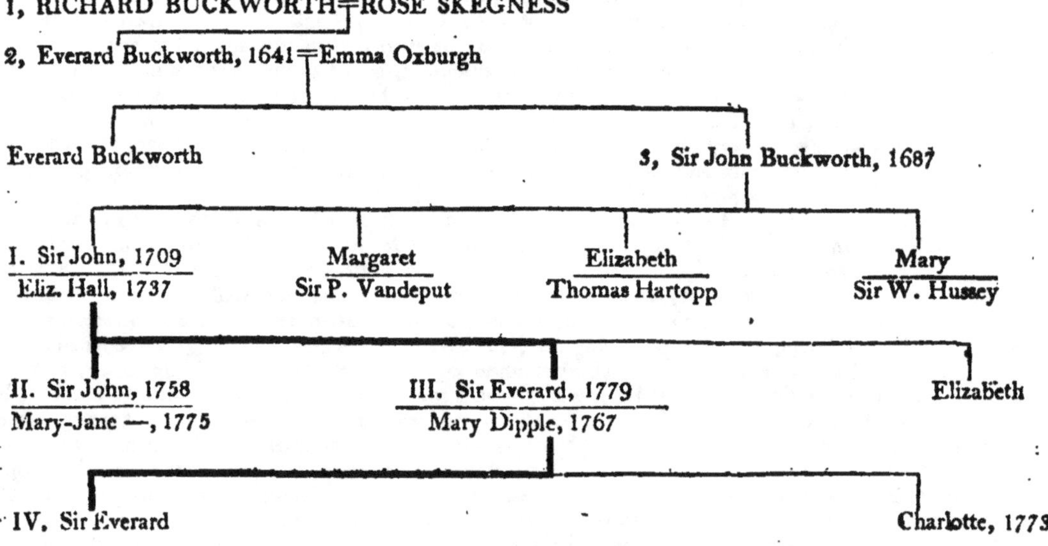

217. CLARKE, of SNAILWELL, Cambridgeshire.

Created Baronet, July 25, 1698.

1, JOHN CLARKE, of Bocking, in Essex *, descended from a family of that name in Kent, had one son,

2, John Clarke, of Bury, in Suffolk, who married Margaret, daughter of —— Bourne, of Bury, and died about 1681, leaving a daughter, ——, wife of Thomas Barnardiston, of Hackney, in Middlesex, Esq. and a son,

I. SAMUEL CLARKE, of Snailwell, in the county of Cambridge, Esq. who was advanced to the dignity of an English Baronet in the tenth year of the reign of his Majesty King William III. He married Mary †, daughter of Major Robert Thomson, of Newington-Green, in the county of Middlesex, who, in the late Civil Wars, distinguished himself for the liberty of his country; he had two sons, Sir Robert, his successor, and Samuel, who died unmarried; and three daughters ‡, Frances, wife of Thomas Lucke, Esq. barrister at law, (she died Nov. 1, 1718;) Margaret, wife of the Rev. —— Malabar, rector of Barton-Togry, in Suffolk; and Mary, who died unmarried. Sir Samuel died March 8, 1719, and was succeeded by his son,

II. Sir ROBERT CLARKE, Bart. who in the year 1717, was chosen representtative in parliament for the county of Cambridge§. He married Mary, the only surviving daughter of Arthur Barnardiston, Esq. (youngest son of Sir Nathaniel Barnardiston, of Barnardiston, in the county of Suffolk, the twenty-third knight, in a lineal descent, of that family) by whom he had ten children; seven whereof lived to maturity; viz. 1, Sir Samuel, his successor, born May 21, 1712; 2, Sir Robert, successor to his brother, born Jan. 22, 1714; 3, Sir Arthur, the present Baronet, born Feb. 6, 1715; 4, John, born May 15, 1717; 5, Mary, born April 15, 1720; 6, Anne, born Feb. 4, 1724; and 7, Jane, born April 7, 1727. Lady Clarke died Jan. 1732-3. One of the daughters was wife of Benjamin Lane, of Hampstead, Esq. Sir Robert died 1746, and was succeeded by his eldest son,

III. Sir SAMUEL CLARKE, Bart. who served the office of high-sheriff for the counties of Cambridge and Huntingdon in 1753, and dying unmarried Nov. 1758, was succeeded by his brother,

IV. Sir ROBERT CLARKE, Bart. who married Elizabeth, daughter of —— Littel, by whom he had one son John. Sir Robert died Aug. 18, 1770, and was succeeded by his son,

V. Sir JOHN CLARKE, Bart. who died young, Nov. 8, 1782, and was succeeded by his uncle,

VI. Sir ARTHUR CLARKE, Bart. whose lady died Oct. 24, 1792.

* Le Neve's MSS. vol. iii. p. 304.

† Ex inf. Dom. Rob. Clarke, Bar. 1727.

‡ Le Neve, ibid.

§ Ex inf. Dom. Rob. Clarke, Bar. 1727.

ARMS—Or, on a bend, engrailed, azure, a mullet, argent.
CREST—On a wreath, a Talbot's head, erased, or.
SEAT—At Snailwell, near Newmarket, in Cambridgeshire.

TABLE.

1, JOHN CLARKE

2, John Clarke = Margaret Bourne

I. Sir Samuel, 1709 = Mary Thomson — —— = Tho. Barnardiston

II. Sir Robert, 1746 = M. Barnardiston, 1732 — Samuel — Frances, 1718 = Thomas Lucke — Margaret = Rev. — Malabar — Mary

III. Sir Samuel Clarke, 1758 — IV. Sir Rob. 1770 = Eliz. Littel — VI. Sir Arthur = ——, 1792 — John — Mary — Anne — Jane

V. Sir John, 1782 (son of IV. Sir Rob.)

---

218. ROGERS, of Wisdome, Devonshire.

Created Baronet, Feb. 21, 1698.

1, The Rev. JOHN ROGERS *, the first martyr in Queen Mary's reign, is the first we find of this family; he is supposed to be the father of,

2, Vincent Rogers, minister of Stratford-le-Bow, Middlesex, who married Dorcas, relict of —— Young, by whom he had,

* Ex inf. Dom. Jo. Rogers, Bar. 1726.

3, Nehemiah Rogers *, prebendary of Ely, and rector of Bishopsgate, who was buried at Messing, in Essex, 1660: he was a great loyalist, and had two sons, 1, Nehemiah Rogers, of London, who belonged to the Custom-House, and married Mary †, daughter of Edmund Porter, D. D. sister to Sir Charles Porter, Knt. lord-chancellor of Ireland, and had issue Edmund Rogers, of London, living 1701, and John, who was imprisoned in Carisbrook-Castle, in the Isle of Wight, and suffered much for his loyalty to King Charles I. and II.; he married Elizabeth ‡, daughter of Sir Robert Payne, of Midlow, in Huntingdonshire, by whom he had two sons, Sir John, and Prisonborn (so called from being born in prison), who had a commission in King Charles the Second's army, and was killed in a duel in France.

I. Sir JOHN ROGERS, Bart. the eldest §, was bred a merchant, and lived as such many years in the town of Plymouth, in the said county of Devon, near which place he purchased a considerable estate, and about the year 1698, was chosen a representative in parliament for that town; during which parliament, his Majesty King William was pleased to confer the dignity of a Baronet on him, in the eleventh year of his reign. He was appointed high-sheriff of the county of Devon, 1701, and married Mary ||, daughter of Mr. William Vincent, of London, (who, after his decease, became wife of Sir Edmund Prideaux, of Netherton, in the said county, Bart.) and died in the year 1710, leaving issue one son,

II. Sir JOHN ROGERS, Bart. who, after his father's decease, was by the said town of Plymouth, chosen representative in parliament, and also their recorder, and for which corporation he was again chosen the last parliament of Queen Anne, and the first of King George I. He married Mary ¶, daughter of Sir Robert Henley, of the Grainge, in the county of Southampton, Knt. by whom he had seseveral sons and daughters, and dying in Jan. 1743-4, was succeeded by his eldest son,

III. Sir JOHN ROGERS, Bart. who served the office of high-sheriff for the county of Devon in 1755, and in 1759, was appointed colonel of the Devonshire militia. He married ———, daughter of ——— Trefusis, and was succeeded in title and estate by his brother,

IV. Sir FREDERICK-LEMON ROGERS, Bart. who was recorder of Plymouth, and a commissioner of the navy; he died in June, 1797, and was succeeded by

V. Sir JOHN LEMON ROGERS, Bart.

* Nehemiah Rogers, vicar of Messing, in Essex, 1620, and rector of Tay Magna, in Essex, 1632; where, in 1647, as rector of that church, he presented to the vicarage (which is a *sinecure*), was rector of St. Botolph, Bishopsgate, 1642; and, after the rebellion broke out in 1642, he was sequestered of his church of St. Botolph, and, I suppose, of such other church preferments as he then had.—*Newcourt's Repertorium*, vol. i. p. 313.

† Le Neve's MSS. vol. iii. p. 302.

‡ Ex inf. Dom. Jo. Rogers, Bar. 1741.

§ Ibid.

|| Ibid.

¶ Ibid.

ARMS—Argent, a cheveron, gules, between three roebucks current, sable, attired and gorged with ducal coronets, or.

CREST—On a mount, vert, a roebuck current, proper, attired and gorged with a ducal coronet, or, between two branches of laurel, vert.

MOTTO—*Nos nostraque Deo.*

SEAT—At Wisdome and Blachford, both in Devonshire.

TABLE.

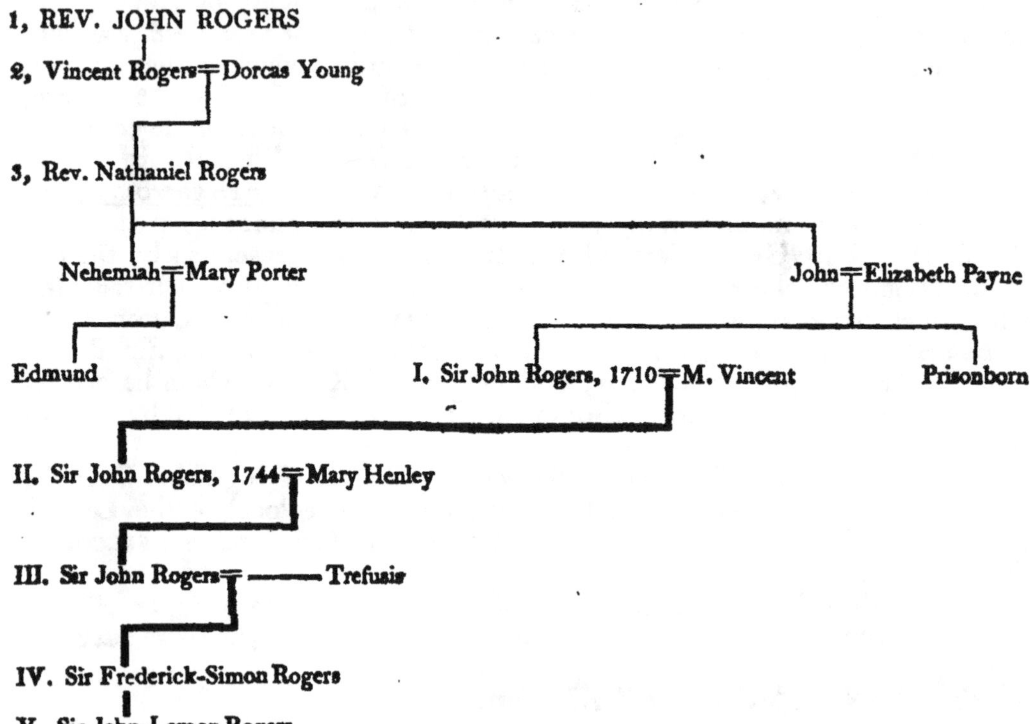

219. WESCOMBE, Consul, at Cadiz.

Created Baronet, March 19, 1699.

I. Sir MARTIN WESCOMBE, the first Baronet of this family, was agent and consul at Cadiz, in the reign of King William III. and resided many years in Spain. His daughter Mary was wife of Bernard Granville, Esq. brother to George, Lord Lansdown.

II. Sir ANTHONY WESCOMBE, Bart. his son, was deputy-commissary general and deputy-judge advocate, commissary of the musters at Minorca, and finally, deputy-muster-master-general of the forces, which he enjoyed till his death. He married, in April 1736, ——, daughter and heiress of —— Calmady, Esq. by his second wife Jane, daughter of Sir John Rolt, of Milton, in Bedfordshire, Knt. He died Dec. 6, 1752, and was succeeded by his son,

III. Sir ANTHONY WESCOMBE, who perhaps is the present Baronet.

ARMS—Sable, two bars, or, and a canton, ermine.
CREST—Out of a mural coronet, or, a griffin's head of the last.
MOTTO—*Festina lente.*

220. CHETWODE, of Oakley, Staffordshire.

Created Baronet, April 6, 1700.

THIS family was seated at Chetwode, in Buckinghamshire, long before th conquest.

1, John Chetwode, from whom this pedigree is clearly deduced, was a person of note, being a knight, and lord of the manor of Chetwode. This John had one son,

2, Robert Chetwode, lord of Chetwode, who founded the priory of Chetwode *, in the lifetime of his father; and the said John, and Robert, with ——, his wife, lie buried in the church, belonging to the said priory, as appeared by an ancient monument †, which was defaced after the suppression of the said priory.

3, Sir Raufe Chetwode, Knt. § his son and heir, had issue,

* Dugdale's Monast. Angl. Vol. II. fo. 339.
† Deposition taken by virtue of a Com. in Chancery, 25 Eliz.

4, Robert Chetwode, Lord of Chetwode, who lived 5 Hen. I, and married Sibell, daughter of Thomas Strange. He attended king Richard I. into Syria, and for his atchievement in arms, received the honour of knighthood, from that prince, in Palestine*, and on his return from the holy wars, received other marks of that monarch's favour. He had two sons, John and William, who was seized of lands in Horton, in Kent †.

5, Sir John Chetwode, Knt. the eldest son, had one son,

6, Sir Robert de Chetwode, Knt. lord of Chetwode, who lived 10, Ed. I. and 14 Ed. I. he married Lucie, lady of Hockliffe, and had a grant from William his uncle ‡, of forty shillings per annum, to be issuing out of lands in Horton, in Kent. He exchanged his manor of Paddleworth, in Kent, with Sir Hamond Gatton, Knt. for the manor of Hockliffe, and certain lands and tenements in Battlesdon and Cotesgrave, in Bedfordshire, and a wood called Linwood.

7, John Chetwode, Knt. his son and heir, was lord of the manors of Chetwode and Hockliffe, who lived 10 Ed. I. and 6 Ed. II. and was knight of the shire for the county of Bucks §, in the parliament then held at York; and 30 Ed. I. he served in parliament, as knight of the shire for the same county, then held at London. He married, first Johanne, daughter of ——; secondly, Amicia de Cugentio, by whom he had no issue.

8, John Chetwode, his son and heir, by his first wife, lived 27 Ed. I. and 10 Ed. II. and married Lucia, daughter of ——, who was living 15 Ed. II. by whom he had,

9, John, who lived 6 Ed. III. and married Johanne, daughter of ——, by whom he had two sons, John, and Robert, of whom hereafter.

Sir John Chetwode, Knt. who lived 19 and 22 Ed. III. left one son,

Sir Nicholas Chetwode, Knt. lord of Chetwode and Hockliffe, living 20 and 30 Ed. III. who married Elizabeth, daughter and heiress of Sir John Lyons, by whom he had

Sir John Chetwode, Knt. lord of Warkworth, Chetwode, and Hockliffe, who married, first, Mary, daughter of ——, who was living 45, Ed. III. and

* Cart. sans date, penes J. Chetwode, Bar.

† He assumed for his arms, quarterly, argent and gules, four crosses, formée, counterchanged; and for his motto, *Corona mea Christus*, and released from him and his heirs, to the prior and canons of Chetwode, and their successors (*a*), in free alms, all rents, duties, and service-customs, due to the said Robert and his heirs, which they held of his fee, and had in the town and field of Chetwode; for which release, the prior and convent did grant yearly, to pay to the said Robert, and to his heirs, a mark of silver, in the parish church of Chetwode. Sibell, who survived her husband, did, in her widowhood, grant in free alms, two yard land, with the appurtenances, to the hermitage of Chetwode, and to the brethren there abiding.

‡ Cart. penes J. Chetwode, Bar.

§ Willis's Not. Parl. in Bucks.

(*a*) Cart. temp. Hen. I. penes J. Chetwode, Bar.

12 Ric. II *. After the death of Mary, Sir John married Amabell, the daughter of Thomas Green, of Greens Norton, who surviving him, afterwards married Sir Thomas Strange, Knt. and died anno 1430. By Mary, his first wife he had one son John, who died without issue, and was buried at Warkworth, 1420, and Margery, wife of John Browning, and likewise died 1420, and lies buried in Warkworth church †. By Amabell, his second wife, he had one son,

Sir Thomas Chetwode, Knt. lord of Warkworth, Chetwode, and Hockliffe, living 1458, and Elizabeth Chetwode, who married first, Sir Thomas Wodhull, Knt. Baron of Wodhull, who died 9 Hen. V. and afterwards William Ludsup, Esq. who died Oct. 27, 1454; she surviving, died 1475, and lies buried in Warkworth church.

Sir Thomas Chetwode, Knt. was, in the year 1428, 7 Hen. VI. created a knight-banneret by John, Duke of Bedford, then regent of France; and further‡, had, by charter under the great seal, granted unto him in the same year, for his services done in France under the said Duke, all the lands, fees, tenements, rents, revenues, and possessions, belonging to Tagni de Chastell, chevalier, and Robert Connel, situate and lying in the town, provost, and vicounte of Paris, which were forfeited, and came to the king by the rebellion and disobedience of the said Tagni, Robert, and others §. He married Agnes, daughter of ——, who survived her said husband, and in her widowhood, *concessit Rado Legh, arm' un' annual. reddit. 5 marc. percipiend. pro termino vite pd. Agne de & in manerio suo de Chetwode, in com. Bucks*; and by whom he had two daughters, viz. Alice, who died without issue, and Johanne, who was married to Elias Langworth, Esq. and died without issue.

The heirs of this branch of the family being extinct, upon the death of Sir

* Esc. in Tur. Lond. 12 Ric. II: N. 133.——I find, *Jobes Cbetwode, Cbivalier, & Maria, uxor ejus, concesser' priori de Cbetwode, un' acr. ter. & advoc. ecclie de Cbetwode; & Jobes Cbetwode, cbivalier, & al.* (a) *concess. priori de Cbetwode, 60 acr. Bosci, in Letbingburgb, 2 mess. & 2 virgat. ter. in Barton, juxta Cbetwode, terr. & ten' in Cbetwode, Covele, Hockleve, Buckingbam, Bourton, & Lekamsted.*

† This John, by his grant, dated 16 Ric. II. 1392, confirmed certain lands theretofore granted, by Sir John Lyons, then Lord of Warkworth, to the priory of Chacomb, for the finding two priests, in which grant the said Sir John Chetwode calls himself cousin and heir of the said Sir John Lyons, and possessor of his lands, tenements, and rents, in Warkworth and elsewhere.

‡ Rot. Norman. 7 Hen. VI. pars prima, m. 67, in Turri Londini.

§ Northt. Claus. in Tur. Lond. 11 Hen. VI. m. 19. dorso.——*Tbo. Strange, mil. concessit Tbo. Cbetwode, mil. annual. reddit.* 20 *marc. percipiend. de manerio suo de Warkwortb.* And by inquisition I find, *Tbo. Cbetwode, mil. filius & beres Jobis Cbetwode, militis, fil. & beres, Nicbi Cbetwode, milit. & Eliz. ux. sue fil. & bered. Jobis de Lyons, milit. & Alicie, ux. sue, fil. & bered. Willi de Sco Licio, Ar. relaxavit, Robto Large, alderman' Lond. & Tbom. Morsted, civi London' & bered. suis totum jus in omnibus terris & ten' &c. in villa, campis & parocbiis de Magno Stucle, in com. Hunt.* (a) *que sibi jure bereditat. accidebant post mortem dci. Jobis Cbetwode, patris sui* (b). And further, *Tbo, Cbetwode, mil. remisit Jobi Watkins, totum jus in omnibus terrie gurgitibus & ten' suis in Harwick.*

(a) Esc. in Tur. Lond. 15 Ric. II. n. 85.
(b) In Tur. Lond. Hunt. Claus. 23. 18 Hen. VI. pars unica.
(c) Ibid, Essex. Claus. 21 Hen. VI. m. 19, dorso.

Thomas Chetwode, and of his two daughters, Alice and Johanne, the manor of Chetwode descended upon the heirs male of

10, Robert Chetwode, second son of John, and brother of John, had lands in Chetwode given him by his father; he married, and left one son,

11, John Chetwode, who was living 36 Edw. III. and 18 Rich. II. in which year he served as knight of the shire for Bucks*, at the parliament held at Westminster, and married Elizabeth, sister and heiress of William de Okeley, in Staffordshire, and daughter of Stephen de Okeley, lord of the manor of Okeley, by Maude, his wife, by whom he had,

12, John Chetwode, who lived 19 and 22 Rich. II. and married Margery, daughter of ——, by whom he had,

13, Roger Chetwode, of Okeley, who married Margery, daughter and one of the coheiresses of David Crew, of Pulcroste, by which marriage, the said Roger became entitled to sundry lands, in Cheshire, and had,

14, Thomas Chetwode, of Okeley and Worleston, who lived 1 Hen. VI. 33 Hen. VI. 37 Hen. VI. and 22 Edw. IV.† He married Margaret, daughter and heiress of —— Sounde, Lord of Sounde, in Cheshire, by whom he had,

15, Roger Chetwode, living 3 Rich. III. and 1 Hen. VII. and married Ellen, daughter and heiress of William de Ree, by whom he had,

16, Thomas Chetwode, of Warleston, in Cheshire, who married, first, Ellen, daughter of Thomas Beresford, of Bentley, in Derbyshire, Esq. and secondly, Ellen, daughter of John Spurstow, of Spurstow, in Cheshire, Esq. by whom he had, Ellen, John, and Raufe, who died without issue. By Ellen Beresford he had issue,

17, Roger Chetwode, who married Ellen, daughter of Thomas Masterson, of Namptwich, in Cheshire, Esq. (living 14 and 27 Hen. VIII.) by whom he had four sons and two daughters, viz. 1, James Chetwode, of Okeley and Warleston, living 28 Hen. VIII. who married Catharine, daughter of Philip Hulse; 2, John, who died without issue; 3, Richard, who married Agnes, daughter and heiress of Anthony, Baron of Wodehull, and left issue, Sir Richard, his son and heir, she surviving her husband, married secondly ‡, Sir George Calverly, Knt. by whom she had two sons that died before her: she died at Hockliffe, March 20, 18 Eliz. Sir Richard Chetwode, Knt. son and heir, married first, 1, Jane, daughter and coheiress of Sir William Drury, Knt. by whom he had two sons, Richard and William, who died young; also three daughters, Catharine, wife of Sir William Skeffington, of Skeffington, in Leicestershire, Knt.; Elizabeth; and Anne, wife of Sir Giles Bray, of Barrington, in Gloucestershire, Knt. Sir Richard married secondly, Dorothy, daughter of Robert Needham, of Sharrington, in Shropshire, Esq. who was great-grandfather to Thomas, Lord Vis-

* Willis's Not. Parl.

† *Thomas Chetwode, rem' &c. Wo. Boerley, de Bromecroft, & al. totum jus, &c. in omnibus terris ten. &c. suis in Norton, in Hales, in com. Salop. & in Moten, Dni. de Oakley, in com. Staff.* (*a*).

‡ Extinct Peerage, Vol. II. p. 21.

(*a*) Tür Lond. Staff. Claus. rot. 6 Hen. VI. pars prima.

count Kilmurry, and by her had issue, Robert, Thomas, John, and Tobias; Frances, Mary, Dorothy, Jane, Grace, Abigail, and Beatrice. Richard Chetwode, Esq. eldest son of Sir Richard, by his first wife, died *vita patris*; but having married Anne*, daughter and coheiress of Sir Valentine Knightley, of Fawesley, in Northamptonshire, Knt. and had issue, Knightley, Dorothy, Anne, Catharine, Richard, Jane, Valentine†, Elizabeth, Susan, John, Thomas, and Mary. The fourth son of Roger Chetwode, Esq. (before-mentioned), by Ellen Masterson, was Roger, of whom hereafter. His daughters were, Ellen, wife of John Hankey, of Churton, in Cheshire, and Margery, who died without issue.

18, Roger, the fourth son of Roger, married ——, daughter of —— Taylor, by whom he had one son,

19, James Chetwode, Esq. who, by Catharine, his wife, had two sons, Thomas and John, who died without issue; and five daughters, 1, Amy, wife of Roger Colley; 2, Ellen, of John Webb, of Shrewsbury; 3, Beatrix, of Anthony Dorrington; 4, Elizabeth, of Thomas Huton, of Drayton, in Shropshire, clerk: and 5, Margaret, who was wife first, —— Dorrington, of Stafford; and secondly, Hugh Beeston, Esq.

20, Thomas, eldest son of James Chetwode, married first, Anne, daughter and heiress of John Leech, of Namptwich, by whom he had John, and one daughter Anne, wife of Richard Woodward, of the county of Derby.

21, John married Bridget, daughter of Henry Birkenhead, of Huxley, in Cheshire, Esq. by whom he had four sons and four daughters, 1, John,

* Bridge's Northamptonshire.

† In the Extinct Peerage, Vol. II. p. 19, it mentions, "That Valentine Chetwode was son and heir to Richard, and married Mary, daughter of Francis Shute, of Upton, in Leicestershire, Esq. and had four sons, 1, Knightley; 2, John; 3, James; and 4, Benjamin, now living in Ireland: and one daughter, Catharine. Knightley Chetwode, his eldest son and heir, is now (1714) dean of Gloucester, and hath issue one son and a daughter, both which died unmarried. This barony of Wodehull (formetly called Wahull, and now Odell, the seat of Sir Rowland Alston, Bart.) is claimed by Knightley Chetwode, Esq. who is now suing for the same, being son and heir of Dr. John Chetwode, who was beneficed in Ireland, who was fourth son of Richard, only surviving son of Sir Richard by the first venter, who was only son and heir of Richard, by Agnes, daughter and heir of Anthony, baron of Wodehull; which Sir Richard claimed the barony of Wodehull, temp. Jac. I. His petition was referred to a committee of lords, who returned the following certificate: "According to your Majesty's direction, we have met, and considered the petition of Sir Richard Chetwode, and find that the petition is true: and that, before any usual calling of barons, by writ, his ancestors were barons in their own right, and were summoned to serve the kings in their wars, with other barons, and were also summoned to parliaments. And we conceive the discontinuance to have risen from the lords, of the honour dying at one year of age, and the troubles of the time ensuing: but still the title of baron was allowed in all the reigns, by conveyances of their estates, and by pardon of alienation from the crown, by the king's own officers, and 9l. per ann. being the ancient fee for the castle-guard of Rockingham, was coustantly paid, and is paid to this day; so that, though there has been a disuse, yet the right so fully appearing, which cannot die, we have not seen or heard of any one so much to be regarded in grace, and in consideration of so many knights fees held, from the very time of the conquest, and by him held at this day, and a pedigree both on the father and mother's side, proved by authentic records from the time of the Conqueror (which in such cases are very rare), we hold him worthy the honour of a baron, if you Majesty thinks meet. LENOX, HOWARD, NOTTINGHAM.

Vide Extinct Peerage, Vol. II. P. 18, where it is said, that King James offered Sir Richard a patent for the said barony, which he thinking a derogation to his claim, refused to accept, and the title has lain dormant ever since.

who married Eleanor, daughter of William Steventon, of Dothill, in Shropshire; 2, Thomas, who married ———, daughter of ——— Wake, by whom he had issue, Thomas, Isaac, Bridget, and Anne: 3, Henry, who married ——, daughter of ——— Harris, by whom he had ——, John, Arthur, Thomas, and James; 4, James, who went to Virginia; Anne, his eldest daughter, died without issue; Bridget, was wife of Arthur Mainwaring, of Namptwich, in Cheshire, Gent.; Elizabeth, of —— Harris, who was father to her brother Henry's wife; and Margaret, of Thomas Wood, of Dorrington, in Shropshire, Gent.

22, John, by Eleanor, his wife, had two sons and two daughters, John, who died in his minority; Philip; Sarah, wife of Sir Thomas Bunbury, Bart.; and Abigail, of Peircy Leigh, of Britch, in Lancashire, Esq.

23, Philip Chetwode married Hester, daughter and heiress of William Touchett, of Whitby, in Cheshire, Esq. by whom he had three sons and four daughters. viz. John; William, a doctor of physic, who lived at Chester, and died unmarried; and Thomas, a captain; Martha, who died young; Eleanor, who died without issue; and Mary, wife of William Grimbaldston, a doctor of physic in London, and died without issue.

I. Sir JOHN CHETWODE, the twenty-fourth in direct lineal succession from his great ancestor Sir John Chetwode, Knt. lord of the manor of Chetwode, in Bucks, whose son Robert founded the priory of Chetwode, was created a Baronet the sixth day of April, 1700; which, however, was conferred without payment of any fine, fee, or reward. He married first, Mary, daughter of Sir Jonathan Raymond, Knt. alderman of London, who died Jan. 12, 1702, leaving one son and three daughters, 1, Philip-Touchet, his successor; 2, Anne, wife of Thomas Whitby, of Aston, in Flintshire, Esq.; 3, Mary, died unmarried; 4, Abigail, wife of Thomas Jones, of Churton, in Cheshire, Esq. Sir John married secondly, Catharine, daughter of John Tayleur, of Rodington, in Shropshire, Esq. who died without issue, Oct. 14, 1717. He died April 22, 1733, and was succeeded by his only son,

II. Sir PHILIP-TOUCHET CHETWODE, Bart. who married, in 1727, Elizabeth, only daughter and heiress of George Venables, of Agdon, in Cheshire, Esq. descended from the barons of Kenderton, and who died Sept. 14, 1745, by whom he had twelve children, six of whom only survived their infancy; 1, John, his successor; 2, Philip, a clergyman, who married Anne, daughter of William Dickenson, and relict of Thomas-Gunter Brown, Esqs. and died 1769, leaving a daughter Anne, born 1766, and a son Philip, born 1767, who was in the memorable engagement between Rodney and Compte de Grasse, April 12, 1782, and perished in the Ville de Paris, a captive French ship, which foundered at sea; 3, George-Venables, an officer in the army, who died 1761; 4, Charles, who married Anne, only daughter of William Bates, of Bloor, in Staffordshire, and died 1768, leaving one daughter Anne, born 1768; 5, Anne, wife, first, of Robert Davison, of Brand, in Shropshire, Esq.; and secondly, of Edward Mainwaring, of Whitmore, in Staffordshire, Esq.; 6, Elizabeth died unmarried 1776. Sir Philip died Nov. 15, 1764, and was succeeded by his son,

III. Sir JOHN CHETWODE, Bart. who married, 1756, Dorothy, third daughter and coheiress of Thomas Bretland, of Thorncliffe, in Cheshire, Esq.

TABLE.

1, Sir JOHN CHETWODE

2 Robert Chetwode

3, Sir Raufe Chetwode

4, Sir Robert=S. Strange

5, Sir John William

6, Sir Robert=L. Hockliffe

7, Sir John Chetwode
Joanna | A. Cugentio

8, John=Lucia

9, John Chetwode=Johanne

Sir John Chetwode 10, Robert Chetwode

Sir Nicholas=E. Lyons 11, John=Elizabeth de Okeley

Mary=Sir John=A. Green 12, John=Margery

John, 1420 Margery J. Browning Sir Thos. Agnes &c, 13, Roger Chetwode Margery Crew

Alice Johanna E. Langworth 14, Thomas M. Pounde

15, Roger=Ellen de Ree

E. Beresford=16, Thomas=E. Spurstow

17, Roger=Ellen Masterson Ellen John Raufe

James=C. Hulse John Richard=A. Wodehull 11, Roger=— Taylor Ellen=J. Hankey Margery.

Jane Drury=Sir Richard=D. Needham 19, James=Catharine

Richard A.Knightley Wiliam. Elizabeth Catharine SirW.Skeffington Anne SirG.Bray 4 sons 7 drs 20, Thomas A.Leech | ——— John, 5 drs

13 children 21, John Chetwode=B. Birkenhead Anne=R. Woodward

22, John Eleanor Thomas — Wake Henry — Harris James, Anne Bridget A. Mainwaring Elizabeth — Harris Margaret T.Wood

John 23, Philip=H. Touchet Sarah=Sir T. Bunbury Abigail=P. Leigh

M. Raymond=I. Sir John, 1733=C.Tayleur Wm. Thomas Martha Eleanor Mary=W. Grimbaldston
1702 1717

II. Sir Philip, 1764=E. Venables, 1745 Anne=T. Whitby Mary Abigail=T. Jones

III. Sir John, 1779 D. Bretland, 1769 Phiilp, 1769 A. Dickenson George-Venables Charles, 1768 A. Bates Anne R. Davison | E. Mainwaring Elizabeth, 1776

III. Sir John, Bart.=Henrietta Grey

John William George Charles Hen-Dorothy A. Maria Eliz. Louisa

who died 1769, by whom he had eight children, who all died in the lifetime of their father, except John, his successor. Sir John died May 25, 1779, and was succeeded by his only son,

IV. Sir JOHN CHETWODE, Bart. born May 11, 1764, and married, Oct. 26, 1785, Henrietta, eldest daughter of George-Harry Grey, Earl of Stamford, of Dunham-Massey, in Cheshire, by whom he has eight children now living, 1, John; 2, William; 3, George; 4, Charles; 5, Henrietta-Dorothy; 6, Anne-Maria; 7, Elizabeth; 8, Louisa.

ARMS—Quarterly, argent, and gules, four crosses, formé, counterchanged.
CREST—Out of a ducal coronet, proper, a demi-lion, rampant, issuant, gules.
MOTTO—*Corona mea Christus.*
SEATS—Oakley, in Staffordshire, Chetwode and Agden, in Buckinghamshire, and Whitley, in Cheshire.

BARONETS

CREATED BY

QUEEN ANNE.

221. WEBSTER, of COPTHALL, Essex.

Created Baronet, May 21, 1703.

THE Websters are descended from an ancient family of that name, seated at Lockington, in Yorkshire, before the reign of King Richard II. which seat and estate, in the 12th of that king's reign, 1388, was, by Alice, daughter and heiress of William Webster (then in her widowhood, as she writes in her deed), conveyed to John Herynge, of South Burton, and Joan, his wife, whereunto William Abel, of Lockynton, William Ward, of the same place, Adam de Rygeton, of South Burton, and others, are witnesses.

But in 12 Hen. VI. John Webster, of Bolesover, in Derbyshire, was returned into chancery among the gentlemen of that county, who made oath for themselves and retainers, for the observance of the peace, and of the king's laws; part of which estate, in 1741, was in possession of Peter Webster, Esq. the chief heir male of the family, a younger son whereof was,

Sir Godfrey Webster, of Nelmes, in Essex, Knt. who married Abigail, daughter and coheiress of Thomas Gorden, of the Mere, in Staffordshire, Esq. by whom he had,

I. Sir THOMAS WEBSTER, who was created a Baronet in the second year of Queen Anne; and, in the year 1705, was returned a member for the borough of Colchester, to the parliament then called; for which place he served again, in the first and second parliaments of Great Britain (after the Union), 1708 and 1710, and also again in the second parliament of King George II. also, about the year 1717, he was, by the freeholders of the county of Essex, elected verdurer of the ancient forest of Waltham, in the said county. He married Jane, daughter and heiress of Edward Cheek, of Sampford-Orcas, in the county of Somerset, Esq. (by his wife Mary, daughter and coheiress of Henry Whistler, of Ebsham, vulgo Epsom, in Surry, Esq. by whom he had two sons, Sir Whistler, his successor, and Sir Godfrey, successor to his brother; and three daughters, Abigail, wife, first, of William Northey, of Compton-Basset, in Wiltshire, Esq. son and heir of Sir Edward Northey, Knt. attorney-general; she was secondly the wife of Sir Edmond Thomas, of Wenvoe, in Glamorganshire, Bart. member of parliament for Chippenham, in Wilts; Jane, wife of the Rev. —— Bluett, of Devonshire; and Elizabeth, of —— Webster, an officer of the army, bearing the same arms, but not acknowledged by her family as a relation, being a stolen match*. Sir Thomas died in 1750, and his relict in 1760. He was succeeded by his eldest son,

II. Sir WHISTLER WEBSTER, Bart. who represented the borough of East Grinstead in parliament. He died Sept. 1776, and was succeeded by his brother,

III. Sir GODFREY WEBSTER, Bart. who married ——, daughter of —— Gilbert, by whom he had one son, Sir Godfrey. He died in 1780, and was succeeded by his son,

IV. Sir GODFREY WEBSTER, Bart. who, in 1786, married ——, daughter of —— Vassal, a rich planter in Jamaica, by whom he had two sons and one daughter. They resided in Florence, and on his coming to England on business, she quitted him, and afterwards being divorced, was married to Lord Holland, who, by Sir Godfrey's death, succeeded to 7000l. a-year, which, though an alienable property of his lady, he gave up to Sir Godfrey for his life. Sir Godfrey shot himself with a pistol, June 3, 1800, at his house in Tenderden-street, Hanover-square. For five or six weeks before, he had betrayed evident symptoms of a troubled mind, in consequence of ill luck at play, whereupon the coroner's inquest brought in a verdict of lunacy. He is succeeded by his son,

V. Sir GODFREY-VASSAL WEBSTER, Bart.

ARMS—Azure, on a bend, argent, cottized, or (between two demi-lions, rampant, ermine), a rose gules, seeded and leaved, proper, between two boar's heads, couped, sable, langued, gules.

CREST—A dragon's head, couped, reguardant, quarterly per fess, embattled vert, and or, with flames of fire issuing out of his mouth, proper.

SEATS—Nelmes and Copthall, in Essex, and Battel-Abbey, in Sussex.

* By the information of the Rev. Robert Raynald, at Mr. Markwich's, at Catsfield, near Battle-Abbey, Sussex, dated Dec. 24, 1752.

TABLE.

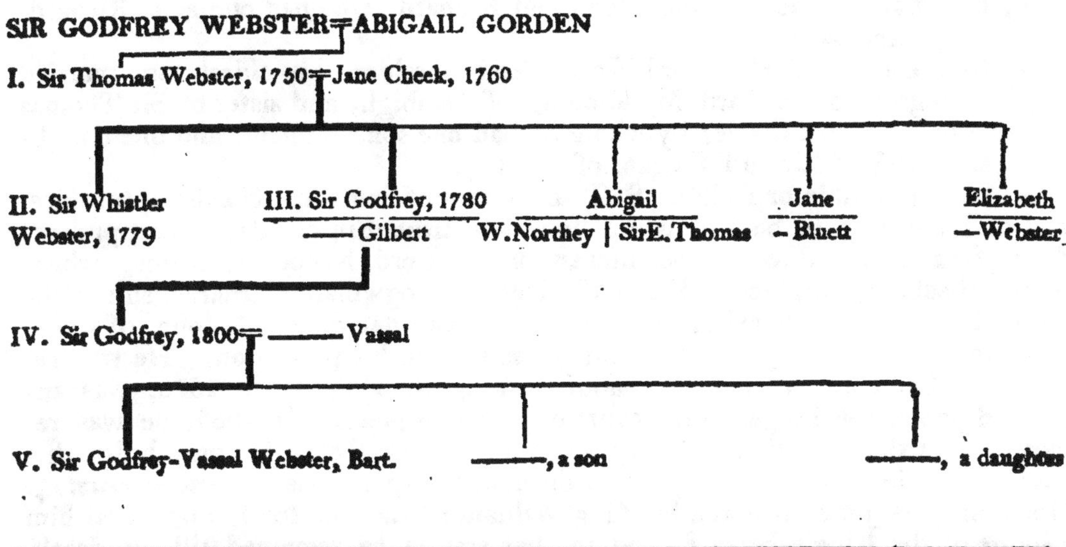

222. DOLBEN, of THINGDON, alias FINEDON, Northamptonshire.

Created Baronet, April 1, 1704.

THIS family is very ancient in Derbyshire, and has branched into several houses*. The name is supposed to be taken from Dolben Maer, a place between Carnarvon and Penmorfa, and from the spelling of it in the Herald's College, it might seem to be from the family of D'Albini, of whom was an Earl of Sussex, during the Norman dynasty: it is now written Doulben, in Wales, which the Rev. John Williams, of Llanrwst, says is wrong.

1, William Dulbin, of Denbigh, in North Wales; descended from those of Segrywd, (not Segrayd or Segroit) in that county, married —— daughter of —— Conway, by whom he had,

* David Dolben, bishop of Bangor, who died November 27, 1767, was of this family. And so was Robert Dolben, of Denbigh, the father of Robert Dolben, of Denbigh, the father of Robert-Wyn Dolben, of Denbigh, the father of John Wyn Dolben, of Denbigh, who married Katherine, daughter of Hugh ap Rees, ap William, ap Ithell Vychan, of Disser or Disserts, by whom he had eight sons; 1, John-Wyn Dolben, who married Margaret daughter of William Myddleton, of Gruneah; 2, William; 3, Henry; 4, Peter; 5, David; 6, Richard; 7, Robert; 8, John, *M. S. of Anthony a Wood*, marked F ½, fol 68.

2, Hugh Dalbin, who married——, daughter of——, Dutton, of Cheshire, by whom he had one son,

3, Humphrey Dalbin, who married Elizabeth, daughter of Lewys, of Nantconway, by whom he had two sons, John and Richard, who had one son, Richard, and a daughter, Jane.

4, John Dalbin, of Haverford West, Pembrokeshire, his eldest son, married Alice, daughter of Richard Myddleton, of Denbigh, and sister of Sir Thomas Myddleton, of Chirk Castle, by whom he had one son, William, and one daughter, Jane, wife of Richard Wogan, of Bolston.

5, William Dalbin or Dolbin, S. T. D. rector of Stanwich, Northamptonshire, and of Benefield; to both of which he was instituted in one day*, and prebendary of Lincoln†, through the interest of the Lord Keeper Williams, whose niece, Elizabeth, daughter of Hugh Williams, of Cogwillan, Carnarvonshire; he married ———, by whom he had three sons and two daughters; 1, John, of whom hereafter; 2, William, who was highly eminent in his profession. He was recorder of London, received the honour of knighthood; and in 1678, was appointed one of the judges in the court of common pleas. In 1683, he was removed from that situation, very highly to his honour, being the only judge that gave his opinion against the legality of disolving corporations by *quo warranto*‡. His rank was justly restored by King William; who, in 1689, appointed him a judge of the King's-Bench §, and in that station he remained till his death, which happened in 1693, the 65th year of his age. He was buried in the Temple-church, and left a character of high estimation, for strict integrity, and the most penetrating discernment ||; and 3, Rowland, a sea-officer; the two last died unmarried. Of the two daughters, ———, the eldest was wife of Dr. Stephen Luddington, archdeacon of Stow, in the diocese of Lincoln, and had a son, Stephen, a clergyman, who died unmarried, and four daughters; —, the eldest, was wife of Dr. Nicholas Stratford, bishop of Chester, by whom she had one son, Dr. William Stratford, canon of Christ-church, who died unmarried, and one daughter, ——, wife of Dr. Entwizle, Dean of Chester, by whom she had two daughters, unmarried, in 1741; the second was wife of Dr. Dickenson, of St. Martin's lane, by whom she had one only daughter, who was married to the Baron Blombergh, a nobleman of Courland, by whom she had several sons; the eldest of which, Edmund-Charles, was equerry to his majesty, and the second ——, rector of Fulham, in Middlesex, and married ——, daughter of Dr. Bland, dean of Durham; the third was wife of Mr. Wheler, by whom she had, Dr. Wheler, a physician, at Chester, and one daughter; ——, the fourth, was wife of Mr. Fox, by whom she had a numerous issue. Dr. Dolben's second daughter was first, the wife of——, a wealthy citizen of London, by whom she had no issue; secondly of Dr. James, warden of All-Souls college, Oxon, by whom she had a son, Gilbert, who was

* Kennet's Chron. and Magn. Brit. North.

† Willis Cathed.

‡ Baronetage.

§ Pointer's Chronol. Vol. II.

|| From the information of lord chief baron Parker.

captain of a man of war, and died (was cast away at sea) unmarried; and three daughters; —— the eldest, was wife of Mr. Richardson, merchant, in Basinghall street, and had no issue; ———, the second, was wife of Mr. Benson, of Salter's-hall, late secondary of the compter, and several other children; the third, Mary, who died unmarried. Dr. William Dolben, however, neither lived to see the eminence of his sons, nor to complete his own career of advancement: for he died in 1631, when his eldest son John, was only six years old, being himself nominated, at the time, for the succession to a vacant bishopric*: but his death produced an affecting testimony to his merit, of no small value in the moral estimate of honours. This was conferred by his parishioners of Stanwich, by whom he was so sincerely beloved, that at his falling ill at London, of the sickness which proved fatal to him, they ploughed and sowed his glebe lands at their own expence, that his widow might have the benefit of the crop; which she accordingly received after his decease; an anecdote more felt and valued by his family, than any thing that usually adorns the page of the biographer.

6, John Dolben, afterwards archbishop, was educated at Westminster school, where he was admitted a king's scholar in 1636; and in 1640, was elected to Christ's church, Oxford, where he was admitted, in the same year, a student on Queen Elizabeth's foundation. It has been thought worthy of remark, as a strong instance of hereditary attachment to those seminares, that he was the second in order, of six succeeding generations, which have passed through the same steps of education†.

When the civil wars broke out, Mr. Dolben, took arms for the royal cause in the garrison of Oxford, and served as an ensign in the important battle of Marston Moor, in 1644, where he received a dangerous wound in the shoulder from a musket-ball; but this was not the worst of his sufferings; in the defence of York, soon after, he received a severe wound of the same kind in the thigh, which broke the bone, and confined him twelve months to his bed. In the course of his military service, he was advanced to the rank of captain, and (according to Wood) of Major.

In 1646, when there appeared no longer any hope of serving the king's cause by arms, when Oxford, and his other garrisons were surrendered, and himself in the hands of his enemies, Mr. Dolben retired again to his college, and renewed his studies; a sense of duty had made him an active soldier; inclination and natural abilities rendered him at all times a successful student. In 1647, he took the degree of master of arts, and remained at college till ejected by the parliamentarian visitors in 1648.. In the interval between this period and the year 1656, when he entered into holy orders, we have no account of him; but it is most probable that his time was, in general, studiously employed, and especially from the moment when he took up that design. From 1657, when he married

* Kimber's Baronetage names Gloucester as the see to which he was to have succeede d; but this must be an error, as Gloucester was not then vacant: it was probably Bangor, to which his relation David Dolben was then appointed.

† List of Westmin. Schol. Anno. 1768.

Catherine daughter of Ralph, eldest brother of archbishop Sheldon*, to the time of the Restoration, he lived at Oxford, at the house of his father in-law, in St. Aldate's parish; and throughout that interval, in conjunction with Dr. Fell, and Dr. Allestry†, constantly performed divine service, and administered the sacraments, according to the liturgy of the church of England, to the great comfort of the royalists then resident in Oxford; particularly the students ejected in 1648, who formed a regular and pretty numerous congregation. The house appropriated to this sacred purpose, was the residence of Dr. Thomas Willis, the celebrated physician, and is yet standing opposite to Merton college. The attachment of Mr. Dolben to what he considered as the right cause, had before been active and courageous: it was ever firm and unwearied, with equal merit, and with better success.

When the regal government was restored, for the sake of which, Mr. Dolben had so often hazarded his life, his zeal for the cause and sufferings in it, were not forgotten by the king. In that very year, 1660, he took his degree of doctor in divinity, on being appointed a canon of Christ Church, Oxford. In the same year he was also presented to the rectory of Newington-cum-Britwell, in Oxfordshire‡, in the gift of the archbishop of Canterbury. His preferments and honours now succeeded each other rapidly; the time of trial was past, and the time of reward had arrived. In 1661, he became a prebendary of St. Paul's, and was one of those who signed the revived liturgy, which passed the house of convocation, Dec. 20, in that year. In 1662, he was appointed archdeacon of London, and presented to the vicarage of St. Giles's Cripplegate; but resigned the latter a short time after, with his other parochial preferment, on being installed Dean of Westminster. He was chosen prolocutor of the lower house of convocation in 1664, and soon after became clerk of the closet to the king. In 1666, he was consecrated bishop of Rochester, and allowed to hold the deanery of Westminster in *commendam*. In 1675, he was appointed Lord Almoner; an office, says Wood, which he discharged with such justice and integrity, as was for the great benefit of the poor. It would betray great ignorance of the ways of events to suppose, that in all these steps he was not, in fact, indebted to the interference and interest of archbishop Sheldon; yet, where merit is conspicuous, the effect of patronage is greatly facilitated, which appears to have been the case in the instance now before us.

Translation to the see of York, was the final gradation of his honours, and enjoyed only for a short time, as between the last advancement and his death, something less than three years intervened. He was translated to York, in August, 1683, and then became, by an unusual transition, the ecclesiastical governor of that place, which he had formerly assisted, in defending by military force. His activity was not yet exhausted, though exerted in a different line §; he diligently contributed to the good administration of the service in his cathedral, and in 1685, made a new regulation of archbishop Grindal's order of preachers, and

* Dolben M. S. S.
† A. à Wood, Vol. II.
‡ Le Neve's lives of the Archbishops.
§ Drake's York.

appointed a weekly celebration of the holy sacrament; and was, in all respects, as his epitaph expresses it, "An example both to the flock and to the pastors under him."

The death of archbishop Dolben, was occasioned, not by natural decay, but the criminal neglect of persons who have escaped from the disgrace they deserved, by mere obscurity. At an inn in the north road, he was suffered to sleep in a room where the infection of the small-pox remained; he there caught the disorder, which put an end to his life at Bishopthorp, on the 11th of April, 1686, in the 62d year of his age; after a confinement to his bed of only four days. That so valuable a life should have been cut off thus prematurely, is a matter of great regret, and of indignation against those who were the causes of it; but providence, in permitting such events, instructs us very forcibly, on how precarious a tenure we hold all worldly blessings. The body of the archbishop was deposited in the cathedral of York, where a handsome monument, records his merits, and the principal circumstances of his life*. By Catherine his wife, who died 1706, in her 86th year, he had two sons,

* Anthony Wood, says of archbishop Dolben, that "He was a man of a free, generous and noble disposition, and of a natural bold, and happy eloquence." The latter circumstance is confirmed by the testimony of his epitaph; and by another which we shall presently cite at large. The former, by the following instances of his liberality, at the different places with which he was connected. The pulpit at Stanwich is inscribed as his gift, when Bishop of Rochester. He contributed one hundred pounds to the re-building of St. Paul's cathedral, and two hundred and fifty pounds to the repairs of Christ-Church, Oxford. He rebuilt that part of the episcopal palace at Bromley, which the present liberal improver has left standing; and when dean of Westminster, influenced the chapter to assign an equal share with their own, in the dividends of fines, to the repairs and support of that venerable church *(a)*. At York he gave one hundred and ninety-five ounces of plate for the use of the cathedral *(b)*.

But the fullest account of his person, talents, and character, was drawn up by his friend Sir William Trumbull, and is still extant in his own hand writing; which, as it proceeds from a person who had the fullest knowledge of him, and is certainly authentic, we shall preserve the original words *(c)*.

"He was an extraordinary comely person, though grown too fat; of an open countenance, a lively piercing eye, and a majestic presence. He hated flattery, and guarded himself with all possible care against the least insinuation of any thing of that nature, how well soever deserved; he had admirable natural parts, and great acquired ones; for whatever he read he made his own, and improved it. He had such a happy genius, and such an admirable elocution, that his extempore preaching was beyond, not only most of other men's elaborate performances, but (I was going to say) even his own. I have been credibly informed, that in Westminster abbey, a preacher falling ill after he had named his text, and proposed the heads of his intended discourse; the bishop went up into the pulpit, took the same text, followed the same method, and I believe, discoursed much better on each head than the other would have done."

"In the judgment he made of other men, he always preferred the good temper of their minds above all other qualities, they were masters of: and it was this single opinion he had of my integrity, which made him the worthiest friend to me I ever knew. I have had the honour to converse with many men, at home and abroad, but I never yet met with one that in all respects equalled him. He had a large and generous soul, and a courage that nothing was too hard for. When he was basely calumniated, he supported himself by the only true heroism, if I may say so phrase it, I mean by exalted christianity, and by turning all the slander of his enemies into the best use of studying and knowing himself, and keeping a constant guard and watch upon his words and actions, practising ever after, (though hardly to be discovered, unless by nice and long observers) a strict course of life, and constant mortification."

"Not any of the bishops bench, I may say not all of them, had the interest and authority in the House of Lords which he had. He had easily mastered all the forms of proceeding. He had studied much of our

(a) Widmore's Westm. Abbey.
(b) Drake's York.
(c) M. S. of the Rev. Brook Birdges, of Orlingbury.

Gilbert, of whom hereafter; and John; and a daughter, Catherine, who died an infant. John, married Elizabeth, second daughter and coheiress of Tanfield Mulso, of Finedon, aforesaid, who died the 4th of March, 1736, by whom he had two sons, William, and John, who both died young; and three daughters, 1, Catherine, wife of Samuel Whitlock, of Chilton Foliot, in Wilts, Esq. (grandson and heir to the famous Bulstrode Whitlock, Esq.) by whom she had three sons, John, Samuel, and Gilbert, and nine daughters; (Catherine, Anne, wife of the Rev. Mr. Gyfford, rector of Nuffield, in Oxon. Elizabeth, Neeltice, Mary, Harriot, Mulso, Charlotte, and Judith; all living in 1741); 2, Elizabeth; 3, Anne, wife of Gilbert Affleck, of Dalham-hall, in Suffolk, Esq. by whom she had twelve sons; 1, John; 2, another John, who married —, only daughter and heiress of James Metcalfe, of Roxton-abby, in Bedfordshire, Esq. and had issue; 3, Gilbert; 4, Charles; 5, Thomas; 6, James; 7, William; 8, Samuel; 9, Robert; 10, Edmund; 11, Philip; and 12, Jermyn; and six daughters, Anne, Elizabeth, (wife of Robert Trefusis, Esq. member of parliament for Truro, and had issue); Catherine, (wife of William Metcalfe, of Fordham, in Cambridgeshire, Esq. and had issue); Mary, Louisa, and Charlotte. This John Dolben, Esq. was member of parliament for Leskeard, in Cornwall, at the time of his death, which happened at Epsom, in Surry, May 29, 1710.

I. Sir GILBERT DOLBEN, eldest son and heir of the archbishop, was advanced to the dignity of baronet by Queen Anne. He was one of the justices of the court of common pleas, in Ireland, near twenty years, in the reigns of King William III. Queen Anne, and George I. which post he resigned on account of ill health, 1720; and was a representative in parliament for Rippon, in Yorkshire, Peterborough, in Northamptonshire, and South-Yarmouth, in the Isle of Wight, thirty years; he married Anne, eldest daughter and co-heiress of Tanfield Mulso, of Finedon, in Northamptonshire, Esq. by whom he had only one son, Sir John, his successor, and died Oct. 22, in the sixty-fourth year of his age, 1722, whereupon the dignity and estate devolved upon his only son,

II. Sir JOHN DOLBEN, Bart. D. D. and prebendary of Durham, who was born at Bishops-Thorpe, near York, Feb. 12, 1683-4, and married the honourable Elizabeth Digby, second daughter of the right honourable William, lord Digby, baron of Geashill, in the kingdom of Ireland, by whom he had one son, Sir William, his successor; and three daughters, Elizabeth, widow of John-Nicholls Raynsford, of Brixworth, in Northamptonshire, Esq. Francis, and

laws, especially those of the parliament, and was not to be brow-beat or daunted by the arrogance or titles, of any courtier or favourite(a). His presence of mind and readiness of elocution, accompanied with good breeding and an inimitable wit, gave him a greater superiority than any other lord could pretend to from his dignity of office. I wish I had a talent suitable to the love and esteem I have for this great and good man; to enlarge more upon the subject, and when I think of his death, I cannot forbear dropping some tears, for myself as well as for the publick; for in him, we lost the greatest abilities, the usefullest conversation, the faithfullest friendship, and one who had a mind that painted the best virtues itself, and a wit that was best able to recommend them to others; as Dr. Sprat expresses it in his life of Mr. Cowley(b)."

(a) Burnet seems to commend his spirit beyond his discretion; but allows that he was latterly more reserved. Widmore speaks more favourably.

(b) Printed also in the Hist. of Rochester. 8vo. or 1772.

Anne, unmarried. Sir John had other children, but they all died under ten years of age, and the dates are not ascertained; two of them (James, and a second Gilbert) are buried in the cathedral, at Aix, in France; an unprecedented permission granted to him as a protestant, who then resided there. Lady Dolben died at Aix, where Sir John went for the recovery of his health, Nov. 4, 1730. Sir John died Nov. 20, 1756, aged seventy-three years, and was succeeded by his only surviving son,

III. Sir WILLIAM DOLBEN, Bart. who married May 17, 1748, Judith, only daughter and heiress of Somerset English, Esq. (by Judith his wife, daughter and coheiress of Hugh Reason, of Hampnet, in Sussex, Esq. by ——, his wife, daughter and heiress of Sir Joseph Sheldon, Knt. Lord Mayor of London) who died in 1771, aged 40. He married secondly, Oct. 14, 1789, Charlotte, daughter of Gilbert Affleck, Esq. and widow of John Scotchmer, Esq. by whom he has no issue. By his first lady, he had only two children, who lived to adult age. John English, and one daughter Anne Juliana, born 1764.

H. S. E.
Johannes Dolben, filius Guielmi, S. Th. Professoris,
Ex antiquâ Familiâ in Cambriâ Septentrionali oriundus,
Natus Stanvici, in Agro Northampton. Mart. 20, A. D. 1624.
Anno ætatis 12 Regiam Scholam Westmonast. Auspicato ingressus,
Singulari istius loco genio plenus 15 exivit,
In numerum Alumnorum Æd. Christ. Oxon. electus.
Exardente Bello Civili
Partes Regias secutus est, in Pugnâ Marstonensi Vexillarius,
In Defensione Eboraci graviter vulneratus
Effuso sanguine consecravit locum,
Olim morti suæ destinatum.
A. D. 1656, a Rev. Episc. Cicestrensi sacris ordinibus initiatus,
Instaurata Monarchia factus est æd. Christi canonicus;
Deinde Decanus Westmonasteriensis;
Mox CAROLO II. Regi optimo ab Oratorio Clericus,
Episcopus postea Roffensis,
Et post novennium Regis Eleemonsynarius.
Anno denique 1683, Metropol. Eborens. honore cumulatus est.
Hanc Provinciam ingenti Animo et pari industria administravit,
Gregi et Pastoribus exemplo;
Intra 30 circiter menses, seculi laboribus exhaustis,
Cœlo tandem maturus
Lethargiâ et Variolis per quatriduum lecto affixus,
A. D. 1686, Æt. 62. Potentis. Princ. Jac. II. altero, Die Dominico,
(Eodem die quo præeunte anno sacras Synaxes
In eccles. sua Cathed. septimanatim celebrandas instituerat,
Cælo fruebatur.
Mœstissima Conjux, Magni Gilberti, Cantuar. Archiep. Neptis,
Ex quâ tres Liberos suscepit Gilbertum, Catharin. et Johan.
Monumentum hoc posuit
Desideratissimo Marito.
In æde Christi sub illius auspiciis partim extructâ,
Bromleiensi palatio reparato, cœnob. Westmonas. conservato;
In Senatu & Ecclesiis eloquentiæ gloria; in Diocecebus suis
Episcopali Diligentiâ;
In omnium piorum animis, insta veneratione semper victuro.

TABLE.

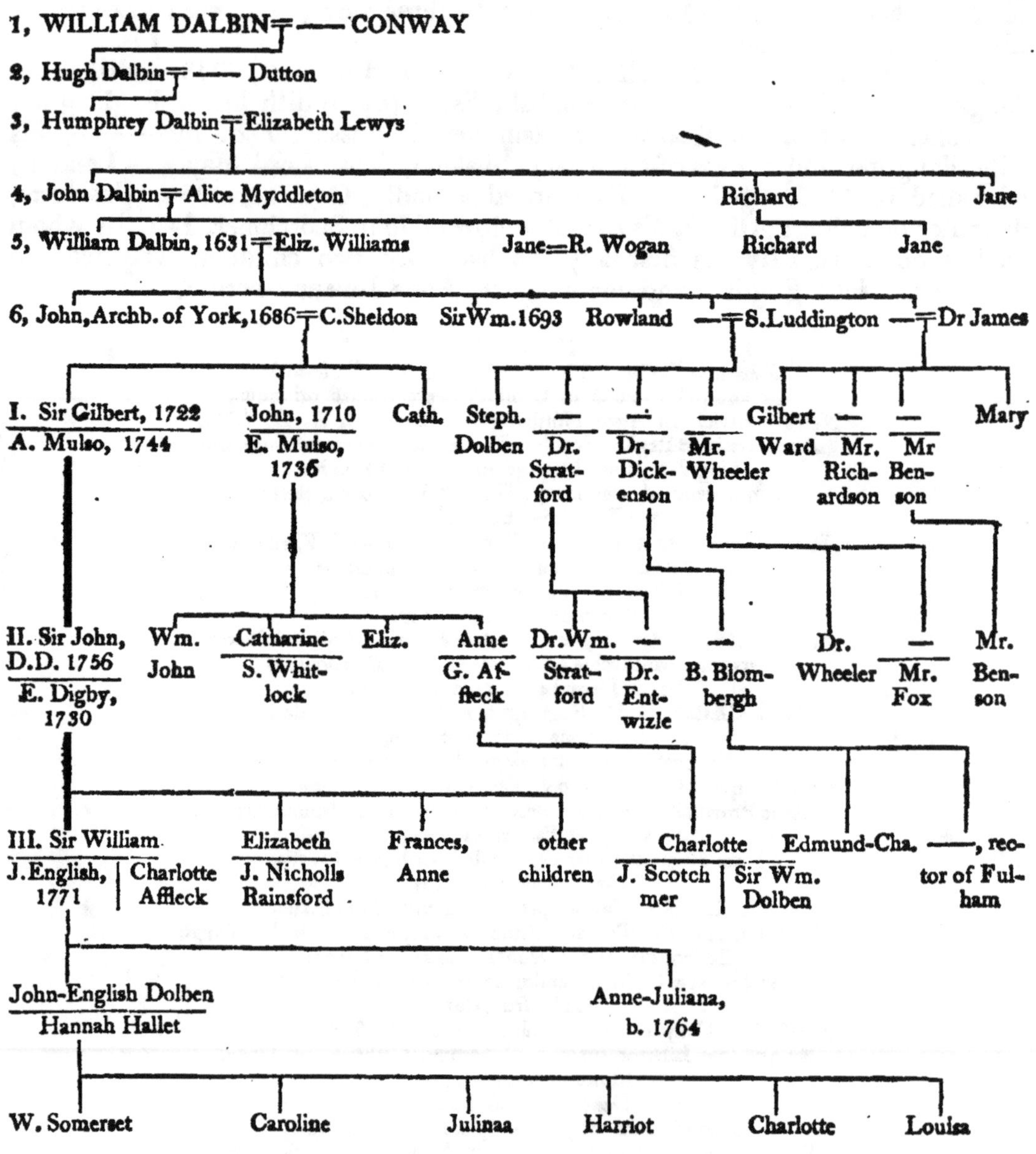
1, WILLIAM DALBIN = —— CONWAY
2, Hugh Dalbin = —— Dutton
3, Humphrey Dalbin = Elizabeth Lewys
4, John Dalbin = Alice Myddleton
Richard
Jane
5, William Dalbin, 1631 = Eliz. Williams
Jane = R. Wogan
Richard
Jane
6, John, Archb. of York, 1686 = C.Sheldon
SirWm.1693
Rowland
— = S.Luddington
— = Dr James
I. Sir Gilbert, 1722
A. Mulso, 1744
John, 1710
E. Mulso, 1736
Cath.
Steph. Dolben
—
Dr. Strat-ford
—
Dr. Dick-enson
—
Mr. Wheeler
Gilbert Ward
—
Mr. Rich-ardson
—
Mr Ben-son
Mary
II. Sir John, D.D. 1756
E. Digby, 1730
Wm. John
Catharine
S. Whit-lock
Eliz.
Anne
G. Af-fleck
Dr.Wm. Strat-ford
—
Dr. Ent-wizle
—
B. Blom-bergh
Dr. Wheeler
—
Mr. Fox
Mr. Ben-son
III. Sir William
J.English, 1771
Charlotte Affleck
Elizabeth
J. Nicholls Rainsford
Frances, Anne
other children
Charlotte
J. Scotch mer
Sir Wm. Dolben
Edmund-Cha.
——, rec-tor of Ful-ham
John-English Dolben
Hannah Hallet
Anne-Juliana, b. 1764
W. Somerset
Caroline
Julinaa
Harriot
Charlotte
Louisa

John English Dolben, Esq. married 1779, Hannah, daughter of William Hallet, jun. of Cannon, in Middlesex, Esq. and heiress to her mother, one of the coheiresses of John Hopkins, of Brittons, in Essex, Esq. by whom he has had, 1, William Somerset, born 1780; 2, Caroline, born 1781, died 1789; 3, Juliana, born 1783; 4, Harriot, born 1785, died 1786; 5, Charlotte, born 1787; 6, Louisa, born 1789.

ARMS—Sable, a helmet, close, between three pheons, argent.
CREST—On a wreath, a griffin, sejant.
SEAT—At Thingdon, alias Finedon, in Northamptonshire.

---

223. FLEMING, of RYDAL, Westmorland.

Created Baronet, Oct. 4, 1705.

THIS family derives its descent from Sir Michael le Fleming, Knt. who being related to Baldwin V. earl of Flanders, was sent to assist William the Conqueror, his son in law; who sent him some years after, with some of his countrymen, into Cumberland, to oppose the Scots. For which services, he had given him, by the said Conqueror, the castle of Gleaston, and manor of Aldingham, ; and other lands in Furness, in Lancashire; and also the castle of Caernarvon, and the lordship and manor of Beckermet; with other estates in the county of Cumberland, which have, ever since, continued in the family.

He, and some of his descendants, were often called le Flemiug, Flameng, Flemengus, Flandrensis, and sometimes de Furness, from their dwelling at Gleaston castle, beforementioned; they had commonly *le* prefixed to their surname, until the time of Edw. IV. which helps to confirm the observation of Camden, that *de* and *le* were strictly observed in some local names, until abont that time.

When, Stephen, Earl of Bologne, who was afterwards king of England, founded the abbey of Furness, in 1126, he granted to the said abbey, whatsoever was in Furness, except the land of Michael Flameng. Which grant was confirmed by Pope Eugenius, with the like exception.

In the 19th year of King Stephen, he granted Fordebote to the said abbey of Furness; and soon after died and was buried there, wherein most of the nobility and gentry in those parts were interred, as was very usual also in other places, many bequeathing their bodies, together with a legacy, to the religious houses; and others desiring not only to be buried near the monks habitations, but in their very robes. He had issue five sons and one daughter, 1, William, to whom, at his death, he left Gleaston castle, the manor of Aldingham, and all other, his lands in Furness, in Lancashire; 2, Richard, to whom he gave his castle of Caernarvon and manor of Beckermet, with the homage and service, wards and reliefs, of all the freeholders, of and in Frisington, Rottington, Weddikar, Kelton, Salter, Arlochden, and Burnrigg, in the county of Cumberland, with other possessions in that county, and in the county of Lancaster, which are yet enjoyed by his posterity and issue male, lineally, for the most part, and sometimes collaterally, for want of issue male in the elder branch; 3, Daniel, a clergyman, who had the church of Urswic, reserved for him, upon his father's exchange of Ros and Crimelton, for Bardsey, and Urswic, with the abbot of Furness; 4, Anselm, from whom the barons Fleming, of Slane, in Ireland, derive their descent *, and from whom, according to an old tradition in the family, of Rydal, the Earls of Wigton, in Scotland, are likewise descended, he assumed the surname de Furness, and was living in the 13th King John. He married Agnes, daughter of Alice, wife of Edgar, and had half of Yanewith for her marriage portion; 5, Jordan, who also took the name of Furness; 6, Godith, a daughter, with whom her father gave in marriage, to William de Essenby, three carucates of land in Adgaresslith, and who was a benefactor to the priory of St. Bees †, in Cumberland.

The present family at Rydal proceeds from Richard, the second son, who was settled in Cumberland. And it is this branch that we are now to pursue. The elder branch who enjoyed the Lancashire estates, continued owners thereof, in a regular heredatary succession of males and females, till it arrived as it were, at the foot of the throne, in the person of Henry Grey, Marquis of Dorset, and afterwards Duke of Suffolk, father of the Lady Jane Grey; ‡

* Irish Compenddium, Baron Slane.

† Rog. Dodsworth, MS. collect. in bibl. Bodl. Oxon. vol. 127. p. 49.

‡ 1, Sir William, the eldest son of Sir Michael le Fleming, of Furness, Knt. after the death of his father enjoyed the manor of Aldenham, the castle and manor of Gleaston, with other lands in the county of Lancaster, and elsewhere.

2, Sir Michael le Fleming, of Furness, Knt. son and heir, left a son,

3, William le Fleming, who had one son,

4, Sir Michael le Fleming, Knt. who in the reign of Hen. III. was drowned in the Leven, and died without issue, and left his whole estate to his sister,

5, Alice, the wife of Richard de Cancefield, by whom she had one son, William, and one daughter, Alice,

6, William de Cancefield, died without issue, and was succeeded in his estates, by his sister,

7, Agnes de Cancefield, the wife of Robert de Harrington, of Harrington, in Cumberland, temp. Edw. I. carried the estate into that family. They had issue.

8, John de Harrington, who in 34, Edw. I. was knighted; and was summoned to parliament as a baron from 18, Edw. II. to 23, Edw. II. he died in that year. This John, had a son,

9, Robert de Harrington, who died before his father, having married Elizabeth, sister and coheiress of John de Multon, of Egremont, and by whom he had a son and heir.

10, John de Harrington, who succeeded his grandfather, and died 37, Edw. III. leaving one son,

11, Robert de Harrington, who residing at Aldingham, in the first year of Richard II. was knighted

2, Richard le Fleming, of Beckermet, in Cumberland, Knt. second son of the first Sir Michael, was knight, and was stiled, Flandrensis, and Flameng, as well as le Fleming, which appears by divers fair old deeds, still in the possession of the family, many of which are without date. To this Sir Richard, William de Skelsmeresergh, by several deeds without date, granted divers lands in Lancaster, with the fishery of Thurston; to which deeds his elder brother William de Furness is a witness. He died in the reign of King John, and was buried with his father, and brother, in Furness-abby, and was succeeded by his only son,

3, Sir John le Fleming, of Beckermet, Knt. who by a deed without date, conveyed to his son Richard, all the land, which his father had given him in Coupland, with the homage and services of certain freeholders which then held of the said John, viz. the homage and service of Sir Alan de Peninton, and his heirs for Rotinger, of Sir Robert de Lamplugh, for half of Harlofden and for Brunrigg, of William de Wedacre, for two parts of Wedacre, of Sir Adam Haverington, for the third part of Wedacre, and of Ralph de Frisington, for Frisington, with wards and reliefs, and all other liberties thereunto belonging, and by several other deeds be conveyed to him, other lands in Cumberland. He gave also the patronage of the rectory of Arloghden, and land in Great Beckermet, to the abbey of Caldre, 26, Hen. III. The advowson of the church of St. John Baptist, of Beckermet, was granted to the said abbey, either by him or his father; which was confirmed by the archbishop of York, about the year 1262. He also conveyed other lands in Lancashire to divers persons; witnesses were the prior of Kertmel, John, prior of Cunningsheved, Sir William de Furnes, William, son of Orme, Matthew de Redeman, Thomas de Betham, Richard de Preston,

at his coronation; he married Isabel, daughter and coheiress of his Sir Nigel Loring, Knight of the Garter, by whom he had two sons, John and William,

12, Sir John Harrington, his eldest son, died 5, Hen. IV. without issue, and was succeeded by his brother,

13, Sir William Harrington, Knt. who married Margaret, daughter of Sir Robert Nevil, of Hornby. He was summoned to parliament, from 8, Hen. V. to the 15, Hen. VI. he had only one daughter,

14, Elizabeth, the wife of William Lord Bonvile, who died in his father's lifetime, leaving a son,

15, William Bonvile, junior, commonly called William Lord Harrington, who married Catherine, daughter of Richard Nevil, Earl of Salisbury, and was slain at the battle of Wakefield, on the part of the house of York, in 39. Hen. VI. leaving only a daughter,

16, Cecilie, wife of Thomas Grey, Marquis of Dorset, and afterwards of Henry Stafford, Earl of Wiltshire, by the former of which she had one son,

17, Thomas Grey, Marquis of Dorset, who married Margaret, daughter of Sir Robert Wotton, Knt. widow of William Medley, and died 22, Hen. VIII. leaving one son,

18, Henry Grey, Marquis of Dorset, who married Katherine, daughter of William Fitz-Alan, Earl of Arundel, by whom he had no issue; he married secondly, Frances, eldest daughter of Charles Brandon, Duke of Suffolk, by his wife Mary, the French Queen; and, as her two brothers died without issue, this Henry, her husband, was created Duke of Suffolk; by her he had three daughters, Jane, Katherine, and Mary; Jane, the eldest, was proclaimed Queen, after the death of Edw. VI. and soon after beheaded. Her father, for countenancing the said proclamation, was beheaded on Tower hill, on the second of Queen Mary, and the whole estate, in Cumberland, Lancashire, and elsewhere, became forfeited to the crown, and was granted out to divers persons, whose posterity or assignees enjoy the same to this day.—*Dugdale's Baronetage.*

* Remains concerning Britain, edit. 1674, p. 151.

Adam, son of Gamel, John de Cancefield, Michael de Hurswic, and others. He died in the reign of Hen. III. and was buried in the abbey of Calder, to which he had been a benefactor. Sir Daniel Fleming says, there was to be seen in his days at the said abbey, a very ancient statue, in freestone, of a man in armour, with *a frett, of six pieces*, upon his shield, lying upon his back, with his sword by his side, his hands elevated in a praying posture, and his legs across, which probably are so placed, from his taking upon him the cross, and being engaged in the holy war; which statue was placed there, most probably, in memory of this Sir John le Fleming, he was succeeded by his son,

4, Sir Richard le Fleming, of Beckermet, Knt. who married Elizabeth, sister and heiress of Adam de Urswick, and John de Urswick, her two brothers; whose father was Adam de Urswick, son of Gilbert, son of Adam, son of Bernulph; with whom he had the manor of Coningston (King's-town); and other possessions in Lancashire; which have continued in his heirs male to this day*.

After this marriage, the castle of Caernarvon was suffered to go to decay, and at last demolished; and the family returned to Coningston-hall, where they resided for several generations; he left a son,

5, John le Fleming, of Coningston; who in the 28 Edw. I. was in the expedition then made into Scotland, with the king when he was at Carlaveroke, situate upon the very mouth of Solway, accounted an impregnable fortress; which King Edward, accompanied with the flower of the English nobility and gentry, besieged, and with difficulty took. During his absence out of the kingdom, John had a protection from the king, dated at Carlaveroke, 10th July, 28, Edw. I. of his people, lands, goods, rents, and other possessions, and freedom from all suits and plaints, until Easter following; He left two sons, Raynerus, and Hugh, who had a daughter, Mary, the wife of Ralph de Frisington.

6, Rainerus le Fleming, of Coningston, gave to the abbot of St. Mary's York, two oxgangs of land in Rotington, and also one villein in the same town; which was confirmed by Edw. II. in the first year of his reign: he had the appellation of *Dapifer*, added to his name; perhaps as being purveyor of the king in the north, he left one son,

7, Sir John le Fleming, of Coningston, Knt. By an inquistion *post mortem*, of Thomas de Multon, of Egremont, in 15, Edw. II. it appears, that Richard de Hodleston, and Gilbert de Culwen, did then hold Millum and Workington, of the said Thomas; and that John, son of Rayner le Fleming, held of the said Thomas, the hamlets of Beckermet, Frisington, Rotington, Wedacre, Arlockden, by homage and fealty, and suit of court of Egremont, and by the service of the ninth part of one knight's fee, and 5s. 6d. a year for cornage, and 2s. 5d. for

* By a deed without date, John, brother of the said Elizabeth, granted to the said Richard le Fleming, and the said Elizabeth, all the lands which had been Adam de Urswick's, his brother, in Urswick, Coningston, Caughton, and Kerneford, in exchange for other lands. Witnesses Roger de Lancastre, John de Cancefield, John de Kirby, Richard de Kirby, and others.

In 52, Hen. III. a writ of trespass was brought by Isabel de Fortibus, Countess of Albemarle, against Roger de Lancaster, Richard le Fleming, Gilbert de Culwen, Ranulph de Docre, and others.

watch of the sea, and by the puture of two serjeants of the said Thomas, every ninth day, at his manor of Egremont.

The lords of the manor of Beckermet, do yet pay yearly 3s. 4d. of the free rents above mentioned, to the owner of Egremont Castle; and all the residue of the aforesaid rents, are yearly paid by the freeholders of Frisington, Rotington, Wedacre, and Arlocden.

He had two sons, and one daughter, Joan, the wife of John le Towers, of Lowick, whose arms were, *argent, on a bend, gules, three towers or.* William, the elder son, died without issue, either before or soon after his father, for,

8, Sir John le Fleming, of Coningston, Knt. second son of the last Sir John, appears to hove been heir to to his father, 7, of Edw. III. by an inquistion taken at Ulverston, after the death of this Sir John, it appears, that he died 27, Edw. III. and that on the day on which he died, he held of the king *in capite*, (which had been of the fee of William de Coucy) the manor of Coningston, with the appurtenances, and a certain fishing then in Thurstan water; that he had two marks rent, issuing out of Claugton, holden of John de Croft; forty acres of land at the water-end, holden of John de Haverington, by a pair of white gloves for all services; he had two sons, Richard le Fleming, his heir, then of the age of thirty years, and Robert,

9, Sir Richard le Fleming, of Coningston, Knt. the elder son of the last Sir John, married Catherine, daughter, or sister, of Sir John de Kirby, in Lancahire, Knt. by whom he had three sons, 1, Thomas; 2, John; 3, James; and a daughter, Joan*; which Joan, 44, Edw. III. released unto her father all her lands in Cumberland and Lancashire, which had been her grandfather's; which deed, she concludes thus, "And because my seal is not known to many, I have procured to be set to these presents, the seal of the official of the deanry of Coupland, together with the seals of William de Cleter, and Thomas de Lamplowe. In 6, of Richard II. Nicholas de Boweness, parson of the moiety of the church of Ayketon, granted to William del Dykes, all his lands in Dystington, in Coupland, which he had of the feoffment of John, son of Hugh de Dystington. One of the witnesses was Richard le Fleming, Knt. He appears to have been witness afterwards to several deeds; the latest of which was 16, Richard II. at which time, he was of the age of 69 years. He died at Coningston-hall not long after; and was succeeded by,

10, Sir Thomas le Fleming, of Coningston, Knt. his eldest son, who married, first, Margaret daughter of William de Berdesey, as appears by a deed, 47, Edw. III. wherein Sir Richard, father of the said Thomas, grants to him and Margaret his wife, daughter of William de Berdesey, and to the heirs of their bodies, the manor of Beckermet, remainder to his own right heirs. By her he had no issue. He married, secondly, Isabel, daughter of Thomas Layburne, Knt. by whom he had two sons, Thomas, and John; Sir Thomas Layburne, in the marriage articles, coventanted to give with his said daughter, for her portion, eighty marks in silver, and sufficient rayment; whereupon the manor of Beckermet and lands

* To these, have usually been added, Richard le Fleming, Bishop of Lincoln, and 1427, Founder of Lincoln College, Oxford, and Robert le Fleming, at the same time Dean of Lincoln.

in Urswick, were intailed upon the said Sir Thomas le Fleming, and Isabel, his wife, and their heirs male; and for want of such, then upon John Fleming, his brother. There appears a release to have been executed by him, 12, Hen. IV. How soon after he died, is not known; but he was dead, 6 Hen. V. his wife Isabel being then a widow.

11, Sir Thomas le Fleming, of Coningston, Knt. the elder son, married, in his father's lifetime, Isabel, daughter and coheiress of Sir John de Lancaster, of Rydal and Howgill castle, and this was the first introduction of the Flemings into Westmorland. In the marriage articles it was covenanted, that John, her father, should pay eighty marks for his daughter's portion, and that Sir Thomas, father of the said Thomas, should settle the manor of Coningston, and all other his lands, on his said son and his heirs male; and for defect of such, then upon John le Fleming, younger brother of the said Thomas, and his heirs male; for want of such, then upon the right heirs of the said Sir Thomas; and that if the said Thomas the son should die, without heirs of the body of the said Isabel, then that John, his younger són, aforesaid, should marry another daughter of the said Sir John de Lancaster, without any other portion or settlement. But the said Thomas, and Isabel had children; and the other three daughters of Sir John de Lancaster married other persons, and after his decease, his estate was divided amongst them; in which division, the manor of Rydal and all the said Sir John's lands and tenements in Rydal and Loughrigg, acceeded to the two daughters, Margaret, wife of Sir Matthew Whitfield, and Isabel, wife of the said Sir Thomas le Fleming. They afterwards purchased the Whitfield moiety, and Rydal, from thenceforth became the chief seat of the Fleming family. The said Sir Thomas, by his wife, Isabel de Lancaster, had two sons John and William.

12, John Fleming, of Rydal, Esq. after the decease of his father and mother, became possessed of the manors of Beckermet, Coningston, and Rydal, and all other their estates in the counties of Cumberland, Lancaster, and Westmorland, and who is sometimes stiled, John Fleming, senior, to distinguish him from his eldest son of the same name *. This John, married, first, Joan, daughter of Sir —— Broughton, of Broughton-Tower, in Lancashire, Knt. by whom he had one son, John Fleming, his heir: he married another wife, whose name was, Anne, by whom he had no issue.

He appears to havc been dead 2 Rich. III. for in that year, there was an award,

* This John, 9 Edw: IV. was retained by indenture, according to the custom of those times, to serve the lord of Graystock, who was often employed in the king's service against Scotland, the form of which retainer was as follows.—

This indenture, made the 9th day of December, in seventh year of the reign of King Ed. IV. between Rauff, Lord of Greystock, and Wemm, on the ton party, and John Fleming, Esq. of the todir party, Witness, that the said John, is retained, and behest (*a*) with the said lord, for terme of his life, as well in were as in peace, against all manner of men, except his legeance, the said John, taking yearly of the said lord, four pound, of lawful money of England. And in the time of were, such wages as the king gyffs to such men, of such degree. And, (i. e.) if he go with the said lord. And the said John, to take his said fee be the hands of the receiver of Graystock, that is, or shall be, that is to say, at Whit-sunday, and Mar, tynmes. And if the said John, go with the said lord, over the sea, or into Scotland, and then it happyn.

(*a*) It is an Anglo Saxon word, from *best*, a command; as much as to say, he had put himself under his command. So *begiht* signifies promised or engaged.

whereby it was ordered, that Ann Car, wife of John Fleming, should enjoy for her dower, lands in Claughton, in Lonsdale, and one tenement in Coningston and yearly during her life, one buck or doe out of Coningston park; and that John Fleming, son and heir of the said John, deceased, enjoy all the rest of his father's lands.

13, John Fleming of Rydal, Esq. son and heir of John, married Joan*, daughter of Sir Hugh Lowther, of Lowther, Knt. by whom he had Hugh, his heir, and five daughters; 1, Agnes, wife of Richard Ducket, of Grayrigg, in Westmorland, Esq. 2, ——— of Richard Kirby, of Kirby. in Lancashire, Esq. 3, Margaret, wife of Tho. Stanley, of Dale Garth, in Cumberland, Esq.; 4, ———, married to William Bardsey, of Bardsey, in Lancashire, Esq. and 5, ——— of ——— Thwaites, of Thwaites, in Cumberland, Esq.

In 4 Hen. VIII. there was an award between Alexander Abbot, of Furness, of the one part, and this John Fleming, of the other part, made by Brian Tunstal, John Lowther, of Lowther, John Lamplugh, of Lamplugh, and William Redmayne, of Thwysel-townes, Esqrs. which was, that they should each shew their writings to the next judge of assize, at Lancaster, who should determine, whether the said John Fleming held the manor Coningston, by knights service, and a certain rent of the said monastery; and also that the said Abbot should pay to the said John Fleming, for all such titles and tenant-rights as the said Abbot claims in Furness Fells, except Crag-house, the sum of forty pounds.

In 6 Hen. VIII, this John was escheator for the counties of Cumberland and Westmorland.

He died before 24 Hen. VIII. and was buried at Gresmere Church, in the burying-place belonging to the lords of Rydal, and was succeeded by his son,

14, Hugh Fleming, of Rydal, Esq. who married Joan, or Jane, one of the two sisters and coheiresses of Richard Hodleston, Esq. being also one of the daughters and coheiresses of Sir Richard Hodleston, of Millum Castle, in Cumberland, Knt. Margaret Hodleston, the other daughter, was wife of Lancelot Salkeld, of Whitehall, in the caid county, Esq. The said Sir Richard Hodleston, quartered the arms Millum, Boyvell, Fenwick, Stapleton, Faulconbridge, Fitz-Alan, Marltravers, Ingham, De la Pole, and Chaucer. All which arms, together with their estates which were not intailed upon the males of that family, came to

the said John Fleming, or any of his servants, to take any prisoners, that then the said lord to have the third and the third of thirds. And if it happyn that the said lord send for the said John, to come to him, and to ryde with him to London, or for any other matter, that then the said lord to pay for his costs, and to gyfe him bouchecourt (*a*), for him and his fellowship.

In witness hereof, ayther party to the partyes of these indentures, enterchangably hath set to their seals. Wretyn the day and the yere aforesaid.

(*a*) Meat and drink (from *bouche*, a mouth) scot free. For so in the French *avoir bouche a court*, to be in ordinary at court, and this extended as well to the court of noblemen, who were subjects, as to the king's court.

* After his death she is called *Janet*: for the reconciling of which, it is to be observed, that according to Camden, in late years, some of the better and nicer sort, misliking *Joane*, have mollified the name into *Jane*; for *Jane* is never found in old records, and (as some will have it) not before the time of Hen. VIII. In 32 Eliz. it was agreed by the court of king's bench, that *Jane* and *Joan*, are the same. *Janet*, is a diminutive of *Joan*, as, little or pretty *Joan*.

the said Hugh Fleming, and Lancelot Salkeld, in right of their wives, and descended upon their heirs; and the said arms have been ever since, quartered by the two families of Fleming and Salkeld.

In 33 Hen. VIII. he was made escheator for the counties of Westmorland and Cumberland, and died in 4 Phil. and Mary, being then an old man, and survived most of his children: he had four sons, 1, Anthony; 2, Thomas, who had two sons, Richard, who married ———, heiress of Troughton-hall, by whom he had many children, who spread out into several branches, and John, who had issue Thomas, John, Richard, Roger, Jane, Margaret, Agnes, and Bridget, most of whom married and had children; 3, David, who was steward to Lord William Parr, Marquis of Northampton, and married ———, daughter of Sir John Lamplugh, by whom he had, 1, John, who had a son, Richard; 2, Thomas; 3, Henry; who had a son John; 4, Eleanor; 5, Nicholas, who had issue Robert, Thomas, and Ralph; 6, Robert, who had a son John; 7, David, who was one of Queen Elizabeth's falconers; 8, Adam. 4, Daniel, the fourth son, died without issue. The said Hugh had also a daughter Joan, the wife of Lancelot Lowther, of Sewborwens, in Newton Regney, in Cumberland, gentleman; and by their marriage articles, May 30, 29 Hen. VIII. it was stipulated, that each of the parties should pay for their own marriage apparel, that the meat and drink should be at the charge of the said Hugh, and also the licence; that the said Hugh should give to the said Lancelot and Joan, bedding and in seyghe; as shall stand with his worship to give; and that the portion should be 66l. 13s. 4d. to be paid at the parish church of Lowther.

15, Anthony Fleming, of Rydal, Esq. son and heir of Hugh, married first, ———, daughter of Sir Geffrey Middleton, of Middleton-hall, Knt. by whom he had no issue; secondly, Elizabeth, daughter of William Hoton, of Hoton, in the forest, Esq. and by the marriage articles, May 28, 24 Hen. VIII. it was covenanted, that each party should buy their own wedding cloaths; and that the marriage should be in Hoton Church; and that the said William, should find meat, drink, and other things necessary for the marriage feast; that whereas the said Anthony and Elizabeth, were of cousinage in the fourth degree, a dispensation should be pursued and obtained for the same, at the equal charge of the said Hugh and William, that the whole estate should be intailed upon the issue of the said marriage; and that in consideration thereof, the said William should pay 120l. at several days; and if the said Elizabeth should die without issue, before any of the said days, respectively, so much was agreed not to be paid. By this lady he had one son, William. This Anthony Fleming, married, thirdly, Jane, daughter of John Rigmaden, of Weddicre, in the county of Lancaster, Esq. by whom he had Thomas and Charles.

16, William Fleming, of Rydal, Esq. after the decease of his father, and of Hugh Fleming, his grandfather, became heir to the whole estate.

In 3 Edw. VI. Gabriel Croft, parson of Gresmere, in consideration of the sum of 58l. 11s. 5d. ½ granted a lease of the rectory and tithes of Gresmere to Marian Bellengham, of Helsington, widow, for the term of ninety-seven years, paying yearly to the parson there 18l. 11s. 7d. which lease was confirmed by John Bishop, of Chester, as Ordinary, and by Alan Bellingham, of Helsington, Esq. son of the said Marian, as patron. For until the disabling statue of 13 Eliz. the incumbents of livings with the consent of patron, and ordinary, might grant such leases, and they were valid in law; but by the said statue, they are restrained, (although with such consent) from granting such leases for a longer term than twenty-one years, or three lives.

In 16 Eliz. the said Alan sold to this William Fleming, for the sum of 500l. his interest in the said lease, which had come to him as executor to his said mother deceased.

There had some little time before, been a suit between the said Alan and William, concerning the tithes of the demesne of Rydal, wherein the said William obtained a verdict for a prescription of 20s. a year, to be paid at Easter, or upon demand, for all manner of tithes for the said demesne; which verdict was exemplified under the great seal, 8, Feb. 18 Eliz.

In the same year, the said William sold some tenements, at Lothrigg into freehold.

He married, first, Margaret, daughter of Sir John Lamplugh, of Lamplugh, Knt. by whom he had, 1, Jane, wife of Richard Harrison, of Martindale, gentleman; 2, Margery, of Nicholas Curwen, of Clifton, in Cumberland, gentleman; 3, Elizabeth, of William Carter, of Broughton, in Lancashire, gentleman.

He married secondly, Agnes, daughter of Robert Bindloss, of Borwick, in Lancashire, Esq. by whom he had nine children; 1, John; 2, Thomas, who died without issue; 3, William, who died without issue; he was a stout man, above six feet high, and was in the ship which first descried the Spanish Armada, in 1588, and therein behaved gallantly; 4, Daniel, whose son succeeded as heir in tail, after-failure of heirs male from his eldest brother, John; 5, Joseph, who died without issue; 6, Dorothy, wife of John Ambrose, of Lowick, in Lancashire, Esq.; 7, Mary, wife of John Senhouse, of Seascales-hall, in Cumberland, Esq.; 8, Grace, of Anthony Barwise, of Hyldekirk, in Cumberland, Esq.; 9, Eleanor, of Sir John Lowther, of Lowther, Knt. one of his Majesty's council, at York, for the northern parts; with whom her mother, being then a widow, gave 1000l. for her portion.

17, John Fleming, of Rydal, Esq. son and heir of William, married first, Alice, daughter of Sir Francis Ducket, of Grayrigg, Knt. by whom he had no issue, her portion was 666l. 13s. 4d. Secondly, Bridget, daughter of Sir William Norris, of Speke, in Lancashire, Knt. by whom he had no issue. He married, thirdly, Dorothy, daughter of Sir Thomas Strickland, of Sizergh, K. B. by whom he had one son, William, and two daughters, 1, Bridget, wife of Sir John Crosland, of Haram-how, in the county of York, Knt.; 2, Agnes, of George Collingwood, of Elsington, in Northumberland, Esq.

In 4 James I. his mother Agnes, purchased the manor of Skirwith, and one-third of the manor of Brougham; with divers lands, in Skirwith, Owseby, Crosfell, Langwathby, and Gulgaith. And in the 8th year of the same king, she entailed the same upon her son, Daniel, and his issue, male.

She also purchased Monk-hall, and divers other messuages and tenements in Cumberland; all of which, after her decease or before, came into the family estate. He was justice of the peace for Westmorland, from 7 Jac. (which is the first time that the rolls make mention of him) to 22 Jac. about which time he turned roman catholic. In the 5th year of Charles the first, he procured a supersedeas for his recusancy; and an acquittance for his knighthood money. In the 7th year of the same king, he obtained a licence (being a popish recusant convict) to travel above five miles from Rydall. In the same year he paid to the king for his recusancy, after the rate of 30l. a year; and two years after, according to the proportion of 50l. a year. He died 18 Car. aged about sixty-eight; and was buried at Gresmere Church, in the burying place, belonging to the lords of Rydal. He gave by his will, 2000l. each, to his two daughters for their portions.

William, his son and heir, only fourteen years of age at the time of his death, died of the small pox before he was twenty-one, and unmarried, 1649. By whose death, without issue, his two sisters portions became augmented to 10,000l. each; but the family estate went over to his uncle Daniel, the next heir male.

Young as this William was, he appeared in arms on the king's party; and after his death, the sequestrators put both his and his father's name into their bill of sale, in 1652; which put his heirs to great charge and trouble afterwards, to get the estate cleared from the commonwealth's title. Sir Wilfrid Lawson, of Isel, one of Cromwell's party, plundered and stripped Rydal-hall, of all that was valuable, and tore up the floors to search for hidden treasure.

18, Daniel Fleming, of Skipwith, Esq. married Isabel, daughter of James Brathwaite, of Ambleside, Esq. by whom he had eight children; 1, William; 2, John, who died without issue, and was buried in the chancel of Kirkland Church, May 30, 1662, as appears by the inscription on his tombstone there; 3, Thomas; 4, Joseph; 5, Daniel, who was lieutenant of a troop of horse in the service of Charles I. under the command of the Earl of Newcastle, he died without issue; 6, Agnes, wife of Christopher Dudley, of Yanewith, Esq.; 7, Dorothy, of Andrew Huddeston, of Hutton-John, Esq.; 8, Mary, of Thomas Brougton, of Scales-hall, in Cumberland, Esq. In 9 Jac. he purchased one-third of the manor of Kirkland, and in the next year another third of it, and died Aug. 2, 1621, and was buried in the quire of Kirkland Church, as appears by an inscription engraved in brass on his tomb-stone there.

19, William Fleming, of Skirwith and Rydal, Esq. son and heir of Daniel, on the death of the last William, without issue, succeeded as next heir male to the whole estate; he married Alice, daughter of Roger Kirkby, of Kirkby, in Lancashire, Esq. by whom he had seven children; 1, Daniel; 2, Roger; 3, William, major of a regiment of militia, in Lancashire; 4, John, who died young; 5, John, who was lost on the coast of Africa, on a trading voyage; 6, Alexander, a merchant, at Newcastle, who died without issue; 7, Isabel, who died unmarried.

In 1642, he was major of a regiment of foot, and raised in the neighbourhood, ninety-eight men, which he commanded as captain, to the latter end of 1644, when the counties of Westmorland and Cumberland were totally subdued, except the city of Carlisle, which surrendered to David Lesley, about nine months after, having first endured all the extremities of famine. On the coming in of Duke Hamilton, he again accepted a commission of lieutenant colonel of a regiment of horse, but before the troop was raised, the king's party was routed by Cromwell, near Preston, in Lancashire. He died at Coningston-hall, in 1653, in the forty-fourth year of his age.*

20, Daniel Fleming, of Rydall, Esq. afterwards Knt: heir of William; author of the Memoirs, from which this account is chiefly taken, was entered commoner, in Queen's College, Oxford, 1650, under the Rev. Thomas Smith, afterwards Bishop of Carlisle. In 1653, he got possession of the manors of Rydall, Coningston, and Beckermet, which had for some time been under sequestration; Rydal had been leased out by Mr. John Archer and other committee-men, at Kendal, to Walter Strickland, Esq. uncle to the two daughters of John Fleming, Esq. sisters of William aforesaid, who died without issue; those two daughters claiming, as heirs to their father and brother, against this colateral branch, who claimed by virtue of the intail. In 1655, he purchased the remaining part of the manor of Kirkland, which had not been completed by his father. He was the first sheriff of Cumberland, after the restoration of Charles II. and was knighted by that king, in 1681, for which he paid as the usual fee to the officers, 78l. 13s. 4d. He continued in the interest of that family, till the reign of James II. when, finding the established religion in danger, he joined with the party that opposed his measures, and being one of the burgesses in parliament for Cockermouth, in the first year of the said king, he voted against the court. His election to that borough was contested, yet such was the moderation of those times, that the whole expence did not amount to 20l.

In 1655, he married Barbara, eldest daughter of Sir Henry Fletcher, Bart. (who was killed in the king's party at Routon Heath battle, near Cheshire, 1645),

* He was buried at Gresmere, in the same place where his grandmother Agnes had been buried about twenty years before. His epitaph is on a square piece of brass fixed in the wall, near his grave, on the east side of the church; and on an oblong piece of glass in the east window was this inscription:

Deo trino et uni
Sacrum
Secundum Christi Redemtoris
Adventum hoc templo expectat
Gulielmus Fleming,
Armiger.
Qui pio in Christo expiravit
Conistoniæ, et quicquid mortale
Habuit hic deposuit,
25° Maii,
Anno Epochæ Christinæ,
MDCLIII.

and underneath, the arms of Fleming and Kirby impaled; and above, in the same window, the several coats in colours quartered by the family of Fleming.

TABLE.

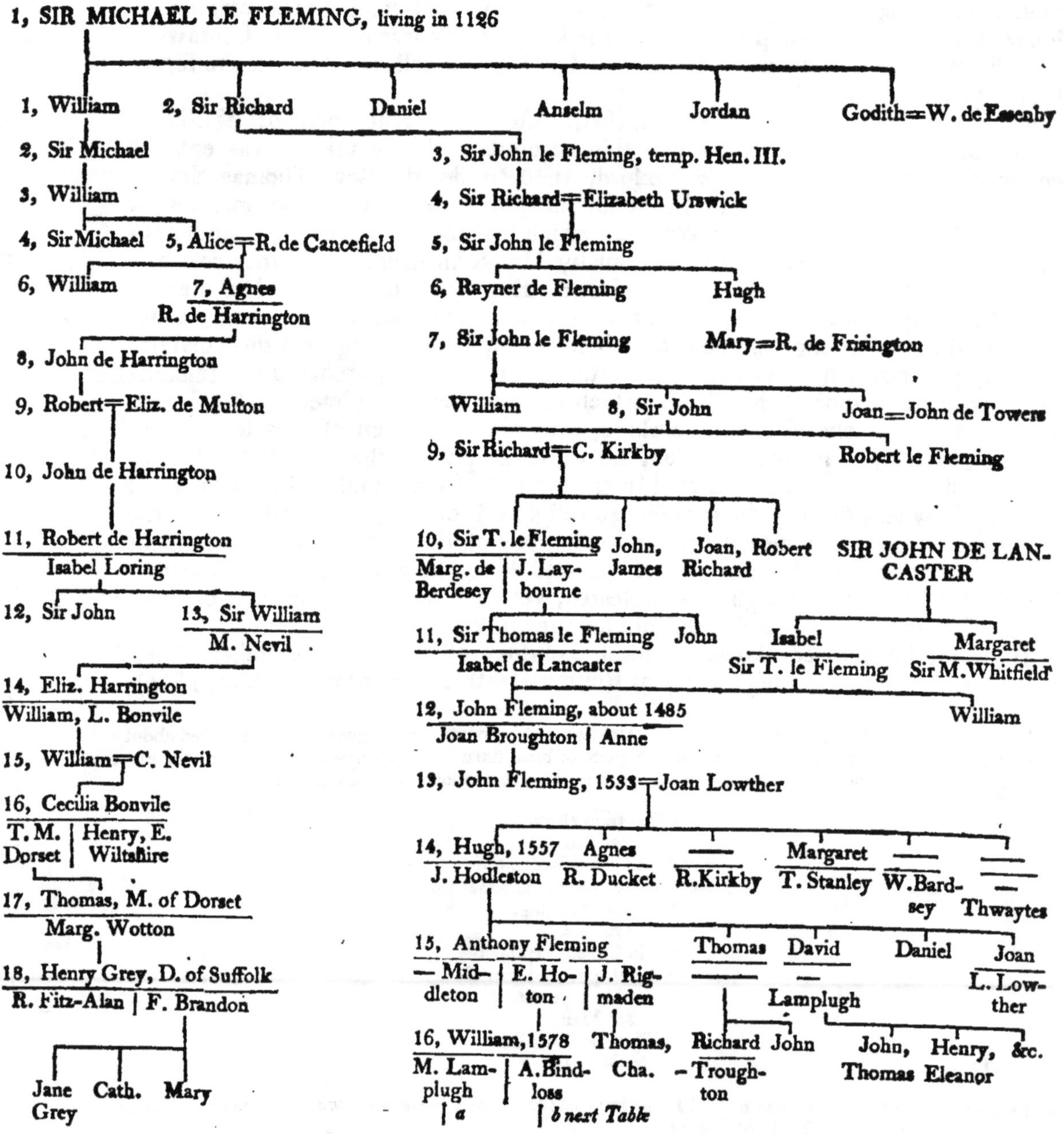
1, SIR MICHAEL LE FLEMING, living in 1126
1, William
2, Sir Richard
Daniel
Anselm
Jordan
Godith=W. de Essenby
2, Sir Michael
3, Sir John le Fleming, temp. Hen. III.
3, William
4, Sir Richard=Elizabeth Urswick
4, Sir Michael
5, Alice=R. de Cancefield
5, Sir John le Fleming
6, William
7, Agnes
R. de Harrington
6, Rayner de Fleming
Hugh
8, John de Harrington
7, Sir John le Fleming
Mary=R. de Frisington
9, Robert=Eliz. de Multon
William
8, Sir John
Joan=John de Towers
9, Sir Richard=C. Kirkby
Robert le Fleming
10, John de Harrington
11, Robert de Harrington
Isabel Loring
10, Sir T. le Fleming
Marg. de Berdesey
J. Lay-bourne
John, James
Joan, Richard
Robert
SIR JOHN DE LANCASTER
12, Sir John
13, Sir William
M. Nevil
11, Sir Thomas le Fleming
Isabel de Lancaster
John
Isabel
Sir T. le Fleming
Margaret
Sir M. Whitfield
14, Eliz. Harrington
William, L. Bonvile
12, John Fleming, about 1485
Joan Broughton | Anne
William
15, William=C. Nevil
13, John Fleming, 1533=Joan Lowther
16, Cecilia Bonvile
T. M. Dorset
Henry, E. Wiltshire
14, Hugh, 1557
J. Hodleston
Agnes
R. Ducket
R. Kirkby
Margaret
T. Stanley
W. Bard-sey
Thwaytes
17, Thomas, M. of Dorset
Marg. Wotton
15, Anthony Fleming
— Mid-dleton
E. Ho-ton
J. Rig-maden
Thomas
David
Daniel
Joan
L. Low-ther
Lamplugh
18, Henry Grey, D. of Suffolk
R. Fitz-Alan | F. Brandon
16, William, 1578
M. Lam-plugh
A. Bind-loss
Thomas, Cha.
Richard
— Trough-ton
John
John, Thomas
Henry, Eleanor
&c.
a
b next Table
Jane Grey
Cath.
Mary

TABLE.

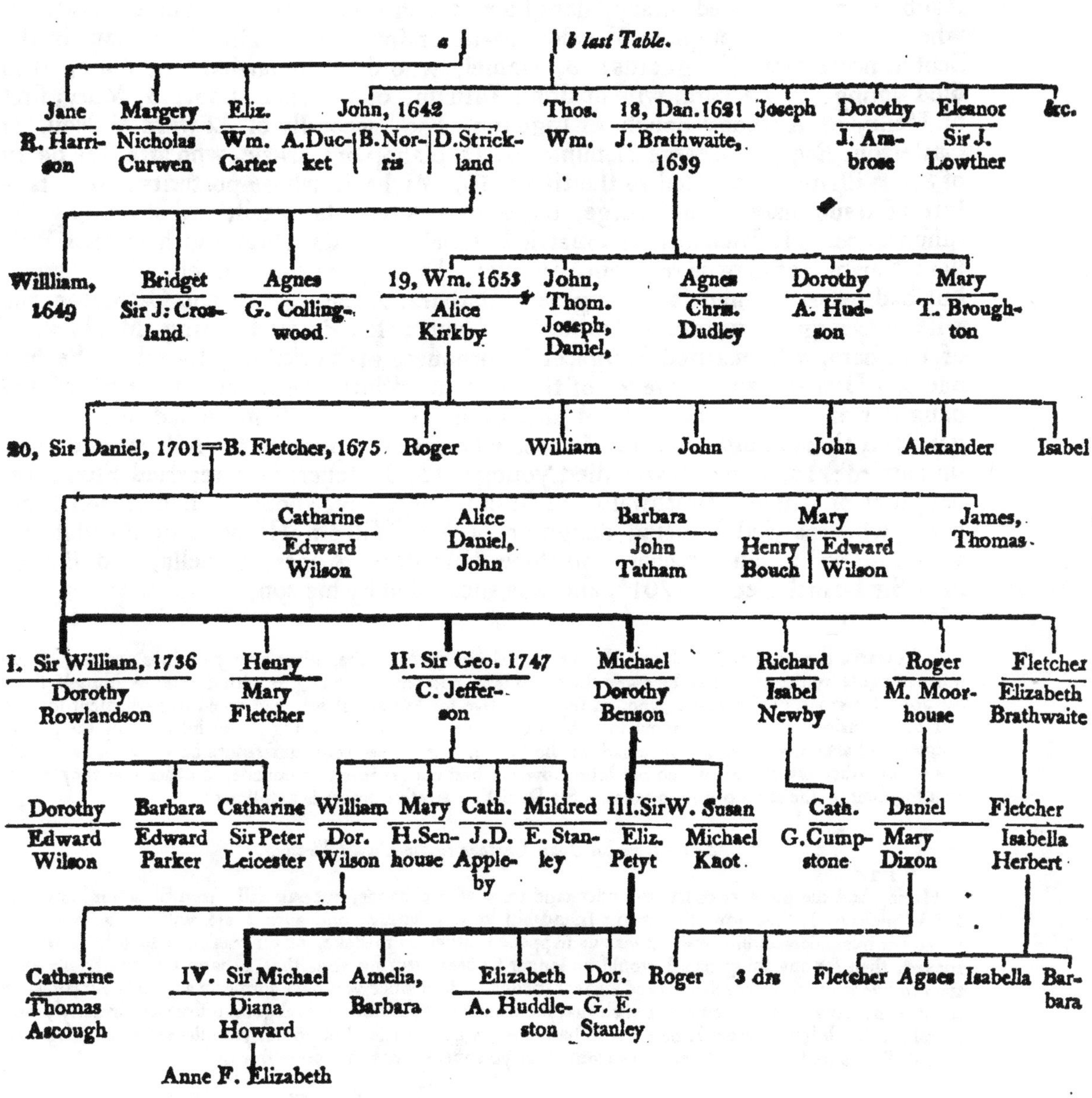
a
b last Table.
Jane
R. Harrison
Margery
Nicholas Curwen
Eliz.
Wm. Carter
John, 1642
A. Ducket
B. Norris
D. Strickland
Thos.
Wm.
18, Dan. 1621
J. Brathwaite, 1639
Joseph
Dorothy
J. Ambrose
Eleanor
Sir J. Lowther
&c.
William, 1649
Bridget
Sir J. Crosland
Agnes
G. Collingwood
19, Wm. 1653
Alice Kirkby
John, Thom. Joseph, Daniel,
Agnes
Chris. Dudley
Dorothy
A. Hudson
Mary
T. Broughton
20, Sir Daniel, 1701=B. Fletcher, 1675
Roger
William
John
John
Alexander
Isabel
Catharine
Edward Wilson
Alice
Daniel, John
Barbara
John Tatham
Mary
Henry Bouch
Edward Wilson
James, Thomas
I. Sir William, 1736
Dorothy Rowlandson
Henry
Mary Fletcher
II. Sir Geo. 1747
C. Jefferson
Michael
Dorothy Benson
Richard
Isabel Newby
Roger
M. Moorhouse
Fletcher
Elizabeth Brathwaite
Dorothy
Edward Wilson
Barbara
Edward Parker
Catharine
Sir Peter Leicester
William
Dor. Wilson
Mary
H. Senhouse
Cath.
J.D. Appleby
Mildred
E. Stanley
III. Sir W.
Eliz. Petyt
Susan
Michael Knot
Cath.
G. Cumpstone
Daniel
Mary Dixon
Fletcher
Isabella Herbert
Catharine
Thomas Ascough
IV. Sir Michael
Diana Howard
Amelia, Barbara
Elizabeth
A. Huddleston
Dor.
G. E. Stanley
Roger
3 drs
Fletcher
Agnes
Isabella
Barbara
Anne F. Elizabeth

and of the lady Catherine, his wife, eldest daughter of Sir George Dalston, of Dalston, in Cumberland, Knt. by whom he had fifteen children; 1, William; 2, Catherine, wife of Edward, son of Edward Wilson, of Dalham-tower, Esq. 3, Alice, who died unmarried; 4, Henry Fleming, D. D. rector of Gresmere and of Ashby; who married Mary, daughter of John Fletcher, of Hunslet, Esq. by whom he had one daughter, Penelope, wife of John Keate, Esq. lieutenant in the Scotch horse grenadier guards; 5, Daniel, who died unmarried; 6, John, who died young; 7, Barbara, wife of John Tatham, of Overhall, Esq.; 8, Mary, first of Henry or Anthony Bouch, of Ingleton, Esq. secondly of Edward Wilson, of Casterton, Esq.; 9, George Fleming, D. D. bishop of Carlisle, who after the death of Sir William. succeeded to the title; 10, Michael, whose posterity, after failure of issue male from George, succeeded as tenants in tail, and still enjoy the inheritance; 11, Richard, who married Isabel, only daughter and heiress of William Newby, of Cawmere, Gent. by whom he had one son Daniel, who married, but had no issue: and four daughters, Barbara, Anne, Isabel, and Catherine, the wife of George Cumston, of Ambleside, Gent.; 12, Roger Fleming, M. A. vicar of Brigham, who married Margaret Moorhouse, of Yorkshire, by whom he had one son Daniel, land-surveyor of the port of Whitehaven, who married Mary, daughter of Joseph Dixon, of Whitehaven, Gent. by whom he had one son Roger, and three daughters; 13, James, who was a captain in the militia, and died unmarried; 14, Thomas, who died young; 15, Fletcher, who married Elizabeth, daughter of Thomas Brathwaite, of Windermere, by whom he had a son Fletcher, who married Isabella, daughter of Mr. William Herbert, of Kendal, by whom he had a son Fletcher, and three daughters, Agnes, Isabella, and Barbara. Sir Daniel died in 1701*, and was succeeded by his son,

* Towards the latter end of James II. Sir Daniel, in his Memoirs, gives a very curious account of the attempt made by the court to take away the penal laws and test. He begins with a letter to himself from Sir John Lowther, of Lowther, who, as representative for Westmorland, had voted in parliament for the bill of exclusion, and was strenuous in opposing the measures then carrying on for introducing the popish religion and arbitrary power. There had, in the former reign, been some differences between the two families of Lowther and Rydal, which Sir John Lowther first endeavours to reconcile, in order that they might join together in the same common cause. Sir Daniel's narrative proceeds as follows:

Letter from Sir John Lowther to Sir Daniel Fleming.

SIR,

Having had the pleasure of late to understand from several hands, but especially from Sir John Lowther, (of Whitehaven), that you still retain a friendship for our family; and sure I am willing to hope, that whatever misunderstanding was betwixt us happened rather by mistake, or for reasons which are now removed, than for any thing else, I would no longer forbear assuring you, that I have no greater pleasure than to live well with my relations and ancient friends. And since you have formerly shewed yourself such upon many occasions, I cannot but wish that there may be the same mutual good offices as formerly; and if, whilst Sir John Lowther is here, who hath always been a friend of yours, you please to visit this place, you shall be sure to find that hearty welcome that you were wont to receive from,

Sir,
Your most affectionate Kinsman,
and humble Servant,
JOHN LOWTHER.

Lowther, Aug. 24, 1687.

I. WILLIAM FLEMING, of Rydal, Esq. who, in 1695, on Sir John Lowther's being made a lord, was chosen to represent the county of Westmorland in

At the same time, Sir John Lowther of Whitehaven, writ to Sir Daniel by the same messenger as followeth:

SIR,

I cannot leave the country without returning you my acknowledgments for your great civilities to both me and my son at the assizes, and for the continued testimonies of your friendship upon all occasions; and if our whole family have not had of late the same advantages thereof that I have enjoyed, it is not unknown how great a trouble it has been to me, nor how often I have wished to be the happy instrument of restoring the good correspondence betwixt so near relations. This, Sir, not I alone, but the whole country, I find, and all good men, have equally desired, and I doubt not to see the wished success; since I can assure you, the same friendship that ever was on our side we do desire may be renewed, and continue as long as the families; which, by the freedom wherewith you were pleased to declare yourself to me at Carlisle upon this subject, is, I hope, what will be most welcome to you. The inclosed, from Sir John himself, will spare me the adding any more, and, I hope, bring you over whilst I stay, which will be till Monday next; and I pray bring your son with you, that the young men may fix their acquaintance.

I am, Sir,
Your most affectionate Kinsman,
and humble Servant,
JOHN LOWTHER.

Lowther, Aug. 24,
1687,

These letters arriving late in the evening, and Sir Daniel's two sons being gone two days before to visit their sisters in Lancashire; and Sir Daniel thinking it necessary to speak with Sir Christopher Musgrave, who was lately come into the country from London, and had writ to Sir Daniel to meet him at Carlisle the week following, he returned the following answers:

SIR, *Rydal, Aug.* 24, 1687.

I thank you for your very obliging letter. which I have this evening received, and for your kind invitation unto Lowther; and I should now have waited upon you and Sir John Lowther according to your desires, had not my two sons, William and Daniel, been gone to Lancashire with my servants and horses. I do concur with you, that whatever misunderstanding was betwixt us, happened rather by mistake than for any thing else; for I ever had a friendship for yourself and family; and without taking any further notice of what is past, upon my part shall be performed the same mutual good offices as formerly. My humble service unto my good lady and all my cousins.

I am, Sir,
Your very affectionate Kinsman,
and most humble Servant,
DANIEL FLEMING.

In answer to Sir John Lowther's, of Whitehaven, he writ as follows:

SIR, *Rydal, Aug.* 24, 1687.

I have even now received yours, with one from Sir John Lowther, and I have made him such a return as I hope will be satisfactory unto you both. I am troubled that I cannot wait on you before you leave this country, and that my son is no better acquainted with my cousin Lowther. I shall ever acknowledge my great obligation unto you for your constant friendship, and for the many favours which I have received from you; and if I may be any way serviceable unto you here in the country, I hope you will favour me with your commands. My humble service unto yourself and my cousin, your son, heartily wishing you both a safe return unto London. My son William and his brother Daniel are now in Lancashire, which hinders me from telling you in person, that I am, Sir,

Your very affectionate Kinsman,
and most faithful Servant,
DANIEL FLEMING.

parliament, and again in 1698, 1702, 1705, and 1707. In 1705, he was created a Baronet, with remainder, for want of issue male of his body, to the issue male

In the mean time, Sir Daniel Fleming had an interview with Sir Christopher Musgrave, who had been displaced some time before from the office of lieutenant of the ordnance, for refusing, as it was said, to promise the king to give his vote for taking away the test and penal laws. About the same time, the king had removed the Earl of Derby from being lord-lieutenant of the county of Lancaster, and put into his place the Lord Molineux; and also removed the Earl of Thanet from being lord-lieutenant of the counties of Westmorland and Cumberland, and put in his place Lord Preston; and that the king's declaration for liberty of conscience might the more easily pass into a law, the council agreed on the three questions following:

1. If in case you shall be chosen knight of a shire, or burgess of a town, when the king shall think fit to call a parliament, whether will you be for taking off the penal laws?

2. Whether you will assist and contribute to the election of such members as shall be for taking off the penal laws and tests?

3. Whether you will support the king's declaration for liberty of conscience, by living friendly with those of all persuasions, as subjects of the same prince and good christians ought to do?

The several lords-lieutenants were ordered to desire the answers of all deputy-lieutenants, to each of the aforesaid questions in particular; but not meeting with the expected success, the following declaration was printed:

WHITEHALL, Dec. 11, 1687.

His Majesty having, by his gracious declaration of the 4th of April last, granted a liberty of conscience to all his subjects: and resolving not only to maintain the same, but to use his utmost endeavours that it may pass into a law, and become an established security to after ages, hath thought fit to renew the lists of the deputy-lieutenants and justices of the peace in the several counties, that those may be continued who shall be ready to contribute, what in them lies, towards the accomplishment of so good and necessary a work, and such others added to them, from whom his Majesty may reasonably expect the like concurrence and assistance.

The Lord Preston's occasions would not give him leave to make such haste into the country as many other lord-lieutenants did; but, in January following, he writ letters to every deputy-lieutenant and justice of the peace within the counties of Westmorland and Cumberland, as followeth:

SIR,

I desire you will meet me at Penrith upon Tuesday, the 24th of this month, about ten of the clock in the morning, having some matters to impart to you by his Majesty's command.

I am, Sir,
Your humble Servant,
PRESTON.

To the letter sent to Sir Daniel Fleming, his lordship added this postscript:

I should be very glad to see you at Hutton, before the meeting at Penrith. I hope to be there on Thursday come se'nnight. My humble service to Mr. Fleming, and believe me to be, Sir,

Your most affectionate and humble Servant,
PRESTON.

Sir Daniel Fleming having not visited Lowther since Sir John Lowther and he were made friends, he thought it right to take Lowther in his way to Penrith, which he did on Jan. 21, being accompanied by his sons, William and Daniel, and his cousin John Brougham, where they were all kindly entertained, and where Sir John and Sir Daniel agreed on their answers to the aforesaid questions.

On the 23d, Sir Daniel Fleming went early to Hutton, and on the day following attended his lordship to Penrith, when they were met by Sir John Lowther in his coach and six, attended by most of the deputy-lieutenants and justices of the peace for Westmorland and Cumberland. After Lord Preston had acquaint-

of Sir Daniel Fleming, his father. He married Dorothy, daughter of Thomas Rowlandson, of Kendal, by whom he had three daughters, 1, Dorothy, wife of Edward Wilson, of Dolham-Tower, Esq.; 2, Barbara, of Edward Parker, of Brodsholm, Esq.; 3, Catharine, of Sir Peter Leicester, of Tabley, Bart. Sir William died at Rydal-Hall, Aug. 29, 1736, was buried at Gresmere, and was succeeded by his brother,

II. Sir GEORGE FLEMING, Bart. the fifth son of Sir Daniel Fleming, Knt. he was entered commoner of Edmund-Hall, Oxford, June 1688. In 1690, he, amongst others of the university, printed congratulatory verses upon his Majes-

ed them with the reasons of their being called together, he desired them either to deliver their answers in writing, or that they would permit his lordship to call in his secretary to write them. Upon which Sir John Lowther replied, that he conceived it would be more for his lordship's ease to permit every gentleman to write his own answer, which was seconded by Sir Daniel Fleming; adding, that if his lordship would give leave to the gentlemen to withdraw, they would return with their several answers in writing. The Protestants went into one room, and the Papists into another. On their return, Sir John Lowther read his answer as follows:

1. If I be chosen a member of parliament, I think myself obliged to refer my opinion concerning the taking away the penal laws and tests, to the reasons that shall arise from the debate of the house.

2. If I give my interest for any to serve in the next parliament, it shall be for such as I shall think loyal and well-affected to the king and the established government.

3. I will live friendly with those of several persuasions, as a loyal subject and a good christian ought to do.

After which, Sir Daniel Fleming and many others gave in the same answers. The papists, with a few others, were for taking away the tests.

Lady Barbara Fleming died before her husband, and on an oblong piece of brass fixed in the wall, at the east end of Gresmere church, he caused the following inscription to be engraved:

Barbaræ Fleming,

Henrici Fletcher, de Hutton, in comitatu Cumbriæ, Baronetti, et Catherinæ, uxoris ejus, (Filiæ primogenitæ Georgii Dalston, de Dalston, in eodem comitatu, equitis Aurati) Filiæ natu maximæ, et Danielis Fleming, de Rydal, in comitatu Westmerlandiæ, Armigeri, amantissimæ, amabilissimæ, fidelissimæque conjugi, in ipso ætatis Flore Morte immaturâ præreptæ;

Quæ
ob felicissimam Indolem, insignem Pietatem,
ingentem charitatem, singularem Modestiam,
summam Probitatem, generosam Hospitalitatem,
vigilantem bonæ Parentis curam,
moresque suavissimos,
magnum sui apud omnes Desiderium relinquens;
Corpus Humo, amorem sponso et amicis,
Benedictionem quatuordecim liberis,
(decem nempe pueris, ac quatuor puellis,)
Cœloque animam legavit;
Monumentum hoc, amoris et mœroris perpetuum testem,
Charissimus posuit maritus.
Nata est apud Hutton, 25 Julii, A. D. 1634.
Nupta ibidem 27 Aug. A. D. 1655.
Confirmata apud Withenslack, 22 Junii, A. D. 1671.
Mortua apud Rydal, de xvtâ Prole)
13 Apr. A. D. 1675.
Lector,
Si lugere nescias, (quod præstat) æmulare.

ty's happy return from Ireland; and, in the beginning of March, 1694, took his master's degree. In 1699, he was made chaplain to Dr. Smith, bishop of Carlisle. March 12, 1700, he was installed prebendary of Carlisle; and April 12, 1705, archdeacon of the said diocese. He was created doctor of laws, by diploma, at Lambeth, March 10, 1726, and installed dean of Carlisle, April 27, 1727. On the 30th of October, 1734, he was nominated to the see of Carlisle. He married Catharine, daughter of Robert Jefferson, and one of the coheiresses of Thomas Jefferson, of the city of Carlisle, Gent. by whom he had issue, 1, William Fleming, M. A. archdeacon of Carlisle, who married Dorothy, daughter of Daniel Wilson, of Dalham-Tower, Esq. by whom he had one daughter Catharine, wife of Thomas Ascough, Esq. This William died in the lifetime of his father, without other issue, whereby the inheritance became transferred to another collateral male branch; 2, Mary, wife of Humphrey Senhouse, of Nether-Hall, Esq.; 3, Barbara, died young; 4, Catharine, wife of Joseph-Dacre Appleby, of Kirklington, Esq.; 5, Mildred, of Edward Stanley, of Ponsonby, Esq.; 6, Elizabeth, who died in her infancy. The direct male line failing again on the death of George, we have recourse to his next brother Michael, who was major of a regiment of foot, and the tenth child as aforesaid of Sir Daniel. He married Dorothy Benson, of Yorkshire, and dying before his brother George, he left issue a son William, and a daughter Susan, wife of Michael Knott, of Rydal, Gent. Sir George died July 2, 1747, aged 81.

III. Sir WILLIAM FLEMING, of Rydal, Bart. succeeded his uncle, and married Elizabeth, daughter of Christopher Petyt, of Skypton, Gent. by whom he had issue, 1, Michael, the present Baronet; 2, Amelia; 3, Barbara, both of whom died unmarried; 4, Elizabeth, wife of Andrew Huddleston, of Hutton-John, in Cumberland, Esq.; 5, Dorothy, of George-Edward Stanley, of Ponsonby-Hall, in Cumberland, Esq. This Sir William, from his veneration for antiquity, was desirous to restore the primitive orthography of the family name, by inserting the particle *le*; and in this instance, effectually performed it, by incorporating the particle with his son's christian name at his baptism, who thereby bears the same name with the first founders of the family after the conquest. Sir William was succeeded by his son,

IV. Sir MICHAEL LE FLEMING, Bart. who has been knight of the shire for the county of Westmorland ever since 1774. He married Diana, only daughter of Thomas, Earl of Berkshire, by whom he has one daughter Anne-Frederica-Elizabeth le, born about 1785.

ARMS—Gules, a fret, argent.

CREST—A serpent, nowed, holding in his mouth a garland of olives and vines, all proper.

MOTTO—*Pax, copia, sapientia,* all relating to the crest, as peace to the olive branches, plenty to the vine, and wisdom to the serpent.

SEAT—Rydal Hall, Westmorland.

224. MILLER, of CHICHESTER, Sussex.

Created Baronet, Oct. 29, 1705.

I. THOMAS MILLER, Esq. representative in parliament for the city of Chichester 1688 and 1690, had a large fortune left him by his uncle, was knighted, and advanced to the dignity of a Baronet by Queen Anne, in the fourth year of her reign. He married Hannah, daughter of ——, by whom he had Sir John, his successor, and other children; for one of his daughters was wife of John Farrington, of Chichester, Esq. eldest son of Sir Richard Farrington, of Chichester, Bart. Sir Thomas died Dec. 2, 1705, aged 70, and his lady Jan. 11, 1706, aged 70.

II. Sir JOHN MILLER, Bt. eldest son and successor to his father, represented the city of Chichester in several parliaments, in the reigns of K. William and Q. Anne. He married first, Margaret, daughter of John Peachy, of Chichester, who died Sept. 23, 1701, aged 38, by whom he had one son Thomas, who died young, and a daughter Emblem, who died Jan. 6, 1718, aged 17. He married secondly, Anne, daughter of William Elson, of Groves, in Sussex, Esq. by whom he had two children that died young; thirdly, ——, eldest daughter of Sir William Meaux, of Kingston, in the Isle of Wight, Bart. Sir John died Nov. 29, 1721, aged 56, and lies buried in Chichester cathedral, leaving, by his marriage, Sir Thomas, his successor. Besides Sir Thomas, he had other children, for one of his daughters was wife of the Rev. Dr. Gooch, Bishop of Norwich; another, of the Rev. Dr. Manningham; another, of the Rev. —— Blackshall, one of the residentiaries of Chichester, and fellow of Winchester-College; and another, of Thomas Yates, Esq. member of parliament for Chichester; and another, of Mr. Dutton, near Guildford.

III. Sir THOMAS MILLER, Bart. eldest son and successor to Sir John, was likewise representative in parliament for Chichester, in the reigns of Queen Anne and King George I. and married ——, daughter of alderman Gother, of Chichester, by whom he left three sons, 1, Sir John; 2, Thomas, who died unmarried, aged about 21; and 3, Henry: and one daughter Jane, wife of —— Bye. Sir Thomas died at Lavent, near Chichester, Nov. 1733, and was succeeded in dignity and estate by his eldest son,

IV. Sir JOHN MILLER, Bart. who married ——, daughter of Dr. Combes, a physician of Winchester, by whom he had two sons and four daughters, Sir Thomas, his successor, George, Jane, Mary, Susanna, and Anne, who was the wife of George, Earl of Albemarle. Sir John was succeeded by his eldest son,

V. Sir THOMAS MILLER, Bart.

ARMS—Argent, a fess wavy, azure, between three wolve's heads erased, gules.

CREST—On a wreath, a wolf's head erased, argent, gorged with a fess wavy, azure.

Not being able to procure any information from this family, I am obliged to give it as it stands in Kimber and Johnson.

TABLE.

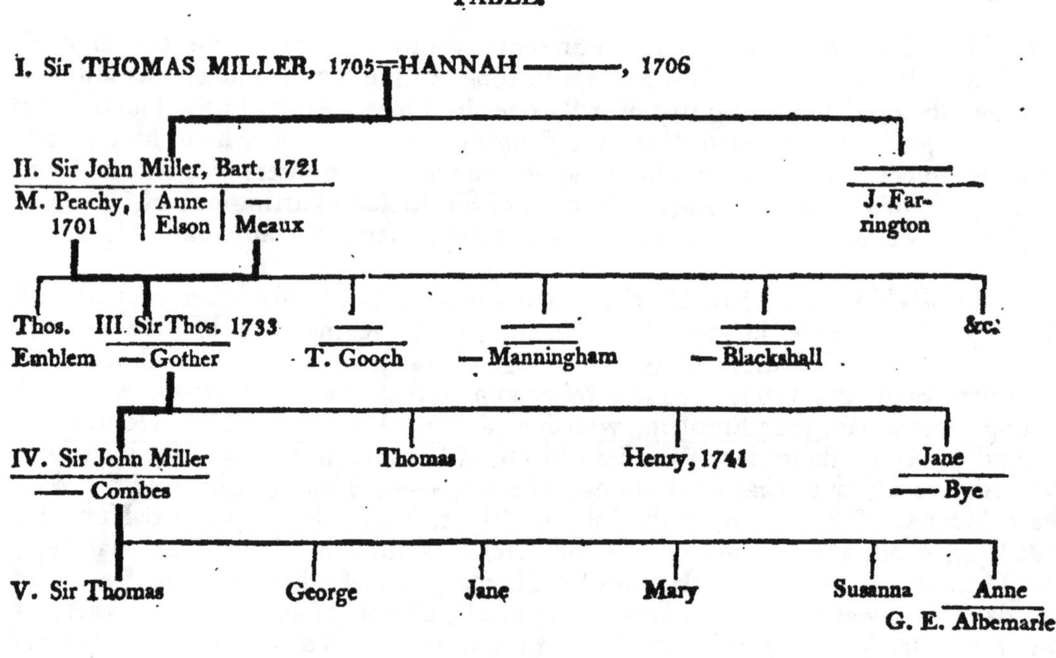

225. DASHWOOD, of West-Wycombe, Bucks.

Created Baronet, June 28, 1707.

THIS family was originally of Dorsetshire, and from thence removed into Somersetshire.

1, Samuel Dashwood, of Rowney, near Taunton, in Somersetshire, Esq. He married ——, daughter of ——, by whom he had four sons, 1, John, ancestor to the Dashwoods of Essex and Suffolk; 2, Francis, of whom hereafter; 3, Richard, who left issue; 4, William, who fined for alderman, and lived at Cheshunt, in Hertfordshire, and left issue. He married secondly, ——, daughter of ——, by whom George Dashwood, Esq. ancestor to Sir Henry-Watkin Dashwood, Bart. of whom we have already treated, *Vol.* III. *P.* 68.

2, Francis Dashwood, Esq. second son of Samuel aforesaid, was a Turkey merchant, and alderman of London. He married Alice, sister to alderman Sleigh, by whom he had three sons and four daughters, 1, Elizabeth, wife of Thomas

Lewis, Esq.; 2, Mary, of John Coppin, of Hertfordshire, Esq.; 3, Martha, of William Roberts, merchant; 4, Sarah, of Fulk Grevile, Lord Brooke. Of the sons, 1, Sir Samuel, was lord-mayor of London, who married Anne, daughter of John Smith, of Tedworth, in Hants, Esq. and sister of the late speaker Smith, by whom he had George, Thomas, Elizabeth, wife of Andrew Archer, of Umberslade, in Warwickshire, Esq. ancestor to Lord Archer; Sarah, of Richard Crawley, Esq.; Annabella, Henrietta, and Sophia; 2, Thomas, married Penelope, daughter of —— Hillersdon, Esq. and left issue. His third son was,

I. Sir FRANCIS DASHWOOD, Bart. so created June 28, 1707. He married first, Mary, only daughter of John Jennings, of Westminster, Gent. by whom he had two daughters, Mary, wife of Sir Fulwar Skipwith, of Newbold-Hall, in Warwickshire, Bart.; and Susanna, of Sir Orlando Bridgeman, of Ridley, in Cheshire, Bart. He married secondly, Mary, daughter of Vere, Earl of Westmorland, by whom he had one son Sir Francis, his successor, and one daughter Rachel, who was the wife (Nov. 1738) of Sir Robert Austen, of Bexley, in Kent, Bart.: she died Aug. 19, 1710*. He married thirdly, Mary, daughter of major King, niece to Dr. King, master of the Charter-House, by whom he had Sir John-Dashwood King, the late Baronet; Charles, born Nov. 4, 1717, and died at Paris unmarried; Henrietta, who died young; and Mary, wife of John Walcot, of Walcot, in Shropshire, Esq. He married fourthly, Elizabeth, daughter of Thomas Windsor, Earl of Plymouth, by whom he had no issue. Sir Francis died Nov. 4, 1724, and was succeeded by his eldest son,

II. Sir FRANCIS DASHWOOD, Bart. who was born Dec. 1708. He served in two parliaments for New Romney, and in 1761, for Melcomb Regis. On the death of John, Earl of Westmorland, Aug. 15, 1762, he succeeded in right of

* She lies buried in the church upon the hills of West Wycombe, with this inscription:

Here rests, in hope
Of a glorious resurrection of the just,
The R[t] Hon. the Lady Mary Dashwood,
Eldest daughter
To the R[t] Hon. Vere Fane, Earl of Westmorland,
And wife to Sir Francis Dashwood, Knt. and Bart.
A lady whose high birth
Received a greater lustre from her eminent virtues,
And whose piety, humility, and prudence,
Made her life and character
Truly noble, truly good.
She was
A most loving and obedient wife,
A tender and indulgent parent,
A careful and kind mistress to her family:
Her diffusive charity made her a refuge for the poor,
And her devout life an illustrious example
To the best of her sex.
Hence learn
To imitate her virtues,
And lament her loss.
She left issue one son Francis, and one daughter Rachel,
And died the 19th Day of August, 1710, in the 35th year of her age.

his mother to the barony of Le Despencer, but he had not the confirmation of the barony and writ of summons until April 19, 1763. He was made keeper of the grand wardrobe April 29, 1763, and on May following, lord-lieutenant of the county of Buckingham. He was likewise chancellor of the exchequer from May 29, 1762, to April 16, 1763, and joint paymaster-general for many years. He married Sarah, daughter of Thomas Gould, of Iver, Esq. and widow of Sir Richard Ellis, who died Jan. 19, 1769 *, but had no issue; and dying Dec. 11, 1781, was succeeded in the barony by his sister, Lady Austen, on whose decease, in May 1788, Sir Thomas Stapleton, descended from Catharine, third daughter of Vere, Earl of Westmorland, became Baron Le Despencer, and the baronetage and manor of West Wycombe descended to his half brother,

III. Sir JOHN-DASHWOOD KING, Bart. who was born Aug. 4, 1716, and married Sarah, daughter of Blundel Moore, of Byfleet, in Surry, Esq, by whom he had two sons, Sir John-Dashwood King, the present Baronet; George, who married ——, daughter of —— Callender: and two daughters, Elizabeth, wife of Captain Lechmere; and Sarah, of Thomas Walcot, Esq. by whom he had George, Francis, Mary, Elizabeth, and John. Sir John died Dec. 6, 1793, and was succeeded by his eldest son,

IV. Sir JOHN-DASHWOOD KING, Bart. who married Mary-Anne, daughter of Theodore-Henry Broadhead, Esq. by whom he has issue Mary, George-Henry, Francis, Elizabeth, John, Edwin, and Henry.

* At the east end of West Wycombe Church, Lord Le Despencer erected an extensive mausoleum of flint, with a frize and cornice, supported by Tuscan pillars. Its form is hexagonical, without any roof. On the inside cornice is this inscription:

TO JOHN, EARL OF WESTMORLAND.
On the other side:
To GEORGE DODDINGTON, BARON of MELCOMB-REGIS, whose legacy to LORD LE DESPENCER, to erect a Monument to him, was the motive that induced his Lordship to plan this singular Structure.

There are recesses for monuments, and smaller hitches for the reception of urns and busts: a few only at present are filled up.

In the centre, a beautiful altar monument of marble under a canopy, supported by four stone pillars:

May this Cenotaph,
Sacred to the virtues and graces
That constitute
Female excellence,
Perpetuate
The memory of
Sarah,
Baroness Le Despencer,
Who finished a most
Exemplary life
January 19th, 1769.

On the other side:
Mors solamen miseris.

ARMS—Argent, on a fess double cottised, gules, three griffin's heads erased, or.

CREST—On a wreath, a griffin's head erased, per fess, erminois, and gules.

SEAT—At West-Wycombe, in Buckinghamshire.

TABLE.

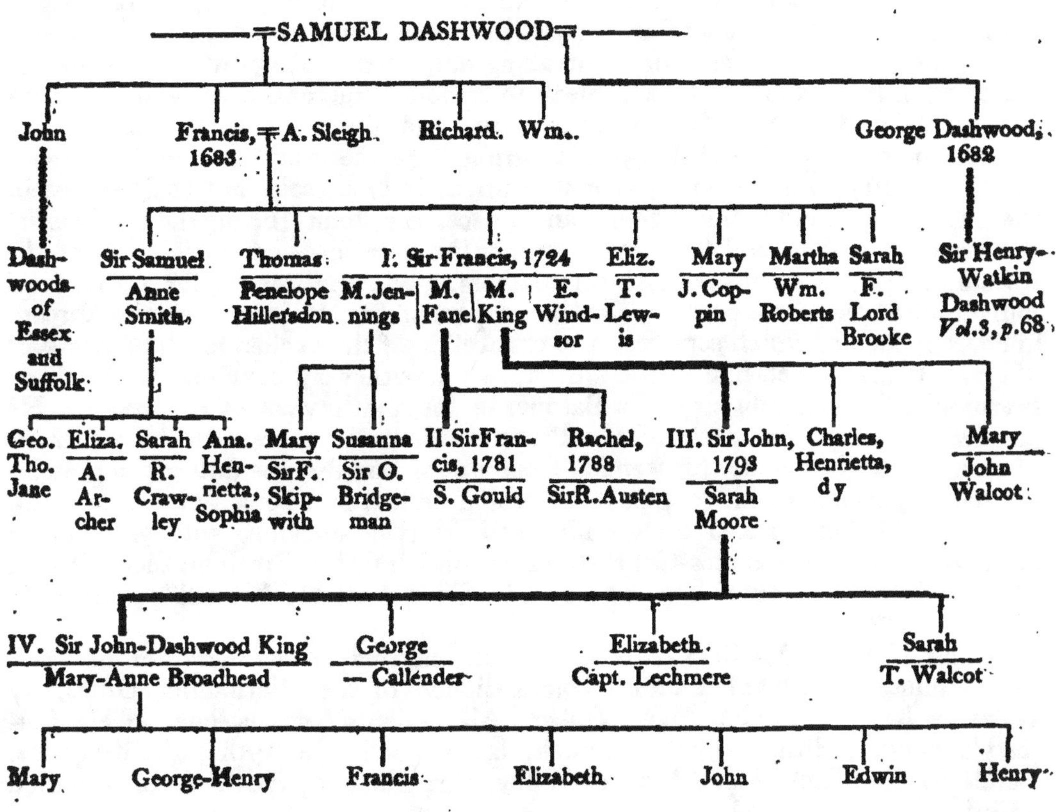

226. LAMBERT, of LONDON.

Created Baronet, Feb. 16, 1710–11.

THIS family is descended from John Lambert, of the Isle of Rhe, who lived in good reputation in that country, being bred to the law, though he came originally from the county of Devon, in England.

John Lambert, his son, was a merchant at St. Martin's, in the said island, and was greatly esteemed by the governor and others, the chief of that country; and so well beloved, that notwithstanding his being a Protestant, yet he lived unmolested in the times of the hottest persecution; and, to prevent his children being perverted to the popish religion, he sent them into England, and continued himself in France, where he died, and was buried in the year 1702, leaving issue by Mary Le Fevre, John, James, who died in Jamaica, and a daughter, who married in Holland.

I. JOHN, the eldest son, was born in 1666, and at fourteen years of age came over to England to be educated and instructed in the English language; and, after being at school at Camberwell for some time, returned to France in 1684; and, upon the persecution breaking out, returned again to England in 1685; and, soon after, he took himself to trade and merchandize, and was very serviceable in promoting our manufactures, and the trade to the plantations, wherein he made great addition to his fortune. In the year 1710, in the changes of the ministry, when monied men shut up their cash, sold out their shares in the pablc funds, and national credit sunk apace, Sir John (being then a knight) was the most zealous and forward to supply the new lords commissioners of the treasury; and, in company with some others, made remittances for upwards of four hundred thousand pounds, for the support of her Majesty's armies abroad, in consequence of which services, the chancellor of the exchequer (the late Earl of Oxford) introduced him to the Queen, who, with very gracious expressions, bestowed on him the dignity of a Baronet in the ninth year of her reign. He married Madelaine, daughter of Mr. Benjamin Beuzelin, a considerable merchant of Rouen, in Normandy (descended from a noble family, his father being disinherited on account of his religion), by whom he had four sons, John, Benjamin, Francis, and James: also three daughters, Mary-Madelaine, wife of Mynheer Hop, envoy from the States-General, Susan, and Judith. Sir John died Feb. 4, 1722-3; his lady survived him, and died in Clarges-street, Piccadilly, in April, 1737, aged 70.

II. Sir JOHN LAMBERT, his eldest son, married Mary, daughter of Tempest Holmes, Esq. late one of the commissioners of the Victualling Office, by whom he had issue, John, Mary, Robert, Alexander, a commissioner of his Majesty's navy, Judith, Benjamin Liddeh, late major in the 19th light dragoons, Berkley-Fitzwilliam, Anne, Frances-Wilhelmina-Massam, and George, who died an infant.

III. Sir JOHN LAMBERT, his successor, was born and baptized in the parish of St. Peter-le-Poor, in Broad-street, Oct. 11, 1728. He married (Aug. 9, 1752) Miss Le Nieps, by whom he had issue John, born May 1, 1755, and died at the age of five years; and Henry. Sir John died May 21, 1799, aged 71, and was succeeded by his son,

IV. Sir HENRY LAMBERT, the present Bart. who married Miss Whyte, by whom he has issue, Henry-John, Frederick-Robert, Francis-John, and Lionel-Hyde.

ARMS—Argent, on a mount, an oak-tree, vert, and, a greyhound passant, gules.

CREST—Three white plumes issuing from a ducal coronet.

MOTTO—*Seguitando si Giunge.*

SEAT—Mount Ida, Norfolk.

TABLE.

JOHN LAMBERT

John Lambert, 1709 = Mary Le Fevre

I. Sir John Lambert, 1722 = M. Benzelin, 1737 | James | ———, a dr

II. Sir John Lambert = Mary Holmes | Benjamin | Francis | James | Mary = M. Hop | Susanna | Judith

III. Sir John Lambert, 1799 = Mary Le Nieps | Mary, = R. Alex. | Judith, = B. Liddell | B. Fitzwilliam, = Agnes | F. Wilhelmina = Massam | George

John | IV. Sir Henry Lambert = Sophia Whyte

Henry-John | Frederick-Robert | Francis-John | Lyonel-Hyde

227. LAKE, of the MIDDLE-TEMPLE, London.

Created Baronet, Oct. 17, 1711.

FROM an ancient manuscript pedigree now before me, it appears that this family is descended from Hugh de Caley, of Owby, in the county of Norfolk, who died in 1286, and by Agnes, his wife, daughter and heiress of Hamo de Hamsted, had one son,

Sir William Cayley, of Owby, Knt. the father of

John Cayley, of Owby, Esq. who had two sons, Sir William and

John Cayley, of Normanton, in Yorkshire, who had three sons, Hugh, who died S. P. William, and John.

William Cayley, the second son, was of Normanton, and had one daughter and heiress,

1, Jennet, the wife of John Lake, Esq. by whom she had,

2, John Lake, of Normanton, Esq. the father of,

3, John Lake, of Normanton, Esq. the father of,

4, John Lake, of Normanton, Esq. who had two sons, John, who died without issue, and,

5, Lancelot Lake, of Normanton, who married Margaret, daughter of Henry Twisleton, of Cryde-Cynge-Park, and Elizabeth, his wife, by whom he had one son,

6, John Lake, of Normanton, who married Catharine, daughter of John Pake, of Wakefield, in Yorkshire, by whom he had ten children, 1, John Lake, of Normanton, living in 1585, who married Mary, daughter of William Beane, widow of John Colthurst, of Ownsby, in Lincolnshire, and died without issue; 2, Beatrix, wife, first, of Robert Jackson, of Tuxford; secondly, of John Barley, of Tuxford; 3, Thomas Lake, of Barley, living in 1585, who married Anne, daughter of Christopher Twisleton, of Barley, by whom he had one daughter Anne, seven years old in 1585, wife of Oliver Beale, of Woodhouse, in the parish of Drax, in Yorkshire, with whom he had Normanton, and by her had six sons, George, Paul, John, Amyel, Thomas, and Joseph; and two daughters, Anne and Mary; 4, Lancelot, of whom hereafter; 5, Alexander; 6, Robert, who died without issue; 7, Catharine; 8, Jane; 9, Bridget; 10, Elizabeth.

7, Lancelot, the third son of John, married Emma, daughter of Robert Northend, of Hallifax, in Yorkshire, by whom he had three sons, 1, John; 2, Thomas; 3, Lancelot; and three daughters, Beatrix, Thomasine, and Ellen.

8, John, the eldest, son of Lincelot, is, I suppose, the John Lake, of Erby, Lincolnshire; who married ——, daughter of ——, Osgarby, by whom he had one son,

9, Richard Lake, of Erby, who married, first, Anne, youngest daughter and coheiress of Edw. Wardell, of Keelby, in Lincolnshire, by whom he had one son,

I. Sir EDWARD LAKE, Bart. chancellor of the diocese of Lincoln *, who

* His loyalty to Charles I. was very remarkable, as appears by the following grant.

G. R. Whereas, our trusty and well-beloved Edward Lake, doctor of laws, our advocate-general for our kingdom of Ireland, in all causes, ecclesiastical, civil, and military, hath performed to us good faithful service, both in Ireland and England, and thereby suffered the loss of his estate in both kingdoms, which, when God shall enable us, we intend to repair, and further reward him: Our will and pleasure therefore is, that we do hereby grant to the said Edward Lake, the nominating and making of a Baronet, being confident, that he will nominate a man of meet and fitting qualities and condition for that dignity. And for his further encouragement, and as a special mark of our gracious acceptation of his good services, and more particularly at the battle of Edge-Hill, where he received sixteen wounds, to the extreme hazard of his life, and his left arm being then disabled by a shot, he held his bridle in his teeth.

We do therefore confer upon him a baronetship, and do hereby create him a Baronet, and do give him for a coat of augmentation to be borne before his own, viz. In a field, *gules, an armed right arm, carrying upon a sword a banner, argent, charged with a cross between sixteen shields of the first, and a lion of England in the fess point:* and for a crest, *a chevalier in a fighting posture, his scarf red, his left arm hanging down useless, and holding his bridle in his teeth; his face, sword, armour, and horse, cruenated.* The said baronetship to the said Edward, and his heirs male of his body lawfully begotten; and for want of such heirs male, to the heirs male of the said Edward; the said coat of augmentation, and the crest, to him the said Edward and his heirs, and to all descending from him or them for ever: all this to be put in form in his patent.

Given at our court, at Oxford, the 30th day of December, the 19th year of our reign.

Notwithstanding the above grant, none of the heirs of the above Edward took out the patent, till Sir Bibye Lake, in 1711, laid the said grant before the Earl of Oxford, in order for a patent; but the said Earl, lost it. Her Majesty being well satisfied with the servicies of Edward Lake, granted a new one, though with precedency only from the date thereof.

married Anne, daughter and coheiress of Simon Bibye, of Bugden, in Huntingdonshire, by whom he had one son, Edward, who died young. Sir Edward died in 1674, and lies burried in the Cathedral of Lincoln †. Richard Lake, the father of Sir Edward, married to his second wife Anne, daughter of —— Morelly, of Claxby, in the county of Lincoln, by whom he had two sons Thomas and John.

Thomas Lake, the elder son, married Mary, daughter of Stephen Goodyer, of London, goldsmith, by whom he had one son,

Thomas Lake, of Bishop's Norton, in Lincolnshire, and of the Middle Temple, Esq. barrister at law, heir to his uncle Sir Edward; he married Elizabeth, daughter of John Storey, of Kniveton, in Derbyshire, Esq. and died May 22, 1711, leaving one son, Bibye, and a daughter, Mary ‡.

† Over him is this Inscription.

Depositum D. Edri Lake, de Norton Episc. in Agro Lincoln. Bar[ti] LL.D. Dioces. Linc. Cancellar Regiæ Majestat. p. Rno suó Hiberniæ Advocati General. ex antiqua familia ejusdem Cognomin. Normantoniæ juxta Pontefract, in Agro Eboracensi, hic subtus jacet. Qui Deo, Ecclisæ. Regi, & Patriæ suæ, Pacis & Belli tempore, fideliter inservijt. Honor inde adeptum Cristæ & Insignior. Augmentatio honoraria Die Anno a Partwf Virgineo 16 Animam demonstrat ad Annum Ætat sue pvectds. Deo reddidit in Uxor. habuit hic juxta contumulatam Annam Filiam Natu maximam & Cohæredem Simon. Bibye, Armigeri, Fæminam lectissimam, pijssimam Fortunæ Conjugalis, Temporibus durissimis Comitem, Participem patientem, constantem, fidelem maxime.

Un Dieu, un Roy, un Cœur.
Patruo suo charissimo Thomas Lake posuit.

In Normanton church is this inscription.

Edwardus Lake de Norton Episcopo, in
Comitatu Lincolniensi Eques Auratus,
L. L. D. Dioceseos Lincolniensis Cancellarius,
In Majorum memoriam qui olim in hoc oppido
Normantoniæ habitaverunt, hoc Horologium
Dedit, ac etiam decem solidos ad reparationem
Ejusdem annuatior in perpetuam solvendos,
Deo et Carolis Regibus dominis suis
Presertim, Carolo Martyri Pacis et Belli
Tempus fideliter nec non insigniter inserviet.
Et animam Deo pie reddidit 18 die Julii anno
Etatis suæ, 77 Annoq. Domini 1674.
El Ecclesia Cathedrali Beatæ Mariæ Lincoln
Sepultus jacet.

‡ He lies buried in the Temple church, where is a monument, near the north corner of the middle east window, with this inscription:

M. S.
Neer this place lye interred,
The remains of Tho. Lake, Esq;
Utter Barrister of the
Hon. Society of the middle Temple;
Nephew and heir of
Sir Edw. Lake.

II. Sir BIBYE LAKE, Bart. subgovernor of the African company, married Mary, daughter and heiress of William Atwell, of London, Esq. who died in 1769, by whom he had three sons and one daughter, Anne, born Nov. 1, 1715, wife of Samuel Jones, of Stepney, who died June 27, 1736, and was buried under a neat marble monument on the north side of the burial ground of Poplar chapel, near Limehouse, Middlesex, on which monument are several inscriptions for the Jones family; 1, Sir Atwell, his successor; 2, Bibye, who married Anne, daughter of ———, Sperling; 3, William, married Susanna, daughter of ———, Pinkerton, and died 1779; Sir Bibye died 1744, and was succeeded by his eldest son,

III. Sir ATWELL LAKE, Bart. who married Mary, only daughter of James Winter, of Mile-End, Esq. by whom he had seven children, 1, Sir James; 2, Mary, wife of William Webb; 3, Edward; 4, Anne; 5, Atwell; 6, Jane; 7, William. Sir Atwell died ———, and was succeeded by his son,

IV. Sir JAMES WINTER LAKE, Bart. who married Joyce, daughter of John Crowther, of Bow, in Middlesex, Esq. by whom he has had thirteen children; 1, Mary, wife of John Wigston, Esq.; 2, Jessie; 3, Edward; 4, Charlotte, wife of Henry-Hare Townshend, Esq.; 5, James; 6, Samuel; 7, William; 8, Willoughby-Thomas, who married Charlotte, daughter of the Vice Admiral Macbride; 9, Atwell; 10, Susanna; 11, Anne; 12, Andrew; 13, Henry.

ARMS—1, By augmentation, *vide* the grant; 2, Sable on a bend, between six cross crosslets, argent, a cheveron between three boars heads couped, sable; 4, Quarterly, argent, and sable, on a bend of the last, three Fleurs-de-Lis, Argent.

CREST—By augmentation, *vide* grant.

MOTTO—*Un dieu, un roy, un cœur.*

SEAT—Edmonton, Middlesex.

Late of Bishop's Norton in the
County of Lincoln, who for
His Loyalty and Valour, signalized
At Edgehill Fight, was created Baronet,
By K. Charles I.
He died May 28, in the 54th
Year of his age.
An. Dom. MDCCI.

TABLE.

HUGH DE CALEY = AGNES, dr. of Hamo de Hamsted

Sir William de Caley, Kt.

John Caley, of Owby

Sir William | John Caley

Hugh Caley | William Caley | John Caley

Jennet Caley = 1, John Lake

2, John Lake

3, John Lake

4, John Lake

John Lake | 5, Lancelot Lake = Marg. Twisleton

6, John Lake = Catharine Pake

John, 1585 = Mary Bearn | Beatrix = Robert Jackson \| John Barley | Thomas = Anne Twisleton | Lancelot = Emme Northend | Alexander, Robert, Catharine | Jane, Bridget, Elizabeth

Anne = A. Beale | 8, John = — Osgarby | Thomas, Lancelot | Beatrix, Thomasine | Ellen

George, Paul | John, Amyel | Thomas, Joseph | Anne, Mary | 9, Richard Lake, of Erby = Anne Wardell \| Anne Morelly

I. Sir Edward, 1674 = Anne Bibye | Thomas = M. Goodyer | John

Edward, d y | Thomas, 1711 = Elizabeth Storey

II. Sir Bibye Lake, 1744 = Mary Atwell, 1762 | Mary

III. Sir Atwell Lake, Bart. = Mary Winter | Bibye = A. Sperling | William, 1779 = S. Pinkerton | Anne = Samuel Jones

IV. Sir James-Winter = Joyce Crowther | Mary = W. Webb | Edward, Anne | Atwell, Jane | William

Mary = J. Wigston | Jessy, Edw. | Charlotte = H.H. Townsend | James, Samuel | Wm. | Willo.-Thos. = C. Macbride | Atwell, Susanna | Anne, Andrew | Henry

228. FREKE, of West Bilney, Norfolk.

Created Baronet, June 4, 1713.

1, FRANCIS FREKE, Esq. a person of good repute in Somersetshire, was father of,

2, Robert Freke, Esq. who was auditor of the treasury, in the reigns of King Hen. VIII. and Queen Elizabeth; and died worth upwards of one hundred thousand pounds. He left two sons; 1, Sir Thomas Freke, Knt. who settled in Dorsetshire, and was ancestor to the Frekes, of Hannington, Upway, and Farringdon, in that county.

3, William Freke, the second son was of Sareen in Hampshire, Esq. and married ——, daughter of Arthur Swaine, Esq. and removed with his son Arthur, to Ireland, which

4, Arthur Freke, Esq. his son and heir, lived near the City of Cork, in Ireland, and married Dorothy, daughter of Sir Piercy Smith, of Youghall, Knt. by whom he had,

5, Piercy Freke, Esq. who succeeded to his father's estates in Ireland, and coming into England, he married Elizabeth, daughter of Raufe Freke, Esq. (his kinsman) with whom he had a considerable fortune, and purchased the estate at Bilney, in Norfolk, which he left to his son and heir,

I. RAUFE FREKE, Esq. who was advanced to the dignity of an English Baronet, 12th of Queen Anne, and by his wife ——, left three sons; 1, Sir Peircy, his successor; 2, Raufe, who died at Richmond, in Surry, 1727, unmarried; and 3, Sir John, successor to his brother.

II. Sir PEIRCY FREKE, Bart. eldest son, and successor to Sir Raufe, was member of parliament for Baltimore, in Ireland, and dying unmarried, at Dublin, April, 1728, was succeeded in dignity and estate by his next surviving brother,

III. Sir JOHN FREKE, Bart. who married 1739, Mary, fourth daughter of Alan Broderick, Esq. of the Lord Viscount Middleton's family, by whom he had no issue; she died at Castle Freke, June 20, 1761, and was interred at Middleton; he married, secondly, 1765, Elizabeth Gore, daughter of Sir Arthur, first Earl of Arran, by whom he had one son,

IV. Sir JOHN FREKE, Bart. who represented the borough of Donegal, in parliament, and Jan. 25, 1783, married Catherine Charlotte, third daughter of his uncle, the Earl of Arran.

ARMS—Sable, two bars, and in chief, three mullets, or.
CREST—On a wreath, a bull's head, or, collared, argent.
SEAT—Saunder's Court, Ireland.

TABLE.

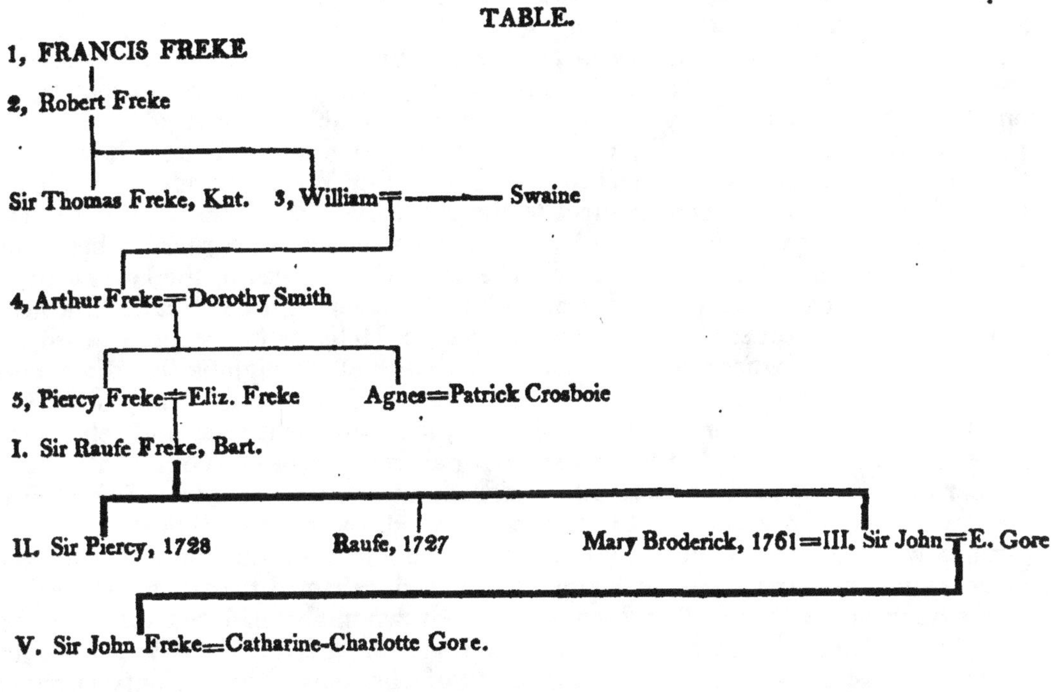

229. EVELYN, of Wotton, Surry.

Created Baronet, August 6, 1713.

THIS family flourished originally in the county of Salop, at a place which is still called Evelyn*, though formerly written Avelyn and Ivelyn, which might be confirmed by a variety of instances. A branch of this family also flourished in France, one of which was taken prisoner at the battle of Agincourt. But what has more certainty and deserves more to be depended upon, is taken from the tradition of the family, that they came from Long Ditton, into Surry, and to Long Ditton, from Harrow on the hill; and that originally they were seated at the town of Evelyn, in the hundred of South Bradford, in the county of Salop.

1, John Evelyn, Esq. descended from William Evelyn, of Harrow on the hill, in Middlesex, where the family had been settled ever since the reign of Hen. IV. removed to Kingston, in Surry, in Hen. VIII's time.

* Additions to Camden's Britannia, by Gibson. Vol. I. Col. 649.

2. George Evelyn, Esq. his son, the founder of this branch of the Evelyns, in Surry, first carried the art of making gunpowder to perfection in England, and for the conveniency of his works in the neighbourhood, purchased an estate at Wotton, i. e. Woodtown, from the groves and plantations that were about it, of one Mr. Owen. This George Evelyn had a considerable interest at court, and procured from queen Elizabeth, a grant, in conjunction with Thomas Reeves, of the rectory of St. Nicholas Coleabby, in Queenhithe Ward, London, which afterwards came by mesne conveyances to the family of the Hackers, and by the attainder of Colonel Francis Hacker, who commanded the guard when king Charles I. was murdered, came again the crown*. It was in the latter part of his life that he came to live at Wotton, which however, did not hinder him from planting there, as appears from what his grandson tells us†. "In a word, to give an instance of what store of woods and timber of prodigious size there were growing in our little county of Surry, the nearest of any to London, and plentifully furnished, both for profit and pleasure, with sufficient grief and reluctancy I speak it, my own grandfather had standing at Wotton, and about that estate, timber that now were worth one hundred thousand pounds; since, of what was left my father, who was a great preserver of wood, there has been thirty thousand pounds worth of timber fallen by the axe and the fury of the late hurricane and storm; now no more; Wotton striped and naked, ashamed to own his name".

He married first, ——, daughter of——, by whom he had ten sons and six daughters, three of which sons, survived him; he married secondly, ——, by whom he had six sons and two daughters, of the sons, Richard only survived him.

Thomas Evelyn, Esq. the eldest, was the ancestor of Edward Evelyn, of Long Ditton, Esq. created a Baronet in 1682, who died in 1692, without issue male, when that title became extinct, as John, the second, was of John Evelyn, of Godstone, in the same county, Esq. created a Baronet 1660, who left no issue male, and that title became likewise extinct; and of George Evelyn, Esq. father of George Evelyn, Esq. colonel Edward Evelyn, of Felbridge-water, near Godstone, in Surry, who married a natural daughter of James, duke of Ormond, and had one son, James, and a daughter, Julia, of Thomas and William, who upon his marriage with the daughter and heir of William Glanvil, Esq. took that name.

From the same John Evelyn, by his eldest son, George, was descended Sir John Evelyn, of West Dene, in Wilts, Knt. grandfather, by Elizabeth, his daughter and coheiress, of Evelyn Pierpoint, duke of Kingston.

The first mentioned George Evelyn, Esq. departed this life, May 30, 1603, in the seventy-third year of his age, and left his estate at Wotton to his youngest and only surviving son, by his second wife‡.

3, Richard Evelyn, Esq. who married Eleanor, only daughter and heiress of John Stanfield, of Lewis, in Sussex, Esq. by whom he had three sons, 1, George;

* Newcourt's Repertor. Vol. I. page 425, 506.
† Camden's Brit. by Gibson. Vol. I. col. 186.
‡ Aubrey's Antiq. of Surry. Vol. IV. page 126.

2, John; 3, Richard; and two daughters, Elizabeth, wife of Edward Darcy, of Dartford, in Kent, Esq. and Jane, of William Glanvil, Esq. He died in 1640, and was burried at Wotton.

George Evelyn, Esq. the eldest son, enjoyed the family estate at Wotton, fifty-eight years, and dying in 1698, at the age of eighty-three, he left it to his brother, John. He was a person of great worth, and generally esteemed by his neighbours, as appeared from his being frequently elected knight of the shire for the county of Surry *; Richard, the third son married ——, daughter and coheiress of George Mynne, of Woodcot, in Surry, Esq. and died in 1669, leaving one daughter, Anne, wife of William Montague, Esq. only son of the lord chief baron Montague.

4, John Evelyn, Esq. the second son of Richard, was born October 31, 1620, at his father's house, at Wotton, and was carefully educated in his tender years, receiving the first elements of learning, at the free school at Lewes, in Sussex, whence he removed in 1637, to Baliol's college, Oxford, where, as a gentleman commoner he remained till the breaking out of the civil war, when he obtained leave from Charles I. under his own hand, to travel beyond the seas for his improvement. In 1644, he left England, in order to make the tour of Europe, which he performed very successfully, making it his business to enquire carefully into the state of the sciences, and the improvments made in all useful arts, wherever he came; concerning which, he made very large and valuable collections. He improved himself in architecture, painting, the knowledge of antiquities, medals, and other branches of polite literature, and indeed, left nothing unexamined that could contribute to the understanding of natural philosophy, to which, beyond all other sciences, he was passionately addicted.

In 1647, he came to Paris, where being recommended to Sir Richard Browne, Bart. the king's minister there, he made his addresses to his only daughter, whom he married, and in her right, became possessed of Saye's Court, near Deptford, in Kent. He had before that time recommended himself to the notice of the learned world, by publishing several treatises which were extremely well received.

* Camden's Brit. by Gibson, col. 154, edit. 1695.

In his time, there was a very extraordinary discovery made upon opening the family vault, of which there is a full account in the additions to the English Britannia, which there is so much the more reason to credit, as these additions came from John Evelyn, his brother, after describing the ridge of the hills that divide Surry from Sussex, and that he proceeds thus *(a)*, "Not far from the bottom, stands an ancient seat of the Evelyns, of Wotton, among streams gliding through the meadows, adorned with gentle risings and woods, which as it were, encompass it. And these together with the gardens, fountains, and other horterlane ornaments, have given it a place and name amongst the most agreeable seats. In opening the ground of the church-yard, of Wotton, to enlarge a vault belonging to this family, they met with a skeleton, which was nine feet and three inches long; as the worthy and famous Mr. John Evelyn had it *(b)* attested, by an ancient and understanding man then present, who accordingly measured it, and marked the length on a pole, with other workmen, who affirmed the same. They found it lying in full length between two boards of the coffin, and measured it before they had discomposed the bones, but trying to take it out, it fell all to pieces; for which reason they flung it amongst the rest of the rubbish, after they had separately measured several of the more solid bones.

(a) Ibid. Vol. I. col. 186.

(b) These epithets added since his death.

After the death of Oliver, and the deposition of Richard Cromwell, there were many of the commanders in the army that shewed an inclination to reconcile themselves to the king, which disposition was very much encouraged by such as had his majesty's interest truly at heart. Amongst these, Mr. Evelyn had a particular eye upon Colonel Herbert Mosley *, an old experienced officer in the parliament army, who had two regiments entirely at his devotion, was very much esteemed by his party, and had the general reputation of being a person of probity and honour. It was a very dangerous step, as things then stood, to make any advances to one in his situation; yet Mr. Evelyn, considering how much it might be in that gentleman's power to facilitate the king's return, fairly ventured his life, by advising the colonel to make his peace with, and enter into the service of the king. The colonel, as might well be expected, acted coldy and cautiously at first, but at last accepted Mr. Evelyn's offer, and desired him to make use of his interest to procure a pardon for himself, and some of his relations and friends whom he named, promising in return, to give all the assistance in his power to the royal cause.

On the king's return, Mr. Evelyn was introduced and graciously received, and began to enter into the active scenes of life, but yet without bidding adieu entirely to his studies. About the close of the year, 1662, when his majesty was pleased, by letters patent, to erect and establish the royal society for the improvement of natural knowledge, John Evelyn, Esq. was appointed one of the first fellows and council. In 1664, upon the first appearance of the nation's being obliged to engage in a war with the Dutch; the king thought proper to appoint him a commissioner to take care of the sick and wounded.

As there is nothing more natural than for men of true learning to preserve a lasting regard and affection for the academies where they first pursued their studies; so Mr. Evelyn gave a noble testimony of his respect for Oxford, by using his utmost endeavour with Lord Henry Howard, in order to prevail upon him to bestow the Arundelian marbles, upon the university, in which he happily succeeded, and obtained in consequence of it, all the reward he desired, which was the thanks of that learned body, delivered by delegates appointed for that purpose.

In July 15, 1699, he was honoured with the degree of doctor of civil law, as a mark of the gratitude of that learned body †, and of the just sense they had of the credit derived to them from his being educated at Baliol College. It was, indeed, a singular point of Mr. Evelyn's felicity, that all the honours he obtained, and all the posts to which he was raised, were the mere rewards of his merit, and bestowed upon him without the least solicitation. In December, 1685, he was appointed, with the Lord Visc. Tiviot and Colonel Robert Philips, one of the commissioners for executing the great office of lord privy-seal, in the absence of Henry Earl of Clarendon, lord-lieutenant of Ireland, which he held till March 11, 1686. After the Revolution, he was treasurer of Greenwich-Hospital; and, though he

* Baker's Chron. Lond. 1696. page 661.

† Wood's Fasti, Oxon, Vol. II. col. 180.

was then much in years, yet he wrote some and translated other pieces, which will do lasting honour to his country.

When we consider the number of books he published, and the variety of subjects upon which he employed his time, it is impossible to forbear wondering at his industry and application, which must be greatly heightened when we reflect how careful he was in reviewing, correcting, and augmenting, all his original works; whence it is evident, that whatever subject appeared weighty enough to attract his attention, it never lost its place in his thoughts, but on the contrary, was often reviewed, and reaped the continual benefit of the new lights he received, as well as of his future meditations, which is the reason that his treatises are so perfect in their kind, and continue as much esteemed by posterity as they were by the inquisitive and judicious part of the world at the time they came from the press.

The history of this learned person's life and labours terminated together; for, in a short time after he had fitted the fourth edition of his Silva for the press, he departed this life in the 86th year of his age, Feb. 27, 1705-6, and was interred at Wotton, in a tomb of about three feet high, shaped like a coffin, with an inscription upon a white marble with which it is covered, expressing, according to his own intention, "that living in an age of extraordinary events and revolutions, he had learned from them this truth, which he desired might be thus communicated to posterity, that all is vanity which is not honest, and that there is no solid wisdom but in real piety."

By Mary, daughter of Sir Richard Browne, Bart.* who was the companion of

M. S.

* Near this place are deposited the bodys of Sir Richard Browne, of Sayes-Court, Deptford, Kent.

Of his wife Dame Joanna Vigornis, of Langham, in Essex, deceased in November, 1618, aged 74 years.

This Sir Richard was youngest son of an ancient family of Hitcham, in Suffolk, seated afterwards at Horseley, in Essex; who, being student in the Temple, was, by Robert Dudley, the great Earl of Leicester, taken into the service of the crown, when he went governor of the United Netherlands, and was afterwards by Queen Elizabeth made clerk of the green cloth, in which honourable situation he also continued under King James, unto the time of his death. May, 1604, aged 65 years.

Of Christopher Browne, Esq. son and heir of Sir Richard, who died 1645, aged 70 years.

Of Thomasin, his wife, daughter of Benjamin Courson, of Much-Bado, in Essex, Esq. whose grandfather, William Courson, and father Benjamin, were successively treasurers of the navy to Henry VIII. and Edw. VI. to Queen Mary, and Queen Elizabeth, and died June 1638, aged 75 years.

Of Sir Richard Browne, Knt. and Bart. only son of Christopher.

Of his wife Dame Elizabeth, daughter of Sir John Pretiman, of Dryfield, in Gloucestershire, who died October 6, 1652, aged 42 years. This Sir Richard was gentleman of the privy-chamber to K. Charles I. and II. and several foreign and honourable employments, continued resident at the court of France from King Charles the First, and from King Charles the Second to the French Kings Louis the Thirteenth and Fourteen, from the year, 1641, till the beginning of the unnatural civil wars until the happy restitution of King Charles the Second, in 1660. He died Feb. 12, 1682-3, æt. 78 years, at St. Nicholas's Church, Deptford, Kent.

his fortunes, and in some measure also of his studies, for almost threescore years; he had five sons and three daughters. Of the former, all died young except one, John, of whom hereafter; of the latter, only one survived him, Susanna, wife of William Draper, of Adscomb, in the county of Surry, Esq. His excellent widow died Feb. 9, 1709, and was, according to her own desire, deposited in a stone coffin near her husband, on which a white marble stone is placed, with a short inscription, which informs us, that she was in the 74th year of her age, and that she was esteemed, admired, beloved, and regretted, by all who knew knew her.

5, John Evelyn, Esq. was born at Sayes-Court, Jan. 14, 1654, and was there tenderly educated, being considered (after the death of his brother Richard, Jan. 27, 1657, who, though but five years of age, was esteemed a kind of prodigy) as the heir of the family. He was likewise universally admired for the pregnancy of his parts, which induced his father to send him, in 1666, to Oxford, where he remained in the house of the most ingenious and learned Dr. Ralph Bathurst, then president of Trinity College, before he was admitted a gentleman-commoner, which was in Easter term 1686. It is not clear at what time he left Oxford, but Mr. Wood seems to be positive that he took no degree there, but returned to his father's house, where he prosecuted his studies under the direction of that great man. There is, however, good reason to believe, that it was during his residence in Trinity College, and when he was not above fifteen years of age, that he wrote that elegant Greek poem which is prefixed to the second edition of his Silva, and is a noble proof of the strength of his genius, and wonderful progress in learning in the early part of his life. He discovered his proficiency soon afterwards, both in the learned and modern languages, by his elegant translations, as well as his intimate acquaintance with the muses in some original poems which were justly admired. He married Martha, daughter and coheiress of Richard Spencer, Esq. and having a head as well turned for business as study, became one of the commissioners of the revenue in Ireland, and would probably have been advanced to higher employments, if he had not been cut off in the flower of his age, dying at his house in London, March 24, 1698, in the 45th year of his age. He had by his wife, two sons and three daughters; Richard died an infant, as did his eldest daughter Martha-Mary; Elizabeth was wife of Simon Harcourt, Esq. eldest son and heir of Simon, Lord Viscount Harcourt, lord high-chancellor of Great Britain, by whom she became mother to the late Earl Harcourt; Jane, the third daughter, died an infant, and was interred at Kensington.

I. JOHN EVELYN, his second and only surviving son. born at Sayes-Court, March 2, 1681, succeeded to his grandfather's estate. He married at Lambeth, Sept. 18, 1705, Anne, daughter of Edward Boscawen, of Worthivil, in the county of Cornwall, Esq. and sister of Hugh, Lord Viscount Falmouth. He was created a Baronet July 30, 1713. He inherited the virtue and learning, as well as the patrimony of his ancestors, made several alterations and additions to the family seat at Wotton, in 1717, one of which was the erecting a beautiful library, forty-five feet long, fourteen feet broad, and as many high, for the reception of that large and curious collection of books made by his grandfather, his father, and himself. He was long one of the commissioners of the customs, a fellow of the Royal Society, and was blessed with a numerous posterity. viz. six sons, two of which died young, and two daughters, 1, Sir John, his successor; 2, Charles, who married Susanna, daughter and heiress of Peter Prideaux, Esq. by whom he had two sons, Charles, and Edward, who died in his infancy; Charles, the eldest son, married Philadelphia, daughter of the late Fortunatus Wright, of Liverpool, captain of the Fane and King George privateer, by whom he had nine children, 1, Susanna, wife of John-Fortunatus Wright, a lieutenant in the royal navy, and has issue; 2, John, a lieutenant in the Portsmouth division of marines, and heir-apparent to Sir Frederick; 3, Martha-Boscawen, born 1759, wife of Nicholas Vincent in 1786: she died in 1794, leaving issue two sons, Nicholas, and Hugh, in America; 4, Edward, died young; 5, Philippa, born 1760, wife of Daniel-Francis Houghton, Esq. formerly a captain in the 69th regiment of foot, having three children, Charles-Evelyn-Daniel-Francis-Poplet-Houghton, born 1784, Frederick-Hugh-Evelyn-Houghton, and Philippa; 6, Charles, died in the East-Indies, a lieutenant in the Honourable East-India Company's service, beloved and respected by all his acquaintance, leaving his friend, John Evelyn, Esq. his cousin, administrator to his property in the East-Indies: General Evelyn left him a property which never came to his knowledge; 7, Maria Evelyn died at a convent, where she was sent for education; 8, Frances-Louisa, born 1767, wife of the Rev. John Griffith, of Manchester, in Lancashire, son of the Rev. Dr. Griffith, by whom he has issue; 9, Hugh Evelyn, born at Totness, in Devonshire, Jan. 31, 1769.

Sidney, the third son of Sir John; 4, William, was a lieutenant-general, and died Aug. 15, 1783. His daughters were Anne and Mary. Sir John died July 14, 1763, and was succeeded by his son,

II. Sir JOHN EVELYN, Bart. who, in 1732, married Mary, daughter of Hugh, Viscount Falmouth, who was born March 12, 1705, and died in 1749, by whom he had one son, Sir Frederick, the present Baronet, and two daughters, Mary and Augusta. Sir John died July, 1767, and was succeeded by his only son,

III. Sir FREDERICK EVELYN, the present Bart.

ARMS—Azure, a griffin, passant, and chief, or.

CREST—A griffin passant, or, beak and fore-legs azure, ducally gorged of the last.

SEATS—At Wotton, in Surry, and Sayes-Court, in Kent.

TABLE.

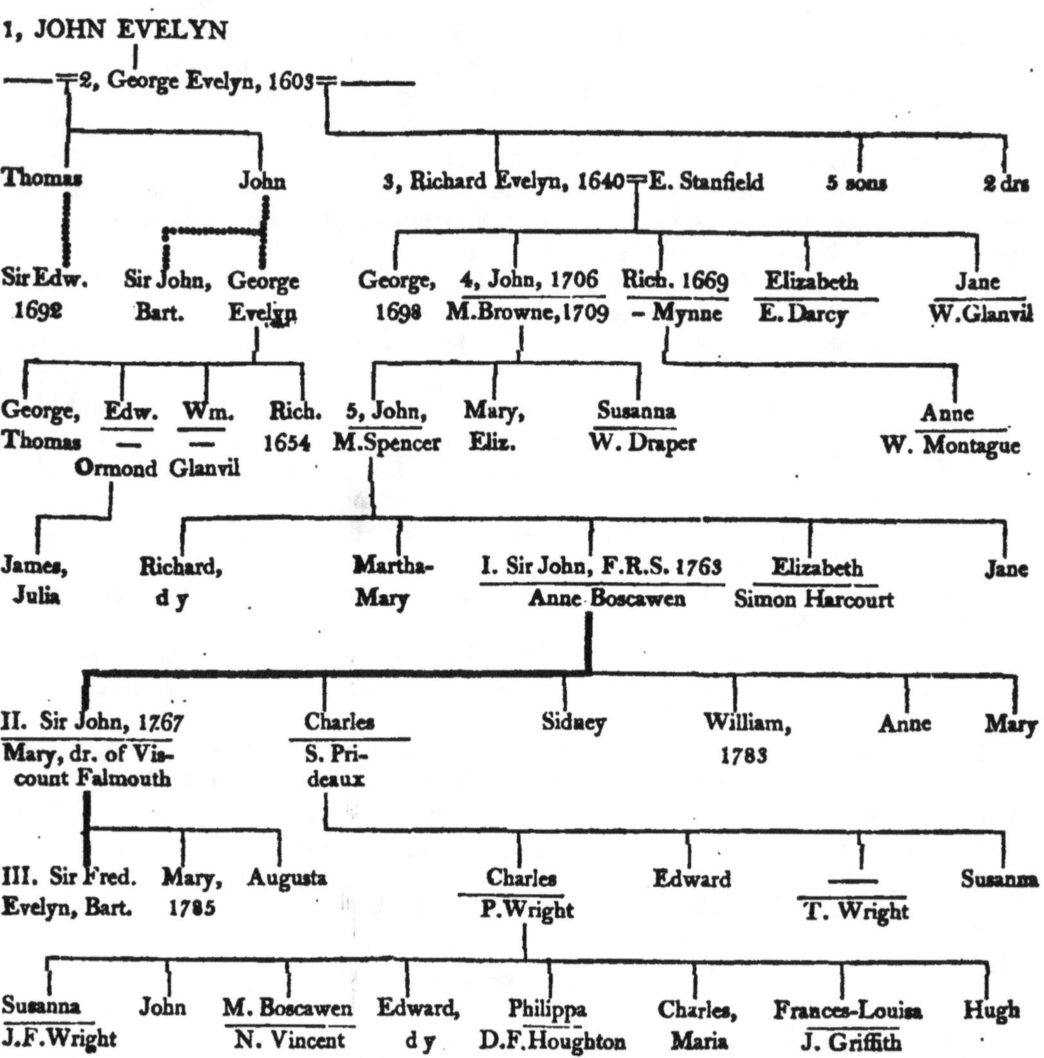
1, JOHN EVELYN
2, George Evelyn, 1603
Thomas
John
3, Richard Evelyn, 1640 = E. Stanfield
5 sons
2 drs
Sir Edw. 1692
Sir John, Bart.
George Evelyn
George, 1698
4, John, 1706
M.Browne, 1709
Rich. 1669
– Mynne
Elizabeth
E. Darcy
Jane
W. Glanvil
George, Thomas
Edw.
—
Ormond
Wm.
—
Glanvil
Rich. 1654
5, John,
M.Spencer
Mary, Eliz.
Susanna
W. Draper
Anne
W. Montague
James, Julia
Richard, d y
Martha-Mary
I. Sir John, F.R.S. 1763
Anne Boscawen
Elizabeth
Simon Harcourt
Jane
II. Sir John, 1767
Mary, dr. of Viscount Falmouth
Charles
S. Prideaux
Sidney
William, 1783
Anne
Mary
III. Sir Fred. Evelyn, Bart.
Mary, 1785
Augusta
Charles
P.Wright
Edward
—
T. Wright
Susanna
Susanna
J.F.Wright
John
M. Boscawen
N. Vincent
Edward, d y
Philippa
D.F.Houghton
Charles, Maria
Frances-Louisa
J. Griffith
Hugh

230. COPE, of Brewern, Oxfordshire.

Created Baronet, March 1, 1713.

FOR the antiquity and descent of this family, see Cope, of Hanwell, already treated of, Vol. I. p. 87.

1, Jonathan Cope, Esq. second son of Sir William Cope, by Elizabeth, his wife, daughter and heiress of Sir George Chaworth, Knt. married Anna, daughter of Sir Hatton Farmer, of Easton, in Northamptonshire, Knt. and left one son,

2, Jonathan, who married Susan, daughter of Sir Thomas Fowle, of London, Knt. and goldsmith, by whom he had three sons, 1, Sir Jonathan; 2, William, who died unmarried; and 3, Anthony, who married Anne, youngest daughter of Sir Robert Dashwood, of Northbroke, in Oxfordshire, Bart. by whom he had no issue.

I. JONATHAN COPE, Esq. the eldest son, was advanced to the dignity of a Baronet the twelfth of Queen Anne; he represented the borough of Banbury, in Oxfordshire, in the last parliament of Queen Anne, and the first of King George the First. Sir Jonathan was possessor of the ground on which the Custom-house, &c. stands, which lease being out, he let it again for ninety-nine years, at 1600l. per annum. He married ——, daughter of Sir Robert Jenkinson, of Walcot, in Oxfordshire, Bart. (sister to Sir Robert-Banks Jenkinson, Bart.) by whom he had one son Jonathan, who married first, in 1741, Arabella Howard, eldest daughter of Henry, Earl of Carlisle, by whom he had Sir Charles, his successor. He married secondly, in 1752, ——, daughter of Francis Leighton, Esq. a lieutenant-general in the army, and widow of Shaw Cathcart, Esq. by whom he had one son Jonathan, the present Baronet, and two daughters, ——, was married in January, 1780, to John Cowper, Esq.; ——, the other daughter, in 1775, to Charles Pigot, Esq. Sir Jonathan had also four daughters, 1, Anna, wife of Sir Thomas Whitmore, of Apley, in Shropshire, Knight of the Bath, by whom he had two daughters, Maria and Sophia; 2, Henrietta-Maria; 3, Mary, wife of Sir Henry-Banks Jenkinson, of Walcot, in Oxfordshire, Bart. who died at Northend, near Fulham, Middlesex, in 1765; 4, Susanna, of William Chetwynd, Esq. Lady Cope died Feb. 27, 1755, and Sir Jonathan March 28, 1765, and was succeeded in title and estate by his grandson,

II. Sir CHARLES COPE, Bart. who married, in 1767, Catharine, youngest daughter of Sir Cecil Bishop, of Parham, in Sussex, Bart. by whom he had one son ——, his successor, and two daughters, Arabella-Diana, wife, June 4, 1790, of John-Frederick, Duke of Dorset; and Catharine, of ——, Earl of Aboyne. Sir Charles died at Orton, in Huntingdonshire, June 13, 1781, and his lady, in 1782, became the wife of the Right Hon. Charles Jenkinson, now Earl of Liverpool. Sir Charles was succeeded by his only son,

III. ——————, Bart. who died Dec. 25, 1781, aged about twelve years, and was succeeded by his uncle,

IV. Sir JONATHAN COPE, Bart. LL.D. who is married and has issue.

ARMS—Argent, on a chevron, azure, between three roses, gules, sliped proper, as many fleur-de-lis, or.

CREST—On a wreath, a fleur-de-lis, or, a dragon's head issuing from the top thereof, gules.

SEAT—Norton, Huntingdonshire.

TABLE.

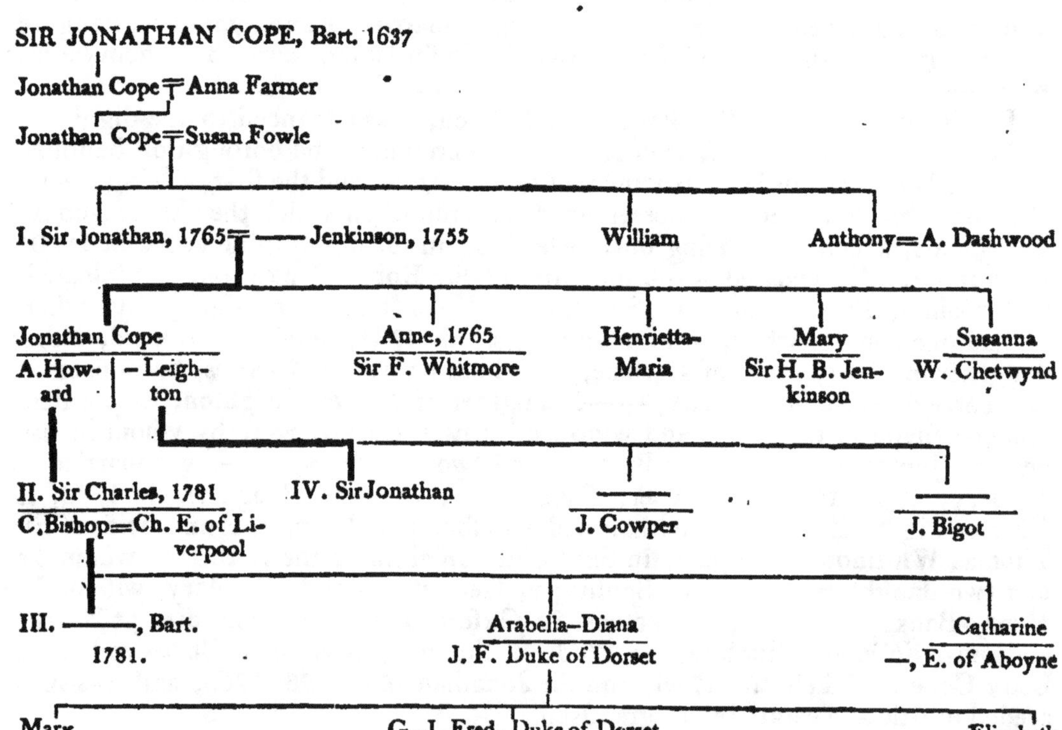

BARONETS

CREATED BY

KING GEORGE I.

231. EYLES, of LONDON.

Created Baronet, Dec. 1, 1714.

THIS family has been a long time seated in Wiltshire. —— Eyles, Esq. left two sons, John and Francis, of whom hereafter.

John, the eldest son, received the honour of knighthood from K. James II. in the last year of whose reign he was lord-mayor of London, which place he resigned upon the news of the Prince of Orange's coming; he married —, daughter of — Cowper, of London, and had three daughters, 1, Sarah, wife of Joseph-Haskyn Styles, of London, Esq.; Mary, of Sir John Smyth, of Isleworth, in Middlesex, Bart.; and ——, of James Montague, of Lackham, in Wilts, Esq. besides sons. Francis, second son of Sir John, died at Earnshill, in Somersetshire, Dec. 1735, and left his estate to his nephew, Francis Eyles, Esq. member of parliament for the Devizes, in Wiltshire, son of his brother, —— Eyles, Esq.

I. FRANCIS EYLES, Esq. the second son, and brother to Sir John, was an eminent merchant, many years a director of the East-India Company, &c. alderman of Bridge Ward, and created a Baronet 1 King George I. He married Elizabeth, daughter of Mr. Ayley, of London, merchant, who died April 6, 1735, by whom he had four sons, 1, James, died unmarried; 2, Sir John, his successor; 3, Edward, who died a bachelor; 4, Sir Joseph, knight and sheriff of London in 1726, and chosen alderman of Cheap Ward in 1738-9, and member in the last parliament of King George I. for the Devizes, in Wiltshire; and in the first parliament of King George II. he served for the borough of Southwark, and in the second for the Devizes again, and married Sarah, daughter of Sir Jeffrey Jeffreys, Knt. alderman and lord-mayor of London, and died Feb. 8, 1739-40, leaving one son Joseph, who died Jan. 28, 1744, and two daughters; and two Samuels. Sir Francis had also four daughters, 1, Elizabeth, wife of Sir Thomas Clark, of Brickendonbury, in Hertfordshire, Knt.; 2, Mary, died an infant; 3, Frances, wife of Nicholas, second son of Sir Jeffrey Jeffreys, Knt.; and 4, Mary, of William Richardson, of Somerset, in the county of Londonderry, Esq. Sir Francis died June 1716, and was succeeded in dignity and estate by his eldest surviving son,

II. Sir JOHN EYLES, Bart. who was sub-governor of the South-Sea Company, and was member, in the last parliament of Queen Anne, and in the first and second parliament of King George I. for Chippenham, in Wiltshire; and in the first parliament of King George II. he represented the city of London. He was first alderman of Vintry Ward, lord-mayor in 1727, alderman of Bridge Ward Without, commonly called Father of the City, and post-master general, being so appointed April 1739, on the death of Edward Carteret, Esq.; and by Mary, his wife, daughter of Joseph-Haskyn Styles, of London, Esq. and Sarah, his wife, daughter of Sir John Eyles aforesaid, had one son, Francis Haskin Eyles Styles, his successor, (he was heir to his uncle, Benjamin-Haskin Styles, Esq. and took the surname of Haskin-Styles); and one daughter Mary, wife of William Bumstead, of Upton, in Warwickshire, Esq. Lady Styles died Nov. 1735, and Sir John March 11, 1745, and was succeeded by his son,

TABLE.

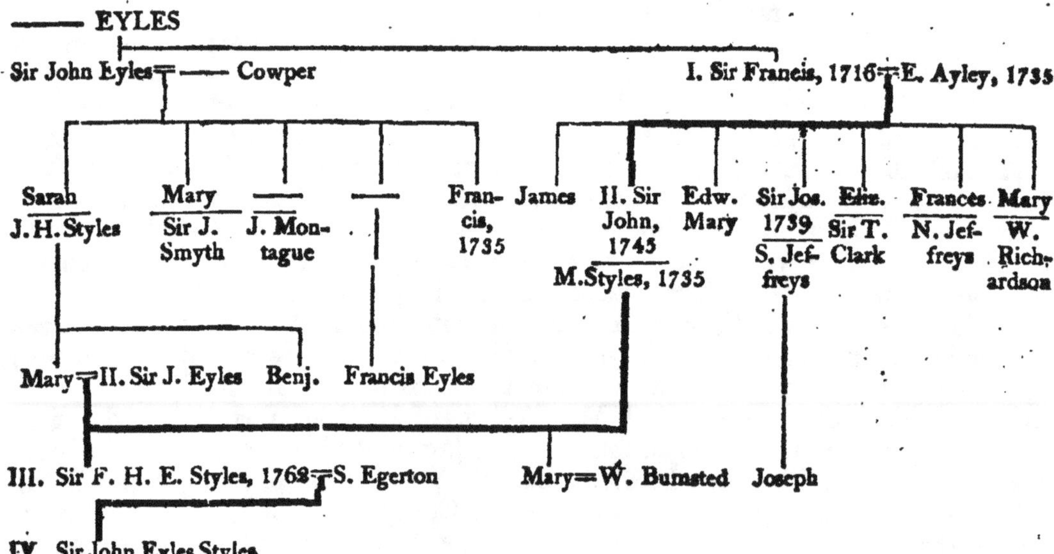

III. Sir FRANCIS-HASKIN EYLES STYLES, Bart. who was appointed a commissioner of the navy in 1747, one of the commissioners for victualling his majesty's navy, Jan. 1751-2, re-appointed March 21, 1761. Sir Francis married, March 8, 1739-40, Sibilla, daughter of Dr. —— Egerton, rector of Astbury, in Cheshire, by whom he had one son Sir John, his successor, and one daughter ——, born Jan. 16, 1745. Sir Francis died Jan. 26, 1762, and was succeeded by his son,

IV. Sir JOHN EYLES STYLES, Bart. born April 16, 1741.

ARMS—Argent, a fess engrailed, sable, in chief, three fleur-de-lis of the second.

SEAT—Hessek, Wiltshire.

232. SMYTH, of ISFIELD, Sussex.

Created Baronet, Dec. 2, 1714.

THIS family is descended from James Smyth, Esq. second son of Sir Robert Smyth, of Upton, in Essex, Bart. (vide Vol. II. p. 371.) He was knighted by King Charles II. and lord-mayor of London the first of King James II. He married first, Mary, daughter of Sir William Peak, Knt. lord-mayor of London, by whom he had no issue; secondly, Elizabeth, daughter and coheiress of Arthur Shirley, of Isfield, in Sussex, Esq. by whom he had one son James; and thirdly, Philadelphia, daughter of Sir William Wilson, of Eastborne, in Sussex, Bart. by whom heleft no issue. Sir James died Dec. 9, 1706, aged 73.

I. JAMES SMYTH, Esq. son and heir, was advanced to the dignity of a Baronet the first year of King George I. He married Mirabella, one of the daughters of Sir Robert Legard, Knt. then one of the masters of the high court of chancery, and dying Feb. 28, 1716-17, left one son*,

* He was buried at Westham-Church, in Essex, with his father, to whose memories there is a monument at the east end of the south aisle, of white marble, with these inscriptions:

First Column.

Near this place lies interred the bodies of
Sir James Smyth, Knt. sometime lord-mayor of London,
who was the second son of Sir Robert Smyth, of Upton,
Knt. and Bart. (who also lies interred near this place), and
departed this life the 9 of December, 1706, in tne 73d year of his age,
and of
Elizabeth, wife of the said Sir James, who was

II. Sir ROBERT SMYTH, Bart. only son and successor to his father, married the Lady Louisa-Carolina-Isabella Hervey, second daughter of John, Earl of Bristol, who died May 11, 1770, by whom he had Sir Hervey, his successor, and one daughter, Anna-Mirabella-Henrietta, born 1738, wife, in 1761, of William-Beale Brand, of Polsted-Hall, in Suffolk, Esq. Sir Robert died Dec. 10, 1783, and was succeeded by his son,

III. Sir HERVEY SMYTH, Bart. born 1734. He was page of honour to the late king, aid-de-camp to General Wolfe at the siege of Quebec, and afterwards colonel in the foot-guards.

ARMS—Azure, two bars, unde, ermine, on a chief, or, a demi-lion, issuant, sable, with due difference.

CREST—On a wreath, an ostrich's head, couped, with a horse-shoe in his mouth, proper.

SEAT—Farnham, Suffolk.

The elder daughter, and one of the coheirs of
Arthur Shirley, Esq. of an ancient family at
Isfield, in Sussex, and departed this life the 28 of
January, 1639, in the 29th year of her age, and of

Second Column.

Elizabeth, and —— Shirley, their 2 daughters,
who dyed in their minority, and of
Sir James, (their son), who was created a Bart. of
Great Britain, the 2d day of December,
In the first year of King George, and dyed
28 of February, 1716, in the 32d year of his age, and of
Mirabella, his wife, who was one of the daughters
of Sir Robert Legard, Knt. and dyed the 21 day
of February, 1714, in the 30 year of her age.

Nostris vixerunt placitoq. ligamine vincti
Ædibus; ac animi sua corpora juncta tenebant;
Supposito Tumulo fatis connecta videntur,
Ut Celis iterum socientur fœdere firmo.

TABLE.

SIR ROBERT SMYTH, of Upton

Sir James, Bart. — Sir James Smyth

Sir James Smyth = M. Peak | E. Shirley, 1689 | P. Wilson

I. Sir James, 1716 = Mirabella Legard, 1714

II. Sir Robert Smyth, 1783 = Louisa C. J. Hervey

III. Sir Henry — Anne = Wm. B. Brand.

233. WARRENDER, of LOCHEND, in the County of East-Lothian, North-Britain,

Created Baronet, June 2, 1715.

THIS family draws its original descent from one De Warren, of a family of that name in Durham*, or the north-riding of Yorkshire; Robert de Warren settled his family in East-Lothian, or in the county of Hadington, and he and his descendants, by a sudden transposition, came to use the name of Warrender, as at present.

Sir George Warrender, of Lochend, married Margaret Cunninghame, a relation of Sir David Cunninghame's, of Milncraig, Bart. of Scotland, and by her mother descended of the family of M'Dowal, of Frewch, by whom he had,

I. GEORGE WARRENDER, who was put out to business as a merchant †, and came to be a very considerable dealer in foreign trade before the Revolution, and acquired, with a fair character, an handsome estate. He was always attached to the interest of his country, and was distinguished amongst his fellow citizens of Edinburgh, and filled the several offices in the magistracy of that city, till he was called to serve as lord-provost, or mayor of Edinburgh, and had the honour to represent the city in the first parliament of King George I. ‡. He was in the provost's chair the last year of Queen Anne, and being firm to the Hanover succession, did all in his power to oppose the violent spirit that then ran so high, and on the 5th of August, when King George I. was proclaimed in Edinburgh, he, as chief magistrate and high-sheriff in the place, discharged that part of his office with the most sincere affection, in proclaiming the king. He represented the city of Edinburgh in parliament from the year 1715, to the time of his death in 1721-2 §, as he appeared zealous for the interest of his country in the year 1715, and opposed the rebels being admitted into the city and the castle, and

* Ex inf. Dom. J. Warrender, Bar. 1741.

† Ibid.

‡ Ibid.

§ He lies buried in the Dissenting Ground in Bunhill-Fields, with the following inscription on a marble grave-stone:

> Hic in spem beatæ Resurrectionis reconditæ jaceat Exuviæ D. Geo. Warrender, de Lochend, Barroneti Civitatis Edinburgenæ nuper Pretoris qui Senatus Edenensis Suffragiis in Regni Comitiæ ante Saxenium cooptatus et in iisdem Principi et Patriæ inservens Mortem. Obiit Londini die 4to Martii, Anno D. 172½, Ætatis 65.
>
> Quam sincero fuerat purioris Religionis Studio quantaq. Vitæ morumq. integrita. Dies docebit.

strenuously asserted the Hanover succession. It was for these and his other services to his country, and to the king ||, he had the honour of his patent from King George I. June 2, 1715. Sir George married first, Margaret Lawrie ¶, a merchant's daughter in the city, by whom he had Sir John Warrender, his successor, and one daughter. Sir George's second wife was Grissel **, daughter of Hugh Blair, merchant, and one of the magistrates of Edinburgh, by whom he had three sons, George Warrender, of Brunsfield, Esq. David, who followed the law in Edinburgh; and Hugh, a counsellor at law in the Temple, London: and five daughters, Jane, wife of Mr. Archbald Stewart, advocate, son of Sir Thomas Stewart, of Coltness, Bart. by whom he had a son Thomas, and one daughter.

II. Sir JOHN WARRENDER, of Lochend, Bart. his eldest son and successor, married Henrietta ††, daughter of Sir Patrick Johnston, lord-provost or mayor of Edinburgh, and member of the last Scots parliament from 1703 to 1706, when the union was concluded between the two kingdoms; and he was one of the commissioners nominated for and did attend that treaty of union, and was amember of the first British parliament.

Sir Patrick was a younger son of the family of Hellon, in the county of Berwick, and died June 14, 1799.

Sir John Warrender, by Henrietta Johnston, his wife, had two sons and five daughters: the sons are George and Patrick.

TABLE.

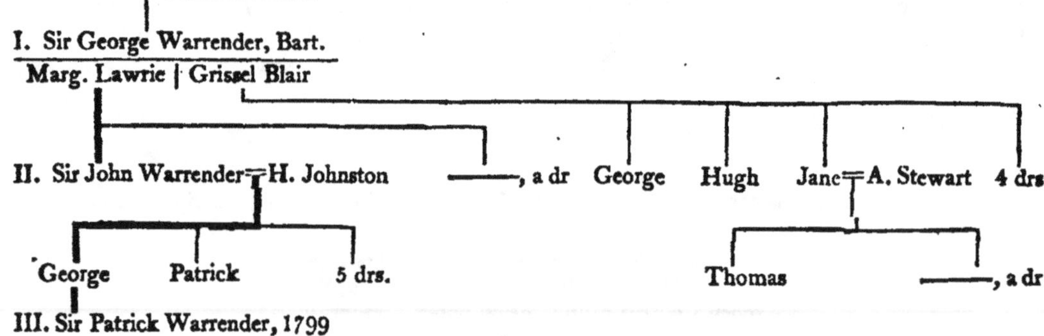

|| Ex inf. Dom. J. Warrender, Bar. 1741.
¶ Ibid.
** Ibid.
†† Ibid.

ARMS—Argent, on a bend, wavy, between six roses, gules, three plates.
CREST—On a wreath, a hare, sejeant, proper.
MOTTO—*Industria.*
SEAT—At Lochend, in the county of East Lothian, Scotland.

---

234. D'AETH, of Knowlton, Kent.

Created Baronet, July 16, 1716.

THIS family was originally of Aeth, in Flanders*, from whence they derive their name, but long settled in England, and were of Charles-Place, Dartford, in the county of Kent.

1, William Death, or D'Aeth, of Dartford, Gent. married first, Elizabeth, by whom he had six children: he married secondly, Anne, daughter and heiress of —— Vaughan, of Erith, Esq. temp. Edward VI. by whom he had nine children, as appears by his tomb-stone still remaining in Dartford church †.

2, Thomas, his third son, the two first dying without issue male, married Joan‡, daughter of William Head, by whom he had several children.

3, Thomas, his eldest son, married Mary §, daughter of —— Barton, Esq. serjeant at law, by whom he had three sons, Adrian, Abel, and Thomas: the two first died without issue; but Thomas, the youngest, was an eminent merchant of the

* Ex inf. Dom. Tho. D'Aeth, Bar. 1741.

† On a grave-stone in the south cross isle of Dartford Church, in Kent, are the effigies of a man in brass between two wives, and beneath them fifteen children, with this inscription in black letter:

> Here under lyeth buryed the bodye of William Death, Gentleman, pryncipall of Staple Inne, and one of the attorneys of the Common Pleas at Westmynster, who had two wives, Elizabeth, and Anne; and had yssue by Elizabeth ten sonnes and six daughters; which Willyam beynge of the age of sixty-three yeares, deceased the first of March, 1590, and Elizabeth, being of the age of XL yeares, deceased the XIII of Aprill, 1582, unto whose soules Almighty God graunt a joyful resurrection.

Above are these quarterings in brass:

1, A griffin passant, between three crescents, argent, for Death; 2, A chevron between three children's heads, couped at the shoulders, inwrapped about the necks with snakes, for Vaughan; 3, A chevron; 4, Obliterated; 5, Three lions rampant; 6, As the first.—*Dr. Harris's Hist. of Kent, p.* 93.

‡ Ex inf. Dom. Tho. D'Aeth, Bar. 1741.

§ Ibid.

city of London. He married Elhanna*, daughter of Sir John Rolt, of Milton-Earnest, in the county of Bedford, Knt. by whom he had two sons, Sir Thomas, and Adrian, who died an infant.

I. Sir THOMAS D'AETH, Bart. who married first, Elizabeth†, daughter of Sir John Narbrough, Knt. admiral, and one of the commissioners of the navy to Kings Charles and James II. and sole heiress to her brother, Sir John Narbrough, of Knowlton, in the county of Kent, Bart. so created 1688, by King James, after his father's decease. He, with his only brother, James Narbrough, Esq. were unfortunately cast away, with their father-in-law, Sir Cloudesly Shovel, on the rocks of Scilly, Oct. 22, 1707‡. Sir Thomas had twelve children by his first wife, of whom two sons, Sir Narbrough, his successor, Henry, and Thomas, survived him; and five daughters, 1, Elizabeth, wife of the Hon. Henry Dawney, one of the prebendaries of Canterbury, son of Henry, second Lord Viscount Downe, of the kingdom of Ireland; 2, Elhanna; 3, Sophia; 4, Bethia, wife, first, of Herbert Palmer, Esq. who died in 1760; secondly, of lieutenant-colonel John Cosnan, who died in 1797, aged 80; and 5, Harriot. By his second wife, Jane§, daughter of Walter Williams, of Dingestow, in the county of Monmouth, Gent. he had one son Francis. He was chosen member to serve in parliament for the city of Canterbury in 1708, and also for the town and port of Sandwich in 1714. Sir Thomas died Jan. 4, 1745, and was succeeded by his son,

II. Sir NARBROUGH D'AETH, Bart. who married, in 1738, Anne, the daughter of John Clarke, of Blake-Hall, in the county of Essex, Esq. by whom he had one son, Thomas-Narbrough, who died a few weeks after his birth in 1739. Sir Narborough died Oct. 8, 1773, and was succeeded by his grandson

III. Sir NARBOROUGH D'AETH, the present Baronet.

ARMS—Sable, a griffin, passant, or, between three crescents, argent.
CREST—A griffin's head, or, with a trefoil in his mouth, vert.
SEATS—Knowlton-Court, and North-Cray Place, both in the county of Kent.

* Ex inf. Dom. D'Aeth, Bar. 1741.

† Ibid.

‡ She lies buried under a handsome monument, in St. Margaret's Church, Westminster, with this inscription:

> The Lady Elizabeth D'Aeth, only daughter of that famous admiral, Sir John Narbrough, Knt. and sister and heir to those two unfortunate young gentlemen, Sir John Narbrough, Bart. and James Narbrough, Esq. She was the fruitful mother of twelve children, by her husband, Sir Thomas D'Aeth, Bart. of whom seven survived her, two sons, Narbrough and Thomas, and five daughters, Elizabeth, Elhanna, Sophia, Bethia, and Harriot. She died in childbed the 24th day of June, in the year of our Lord, 1721, in the 39th year of her age, and lies interred in the vault underneath.

§ Ex inf. Dom. Tho. D'Aeth, Bar. 1741.

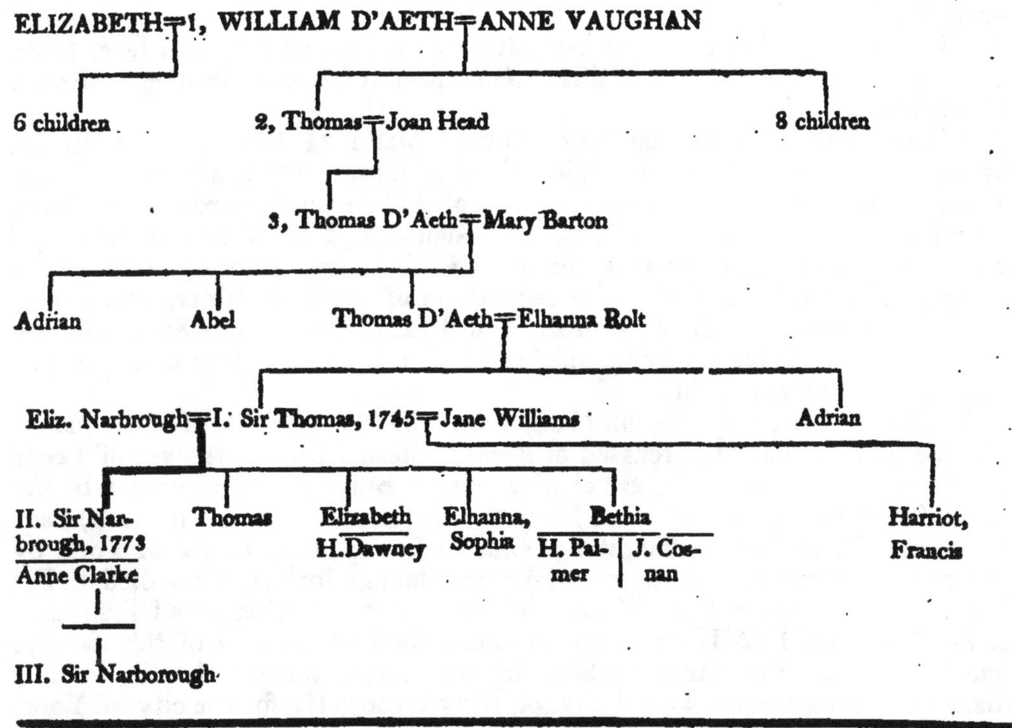

235. MILNER, of NUN-APPLETON HALL, Yorkshire.

Created Baronet, Feb. 26, 1716.

THIS is originally a Yorkshire family*; the Milners, of Wickerby, in Lincolnshire, Harlington, in Bedfordshire, and Farningham, in Essex, are all from this county, as appears by an entry in the Heralds-Office, 1634†. They were with the Earl of Surry at Flodden-Field, temp. Hen. VIII.

* Thoresby's Leeds, p. 215.

† George Milner, of Farningham, in Essex, who was at the battle of Flodden Field with the Earl of Surry, had three sons, George, Henry, and Michael. George had one son, Henry Milner, of Harlington, in Bedfordshire, who married Cecily, daughter of Edmund Gostwick, auditor to Henry VIII. Edward VI. and Queen Mary, by whom he had two sons, Henry and Edward, and one daughter Anne wife of Philip Lewgers, of Bedford, Clerk.

Henry Milner, the elder son, was of Wickinbye, in Lincolnshire, and married Anne, daughter of William Hardinge, alias Cawd, by whom he had one son Clinton, aged 19, 1634, and three daughters, Elizabeth, Mary, and Anne.

Henry Chyttinge, Chester.
Thomas Thompson, Rouge Dragon.

1, Marmaduke Milner*, the first we find in the registers, was of Calvet-House, near Mewker, in Swaledale, where the estate descends according to the custom of gavel-kind.

2, Richard Milner†, his son and heir, alderman of Leeds 1652, died Dec. 1659, leaving by Alice, daughter of William Jenkinson, of Leeds, brother to Josias, the benefactor,

3, William Milner, his son and heir, baptized March 24, 1630, married Ruth‡, daughter of John Belton, of Rawcliffe: she died Dec. 9, 1701, and he died Oct. 5, 1691, by whom he had three sons, 1, Joseph Milner, of Rotterdam, merchant, who married Anne§, daughter of Smart Goodenough, Esq. sheriff of Somersetshire, by whom he had three sons, Francis, William, and Henry; he died June 15, 1700, and his wife in 1698. The second son of William Milner, was Benjamin, of Amsterdam, merchant, who married Sarah||, daughter of Smart Goodenough, Esq. sister to his brother's wife, and had one son Goodenough, that died an infant, and several daughters.

4, William Milner, Esq. the third son, born Nov. 29, 1662, lord of the manor of Cat-Beeston, which he purchased of Richard Sterne, Esq. was mayor of Leeds in 1697, and a gentleman of great charity, and a considerable promoter of the welfare of that town. He married Mary¶, daughter of Joshua Ibbetson, Esq. mayor of Leeds, by Mary, daughter of Charles Breary, Esq. mayor of York, by whom he had Joseph and Richard, who died infants, Joshua, who died S. P.; William, Mary, Jane, wife of William Whitton, Esq. Elizabeth, and Frances.

I. Sir WILLIAM MILNER, son and heir, the first Baronet of this family, so created in the third year of his late Majesty's reign, was member in the last parliament of King George I. and first of King George II. for the city of York. He married Elizabeth, daughter of Sir William Dawes, Bart, archbishop of York, who died March 9, 1782, aged 82, by whom he had Sir William, his successor, and a daughter Mary. Sir William died Nov. 23, 1745, and was succeeded by his only son,

II. Sir WILLIAM MILNER, Bart. who, in 1747, married Elizabeth, youngest daughter and coheiress of the Rev. George Mordaunt, who was younger brother to Charles, Earl of Peterborough, who died his widow in 1785, by whom he had seven children, 1, Elizabeth; 2, Anastasia-Maria; 3, William-Mordaunt, his successor; 4, George, in the foot-guards, and married, in 1786, Mrs. Fitzgerald, 5, Louisa-Sarah, wife, in 1789, of the Rev. Edward Townshend, nephew to the late Charles Viscount Townsend; 6, Henry-Stephen; 7, Henrietta-Maria. One of the daughters was married, on Sept. 19, 1768, to Sir John Lindsay, Bart. of Scotland. Sir William was many years receiver-general of the excise: he was succeeded by his eldest son,

III. Sir WILLIAM-MORDAUNT MILNER, Bart. who, in 1776, married ———, daughter of Humphrey Sturt, Esq.

* Thoresby's Leeds, p. 215.
† Ibid. ‡ Ibid. § Ibid || Ibid. ¶ Ibid.

ARMS—Parted per pale, or and sable, a chevron, between three horse's bits, counterchanged.

CREST—On a wreath, a horse's head, couped, sabled, bridled and maned, or, and charged on the neck with a bezant.

SEAT—At Nun-Appleton, near Tadcaster, Yorkshire.

TABLE.

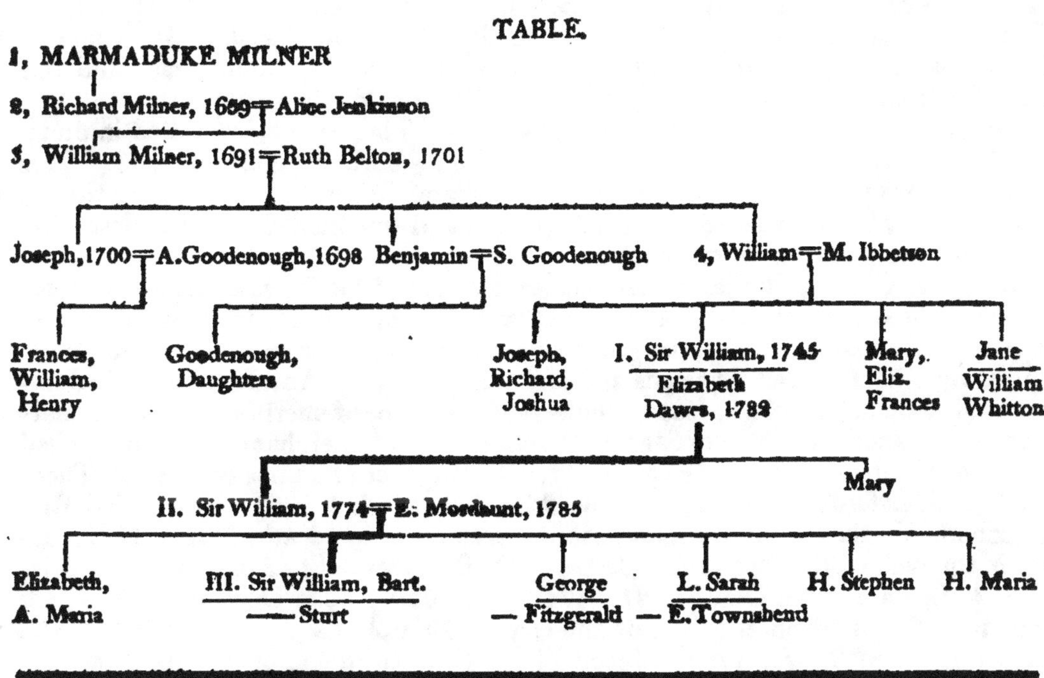

236. ELTON, of the City of BRISTOL.

Created Baronet, October 31, 1717.

THIS family is descended of an ancient family (till lately) of the Hazle *, in Herefordshire, and Gloucestershire.

I. Sir ABRAHAM ELTON, the first baronet, was advanced to the dignity by his majesty King George I. and was member of parliament for Bristol, in the second parliament of that king. He likewise served the office of one of the sheriffs of the city of Bristol, in 1702, and that of mayor in 1710. He married †

* Ex. inf. Dom. Ab. Elton, Bar. 1727.

† Ibid.

Mary, the daughter of Mr. Robert Jefferies, of Pile-Green, in Gloucestershire, by whom he left three sons, 1, Sir Abraham, his successor; 2, Isaac, who was a merchant, and died October 22, 1714, aged thirty-four and was buried at St. Philip's, Bristol. He had two daughters, named Mary, who were both buried with him. 3, Jacob Elton served the office of one of the sheriffs of Bristol, in 1720, and that of mayor in 1733. He died June 15, 1765, and was buried St. Philip's, having been twice married. His first wife was ———, daughter of ——— Small, of the city of Gloucester. He married secondly, April 1739, Elizabeth, relict of George Bridges, of the city of Bristol, distiller, by whom he had no issue. By his first wife he had two sons, Abraham and Isaac, and one daughter Mary, wife of George Prescott, of Theobalds, in Herts, Esq.

Abraham, married Mary, daughter of ———, Thrubshaw, who died in June, 1768, by whom he had one daughter, Mary, born in August 1739. This Abraham served the office of one of the sheriffs of Bristol, in 1736, and that of mayor in 1753. He died August 15, 1762, and was buried with his first wife, at White Staunton, in Somersetshire.

Isaac, of Clifton, in Gloucester, the second son of Jacob, also served the office of one of the sheriffs of Bristol, 1743, and that of mayor in 1761, and was likewise an alderman, he married Mary, daughter of Edward Mortimer, of Trowbridge, Wiltshire, by whom he had four sons and two daughters, 1, Abraham, who died unmarried, Jan. 30, 1762; 2, Isaac, who served the office of sheriff in 1765, and married first, Sarah, daughter of Samuel Peach, of Bristol, merchant, by whom he had one son Abraham. He married secondly, —, daughter of James Ferney, of Theobalds, in Hertfordshire, Esq.; 3, Jacob, who died March 8, 1762. He married Miss Elizabeth Matthews, of Glamorganshire, who after his death, March 1762, became the wife of the Rev. John Casberd, D. D. vicar of St. Augustines, in Bristol; 4, Edward, born October 21, 1742; 5, Mary, born December 10, 1743, wife in 1762, of Michael Miller of the city of Bristol, Esq.; 6, Elizabeth, who died unmarried, March 1767. Jacob Elton, Esq. third son of Sir Abraham, had also a daughter, Mary, wife of George Prescot, of Theobalds, in Hertfordshire, Esq.; and has issue. Sir Abraham Elton, Bart. had also one daughter, Elizabeth, wife of Peter Day, of the city of Bristol, Esq. She died November 6, 1718, aged twenty-six, and was buried at St. Philip's. Sir Abraham died February 9, 1727-8, and was succeeded by his eldest son,

II. Sir ABRAHAM ELTON, Bart. who at the last parliament of King George I. was elected for Taunton, and afterwards for the city of Bristol, which he represented till his death; he was alderman of Bristol, and served the office of mayor. He married ——, daughter of ——, by whom he had three sons; 1, Sir Abraham, his successor; 2, Jacob, a captain in the navy, who was killed in a sea fight, March 29, 1745. He married Caroline, daughter and coheiress of Charles Yate, of Culthorp, in Gloucestershire, Esq. by whom he had no issue; 3, Sir Abraham Isaac, successor to his brother. Sir Abraham had also two daughters; 1, Mary, widow of James Heywood, of Mariston, in Devonshire, Esq. and Elizabeth, wife of captain Foster. Sir Abraham died October 1742, and was succeeded by his eldest son,

III. Sir ABRAHAM ELTON, Bart. who served the office of mayor of Bristol, where he was a merchant, and died unmarried, November 29, 1761, and was succeeded by his only surviving brother,

IV. Sir ABRAHAM ISAAC ELTON, Bart. barrister at law, and town clerk of Bristol. He married, Dec. 26, 1747, Elizabeth, daughter of James Read, of Bristol, merchant, by whom he had one son, Abraham, and three daughters, Mary, born in 1751, wife, in 1770, of Oldfield Bowles, of North Aston, in Oxfordshire, Esq. Sarah, born 1752, wife of the Rev. Hector Munro, of Ireland. Elizabeth died an infant. Sir Abraham-Isaac died at Bath in 1790, and was succeeded by his only son,

V. The Rev. Sir ABRAHAM ELTON, the present Baronet, who married, Nov. 7, 1776, Elizabeth, eldest daughter of Sir John Durbin, of Walton, in Somersetshire, Knt. late mayor of Bristol, merchant, by whom he has one son son Charles-Abraham, born at Bristol Oct. 31, 1778, and one daughter Julia, born at Clifton, March 23, 1783.

ARMS—Paly of six, and gules, or, on a bend, sable, three mullets of the second.

CREST—On a wreath, an arm embowed in armour proper, holding in the gauntlet a scymitar argent, and pommel, or, tied round the arm with a scarf, vert.

SEAT—At Cleveland, near Bristol.

TABLE.

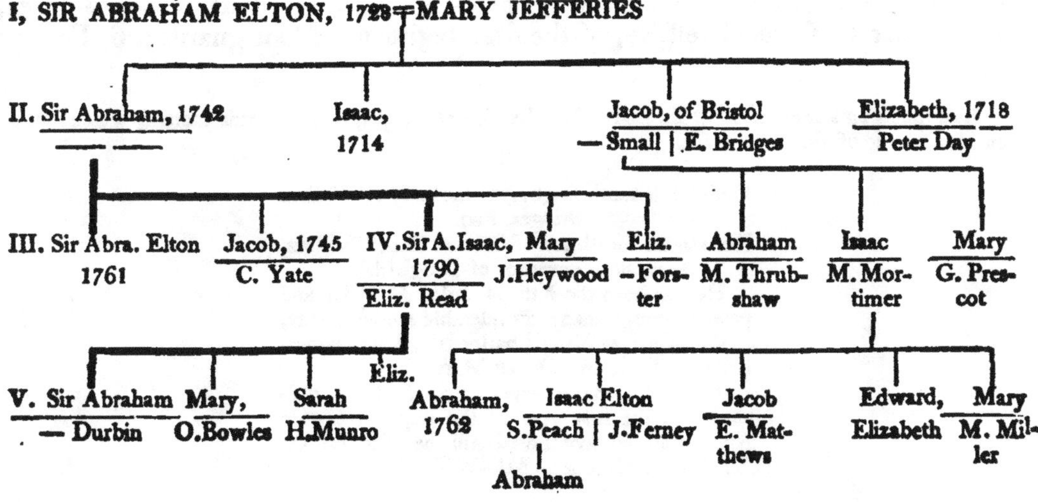

237. BRIDGES, of Goodneston, Kent.

Created Baronet, April 19, 1718.

THIS family is of considerable antiquity in Ireland, where several of the branches thereof have now considerable estates, but the first that settled in England, was,

1, John Bridges, of South Littleton, in Worcestershire, who, on the 14th of November, 1578, purchased a house and lands at Alcester, in Warwickshire; and, in 1592, settled them on himself for life, afterwards on Abraham, his son, with remainder to John, his grandson. He died at Westchester, in his passage to Ireland, and lies buried in the cathedral there.

2, Abraham Bridges, his son, had one son,

3, John Bridges, who was a counsellor, and usually lived at Hackney, near London, where he lies buried. He married Elizabeth Holyoake, by whom he had seven sons, and two daughters; 1, Colonel John Bridges, of whom hereafter; 2, Robert Bridges, who, by Mary Woodcock, his wife, had eight sons, and two daughters; several of whom were married, and their descendents are settled in Holland, Ireland, Wallington, in the parish of Bedington, in Surry, and elsewhere; amongst whom were William Bridges, Esq.; many years surveyor of the ordnance, at the Tower * in the chapel whereof he lies buried, and member of parliament for Leskard, in Cornwall; and, Sir Mathew Bridges, Knt. who married ——, daughter of Sir —— Rooth, Knt. admiral of his Majesty's, navy, and died October 30, 1714. His son Brooke Bridges, Esq. was one of the deputed searchers of the customs, upwards of twenty years, and died in April 1737, he left one son, Brooke Bridges, late of James-street, Bedford-row, Esq. who has left one son, William Bridges, Esq. and four daughters, all unmarried; 3, Elisha, who died young; 4, William, who had one daughter, wife of Robert Pauncefort, of Herefordshire, Esq.; 5, Mathew, who married ——, daughter of —— Temple, of Bucks, and had issue, one daughter, ——, wife of —— Jeffries, Esq.; father of Colonel Jeffries, of the first regiment of foot guards; 6, Francis

* Inscription on a monument at the east end of the Tower Chapel, on the outside thereof, which monument is at the end of the broad walk.

> Under this tomb lies buried the body of William Bridges, Esq.
> He was the fourth son of Colonel Robert Bridges, some time governor of Droghedah.
> He was born the Xth of July, MDCL. and passed through many considerable employments, in the reigns of King Charles II. King James, King William, and Queen Mary.
> He was made surveyor general of the ordnance, in the first year of the reign of Queen Anne, and so continued till he died on the XXXth of October, MDCCXIIII.

Bridges, Esq.; who left issue, Brooke Bridges, of Hatton-garden, Esq. who left issue one son, Brooke Bridges, Esq. who died May 21, 1740; and three daughters; Elizabeth, wife of Nathaniel Carpenter, Esq. secondly of Jasper Mauduit, of London, merchant, and of Hampstead, in Middlesex, which Mr. Mauduit's brother was thought to be the author of a pamphlet, published in 1760, intitled, "Considerations on the present German war" who died May 18, 1768. Mary, of the Rev. Mr. William Bush; and Anne; 7, Brooke Bridges, Esq. who was a commissioner of the forfeited estates in Ireland, where he acquired great estates, which he disposed of to the other branches of the family by his will, dying at Holland-house, near Kensington, a batchelor, April 8, 1702, and was buried at Wadenhoe, in Northamptonshire, one of his estates. The daughters were, Elizabeth, the wife of —— Joyce, Esq. and Mary of Nathaniel Taylor, Esq. barrister at law, from whom are descended the Taylors, of Bifrons, in Kent.

4, Colonel John Bridges, of Alcester, in Warwickshire, eldest son and heir of John Bridges, and Elizabeth Holyoake; married Mary, daughter of Bartholomew Beale, of Walton, in the county of Salop, Esq. by whom he had four sons, and several daughters; 1, John Bridges, Esq. who purchased Barton Seagrave, in Northamptonshire, and settled there, and who married Elizabeth, daughter of William Trumball, LL.D. father of Sir William Trumball, Knt. secretary of state, by whom he had seven sons, and five daughters; 1, John Bridges, Esq. his eldest son and heir, who, in the reign of her majesty Queen Anne, for several years, was one of the commissioners of the customs, which was continued to him in the beginning of the reign of his majesty George I. and he was afterwards appointed treasurer of the excise. He was a gentleman truly valuable, in all respects, of superior parts and learning, a great encourager of ingenious and learned men, and a diligent, exact, and curious searcher out of antiquities; in collecting of which, in his native county of Northampton, he had made so great progress, that, had providence spared his life, but some few years longer, Northamptonshire would have had no temptation to have envied Hertfordshire, her Chauncey, or Warwickshire, her Dugdale. He died at his chambers in Lincoln's-Inn; of which he was a bencher, March 16, 1723-4: he was also F. R. S. and was buried in his family vault, at Barton Seagrave, aforesaid; 2, William Bridges, Esq. secretary to the stamp-office, married Martha, daughter of Robert Hart, of Brill, in the county of Bucks, Esq. by whom he had one son, John Bridges, Esq. of Barton Seagrave, who married Margaretta, daughter of John Horton, of Gumley, in the county of Leicester, Gent. and died July 1741; 3, Brooke Bridges, who died unmarried; 4, Charles Bridges, who was twice married, but had no issue that lived to maturity; 5, George-Rodolph Bridges, who died young; 6, Nathaniel Bridges, rector of Wadenhoe, who married Sarah, daughter of the Rev. Mr. Sawyer, of Ashley, in the county of Northampton, by whom he had one son, Brooke Bridges; and two daughters, Elizabeth, and Anne, and 7, Ralph Bridges, D. D. rector of South Weale, in Essex, and proctor for the clergy in the diocese of London, in convocation; he died Nov. 23, 1758, having held the rectory of South Weale forty-five years. The daughters of John Bridges, of Barton were, 1, Elizabeth, wife of Richard Bynns, of

Cheadle, in the county of Stafford, D. D. 2, Margaret, of John Horton, of Gumley aforesaid, Gent.; 3, Catherine, of the Rev. John Woods, rector of Wilford, in the county of Nottingham; 4, Anne; and, 5, Deborah, who both died unmarried. We come now to the younger children of Colonel John Bridges, by Mary Beale, his wife, who were as follow; 2, Brooke, of whom hereafter; 3, Elisha; 4, Nathaniel, who both died unmarried: of his daughters, Elizabeth, was wife of the Lord Lambert, eldest son and heir of the Earl of Cavan, in the kingdom of Ireland; and Mary, of John Smith, of Thedilthorpe, in the county of Lincoln, Esq.

5, Brooke Bridges, of Grove, in the county of Middlesex, Esq. auditor of the imprest, second son of Colonel John Bridges, before-named, purchased Goodneston, in Kent, of Sir Thomas Engham, Knt. and built a very handsome house, and very much improved the gardens, and along the sides of the terrace walks, stand the busts of the twelve Cæsars, in marble, larger than the life; they were brought from Rome, and cost about 600l. He married Mary, daughter of Sir Justinian Lewen, Knt. by whom he had Sir Brooke Bridges, of Goodneston, in the county of Kent, the first baronet, so created 4 George I. and John Bridges, of Cobham, in the county of Surry, Esq. who married first, Mrs. Anne Lewen, by whom he had two children, who died infants; and, secondly, ———, the widow of ——— Westerne, Esq. and died December 23, 1717, aged seventy-four.

I. Sir BROOKE BRIDGES, of Goodneston, Bart. the eldest son, who was, for many years, one of the auditors of the impost of the treasury, married in 1707, Margaret, daughter of Sir Robert Marsham, Bart. since Lord Romney, by whom he had Sir Brooke Bridges, his successor; and Margaret*. His second lady was Mary, second daughter of Sir Thomas Hales, of Beakesborne, in the county of Kent, Bart. by whom he had one son, Thomas, who died an infant. Sir Brooke died March 16, 1727-8.

II. Sir BROOKE BRIDGES, Bart. the only son and successor, married Anne, daughter, and one of the three coheiresses of Sir Thomas Palmer, of Wingham, in the county of Kent, Bart. (by his first lady, daughter of Sir Robert Marsham, Bart.) by whom he had one posthumous son, Sir Brooke Bridges, Bart. and died May 23, 1733, in the 24th year of his age, being at the time of his death, high sheriff of the county of Kent. Sir Brooke's widow remarried to Colonel Charles Fielding, brother of the right honourable the earl of Denbigh.

III. Sir BROOKE BRIDGES, Bart. only son and successor to his father in dignity and estate, was chosen in 1762, to represent the county of Kent, in parliament, and was re-elected in 1768. He married, in 1765, Fanny, daughter of Edmund Fowler, of Danbury, in Essex, by whom he had seven sons, and six daughters; 1, Brooke, born Aug. 14, 1766, and died July 9, 1781; 2, Charles, died young; 3, William, born June 22, 1767, of whom hereafter; 4, Henry, born June 4, 1769; 5, Edward-Brook, born Sep. 7, 1779; 6, Brook-John, born

* Qu. If this Margaret did not die unmarried in April 1736, or whether she was the wife of John Plumbtree, of Fredville, in Kent, Esq. in September 1750, or of the Rev. ——— Potwin, rector of Sanbury and Woodham Ferry, Essex.

TABLE.

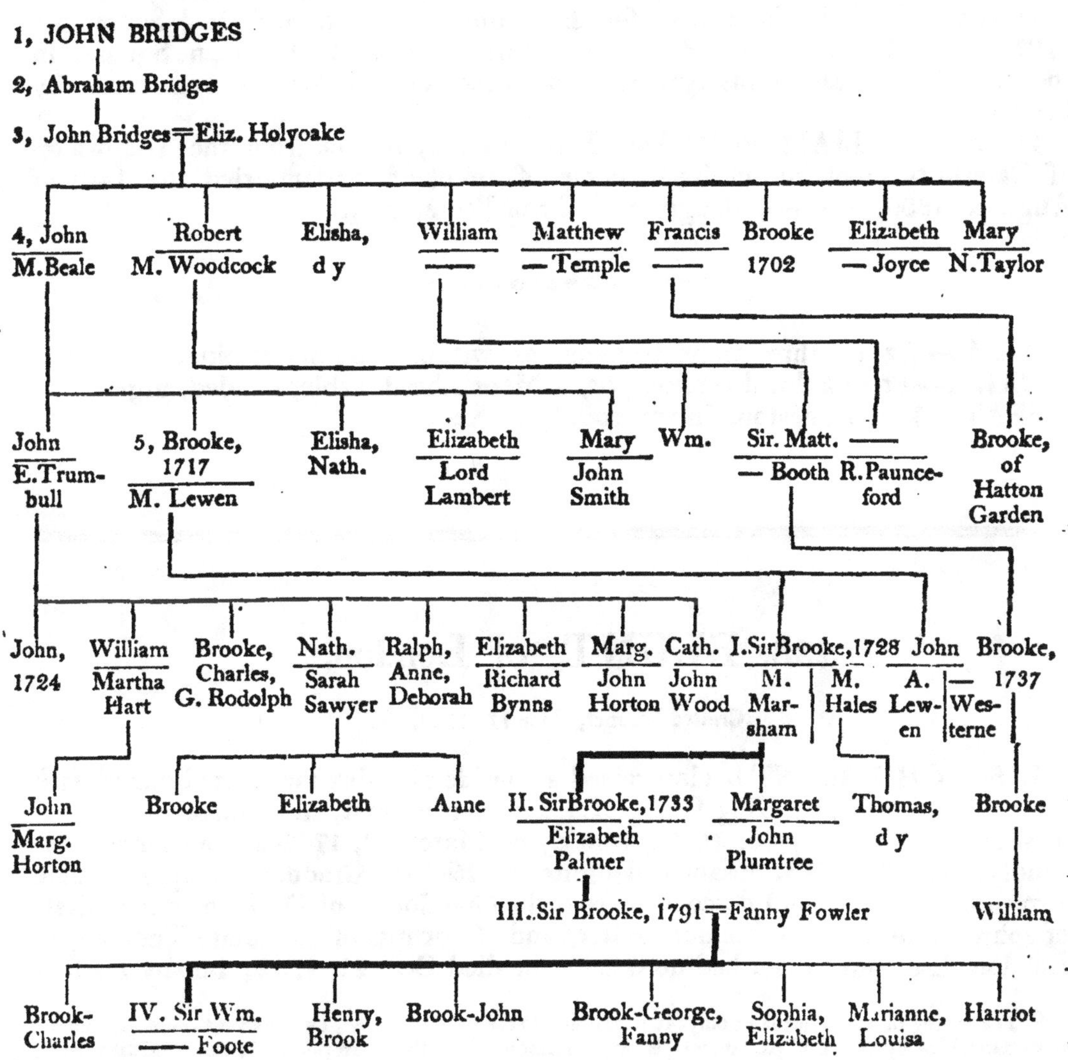
1, JOHN BRIDGES
2, Abraham Bridges
3, John Bridges=Eliz. Holyoake
4, John
M.Beale
Robert
M. Woodcock
Elisha,
d y
William
——
Matthew
— Temple
Francis
——
Brooke
1702
Elizabeth
— Joyce
Mary
N.Taylor
John
E.Trumbull
5, Brooke,
1717
M. Lewen
Elisha,
Nath.
Elizabeth
Lord
Lambert
Mary
John
Smith
Wm.
Sir. Matt.
— Booth
——
R.Paunceford
Brooke,
of
Hatton
Garden
John,
1724
William
Martha
Hart
Brooke,
Charles,
G. Rodolph
Nath.
Sarah
Sawyer
Ralph,
Anne,
Deborah
Elizabeth
Richard
Bynns
Marg.
John
Horton
Cath.
John
Wood
I.SirBrooke,1728
M.
Marsham
M.
Hales
John
A.
Lewen
Brooke,
1737
—
Westerne
John
Marg.
Horton
Brooke
Elizabeth
Anne
II. SirBrooke,1733
Elizabeth
Palmer
Margaret
John
Plumtree
Thomas,
d y
Brooke
III..Sir Brooke, 1791=Fanny Fowler
William
Brook-
Charles
IV. Sir Wm.
—— Foote
Henry,
Brook
Brook-John
Brook-George,
Fanny
Sophia,
Elizabeth
Marianne,
Louisa
Harriot

Nov. 28, 1782; 7, Brook-George, born Nov. 7, 1784. The daughters were, 1, Fanny, born June 20, 1771; 2, Sophia, born May 9, 1772; 3, Elizabeth, born May 23, 1773; 4, Marianne, born Nov. 19, 1774; 5, Louisa, born Aug. 1777; 6, Harriot, born Feb. 20, 1781. Sir Brooke, was, for several years, receiver-general of the land tax, for the county of Kent, and died September 1791, at the house of the Honourable Mrs. Hatton, in Portman Square, in the fifty-eighth year of his age, and was succeeded in dignity and estate by his son,

IV. Sir WILLIAM BRIDGES, Bart. who by licence from the Archbishop of Caterbury, took the christian name of Brooke*, and married the 14th of August, 1800, ———, daughter of John Foote, Esq.

ARMS—Azure, three water bougets, or, within a border ermine.
CREST—From a ducal coronet, or, a Moor's head, sable, banded, argent.
SEAT—At Goodneston, in the county of Kent.

238. BLUNT, of London.

Created Baronet, June 17, 1720,

I. Sir JOHN BLUNT having raised a considerable fortune, was dignified with the title of Baronet by King George I. He married first, Mrs. Elizabeth Court, of Warwickshire, July 16, 1689; who dying March 22, 1707-8, he married secondly, Dec. 22, 1713, Susanna, daughter of Richard Craddock, Esq. sometime governor of Bengal, and descended from the Craddocks, of Durham, relict, first, of John Banner, late of London, salter, and afterwards of Benjamin Tudman, of London, Esq. but by her had no issue: she died Dec. 21, 1752; but by his first

* The taking of a new surname only, or in addition to the paternal name, by a warrant under the king's sign-manual, or by an act of parliament, is very common; but the assumption of a new christian name, by licence from the bishop of the diocese, as the present Sir Brooke (William) Bridges, has done, is an incident that now rarely occurs. In former days, to have made this alteration without consent of the ordinary, would have exposed the offending party to ecclesiastical censures; for in the consistorial acts of the bishop of Rochester, it is recorded, "October 13, 1515, that Agnes Sharpe appeared, and confessed her having of her own motion and consent, voluntarily changed at confirmation, the name of her infant son, to Edward, who was, when baptized, named Henry; for which she submitted to penance. The penance enjoined, was, to make a pilgrimage to the rood at Boxley, and to carry in procession, on five Lord's days, a lighted taper, which she was to offer to the image of the blessed Mary."

wife he had thirteen children, whereof five sons and two daughters survived him, viz. 1, John, born July 23, 1694, who died unmarried; 2, Sir Henry, his successor; 3, Charles, born Nov. 4, 1700, lieutenant in brigadier Bisset's regiment of fusileers; 4, William, born July 4, 1704; 5, Thomas, born March, 1707-8; Rachel, the eldest daughter, born Jan. 21, 1697-8, wife of Samuel, son of Charles Blunt, of London, Esq. which Charles was cousin-german to Sir John, and surviving him, was remarried in May, 1739, to John Parkes, of London, merchant; Elizabeth, another daughter of Sir John, was born Dec. 9, 1705. Sir John died Jan. 24, 1732-3, and was succeeded in dignity and estate by his eldest son,

II. Sir HENRY BLUNT, Bart. who married, in 1724, Dorothy, eldest daughter of William Nutt, late of Walthamstow, in Essex, Esq. by whom he had several children, and dying Oct. 12, 1759, was succeeded by his son,

III. Sir CHARLES WILLIAM BLUNT, Bart. married, July 22, 1764, Elizabeth, only daughter of Richard Peers, Esq. alderman of London, and sister and heiress of Sir Richard Peers, Bart. who assumed the surname and arms of Symons, by whom he has three sons, 1, Charles-Richard, born Dec. 6, 1775; 2, Richard-Charles, born June 2, 1776; 3, William, born Dec. 7, 1780: and nine daughters, 1, Anna-Sophia, born May 13, 1765; 2, Elizabeth, born April 1766, died the day after; 3, Louisa, born May 31, 1767; 4, Maria-Tryphena, born June 6, 1768. wife of Charles Cockerell, and died Oct. 8, 1789; 5, Elizabeth, born Sept. 1769; 6, Charlotte, born Sept. 1772; Lydia, born Sept. 25, 1773; 8, Anna-Maria, born Aug. 19, 1774; 9, Dorothea, born Nov. 23, 1778.

ARMS—Barry nebulée of six, or, and sa. a crescent for difference.

CREST—The sun in glory, charged on the centre with an eye issuing tears, all proper.

SEAT—Clery, Hants.

TABLE.

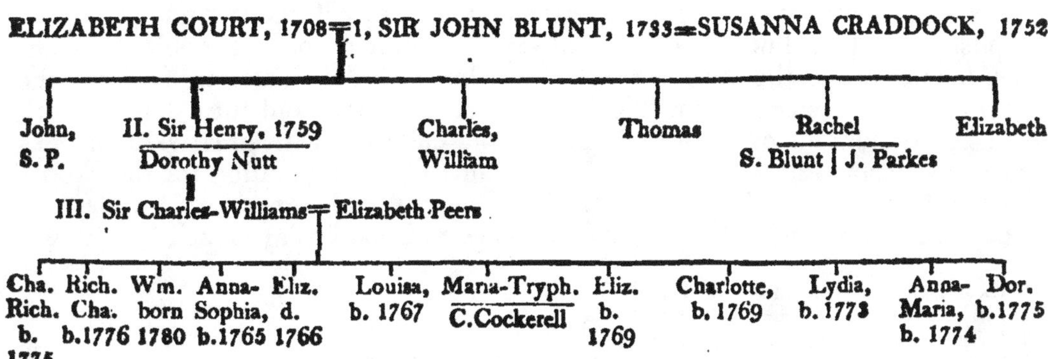

239. CODRINGTON, of Dodington, Gloucestershire.

Created Baronet, April 21, 1721.

THIS family is a younger branch of the Codringtons, of Codrington*, in the county of Gloucester†, which was a family of good note in this county in the time of Henry IV. John Codrington, Esq. being standard-bearer to K. Henry V. in his wars with France‡, and, as it appears by the Heralds Books, was then armed in a coat with lions, in the service of the said king in battle, watch, and ward, under his banner; and for the good services that the said John Codrington had done, or should do, and to the worship of knighthood, as it is there expressed, a farther addition was made to his arms in the twenty-third of Hen. VI.

1, Christopher Codrington, a younger son of this family, went with his fortune into Barbadoes, in the reign of King Charles I. where he married, and died §, leaving two sons, Christopher and John. Christopher became lieutenant-governor of the Island of Barbadoes, and afterwards captain-general of the Leeward Islands, in which post he died ||, leaving only two sons, one of them of his own name.

2, John, his brother, was colonel of the life-guards in Barbadoes, treasurer, and privy-counsellor. He married —— ¶, daughter of Colonel Bates, of that island, by whom he had two sons, Sir William and John.

Christopher, the son of the aforesaid Christopher, the captain-general of the Leeward Islands, was bred up at Oxford, and chosen fellow of All Soul's College there, but afterwards betaking himself to a martial life, attended King William in the wars in Flanders, where he so eminently signalized himself at the siege of Huy, that he was particularly taken notice of by that prince **, and was soon advanced to be colonel of his guards, and afterwards succeeded his father in the government of the Leeward Islands.

This gentleman was a person famous for personal merit and great accomplishments ††; but he will be always celebrated for his noble benefactions, having bequeathed to the aforesaid college of All Souls, in Oxford, the sum of 10,000l. sterling, for the building of a library, and furnishing it with books ‡‡, besides his own inestimable library, collected with great skill and expence; as also an estate of 2000l. per annum to the Corporation for the Propagation of Christian Knowledge, for the building and endowment of a college at Barbadoes. "He died at his seat in Barbadoes on Good Friday, April 7, 1710 §§,

* Ex inf. Dom. Wil. Codrington, Bar. 1726.
† Sir Robert Atkins's State of Gloucestershire, p. 391.
‡ Ex inf. Dom. Wil. Codrington, Bar. 1726.
§ Ibid. || Ibid. ¶ Ibid. ** Ibid. †† Ibid.
‡‡ Ayliff's History of Oxford, Vol. I. P. 340.
§§ Memorials and Characters of Eminent Persons, P. 444.

and was buried the day following in the parish church of St. Michael, in that island; but his body was afterwards brought over to England, and interred in the chapel of All Soul's College, Oxford, where two Latin orations were spoke to his memory by two fellows of that college. He was a gentleman of great parts *, of a quick and piercing comprehension, a strong, solid, and distinguishing judgment, a retentive memory, a warm imagination, a sublime way of thinking, a methodical way of reasoning, and a voluble distinct utterance: he had his education first at Christ Church, Oxford, but afterwards removed to All Soul's College, and was chosen fellow there, and soon acquired the deserved character of an accomplished well-bred gentleman, and universal scholar. He afterwards betook himself to the army, but without quitting his fellowship, where his merit and impregnable courage soon recommended him to his prince's favour, who rewarded him with the government of the Leeward Caribbee Islands; after the resignation of which, he led a very retired life, and applied himself to study, particularly church-history and metaphysics; of the latter, he was esteemed the greatest master in the world. In a word, he had, in his West-India retirement, made so wonderful a progress in his studies, that, had Providence spared him to have returned to his beloved university, he would have been as much the object of their admiration as he deserved to be the object of their delight †." The remainder of this great man's fortune descended to his nephew and heir at law,

I. Sir WILLIAM CODRINGTON, who was advanced to the dignity of a Baronet by King George I. in the eighth year of his reign, and married Elizabeth, daughter of William Bethel, of Swindon, in the county of York, Esq. who died Feb. 7, 1761, by whom he had three sons, Sir Richard, his successor, ——, and Edward, who died in France Jan. 1775; and two daughters, ——, wife of William Dowdeswell, M. P. for Tewksbury in 1747, and ——, of J. Perriman. Sir William was member of parliament for Minehead, in Somersetshire, and one of the gentlemen of his Majesty's privy-chamber at the time of his death, which happened Dec. 17, 1738, at Dodington, and was succeeded by his eldest son,

II. Sir WILLIAM CODRINGTON, Bart. who married Anne, daughter of ———, by whom he had one son Sir William, his successor. Sir William was representative in parliament for Tewksbury, in Somersetshire, and lieutenant-colonel of the militia of that county. He died March 11, 1792, and was succeeded by his son,

III. Sir WILLIAM CODRINGTON, Bart. who married, in 1776, Mary, daughter of the late Hon. Mr. Ward.

ARMS—Argent, a fess embattled and counter-embattled, gules, between three lioncels passant, sable.

CREST—On a wreath, a dragon's head couped, gules, between a pair of (dragon's) wings, chequy, or, and azure.

SEAT—At Dodington, in the county of Gloucester.

* Memorials and Characters of Eminent Persons, P. 444.

† He wrote four poems on the Musæ Anglicanæ.

TABLE.

CODRINGTON

1. Christopher Codrington

2, Christopher Codrington, governor of Barbadoes — John

Christopher — 3, John Codrington = —— Bates

Christopher — I. Sir William, 1738 = E. Bethel, 1761 — John

II. Sir William, 1792 = Anne — —— — Edward, 1775 — —— = W. Dowdeswell — —— = J. Perriman

III. Sir William = Mary Ward

---

240. FREDERICK, of WESTMINSTER.

Created Baronet, June 10, 1723.

THIS family is descended from Sir John Frederick, Knt. son of Christopher Frederick, citizen of London, lord-mayor of the city of London in 1662, who was one of the most considerable traders in the said city, though I do not find that he ever was sheriff for the city of London, which is very remarkable. He was president of Christ's Hospital, and rebuilt the dining-hall there after the fire of London, and his picture is in the court room of the said hospital. He left issue Thomas Frederick, of Downing-street, Westminster, Esq. who, I believe, is the person who gave 500l. to St. Thomas's-Hospital, Southwark; he had three sons, 1, Sir John Frederick, Bart. of whom hereafter; 2, Sir Thomas Frederick, Knt. who went to the Indies, and acquired a considerable fortune, but of him hereafter; 3, Charles Frederick, Esq. third son of Thomas, died unmarried: also three daughters, Mary, the eldest, was wife of Thomas Powel, of Nanteos, Cardiganshire, Esq.; Leonora, wife of Rumney Diggle, of Gray's-Inn, Esq.; and Jane, wife, first, of James Lannoy, of Hammersmith, in Middlesex, Esq. secondly, of the Duke of Athol.

I. Sir JOHN FREDERICK, Bart. the eldest son, was advanced to the dignity of a Baronet in the ninth year of King George I. He married, July 1727, ——, daughter of —— Kinnersley, Esq. by whom he had two sons, Sir John, his successor, and Sir Thomas, successor to his brother. His lady died Aug. 31, 1749, and Sir John in Oct. 1755. He was succeeded by his eldest son,

II. Sir JOHN FREDERICK, Bart. who died unmarried March 24, 1757, and was succeeded by his brother,

III. Sir THOMAS FREDERICK, Bart. who married Elizabeth, daughter of Peter Bathurst, of Clarendon-Park, in Wiltshire, Esq. by whom (who died Sept. 11, 1764) he had two daughters; 1, Elizabeth, born 1758, wife of John Morshead, of Carhither, in Cornwall, Esq. by whom she had one daughter Selina; 2, Selina, born Jan. 30, 1760, wife of Robert Thistlewaite, of Norman Court and Southwick, in the county of Hants, Esq. brother to the Countess of Chesterfield; he dying without issue male, the title descended to the issue of

Sir Thomas Frederick, Knt. brother of Sir John, the first Baronet. Sir Thomas was baptized Jan. 22, 1680-1, married Jan. 11, 1704-5, at Fort St. George, in the East-Indies, Mary, daughter of —— Moncrief, of Scotland, cousin of Sir Thomas Moncrief (after his death she became the wife of William Pointz, Esq. receiver-general of the excise, brother of Stephen Pointz, Esq. preceptor of William, Duke of Cumberland), by whom he had four sons and six daughters, 1, Thomas, born at Fort St. George, Oct. 25, 1707, M. P. for Shoreham, in Sussex, and died Aug. 29, 1740, at St. Olave, in the Old Jewry, unmarried; 2, Sir John, successor to the title, of whom hereafter; 3, Sir Charles, Knt. born at Fort St. George, Dec. 21, 1709, M. P. for Queenborough, in Kent, K. B. surveyor-general of the ordnance. He married, Aug. 18, 1746, Lucy, daughter of Hugh, Viscount Falmouth, born May 6, 1719, by whom he had four sons and two daughters, 1, Charles, born Oct. 9, 1748; 2, Thomas-Lenox, born March 25, 1750, a captain in the navy, who married Anne Greigson, of Plymouth; 3, John-Montague, born Feb. 21, 1754, died July following, and was buried at St. Oalve, in the Old Jewry; 4, Edward-Boscawen, born May 23, 1762, an officer in the army, one of the esquires to Prince Frederick, Bishop of Osnaburgh, at the installation of the Order of the Bath, June 15, 1772. The daughters were, 1, Lucy, born July 7, 1752; 2, Augusta, born July 25, 1747, wife of Thomas, son of Sir George Prescott, of London, merchant. The fourth son of Sir Thomas, Knt. was Marescoe, of Welbeck-street, a major-general, born Dec. 7, 1725, and married first, June 12, 1760, Sarah, daughter of Robert Pickering, of Rochester, in Kent, by whom he had two sons, Thomas, born at Rochester, April 22, 1761, and Robert, born 1774. He married secondly, Sarah, daughter of —— Davis.

The daughters of Sir Thomas Frederick, Knt. were, 1, Leonora, born at Fort St. George, April 29, 1706, died May following; 2, Mary, born at Fort St. George Nov. 9, 1711, wife of Alexander Hume, Esq. eldest brother of Sir Abraham Hume, Bart. who died Sep. 15, 1765, aged 73, by whom she had a daughter Mary, who died unmarried, May 5, 1763; 3, Henrietta, born at Fort St. George, Sept. 10, 1717, wife of Luke Spence, of Malling, in the county of Sussex, and died 1777, by whom she had one son Henry, who married Philippa, daughter of Robert Butts, Bishop of Ely; 4, Leonora, died young; 5, Jane, died young; 6, Hannah, who, in Aug. 25, 1772, became the wife of Sir Abraham Hume, of Wormlybury, Herts, Bart. by whom she had two sons, 1, Abraham, successor to his father, born Feb. 20, 1748-9, who married, March 20, 1771, Amelia, daughter of John Egerton, Lord Bishop of Durham; they were married by the Archbishop of Canterbury; 2, Alexander, born Oct. 19, 1758; and 3, Hannah, born May 30, 1752, wife, in 1773, of Joseph Hare. Sir Thomas died Dec. 16, 1770, and was succeeded by his cousin-german,

IV. Sir JOHN FREDERICK, of Burwood, Bart. He was one of the commissioners of his Majesty's customs, born Nov. 28, 1708, at Fort St. George, and F. R. S.; he succeeded his brother also in estates, and as M. P. for West Looe. He married, Oct. 22, 1741, Susanna, daughter of Sir Roger Hudson, of Sunbury, in Middlesex, Knt. coheiress to her brother, Vansittart Hudson, Esq. who died June 29, 1787, by whom he had two sons and three daughters, 1, ——, born March 1748, died young: 2, Sir John, of whom hereafter: the daughters, Susanna, Mary, and Anne, all died young. Sir John died April 9, 1783, and was succeeded by his son,

V. Sir JOHN FREDERICK, the present Baronet, born March 18, 1749, and was on his travels abroad in 1771. He married Mary, youngest daughter and coheiress of Richard Garth, of Morden, Esq. by whom he had a son John, born Sept. 20, 1779. Sir John represented the county of Surry in the last parliament, and is returned again for the present.

ARMS—Or, on a chief, azure, three doves, argent.

CREST—On a chapeau, azure, turned up ermine, a dove, as in the arms, holding in his beak an olive branch, proper.

SEAT—Burwood, Surry.

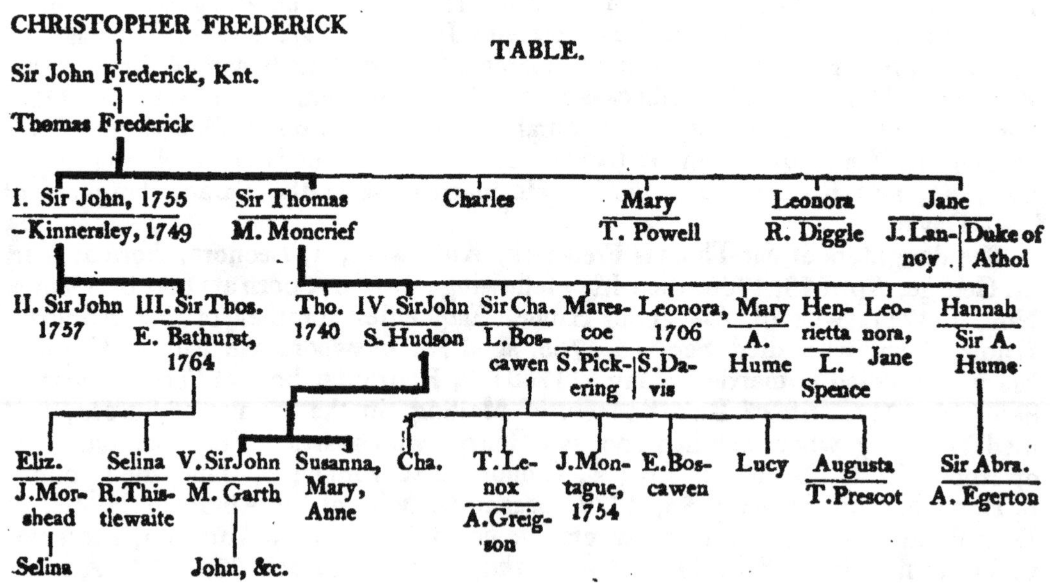

241. VANDEPUT, of TWICKENHAM, Middlesex.

Created Baronet, Nov. 7, 1723.

THIS family hath been of great eminency in the Netherlands, and the present Sir George Vandeput, Bart. is the eighth, in a lineal descent, from Henry Vandeput, of Antwerp*, who fled from thence with several wealthy families in 1568, the 11th of Elizabeth, on the persecution of the Duke d'Alva to extirpate the Protestant religion in the Netherlands, and brought over with him a good estate, though several branches of this family are still remaining in the Low Countries.

1, Giles Vandeput, Esq. son of the above Henry, married Sarah, daughter and heiress of John Jaupin, Esq. by whom a considerable estate came into this family. He died Mar. 24, 1646, leaving

2, Peter, his son and heir, who married Jane, daughter of Theodoric Hoste, of London, merchant, by whom he had seven children, whereof only two survived him, Sir Peter, his son and heir, and Jane, wife of Sir Edward Smijth, of Hill-Hall, in Theydon, Essex, Bart. †

4, Sir Peter Vandeput, Knt. son and heir, great-grandfather of the present Baronet, held the sheriffalty of London in 1684, by commission, jointly with Sir William Gosselin, which is the only instance of that kind in history. He married Margaret, daughter of Sir John Buckworth, of West-Sheen, in Richmond, Surry, Knt. by whom he had several children, of which Peter was his heir; —, the eldest,

* Ex stem. penes Pet. Vandeput, Bar. 1741.

† In St. Margaret Patten's church, in London, is a monument erected by Sir Peter Vandeput, Knt. to the memory of his parents, with this inscription (a):

H. S. E.

Ægidius Vandeput, Antwerpiensis, inter Mercatoris Londini, fide opt. ubi mortuus est 24 Kal. Mar. Anno 1646, Ætat. 70. Sara, Ægidii Uxor, Fœmina lectissima, Iprensis, defuncta est Lond. 3 Non. Mar. Anno 1656, Ætat. 67. Petrus, Ægidii Filius, variarum Gentium Linguis & Literis instructus, Probitate, Prudentia, Integritate, Mercat. plane eximius: Obiit Lond. 5 Id. Feb. Anno 1668. Ætat. 57. Jana, Filia Theodorici Hoste, Merc. Lond. Petri Uxor fidissima. Septem Liberis infra sepultis, superstite Petro e Jana, enupta Edw. Smith, de Theydon-Mount, in com. Essex, Bar. decessit 4 Non. Feb. Anno 1672, Ætat. 53.

Petrus Vandeput, Eq. Aur. Petri, Filius H. M. P. Parentibus chariss. Anno 1686, juxta quos ipse & Ux. Margareta, Filia, Joh. Buckworth, Eq. Aur. Suas exuvias poni statuerunt.

(a) Maitland's Hist. of London, P. 442.

was wife of Sir Peter Jackson, Knt. a Turkey merchant in London; she died his widow August 14, 1731 *. Sir Peter died April, 1708, and was buried with his ancestors in St. Margaret Pattens †.

I. PETER VANDEPUT, Esq. son and heir of Sir Peter, was advanced to the dignity of a Baronet, by letters-patent, Nov. 7, 1723. He married

* Historical Register.

† Dr. Brady, minister of Richmond, in Surry, in which parish Sir Peter lived some years, has given this account of him in a sermon preached in that church, May 2, 1708 (*b*). "I am, I confess, no friend to those funeral panegyricks, which are promiscuously dispensed to the deserving and undeserving; but, since to rob the dead is a sort of sacrilege, since the righteous should be had in everlasting remembrance, I think myself obliged to do some sort of justice to the extraordinary merit of our lately deceased brother; and I cannot but avow, that I never met with any one who had a better title to a character of distinction. For,

"If, as we ought in the first place, we consider him as a christian, his piety was serious and unaffected, deeply imprinted upon his heart, and decently conspicuous in all his actions. He was a true son of the Church of England, unmoveable in his adherence to her doctrine and her discipline; a constant frequenter of her worship and her ordinances; and nothing so much disturbed him in his tedious distemper, as its hindering him from attending on them so constantly as he would have done: and all this was the result of a mature judgment, and not owing to the happy prejudice of education; he understood his religion, and therefore he valued it, being determined to persevere in it both by choice and inclination. And his affection to the church extended also to her ministers, whom he highly esteemed in love for their works' sake; nay, it even descended to the meanest of her members, by his exemplary beneficence, and charity to the poor.

"If we look upon him as an Englishman, and as a man of business, he was extremely useful in his generation, having discharged several offices of great trust and honour with an unbiassed honesty, and irreproachable integrity; and that, in such times of difficulty and danger, as nothing could have stemmed but a consummate wisdom, and the dictates of a conscience that was void of offence. He was a hearty friend to our present best of governments, into the interests of which, though he entered very early, yet was it without rashness or inconsideration, having first taken the advice, and then followed the opinion of the most eminent divines and lawyers in the kingdom; but as he was thus cautious in fixing his principles, so was he steady and unalterable in his practice accordingly, laying hold upon all occasions, and improving all opportunities, to advance and support the great cause he was engaged in.

"If we reflect upon him further, as a gentleman, he was an exact pattern of true good breeding; his conversation was innocent, entertaining, and improving; his behaviour modest and engaging; his notion of things solid, and his reasonings upon them clear; and the society of his friends was so dear and pleasing to him, as would always inspire him with such an air of cheerfulness, as made him seem to forget the infirmity he laboured under; an infirmity which few others would have borne so contentedly, and of which he supported the burden for several years, with a great deal of christian patience, and resignation to the will of God.

"What shall I say of him, as a husband, as a father, as a relation, as a neighbour, as a friend! How regularly did he govern his numerous family, and how happy was he in finding the good effects of his care! How just and faithful was he to his excellent lady! how tender and indulgent to his well-deserving children! how kind and respectful to his other relations! how obliging and serviceable to all his acquaintances! how sincere and open-hearted to his more intimate friends! These are qualities of which there are so many witnesses present, that no one can suspect me in what I have said of him, to have been biassed by friendship, or by the many obligations which shall ever make his memory be dear and precious to me, when he is nothing else but dust and ashes.

"Let, then, a due remembrance of his uncommon accomplishments, be a pomp more lasting than his funeral solemnity; and instead of those escutcheons which have adorned his hearse, be these the odours to embalm his reputation; and to conclude, let his memory still live in this durable character, of a serious christian, a true churchman, a lover of his country, a complete gentleman, an affectionate husband, a loving father, a kind relation, a valuable acquaintance, and an admirable friend."

(*b*) Memorials and Characters of Eminent Persons, p. 405.

Frances*, daughter of Sir George Matthews, of Southwark, Knt. who died March 3, 1764, by whom he had issue Peter, who died before his father, Sir George, his successor, and Frances, who died unmarried. Sir Peter died at Mentz, in Germany, Aug. 25, 1748, and was buried there, being succeeded in title and estate by his only surviving son,

II. Sir GEORGE VANDEPUT, Bart. who had the remarkable contest with Lord Trentham as candidates for the city of Westminster in 1750. He married first, ——, daughter of —— Schutz, by whom he had issue. He married secondly, Aug. 19, 1772, at Kelvedon, in Essex, Philadelphia, youngest daughter of the late Lieutenant-Colonel Gery, by whom he had issue, Sir George, his successor; Philadelphia, wife of Captain Charles Smijth, brother of Sir William Smijth, of Hill-Hall, Essex, Bart.; and ——, wife of Richard Vere, an officer in the army, son of the Rev. George Drury, of Claydon, Suffolk. Sir George died Dec. 1784, and was succeeded by his son,

III. Sir GEORGE VANDEPUT, the present Baronet.

ARMS—Argent, three dolphins, hauriant, azure.

CREST—On a wreath, a dolphin, hauriant, azure, between two wings, expanded, or.

SEAT—Bessington, Middlesex.

TABLE.

1, HENRY VANDEPUT

2, Giles Vandeput, 1646=Sarah Jaupin

3, Peter Vandeput, 1668=Jane Hoste, 1672

4, Sir Peter Vandeput, 1708=Marg. Buckworth — Jane=Sir Edward Smijth

I. Sir Peter Vandeput, Bart. 1748=Frances Matthews, 1764 — ——=Sir Peter Jackson

Peter — —Schutz=II. Sir George, 1784=P. Gery — Frances

III. Sir George — Philadelphia=C. Smijth — ——=R. V. Drury

Jane, daughter of —— Vandeput, wife of Abraham Fortrie, son of John, and grandson of Nicholas de la Fortrie, of Flanders, which family, in the reign of Elizabeth, came over to England on account of their religion.—*Visit. of London*, 1634, *marked* C. 24, *Coll. of Arms*, *Pedig. of Fortrie*, *p.* 151.

* Ex inf. Dom. Pet. Vandeput, Bar. 1741.

242. MITCHELL, of West-Shore, Scotland.

Created Baronet, June 19, 1724.

THE present Baronet is the lineal representative of the Mitchells*, of Bandeth, the principal family of that name in Scotland.

They were considerable in the reign of King James VI. who, for a reward of their loyalty and good services, granted to William Mitchell †, son of John Mitchell, of Bandeth, and to his heirs for ever, a charter of the lands of Bandeth, in the county of Sterling, with all the usual privileges, *cum curiis*, *mulierum merchetis*, *aucupationibus*, *venationibus*, *&c.* And that the said William's predecessors were very ancient possessors of these lands, is implied by these words in the charter; *Dilecto nostro Willielmo Mitchell, veteri nativo possessori.* In the seisin, the said William is stiled, *Vir honorabilis Willielmus Mitchell, de Bandeth*; and the witnesses thereto are, James, Earl of Arran, and Patrick, Lord Archbishop of St. Andrews, &c. The charter bears date at Holy-Rood House, Feb. 8, 1584, under the great seal. There was also in the custody of the late Sir Andrew Mitchell, Bart. ‡, a presentation to the archdeaconry of Tingwall, in Zetland, granted by King Charles I. to Mr. John Mitchell, of Bandeth, son of James Mitchell, grandson to the aforesaid William, which bears date Nov. 21, 1629, since which time the family has been settled in the north of Scotland.

This Mr. John Mitchell, eldest son of James Mitchell, of Bandeth, by Grizel, his wife, eldest daughter of —— Colvill, of Cleish, Esq. afterwards Lord Colville) had, by Margaret, his wife, eldest daughter of Robert Forrester, of Queen's-haugh, one son,

John, who married Jean, the only daughter and heiress of Andrew Umphray, of Berrie, and had issue by her four sons and several daughters; 1, John, of whom hereafter; 2, James Mitchell, of Girlesta, who had by Lillias Sinclair, his first wife, one son John, who died young, and one daughter Grizel, wife of John Scott, of Gibleston, Esq.; and by his second wife Barbara, daughter of —— Sinclair, of House, he had one daughter Elizabeth, wife of Magnus Henderson, of Gardie; 3, Charles, of Pitteadie, who married first, Jean, sister to Sir Robert Blackwood, Knt. who died without issue; secondly, Margaret, daughter of Sir Henry Wardlaw, of Petrivie, Bart. by whom he had issue one son and three daughters; and 4, Andrew Mitchell, apothecary, in London.

I. JOHN MITCHELL, Esq. the eldest son and heir, was advanced to the dignity of a Baronet of Great Britain, 10 K. George I. He married Margaret, eldest daughter of Francis Murray, Esq. son of John Murray, Baron of Penni-

* Ex inf. Dom. Jo. Mitchell, Bar. 1726.

† Ibid.

‡ Ibid.

land, in the shire of Caithness, whose ancestor was Walter Murray, of Penniland, lawful son to Andrew Murray, of Tullibardin, progenitor to his Grace the Duke of Athol, by whom he had issue seven sons, 1, John; 2, Charles; 3, James; 4, Charles; 5, Sir Andrew; 6, Erancis; and 7, John-Charles, whereof only three were living in 1741, Sir Andrew, Francis, and John-Charles; and —— daughters, the eldest whereof, Elizabeth, was wife of Thomas Gifford, of Busta, Esq.; and 2, Jean, of Charles Neven, of Windhouse, Esq. who died without issue; 3, Barbara, of Alexander Sinclair, jun. of Brou. Sir John Mitchell, Bart. died in June, 1739, and was succeeded by his eldest surviving son and heir,

II. Sir ANDREW MITCHELL, Bart. who was one of the honourable faculty of advocates in Scotland. He married ——, who died his widow Aug. 14, 1789. Sir Andrew died in 1764, and was succeeded by

III. Sir JOHN MITCHELL, who married, Dec. 28, 1771, Elizabeth, daughter of John Bruce Stewart, Esq. who died his widow, Feb. 1791. Sir John died Dec. 5, 1783, but who he was succeeded by I cannot pretend to say, not having been able to procure any information from this family.

ARMS—Sable, a fess between three mascles, or, within a bordure, chequy of the second and first,

CREST—On a wreath, three ears of barley, conjoined in the stalk, proper.

MOTTO—*Sapiens qui assiduus.*

SEAT—At West-Shore, in Zetland, Scotland.

TABLE.

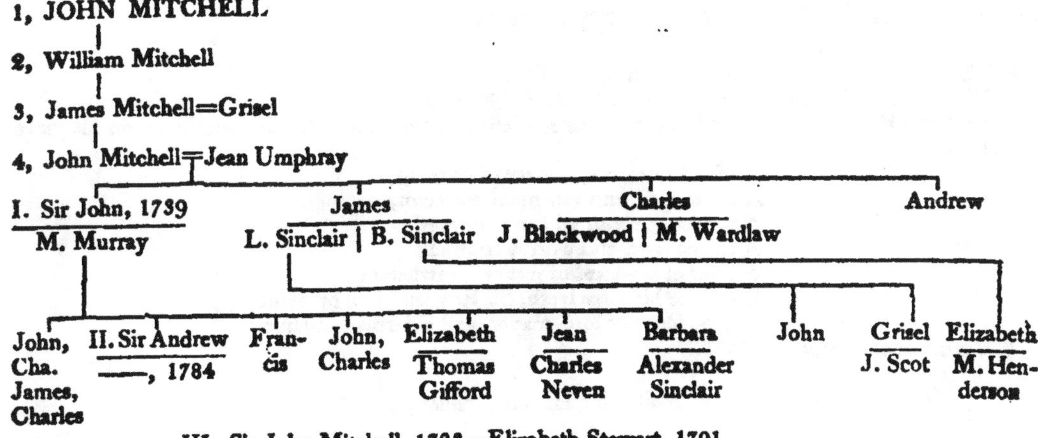

243. HILL, of HAWKESTONE, Shropshire.

Created Baronet, Jan. 20, 1726–7.

OF this ancient family of Hull, or Hill *, of Court-Hill, Wlonkeslowe, Blore, Buntingsdale, Malpas, Soulton, and Bleckley, was,

1, —— Hull, father of

2, —— Hull, whose son,

3, Hugh Hull, alias Hill, of Hull and Wlonkeslowe, in Shropshire, Esq. who lived in the time of Edward II. married Eleanor, daughter and coheiress of Hugh Wlonkeslowe, Esq. and had issue,

4, William, who lived in the time of King Richard II. and was father of

5, Geoffry Hill, Esq. who lived in the time of King Henry IV. and married ——, daughter of —— Warren, Lord of Ightfield, by whom he had,

6, Humphry Hill, Esq. who lived in the time of Henry V. and Henry VI. who, by Anne, his wife, daughter and coheiress of John Bird, of Charleton, (niece and heiress of David de Malpas), had three sons, 1, William, ancestor to the Hills, of Court-Hill, Blore, Wlonkeslowe, and Buntingsdale; 2, Ralph, of whom hereafter; and 3, Thomas, of Malpas and Hodnet, whose issue male failed in his son, Sir Rowland Hill, lord-mayor of London, 4 Edw. VI. who was one of the richest and most considerable merchants of his time †. He did great acts of generosity, was an eminent benefactor to the public, founded Drayton, and other free-schools, and built Stoke and Hodnet churches, Atcham and Terne bridges, at his own expence ‡. Sir Rowland left his large acquisitions amongst his four sisters, 1, Agnes, wife of John Cowper, Esq.; 2, Joan, of George Dormayne, Esq. from which family are descended the Cholmondeleys and Leechs; 3, Jane, of John Gratwood, Esq. from which family are descended the Levesons, of Wolverhampton, and the Corbets, of Stoke, Baronets; 4, Elizabeth, of John Barker, of Haughtmond, in Shropshire, Esq. § from whom are descended the Leighs, Barons of Stoneley, in Warwickshire.

* This account of Hill was chiefly from the family, in 1727.

† Vide Stowe's Survey of London, edit. 1633, fo. 90. 245.

‡ He died 1561, and lies buried in St. Stephen's, Walbrook, with the following inscription on his grave stone (a):

A friend to vertue, a lover of learning,
A foe to vice, and vehement corrector,
A prudent person, all truth supporting,
A citizen sage, and worthy counsellor,
A lover of wisdom, of justice a furtherer:
Loe, here his corps lyeth, Sir Rowland Hill by name,
Of London, late lord-mayor, and alderman of fame.

§ Visitation of Shropshire, 1623.

(a) Maitland's Hist. of London, p. 507.

7, Ralph Hill, Esq. above-mentioned, second son of Humphry, married——, daughter of Thomas Green, of Norton, Esq. by whom he had two sons, 1, William, ancestor to the Hills, of Soulton and Bleckley; and

8, Humphry Hill, of Adderley, Esq. who, by his wife, Alice, daughter of — Bulkley, of Stanlow, Esq. had three sons, 1, Rowland Hill, of Hawkestone, Esq. of whom hereafter; 2, Thomas, who married Elizabeth, daughter of — Dancey, Esq. of Lancashire, and left no issue; and 3, Robert Hill, of Adderley, who left issue Humphry Hill.

9, Rowland Hill, of Hawkestone, Esq. eldest son of Humphry and Alice, married Mary, daughter of Thomas Dycher, of Muckleton, in Shropshire, Esq. by whom he had

10, Rowland Hill, of Hawkestone, Esq. who, by Elizabeth, his wife, daughter of William Jolliffe, of Leek, in Staffordshire, Esq. was father of

11, Rowland Hill, of Hawkestone, Esq. a gentleman remarkable for his great wisdom, piety, and charity, who suffered very much by the rebels in the Civil Wars, temp. Car. I. by coming to the relief of his father, whom they had detained prisoner in the castle near Hawkestone; and by Margaret, daughter of Richard Whitehall, of Whitchurch, in Shropshire, Esq. had seven sons and four daughters; 1, Rowland, the eldest, who died unmarried; 2, the Hon. and Rev. Richard Hill, LL.D. who died unmarried at Richmond, in Surrey, June 11, 1727, aged 73, and was buried at Hodnet, in Shropshire. He was, in the time of King William III. envoy extraordinary to the court of Brussels, as also in that reign and Queen Anne's, to the courts of Turin, and of all the other Italian princes, except the Roman pontiff. In the time of King William, he was paymaster of his Majesty's armies in Flanders, where, by his remarkable, punctuality, and just dealings, he acquired so great credit, as to be able by it to subsist the armies there, when remittances came too slow for that purpose from England; which great service gained him the favour of the king his master, who, soon after the conclusion of the peace, appointed him to be one of the lords commissioners for executing the great office of lord-high-treasurer of England. His merit also recommended him to the favour of Queen Anne, who, soon after her accession to the throne, appointed him one of the council to his Highness Prince George, of Denmark, as lord-high-admiral of England; and in 1705, sent him to the Duke of Savoy, a prince remarkable for his politics, with whom he succeeded so well as to bring him into the grand alliance.

In the reign of George I. he retired from civil employments, and became fellow of Eton College, which fellowship he held till the time of his death. He was a statesman of great abilities and eminent integrity, a man of general knowledge, and remarkable for his fine address and good breeding. He added much to his own private estate and fortune, which was of itself considerable, great part of which he gave among his relations in his life-time, and the rest at his death. He augmented many poor livings, and was a considerable benefactor to St. John's College, Cambridge, where he had his education, and an ornament to that society. He left them five rectories, viz. Ditchingham, South and North Lopham united, the two Forncetts united, Sturston, and Alborough; his heir to present, but always a fellow of that college. He subscribed largely to public works of charity, and did a great many private ones in a wise and well-chose manner. Not long before he died, by the favour of his Majesty King George I. in the 13th of his reign, he obtained for his family this creation, to the dignity of a Baronet of this kingdom, in the person of his nephew and heir at law, Rowland Hill, of Hawkestone, Esq. to him and to the heirs male of his body; in default of such, to his nephew Samuel Hill, of Shenston-Park, in Staffordshire, Esq. (who was made secretary for the Latin tongue, Oct. 7, 1714, and elected M. P. for Litchfield in 1715), and the heirs male of his body; in default of such, to his nephew, Thomas Hill, of Tern-Hall, in Shropshire, Esq. M. P. for Shrewsbury in several parliaments. He married Mary, daughter of William Noel, Esq. by whom he had one daughter Mary, wife of Sir Bryan-Broughton Delves, but had no issue: she was remarried to —— Errington, Esq. of Northumberland), and the heirs male of his body; and in default of such, to his nephew, the Rev. Mr. Rowland Hill, rector of Forncett, in Norfolk, and the heirs male of his body; which Rowland was afterwards rector of Hodnet, in Shropshire, and died unmarried, July 11, 1733.

John Hill, of Leighteich, Esq. third son of Rowland, by Margaret, daughter of Richard Whitehall aforesaid, married ——, daughter of —— Stubbs, of Shaw, in Staffordshire, Esq. by whom he had one son, Sir Rowland Hill, the first Baronet, and five daughters; Margaret, the eldest, was wife of Richard, eldest son of Sir Thomas Brooke, of Norton, in Cheshire, Bart. who left issue by her one son, Sir Richard Brooke, Bart.; 2, Eleanor, of Borlace Wingfield, of Preston, in Shropshire, Esq. and had issue; and three other daughters.

I. Sir ROWLAND HILL, Bart. was high-sheriff of Shropshire in 1732, and in the second parliament of King George II. summoned to meet June 13, 1734, and was elected member of parliament for the city of Litchfield. He married, May 27, 1732, Jane, daughter of Sir Brian Broughton, of Broughton, in Staffordshire, Bart. who died Jan. 1774, by whom he had ten children, 1, Sir Richard, his successor; 2, Jane, died unmarried; 3, Elizabeth, born Feb. 26, 1734, wife, June 7, 1762, of Clement Tudway, who has in several successive parliaments represented the city of Wells, in Somersetshire; 4, John, who for thirteen years was returned M. P. for Shrewsbury, married Mary, one of the daughters and coheiresses of John Chambre, Esq. of Pettow, in Shropshire, by whom he has had sixteen children, thirteen of whom are now living; 5, Thomas, yet unmarried; 6, Rowland, who married Mary, sister of Clement Tudway, Esq. M. P. for Wells, by whom he has issue; 7, Robert, who married Mary, daughter and heiress of J. Wilbraham, of Hough, in Cheshire, Esq. by whom he has fourteen children, twelve of whom are living; 8, Brian, still unmarried. Sir Rowland died August 7, 1783, and was succeeded by his eldest son,

II. Sir RICHARD HILL, the present Baronet, who has now been elected one of the knights of the shire in five successive parliaments, during which his loyalty, integrity, and independency, have always gained him the esteem and good will of his constituents, and he has never met with any opposition in that situation.

TABLE.

1, —— HULL

2, —— Hull

3, Hugh Hull, or Hill, temp. Edw. II. = Eleanor Wlonkeslowe

4, William Hill, temp. Rich. II.

5, Geoffry Hill. temp. Hen. IV. = —— Warren

6, Humphry, temp. Hen. V. and VI. = Amy Bird

William — Hills, of Court-hill, &c.

7, Ralph = —— Green

Thomas Hill

William — Hills, of Soulton and Bleckley

8, Humphry = A. Bulkley

Sir Rowland

Agnes = J. Cowper

Joan = G. Dormayne — Cholmondeleys and Leechs

Jane = J. Cratwood — Levesons and Corbets

Elizabeth = J. Barker — Leighs, Barons of Stoneley

9, Rowland = M. Dycher

Thomas = —— Dancy

Robert — Humphrey

10, Rowland Hill = E. Joliffe

11, Rowland = Margaret Whitehall

Rowland

Richard

12, John Hill = —— Stubbs

I. Sir Rowland Hill, 1783 = J. Broughton = J. Farham, 1785

Margaret = R. Brooke

Eleanor = B. Wingfield

Samuel

Thomas

II. Sir Richard

Rowland, d y

John, d y

Jane

Elizabeth = C. Tedway

John = M. Chambre

Thomas

Rowland = M. Tudway

Robert = M. Wilbraham

Brian

ARMS—Ermine, on a fess, sable, a castle triple-towered, argent.

CREST—On a wreath, a tower, argent, surmounted with a garland of laurel, proper.

SEAT—At Hawkestone, near Hodnet, in Shropshire.

Quarterings—Second (Wlonkeslowe), sable, a lion rampant, crowned, or, between three crosses, patee fitchee, argent.—Third (Bird), per pale, or, and argent, an eagle displayed, sable.—Fourth (Malpas), gules, a cheveron, between three pheons, argent.

BARONETS

CREATED BY

KING GEORGE II.

244. CLAYTON, of Marden, Surrey.

Created Baronet, Jan. 13, 1731–2.

THIS family is descended from the Claytons, in Northamptonshire *. Sir Robert Clayton, Knt. a gentleman, not more remarkable for his application to business than his integrity in the discharge of it: qualities that equally procured him success and honour; for, in 1670, he was nominated to serve the office of sheriff for the city of London, and the same year had the honour of knighthood conferred upon him by King Charles II. who, besides many other instances of his royal favour, even admitted him to some share of his confidence and friendship; but he willingly relinquished that honour, when it was no longer consistent with the safety of religion and the rights of his country.

In 1679, he was elected lord-mayor, and discharged that high office agreeably to the trust reposed in him, supporting the character of a magistrate with a form suitable to the dignity, and, at the same time, preserved such an unalterable steadiness, as was not to be shaken by threats, or moved by promises.

* Ex inf. Dom. William Clayton, Bar. 1741.

He served in several parliaments for the borough of Blechingley, but was, for near thirty years, one of the representatives for the city of London, being often returned without either the charge or trouble of canvassing; and about the year 1681, many, who were in the real interest of their country, being of opinion that a bill to exclude a popish successor was the only means to preserve it, he readily went into those measures, and not only voted for the bill in the parliament then held at Westminster, but also seconded the motion for it in that held the February following at Oxford; an attempt that drew on the hasty dissolution of both those parliaments, and proved fatal to Lord Russel, by whom the bill was brought in.

The king dying soon after, and the duke, his brother, notwithstanding all the efforts made for his exclusion or limitation, succeeding to his crown and kingdoms, Sir Robert, who knew him to have an inclination equal to his power of resenting injuries, prudently retired from a public life, and filled up this interval from business with building and planting upon his estate at Marden, which, from a naked and uncultivated soil, he, by much labour and expence, converted into the beautiful and pleasing form it now wears.

This retreat proved his security, for most of those who had rendered themselves obnoxious by their former behaviour, being now become objects of the royal displeasure, his then peaceful retirement was successfully urged in his favour, by one who had a large share both in the design and execution of those black counsels.

Having happily escaped this danger, he enjoyed his rural solitude with as much tranquillity as the convulsions of the times would permit; till finding that the arbitrary proceedings of the government tending to nothing less than the enslaving the consciences, as well as persons of the people, he readily joined with those great men who appeared in defence of their civil and religious liberties; and, as he had ventured the greatest part of his personal estate in support of those measures, he was judged a fit person to compliment his Royal Highness the Prince of Orange (who was then at Henley-upon-Thames) in the name of the city of London, on his happy arrival in this kingdom. But while he was thus contributing to the security of other people's fortunes, he saw himself in danger of losing part of his own; for, being attainted in Ireland during the residence of the unfortunate king in that kingdom, a large estate which he was there possessed of was, in consequence of that attainder, seized upon, and put into hands from which it was impossible ever after to recover it.

When the tranquillity of the nation was happily settled, he again took his share in the public transactions; and their Majesties, in approbation of his conduct, appointed him one of the commissioners of the customs, which post he held till his decline of life made a quiet retreat more desirable than public employments. This he spent in several well-judged acts of charity and benevolence, contributing not only to the relief of particulars, but to the distresses of mankind in general*. He married Martha, daughter of Mr. Perient Trott, of London, merchant, by whom he had only one son Robert, who died an infant. He died at Marden, in Surrey, July 16, 1707, in the 78th year of his age, and was buried in the vault of the chancel belonging to the family, in the parish church of Bletchingley, under a stately monument of white marble of the Corinthian order, with suitable decorations; the figures of himself, in his habit of lord-mayor, and his lady, standing upon the projection of the base, with that of an infant lying between†. Sir Robert leaving no issue, was succeeded in his estate by his nephew,

* A noble instance of which was his benefaction to the hospital of St. Thomas, in Southwark, as appears by the following inscription upon the pedestal of the statue there erected to him:

> "To Sir Robert Clayton, Knt. born in Northamptonshire, citizen and lord mayor of London, president of this hospital, and vice-president of the New Workhouse, and a bountiful benefactor to it; a just magistrate, and brave defender of the liberty and religion of his country. Who (besides many other instances of his charity to the poor) built the Girl's Ward in Christ's Hospital; gave first, towards the rebuilding of this house, 600*l*. and left, by his last will, 2,300*l*. to the poor of it.
>
> This Statue was erected, in his life-time, by the Governors, A. D. 1701, as a monument of their esteem of so much worth, and to preserve his memory after death, was by them beautified, A. D. 1714."

† At the upper end of the north aisle of Bletchingley Church, in Surrey, railed in with blue and gold rails, on a handsome pavement of black and white marble, is a fair large monument reaching to the top of the chancel, being an arch supported by twelve corinthian pillars; over them are two angels, and above, on the top, are three urns. Under the arch is Sir Robert Clayton, in his lord mayor's habit, in his left hand a roll, on his right hand his lady, both at full length, standing upright, she holding her right hand on her breast, and with her left supporting her gown; between them is a young child cumbent. Under Sir Robert:

Non vultus instantis tyranni.

Under the lady:

Quando ullam inveniet parem.

On each side a boy weeping; under that, on the right hand:

Ric. Crutcher, fecit.

On it are these arms. Per pale baron and femme, the first argent, a cross sable; the second, paly of six, or, and gules, on a canton, argent, a bear rampant, sable.

Between them, on a marble curtain, adorned with cherubims, is this inscription:

> Here rests what was mortall of Sir Thomas Clayton, Kt. in the year MDCLXXX. Lord Mayor, and at his death Alderman and Father of the City of London, and near xxx years was one of its representatives in parliament.
>
> By the justest methods and skill in business, he acquired an ample fortune, which he applied to the noblest purposes, and more than once ventured it all for his country. He fixed the seat of his family at Marden, where he hath left a remarkable instance of the politeness of his genius, and how far nature may be improved by art, his relations, his friends, the hospital of St. Thomas, in Southwark, of which he was president, Christ Church Hospital, and

I. WILLIAM, (the only surviving son of William Clayton, of Hambleton, in Bucks, Esq. for many years in the commission of the peace for that county), who, in the first parliament of King George I. was elected for the borough of Bletchingley, for which he was returned in all the succeeding elections till his death. He was also president of Guy's Hospital, and in the fifth year of his late Majesty's reign, had the grant of a Baronet's patent. He married Martha *, eldest daughter of Mr. John Kenrick, of London, merchant (and niece to the late Lady Clayton), by whom he had five sons and five daughters; Robert and William died young; Kenrick, his successor; and William, who married first, Mary, daughter of John Wood, of Skerries, near Westram, in Kent, Esq. who died in childbed, Jan. 2, 1760. He married secondly, ———, daughter and coheiress of Rice Lloyd, of Atty-Cadno, in Carmarthenshire, Esq. and one of

> the Workhouse in London, were large sharers of his bounty. He lived in the communion of the church of England, and in perfect charity with all good men, however divided amongst themselves in opinions. The welfare of his country was the only aim of his public actions; and in all the various efforts that were made in his time for preserving its constitution he bore a great share, and acted therein with a constancy of mind which no prospect of danger could ever shake. Its but just the memory of so good and great a man should be transmitted to after-ages, since in all the public and private transactions of his life he hath left so bright a pattern to imitate, but hardly to be outdone. He was born at Bulwick, in Northamptonshire, the xxixth day of September. An. Dom. MDCXXIX, and died at Marden, the xvith day of July, MDCCVII. Gulielmus Clayton, nepos et Hæres, D. D.

On another tablet below the last, is this inscription:

> To the pious memory of Dame Martha Clayton, daughter of Mr. Perient Trott, of London, merchant, and wife of Sir Robert Clayton, Knt. alderman and sometime lord-mayor of the city of London. This Monument is erected by her surviving husband, in testimony of her many admirable endowments and uncommon strictness in all moral virtues, of her unfeigned piety towards Almighty God through the course of her whole life, of her true conjugal affection during a happy partnership of xlvi years, and of her diffusive charity to all those whom poverty or other necessities made them any way the object of her relief, having had only one son, who was christened Robert, and died very young. She departed this life the xxvth day of December, Anno Dom. MDCCV. in the LXIIId year of her age, and is deposited in the adjoining vault, where the late dear companion of her life, when God shall call him out of this mournful state, desires to be interred by her.

Aubrey's Hist. of Surrey, Vol. III. p. 77, &c.

On a black marble grave-stone in the same church.

> Under this stone lyeth the body of Thomas Clayton, Gent. a native of Bulwick, in Northamptonshire, and for many years an inhabitant of this borough; where by a kind and obliging deportment, and readiness to serve every one to whom he would in any manner be useful, he obtained the love of all that knew him, and died much lamented the iv day of May, Anno Dom. MDCCVII. and in the LXX year of age.

Aubrey's Surrey, Vol. III. p. 80.

* Ex inf. Dom. Wil. Clayton, Bar. 1741.

the most ancient families in Wales, who owned a very considerable property, which many years ago was divided into eleven portions to eleven brothers, many of whom served their country in the former wars; but the grandfather of the present Baronet being the eldest, he possessed Atty-Cadno, the old family seat of the Lloyds, by whom it descended to Sir William Clayton. By this lady he had one son Sir William, the present Baronet, and two daughters, Catharine, wife of, June 11, 1765, John Griffin Whitwell, late Lord Howard, of Walden; and Mary, Feb. 14, 1786, of Lt. Gen. Henry-Edward, brother to Charles-James Fox. He married 3dly, in Sept. 1767, Louisa Fermor, sister to George, Earl of Pomfret, and served in several parliaments for Bletchingley, in Surrey, and Marlow, in Bucks. Sir William's daughters were Martha and Susanna, who both died young; Mary, wife of Jonathan Rushley, of Menabilly, in Cornwall, Esq.; Anne, of Sir Charles Blackwell, Bart. secondly, of Dr. Thomas, Bishop of Rochester, she died July 7, 1772; and Sarah. Lady Clayton died Dec. 14, 1739, and Sir William in Dec. 1744, and was succeeded by his son,

II. Sir KENRICK CLAYTON, Bart. who served in six parliaments for Bletchingley. He married Henrietta-Maria, eldest daughter of Henry Herring, Esq, who died July 25, 1774, aged 65*, by whom he had one son Sir Robert, his successor, and two daughters, Mary, wife of Sir John Gresham, Bart. and Henrietta. Sir Kenrick died March 10, 1769, and was succeeded by his only son,

III. Sir ROBERT CLAYTON, Bart. who married, June 1, 1767, Elizabeth, eldest daughter of Frederick Standish, of London, merchant, by his wife Mary, daughter of Sir Harcourt Masters, of London, Knt. He died May 10, 1799, in his 60th year, and was buried in the family vault at Bletchingley: he lived in great hospitality, and acquired the love of his tenants and the respect of his neighbours. The weight of his influence was found in all the county elections, to which he was always attended by a numerous train of the most respectable freeholders. Sir Robert was succeeded by his cousin †,

* On a brass plate upon her coffin:

> Dame Henrietta Maria Clayton, relict of Sir Kenrick Clayton, Bar^t. died July 25th, 1774, in the 65th year of her age.—Arms of Clayton, in a lozenge, with Herring in pretence, viz. 1st and 4th, or, on a pale cottized, azure, three eagles displayed; 2d and 3d, azure, two bendlets, or, surmounted by a fess ermine.

† All the former part of his life he represented Bletchingley, but in the late parliament he was returned for Ilchester. Without gaming himself, it was supposed he had play debts to pay, which, with his hospitality, involved him in some pecuniary difficulties about the year 1778, when a relation of his purchased of him the reversion of his interest in the borough of Bletchingley, one means of extricating him. Sir Robert aftewards attempted to set aside the transaction, but could not substantiate his case, and the bargain was confirmed. Sir Robert was a steady opponent of Lord North's administration; but when a part of that opposition joined Mr. Pitt, he remained attached to Mr. Fox, and continued so till his death. Notwithstanding his being in opposition when Dr. Thomas, who had been presented to the living of Bletchingley, was made Bishop of Rochester, by which the crown had a right to present to the living, Lord North very handsomely gave it to Sir Robert's relation, Dr. Kenrick, the present rector. If Sir Robert's abilities were not of the first class he was certainly an honest man, and acted on principle. He has given his Surrey estate to his cousin William Clayton, his successor.

IV. Sir WILLIAM CLAYTON, the present Baronet, son of William, second surviving son of Sir William, the first Baronet, by his second lady. He was of Harleyford, in Bucks, and of Marden Park aforesaid. He was born in Stanhope-street, May Fair, April 16, 1762, and married, July 16, 1785, Mary, daughter of Sir William East, of Hall Place, in Berks, Bart. by whom he has five sons and two daughters, 1, William-Robert, born Aug. 28, 1786; 2, Catharine-Emilia, born Nov. 13, 1789; 3, East-George, born April 9, 1794; 4, John-Lloyd, born Aug. 19, 1796; 5, Rice-Richard, born Nov. 15, 1797; 6, Augustus-Philip, born 1799; 7, Mary-Caroline, born 1800.

ARMS—Argent, a cross, sable, between four pellets.

CREST—In a mural crown, gules, a leopard's paw erect, argent, grasping a pellet.

MOTTO—*Virtus in actione consistit.*

SEATS—At Marden, near Godstone, in Surrey; and Harleyford, near Great Marlow, Bucks.

Aug. 5, 1745, Colonel Clayton, son of the late General Clayton, married ——, daughter of Everard Buckworth, Esq. and niece of Sir John Buckworth, with 20,000l. fortune.

TABLE.

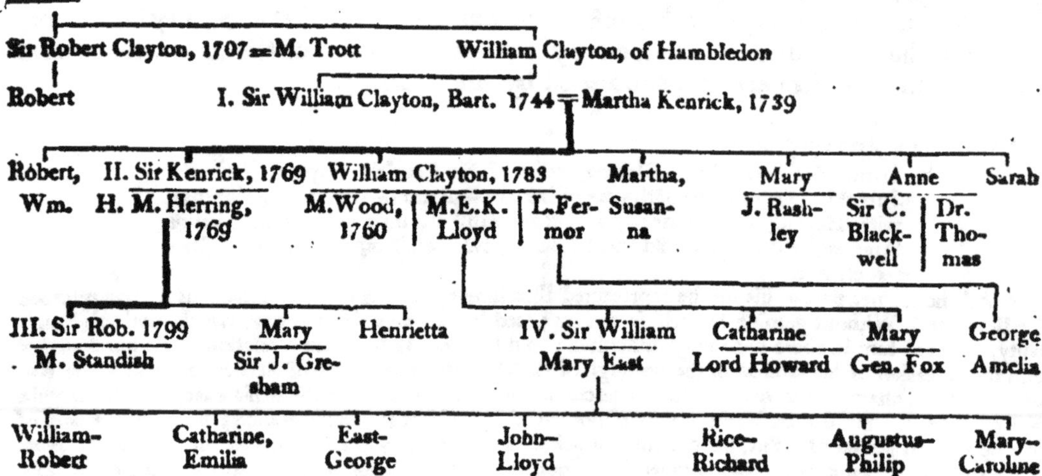

245. BROWN, of WESTMINSTER.

Created Baronet, March 11, 1731-2.

I. ROBERT BROWN, a merchant at Venice, having been his majesty's resident abroad, was advanced to the dignity of a Baronet, 5 Geo. II. with a remainder in his patent, in case of failure of issue male of his body lawfully begotten, to his brother Colonel James Browne, Esq. and his heirs male; and in default of such issue, to Edward Brown, Esq. another brother of the said Robert, and the heirs male of his body, lawfully begotten.

Sir Robert was elected in the eighth and ninth parliament of Great Britain for Ilchester, in Somersetshire, and in May, 1741, was appointed pay-master of his Majesty's works, concerning the repairs, new buildings, and well keeping of any of his Majesty's houses of access, and others, in time of progress. He married Margaret Cecil, sister of the Right Rev. Dr. Cecil, rector of Hatfield, in Hertfordshire, and bishop, first of Bristol, and afterwards of Bangor, by whom he had two daughters, who died unmarried. Lady Brown died on Ash-Wednesday, Feb. 13, 1782, aged 84, and was buried at Audley-street Chapel, as was her husband and two daughters. Sir Robert died Oct. 5, 1760, and was succeeded by his nephew,

II. Sir JAMES BROWN, Bart. who married ——, by whom he had one son William-Augustus. Sir James died April 20, 1784, and was succeeded by his only son,

III. Sir WILLIAM-AUGUSTUS BROWN, Bart. who has been a long time insane, and living in the same house with his mother, in 1794, in the absence of his keeper took up a coal-scuttle, and dashed her brains out.—*Gent. Mag.* p. 579.

ARMS—Gules, a cheveron, between three fleur-de-lis, or.

CREST—On a wreath, a demi-lion rampant, gules, holding in its dexter paw a fleur-de-lis, as in the arms.

MOTTO—*Gaudeo.*

PLACE OF RESIDENCE—Westminster.

TABLE.

—— BROWN

I. Sir Robert Brown, 1760 — Margaret Cecil, 1782

James

Edward

II. Sir James Brown, 1784 = ——, 1794

III. Sir William-Augustus Brown

246. HEATHCOTE, OF LONDON.

Created Baronet, Jan 17, 1732-3.

THIS was a private gentleman's family of great respectability in the county of Derby. Gilbert Heathcote married Anne, daughter of Thomas Dickins, Esq. of Chesterfield, by whom he had seven sons; 1, Gilbert; 2, John; 3, Samuel, ancestor to the Heathcotes, of Hursley; 4, Josiah; 5, William; 6, Caleb; 7, George.

I. Sir GILBERT, the eldest son and heir, knighted by Queen Anne, was one of the directors and first founders of the Bank of England; lord-mayor of the city of London, which he represented in four successive parliaments in the reign of Queen Anne. In the year 1714, he was chosen to serve in parliament for Helston, in Cornwall; in 1722, for Lymington, in Hampshire; and, in 1727, for St. Germain's, in Cornwall. He was advanced to the dignity of a Baronet 5 Geo. II. He married Hester, daughter of Christopher Rayner, Esq. by whom he had one son Sir John, his successor; and two daughters, Anne, wife of Sir Jacob Jacobson, Knt.; and Elizabeth, to Sigismond Trafford, of Dunston-Hall, Lincolnshire, Esq. Sir Gilbert died Jan. 25, 1732-3, aged 82, and was buried at Normanton, his seat in Rutlandshire, where a handsome monument, by Mr. Rysbrach, was erected for him*.

II. Sir JOHN HEATHCOTE, Bart. only surviving son and successor to Sir Gilbert, was member of parliament for Grantham, in Lincolnshire, in one parliament, and for Bodmin, in Cornwall, for two others. He was appointed, by the will of Sir Hans Sloane, Bart. to be one of the trustees to the British Museum, and elected one of the vice-presidents of the Hospital for the Maintenance and Education of exposed and deserted Infants, May 14, 1755. He married, July 1720, Bridget, daughter of Thomas White, of Tuxford and Walling Wells, in

* Whereon is the following inscription:

To the memory of Sir Gilbert Heathcote, Knt. and Bart. a person of just natural endowments, improved by long experience, ready to apprehend, slow to determine, resolute to act, and a zealous friend to the rights and liberties of mankind; in offices of power and trust, true to his country's honour; a great instrument in founding and well governing the Bank of England. In the year 1711, was lord-mayor of London, which city he governed with courage and temper, after having represented it in four successive parliaments with dignity and integrity.

A kind landlord, a steady friend, an affectionate relation, and in his character unblemished.

Sir Gilbert Heathcote, born at Chesterfield, in Derbyshire, married Hester, daughter of Christopher Rayner, Esq. left issue Sir John Heathcote, and Ann, married to Sir Jacob Jacobson, Knt.; and Elizabeth, married to Sigismond Trafford, of Lincolnshire, Esq.

Nottinghamshire, clerk of the ordnance, and M. P. for Retford, who died May 5, 1772, and was buried at Normanton, where an elegant monument is erected to her memory. By her he had two sons and five daughters; 1, Sir Gilbert, his successor; 2, John, who married Lydia, daughter of John Moyer, Esq. by whom he had two children; 3, Bridget, wife of James, Earl of Morton; 4, Anne, of Sir Archibald Edmonston, Bart.; 5, Hester, of Sir Robert Hamilton, Bart; 6, Mary, of Charles White, Esq.; and 7, Henrietta, of Henry Calthorp Campion, of Hurst Pierpoint, Esq. Sir John died at Normanton, Sept. 5, 1759, and was succeeded by his eldest son,

III. Sir GILBERT HEATHCOTE, Bart. who married, June 22, 1749, Margaret, youngest daughter of Philip, Earl of Hardwicke, and lord-high-chancellor of England, who died in childbed Aug. 11, 1769. Sir Gilbert married secondly, March 27, 1770, Elizabeth, daughter of Robert Hudson, Esq, of Teddington, in Middlesex, by whom he had three sons and one daughter, 1, Sir Gilbert, his successor; 2, John; 3, Robert; and 4, Elizabeth, wife, in 1797, of Thomas Grosvenor, Esq. a colonel in the third regiment of guards, and nephew to the Earl of Grosvenor. Sir Gilbert died at North-End, near Kennington, Dec. 4, 1785, and was succeeded by his eldest son, then a minor.

TABLE.

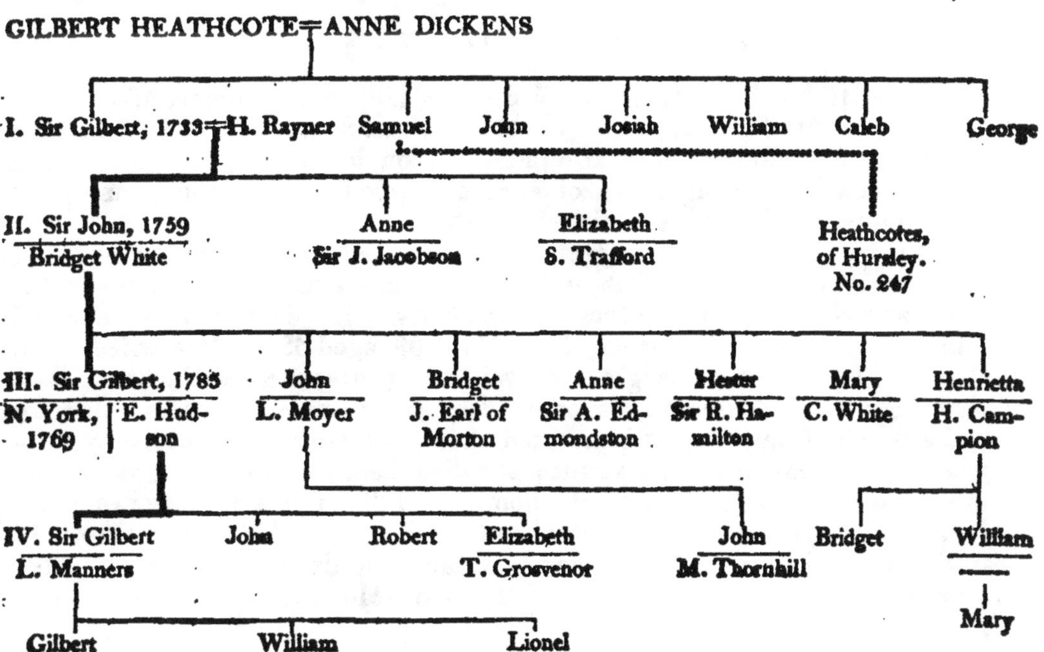

IV. Sir GILBERT HEATHCOTE. Bart. born Oct. 1773. He married Catharine-Sophia, second daughter of John Manners, of Buckminster Park, in the county of Leicester, Esq. by the Right Honourable Lady Louisa, daughter of Lionel, Earl of Dysart, by whom he has issue three sons, 1, Gilbert-John, born Jan. 16, 1794; 2, Lionel-Edward; and 3, William-Henry.

ARMS—Quarterly: first and fourth, ermine, three pomeis, each charged with a cross, or; second and third, azure, a saltire engrailed, ermine.

CREST—On a mural crown, azure, a pomeis, charged with a cross, or, between two wings displayed, ermine.

SEATS—Normanton Park, in Rutlandshire, and Stamford, in Lincolnshire.

247. HEATHCOTE, of Hursley, Hampshire.

Created Baronet, Aug. 16, 1733.

SAMUEL HEATHCOTE, Esq. third son of Gilbert Heathcote, of Chesterfield, in the connty of Derby, Esq. went over a merchant to Dantzic, where he got a considerable estate with great reputation; on his return, he was esteemed by all that knew him, being a man of exceeding good understanding, and great honour and integrity in all his dealings.

He was very intimate with the great Mr. Locke, who advised with * and had great assistance from him in that useful work, the regulating the coin of the kingdom, as well as in several other public affairs. He died greatly lamented by all his relations and acquaintance, Nov. 13, 1708, aged 53. He married, Jan. 22, 1690-1, Mary, second daughter of William Dawsonne, of Hackney, Esq. and sister of the late William Dawsonne, Esq. (who was many years a director of the East-India Company, and executed that trust with the greatest reputation), a lady of great merit and virtue; she died Feb. 10, 1719-20, aged 50, by whom he had issue four sons, two of whom, Sir William, his successor, and Samuel, member of parliament for Boralston in the 8th and 9th parliaments of Great Britain, in Devonshire, survived him; and two daughters, one of whom was wife of Sir Francis-Henry Drake, of Buckland-Monachorum, in Devonshire, Bart.

* Ex inf. Dom. Wil. Heathcote, Bar. 1741.

I. Sir WILLIAM HEATHCOTE, the eldest surviving son of the aforesaid Samuel Heathcote, Esq. was created a Baronet by his late Majesty, Aug. 16, 1733. He was elected in the last parliament of George II. for the town of Buckingham, and in the first and second parliaments of his present Majesty for the town and county of the town of Southampton. He married, April 7, 1720, Elizabeth, only daughter of Thomas, Earl of Macclesfield, sometime lord high-chancellor of Great Britain, on whom and her issue male is entailed the honours of viscount and baron. By his said lady Elizabeth he had six sons, 1, Sir Thomas, his successor; 2, William, a clergyman, who died Dec. 22, 1748, unmarried; 3, Samuel, died S. P. 1797; 4, Gilbert, living in 1799; 5, George; 6, Henry, a clergyman, who married first, ——, daughter of Thomas Diggle, of Hampshire, Esq. by whom he had three children: he married secondly, ——, daughter of —— Stalham, of Liverpool, in Lancashire, Esq. by whom he had five children. He had also three daughters; Mary, wife of Thomas, Earl of Macclesfield; Elizabeth, of Admiral Francis-William Drake; and Gennetta, single in 1799. Sir William died May 10, 1751, and was succeeded by his eldest son,

II. Sir THOMAS HEATHCOTE, Bart. who married first, Elizabeth Hinton, who died Dec. 1749, by whom he had four children; 1, Elizabeth, wife of William Wyndham, of Dinton, in Wiltshire, Esq.; 2, William, his successor; 3, Rev. Thomas, rector of Stonage, Kent, who married, Aug. 20, 1772, Letitia, daughter of Sir Thomas Parker, Knt. lord-chief-justice of the King's Bench, and afterwards lord-high-chancellor of England; and 4, George. Sir Thomas married secondly, Anne, daughter of the Rev. —— Tollet, of Westminster, by whom he had four children; 1, Anna-Sophia; 2, Samuel, who married Elizabeth Stow, by whom he had five children; 3, Gilbert, fellow of New College, Oxon; and 4, Henry, who died young. Sir Thomas died June 27, 1787, and was succeeded by his son,

III. Sir WILLIAM HEATHCOTE, the present Baronet, born 1746, married Frances, daughter and coheiress of John Thorpe, of Embley, in Hampshire, Esq. born 1746, by whom he has six sons and two daughters; 1, Thomas, born Sept. 3, 1769, married, June 27, 1799, Elizabeth, only daughter of Thomas-Edwards Freeman, Esq. deceased, late member for the borough of Steyning, and grand-daughter of Thomas-Edwards Freeman, of Batsford, in Gloucestershire, Esq.; 2, Frances-Sarah, born Sept. 1770; 3, Rev. William, prebendary of Winchester, born 1772, married, 1798, Elizabeth, daughter of Lovelace-Bigg Wither, of Manydown, Hants, Esq.; 4, Samuel, born 1773, married Catharine, daughter of Isaac Pickering, of Foxlease, in the New Forest, Esq.; 5, Harriet-Harsant, born July 1775, wife, April 18, 1798, of Langford Lovel, of the island of Antigua; 6, Henry, captain of the navy, born 1777; 7, Gilbert, in the navy, born 1779; 8, Maria-Frances, born 1787. Sir William has sat in two parliaments for Hampshire.

ARMS—Ermine, three pomeis, each charged with a cross, or.

CREST—On a mural crown, azure, a pomeis, charged with a cross, or, between two wings displayed, ermine.

SEAT—Hursley Lodge, near Winchester, in Hampshire.

TABLE.

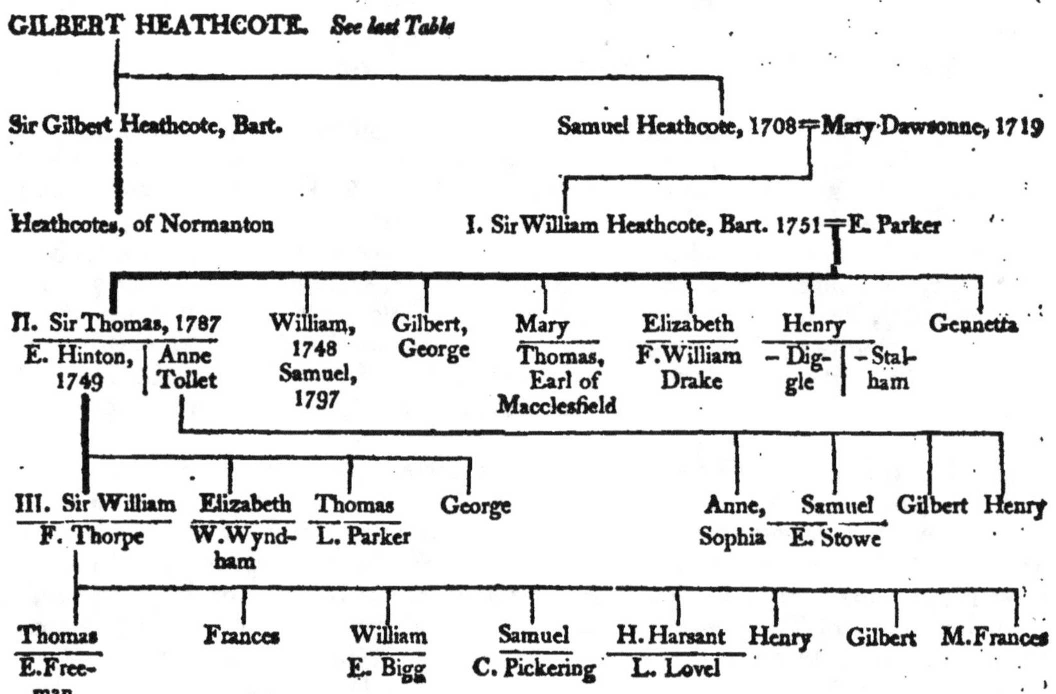

248. PAGE TURNER, of BATTESDEN, Bedfordshire.

Created Baronet, August 24, 1733.

1, JOHN TURNER, a considerable merchant in the town of Leicester, married ——, by whom he had four sons, 1, Elias, who left a daughter Abigail, the wife of —— Montgomery, by whom he had a son George; 2, Edward, who died S. P.; 3, John, of whom hereafter; 4, William, who died S. P.: and two daughters, 1, Elizabeth, the wife of —— Dawes; and ——, the wife of Atherston.

2, John Turner, the third son, was a merchant in London, where he obtained a considerable fortune and reputation; he married ——, daughter of —— Caplin, Esq. by whom he had three sons, 1, John, who married Miss Manners, but dying without issue in 1760, left the bulk of his fortune and his estate at Sunbury, in Middlesex, to his nephew Edward; 2, Edward, of whom hereafter; 3, William, who died without issue: and two daughters, 1, Elizabeth, the wife of —— Guy, Esq. by whom she had three daughters, Elizabeth, Mary, and Sarah, who all died unmarried; 2, Mary, the wife of —— Withers.

I. EDWARD, the second son of John, married, in 1728, Mary, eldest daughter of Sir Gregory Page, of Blackheath, in Kent, Bart. by whom he had three sons, 1, Sir Edward, his successor; 2, Gregory; 3, William: the two last died young. He was advanced to the dignity of a Baronet Aug. 24, 1733. Having been left by his father a considerable fortune for a younger brother, which he improved by commerce, and purchased estates in the county of Oxford. He was a leading director, and afterwards chairman, of the East India Company. He died 1735, and was succeeded in his title and estate by his only surviving son,

II. Sir EDWARD TURNER, Bart. in whom centered a considerable part of his great-uncle and god-father's monied property, which was laid out in land in Oxfordshire: he also succeeded to the bulk of the fortune of his uncle, John Turner, Esq. of Sunbury, in Middlesex. He married Cassandra, eldest daughter of William Leigh, of Addlestrop, in the county of Gloucester, son of Theophilus Leigh, by Mary, daughter of Lord, afterwards Duke of Chandos, by whom, who died in Oct. 1770, he had six sons, 1, John, who died young; 2, John, who died young; 3, Gregory, of whom hereafter; 4, Edward, who died young; 5, William, living 1802; 6, John, who married Elizabeth Dryden, niece of Sir John Dryden, Bart. of Cannons Ashby, in Northamptonshire, and took the name and arms of Dryden, and was created a Baronet in 1795. He died April 1797, leaving issue Sir John-Edward Dryden, the present Baronet, and seven other children. Sir Edward also left two daughters, 1, Elizabeth, wife of Colonel Twisleton, of Broughton Castle, in Oxfordshire, who afterwards claiming by female descent the barony of Say and Sele, that title was confirmed to him by decision in the house of peers: he died, leaving issue; 2. Cassandra, wife of Lord Hawke, by whom she has issue.

Sir Edward was elected member for Great Bedwin, in Wiltshire; and at the general election in 1755, after a severe contest, which terminated in the return of all the four candidates, Lord Parker, Sir Edward, Sir J. Dashwood, and Lord Wenman ; he, with his colleague, Lord Parker, were adjudged the legal representatives, by decision of the house of commons, for the county of Oxford. In the general election in 1761, he was chosen M. P. for Penrhyn, in Cornwall, which he represented till his death in October 1766; while he was endeavouring, in his capacity as a magistrate, to serve the poor by lowering and regulating the price of bread, at that time very high. He died of a paralytic stroke, at his seat of Ambrosden, in Oxfordshire, and was succeeded by his eldest son,

III. Sir GREGORY-PAGE TURNER, the present Bart. who, in Aug. 1795, succeeding to the estates of his great-uncle and god-father Sir Gregory Page, by his will, and by virtue of his Majesty's sign-manual, added to his own, the name and arms of Page. He married, in Jan. 1785, Frances, daughter of Joseph Howell, of Elm, in the county of Norfolk, Esq. by whom he has five children, 1, Gregory-Osborne, born Sept. 28, 1785 ; 2, Francis-Stackpole, born Jan. 15, 1787; 3, Edward-George-Thomas, born Sept. 12, 1789 ; 4, Anne-Leigh-Guy, born Aug. 9, 1791 ; 5, Francis-William-Martin, born Feb. 15, 1794. Sir Gregory served the office of high-sheriff for Oxfordshire in the year 1783 ; and at the general election in 1784, was chosen member of parliament for the borough of Thirske, in Yorkshire, which he has represented ever since.

ARMS—Quarterly: 1st and 4th, argent, a fer-de-mouline pierced, sable, for Turner ; 2d and 3d, azure, a fess indented, between three martlets, or, for Page.

CREST—On a wreath, a lion passant, argent, holding in his dexter paw a fer-de-mouline, as in the Arms.

SEAT—Battesden, Bedfordshire, and Ambrosden, near Burton, Oxfordshire.

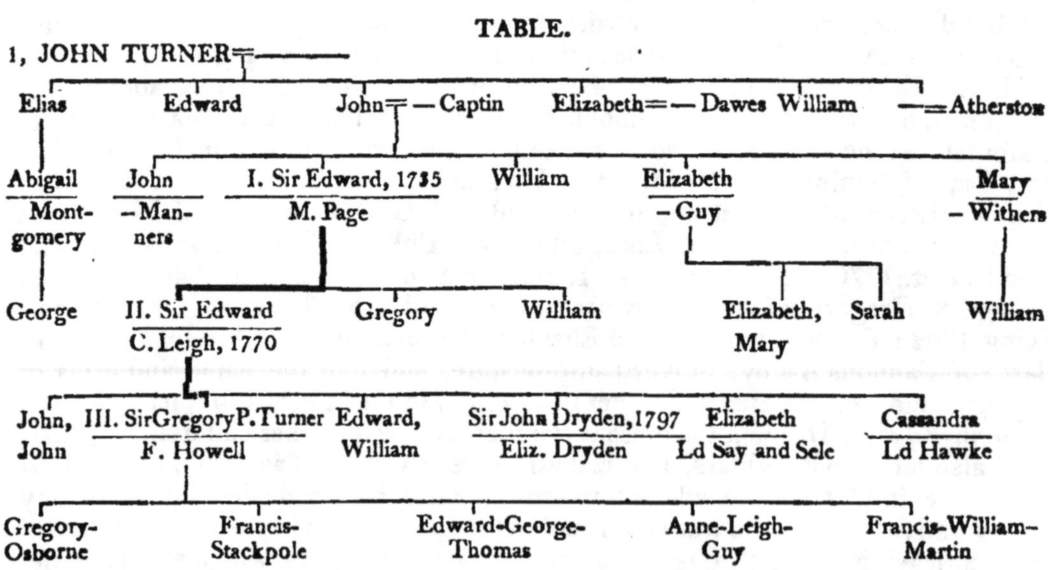

249. PAYNE, of St. Christopher's.

Created Baronet, Oct. 31, 1737.

IT is supposed this family came from Normandy with William the Conqueror; a place in that province, called Payne, seems to have given them, or to have received from them, that name.

1, Abraham Payne, the grandfather of the present Baronet, was of genteel parentage in the county of Devon; he was educated a churchman, but in the Civil Wars engaged himself in the service of Charles I. with whom he continued till that monarch lost his life on the scaffold. Frustrated in his prospects here, he determined to seek his fortune in the West Indies: he married ——, by whom he had three sons, 1, Abraham, ancestor of Sir Ralph Payne, Lord Lavington, in Ireland; 2, Sir Charles, of whom hereafter; 3, Nathaniel; and two daughters.

I. CHARLES, the second son, married ——, daughter and coheiress of John M'Arthur, a Scotch gentleman from the neighbourhood of Aberdeen, who was an officer in the army of the Earl of Argyle, and said to be his relation by a female branch. After the fatal end of the Earl, he found a retreat in the island of St. Christopher, where he afterwards obtained from King William a patent for a forfeited estate there: this patent was confirmed by grant from Queen Anne*. He received the honour of knighthood from the late king, and returned to St. Kitt's the same year. In Oct. 31, 1737, he was created a Baronet. He had seven sons, who received their education at Hackney under Mr. Newcome, and four daughters. Abraham married ——, daughter of Jeffrey Brown, Esq. chief justice of the island of St. Christopher's, by whom he had a posthumous daughter, ——, wife of Mr. Woodley, who died seven or eight years ago, leaving a numerous family. He was general and commander in chief of his Majesty's Leeward Caribbee Islands, of one of which he was a native, and where (St. Christopher's) all his estates are. ——, one of the daughters, was wife of Thomas Butler, Esq. counsellor of law in that island. Sir Charles died in 1744, and was succeeded by his eldest svrviving son,

II. Sir GILLIES PAYNE, Bart. who married ——, daughter of ——, by whom he had eight children living, most of them married. John, the eldest, married ——, daughter of Sir Philip Monnoux, Bart. by whom he has two sons: he is lieutenant-colonel of the Bedfordshire militia. Peter, the second son, in 1789, married ——, daughter of —— Steward, of Stourton Castle, by whom he has two sons and three daughters. Jennet, one of the daughters, was wife, Dec. 14, 1792, of Richard Booth, Esq. of Glendon-Hall, Northamptonshire.

* This estate is now in possession of the present Baronet.

ARMS—Gules, a fess, between two lions, passant, argent.

CREST—On a wreath, a lion's gamb erased and erect, argent, griping a broken tilting-spear, gules.

SEAT—Tempsford-Hall, Bedfordshire.

TABLE.

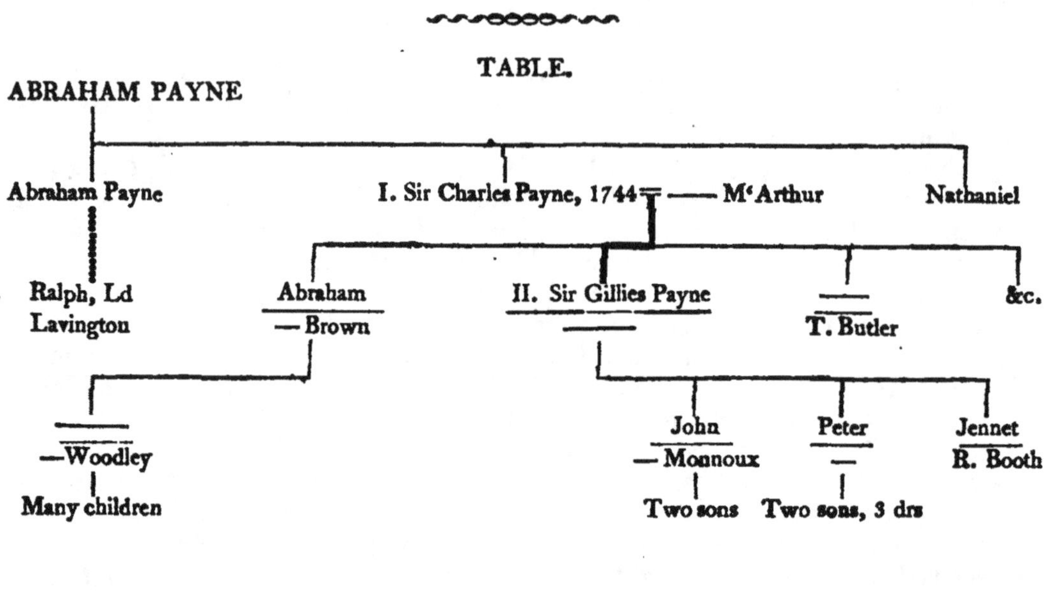

250. ARMYTAGE, of Kirklees, Yorkshire.

Created Baronet, July 4, 1738.

THIS family is of great antiquity, being derived*, according to a pedigree attested by Sir Henry St. George, Norroy King at Arms, Feb. 2, 1637, from John Armitage, of Wrigbowls, living 10 King Stephen; which place, and his arms, are said to be the gift of Roger Omfynes, steward to Remigius, Bishop of Dorchester, and founder of Elsam Abbey, in Lincolnshire.

Descended from John †, after five generations, was

1, William Armitage, father of

2, John, who had issue

3, William Armytage, of Kirklees, in the west-riding of the county of York, who lived temp. Edw. VI. and married Catharine ‡, daughter of Henry Beaumont, of Crossland, Esq. by whom he had,

* Thoresby's Leeds, p. 576. † Ibid. ‡ Ibid, p. 91.

4, John, who, by Elizabeth, daughter of John Kaye, of Lockwood, was father of

5, John Armytage, Esq. justice of the peace in the west-riding of Yorkshire, and treasurer for lame soldiers with Sir Robert Swift, Knt. 41 and 42 Eliz. He married first, Jane*, daughter of Mr. John Gregory, of Kingston-upon-Hull, by whom he had no issue. He married secondly, Margery †, daughter of Richard Beaumont, Esq. by whom he had three sons and one daughter; 1, John; 2, Gregory, who married Isabel, daughter and coheiress of Mr. John Savile, of Netherton, from whom the Armytages, of Netherton, descended; 3, Edward Armytage, of Kerresforth-Hill, near Barnsley, who married Jane, daughter of John Popeley, and was ancestor to the present Baronet; the daughter Anne was wife of Sir Hugh Wirrall, of Loversall, Knt.

6, John Armytage, Esq. son and heir of John, was high-sheriff of Yorkshire, 13 Jac. I. and by Winifred ‡, daughter of Henry Knight, of Knight-Hill, Esq. had, 1, John; 2, Thomas, who died young; 3, Sir Francis; 4, Elizabeth, wife of Sir John Savile, of Lupset, near Wakefield, Knt.; and other children, who died young.

John Armitage, son and heir, married Dorothy §, daughter of Cyril Arthington, of Arthington, Esq. but died without issue.

I. Sir Francis Armytage, brother and heir to John, was created a Baronet by King Charles I. He married Catharine ||, daughter of Christopher Danby, of Farnley, near Leeds, Esq. by whom he had, 1, Sir John, his successor; 2, Francis, who married Mary, daughter of Robert Traps, of Nidd, near Knaresborough, Esq.; 3, William, who married Elizabeth, another daughter of Robert Traps, Esq.; 4, Catharine, who died unmarried; 5, Anne, wife of Mr. Smith, of London; 6, Prudence; 7, Elizabeth, who both died unmarried; and 8, Winifred, who was wife of Thomas Lacy, Esq.

II. Sir John Armytage, Bart. son and heir, was justice of the peace, deputy-lieutenant, and captain of a troop of volunteer horse; he married Margaret ¶, second daughter of Thomas Thornhill, of Fixby, Esq. by whom he had eight sons and five daughters; 1, Sir Thomas, his successor; 2, Sir John, successor to his brother; 3, Michael; 4, Francis; 5, William, who died unmarried; and 6, Sir George, successor to Sir John; 7, Charles, who died unmarried; and 8, Christopher, who married Rebecca, daughter of Thomas Moore, of Austrope, perhaps Awthorp, Esq. and had a son John, who died S. P. Of the five daughters, Alithea, Anne, and Beatrice, died young; Margaret was wife of Francis Nevile, of Chivet, Esq. and Catharine, of Christopher Tancred, of Wixley, near Wetherby, in Yorkshire, Esq.

III. Sir Thomas Armytage, Bart. son and heir, died unmarried in 1693 **, and was succeeded in dignity and estate by his brother,

IV. Sir John Armytage, Bart. who died likewise unmarried, Dec. 1732, aged about 80, and was succeeded by his only brother,

* Ex inf. Dom. Sam. Armytage, Bar. 1741.
† Ibid.
‡ Thoresby's Leeds, p. 92. § Ibid. || Ibid. ¶ Ibid. ** Ibid.

V. Sir George Armytage, Bart. who dying also unmarried, the title in this branch became extinct, and he left his estate to his cousin,

I. SAMUEL ARMYTAGE, Esq.*, son of Mr. George Armytage, late of Kerresforth-Hill, near Barnsley, in the said riding, descended from Edward Armytage, of Kerresforth-Hill, third son of John Armytage, Esq. by his second wife Margery, daughter of Richard Beaumont, of Crossland, in the said riding, Esq. about 41 and 42 Elizabeth, which said Samuel Armytage was advanced to the dignity of a Baronet 12 George II. He married Anne, daughter of —— Griffith, of Montgomeryshire, who died Nov. 1738, and Sir Samuel died 1737, leaving three sons and three daughters, 1, Sir John, his successor; 2, Sir George, successor to his brother; 3, Samuel, died unmarried. Of the daughters, 1, Rachel, wife of James Farrer, of Ewood, now of Barnbrough-Grange, in the said riding, Esq.; 2, Mary, of the Rev. Francis Hull, of Swaith, near Barnsley, in the said riding; 3, Anna-Maria, of Thomas Carter, of the kingdom of Ireland, Esq. who died 1765: since she is become the wife of —— Nicholson, of the kingdom of Ireland, Esq. Sir Samuel was succeeded in title and estate by his eldest son,

II. Sir JOHN ARMYTAGE, Bart. who went a volunteer with General Blythe to the coast of France, and was unfortunately slain at St. Cas, Sept. 1758, in the 27th year of his age, unmarried. He was succeeded in title and estate by his brother,

III. Sir GEORGE ARMYTAGE, Bart. who married, in 1761, Anna-Maria, eldest daughter and coheiress of Godfrey Wentworth, of Wooley-Park and Hickleton, in Yorkshire, Esq. by whom he had three sons and three daughters; 1, Sir George, his successor; 2, John, who married ——, of Northamptonshire, by whom he has issue; 3, Godfrey, who, upon the death of his grandfather, in pursuance of his will, took the name and arms of Wentworth: he married ——, daughter of —— Fawkes, of Yorkshire, and has issue. The daughters were, 1, Anna-Maria, wife, 1787, of William Egerton, of Tatton-Park, in Cheshire, Esq. who died without issue; 2, Harriet, wife, 1786, of Thomas Grady, Esq. by whom she had no issue: after his death, she was the wife of Jacob Bosanquet, Esq. and died, leaving four children; 3, Charlotte, of John Eyre, of Babworth, in Nottinghamshire, by whom she has several children. Sir George represented the city of York in parliament, and died 1783, and was succeeded by his son,

IV. Sir GEORGE ARMYTAGE, Bart. who married, in 1783, Mary Harbord, eldest daughter of Lord Suffield, by whom he had several children: she died in 1790, and one son survived her, but is since dead. Sir George married secondly, 1792, ——, daughter of —— Bowles, by whom he has several children.

ARMS—Gules, a lion's head erased, between three crosslets, argent.

CREST—On a wreath, a dexter arm embowed, couped at the shoulder, habited, or, the cuff, argent, holding in the hand, proper, a sword, gules, garnished of the first.

SEAT—At Kirklees, (formerly a Benedictine nunnery), three miles from Hathersfield, in Yorkshire.

* Ex inf. Dom. Sam. Armytage, Bar. 1741.

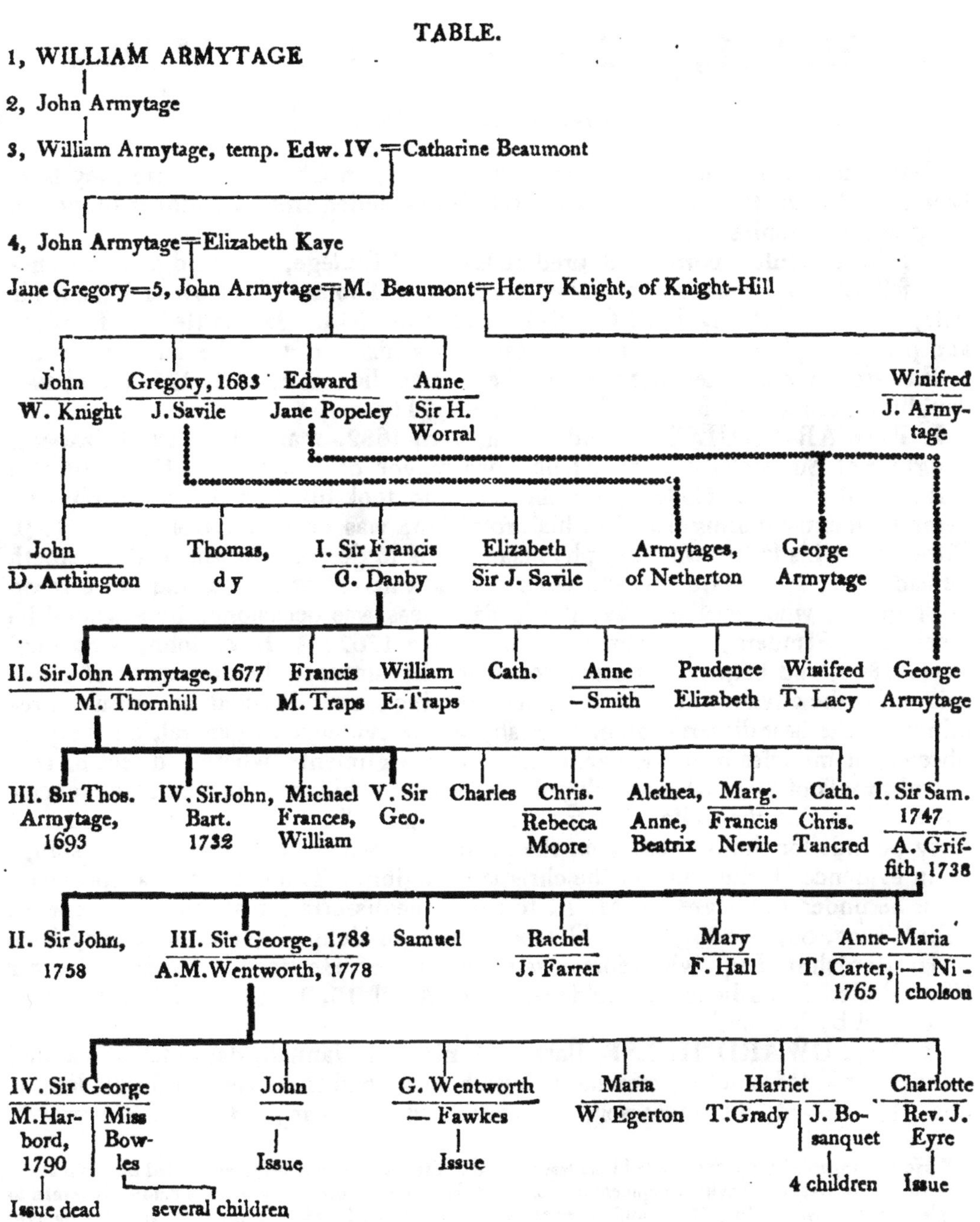
TABLE.
1, WILLIAM ARMYTAGE
2, John Armytage
3, William Armytage, temp. Edw. IV.=Catharine Beaumont
4, John Armytage=Elizabeth Kaye
Jane Gregory=5, John Armytage=M. Beaumont=Henry Knight, of Knight-Hill
John
W. Knight
Gregory, 1683
J. Savile
Edward
Jane Popeley
Anne
Sir H. Worral
Winifred
J. Armytage
John
D. Arthington
Thomas, d y
I. Sir Francis
C. Danby
Elizabeth
Sir J. Savile
Armytages, of Netherton
George Armytage
II. Sir John Armytage, 1677
M. Thornhill
Francis
M. Traps
William
E. Traps
Cath.
Anne
– Smith
Prudence
Elizabeth
Winifred
T. Lacy
George Armytage
III. Sir Thos. Armytage, 1693
IV. Sir John, Bart. 1732
Michael
Frances,
William
V. Sir Geo.
Charles
Chris.
Rebecca Moore
Alethea,
Anne,
Beatrix
Marg.
Francis Nevile
Cath.
Chris. Tancred
I. Sir Sam. 1747
A. Griffith, 1738
II. Sir John, 1758
III. Sir George, 1783
A.M. Wentworth, 1778
Samuel
Rachel
J. Farrer
Mary
F. Hall
Anne-Maria
T. Carter, 1765
— Nicholson
IV. Sir George
M. Harbord, 1790
Miss Bowles
Issue dead
several children
John
—
Issue
G. Wentworth
— Fawkes
Issue
Maria
W. Egerton
Harriet
T. Grady
J. Bosanquet
4 children
Charlotte
Rev. J. Eyre
Issue

251. HULSE, of LINCOLN'S-INN-FIELDS, Middlesex.

Created Baronet, Feb. 17, 1732-3.

THIS family, originally of Northwich hundred, in Cheshire, where they have been seated since the time of Edward III. is descended from a younger branch of the present Cheshire family.

1, Edward Hulse, born 1638, bred at Emanuel College, Cambridge, and sometime fellow there, married Dorothy, daughter of Thomas Westrow and Anne his wife, sister of Arthur, Lord Capel, beheaded in 1648. He settled in London, and practised physic there for forty years. By his said wife he had two sons, 1, Edward, of whom hereafter; 2, William, who died Aug. 22, 1761; and two daughters, Anne and Mary. Edward died 1711.

I. EDWARD HULSE, his eldest son, born 1682, married, 1713, Elizabeth, daughter of Sir Richard Levett, Knt. lord-mayor of London in 1700; he also was bred at Emanuel College, Cambridge, and took his degree there in physic; being eminently distinguished in his profession, was created Baronet in 1738-9. Either he or his father was first physician to his Majesty. By the said Elizabeth he had issue, 1, Edward, his successor; 2, Edward-Westrow, captain of a troop of dragoons, who died Nov. 22, 1746, his illness was occasioned by a wound he received in Flanders; 3, Richard-Thomas, died 1767; 4, Rev. John, who died ——, 1800, and bequeathed some considerable estates to the university of Cambridge for the advancement of religious learning; and directed an annual premium for the best dissertation in English, on the evidence in general, on the prophecies, or miracles in particular, or any other arguments, whether direct or collateral proofs of the christian religion, in order to evidence its truth and excellence. The vice-chancellor and trustees have accordingly offered a premium of forty pounds for the best essay on the prophecies which are now accomplishing, as an evidence of the truth of the christian religion. The successful author, who must be under the degree of M. A. to print the dissertation at his own expence (*Gent. Mag.* Sup. 1800.); and Elizabeth, wife of John Calvert, of Albury-hall, in Hertfordshire, Esq. who represented the town of Hertford in parliament. Sir Edward died at his house in Golden-square, April 10, 1759, aged 74, and was succeeded by his son,

II. Sir EDWARD HULSE, Bart. who married Hannah, daughter of Samuel Vanderplank, of London, merchant, by whom he had three sons and five daughters; 1, Edward, his successor; 2, Samuel, in the army; 3, Rev. Westrow*.

* He accompanied Sir Eyre Coote in his last voyage to the East Indies, being appointed chaplain to the company. He was seized with an epidemic disorder of that climate, not many months before his return to England, which was in July 1784, and never recovered from it. Mr. H. was the first, and it is thought will be the last, chaplain to the East India Company, the directors being of opinion that a chaplain is an unnecessary officer upon their establishment: he was also chaplain to the Prince of Wales. He died in April 1787.

Of the daughters, 1, Hannah, was wife, Sept. 1, 1767, of Richard Benyon, Esq. of Gidea-Hall, Essex, son of Governor Benyon; 2, Elizabeth, of Joseph Berners, Esq. in 1772; 3, Mary-Ann; 4, Dorothy; 5, Charlotte-Matilda. Sir Edward was high-sheriff for Northamptonshire in 1765, died 1780, and was succeeded by his eldest son,

III. Sir EDWARD HULSE, Bart. born 1744, and married, May 1769, Mary, daughter of John Lethieullier, Esq. and heiress of her uncle Smart Lethieullier, of Aldersbrook, in Essex, a lady of immense fortune, by whom he had several children.

ARMS—Argent, three piles, one issuing from the chief, between the others, reversed, sable.

CREST—On a wreath, a buck's head couped, proper, attired, or; between the attires, a sun, of the last.

SEAT—Bremer, in Hampshire.

TABLE.

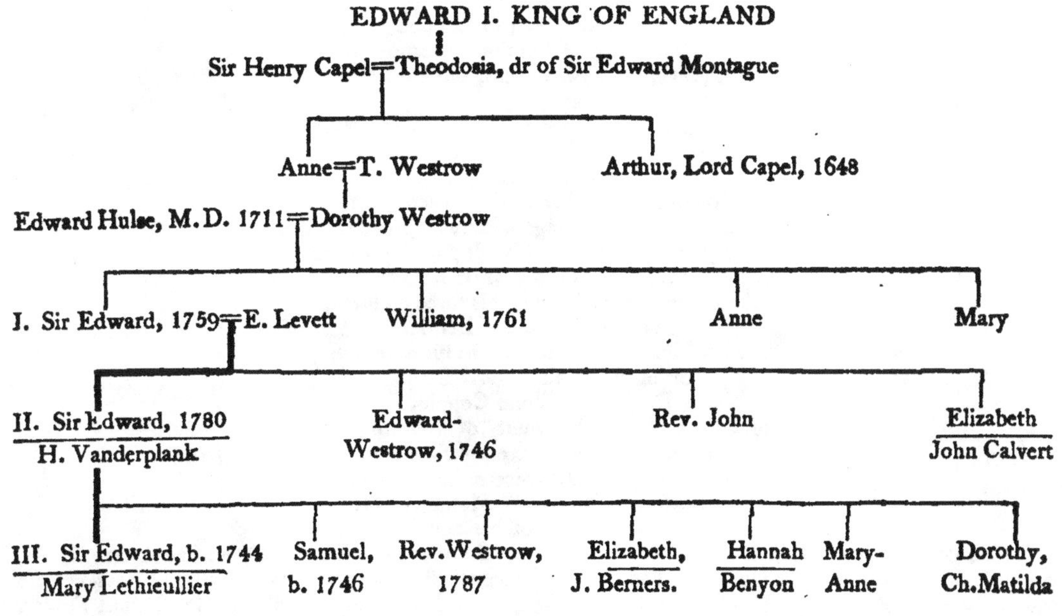

252: BEAUCHAMP PROCTOR, of LANGLEY PARK, Norfolk.

Created Baronet, Feb. 23, 1744-5.

EPHRAIM BEAUCHAMP, of London, Gent. and of Tottenham, in the county of Middlesex, lord of the manor of Boreham, alias Parke, in the parish of Elstree, in the county of Hertford, 1708, and many years one of the governors of Christ-Church, Bethlehem, and Bridewell Hospitals, married Letitia, daughter of John Coppin, of Pollux-Hill, in Bedfordshire, Esq. by whom he had three children, Thomas, Mary, and Letitia, all of whom lie buried at Tottenham. Ephraim Beauchamp died Sept. 16, 1728, in the 68th year of his age*.

Thomas, only son of Ephraim, married Anne, daughter and coheiress of William Proctor, of Epsom, in Surry: this gentleman was killed by a fall from his horse at Epsom, in the lifetime of his father, and was buried Nov. 24, 1725, by Jane, his wife, who died Sept. 20, 1705 †, which William was the son of George

* A black and white marble monument against the north wall, adorned with Ionic pilasters, cornice, and pediments, is inscribed thus:

Near this plate lies interred the body of
Ephraim Beauchamp,
Citizen and Mason of London,
and many years one of the Governors of
Christ Church, Bethlehem, and Bridewell
Hospitals;
Which offices he discharged with honour and integrity.
He was a loving Husband, a tender Father,
and a kind Master,
Pious and charitable without ostentation,
and in all his dealings without reproach.
He departed this life the 16th day of September,
1728, in the 68th year of his age.
And here also lye interred his three children,
Thomas, Mary, and Letitia.
This Monument is erected to his memory
by his mournful widow Letitia,
Daughter of John Coppin,
of Pollux-Hill, in the county of Bedford, Esq.
who, after a life of exemplary piety
and charity, went to receive her eternal
reward the 16th day of March, 1739,
in the 72d year of her age.

† George Proctor, of Barnet, in the county of Herts, had one son William, and five daughters; 1, —, was wife of — Ambrose, by whom she had one son Thomas; 2, Hannah, of — Brattle, by whom she had one son Daniel; 3, —, of — Skinner; 4, —, first, of — Hanbury, secondly, of Christopher Tower,

Proctor, who died before 1671, by whom he left an infant son William, and three daughters, Mary, Jane, and Anne, wife of William Sheldon.

I. Sir WILLIAM was created a Baronet, February 20, 1744, and, in pursuance of the will of his uncle George Proctor, and by virtue of a grant from George II. added the name and arms of Proctor to those of Beauchamp. He was one of the representatives of the county of Middlesex, from 1747 to 1768. He was appointed colonel of the eastern battalion of the Middlesex militia in 1759. In March, 1761, he was elected one of the knights companions of the most honourable order of the Bath, and installed the May following; he was also one of the commissioners of the lieutenancy of London, and was governor of many public charities. Sir William married first, Jane, daughter of Christopher Tower, of Iver, in Bucks, Esq. by whom he had many children, who died young; the surviving are, 1, Anne, born Aug. 8. 1749, wife of Sir Edmund Bacon, P. B. of England, Jan. 28, 1778; 2, Sir Thomas, the present Baronet; 3, Frances, born Nov. 21, 1757, wife of John Constance, of Weston-House, in Norfolk, Esq. by whom she has seven children, Hambleton, George, William, Frances, Emily, John, and Neville; 4, George, born Jan. 22, 1759, married, Oct. 20, 1789, Charlotte, eldest daughter of Robert Palmer, of Sunning, in the county of Bucks, Esq.; 5, Mary, died unmarried, 1776.

Sir William married secondly, Letitia, eldest daughter and coheiress of Henry Johnson, of Great Berkhamstead, in Hertfordshire, Esq. by whom he had five children; 1, Letitia, born March 20, 1763, died March 19, 1780; 2, Henrietta, born Dec. 5, 1764, died an infant; 3, William-Henry, born April 9, 1769, married, June 1790, Frances-Mary Davie, niece of Sir John Davie, Bart.; 4, Christopher, born Sept. 13, 1771; 5, Sidney, born Feb. 10, 1774, died an infant. Sir William Beauchamp Proctor died at his seat at Langley Park, in Norfolk, Sept. 16, 1773, aged 51, and was succeeded in title and estate by his son*,

II. Sir THOMAS BEAUCHAMP PROCTOR, the present Baronet, born Sept. 29, 1756, married Mary, second daughter of Robert Palmer, of Sunning, in Berks, Esq. by whom he has issue, 1, Mary, born Oct 21, 1779, wife, May 5, 1800, of the Rev. Henry Hobart, son of the late M. P. for Norwich; 2, William, born Oct. 11, 1781, in his majesty's navy; 3, Harriet, born Oct. 28, 1782; 4, Thomas, born Jan. 19, 1784, died June 17, 1789; 5, George-Edward, born July 23, 1785; 6, Robert, born April 1, 1787; 7, Thomas-William-Henry, born June 11,

by whom she had one son Christopher, who married Jane, the daughter of his uncle William Proctor, by whom he had two daughters, Jane, wife of Sir William Beauchamp Proctor, Bart.; and Anne, of Sir Nevill Hickman, Bart. who died 1781, leaving two daughters, Anne, and Rose, the wife of — Baker; 5, —, the wife of — Goodwin. George Proctor died before July 11, 1671, when

William Proctor, his son, was bound an apprentice to John Owen, Esq. He married ——, by whom he had nine children, 1, Samuel, baptized July 22, 1691; 2, Anne, baptized Aug. 25, buried Aug. 27, 1692; 3, Anne, baptized Aug. 10, 1693; 4, Hannah, baptized Dec. 2, 1694; 5, William, baptized July 22, 1696; 6, Jane, the wife of Christopher Tower above-mentioned: 7, George, baptized Mar. 7, 1699; 8, Charles, baptized June 3, 1703; 9, Frances, baptized Sept. 5, buried Oct. 16, 1705. Anne, the second daughter, was wife of Thomas Beauchamp.

* His remains were removed to Tottenham, and there interred in the family vault with his ancestors.

1790; 8, Amelia, born Aug. 28, 1791; 9, Richard, born Jan. 30, 1793. Sir Thomas served the office of high-sheriff for the county of Norfolk in 1780.

ARMS—First and fourth, argent, a chevron, between three martlets, sable, for Proctor; second and third, gules, a fess between six billets (three and three barways), or, a canton ermine, for Beauchamp.

CREST—On a mount, vert, a greyhound, sejant, argent, spotted, brown, collared, or.

MOTTO—*Toujours fidele.*

SEAT—Langley Park, Norfolk.

TABLE.

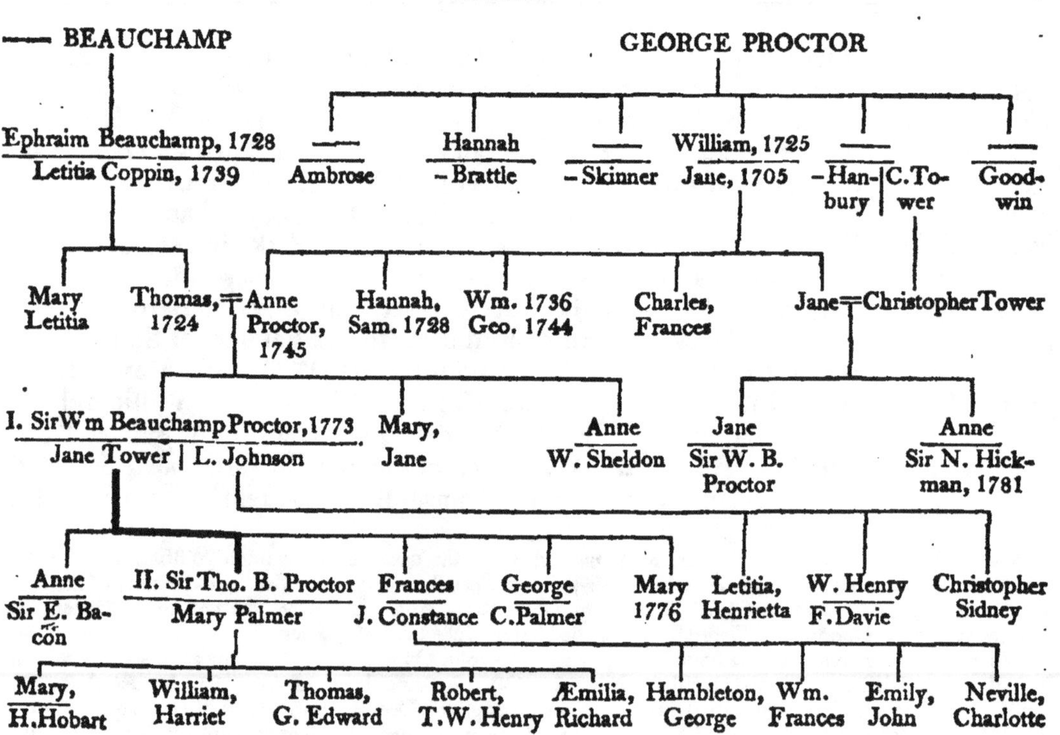

253. GREY, of Howick, Northumberland.

Created Baronet, Jan. 11, 1745-6.

Sir HENRY GREY, the present Baronet, was advanced to this dignity, with limitation to the heirs male of his body lawfully begotten. Sir Henry is married, and has five children, 1, William-Henry, born June 31, 1764; 2, Elizabeth, born Feb. 19, 1765; 3, James-Warton, born Mar. 10, 1766; 4, Ralph, born July 17, 1767; and 5, Henry, born May 24, 1769.

ARMS—Gules, a lion rampant, within a bordure, ingrailed, argent.
CREST—On a wreath, a scaling ladder, argent.
SEAT—At Howick, Northumberland.

John Grey, Esq. of Morwick, near Warkworth, uncle to the present Sir Henry Grey, Bart. and Sir Charles Grey, K. B. of Fallad, in Northumberland, died Oct. 31, 1783.

John Grey, brother to Sir Henry, married, Jan. 28, 1775, ——, daughter of —— Wikett, of Dorset-court, Westminster.

---

254. GOOCH, of Virginia.

Created Baronet, Nov. 4, 1746.

1, ROBERT GOOCH, of Bungay, in the county of Suffolk, is the first of this family we have any particular account of; he left one son,

2, William Gooch, of Mettingham, in Suffolk, armiger, who married Martha, daughter of Christopher Layer, of the city of Norwich, armig. by whom he had two sons and one daughter; 1, William, of whom hereafter; 2, Thomas, who was alderman and thrice bailiff of Yarmouth; he married Joan *, daughter of Tho-

* Inscriptions on grave-stones in St. Nicholas Church, Yarmouth:
Here resteth Joan, the loving wife of Thomas Gooch, alderman of Yarmouth, daughter of Thomas Atkins, Esq. alderman of London, departed this life the 31st of May, 1669, aged 51 years.

mas Atkins, Esq. alderman of London †, by whom he had one son Leonard Gooch, of Earsham, in Norfolk, who left two daughters, Anne, wife of Sir Edward Ward, of Bexley-Hall, Bart. and Mary, of —— Buxton, Esq. of ——, in Norfolk. Barbara, daughter of William Gooch, was wife of Sir Henry Bacon, of Herringfleet, in Suffolk, Bart.

3, William Gooch, the elder son, was of Mettingham, in Suffolk; he was justice of the peace in 1664. He married Elizabeth, daughter and heiress of Richard Baspoole, of St. Margaret's, in Suffolk, by whom he had two sons; 1, Richard, who married Anne, daughter and heiress of Arthur Colman, of St. John's, by whom he had one son William, born 1665, and three daughters, Mary, born 1668, Elizabeth, born 1672, Frances; and two daughters, 1, Martha, wife of Richard Vinor, by whom she had two sons, John and Richard, and one daughter Anne; 2, Barbara, wife of Robert Rogerson, by whom she had one son Thomas, and two daughters, Anne and Margaret. William died in 1685.

4, Thomas Gooch, the second son of William, married Frances, daughter and coheiress of Thomas Lone, of Worlingham, in Suffolk, who died July 25, 1696, aged 44, and was buried at Yarmouth, by whom he had two sons and two daughters; 1, Thomas, Bishop of Ely, of whom hereafter; 2, Sir William, the first Baronet; 3, Frances, wife of Henry Borret, Esq.; 4, Matilda, of the Rev. Matthew Postlethwaite, rector of Denton, and of Redenhall, with Harleston, in Norfolk. Thomas Gooch died 1688.

I. WILLIAM GOOCH, lieutenant-governor of Virginia, served under the great Duke of Marlborough, was wounded at the siege of Carthagena, and was made a Baronet Nov. 4, 1746. He married Rebecca, daughter of Robert Staunton, of Hampton, in Middlesex, Esq. by whom he had no issue, and died Dec. 17, 1751 ‡, whereby the title, agreeable to limitation, devolved on his brother,

† Here resteth the body of Thomas Gooch, alderman and thrice
bailiff of this towne, who departed this life the 27th of February,
anno 1678, aged 79 years.

‡ Inscription on Sir William Gooch's monument in one of the aisles in Yarmouth Church:

Near this marble, his mother and other relations,
are interred the remains of Sir William Gooch, Bart.
Born in this town Oct. 21, A. D. 1681.
He went young into the army, and behaved gallantly
During all Queen Anne's wars, at the end of which
He married
Mrs. Rebecca Staunton, of Hampton, Middlesex, with her he retired,
But not till after he had loyally assisted in
subduing the rebellion in Scotland in 1715.
In 1727, the king made him lieutenant-governor of Virginia,
and of him 'twas justly (and what could be better) said,
That he was the only governor abroad against
whom inhabitant or merchant never once complained.
In 1740, he became colonel of an American regiment,
and was sent with them to the siege of Carthagena,
where, though Providence remarkably preserved him,

II. The Rev. Sir **THOMAS GOOCH**, head of Caius College, Cambridge, 1716, vice-chancellor, 1717, Bishop of Bristol, 1737, translated to Norwich, 1738, and thence to Ely, 1747. The Bishop, during the violence of party in Dr. Bentley's time, was shot at as he was passing from Chapel to Caius Lodge. On the late alterations there, search was made, and a bullet found. He married first, Mary, sister of Bishop Sherlock, by whom he had one son, Sir Thomas, his successor; he married secondly, Harriet, daughter of Sir Thomas Miller, of Sussex, Bart. by whom he had one son, John, D. D. rector of Ditton and Wellingham, Cambridgeshire, and prebendary of Ely. He married Mary, daughter of George Sayer, Esq. by whom he has two daughters, Mary, wife of the Rev. Dr. Ratcliffe, prebendary of Canterbury, and rector of Gillingham, in Kent; and Rachel, of Dr. Beadon, Bishop of Bath and Wells, by whom she has one son Richard, in the army. The Bishop married thirdly, Mary Compton, niece of Bishop Compton and the Earl of Northampton, by whom he had no issue; she died May 14, 1780. The Bishop died 1754, aged 79, and was succeeded in his title of Baronet by his son,

III. Sir **THOMAS GOOCH**, Bart. who married Anne, daughter and heiress of John Atwood, of Saxlingham, in Norfolk, Esq. by —— ||, daughter of ——, and widow of — Bates, by whom he had four sons and one daughter; Matilda, wife, 1776, of Paul Cobb Methuen, of Corsham-House, in Wiltshire, Esq. by whom she has four sons, Paul, Thomas, Charles, and John; and five daugh-

His wounds, and a bad climate, greatly impaired his health.
For this and his other services he was advanced
To the ranks of brigadier and major-general;
But these neither encreasing his fortune,
Nor restoring his health, he returned to England,
Where, after unsuccessful journies to Bath,
He concluded his life Dec. 17, 1751.
To whose memory his much-afflicted widow
Has erected this Monument.

Nothing is unworthy of publication which may convey useful lessons to mankind. Sir William Gooch being in conversation with a gentleman in a street of the city of Williamsburgh, returned the salute of a negro, who was passing by about his business. "Sir," said the gentleman, "does your honour descend so far as to salute a slave?"—"Why, yes," replied the governor, "I cannot suffer a man of his condition to exceed me in good manners."

Perhaps never reprimand was more delicate!—How different an impression the following incident gives us of another governor of Virginia. The laws of that country were formerly oppressive to the Quakers. Lord Howard of Effingham having an aversion to those sectaries, put them rigidly in execution; in consequence of which they suffered many vexations. A deputation of them at length waited upon him at Turky-Island, requesting, with a buckram kind of humility, a mitigation of his severity. On his absolute refusal, "Well," replied their chief, "the Lord's will then be done!"—"Yes, by G—," answered the governor, "and the lord's (*a*) will shall be done, I give you my word."—*Lond. Mag.* 1761, p. 407.

(*a*) Meaning himself.

|| John Atwood was the son of Robert Atwood, Esq. by Anne, his wife, daughter of John Burton, of Yarmouth, Esq, by Anne, his wife, daughter of General Desborow, and Anne, his wife, daughter of Sir Richard Everard, of Much Waltham, in Essex, Bart. and Joan, his wife, daughter of Sir James Barrington, and Joan, his wife, daughter of Sir Henry Cromwell, of Hinchenbrooke, in Huntingdonshire, son of Thomas Barrington, of Barrington-Hall, in Essex, by Winifred Pole, his wife, daughter and coheiress of Henry Pole Montague, lineally descended, by heirs female, from George, Duke of Clarence, youngest brother of Edward IV.—*See Anderson's Genealogical Tables.*

ters, Matilda, Anne, Gertrude-Grace, Catharine, and Cecilia. The sons were, 1, Sir Thomas, the present Baronet; 2, William, who married Elizabeth-Sarah, daughter and heiress of —— Villa-Real, of Edwinston, in Nottinghamshire, Esq. and niece to Lady Viscountess Galway, by whom he has two sons, William, who married ——, daughter of —— More, in the Isle of Man, Esq. and Henry, captain in the army; 3, John, archdeacon of Sudbury, and rector of Benacre, in Suffolk, and Saxlingham-Nethergate, with Thorpe, in Norfolk. He married Barbara, daughter of Ralph Sneyd, Esq. of Keat-Hall, Staffordshire, by Barbara, his wife, daughter of Sir Walter Bagot, of Blithfield, Bart. by whom he has five children, 1, John-Lewis; 2, Henry-Edward; 3, Caroline-Barbara; 4, George-Thomas; 5, Charles-Francis. Robert, the fourth son, died in 1796.

Sir Thomas married secondly, Phœbe, widow of John Birt, consul of Genoa, and daughter of —— Horton, by whom he had one daughter Georgiana, wife of Thomas Farr, of Becles, in Suffolk, Esq. Sir Thomas died Sept. 1781, and was succeeded by his son,

IV. Sir THOMAS GOOCH, the present Baronet, who served the office of sheriff for the county of Suffolk in 1785. He married Anne-Maria, daughter of William Hayward, of Surry, Esq. lineally descended from William Patten, commonly called William of Wainfleet, sole founder of Magdalen College, Oxford, and of a very ancient family in Lancashire, by whom he has five sons and three daughters, 1, Thomas-Sherlock, who married Mariana, sister of Abraham Whittaker, of Lyster-House, Herefordshire, sister to the second wife of John Lord Rous, by whom he has two daughters, and one son Edward-Sherlock; 2, William, married ——, daughter of —— Wilkenson, of Newcastle-upon-Tyne, Esq.; 3, Thomas, lieutenant-colonel in the army, married Hannah, widow of Philip Webb, Esq. of Milford-House, Surrey, daughter of Sir Robert Barker, Bart. late commander in chief in India; 4, Richard; 5, Paul. The daughters are, Elizabeth, Matilda, and Sophia.

ARMS—Parted per pale, argent, and sable, a chevron between three talbots, passant, counterchanged; on a chief, gules, three leopards' heads, or.

CREST—A talbot, passant, per pale, argent, and sable.

MOTTO—*Fide et Virtute.*

SEAT—Benacre-Hall, Suffolk.

The following lines were found by Sir William Gooch, Bart. (great-uncle to the present Baronet) in Williamsburgh church-yard, on a grave-stone, when he went over as lieutenant-governor to Virginia. The person in whose memory they were written was supposed to be one of this family (who at that time lived at Mettingham, near Bungay), who was obliged to flee his country, in consequence of the active part he took against Oliver Cromwell, and was never heard of by his friends, until Sir William found this inscription:

Within this tomb there doth interred lye
No shape, but substance true nobility;
Itself though young in years, just twenty-nine,
Yet grac'd with virtues, moral and divine.
The church from him did good participate,
In counsel rare fit to adorn the state.
William Gooch, Esq. dyed Oct. 29, 1655.

TABLE.

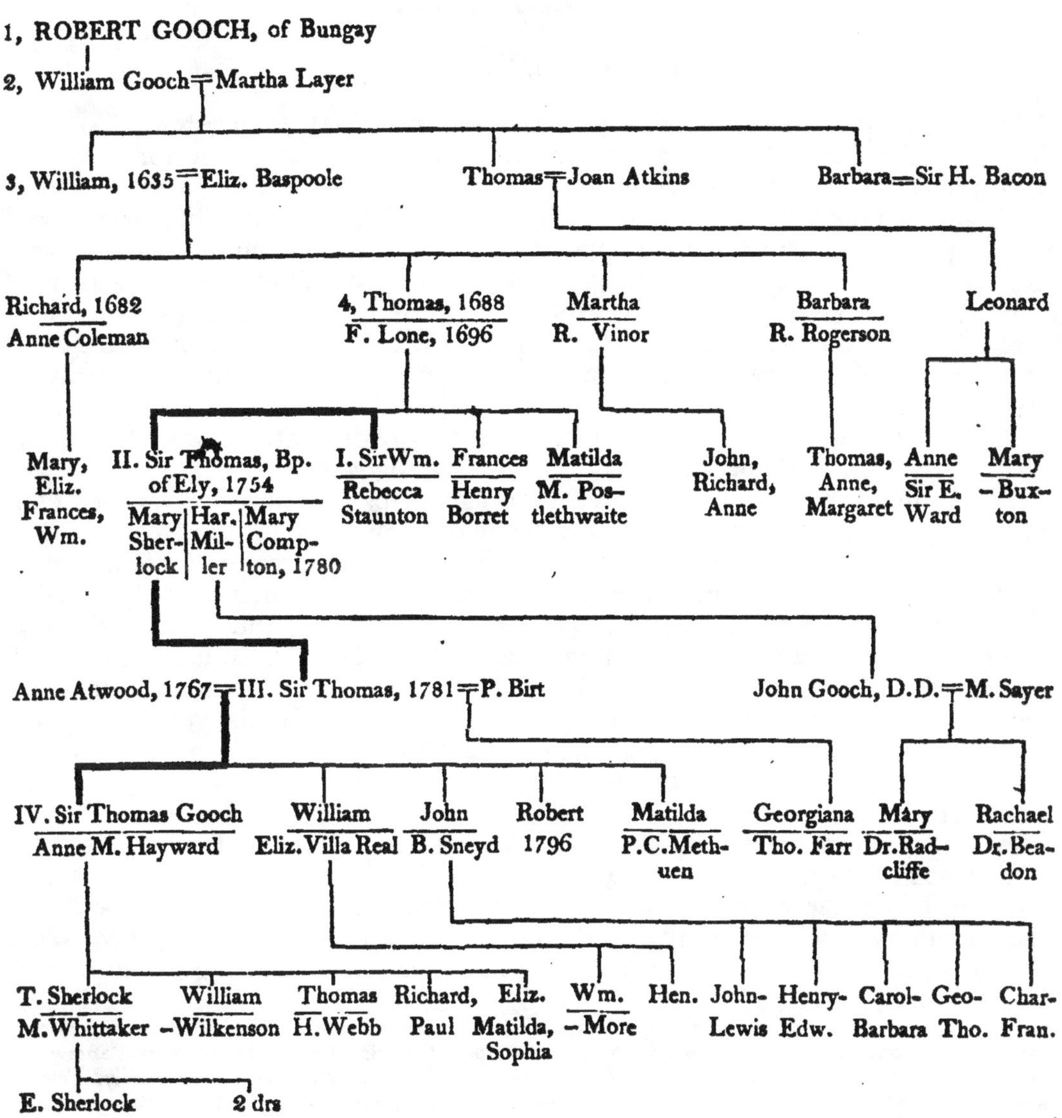
1, ROBERT GOOCH, of Bungay
2, William Gooch = Martha Layer
3, William, 1635 = Eliz. Baspoole
Thomas = Joan Atkins
Barbara = Sir H. Bacon
Richard, 1682
Anne Coleman
4, Thomas, 1688
F. Lone, 1696
Martha
R. Vinor
Barbara
R. Rogerson
Leonard
Mary, Eliz. Frances, Wm.
II. Sir Thomas, Bp. of Ely, 1754
Mary Sherlock
Har. Miller
Mary Compton, 1780
I. Sir Wm.
Rebecca Staunton
Frances
Henry Borret
Matilda
M. Postlethwaite
John, Richard, Anne
Thomas, Anne, Margaret
Anne
Sir E. Ward
Mary
- Buxton
Anne Atwood, 1767 = III. Sir Thomas, 1781 = P. Birt
John Gooch, D.D. = M. Sayer
IV. Sir Thomas Gooch
Anne M. Hayward
William
Eliz. Villa Real
John
B. Sneyd
Robert 1796
Matilda
P.C. Methuen
Georgiana
Tho. Farr
Mary
Dr. Radcliffe
Rachael
Dr. Beadon
T. Sherlock
M. Whittaker
William
- Wilkenson
Thomas
H. Webb
Richard, Paul
Eliz. Matilda, Sophia
Wm.
- More
Hen.
John-Lewis
Henry-Edw.
Carol-Barbara
Geo-Tho.
Char-Fran.
E. Sherlock
2 drs

255. FETHERSTONHAUGH, of Fetherston-haugh, Northumberland.

Created Baronet, Jan. 3, 1747.

THIS family is of Saxon origin, and was seated at Fetherston after the conquest; that part of the county having been allotted to their ancestor, a Saxon officer, for his gallant behaviour against the Britons. They had large possessions, and bore honourable offices, in the county of Northumberland. They were sheriffs, deputy-lieutenants, &c. as appears from records and chronicles, and are registered in King Stephen's reign as gentlemen of coat-armour, resident at Fetherstonhaugh-Castle. It appears, from various deeds and writings, that they were, for some centuries, the owners of several manors and estates near this castle; but none of these remain to the present Baronet, who only inherits the castle itself, and its domains.

This family has, in process of time, been subdivided into several branches, particularly two, of Fetherstonhaugh, and Fetherstonhalge*.

The tradition is, that some hundred years ago, Albany Fetherston married two wives, and had a son by each of them; the elder son inherited the Northumberland estate. The younger son, whose mother was an heiress of a considerable estate in and near Stanhope, in the county palatine of Durham, inherited, in right of his mother, the Stanhope estate. The two brothers being thus separated, they thought proper to distinguish their families, in case they should happen to grow numerous: in pursuance of which intention, to preserve a distinction between them, the elder added *Haugh* to the end of his name, and the younger added *Halge*; the former word signifying a low situation, the latter a high one, which answereth (as may yet be seen) to the real situation of their respective mansions †.

Albany Fetherston-haugh, the descendant of the elder branch, had a second son named Henry, who, in the beginning of King James I.'s reign, was made receiver of all the king's revenues in Cumberland and Westmoreland, and had a son Timothy; which Timothy ‡, in the next reign, espoused the royal party, raised a troop of horse at his own expence, was knighted under the king's banner, and

* Their house, it is said, was formerly upon a hill (where are two stones, called Fether Stones) and was moated about for a defence against the Scots; but upon the ruin of this, the house was afterwards built in the holme or valley under the hill, which they there call *haugh*, and thence it was called Fetherstonhaugh; and the family writ their names de Fetherston, and sometimes de Fetherstonhaugh.—*Machel.*

† William de Monte, so called from his house at Stanhope, situated on Craighill, lived in the time of King Stephen, and in 48 Edw. III. this family took the surname of Fetherstonhalge.—*Herald's College.*

‡ Vide Lloyd's Memoirs of Excellent Persons, p. 559.

fought bravely and successfully till the battle of Worcester, when he was taken prisoner with the Earl of Derby, and beheaded at Bolton, in Lancashire. This event hurt the estate of this particular line, but not irrecoverably, for the descendants of this gentleman are still very respectable, both in character and fortune.

The last-mentioned Albany Fetherstonhaugh, father of Henry, and grandfather of Timothy, had opulent manors and possessions; but they became, in process of time, reduced to the single castle, with its domains, which is now inherited, as before-mentioned, by the present Baronet, who is descended from this branch of the family.

———, great-grandfather of the late Sir Matthew, possessed an estate at Alton Moor, in Northumberland, which was part of the estate belonging to Fetherstonhaugh, and given to his ancestors as a younger brother's fortune. He left a son,

———, who married ———, daughter of Matthew Whitfield, Esq. of Whitfield-Hall, in Northumberland, by whom he had one son,

Matthew Fetherstonhaugh, Esq. who was twice mayor of Newcastle, and married, in 1710, ———, daughter of Robert Brown, Esq. who, upon the death of her only brother, became heiress of a large fortune, and died 1767. He died Feb. 17, 1762, aged 102. He had two sons, Sir Matthew, and the Rev. Ulrick, rector of Stanford-le-Hope, in Essex, &c. who married ——, daughter of —— Stillingfleet Durnford, of the office of ordnance, by whom he left issue, and died Dec. 26, 1708; and two daughters, ———, wife of Captain Day, and ———, of Christopher Richardson, of Randal-Holme-Hall, in Cumberland, Esq. He was succeeded in his estates by his son,

I. MATTHEW FETHERSTONHAUGH, Esq. who, upon the death of the late Sir Henry Fetherstonhaugh, Bart. who died Oct. 1746, without issue, had bequeathed to him the greatest part of his possessions and fortune, wishing him also to obtain a continuation of the title, whereupon he obtained a patent as above-mentioned. Sir Matthew married, Dec. 24, 1746, Sarah, only daughter of Christopher Lethieullier, of Belmont, in Middlesex, Esq. who died Aug. 27, 1788, leaving one son Henry, the present Baronet. Sir Matthew was member of parliament for Morpeth, in Northumberland, and after that for Portsmouth; he was governor of St. Thomas and the Middlesex hospitals, and fellow of the Royal Society. He died May 24, 1774, and was succeeded by his only son,

II. Sir HARRY FETHERSTONHAUGH, the present Baronet.

ARMS—Gules, on a chevron, between three ostriches feathers, argent, a pellet.

CREST—An antelope statant, argent, armed, or.

SEATS—Up-Park, in Sussex; Harringbrook, in Essex; and Fetherstonhaugh Castle, in Northumberland.

TABLE.

— FETHERSTONHAUGH

— Fetherstonhaugh = — Whitfield

Matthew Fetherstonhaugh, 1764 = — Brown, 1767

I. Sir Matthew	Ulrick	—	—
Sarah Lethieullier	— Durnford	Capt. Day	Chris. Richardson

II. Sir Harry Fetherstonhaugh

Of the Stanhope family, who were distinguished by the addition of Halge, were Sir Heneage and Sir Fetherston, Baronets, first so created in 1660.

So also was Colonel Fetherstonhalge, killed at the battle of Blenheim, the last possessor of the Stanhope estate; which was, after his decease, sold to the Earl of Carlisle, and put a period to the name there; he had twice represented the county palatine of Durham.

Cuthbert Fetherston, Esq. great-grandfather of the late Sir Fetherston, Bart. came from Stanhope to London in 1550.

256. IBBETSON, of Leeds, in Yorkshire.

Created Baronet, May 12, 1748.

THIS family is of considerable antiquity in this county, where they have divided into several branches.

I. HENRY IBBETSON, of Leeds, in Yorkshire, Esq. (second son of Mr. Ibbetson, an eminent merchant there) was created a Baronet by letters-patent bearing date May 12, 1748, 21 Geo. II. He married, in 1740, Isabella, daughter of Ralph Carr, of Cocken, near Durham, Esq. by whom he had ten children; 1, Isabella; 2, Harriet; 3, Sir James, his successor; 4, Elizabeth; 5, Henry; 6, Margaret; 7, Carr; 8, Catharine; 9, Denzil, who was killed by an accidental discharge of his gun, when out a shooting in the woods at Cocken, near Durham, the seat of his uncle Ralph Carr, Esq.; 10, Thomasine, wife of James Fenton, of Leeds, Esq. Sir Henry died June 22, 1761, and was succeeded by his eldest son,

II. Sir JAMES IBBETSON, Bart. who, in 1768, married Jenny, daughter of John Caygill, of Halifax, in Yorkshire, Esq. by whom he had four sons and three daughters, 1, Sir Henry-Carr Ibbetson, the present Baronet; 2, Anne-Frances; 3, Isabella; 4, Harriet; 5, Charles; 6, James, who was killed by a fall from his horse; and 7, John-Thomas. (The brother of Sir Henry Ibbetson, the first Baronet, was Samuel, who married ——, by whom he had one daughter Alice, who was wife of Lord Shipbrook.) Sir James Ibbetson died Sept. 4, 1795, aged 48, and was succeeded by his eldest son,

III. Sir HENRY-CARR IBBETSON, the present Baronet, who was captain in the third, or Prince of Wales's dragoon guards, and afterwards lieutenant-colonel of the West York militia; he is unmarried.

ARMS—Gules, on a bend, cottized, argent, between two fleeces, or, three escallops of the field.
CREST—On a wreath, an unicorn's head, erased, per fess, argent and gules, and charged with three escallops counterchanged, two and one, of the last.
MOTTO—*Vixi liber et moriar.*
SEAT—Denton Park, Yorkshire.

TABLE.

MR. IBBETSON

Samuel — I. Sir Henry Ibbetson, 1761 = Isabella Carr

Alice = Lord Shipbrook — II. Sir James, 1795 = Jenny Caygill — Isabella, = Harriet — Elizabeth, = Henry — Margaret, = Carr — Catharine, = Denzil — Thomasine = J. Fenton

III. Sir Hen-Carr Ibbetson — Anne-Fran. — Isabella — Harriet — Charles — James — John-Thomas

257. GIBBONS, of Stanwell-Place, Middlesex.

Created Baronet, April 21, 1752.

I. WILLIAM GIBBONS, Esq. governor of the Island of Barbadoes, was advanced to the dignity of a Baronet, April 21, 1752. He died in May, 1760, and was succeeded by his son,

II. Sir JOHN GIBBONS, Bart. who was elected a knight of the most noble order of the Bath, in March, 1761, and installed the May following, and died at Stanwell, July 9, 1776, aged 59, and was succeeded by his son,

III. Sir WILLIAM GIBBONS, Bart. LL.D. who, July 2, 1789, was appointed a commissioner of the Sick and Hurt Office. He married, Sept. 3, 1771, ——, daughter of Admiral Watson, by whom he has one son John, who, in 1795, married ——, daughter of the late Richard Taylor, of Charlton-House, Esq.

ARMS—Gules, a lion rampant, or, debruised by a bend, argent, charged with a torteaux, between two crosses, formée fitchy, sable.

CREST—On a wreath, a lion's gamb, erased and erect, gules, charged with a bezant, holding a cross, formée, fitchy, sable, on the gamb, a bezant.

SEAT—At Stanwell-Place, Middlesex.

TABLE.

I. Sir WILLIAM GIBBONS, 1760=——, 1758

II. Sir John Gibbons, 1776=——

III. Sir William Gibbons=Miss Watson

John Gibbons=Miss Taylor

---

258. WINNINGTON, of Stanford-Court, Worcestershire.

Created Baronet, Feb. 15, 1755.

THIS family is undoubtedly of great antiquity in the county of Cheshire; for we find, in the reign of Edward I. 1275, they were lords of the manor of Winnington, near Namptwich, in Cheshire, where they continued to reside till the beginning of the last century, and intermarried with many of the principal families in that county.

1, Richard Winnington had one son,

2, Richard Winnington, Esq. who, temp. Edward III. married Emma, eldest daughter of William Mainwaring, Esq. (who was lineally descended from Ranalphus Mainwaring, who came over with the Conqueror), by whom he had one son,

3, Richard-Mainwaring Winnington, who married Catharine, third daughter and one of the coheiresses of Robert le Grosvenor, lord of Hulme, by which marriage he obtained the lordship of Putford, and several other lands, in Cheshire.

4, Richard Winnington, their eldest son, married Joan Smith, by whom he had two daughters, Catharine, who died without issue, 23 Hen. VII. and Elizabeth, wife of Sir Piers Warburton, of Orley, 1511, being then sole daughter and heiress of Richard Winnington, who died 19 Hen. VII. By this match, the Warburtons of Arley became possessed of the manors of Winnington and Putford, and all the estates belonging to the Winningtons, which they continued in possession of till the marriage of the sole daughter and heiress of General Warburton to Samuel Pennant, Esq. late member of parliament for Liverpool.

One of the younger branches of this family settled at Powick, near Worcester, and left one son,

1, Francis Winnington, who was an officer in the army in the reign of Cha. I. and married ——, by whom he had one son,

2, Francis Winnington, born at Worcester, Nov. 7, 1634; he was bred to the law, and had the honour of knighthood conferred on him by Charles II. to whom, as well as to James II. he was solicitor-general. Sir Francis married first, Elizabeth, daughter of —— Herbert, Esq. by whom he had one daughter Elizabeth, wife of William Dodeswell, of Pull-Court, Esq. He married secondly, Elizabeth, third sister and coheiress of Edward Salway, of Stanford-Court, Worcestershire, by whom he had four sons; 1, Salway, who married, July 24, 1690, Anne, sister of Thomas, Lord Foley, of Great Whitby, in Worcestershire, by whom he had eight children, (1, Elizabeth, born Oct. 18, 1692. who died the same year, and was buried at St. Giles's in the Fields, in the county of Middlesex; 2, Francis, born Jan. 15, 1693, who died on his travels, at Vienna, August 19, 1718, and was interred in the burial place of the Protestants of that city; he was a youth of great hopes, and beloved and admired by all that knew him; 3, Thomas, born Dec. 31, 1699, who, Aug. 6, 1719, married Love, the fourth daughter of Sir James Read, of Brocket-Hall, in Hertfordshire, Bart. sister and coheiress of Sir John Read, Bart. by whom he had one son Francis-Read, born July 16, 1720, who died in his infancy; 4, Anne, wife of John Wheeler, of Wooton-Lodge, in Staffordshire, Esq.; 5, Mary, who died April 18, 1730, unmarried; 6, Edward, born April 10, 1704, and died April 18, 1711, and was buried at St. James's, in the county of Middlesex; 7, Helena, born in May, 1705, died Aug. 10, 1725, unmarried; 8, Henrietta, wife of Samuel, Lord Masham). The other sons of Sir Francis Winnington were, 2, Francis, of whom hereafter; 3, John, who died unmarried; 4, Edward, who married ——, daughter of —— Jefferies, of Ham-Castle, by whom he had several children, who all died in their infancy. This gentleman was bred to the law, in the knowledge of which none of his contemporaries excelled him, in his practice none equalled him; for having, by his marriage, acquired a very considerable estate, he often pleaded the cause of the oppressed and indigent without fee or reward: he for many years represented the borough of Droitwich.

Sir Francis had likewise, by his second lady, two daughters; Honora, wife of —— Bruen, of Bruen-Stapleford, in Cheshire, Esq.; and Mary, of John Calvert, of Albury-Hall, Hertfordshire, Esq. Sir Francis was eminent for his knowledge in the laws of England, was a great master of eloquence, and a most zealous defender of the liberties of his country. He for some time represented the county of Worcester, and afterwards that city, as also the boroughs of Tewksbury and Windsor, in parliament, where he gave a remarkable instance of his zeal for the Protestant religion, by resigning his office of solicitor general to James II. that he might act consistently with his conscience, by supporting the exclusion bill. The share this gentleman had in the education of Lord Somers, adds much to the honour of his memory.

Sir Francis died May 1, 1700, and was buried in the chancel of the parish church of Stamford, in Worcestershire, where a monument is erected to perpetuate his name*.

We now return to Francis, second son of Sir Francis Winnington, Knt. who settled at Broadway, in Worcestershire, and married Anne, daughter of Tho. Jackson, of London, Esq. by whom he had four daughters, 1, Martha, wife of the Rev. Dr. Turner, of Newcastle, in Northumberland; 2, Elizabeth, of Reginald Wyniat, of Stanton-Hall, Worcestershire, Esq.; 3, Anne, of John Ingram, of Bewdley, in the same county, Esq.; and 4, Mary, who died unmarried. This Francis Winnington, Esq. had likewise two sons; Francis, who married Susanna Courtenay, nearly related to Lord Courtenay; and Edward, who married Sophia Boot, of ——, near Wantage, in Berkshire.

By this lady, who died Feb. 20, 1779, he had one son,

I. Sir EDWARD WINNINGTON, the late Baronet, (created such by letters-patent, dated Feb. 15, 1755), who married Mary, daughter of John Ingram, of Bewdley, in Worcestershire, by whom he had one son, Sir Edward, the present Baronet. Sir Edward was member of parliament for Bewdley, in Worcestershire, and died Dec. 9, 1791, and was succeeded by his only son,

II. Sir EDWARD WINNINGTON, Bart. born Nov. 14, 1749, member of parliament for the borough of Droitwich. He married Anne, youngest daughter of Thomas Foley, Esq.

* On the south side of the said church is a handsome monument, erected to the memory of the Right Honourable Thomas Winnington, second son of Solway Winnington aforesaid, who was member of parliament for Droitwich from 1725 to 1741, at which time he was chosen to represent the city of Worcester; he was likewise appointed one of the lords of the admiralty, in 1730; of the treasury, in 1736; cofferer of his Majesty's privy-council, in 1740; and lastly, in 1743, paymaster-general of the forces, in which place he died April 23, 1746. On his monument are the following verses:

Near his paternal seat, here buried lies
The grave, the gay, the witty, and the wise:
Equal to ev'ry part, in all he shin'd,
Variously great, a genius unconfin'd!
In converse bright, judicious in debate,
In private amiable, in public great,
With all the statesman's knowledge, prudence, art,
With friendship's open, undesigning heart.
The friend and heir, here join their duty: one
Erects the bust, and one inscribes the stone.
Not that they hope by these his fame should live,
That claims a longer date than they can give.
False to their trusts, the mould'ring busts decay,
And soon the effac'd inscription wears away;
But England's annals shall their place supply,
And while they live, his name can never die.

ARMS—Quarterly: first and fourth, argent, an orle between eight martlets, sable; second and third, sable, a faltier engrailed, or.

CREST—A saracen's head, full-faced, couped at the shoulders, proper, wreathed about the temples, argent, and sable.

MOTTO—*Grata sume manu.*

SEATS—At Stanford-Court, and Ham-Castle, both in Worcestershire.

TABLE.

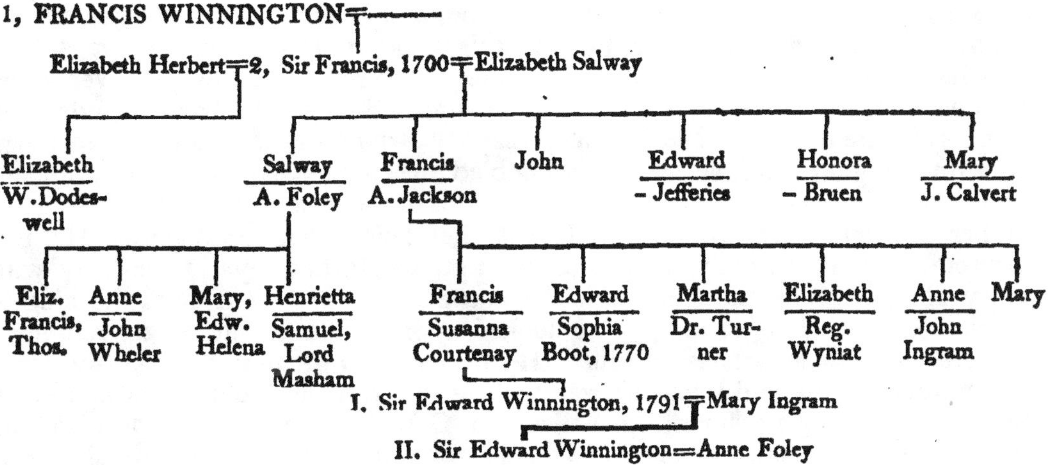

259. SHEFFIELD, of NORMANBY, in Lincolnshire.

Created Baronet, March 1, 1755.

SIR CHARLES SHEFFIELD was the natural son of John Sheffield, Duke of Buckinghamshire, a writer of some name in verse and prose, who was born about 1650; for he tells us, that he was seventeen when Prince Rupert and the Duke of Albemarle jointly commanded the fleet against the Dutch, which was in 1666, so that the author of the "Peerage of England" must be in an error, who places his birth in 1646. He lost his father at nine years of age; and his mother, marrying Lord Ossulston, the care of his education was left entirely to a governor, who travelled with him into France, but did not greatly improve him in his studies. Having, however, fine parts, and a turn to letters, he made up the defects of his education, and acquired a very competent share of learning. He went a volunteer in the second Dutch war; and afterwards, between 1673 and 1675, made a campaign in the French service. As Tangier was in danger of being taken by the Moors, he offered to head the forces which were sent to defend it, and accordingly was appointed commander of them. He was then Earl of Mulgrave, and one of the lords of the bedchamber to Charles II. May, 1674, he was installed knight of the Garter, and began to make a figure at court. An affection to the Princess Anne, and an attempt to be more closely connected with her, involved him at this time in some small disgrace with Charles II. whose favour, however, he soon recovered, and enjoyed ever after. He does not, by his presumption, as it was called, seem to have offended the princess in the least. "Queen Anne," says a certain writer, "undoubtedly had no turn for gallantry, yet so far resembled her predecessor Elizabeth, as not to dislike a little homage to her person. This duke was immediately rewarded on her accession, for having made love to her before her marriage." He understood a court perfectly well, and was apt, as Burnet says, to comply with every thing that he thought might be acceptable. He went with the king to mass, and kneeled at it; and, being looked upon as indifferent to all religions, the priests made an attack on him. He heard them gravely arguing for transubstantiation; he told them, he was willing to receive instruction, he had taken much pains to bring himself to believe in God, who made the world and all men in it; but it must not be an ordinary force of argument that should make him believe, that man was quits with God, and made God again.

He greatly disapproved several measures of King James, yet was not a friend to the revolution; and though he paid his respects to King William before he was advanced to the throne, he was not in any post of government till some years after. Nevertheless, when it was debated in parliament whether the Prince of Orange should be proclaimed king, or the princess reign solely in her own right, he voted and spoke for the former. He was created Marquis of Normanby by King William, and enjoyed some considerable posts under that prince. April, 1702, after the accession of Queen Anne, he was sworn lord privy-seal, appointed one of the commissioners to treat of an union between England and Scotland, and, March 4, created Duke of Normanby first, and then Duke of Buckinghamshire. He was always attached to Tory principles, and was instrumental in the change of the ministry in 1710. In 1711, he was made steward of her Majesty's household, and president of the council, and so continued to the end of her reign. Upon her decease, Aug. 1, 1714, he was one of the lords justices of Great Britain, till George I. arrived from Hanover; after which, he appears to have been laid aside as of principles different from the succeeding ministry, and therefore of no further use. He spent the remainder of his life in indolent retirement*, and died Feb. 24, 1720-1†.

* In a reprinted letter, dated Nov. 10, 1719, he tells a friend, "The Duchess of Buckingham and myself are the greatest eaters of oysters in all England, and pray do what you can for us."

† He was buried in Westminster-Abbey, after lying some days in state at Buckingham-House; and a monument was erected over him with this inscription, as directed in his will, viz. in one place:

Pro Rege sæpe, pro Republica semper.

In another place:

Dubius, sed non improbus vixi.
Incertus morior, sed inturbatus.
Humanum est nescire & errare.
Christum adveneror, Deo confido
Omnipotenti, benevolentissimo.
Ens entium, miserere mei.

The second line of the epitaph stands as follows on the Duke's monument: Incertus morior, non perturbatus;" and the words, "Christum adveneror," are omitted, at the desire, as is said, of bishop Atterbury, who thought the verb *adveneror* not full enough, as applied to Christ. Great clamours were raised against this epitaph, many asserting that it proved the Duke a sceptic; and as great a trifle as it may seem, his grace's orthodoxy became the subject of a controversy: it was, however, defended in form by Dr. Fiddes, in "A Letter to a Freethinker," 1721.

Dryden has given many testimonies of his critical and poetic merit. He dedicated his translation of Virgil's Æneid to him, and gave this reason for it: "Had I not addressed to a poet, and a critic of the first magnitude, I had myself been taxed for want of judgment, and shamed my patron for want of understanding."

Happy the poet! blest the lays!
Which Buckingham has deign'd to praise.
PRIOR'S ALMA.

Nor Tyber's streams, no courtly gallies see,
But smiling Thames his Normanby.
GARTH.

Yet some there were among the sounder few,
Of those, who less presumed and better knew,
Who durst assert the juster ancient cause,
And here restor'd wit's fundamental laws.
Such was the Muse, whose rules and practice tell
Nature's chief master-piece is writing well.
POPE'S ESSAY ON CRITICISM.

This last line is taken from the duke's Essay on Poetry. "We have three poems in our tongue," says Addison, "which are of the same nature, and each of them a master-piece in its kind, the Essay on Translated Verse, the Essay on Poetry, and the Essay on Criticism."—"Our language," says Burnet, "is now certainly proper, and more natural than it was formerly, chiefly since the correction that was given by the Rehearsal." We have been at the pains of transcribing these testimonies, chiefly to shew what a precarious and uncertain thing literary reputation is, and how miserably many an author may flatter and delude himself with dreams and visions of immortal fame; for, hear what two of the present times have said of this so much admired Duke of Buckinghamshire. "The coldness and neglect," (says Warton on Pope), "with which this writer, formed only on the French critics, speaks of Milton, must be considered as proofs of his want of critical discernment, or of critical courage. I can recollect no performance of Buckingham

His grace first married Ursula, daughter of Colonel Stanwell, and widow of Edward, Earl Conway: he married secondly, Catharine, eldest daughter of Fulk Greville, Lord Brook, widow of Baptist Noel, Earl of Gainsborough, who died in 1704-5: his grace had no issue by either of these ladies. He married thirdly, Catharine, eldest daughter of King James II. (by Catharine, daughter of Sir Charles Sedley, Bart. whom that prince created Countess of Dorchester), who was born in 1681, and in 1699, was married to the Earl of Anglesea, but being divorced from that nobleman, his grace's great tenderness compensated for all the injuries she had suffered. By his grace she had several children, who died young, among whom was the Marquis of Normanby, who departed this life Feb. 1, 1714, aged seventeen. She survived the Duke, but had the misfortune to be deprived of her son and heir, Edmund, the last Duke of Buckinghamshire, who being of a weakly constitution, was obliged to reside a great part of his time out of his native country, and the Duchess constantly attended him; but for about half a year he resided at Oxford, and was admitted, 1722, at Queen's College, under the care of Dr. Smith, then provost, whom her grace had placed a great confidence in; but tender as he was, yet, fired with the example of his ancestors, many of whom had signalized themselves in the wars, he went, in 1734, a volunteer under the command of his uncle, the Duke of Berwick, in Germany, whom he served as aid-de-camp at the siege of Fort Kehl and Philipsburgh, till the marshal lost his head by a cannon-ball from the walls of the latter. This catastrophe put an end to his grace's campaign. The next year, intending to try the air of Naples, he advanced as far as Rome, where he died Oct. 30, 1731, of a hasty consumption, and his body being brought to England, was conveyed to Westminster-Abbey with the like funeral solemnity as that of his father, by whose side he was interred; and, in 1742, the Duchess died, upon whose death that noble house (now the Queen's palace) in St. James's Park, which was built by the old Duke, came into the possession of Charles Herbert, together with his whole estate, in pursuance of his will, on his surviving his grace's heir, who should die without issue, and of his taking the name of Sheffield. His grace likewise left, upon the death of the Duchess, one thousand pounds to Mr. Herbert's mother (Mrs. Lambert), by whom his grace had not only this son, Sir Charles Sheffield, but also two natural daughters, Sophia and Charlotte, to whom he left one thousand pounds each, to be raised to five thousand pounds, in case Mr. Herbert should succeed to the estate. On his grace's

that stamps him a true genius: his reputation was owing to his rank. In reading his poems, one is apt to exclaim with our author:

"What woeful stuff this madrigal would be,
In some starved hackney sonneteer, or me!
But let a lord once own the happy lines,
How the wit brightens! how the style refines!

"It is certain," says the other, "that his Grace's compositions in prose have nothing extraordinary in them: his poetry is most indifferent, and the greatest part of both is already fallen into total neglect."

We mean not to rest the Duke's literary merit upon the authority of these two writers, but only to shew the sense the present age has of it, as here represented by them.

death, the Duchess took great care of their education; Sophia was the wife of Dr. Walker, dean of Burien, and afterwards of Jeremiah Griffith, Esq. counsellor-at-law; and Charlotte, wife, first, of Joseph Hunt, D. D. and master of Baliol College, Oxford; secondly, of —— Cole; and thirdly, of the Honourable William Digby, canon of Christ Church, Oxford, who was son of Lord Digby.

I. Sir CHARLES SHEFFIELD, Bart. married first ——, daughter of General Sabine, by whom he had three sons; 1, Sir John, his successor; 2, Charles, who died without issue, 1790; 3, Rev. Robert Sheffield, who married Penelope, daughter of Sir Abraham Pitches, by whom he has one son Robert, and one daughter Penelope. Sir Charles had also three daughters; Anne-Diana, widow of Major-General Cox, who died 1788, by whom she had one son William, and nine daughters; 1, Margaretta-Diana; 2, Caroline-Henrietta; 3, Sophia-Mary; 4, Anne-Maria; 5, Charlotte-Augusta; 6, Louisa-Matilda; 7, Frances-Amelia; 8, Charlotte-Catharine; 9, Julia. Sir Charles died Sept. 5, 1774, and was succeeded by his son,

II. Sir JOHN SHEFFIELD, Bart. who married, April 3, 1784, Sophia-Charlotte, daughter of Dr. Digby, dean of Durham, brother to the late Earl Digby, by whom he has no issue.

ARMS—Argent, a chevron between three garbs, gules, all within a border gobony, argent, and azure.

CREST—On a wreath, a boar's head and neck erased, or.

SEAT—At Normanby, in Lincolnshire.

TABLE.

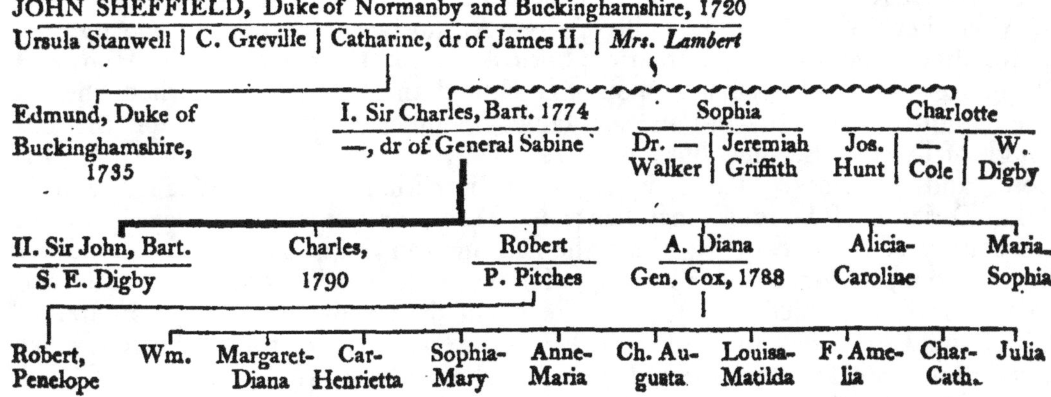

260. MANN, of LINTON, Kent.

Created Baronet, March 3, 1755.

1, **EDWARD MANN**, of Ipswich, in the county of Suffolk, Esq. comptroller of the customs of that place, is the first mentioned in this pedigree. He married ——, daughter of —— Dyer, by whom he had a son,

2, Edward Mann, of Ipswich aforesaid, who married Dorothy, daughter of —— Mannock, of Stoke Nayland, in the county of Suffolk, by whom he had one son,

3, Thomas Mann, of Ipswich aforesaid, and the Inner-Temple, London, usher of the rolls, who married Elizabeth, daughter of William Alston, of Marlesford, in the county of Suffolk, Gent. by whom he had five sons; 1, John; 2, Thomas; 3, Edward; 4, William; 5, Geoffry; and five daughters; 1, Elizabeth; 2, Dorothy; 3, Mary; 4. Margaret; 5, Martha.

4, John Mann, the eldest son, married Mary, daughter of Edward Hinton, of Bourton, in Berkshire, by whom he had one son,

5, Robert Mann, of London, and afterwards of Linton, in Kent, Esq. who died March 12, 1752, leaving by Eleanor, his wife, daughter and heiress of Christopher Guise, of Abbot's-court, in Gloucestershire, Esq. five sons and three daughters, 1, Edward-Louisa, who died at Linton, Dec. 16, 1755, and was succeeded in his estates by his brother; 2, Sir Horatio Mann, of whom hereafter; 3, Galfridus, of Bocton-Malherb, in Kent, member in two or three parliaments for the town of Maidstone, in the said county, who married Sarah, daughter of John Gregory, of the city of London, Esq. by whom he had two sons, 1, Edward, born Jan. 15, 1735, and died Sept. 14, 1737; 2, Sir Horatio, the late Baronet; and five daughters; 1, Eleanor, born Feb. 21, 1736, and died Jan. 26, 1737; 2, Alice, born May 30, 1739, wife of —— Apthorpe; 3, Sarah, born Aug. 10, 1740, died unmarried; 4, Catharine, born Aug. 13, 1742, wife of the Hon. and Right Rev. Dr. Cornwallis, Bishop of Litchfield and Coventry, by whom she has one daughter Elizabeth, and one son James, member of parliament for the borough of Eye; 5, Eleanor, born Aug. 29, 1747, wife of Thomas Powis; 4, Robert; and 5, James. The daughters of Robert Mann were, 1, Eleanor, wife of John Toriano, of London, merchant; 2, Mary, of Benjamin-Hatley Foote, of the county of Kent, Esq. by whom she had one son John, a banker in London; 3, Catharine, of Mr. Hender Foote, (who was first a barrister-at-law, and then took orders, and died 1773), by whom she had three sons, John Foote, of Charlton, Esq. who married and has issue; Robert, rector of Barton, alias Boughton Malherbe, and vicar of Linton, who married Anne, daughter of Dobbins Yate, of Gloucestershire, Esq.; and Edward, of the royal navy; and three daughters, two of whom died unmarried; and Catharine, the second, was wife, first, of —— Ross, and secondly, of Sir Robert Herries, of London, Knt.

I. HORATIO MANN, Esq. second son of the above Robert Mann, of Linton, in the county of Kent, Esq. was advanced to the dignity of Baronet, by letters-patent dated March 3, 1755, 28 Geo. II. to him and his heirs male of his body lawfully begotten; and in default of such issue, to his brother Galfridus, and his heirs male of his body lawfully begotten.

Sir Horatio was appointed, in 1740, his Majesty's envoy extraordinary and minister plenipotentiary at the court of Florence. He was a knight companion of the most honourable military order of the Bath, and died at Florence, advanced in years, Nov. 6, 1786, where he had resided forty-six years, and was succeeded by his nephew, son of his brother Galfridus.

II. Sir HORACE MANN, Bart. succeeded his father in the possession of his estates; and, in Jan. 15, 1774, appeared as proxy for his uncle, Sir Horatio Mann, Bart. at his installation as knight of the Bath, having been knighted previous to that ceremony. He was then called Sir Horace Mann, to distinguish

TABLE.

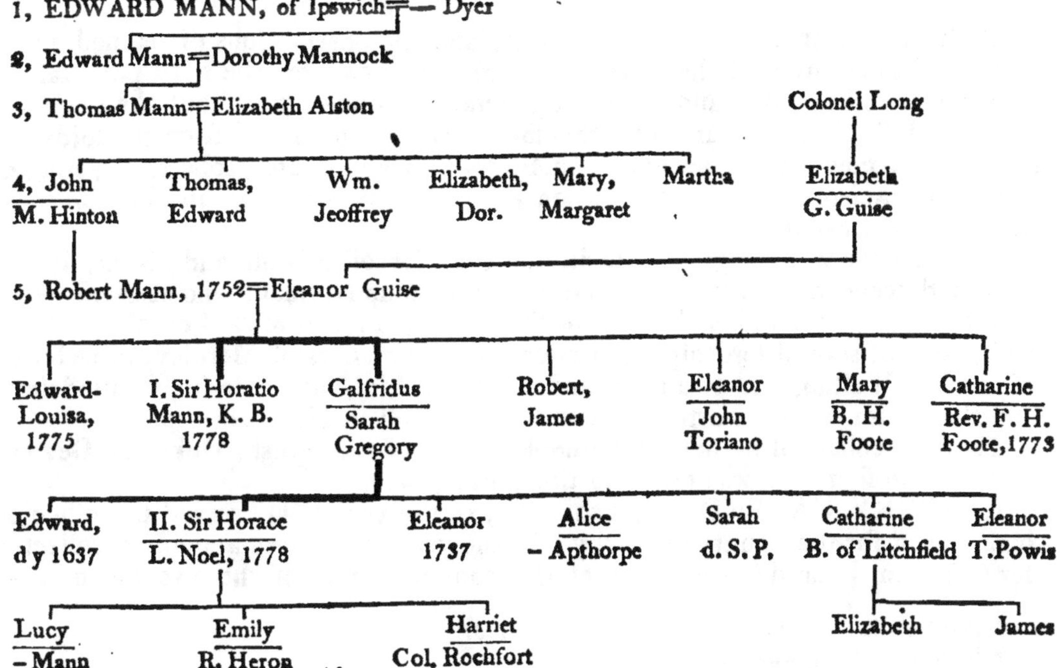

him from his uncle, Sir Horatio. In 1779, he succeeded, by gift from his uncle above-mentioned, to his seat and estate at Linton, where he at times resides. He married, April 13, 1765, Lucy, sister of Thomas, Earl of Gainsborough, who died at Nice 1778, by whom he has three daughters; 1, Lucy, wife, 1786, of —— Mann, Esq.; 2, Emily, Jan. 9, 1792, of Robert Heron, Esq.; 3, Harriet, July 29, 1801, of Colonel —— Rochfort, of Ireland. Sir Horatio has been in two parliaments for Sandwich.

ARMS—Sable, on a fess, counter-embattled, between three goats, passant, argent, as many ogresses.
CREST—A demi-dragon, sable, guttée de l'eau.
MOTTO—*Per ardua stabilis.*
SEATS—At Egerton and Linton, in Kent.

261. CAVENDISH, of Doveridge, Derbyshire.

Created Baronet, May 7, 1755.

AS it is evident from authentic records, and the observations of learned men, that, after the custom of the Normans, surnames were, for the most part, taken from towns, offices, &c. and were not generally assumed till about the reign of Edward II.* So it appears, that this family was denominated from the lordship of Candish, now called Cavendish, in Suffolk, which estate Robert, a younger son of the ancient family of the Gernons, acquired by marriage, and his son took the name of Cavendish.

The Gernons were of great note in the counties of Norfolk and Essex, being lineally descended from Robert de Gernon, a famous Norman, who assisted William the Conqueror in his invasion of this realm; and, in reward of his services, had grants of several lordships†, particularly the manors of Merdley, three hides of land in Wallington, two hides and a half in Aiot, one hide in Wimundeley, and the manor of Lechworth, rated at ten hides, all in Hertfordshire.

This is a collateral branch of the noble family of Cavendish, Dukes of Devonshire. The first that was raised to this dignity was,

I. HENRY CAVENDISH, Esq. who, in the year 1741, served the office of high-sheriff for the county of Derby; in the year 1743, was appointed collector for Cork, in Ireland; made one of the commissioners of the revenues of that

* Camden's Remains, tit. Surnames, p. 109, 115, 143.
† Doomsday Book, folio 137, 138.

kingdom, Aug. 15, 1747; one of the commissioners of excise there, and one of the chief commissioners and governors of all other the revenues in that kingdom, March 25, 1749, which posts he resigned in 1755. In the last parliament for the kingdom of Ireland, he represented the borough of Lismore. Sir Henry had several children; Henry, his successor; ——, his second son, in 1759, was appointed clerk of the quit rents in Dublin.

II. Sir HENRY CAVENDISH, Bart. married Sarah, daughter of — Bradshaw, of Cork, in Ireland, sole heiress of Richard Shaw, Esq.; he was representative, in 1771, for Leostwithiel.

ARMS—Sable, three buck's heads caboshed, argent, attired, or, within a bordure of the second.

CREST—On a ducal coronet, a snake, nowed, proper.

SEAT—At Doveridge, in Derbyshire.

Henry, son of the Right Hon. Sir Henry Cavendish, Bart. in 1789, married —, daughter of — Cooper, and niece to the Bishop of Killaloe.

Oct. 9, 1783, —, daughter of the Right Hon. Sir Henry Cavendish, Bart. was married to Lord Viscount Valentia.

1801. The Hon. J. Cavendish, son of Sir Henry Cavendish, married Lady A. Gore, third daughter of the Earl of Arran, and sister to the Marchioness of Abercorn.

July 23, 1793, Hon. James Caufield Browne, eldest son of Viscount Kilmaine, to the Hon. Miss Cavendish, daughter of the Right Hon. Sir Henry Cavendish, Bart.

TABLE.

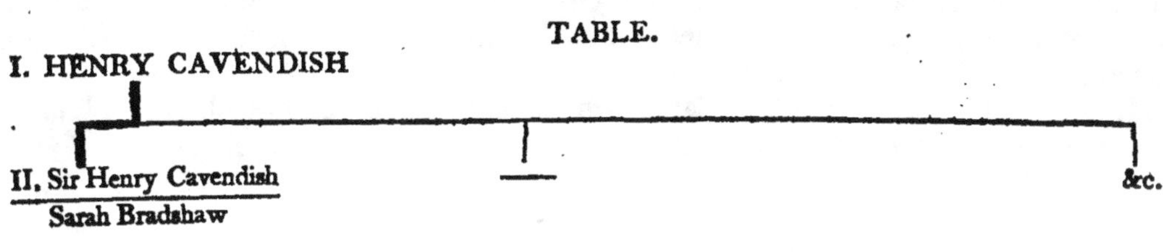

262. JOHNSON, of NEW YORK, North-America.

Created Baronet, Nov 27, 1755.

I. Sir WILLIAM JOHNSON, Bart. was descended from a good family in the kingdom of Ireland, and went to America under the care of his uncle, the late Sir Peter Warren, K. B. In the year 1755, the expedition against Crown Point, in America, was conducted by this gentleman, who was then a colonel, and afterwards a general. He had settled on the Mohawk river, and not only acquired a considerable estate, but was universally beloved, both by the inhabitants and the neighbouring Indians, whose language he had learned, and whose affections he had gained by his faithful and humane behaviour towards them. The honour this gentleman acquired in the battle against the French general, the Baron de Dieskau, is too recent to be soon forgotten, or to stand in need of being mentioned here.

The activity of Sir William in negociations was no less remarkable than his valour in the field; and it is much to be doubted, whether his moderation, and the general good esteem in which he was held, had not a greater share in reducing the rebellious savages to reason, than the force of his arms. He brought the Senecas (one of the revolted tribes of the Iroquois, and the most inveterate enemies of the English) to a treaty, at his house at Johnson's-Hall, where he appeared, April 3, 1764, in the character of his Majesty's sole agent and superintendant of India affairs for the northern parts of America, and colonel of the six united nations, their allies, and dependants. He died at his seat at Johnson's-Hall, in the province of New York, in America, 1774, not more celebrated for his conduct in the war, than remarkable for the ascendancy he had gained over the Indian nations. He left a large sum of money to be employed in presents to the Indians of the Mohawk castles, through whose faithful and inviolable attachment the worthy Baronet was enabled to conduct the business of his department with admirable ability, justice, and humanity. All the inhabitants, men, women, and children, of those castles, had mourning presented to them on the much-lamented death of their beloved patron. He had two sons, Sir John, his successor, and Colonel Grey Johnson, whose only daughter, in 1783, became the wife of Colonel John Campbell, at Quebec. Sir William was succeeded by his eldest son,

II. Sir JOHN JOHNSON, Bart. whose son, Lieutenant-Colonel Johnson, Sept. 30, 1802, married Susan, daughter of Stephen de Lancey.

The Arms and Crest of this family could not be ascertained.
SEAT—Guyot, in Lincolnshire.

TABLE.

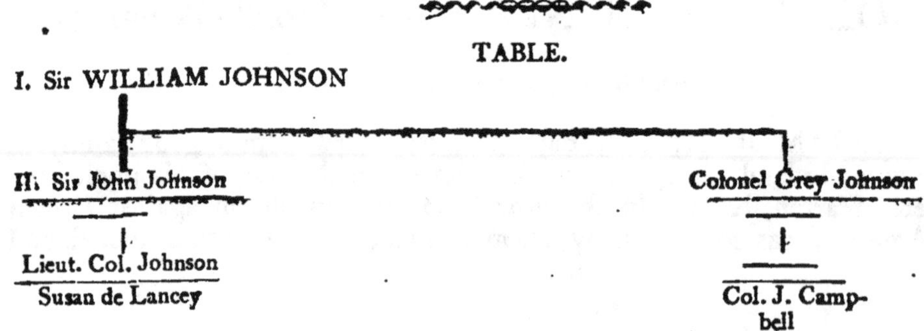

263. RIDLEY, of Heaton, in Northumberland.

(By virtue of the limitation in the Patent to Matthew White, of Blagdon, in Northumberland.)

Created Baronet, May 6, 1756.

THE family of White was originally of the county of Durham.

Matthew White, Esq. was an eminent merchant at Newcastle-upon-Tyne, and alderman and governor of the merchants and hoastman's companies: he married Jane, daughter of Nicholas Fenwick, Esq. and alderman of that town, by whom he had several children, who lived to maturity. Margaret, the eldest daughter, was wife of Richard Ridley, of Newcastle aforesaid, and of Heaton, in the county of Northumberland, Esq. by whom she had several children, of whom hereafter; Elizabeth, the second daughter, was wife of Robert Douglas, of Newcastle-upon-Tyne, Esq. who died without issue; Martha, the third daughter, died unmarried; and Isabella, the fourth daughter, was wife of Thomas Waters, of Newcastle aforesaid, Esq. by whom she had Matthew Waters, of Walls-End, in Northumberland, Esq. and Isabella; Jane died unmarried.

I. MATTHEW WHITE, of Blagdon, in the county of Northumberland, Esq. only surviving son, married Elizabeth, daughter and coheiress of John Johnson, of Newcastle, and of Bebride, in the county of Northumberland, Esq. by whom he had, 1, Matthew; 2, John; 3, Elizabeth, wife of Matthew Ridley, of Heaton, in the said county, Esq. son of Richard Ridley aforesaid, Esq. by whom she had several children, as will appear hereafter; 4, Nicholas; 5, George; 6, Matthew; 7, Jane; 8, Charles; and 9, Mary. They all died unmarried, except Elizabeth above-mentioned.

The last-mentioned Matthew White, of Blagdon, Esq. was high-sheriff of the county of Northumberland in 1756, and was, at presenting an address to his Majesty from the said county, created a Baronet of this kingdom, with limitation in the patent, in failure of issue male, to the heirs male of his sister Elizabeth, wife of the said Matthew Ridley. Sir Matthew White, Bart. died March 21, 1763, and was buried at All Saints Church, in Newcastle-upon-Tyne; on whose death, the title, according to the said limitation, descended to Matthew-White Ridley, eldest son of the said Matthew and Elizabeth Ridley.

We shall now give an account of the family of Ridley, as we find it recorded in the Herald's Office; and it is much to be wished that every family of distinction would be as careful in entering their pedigree in the College of Arms, as the Ridleys have been, many inconveniencies, even to the families themselves, would be thereby avoided.

The family of Ridley has been of long standing in Northumberland, and possessed of several considerable estates in that county (where they still continue) as appears from divers ancient evidences. The principal family seat was at Willymondswyke, on the banks of the river Tyne, which, with the estate, during the troubles in Charles the First's reign, were lost, and are now in the possession of Sir Edward Blacket, Bart. They are supposed to be descended from the Ridleys, of Ridley, in Cheshire: the arms, anciently used by both families, were alike.

1, Nicholas Ridley, of Willymondswyke, in the county of Northumberland, Esq. (about 1400) married Alice, daughter and coheiress of —— Skelton, of Bramford, and was succeeded by his son,

2, Nicholas Ridley, who married Anne, daughter of —— Eglesfield, of Cumberland, by whom he had Sir Nicholas, and Thomasin, wife of Thomas Carnaby, of Halton-Castle, in the county of Northumberland, Esq.

3, Sir Nicholas Ridley, Knt. married Mary, daughter of —— Curwen, of Workington, in the county of Cumberland, Esq. by whom he had issue, 1, Nicholas; 2, Christopher, of Unthank; and Jane, who was the wife of Gilbert Errington, of Errington, in the county of Northumberland, Esq.

4, Christopher Ridley, of Unthank aforesaid, in the county of Northumberland, was father of Nicholas Ridley, Bishop of London, who suffered for the Protestant faith at Oxford, Oct. 16, 1555*.

* He was born about the year 1500, in Tynedale, near the Scottish borders in Northumberland. He received his school-education at Newcastle-upon-Tyne, whence he was removed to Pembroke-Hall, in Cambridge, at the charge of his uncle, Dr. Thomas Ridley, about 1518, when Luther was preaching against indulgences in Germany. Here he acquired a good skill in the Latin and Greek tongues, and in the learning then more in fashion, the philosophy and theology of the schools. His reputation procured him the esteem of the other university as well as of his own; for, in 1524, the master and fellows of University-College, in Oxford, invited him to accept of an exhibition, founded by Walter Skyrey, Bishop of Durham, which he declined. The next year he took his master's degree, and was appointed by the college their general agent in some causes relating to it. His uncle was now willing to add to his attainments the advantages of travel, and the improvement of foreign universities; and as his studies were directed to divinity, he sent him to spend some time among the doctors of the Sorbonne at Paris, and afterwards among the professors at Louvain. Having staid three years abroad, he returned to Cambridge, and pursued his theological studies; and, as his safest guide in them, diligently applied himself to the reading of the Scriptures in the original. In a walk in the orchard at Pembroke-Hall, which is to this day called Ridley's Walk, he got to repeat, without book, almost all the epistles in Greek.

His behaviour here was very obliging, and pious, without hypocrisy or monkish austerity; for, very often he would shoot with the bow, or play at tennis, and he was eminent for the great charities he bestowed. He was senior proctor of the university, when the important point of the Pope's supremacy came before them, to be examined upon the authority of Scripture; and their resolution, after mature deliberation, "that the Bishop of Rome had no more authority or jurisdiction derived to him from God in this kingdom of England, than any other foreign bishop," was signed in the name of the university by Simon Heynes, vice-chancellor, Nicholas Ridley, Richard Wikks, proctors. He lost his uncle in 1536, but the education he had received, and the improvements he made, soon recommended him to another and greater patron, Cranmer, Archbishop of Canterbury, who appointed him his domestic chaplain, and collated him to the vicarage of Herne, in East Kent. He bore his testimony in the pulpit there against the act of the Six Articles, and instructed his charge in the pure doctrines of the Gospel, as far as they were yet discovered to him; but transubstantiation was at this time an article of his creed. During his retirement at this place, he read a little treatise written seven hundred years before, by Ratramnus, or Ber-

The bishop had also a brother, named Hugh, and a sister, Elizabeth, wife of John Ridley, of Wall-Town, in Northumberland, Esq. which John is supposed to be a collateral branch of the family: he died 1562, and was buried at Haltwissle, in Northumberland, where his monument and inscription still remain, a copy of which is preserved in the Herald's-Office, London. Their daughter Elizabeth, and sole heiress, was wife of Thomas Ridley, one of the great-grandsons of Sir Nicholas Ridley before-mentioned, and had issue,

John Ridley, of Wall-Town, son and heir, who was living in 1615, and married Anne, daughter and coheiress of —— Charlton, of Hesleside, in Northumberland, Esq.

This John had two sons and four daughters; 1, John, who married Elizabeth, daughter of Thomas Charlton, of Charlton-Hall, in Cumberland, Esq. by whom he had four sons and four daughters; 2, William Ridley, was of London and Wall-Town, and married Anne, daughter of —— Woodman, by whom he had three sons and one daughter; Elizabeth, the eldest daughter, was wife of William of the Morrelle; 2, Margaret, of Ralph Thurlway; 3, Thomasin, of Daniel Stoughton; and 4, Mary, of Thomas Ridley, of Hardriding, in Northumberland; which Thomas was great-grandson of Nicholas Ridley, Esq. son of the first-mentioned Sir Nicholas Ridley, Knt.

tram, a monk of Corbey. This first opened his eyes, and determined him more accurately to search the Scriptures in this article, and the doctrine of the primitive fathers. His discoveries he communicated to his patron, and the event was the conviction of them both, that this doctrine was novel and erroneous. After he had stayed about two years at Herne, he was chosen master of Pembroke-Hall, and appointed chaplain to the king; and such was his courage and zeal for the Reformation, that next to the archbishop, he was thought to be its greatest support among the clergy. In the reign of Edward VI. when a royal visitation was resolved on through the kingdom, he attended the visitors of the northern circuit as their preacher, to instruct that part of the nation in the principles of religion. In 1547, he was appointed Bishop of Rochester, and consecrated in the usual form of popish bishops, as the new ordinal had not yet taken place. When Bonner was deprived of the bishopric of London, Ridley was pitched upon as a proper person to fill that important see; being esteemed (says Burnet) both the most learned and the most thoroughly zealous for the Reformation. In this high station his behaviour was with great dignity, for it was benevolent, useful, and exemplary. He was very careful to do his predecessor no injury in his goods, and shewed the tenderness of a son to his mother, placing her always at the upper end of the table.

His mode of life was, as soon as he rose and dressed himself, to continue in private prayer half an hour; then he retired to his study, where he continued till ten o'clock, at which hour he came to common prayer with his family, and there daily read a lecture to them. After prayers he went to dinner, where his conversation was always wise and discreet, and sometimes, if the case required, merry and cheerful. This conversation he would indulge for an hour after dinner, or else in playing at chess. The hour for unbending being expired, he returned to his study, where he continued till five, except suitors or business abroad required otherwise. Then he went to common prayers in the evening, after which he supped, then diverting himself for another hour as before, he went back to his study, and continued there till eleven at night, when he retired to private prayer, and then went to bed. A little before the king died, he was named to succeed to Durham; but, great as the honours were which he received or were intended him, the highest were reserved for him under Queen Mary, which were, to be a prisoner for the gospel, a confessor of Christ in bonds, and a martyr for his truth. Some of his writings are lost, some may be seen in Fox, and some are exhibited in his life, written by Dr. Gloster Ridley, 4to; to which we must refer the reader, if he is desirous of a fuller account of this excellent person's life, learning, and sufferings.

Having given an account of the descendants of Christopher, the second son of Sir Nicholas, I shall now return to

4, Nicholas Ridley, Esq. the eldest son of the said Sir Nicholas; which Nicholas married Mary, daughter of —— Musgrave, by whom he had two sons and four daughters, William, and Sir Hugh Ridley, Knt.; Jane, wife of John Heron, of Chipchase, in Northumberland, Esq.; Anne, wife of William Wallis, of Knaresdale; Margaret, of John Fetherstonhaugh, of Stanhope, in the county of Durham; and Mabil, of —— Fenwick, of Little Harle, in Northumberland, and afterwards of Sir John Lumley, Knt.

5, Sir Hugh Ridley, Knt. married Isabel, daughter of Sir John Heron, of Chipchase aforesaid, Knt. by whom he had four sons and one daughter, Dorothy, wife of Henry Jackson; 1, Sir Nicholas; 2, John, who married Jane, daughter of John Errington, brother of Gilbert Errington, of Errington, Esq.; 3, Cuthbert; 4, Thomas, married his cousin, Elizabeth, daughter and heiress of John Ridley, of Wall-Town before-mentioned.

6, Sir Nicholas Ridley, Knt. the eldest son of Sir Hugh, was of Willymondswyke aforesaid, and married Mabel, daughter of Sir Philip Dacres, of Morpeth, Knt. third son of Lord Dacres, by whom he had three sons and six daughters; 1, Nicholas; 2, William, who was of Battersley, in the county of York; 3, Alexander. The daughters were, Jane, Margery, Elizabeth, Anne-Mabil, and Isabel.

7, Nicholas Ridley, Esq. the eldest son, had three sons; 1, Nicholas, from whom were descended the Ridleys, of Craw-Hall; 2, Lancelot; and 3, Thomas, of whom hereafter. Lancelot had one son, Sir Thomas Ridley, Knt. doctor of the civil law, who died Jan. 23, 1628, and was buried in St. Bennet's Church, near Paul's Wharf, London. (This Sir Thomas married Margaret, daughter and heiress of William Boleyn, the son of William, the son of William, who was the son of William, second son of Thomas Boleyn, Esq. father of Sir Geoffry Boleyn, Knt. lord-mayor of London in 1458, the father of Sir William Boleyn, Knt. the father of Thomas Boleyn, Earl of Wiltshire and Ormond, who was the father of Queen Anne Boleyn, mother of Queen Elizabeth), by whom the said Sir Thomas Ridley had two daughters; 1, Anne, wife of Sir Leonard Bosvile, Knt. son and heir of Sir Ralph Bosvile, of Bradborne, in the county of Kent, Knt.; 2, Elizabeth, wife of Mark Cottle, registrer of the prerogative court of Canterbury.

8, Thomas Ridley, the third son of Nicholas, married Mary, daughter of John Ridley, of Wall-Town before-mentioned, and died about the beginning of the reign of King James; and by Mary, his wife, aforesaid, had three sons, 1, John, who died without issue; 2, Cuthbert, was of Ticket, in Northumberland; and 3, Nicholas, which

9, Nicholas was of Hardriding aforesaid, and died about 1618. He married first, Anne, daughter of —— Heron, of Birtley, in Northumberland, by whom he had Elizabeth, and Barbara, who died young; he married secondly, Barbara, daughter of —— Errington, of West-Denton, in Northumberland, Esq. by whom he had two sons and one daughter; Albany, a merchant in London, who died without issue; and Susanna, wife of Michael Stockoe, of Heddon Bridge, in Northumberland; and

10, John Ridley, of Hardriding, Esq. one of his Majesty's justices of the peace in the county of Northumberland. He was aged 51 years, Sept. 1666, and major of a regiment in the army of William, Marquis of Newcastle, for Charles I. as also major in the garrison at Carlisle, Sir Philip Musgrave being then governor, and afterwards major to Sir Marmaduke Langdale, Knt. afterwards Lord Langdale. He married first, Anne, daughter of Sir Ralph Fetherstonhalge, of Stanhope, in the county of Durham, Esq. by whom he had two sons, John, who died unmarried, and Nicholas, of whom hereafter; and one daughter, Barbara, wife of John Bradwood, of Carlisle. By his second wife, Mary, daughter of Edward Lawson, of Brunton, in the county of Northumberland, Esq. he had five sons and four daughters, 1, Elizabeth, wife of Edward Stockoe, of Carlisle; 2, Mary, of Thomas Pate, clerk, vicar of Haltwissle; 3, Jane; 4, Anne, of Christopher Barrow, of Shankfoot, in Northumberland, Gent. The sons were, 1, Nevile; 2, Wilfred; 3, Godfrey; 4, John; 5, Edward, of Lincolnshire, Esq. who was fourteen years old in 1666; he married Dorothy, daughter of —— Chamberlayne, Esq. by whom he had Richard Ridley, Esq. a colonel of the guards, who died unmarried, and was buried at St. Margaret's Church, Westminster; and four daughters, Mary, Eleanor, Dorothy, and Anne.

11, Nicholas Ridley, of Hardriding, Esq. before-mentioned, was of Newcastle-upon-Tyne, and also of Heaton, in Northumberland; he died Jan. 22, 1710, and by Martha, his wife, daughter of Richard March, of Newcastle-upon-Tyne, merchant, who died April 13, 1728, he had five sons; 1, John, died young, April, 1686, and was buried in St. Nicholas Church, in Newcastle-upon-Tyne; 2, Richard, of whom hereafter; 3, Nicholas; 4, Edward; and 5, John: and four daughters, 1, Mary, wife of Gawen Ansley, of Little Harle, in Northumberland, Esq.; 2, Anne; 3, Anne, wife of Joshua Douglas, of Newcastle-upon-Tyne, Esq; 4, Martha, who died unmarried.

12, Richard Ridley, Esq. eldest surviving son, was of Newcastle-upon-Tyne, and also of Heaton, in Northumberland, and died Nov. 2, 1739, and was buried in St. Nicholas Church aforesaid; and by Margaret, his wife, daughter of Matthew White, of Newcastle-upon-Tyne, and of Blagdon, in Northumberland, Esq. had four sons and five daughters, 1, Matthew, of whom hereafter; 2, Richard, was a captain of foot, and married Anne, daughter of George Roach, of Portsmouth, merchant, and died without issue; 3, Nicholas; and 4, Nicholas, died infants: 1, Margaret, was wife of the Rev. Hugh Moyer, M. A. lecturer of All Saints Church, in Newcastle-upon-Tyne; 2, Jane, of Matthew Bell, of Newcastle aforesaid, and of Woolsington, in Northumberland, Esq.; another Jane, Martha, and Mary, died infants.

13, Matthew Ridley (eldest son and heir of Richard Ridley, Esq. aforesaid), of Heaton, in the county of Northumberland, Esq. and member of parliament for the town and county of Newcastle-upon-Tyne, married first, Hannah, daughter of Joseph Barnes, of Newcastle aforesaid, who died Nov. 7, 1741, and was buried in the church of St. Nicholas, in that town, and left an only son, Richard Ridley, Esq. a major of foot, who was born in the parish of St. George the Martyr, Queen-square, London, July 5, 1736.

Matthew Ridley, Esq. married secondly, Elizabeth, eldest daughter, and at length heiress, of Matthew White, of Blagdon, Esq. (which Matthew was brother of Margaret, the wife of Richard Ridley, Esq. aforesaid), they were married at Stannington, in Northumberland, Nov. 18, 1742, by whom he had seven sons and four daughters, 1, Matthew-White Ridley, the present Baronet; 2, Edward, died an infant; 3, Nicholas, of Gray's-Inn, Esq. who married, 1790, Letitia, daughter of —— Atkins; 4, John, a lieutenant in the Welch Fuzileers; 5, Henry, of University-College, Oxford; 6, Edward, died an infant; 7, Charles. The daughters were, Elizabeth-Christiana, probably so called as being born on Christmas-Day; 2, Margaret; 3, Jane; 4, Mary, who died Oct. 1797.

II. Sir MATTHEW-WHITE RIDLEY, Bart. succeeded his uncle, Sir Matthew White, Bart. in title and estate, and is member of parliament for Newcastle; he married, 1777, ——, daughter of —— Cockburne, of Pall Mall, by whom he has issue.

ARMS—Quarterly: first and fourth, gules, on a cheveron, between three falcons, argent, as many pellets, for Ridley; second and third, argent, three cock's heads erased, sable, for White, combed and wattled, gules.

CREST—On a wreath, a bull, passant, the tail turned over the back, gules.

MOTTO on the Crest—*Constans fidei.*

SEAT—At Blagdon, in the county of Northumberland.

Vide the following references to this pedigree in the Herald's Office: Vincent. Northumber. No. 149, fo. 55. Dugdal. Dit. fol. 24. Regist. Howard. fo. 100, and l. 23, fo. 25.

TABLE.

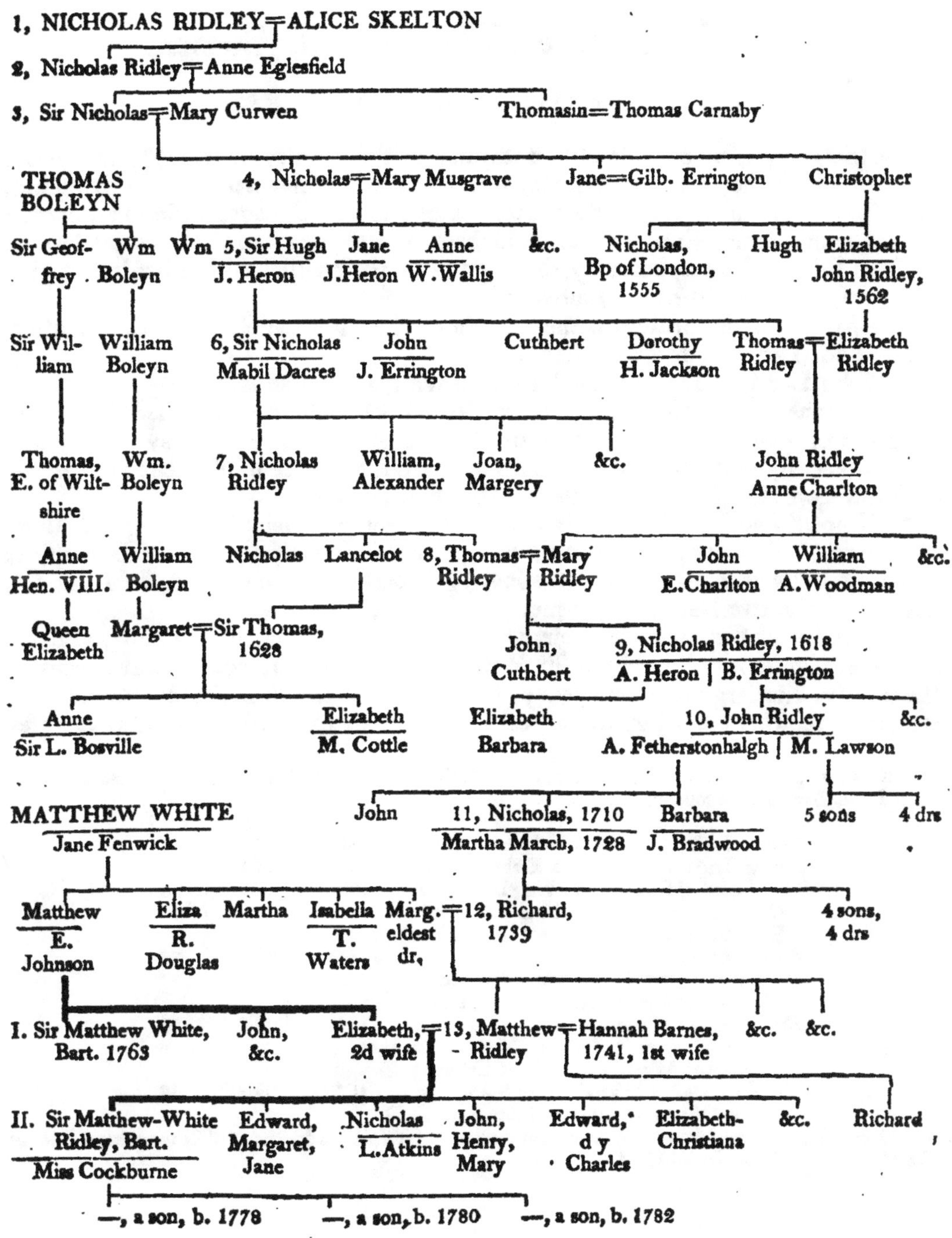
1, NICHOLAS RIDLEY = ALICE SKELTON
2, Nicholas Ridley = Anne Eglesfield
3, Sir Nicholas = Mary Curwen
Thomasin = Thomas Carnaby
THOMAS BOLEYN
4, Nicholas = Mary Musgrave
Jane = Gilb. Errington
Christopher
Sir Geoffrey
Wm Boleyn
Wm
5, Sir Hugh J. Heron
Jane J. Heron
Anne W. Wallis
&c.
Nicholas, Bp of London, 1555
Hugh
Elizabeth John Ridley, 1562
Sir William
William Boleyn
6, Sir Nicholas Mabil Dacres
John J. Errington
Cuthbert
Dorothy H. Jackson
Thomas Ridley = Elizabeth Ridley
Thomas, E. of Wiltshire
Wm. Boleyn
7, Nicholas Ridley
William, Alexander
Joan, Margery
&c.
John Ridley Anne Charlton
Anne Hen. VIII.
William Boleyn
Nicholas
Lancelot
8, Thomas Ridley = Mary Ridley
John E. Charlton
William A. Woodman
&c.
Queen Elizabeth
Margaret = Sir Thomas, 1628
John, Cuthbert
9, Nicholas Ridley, 1618 A. Heron | B. Errington
Anne Sir L. Bosville
Elizabeth M. Cottle
Elizabeth Barbara
10, John Ridley A. Fetherstonhalgh | M. Lawson
&c.
MATTHEW WHITE Jane Fenwick
John
11, Nicholas, 1710 Martha March, 1728
Barbara J. Bradwood
5 sons
4 drs
Matthew E. Johnson
Eliza R. Douglas
Martha
Isabella T. Waters
Marg. eldest dr. = 12, Richard, 1739
4 sons, 4 drs
I. Sir Matthew White, Bart. 1763
John, &c.
Elizabeth, 2d wife = 13, Matthew Ridley = Hannah Barnes, 1741, 1st wife
&c.
&c.
II. Sir Matthew-White Ridley, Bart. Miss Cockburne
Edward, Margaret, Jane
Nicholas L. Atkins
John, Henry, Mary
Edward, d y Charles
Elizabeth-Christiana
&c.
Richard
—, a son, b. 1778
—, a son, b. 1780
—, a son, b. 1782

264. LADE, of Warbleton, Sussex.

Created Baronet, March 17, 1758.

THIS family is of considerable antiquity in the county of Kent*, in several parts of which they had possessions, which still bear their names. In Snodland, near Rochester, and in Acris, there are estates still called Lads, which had owners of that name, temp. Edw. I; and in Eleham, where they were resident at least as early as Edw. IV. as appears by the register of their wills, which begins at that æra; there is one still called Ladwood.

The name was, according to the custom of the times, spelt Le Lad, and afterwards Lad, Ladd, Ladde, and Lade.

1, John Ladd, of Eleham, died 1527, leaving several sons.

2, Thomas Ladd, the youngest, settled at Barham, and married Elizabeth, daughter of —— Mumbray, sister and heiress of Thomas Mumbray, of Sutton, near Dover, by whom he had Vincent, and Silvester, wife of Vincent Nethersole, of Wimingwould, in Kent; and died March 15, 1626.

3, Vincent Lade, of Barham, in Kent, Gent. son and heir, died Aug. 27, 1626. He married Elizabeth, or Agnes, daughter of Vincent Denne, of Denhill, in Kent, Esq. by whom he had four sons, 1, Robert; 2, Thomas; 3, John; and 4, Vincent. The two last left no issue.

Robert Lade, Esq. son and heir, was of Gray's-Inn, barrister at law, and recorder of Canterbury, to whom Sir William Segar, Garter, confirms the arms of the family, viz. Argent, a fess wavy, between three escallops, sable—Crest, on a wreath, a panther's head guardant, sable, bezantee; quartering Mumbray, gules,

* Ex stem. penes Dom. Joh. Lade, Bar. 1739-40, though in an old Bible, late in the possession of Sir John Lade, Bart. are the following entries:

	Born	Died	Aged
Thomas Lade, of Bowich, in Eleham, Kent	1445	1515	70
Vincent Lade, of Bowich, in Eleham . .	1490	1563	73
Tho. Lade, of Barham, in Kent	1527	1603	76
On the tomb stone in Barham. Married Eliz. daughter of Tho. Mombray, of Sutton, Esq.			
Vincent Lade, of Barham	1554	1626	72
On a tomb stone in Barham. Married Eliz. daughter of Vincent Denn, of Denhill, Esq.			
Thomas Lade, of Barham	1586	1660	74
On a tomb stone in Barham. Married Margaret, daughter of Wm. Denwood, of Ebbsfleet, Esq.			
Thomas Lade, of Warbleton, in Sussex .	1620	1668	48
Married Mary, daughter of John Nutt, D. D.			

Which said Thomas and Mary were father and mother of Sir John Lade, born 1662, the present Baronet. Ex inf. Dom. Jo. Lade, Bar. 1739-40.

a lion rampant, argent, collared and chained, sable. This Robert married Mary, daughter of William Lovelace, of the Friars, in Canterbury, and was the ancestor of the Lades, of Canterbury and Barham.

4, Thomas Lade, of Barham, second son of Vincent before-mentioned, married Margaret, daughter of William Denwood, of Ebbsfleet, in Kent, by whom he had three sons, and four daughters, 1, Vincent Lade, of Barham, who, by Elizabeth, daughter of —— Knowler, of Canterbury, left Thomas, Vincent, Elizabeth, and Mary; 2, Thomas Lade, of Warbleton, in Sussex, Gent. of whom hereafter; 3, John, of Adsam, in Kent, who married Hannah, daughter of Walter Cloak, of Winchop, near Canterbury, and left issue. Of the four daughters, Mary was wife of —— Denne, of Canterbury; Sarah, of William Cullen; Anne, of John Roberts, of Warbleton, Gent.; and Margaret, who died unmarried.

5, Thomas Lade, of Warbleton, second son, died Dec. 1668. He married Mary, daughter of John Nutt, of Mayes, in the parish of Selmiston, in Sussex, Gent. by whom he had three sons, and two daughters, 1, Vincent Lade, of Warbleton, who married, and had issue one son Vincent, who died S. P. and four daughters, 1, Anne, wife, first, of Thomas Wandell, of Southwark, druggist; and secondly, of William Nutt, of Marshalls, in Maresfield, in Sussex, Gent. only son of John Nutt, of the same place, Gent. by Philadelphia, his wife, eldest daughter of Sir William Wilson, of East-Bourne Place, in the same county, Bart. a descendant from a collateral branch of the family of Sir Thomas Nutt, formerly of Mays, in the parish of Selmiston, in Sussex, Knt.; 2, Elizabeth, wife of John Whithorne, of Jamaica, by whom she had three sons, 1, Lade Whithorne, who died S. P.; 2, Charles; 3, John Whithorne, who took the name of Lade, and on whom the title of Baronet was entailed by the patent; 3, Mary, wife of John Price, of Richmond, in Surry; and 4, Philadelphia, of John Inskip, of Uckfield, in Sussex, to whose son John, Sir John Lade bequeathed the chief part of his estate; 2, Thomas Lade, who died unmarried 1681; 3, John, of whom hereafter. The daughters of Thomas were Anne, and Catharine, wife of Mr. Hugh Offley, of Possingworth, near Waldron parish, in Sussex.

I. JOHN LADE, Esq. the third and youngest son of Thomas, was brought up to trade, which he carried on many years in the borough of Southwark, whereby he raised a very considerable fortune, which, by his prudent management, he greatly increased. He represented the said borough in the last parliament of Queen Anne, and in the first parliament of King George I.; and was again elected in the second parliament of King George I. on the death of George Meggot, Esq. He acted many years as justice of the peace for the county of Surry with great reputation, being esteemed a very able magistrate. In 3 Geo. II. he was advanced to the dignity of a Baronet, with remainder, for want of issue male of his body lawfully begotten, to his great-nephew John, third and youngest son of John Whitmore and Elizabeth his wife before-mentioned, then called John Lade, and the heirs male of his body lawfully begotten.

† Ex inf. Dom. Jo. Lade, Bar. 1739-40.

Sir John died July 30, 1740, unmarried, near 80, and left his estate to his grand-nephew John, son of John Inskip beforementioned, but he was succeeded in title by his grand-nephew,

II. Sir JOHN LADE (according to the patent), who was a lieutenant of marines, and died unmarried 1747, his grand-uncle only left him fifty-two pounds a year, on whose death the title was extinct.

I. JOHN LADE, of Warbleton, Esq. was created a Baronet, Mar. 17, 1758. (I suppose this to be the person that the first Baronet left his fortune to.) He married Mary, daughter of Ralph, and sister of Henry Thrale, Esq. member for the borough of Southwark, who died his widow, April 22, 1802. Sir John died April 21, 1759, of a mortification, arising from the amputation of his leg, which

TABLE.

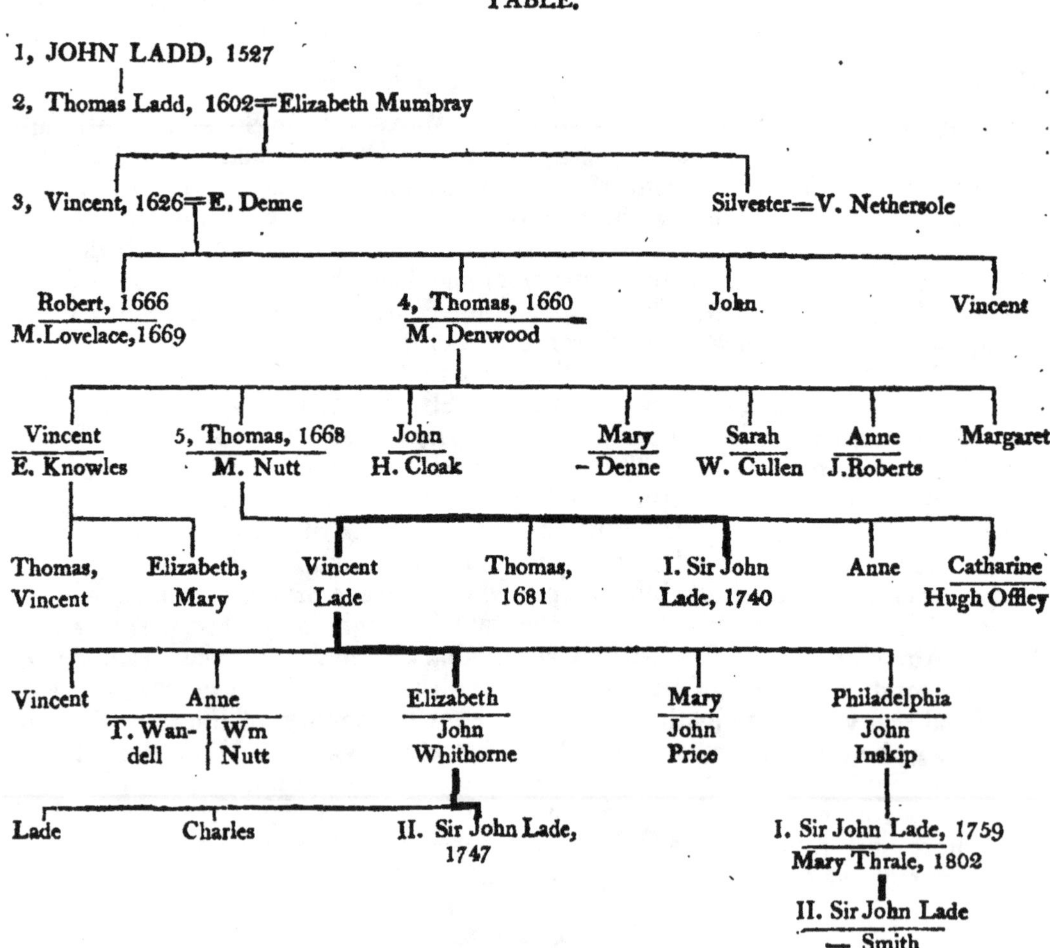

had been broken by a fall from his horse in hunting, leaving her with child of a son,

II. Sir JOHN LADE, Bart. who married Mrs. Smith, by whom he has no issue.

ARMS—Quarterly: 1st and 4th, argent, a fess wavy, between three escallops, sable; 2d and 3d, gules, a lion rampant, or, ducally collared and chained, sable.

CREST—In a coronet, or, a leopard's head, regardant, sable, bezantée.

SEAT—At Warbleton, Sussex.

265. WILMOT, of CHADDESDEN, Derbyshire.

Created Baronet, Feb. 15, 1759.

THE name of Wilmot, or Wylimot, for variously hath it been written, is originally Saxon, and very ancient in England. Speed mentions Wilmot, a nobleman of Sussex, in the reign of King Ethelred.

The family, as we find by deeds now in their possession, settled soon after the conquest at Sutton-upon-Soar, and Bonyngton, adjoining thereto, and since called Sutton Bonyngton, in Nottinghamshire, and about fourteen miles from the town of Derby.

1, Ralph Wylimot is one of the witnesses to a grant of lands in Bonyngton aforesaid, before the custom of dating deeds began. His descendant was,

2, Ralph Wylimot, of Sutton aforesaid, who was witness to a grant of lands there in 1282.

3, Ralph Wylimot.

4, Ralph Wylimot is one of the witnesses to a grant of lands made by William, son of John Chaddesden, in 13—.

5, Robert Wilmot, of Bonyngton, is one of the witnesses to a grant of lands there in 1380.

6, Robert Wilmot, of Bonyngton, is one of the witnesses of a grant of lands there 21 Rich. II. and to another grant of lands 4 Hen. IV.*

7, Richard Wylymot, of Bonyngton, 30th of June, 9 Hen. IV. grants to John Bonyngton and others, a certain messuage and lands in Bonyngton, part of which lands lay adjoining to lands of William Wylymot: another part adjoining to lands of John Wylymot; and, on the 6th of July, 9 Hen. IV. John Bonyngton and others, grant certain messuages and lands to the said Richard Wylymot.

8, Robert Wylymot marrying ———, daughter and heiress of ——— Bonyng-

* See a letter of attorney from Ralph Wyllymot, of Bonyngton, to John Bonyngton, Esq. dated July 4, 9 Hen. IV.

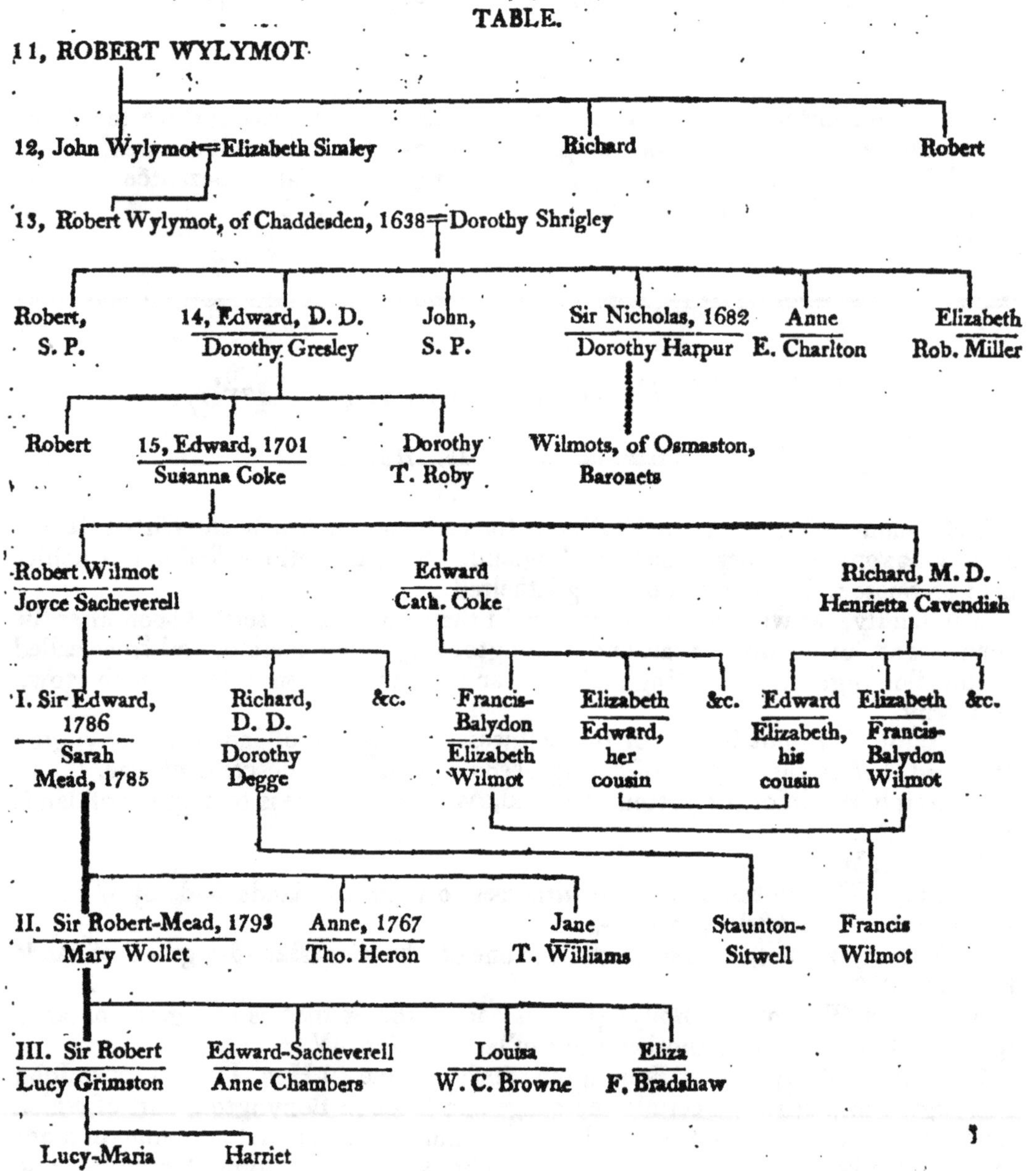
TABLE.
11, ROBERT WYLYMOT
12, John Wylymot = Elizabeth Simley
Richard
Robert
13, Robert Wylymot, of Chaddesden, 1638 = Dorothy Shrigley
Robert, S. P.
14, Edward, D. D. Dorothy Gresley
John, S. P.
Sir Nicholas, 1682 Dorothy Harpur
Anne E. Charlton
Elizabeth Rob. Miller
Robert
15, Edward, 1701 Susanna Coke
Dorothy T. Roby
Wilmots, of Osmaston, Baronets
Robert Wilmot Joyce Sacheverell
Edward Cath. Coke
Richard, M. D. Henrietta Cavendish
I. Sir Edward, 1786 Sarah Mead, 1785
Richard, D. D. Dorothy Degge
&c.
Francis-Balydon Elizabeth Wilmot
Elizabeth Edward, her cousin
&c.
Edward Elizabeth, his cousin
Elizabeth Francis-Balydon Wilmot
&c.
II. Sir Robert-Mead, 1793 Mary Wollet
Anne, 1767 Tho. Heron
Jane T. Williams
Staunton-Sitwell
Francis Wilmot
III. Sir Robert Lucy Grimston
Edward-Sacheverell Anne Chambers
Louisa W. C. Browne
Eliza F. Bradshaw
Lucy-Maria
Harriet

aforesaid; Eliza, of Francis Bradshaw, of Holbrooke, Derbyshire, Esq. Sir Robert died Sept. 9, 1793, and was succeeded by his eldest son,

III. Sir ROBERT WILMOT, Bart. born July 5, 1765, who, in March, 1796, married Lucy, eldest daughter of the late Robert Grimston, of Neswich, in Yorkshire, by whom he has two daughters, Lucy-Maria, born April, 1797, and Harriet, born June, 1798.

ARMS—Sable, on a fess, or, between three eagles' heads, couped, argent, as many escallops, gules, a canton, vaire, ermine, and gules.

CREST—An eagle's head, couped, argent, gorged with a mural coronet, sable, in the beak, an escallop, gules.

SEAT—At Chaddesden, in the county of Derby.

266. CUNLIFFE, of LIVERPOOL, Lancashire.

Created Baronet, March 26, 1759.

THIS family is undoubtedly of very great antiquity, and it is probable they were among the first Saxons who settled themselves in the north of England. Their name seems to corroborate this conjecture, as the word Cunlive, or Cunliffe, in the Saxon language, imports a gift or grant for life, or a competent maintenance, according to the military customs of those times; and certain it is, that a house and lands, bearing the name of Cunlive, or Cunliffe, were granted them, in the early times we are speaking of, at Billington, near Whalley, in Lancashire. This became afterwards the surname of the family; for, in the year 1282, being the eleventh of the reign of Edward I. a writ of inquisition was issued, concerning the extent of the manor of Manchester, in which a jury of twelve principal persons were sworn, among whom was Adam de Cunlive.

The family of Cunliffe continued in the possession of the lands and hall of Cunliffe, till the civil wars between the houses of York and Lancaster; but it appears that, in the reign of Henry VII. they had lost their possessions there, and were seated either at Wicollar or at Hastings, in the same county *.

They are still possessed of Wicollar, but the civil wars between Charles I. and his parliament, like the civil wars of earlier date, were again prejudicial to, and lessened their possessions.

* Vide 5th D. 14, folio 92.—Herald's College.

1, Nicholas Cunliffe, of Hollings, and Robert, his brother, were at first engaged on the side of the parliament; and it appears, from the journals of the House of Commons, that they were employed in 1643 by the parliament, to execute an important trust in Lancashire.

Robert Cunliffe was summoned to parliament in 1653, as one of the representatives of the county of Lancaster; but, as this parliament was not sufficiently subservient to the views of Cromwell, they were hastily dissolved.

2, John Cunliffe, son of the before-mentioned Nicholas, very soon after was active in opposing the ruling power; for which his house at Hollings was plundered, and a garrison put into it, by those who acted under the arbitrary and despotic government that succeeded the protectorship. He also suffered much by sequestration, as appears by written evidences now in being, which obliged him to mortgage his estate at Hollings, and settle his residence at Wicollar.

This John Cunliffe had several daughters and two sons, Nicholas and Ellis; from Nicholas, the elder, are descended the Cunliffes, of Wicollar, near Colne, in Lancashire.

3, Ellis, the second son, was bachelor of divinity, and fellow of Jesus College, Cambridge. He was several years rector of Newmarket, which he resigned for that of Etwall, in Derbyshire; and was so much in favour with Charles II. that he did him the honour of standing sponsor to his son Foster. He married ——, daughter and coheiress of —— Foster, of Airton, in Yorkshire, by whom he had two daughters and one son,

4, Foster, who was a merchant at Liverpool, whose honesty, diligence, and knowledge in mercantile affairs, procured wealth and credit to himself and his country. His life was a scene of business; he sought after no personal honour, but had the pleasure to see his son unanimously returned member of parliament for Liverpool, and died lamented by the wise and good, April 11, 1758.

Foster Cunliffe left two sons, Sir Ellis, Bart. and Sir Robert, successor to his brother; and two daughters, ——, wife of William Shaw, of Preston, Esq. and Mary.

* In the church of St. Peter, in Liverpool, is erected a handsome marble monument, with suitable enrichments of mathematical instruments, and other decorations adapted to his mercantile employ, with this inscription, for the said Foster Cunliffe:

To the memory of
Foster Cunliffe, of Liverpool, son of Ellis Cunliffe, B.D.
A merchant,
Whose sagacity, honesty, and diligence,
Procured wealth and credit to himself and country;
A magistrate,
Who administered justice
With discernment, candour, and impartiality;

I. ELLIS CUNLIFFE, Esq. the elder son, was chosen member of parliament for Liverpool in the life-time of his father, and was first knighted, and afterwards created a Baronet, by his late Majesty George II. 1759. He was a second time elected for Liverpool in 1761, and discharged his duty as a member of the house of commons with integrity and success. He first pointed out to those in power, the probability and benefit of joining the Trent to the Mersey by a canal, which has since been effected, and from which many salutary consequences are derived. He also obtained the extension of the Post-Office, by which the communication of correspondence is accelerated, and a daily post established between Liverpool and London: he was neither venal nor factious, his fortune placed him above the temptation of a bribe, and he had too much discernment to be hurried away by every torrent of opposition. Hence it was no wonder that he was a second time returned to assist in the grand council of the nation. Though Providence had bestowed on him almost every earthly blessing, yet he wanted what neither honour nor riches can procure, health of body. He was obliged, on this account, to remove for some years into the milder climates of Europe, from whence he returned with his health much improved, his understanding untainted with folly, his morals uncorrupted by vice, and his religious principles undebased by the libertine or superstitious notions of the countries he had passed through. After some years, finding his health again declining, he was advised again to go to Naples, but died at Leostwithiel, in his road to Falmouth, where he designed to embark, Oct. 16, 1767, in the 51st year of his age, and was interred in the chapel at Cherton-Heath, in Cheshire. Sir Ellis married Mary, daughter of Henry Bennet, Esq. by whom he had two daughters, Mary, wife of Drummond Smith, of Tring Park, Esq.; and Margaret-Elizabeth, of William Gosling, of Roehampton Grove, in Surry, Esq. He was succeeded in title and estate by his brother,

II. Sir ROBERT CUNLIFFE, Bart. who was high-sheriff for the county of Cheshire in 1770. He married Mary, daughter of Ichabod Wright, of Nottingham, Esq. by whom he had one son, Sir Foster, and three daughters; Elizabeth, wife, March 9, 1782, of S. Courtenay, Esq.; Mary, wife, May 4,

A christian,
Devout and exemplary,
In the exercise of every private and public duty,
Friend to merit,
Patron to distress,
An enemy to vice and sloth;
He lived esteemed by all who knew him,
(Though few have been so extensively known)
and died lamented by the wise and good,
in the 73d year of his age,
11th of April, 1718.

From the monument.

1780, of Richard Broke, Esq.; and Margaret. Sir Robert died, and was succeeded by his son,

III. Sir FOSTER CUNLIFFE, Bart. who married, 1781, Harriet, daughter of Sir David Kinlock, of Glemmerton, Bart. by whom he had ———, a son, born Aug. 24, 1782.

ARMS—Sable, three conies, current, argent, two and one.
CREST—On a wreath, a greyhound, sejant, argent, collared, sable.
MOTTO—*Fideliter.*
SEAT—At Saighton, in Cheshire.

TABLE.

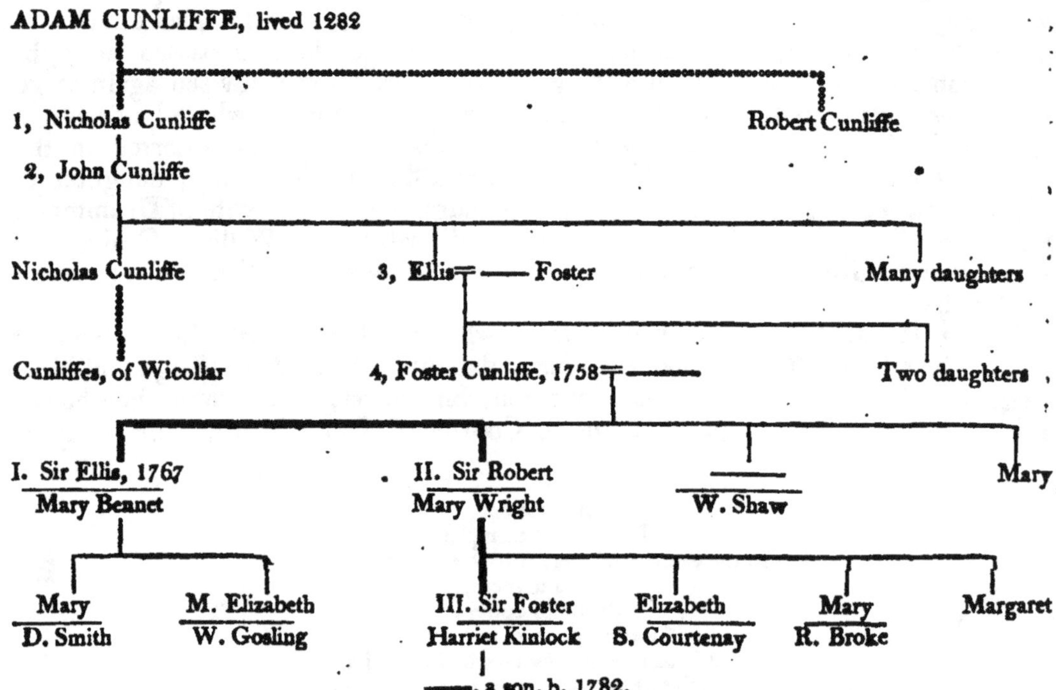

267. YEA, of PYRLAND, Somersetshire.

Created Baronet, June 11, 1759.

1, **DAVID YEA**, of Sturminster-Marshall, in Dorsetshire, Esq. is the first mentioned in this pedigree; he married Ursula, daughter of Edward Hobbes, of Brompton-Ralph, and Stoke-Garscy, in Somersetshire, Esq. by whom he had one son,

2, David Yea, of Oakhampton, and of the parish of Brompton-Ralph, Esq. high-sheriff for the county of Somerset, who married Dorothy, youngest daughter and coheiress of William Lacy, of Hartrow, and of Elworthy, in Somersetshire, Esq. by Sarah, his wife, daughter and coheiress of Michael Hole, of the same county, Esq. by whom he had one son David, and three daughters, Mary and Jenny died unmarried, and Dorothy, wife, first, of —— Tate, Esq. secondly, of Francis Collins, of Wiveliscombe, in Somersetshire, Esq.

3, David Yea, Esq. the son, was of Brompton-Ralph, and of the parish of Wiveliscombe, in Somersetshire; he served the office of high-sheriff, and was one of his Majesty's justices of the peace for the same county. He married Joan, daughter and heiress of Nathaniel Brewer, of Tolland, in Somersetshire, Esq. descended from the Brewers, of Chard, in the same county, by whom he had four sons and five daughters; 1, David, died in December, 1758; 2, Thomas, died unmarried; 3, William, of whom hereafter; 4, Robert, died an infant; Mary, the eldest, and Sally, the youngest, died unmarried. The other daughters were, Dorothy, Jenny, and Betty.

I. **WILLIAM YEA**, Esq. the third and only surviving son, is of Pyrland, in the parish of Taunton St. James; of Burliford, in the parish of Bishop Nymton; of Northwheelborough, in the parish of King's-Carwell; of the manor and parish of Sturminster-Marshal; of Yea's Hundred Acres, in the parish of Cannington, Stockland, and Huntspill; with divers other considerable possessions, all situate in the several counties of Somerset, Devon, and Dorset. He was created a Baronet, June 18, 1759, served the office of high-sheriff in 1760, and is one of his Majesty's justices for the county of Somerset. He married Julia, eldest daughter of Sir George Trevelyan, of Nettlecombe, in Somersetshire, Bart. by Julia, his wife, daughter of Sir Walter Calverley, of Calverley, in the county of York, Bart. by whom he has had six sons; 1, William-Walter, born at Oakhampton, Oct. 8, 1756, who married, May 1, 1783, ——, daughter of Francis Newman, of Cadbury-House, Somersetshire, Esq.; 2, Lacy, born Dec. 14, 1757, died 1758; 3, Lacy, born Jan. 21, 1759; 4, George, born April 1, 1760; 5, Thomas-Frere, born May 12, 1766; and ——, born May 27, 1770.

ARMS—Quarterly: first, vert, a ram, passant, argent; second, gules, two rams, passant, in pale, ermine; third, gules, two bends wavy, or, a chief vaire; fourth, as the first.

CREST—A talbot, passant, argent.

MOTTO—*Esto semper fidelis.*

SEATS—At Pyrland, &c. Somersetshire.

TABLE.

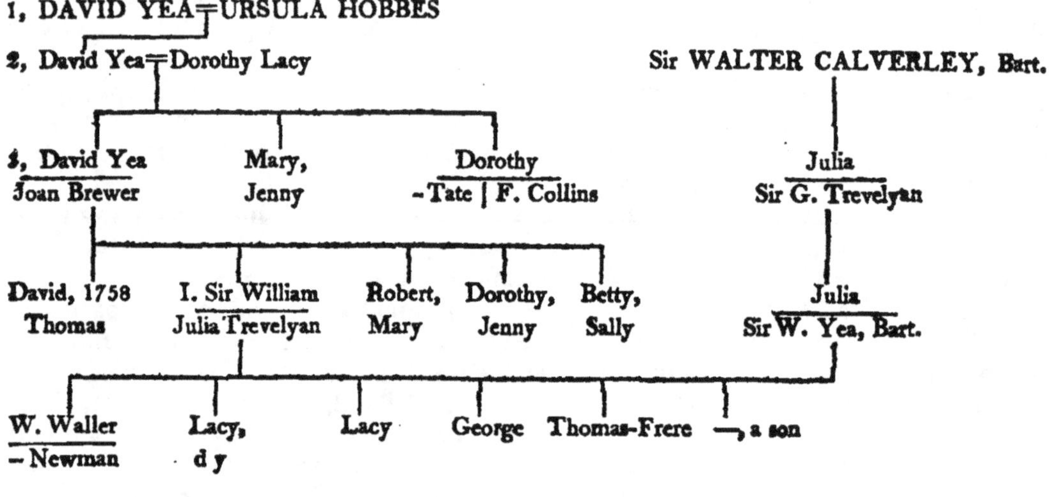

268. GLYN, of LONDON, and of EWELL, Surry.

Created Baronet, Sept. 25, 1759.

THE family of Glyn is paternally descended from Cilmin Droed-tu, or Cilmin with the Black Foot, who was the chief of the fourth tribe of North-Wales, and resided in the county of Carnarvon during the reign of Prince Merfyn Frych, being his brother's son*.

In lineal descent from Cilmin.

19, William Glyn, Esq. of Glyn-Llyfon, in the parish of Landurog, in the county of Carnarvon, married Catharine, daughter of Thomas Mostyn, of Mos-

* Pennant's North Wales. (See No. 141, page 260, Vol. II. of this Work.)

tyn, and had two sons, Thomas Glyn, Esq. of Glyn-Llyfon, and the Rev. Richard Glyn*: in a commission of the 9th of Elizabeth, 1567, to several gentlemen of North-Wales, to admit and regulate the order of Bards and Musicians, this William is inserted.

20, The Rev. Richard Glyn, M. A. was instituted rector of Llanvaethle and chapelry of Llanvwrog, in Anglesey, in 1587, and died in 1617†; he had two sons, William, and Thomas, who resided in London.

21, Thomas Glyn was free of the Merchant-Taylors Company of London, in 1601‡; he had a son,

22, The Rev. Christopher Glyn, who was born in 1596, admitted into Merchant-Taylors School in 1606, at St. John's College, Oxford, in 1615, vicar of Burford in 1632 §, and died in 1668. He married Margerie Needham, by whom he had three sons and two daughters.

23, The Rev. Robert Glyn, M. A. the eldest son, was born in 1623, rector of Little Bissington, in Gloucestershire, in 1652 ||, and died in 1702¶. He married Mary, daughter of —— Davis, of Shillingford, Oxfordshire, by whom he had four sons and four daughters; 1, Christopher, who died unmarried; 2, the Rev. Edward, rector of Broughton Poggs, Oxfordshire, who had three sons, who all died unmarried, and four daughters; the third son was Robert, of whom hereafter; the fourth was Thomas.

24, Robert Glyn, the third son, citizen of London, was born in 1673, died in 1746, and was buried in the family vault at Ewell, in Surry. He married Ann Maynard, niece to Sir William Lewen, lord-mayor of London, by whom he had two sons, William, who died young, and Richard.

I. Sir RICHARD GLYN was born in 1712, alderman and banker in London, lord-mayor in 1758, and created a Baronet in 1759. He represented in parliament the city of London and the city of Coventry, was doctor of laws, president of the royal hospitals of Bridewell and Bethlem, vice-president of the Artillery Company, and colonel of one of the regiments of the city militia; he died in Jan.

* Pennant.
† Rowland's Anglesey.
‡ Records of Merchant Taylors' Company.
§ Records of Merchant Taylors' School, St. John's, Oxford, and parish of Burford.
|| Parish Registers of Burford and Rissington.
¶ In the parish church:

Robtus Glyn, hujus ecclesiæ Rector.
Vir,
Eruditione, Probitate, Candore, Fide & Pietate
spectabilis;
Undè nemini inimicus, inimicum non habuit.
Hic, postquam vitam multâ cum laude, nullis
simultatibus exegesset,
Animâ ad Authorem Dominum remeante
terrena membra terris reliquit,
Tristissimum sui linguens desiderium.
Ætatis LXXIX.
Salutis MDCCII.

1773, and was buried in the vault at Ewell, in Surry. He married first, Susanna, only daughter and heiress of George Lewen, of Ewell, Esq. by whom he had three sons, 1, Robert-Lewen, born in 1737, who died unmarried; 2, Sir George, the present Baronet, of whom hereafter; and 3, Richard, born 1741, who also died unmarried.

By his second wife, Elizabeth, daughter and coheiress of Robert Carr, Esq. he had three sons, Sir Richard-Carr, born 1755, created a Baronet in 1800, and married Mary, daughter of John Plumtre, of Fredville, in Kent, Esq. and has five sons and two daughters; 2, Thomas, born 1756, and married Hen-

TABLE.

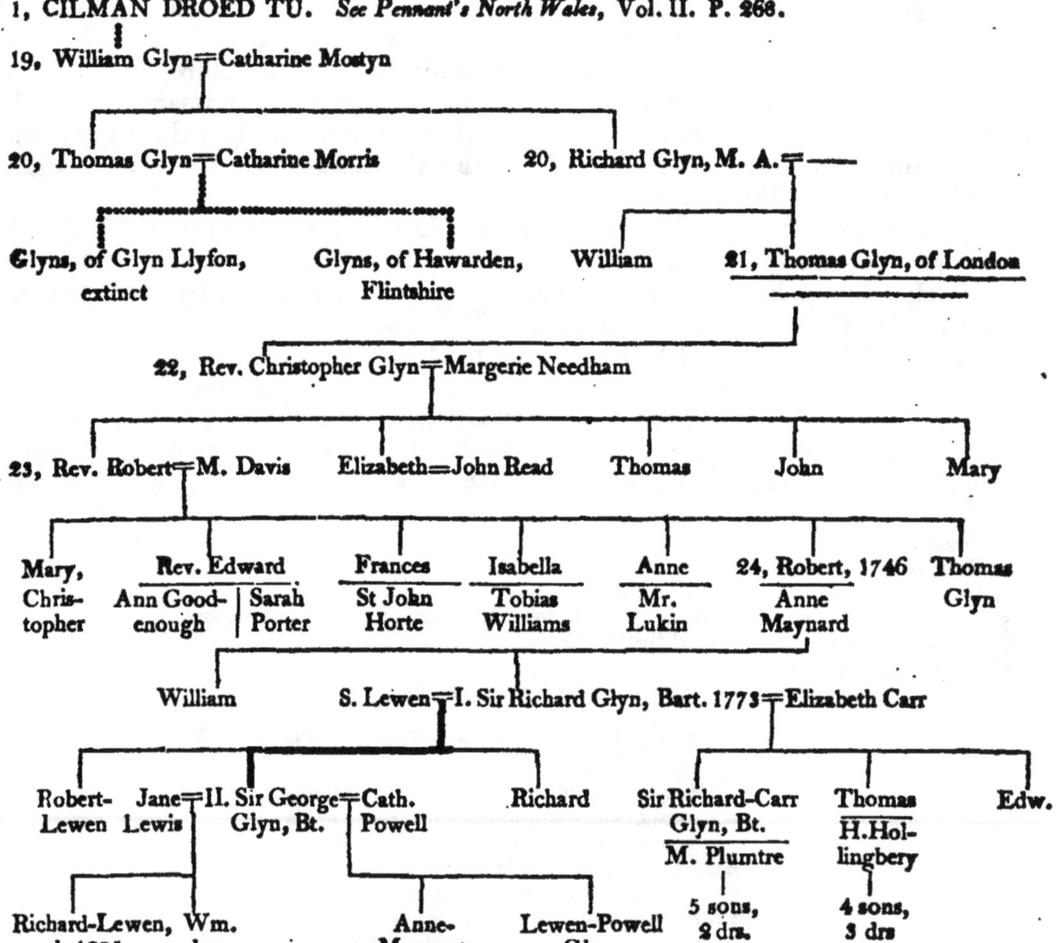

rietta-Elizabeth-Sackville Hollingbery, daughter and heiress of Thomas Hollingbery, archdeacon of Chichester, by whom he had four sons and three daughters; and 3, Edward, born 1757, and died young.

II. Sir GEORGE GLYN, Bart. of Ewell, in Surry, born in 1739, was colonel of the late third regiment of Surry militia, a deputy lieutenant and magistrate for that county. He married first, Jane, youngest daughter of the Rev. Watkin Lewes, of Tredeved, in Pembrokeshire, by whom he had two sons, Richard-Lewen, born 1769, a major in the army, and died unmarried at St. Domingo in the service of his country, in 1795; and William-Lewen, who died an infant. By his second wife, Catharine, youngest daughter and coheiress of the Rev. Gervas Powell, of Lanharan, in Glamorganshire, he has Anna-Margaret, born in 1797, and a son, Lewen-Powell, born Aug. 1801.

ARMS—First and fourth: argent, an eagle displayed, with two heads, sable, guttée d'or, for Glyn; second and third, party per pale, azure and gules, three stags' heads, or, in an inescutcheon surtout, a man's leg and thigh, human, couped, for Lewen.

CREST—On a wreath of the colours, an eagle's head erased, sable, guttée d'or, holding in the beak an escallop, argent.

COUNTRY RESIDENCE—Ewell, Surry.

269. COLEBROOKE, of Bath.

Created Baronet, Oct. 12, 1759.

THAT this family is of considerable antiquity, may be collected from the following circumstance: that it was usual, before the general use of patronymicks, for persons to assume the names of towns in which they first drew breath, had been educated, or executed an office. Not unfrequently a family name was dropped, after it came into use. Thus the celebrated William, Bishop of Winchester, son of John Perot, according to some, and of John Long, according to others, born at Wickham, in Hampshire, was called William Wickham, from the place of his nativity, and by that name only is he known by historians. The predecessor of Wickham, much in favour with Edward III. took his surname from Edindon, in Wiltshire, because he had his birth in it, and was denominated William de Edindon, having relinquished his paternal name.

The learned Camden, and others of our antiquaries, agree, that variations in surnames were usual *; and, as the eldest branches assumed family names from castles, manors, offices, &c. so it was customary for younger sons to denominate themselves from the possessions or abode of their ancestors.

The name of Colebrooke is given to many places in England and Ireland; but we have not been able to trace in which of these the person resided who added Colebrooke in addition to his christian name.

The following are the places which have occurred to us. The parish of Colebrooke, in Dorsetshire; two places of the name in Devonshire; Colebrooke Castle, in Monmouthshire; Colebrooke Dale, in Shropshire; the town of Colebrooke, in Buckinghamshire; and Colebrooke, in the county of Fermanagh, in Ireland.

1, Thomas Colebrooke, who settled in Arundel, in Sussex, and died there Jan. 6, 1690, left four sons and one daughter.

John, the second son, was deputy-paymaster in the expedition under Lord Cathcart in the year 1740. His spirited conduct, and disinterested perseverance in the execution of this trust, were noticed in the further report of the secret committee in 1742, and had the approbation of the house of commons. In 1748, he was appointed his Majesty's Consul at Cadiz, from which post he was dismissed in 1752, and died in October, 1760, unmarried.

2, James, the eldest, was born at Arundel, May 12, 1680, and married, Jan. 2, 1706, Mary Hudson. He died Nov. 18, 1752, and she on the 12th of March following. Their bodies are deposited in a mausoleum at Chilham, in the county of Kent, with an inscription over the entrance †. He died possessed of large estates in Kent, Sussex, and Middlesex, in which last county he built, at Southgate, near Enfield Chace, a large mansion, since called Arno's Grove ‡. He was much attached to Sir Robert Walpole, by whom he had the offer of being created a Baronet. By the said Mary Hudson he had five sons and eight daughters, whereof the two eldest sons and one daughter died in their infancy. The others were, 1, Dionysia, born March 9, 1707-8, wife, 1729, of John Walker, Esq. of Lyneham, in the county of Wilts, who, after the decease of his brother Heneage, succeeded to the office of usher of the Exchequer, granted by Hen. II. to Roger Warenquefort by letters-patent, which office in fee was purchased by an ancestor

* Camden's Remains, in loco Surnames, p. 110.

† M. S.
Jacobi Colebrooke, Armigeri,
et Mariæ conjugis, B. M.
Pietatis Ergo posuere
Tres Filii
et Sibi et Suis;
Robertus Colebrooke,
Jacobus Colebrooke,
Georgius Colebrooke.

‡ See Watts's Picturesque Views of Seats, No. 63.

of the said John Walker in the first year of James I. This John had the offer of being created a Baronet by Mr. Fox, and died in 1758, and lies buried at Woodborough, in Wiltshire. By the said Dionysia (who died 1761, and lies buried in Lyneham) he had three sons and three daughters, 1, John, who was educated at Cambridge, and married, in 1763, Arabella, daughter of Jonathan Cope, Esq. of Orton, in Huntingdonshire, son and heir of Sir Jonathan Cope, Bart. of Brewern Abbey, in Oxfordshire, by Lady Arabella Howard, daughter of Henry, the fourth Earl of Carlisle: they are without issue. This John was of Compton-House*, in the county of Wilts, and after the death of his mother, took the name and arms of Heneage, by the king's licence, being grandson and heir of Cecil, daughter of Sir Michael Heneage, Knt.; he was returned to two parliaments by the borough of Cricklade; 2, James-Button Walker, killed at St. Cas, in Normandy, in 1758†, and Colebrooke Walker, who departed this life in 1756.

Of the daughters, Mary, the eldest, died unmarrried in 1775; Dionysia, the second, was wife of the Rev. Theophilus Meredith, rector of Ross, in Herefordshire, and brother of the Right Honourable Sir William Meredith, Bart. who left a daughter Harriet. Cecil, the youngest, was wife of Lieutenant-General Calcraft, who left a son, John, a colonel in the army, and three daughters, 1, Cecil, unmarried; 2, Arabella, wife of William St. Quintin, Esq. of Scampston, in Yorkshire; and 3, Mary, of the Rev. George Wyld, of Speen, in Berkshire.

2, Mary, the second daughter of James Colebrooke, was born Jan. 27, 1710-11, and died unmarried; 3, Anne, born April 11, 1712, wife of John Symonds, Esq. of the Meende, in Herefordshire, and member for the city of Hereford in the parliament summoned to meet May, 1754, and also in that which met May 19, 1761. He died in 1763, and she in 1764, and both lie interred in the church of the Meende; 4, Anna-Maria, born May 24, 1720; she was wife of William-Paine King, Esq. of Fineshade Abbey, in the county of Northampton, who dying without issue in 1766, bequeathed to her the whole of his fortune, which was considerable. In 1767, she married the Honourable Edwin Sandys, then member for the city of Westminster, who, on the decease of his father, Samuel, Lord Sandys, in 1770, succeeded to the peerage; Edwin, the last lord, departed this life at Ombersley Court, in Worcestershire, on the 11th of March, 1797, and leaving no issue, gave likewise his estate, real and personal, to his wife for ever; 5, Sarah, born May 13, 1724, was married in September, 1746, to Jeremiah Cray, Esq. of Ibsley, in the county of Hants, and verdurer of the New Forest, by whom she had seven children, who all died infants or unmarried, except, 1, Sarah, wife of Alexander, son of Sir Ludovic Grant, of Dalvey, Bart.

* See View in Robertson's Topographical Survey of the Great Road from London to Bath and Bristol, Vol. II.

† James was christened Button, from Mary, eldest daughter of Sir William Button, Bart. having married Clement Walker, of Charter-House, Hendon, Somersetshire, the well-known author of the History of Independency, who was member for Wells in the Long Parliament. Sir William was descended from Sir William de Bitton, 12 Hen. III. whose grandson, Sir John, took the name of De Button. Sir John appears to have possessed lands within the hundred of Bitton, in Gloucestershire, in the fourth year of Richard the Second.

now Sir Alexander Grant; and 2, Margaret, of Percival Lewis, Esq. of Putney, in Surry, and of Downton House, in Radnorshire, son of Edward Lewis, Esq. member for the town of New Radnor in five parliaments, from 1760 to 1790. Jeremiah Cray died on the 4th of November, 1786, and Sarah, his wife, on the 4th of March, 1797, and both lie buried with their daughters Harriet and Margaret Lewis, at Ellingham, in Hampshire.

The sixth daughter of James Colebrooke was Charlotte, born Nov. 12, 1725, she was the wife of John Wicker, of Horsham, in Sussex, who died in August, 1767, and left one daughter, Mary, who was wife, in 1766, of the Rev. Sir Thomas Broughton, Bart. of Broughton, in Staffordshire, and of Doddington Hall, in Cheshire: she died in 1785, leaving eight sons and five daughters, and was interred in the family vault at Broughton. Charlotte Wicker survived her daughter until 1795, when, dying at Bath, she was buried at Weston, near that city, where a monument was erected to her memory by Sir Thomas Broughton *.

The seventh daughter of James Colebrooke is Rachael, born Sept. 22, 1727, who is still unmarried.

The surviving sons of James Colebrooke and Mary Hudson were as follows:

1, Robert Colebrooke, of Chilham Castle, in the county of Kent †, born June 24, 1718, married Henrietta, eldest daughter of Lord Harry Powlett, afterwards Duke of Bolton, and sister of the last two dukes. On her demise in 1753, he married Elizabeth, one of the daughters and coheiresses of John Thresher, of Bradford, in the county of Wilts, and sister of the wife of the late Sir Bourchier Wray, Bart.

Robert was bred at Cambridge, and served in three parliaments, from the year 1741 to 1761, for the borough of Malden. In the year 1762, he was appointed his Majesty's minister to the Swiss Cantons, which post he quitted in 1764,

* To the memory
of Mrs. Charlotte Wicker,
Relict of John Wicker, Esq.
of Horsham, in the county of Sussex,
By whom she left an only daughter,
Mary, the wife of the Rev.
Sir Thomas Broughton, Bart. of Doddington-
Hall, in the county of Chester.
She departed this life Aug. 31, 1795.
Few ever exceeded her in respectability
of character or conduct, or in
unaffected piety towards that God
in whose mercy she confided for
acceptance at the throne of
Grace, through the merit of
Jesus Christ, the
Blessed Redeemer
of mankind.

† See View in Grose's Antiquities, Vol. II.

and dying on the 10th of May, 1784, his remains were deposited in the mausoleum at Chilham with those of his wife Henrietta, leaving no issue *.

I. JAMES COLEBROOKE, of Gatton, in the county of Surry, Esq. born July 21, 1722, was advanced to the dignity of a Baronet by letters-patent, dated Oct. 12, 1759, 33 Geo. II. and, in failure of issue male, with remainder to his brother George. He married Mary, eldest daughter and coheiress of Stephen Skinner, Esq. of Walthamstow, in Essex. (Emma, the second daughter of the said Stephen, was wife of William Harvey, Esq. of Chigwell, knight of the shire for the county of Essex; and Deborah, the third daughter of Thomas Grosvenor, Esq. member for the city of Chester in several parliaments, and brother to Earl Grosvenor.) Mary, wife of Sir James Colebrooke, died in the year 1754, and her body was deposited in the mausoleum at Chilham †.

* The following inscription is on a tablet of black marble, to the memory of the said Honourable Henrietta Colebrooke:

Within this receptacle
deposited, lies the body of
the Honourable Henrietta,
Daughter of
The Right Honourable Lord Harry Paulet, and
Wife
of Robert Colebrooke, of Chilham-Castle, Esq.
In whom the noblest birth, and most perfect beauty,
were surpassed
by sweetness of disposition, and elegance of manners.
For five long lingering years,
with humble fortitude, and devout resignation,
she sustained the gnawing pangs of an inveterate cancer.
Nevertheless,
Tho' true greatness of mind may render the soul
superior to the calamities of nature,
Life must sink under the infirmities of it;
She therefore yielded to mortality,
on the 22d day of December,
in the year of our Salvation, 1753,
in the thirty and seventh year
of her age.

† Sacred
to the Graces,
and to every virtue
which could adorn a Woman,
Let
this Marble be inscribed
to the Memory of
Mary Colebrooke,
Wife of James Colebrooke, of Gatton, in
the county of Surry, Esq.
She was the eldest daughter of
Stephen Skinner, of Walthamstow, Esq.
was born the 12th day of August, 1728,
and married the 7th day of May, 1747,

Sir James was educated at Leyden, in Holland, and was elected a burgess to sit in three parliaments for the borough of Gatton; he died May 10, 1761, aged 87, and his body was deposited at Chilham, leaving only two daughters, 1, Mary, born March 10, 1750, and married John Aubrey, Esq. of Dorton House and Borstall Tower, in Buckinghamshire, the latter descended to him by the tenure of the horn through more than thirty generations, from the reign of Edward the Confessor, without alienation or forfeiture*.

He was returned to serve in several parliaments for different boroughs, and once for the county of Bucks; he succeeded his father in the title of Baronet, and to the estate of Llantrithed, in Glamorganshire, on the 4th of September, 1786. Mary died in 1781, and having had a son who died before her, lies buried with him at Borstall.

The second daughter was Emma, who was born Dec. 22, 1752, wife of Charles, fourth Earl of Tankerville, in 1772, and by him has had four sons and eight daughters, of whom three sons and six daughters are now living. The only one married is Lady Caroline, the eldest, married, in 1795, to Sir John Wrottesley, of Wrottesley, in Staffordshire, Bart.

II. Sir GEORGE COLEBROOKE, the present Baronet, born June 14, 1729, married, July 23, 1754, Mary, only daughter and heiress of Patrick Gaynor, Esq. of Antigua, by Mary Linch, his wife, by whom he has had four sons and three daughters, whereof two daughters and three sons are living; 1, Mary, born Oct. 26, 1757, wife of the Chevalier Charles Adrien de Peyron, in the service of Gustavus, King of Sweden, and by him had one son, Charles-Adolphus-Mary. The chevalier was killed in a duel, in 1784, by the Count de la Marck, upon which melancholy occasion, the king, being at Paris, sent for the mother and child, and not only promised to confer upon the boy, then only three years of age, the office in his household which the father held, but graciously offered to take him into his family, and educate him with his son, the Prince Royal, now King of Sweden. His Swedish Majesty, on his return to Stockholm, ordered a grant of the office of gentleman of his bed-chamber to be transmitted, together with a certificate of the boy's parentage and birth, and of its registration in the list of the nobility, by which he, having attained the proper age, will have a right to a seat in the diet of Sweden.

In 1789, the mother took for her second husband, William Traill, Esq. by whom she has had a son, George-William, born Oct. 2, 1792, and a daughter Harriet, who is dead.

and died in childbed the 14th of May, 1754,
of the small-pox, leaving issue two daughters,
Mary and Emma, and one son James,
who survived her only six days,
and whose ashes are here
likewise deposited.

Heu! minime cum reris, in ipso flore Inventæ
Mors inopina Domus Spem abripit omnem.

* Archæologia, Vol. III.

The second daughter was Louisa, born Jan. 1764, wife of Andrew Sutherland, Esq. captain in his Majesty's navy, to whom the Ardent struck on the 12th of May. He died at Gibraltar in 1795, commissioner of that port, leaving a daughter Louisa, born April 17, 1791, and a son, called James-Charles-Colebrooke Sutherland, born Nov. 6, 1792. Sir George's three sons alive are, 1, George, born Aug. 9, 1759, who is captain of the light company of the Somerset militia, and hereditary keeper of the castle of Crawford; 2, James-Edward, born July 7, 1761, who is judge of appeals at Moorshedabad, in the province of Bengal*.

* When he was Persian translator, Governor Hastings wrote in his commendation the following letter, dated Feb. 8, 1786.

"You desire my opinion of Mr. Colebrooke's capacity for the office: such an opinion given of a son to his father, must of course be favourable, and would be therefore read with distrust, or at least with deductions, on account of the delicacy required by that relation. I wish to preclude such constructions, by declaring, as I do solemnly, that I know few young men in the service, and the service may boast of many who are an honour to it, who possess superior talents, or more cultivated understandings, and few equal to him in the knowledge of the Persian language. I respect his personal character so much, that I feel a regret, almost approaching to self-reproach, in the reflection, that after so many years of official labour bestowed where I may be supposed to have had it in my power to recompence, the only return I can now make to him, is a mere acknowledgment of his merits."

An Extract of a Minute of the Governor-General of Bengal, on his presenting the Translation of the Digest of the Hindoo Law to the Supreme Council.

"I congratulate the Board on the opportunity afforded me of laying before them a translation, by Mr. H. T. Colebrooke, of a Digest of Hindoo Law, on Contracts and Successions, compiled by Native Pundits in the Sanscrit Language, under the superintendance of Sir William Jones. The whole, including the Preface of the Translator, a List of Authorities quoted in the Digest, Notes on the Orthography of Sanscrit Words, and a Table of Contents, is comprised in seven manuscript folio volumes, containing 1614 pages.

The translation has been completed in little more than two years, and has been executed most ably and faithfully, I believe, in the midst of official avocations; it is a proof of literary industry, rarely exceeded, and which zeal and a laudable hope of distinction only could have excited; and although I am persuaded that Mr. Colebrooke would not have undertaken this work without a consciousness of his ability to perform it well, I will not deny myself the satisfaction of recording the unqualified testimony of the natives (who are the most competent judges) to his proficiency in the Sanscrit language.

This work was proposed by Sir William Jones, on the grounds of public utility; I trust that his expectations from it will not be disappointed; that it will long remain a memorial of the judgment and benevolence which dictated it; that it will be received by the natives of these provinces as a proof of the respect of the British government for their jurisprudence; and that, whilst the translator enjoys the satisfaction of having so essentially contributed to promote an object of public utility, he will no less derive that reputation from his labours which they are so justly entitled to."

The Court of Directors thought fit to return the following answer:

We have perused the Minute of the Governor-General, referred to in these paragraphs, on the subject of Mr. Colebrooke's Translation of the Digest of Hindoo Laws, on Contracts and Successions, compiled under the superintendance of the late Sir William Jones. This testimony of the zeal and abilities of Mr. Colebrooke, is highly honourable to him, and pleasing to us; and we desire he may be acquainted, that we entertain a due sense of the merits and disinterestedness of his conduct upon this occasion.

We have the further satisfaction to observe it recorded by the Governor-General, that, during the execution of this laborious work, Mr. Colebrooke continued to discharge his duties as a judge and magistrate, in a mode as creditable to himself, as beneficial to the community.

The third son was Henry-Thomas, born June 15, 1765, who is judge at Mirzapoor. Having made himself master of the Sanscrit language, he undertook, on the death of Sir William Jones, to translate a Digest of the Hindoo Law, for the use of the courts of justice: he has been engaged likewise in a private and much esteemed work, on the Agriculture and Commerce of Bengal. He is now employed in making a Grammar of the Sanscrit.

Sir George's three sons hold the office of chirographer in the court of common pleas, by letters-patent, dated March 18, 6 Geo. III.

The children who are dead were, 1, James, born Sept. 15, 1758, who died on the 26th of September, 1759; and Harriet, born Sept. 19, 1762, who died June 11, 1785: they both lie in the mausoleum at Chilham.

Lady Colebrooke's uterine sister, Sarah Gilbert, was married, in 1766, to Joshua Smith, Esq. of Stoke Park, in the county of Wilts*, and member for Devizes in three successive parliaments, and has had by him four daughters living: the eldest, Mary, wife of Charles, the ninth Earl of Northampton; and the second, Elizabeth, of William Chute, Esq. of the Vine, Hampshire, member for the county in the last and present parliament. The third daughter is Augusta, wife of Charles Smith, of Sutton, in the county of Essex, member of parliament for Saltash: the only unmarried daughter is Emma.

Sir George studied at Leyden, and was chosen fellow of the Society of Antiquaries, and is the author of some pieces of literature. He was elected to serve in three successive parliaments for the borough of Arundel, from 1754 to 1774, and he was appointed deputy chairman of the directors of the East India Company in 1768, chosen chairman in 1769, and was re-elected to that arduous employment in 1771 and 1772.

During the time he presided, he was greatly instrumental in preventing the newly-acquired territories in the East Indies from being annexed to the crown, and, in every respect, to preserve the independence of the company from that interference and controul which have since been established. Lord North, then minister, gave him assurances that it was not his intention that government should interfere with the patronage of the Company, or nominate, by its authority, "so much as a single writer." Lord North deviated from that engagement, by explaining, that such promise was made to the chairman, not as minister, but as a private man; probably, however, the minister was himself over-ruled.

ARMS—Gules, a lion rampant, argent, ducally crowned, or, on a chief of the last, three Cornish choughs, proper.

CREST—On a wreath, a wyvern with wings expanded, or, resting his foot upon a plain shield, gules.

MOTTO—*Sola bona quæ honesta.*

SEAT—Gatton-Place, in Surry.

* See View in Robertson's Topographical Survey of the Great Road from London to Bath and Bristol, Vol. II.

TABLE.

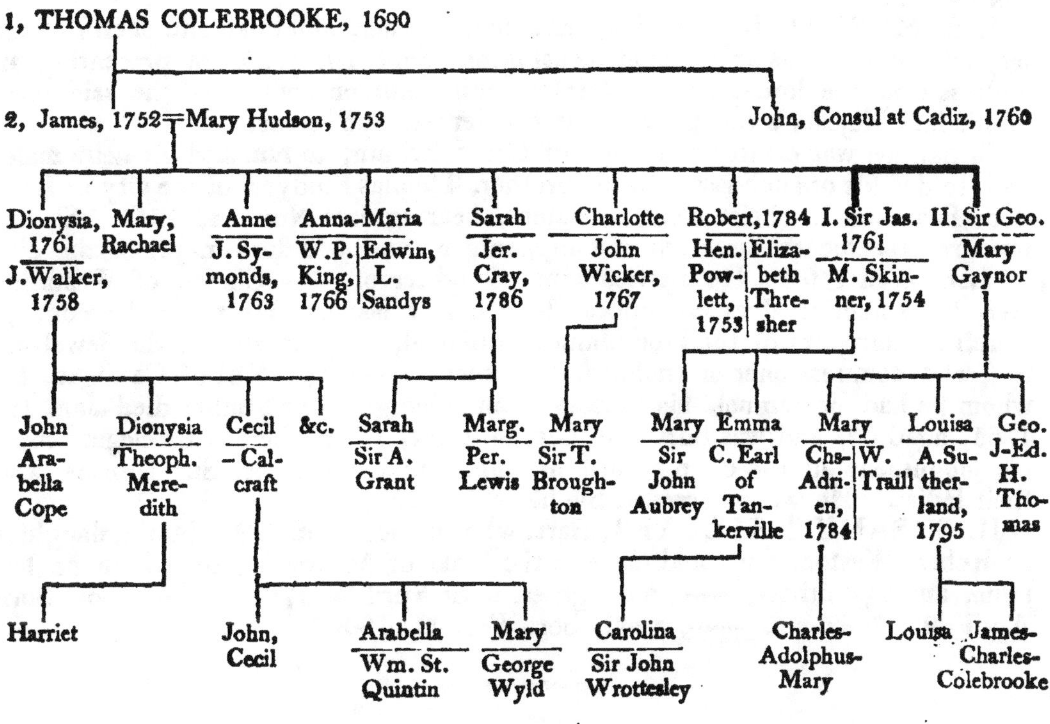

270. FLUDYER, of London.

Created Baronet, Nov. 14, 1759.

SAMUEL FLUDYER followed the clothing business in London, and left two sons, Sir Samuel, and Sir Thomas. Thomas Fludyer, the younger son, of the city of London, Esq. was knighted in the council-chamber of Guildhall, Nov. 9, 1761, when his present Majesty, and several of the royal family, honoured his brother, Sir Samuel (who was then lord-mayor), with their presence, at a feast provided there on the occasion. He was, first, member of parliament for Great Bedwin, and afterwards for Chippenham, in Wiltshire, and fellow of the Royal and Antiquary Societies. Sir Thomas married Mary, daughter of Sir George Champion, Knt. and alderman of London; he died March 19, 1769, aged 57, and was buried at Lee, in Kent, leaving a very considerable fortune to his only daughter and heiress, Mary, born June, 1755, who was wife, March 2, 1773, of Trevor-Charles Roper, son of the Honourable Charles Roper, and nephew to Lord Dacre.

I. SAMUEL FLUDYER, Esq. the elder brother, alderman and sheriff of the city of London, was knighted at Kensington, Sept. 19, 1755, on presenting an address from the lord-mayor, alderman, and common-council of the said city, on his late Majesty's safe arrival from his German dominions.

Sir Samuel was created a Baronet of Great Britain, to him and his heirs male, and, in default of such issue, to his brother, Thomas Fludyer, of the city of London, Esq. and his heirs male, by patent, bearing date Nov. 14, 1759. Sir Samuel represented the borough of Chippenham, and was lord-mayor of the city of London in 1761. He married Jane, daughter of —— Clarke, of Westminster, by whom it does not appear he had any issue. He married secondly, Caroline, daughter of the Hon. James Brudenell, Esq. master of the jewel-office, and commissioner of trade, and brother to George, Earl of Cardigan, by whom he had Sir Samuel, his successor, and George. Sir Samuel died Jan. 18, 1768, aged 63, and was buried at Lee, in Kent, where there is an elegant marble monument in the church-yard for him and his brother, Sir Thomas, and their ladies. He was succeeded by his eldest son,

II. Sir SAMUEL FLUDYER, Bart. who married, Oct. 1784, Maria, daughter of Robert Weston, Esq. and niece to the Duke of Montague, by whom he has issue, amongst others, ——, a daughter, born April 18, 1793; ——, a son, born April 29, 1798; and ——, a son, born Feb. 31, 1800.

ARMS—Sable, a cross, patonce, between four escalops, argent, each charged with a cross, patonce, of the field.

CREST—On a wreath, an escalop, as in the arms, between a pair of wings, elevated, argent.

SEAT—Lee, in Kent.

TABLE.

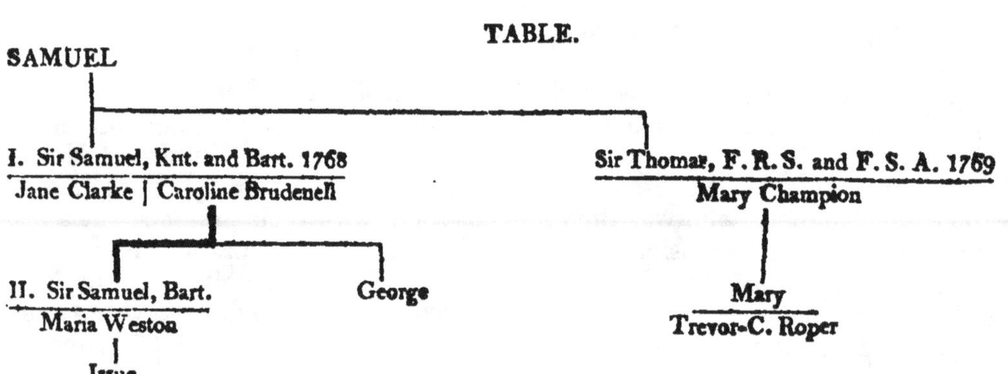

271. WATSON, son to the late Admiral Watson.

Created Baronet, March 22, 1760.

DR. JOHN WATSON, prebendary of Westminster, and rector of Castle-Camps, in Cambridgeshire, married ——, half-sister of Sir Charles Wager, by whom he had Charles, who was born in 1714; he lost his father when he was but nine years old. His uncle superintended his education, and when he was fifteen years old, entered him in the navy. In the year 1735, he was made a lieutenant, and in 1737, a post-captain, being appointed commander of the Garland, of twenty guns.

In 1744, Captain Watson commanded the Dragon, a sixty-gun ship, and one of the fleet under Admiral Matthews in the Mediterranean. He was employed in several cruizes between Toulon and Gibraltar, whilst the British fleet lay there, watching the motions of the combined fleet of France and Spain, which then lay at Toulon. The orders which he received from the admiral were, to proceed to Cadiz, and after cruizing off that harbour for a certain time, to go to Lisbon, and from thence to England. This destination was the most lucrative that could be desired, as the captain was sure of receiving eight hundred moidores freight money; but before he passed the gut of Gibraltar, captain Watson received intelligence of the preparations of the enemy at Toulon, and the likelihood of their coming out to sea, he nobly renounced all views of self-interest, and bent his course to Hieres Bay to join the fleet, which he effected a few days before the battle. So noble an instance of sacrificing private advantage, and choosing a situation of danger, when the interest of his country was at stake, places the character of this gallant officer in a most advantageous point of view. Such ardent zeal! such just and unbiassed sentiments, so uncommon in any rank or profession, deserves to be recorded, not only in justice to so much worth, but as an example to other commanders. It is highly probable that captain Watson, by discontinuing his cruize, missed the opportunity of falling in with a Spanish fleet, valued at three hundred thousand pounds, which was taken by the Solebay on the very station where the Dragon was to have been.

In the several ships he afterwards commanded, he highly distinguished himself, particularly in the action of the 3d of May, 1747, when even the French admiral made the most honourable mention of his ship, the Princess Louisa, and a few others, in the account he sent to his court of that memorable engagement. In the following action, which happened the same year, in which Sir Edward Hawke commanded in chief, captain Watson again displayed his intrepidity; and, on the 12th of May, 1748, "as a reward for his merit," (to use the very words of Lord Anson), he was raised to the rank of rear-admiral of the blue, and sent with some ships to Cape Breton.

At the conclusion of the war, he retired into the country, until he was fixed upon as the commander of the king's ships at Plymouth, where he continued a short time, and was then appointed to the command of the squadron destined for the East Indies. Soon after he arrived on the coast of Coromandel, he received his Majesty's commission, appointing him a rear-admiral of the red, and in that capacity assisted at the reduction of Chandernagore.

After the reduction of the fort of Geriah, the wives and children of Angria became prisoners to the victors. Admiral Watson took an early opportunity of visiting these captives. Upon his entering their house, the whole family made a grand salaam, or reverential bending of their bodies, touching the ground with their faces, and shedding floods of tears. The admiral desired them to be comforted, adding, " that they were now under his protection, and that no kind of injury should be done them. They then again made the salaam. The mother of Angria, though strongly affected with these instances of goodness and humanity, yet could not help crying out, " the people have no king, she no son, her daughters no husbands, their children no father." The admiral replied, " that from thenceforth they must look upon him as their father and their friend." Hereupon the youngest child, a boy of about six years of age, sobbing, said, " then you shall be my father," and immediately took the admiral by the hand, and called him father.

The integrity of this worthy man appeared conspicuously, in his refusing to be a party in the scandalous transaction which deprived Omichund of about three hundred thousand pounds sterling, which he claimed as the price of successful treachery; and in making this the price of his assistance, he might not perhaps be more rapacious than others, who took part in the same business. Mr. Watson, as he rejected the demand, chose to avow his rejection, and could not be prevailed upon to set his hand to an instrument which he did not intend to fulfil; and indeed, it apears to us, that the deed given to Omichund, and executed by Meer Jaffier, Colonel Clive, and other members of the select committee, gave that Armenian a legal right to recover from the parties the sum specified therein, but he must rather have resorted to Westminster-Hall for satisfaction than to the law courts of India.

During his whole stay in India, he had been more or less subject to the overflowings of the bile, which brought on either slight fevers or gripings in the bowels. Aug. 12, 1757, he was seized with an indisposition which increased upon him, but was not attended with any very alarming symptoms. The 15th was intensely hot; both man and beast, and the very fowls of the air, so sensibly felt it, that some of each species fell down dead. Admiral Watson was incapable of supporting it: his pulse became feeble, and his head confused; somnolency followed, and between eight and nine o'clock the next morning he died.

The admiral married, in 1748, ——, eldest daughter of John-Francis Buller, of Merval, in the county of Cornwall, Esq. by whom he had one son, Sir Charles, and two daughters. His widow died at Swaffham, in Cambridgeshire, in 1800.

I. CHARLES WATSON, Esq. in honour of his father, had the dignity of a Baronet conferred upon him by his late Majesty, which was the last in that reign. Sir Charles married, in 1787, Julian, daughter of the late Sir Joseph Copley, Bart. by whom he has issue.

ARMS—Argent, on a chevron, engrailed azure, between three martletts, sable, as many crescents, or.

CREST—A griffin's head erased, argent, ducally gorged, or.

SEAT—At Fulmer, in Berkshire.

The late admiral Watson was handsome in his person, and had a manly commanding countenance. His temper, though naturally warm, was extremely good, and his disposition exceedingly humane. His manners were easy and polite; he was a lover of temperance and sobriety, though he made no scruple at his table, occasionally, to promote a free circulation of the glass; and his sentiments were generous and noble. Few men, who, like Mr. Watson, had been taken from school at so early a period of life, excelled him in epistolary writing: he studied men and things more than books, and was confessedly quick and happy in finding out real characters. He liked and loved the honest man, but detested the hypocrite. Though firm in his resolutions, he was ever open to conviction; and whenever he thought the public service would be benefited by any advice he had privately received, he would be sure to carry it into execution; and, after success had attended it, to declare publicly to whose counsel the success was owing.

The East-India Company, in gratitude for the great and effectual services the admiral rendered to them, erected a monument to his memory in Westminster Abbey. Before his death, Mr. Watson was advanced to the rank of vice-admiral of the red.

This monument is placed over the north door, with the following inscription:

> To the memory of Charles Watson, vice-admiral of the white, commander in chief of his Majesty's naval forces in the East Indies, who died at Calcutta the 16th of August, 1757, in the 44th year of his age. The East-India Company, as a grateful testimony of the signal advantages which they obtained by his valour and prudent conduct, caused this monument to be erected.

Between the pillars, over the centre of the door, is the figure of the admiral in full proportion, standing on a pedestal, with a branch of olive in his right hand, looking towards a beautiful figure of a woman in a kneeling posture, returning thanks for her safe deliverance from imprisonment in the Black Hole; and underneath are the following words:

Calcutta freed, January 11, 1757.

On the other side of the admiral, is the figure of an Indian prisoner sitting chained to a pillar, looking with a dejected countenance, but casts a contemptuous look towards the admiral; over him is written "Chandernagore taken, March 23, 1767; and underneath him is, "Gheriah taken, February 13, 1756." —*Naval History*, Vol. V. p. 410.

TABLE.

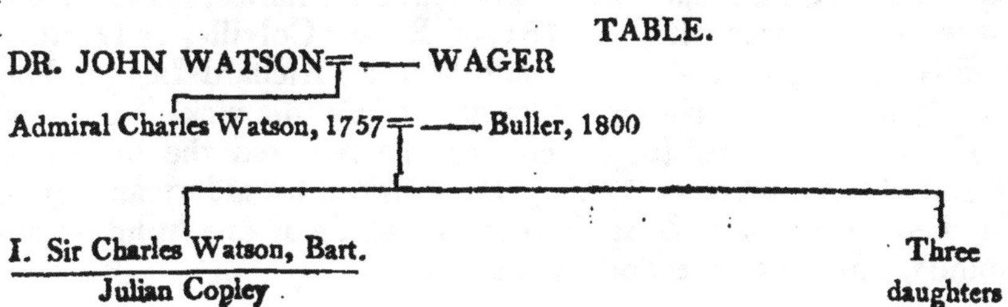

BARONETS

CREATED BY

KING GEORGE III.

272. ASGILL, of London.

Created Baronet, April 16, 1761.

I. SIR CHARLES ASGILL, Bart. was the son of Charles Asgill, Esq. an eminent merchant of the city of London. He was a strong instance of what may be effected even by moderate abilities, when united with strict integrity, industry, and irreproachable character. His first setting out in life was at a banking-house in Lombard-street, as out-door collecting clerk. From this inferior situation he progressively rose, by his merit, to the first department in the house; and soon after married, in 1752, ——, daughter of Henry Vanderstegen, a merchant in London, with whom he had a fortune of twenty-five thousand pounds: he immediately joined his name to the firm. This lady dying Feb. 6, 1754, without issue, Sir Charles married 2dly, ——, daughter of Daniel Pratviel, Esq. merchant, in London, by whom he had several children, Sir Charles, his successor. One of his daughters, ———, was wife, in 1781, of Robert Colville, of Hemingstone-Hall, in Suffolk, Esq.; and ———, another, of Richard Legge, Esq. April 5, 1800. In 1749, he was chosen alderman of Candlewick Ward, and served the office of sheriff in 1756, (in which year he received the honour of knighthood), and that of lord-mayor in 1758. He resigned his alderman's gown July 1, 1777, and died in 1778, it is said worth upwards of one hundred and sixty thousand pounds, and was suceeded by his son,

II. Sir CHARLES ASGILL, Bart. then a captain of the first regiment of guards, and served with much reputation in the American war, and had nearly been hanged for a spy; but by the interposition of maternal tenderness with the French court, he escaped the vindictive justice of the colonists—GENT. MAG. P. 841, 1788. He married, Aug. 28, 1790, Jemima-Sophia, daughter of admiral Sir Chaloner Ogle, Knt.

ARMS—Parted, per fess, argent, and vert, a pale counterchanged in each piece, of the first, a lion's head erased, gules.
CREST—A sphynx, with wings endorsed, ar. crined, or.
MOTTO—*Sui oblitus commodo.*

TABLE.

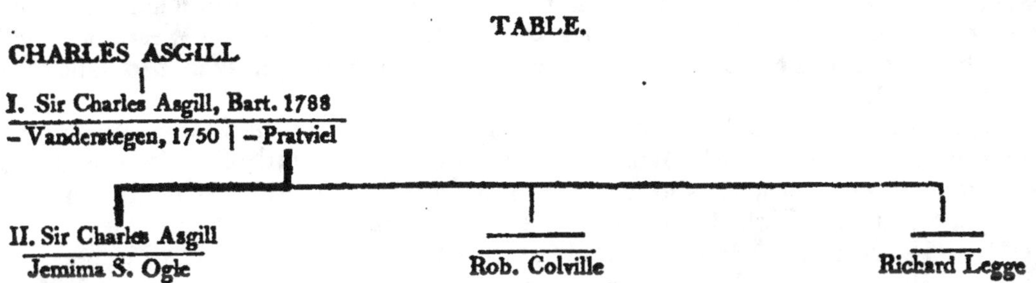

Some of the family were buried in St. Bartholomew Church Yard, behind the Royal Exchange, London, with inscriptions.

273. HESKETH, of RUFFORD, Lancashire.

Created Baronet, May 5, 1761.

THIS family very probably derive their surname from the lordship of Heskaythe, in Lancashire, of which they have been possessed many ages.

1, Robert de Heskaythe left one son,

2, William de Heskaythe, who married Annabella, daughter and heiress of Sir Rowland Stafford, Knt. by whom he had one son,

3, William Heskaythe, who married Elbota, daughter and heiress of Richard de Tottleworth, by whom he had three sons; 1, Sir William; 2, Adam, who married Maud, daughter of William Fleming, Bishop of Bath; and 3, John, of whom there is no farther mention.

4, Sir William Heskaythe, Knt. was lord of Heskaythe and Beconsaw, and married, 4 Edw. I. Dame Maude, daughter and coheiress of Richard de Fitton, lord of Fitton (whose arms being argent, on a bend, sable, three garbs, or, were afterwards used by the Hesketh as their proper armorial ensigns), by whom he had two sons; 1, Thomas: 2, Adam, whose son and heir, William, dwelt at Rufford, where he died.

5, Thomas de Heskaythe was lord of Rufford, &c. and married Alis, daughter of Warin de Bisham, lord of Bisham, by whom he had four sons; 1, Robert, who died S. P.: 2, Sir John; 3, Robert*; and 4, Richard: and one daughter Margaret, wife of Richard Nowell.

6, Sir John de Heskaythe, Knt. succeeded to the family estates, and married Alice, daughter and heiress of Edmund Fitton (with whom he had half the lordship of Rufford), by whom he had one son,

7, Sir John de Heskaythe, lord of Rufford, Heskaythe, Beconsaw, Great Harwood, and Tottleworth, was living in 1355, and married Mariella, daughter and coheiress of —— Twenge, alias Doddingsels, of Kendal, in Westmoreland, by whom he had Thomas, of whom hereafter, and William, who had lands in Beconsaw, 23 Edw. III.

8, Thomas de Heskaythe, lord of Heskaythe, &c. married Margaret, daughter and coheiress of Thomas Banaster, baron of Newton, lord of Walton, and son of Sir Thomas Banaster, who was one of the knights of the most noble order of the garter, temp. Rich. II. by whom he had three sons; 1, Robert, who died 1 Hen. IV. S. P.; 2, Nicholas; and 3, Gilbert, who married, and had issue.

9, Nicholas Heskaythe, Esq. was heir to his brother Robert, and married Margaret, daughter and coheiress of —— Minshull, by whom he left an only son,

10, Sir Thomas Heskaythe, Knt. lord of Rufford, &c. who married Sibill, daughter and coheiress of Sir Robert Lawrence, Knt. by whom he had three sons; 1, Hugh, who left no legitimate issue; 2, Thomas; and 3, Nicholas.

11, Thomas, married Margaret, daughter of Hamond Maseye, of Ryxton, Esq. by whom he had ten sons; 1, Robert; 2, William, a chaplain, who died S. P.; 3, Thomas; 4, John, a priest; 5, Hugh; 6, William, who married two wives, and left issue; 7, Geoffry; 8, Richard; 9, Henry; and 10, Nicholas, a priest.

12, Robert, the eldest son, and heir to the lordships of Heskaythe, Rufford, &c. married Alice, third daughter of Sir Robert Booth, Knt. and of Dunham-Massey, in Cheshire (ancestor to the late Earl of Warrington, and late Lord Delamer); after her husband's death, she professed chastity, and died 1494, leaving three sons and three daughters; 1, Sir Richard, attorney-general to Henry VIII. and died 1520; 2, Thomas; and 3, Hugh, who was bishop of the Isle of Man. The daughters were, 1, Margaret, wife of Henry, son and heir of Richard Keightley, Esq.; 2, Doyce, of John, son and heir of Roger Nowell, of Reade, Esq.; and 3, Alice, of Sir Richard Aughton, Knt. lord of Meales, in Lancashire.

13, Thomas Heskaythe, Esq. was lord of Heskaythe and Rufford, and died

* It was no uncommon thing in former ages to have two children of the same christian name.

Aug. 14, 1523. He married Elizabeth, daughter of William Fleming, baron of Waythe, and lord of Crofton, by whom he had one son,

14, Sir Robert Heskaythe, Knt. who married Grace, daughter of Sir John Townley, of Townley, in Lancashire, Knt. and died Feb. 8, 1539, leaving two sons, Sir Thomas, and Robert, who had several children, and two daughters, Ellen, wife of Richard Barton, of Barton; and Jane, of Richard Asheton, of Crofton, in Lancashire, Esqrs.

15, Sir Thomas Heskaythe, Knt. was lord of Rufford, Holmes, Holmeswood, Howick, Beconshawe, Martholme, and Harwood. He served the office of high-sheriff of the county of Lancaster, 5 Eliz. and served his sovereign in Scotland at the siege of Leith, where he was much wounded, and had his ensign struck out of his hand, which he recovered again: he greatly repaired the house at Martholme and Holmeswood, and the chapel of Rufford. He married Alice, daughter of Sir Thomas Holcroft, Knt. by whom he had three sons and two daughters; 1, Robert; 2, Thomas; 3, Richard; 4, Dorothy, wife of —— Henry, Esq.; and 5, Margaret, of Nicholas Shillicombe, of the Field, Esq. Sir Thomas died at Rufford, 1587, and was succeeded by his son,

16, Robert, who was justice of the peace, and of the quorum, lord of Rufford, &c. He married first, Mary, daughter and heiress of Sir George Stanley, knight-marshal in Ireland, (which Sir George was son and heir of Sir James Stanley, Knt. second son of George, Lord Stanley and Strange, by Joan, daughter and heiress of John, Lord Strange, of Knocking, and of his wife Jacquet, eldest daughter and coheiress of Richard, Lord Woodville, and Earl of Rivers, sister to Elizabeth, queen to Edward IV. and mother to Queen Elizabeth, mother to Henry VIII.), by which marriage the Hesketlis became allied to tne royal and many noble families. This Robert married 2dly, Blanch, daughter and coheiress of Henry Twyford, of Kenwick, Esq. by whom he had no issue, but by the former he had five sons and three daughters; 1, Thomas, who was twice married, but left no issue; 2, Robert, of whom hereafter; 3, Henry, who died without issue; 4, George, who married Jane, widow of —— Shireburne (a younger brother of Shireburne, of Stonyhurst), by whom he had one son Robert; 5, Robert, who married Mary, daughter of —— Hadock, of Pheasantford, Esq. by whom he had a son Robert.

17, Robert Hesketh, Esq. was heir to his father and brother, and married Margaret, daughter of Alexander Standish, Esq. (by his wife Elizabeth, daughter and heiress of Adam Hawarden, of Woston, in Lancashire, Esq.); he died Jan. 1653, leaving one son,

18, Robert, who died in his father's life-time, having married Lucy, daughter of Alexander Rigby, of Middleton, in Goosenarge, Esq. (afterwards wife of John, son and heir of Sir Francis Molineux, of Tevershall, in Nottinghamshire, Bart.) by whom he had two sons; 1, Alexander, who died young; 2, Thomas: and two daughters, Lucy, who died an infant, and Margaret, who died unmarried.

19, Thomas Hesketh, Esq. was heir to his father and grandfather. He married

Sidney, only surviving daughter of Sir Richard Grosvenor, of Eaton, in Cheshire, Bart. (ancestor to the present Earl Grosvenor), by his wife Sidney, daughter o Sir Roger Mostyn, of Mostyn, in Flintshire, Bart. by whom he had two sons, Robert, and Thomas, of whom hereafter; Robert married Elizabeth, daughter of William Spencer, of Ashton, in Lancashire, Esq. (sister to Colonel Spencer, who was second husband to Sidney, widow of the above-named Hesketh, Esq.) but had an only daughter Elizabeth, wife of Sir Edward Stanley, of Bickerstaff, in Lancashire, Bart. at that time heir expectant to, and finally possessed of the title, Earl of Derby. Jane, daughter of Thomas and Sidney, was wife, first, of Henry, second son of Sir Robert Brooke, of Norton, in Cheshire, Bart.; secondly, of Hugh, son of John Warren, of Poynton, in the same county, but died without issue.

20, Thomas, second son of Thomas, was heir to his father and brother, and married Anne, fifth daughter of Sir Reginald Graham, of Norton Conyers, in the county of York, Bart. by whom he had one son,

21, Thomas Hesketh, Esq. lord of Hesketh, Rufford, Holmes and Holmeswood, Martholme, Great Harwood, Howicke, Betton, &c. was one of the representatives for the town of Preston in the sixth parliament of Great Britain, and married Martha, only daughter of James St. Amand, of St. Paul, Covent Garden, London, Esq. (by Elizabeth, daughter of Sir William Juxton, of Little Compton, in Gloucestershire, Bart.) by whom he had four sons; 1, Robert; 2, Thomas, who both died infants; 3, Sir Thomas, of whom hereafter; and 4, Robert, successor to his brother.

I. THOMAS HESKETH, Esq. the eldest surviving son, was advanced to the dignity of a Baronet, by letters-patent, May 5, 1761, with limitation to his heirs male, and in default of such issue, to Robert, his brother, and the male issue of his body lawfully begotten; which Sir Thomas married Harriet, daughter and coheiress of Ashley Cowper, Esq. and died without issue, March 4, 1778, and was succeeded by his brother,

II. Sir ROBERT HESKETH, Bart. who assumed the name of Juxton. He was born April 23, 1728, and married at Preston, in Lancashire, April 19, 1748, Sarah, daughter of William Plumbe, of Waverstree, in Lancashire, Esq. by whom he had issue; 1, Thomas; 2, Anne, born Feb. 28, 1748-9; 3, Robert, born July 23, 1751; and 4, ——, wife, in 1801, of E. Pierson, merchant, at Liverpool. Sir Robert died Dec. 30, 1796, and was succeeded by his son,

III. Sir THOMAS HESKETH, Bart.

ARMS—Argent, an eagle displayed, with two heads, proper.
CREST—On a wreath, a garb, proper.
SEATS—At Rufford, &c. in Lancashire.

TABLE.

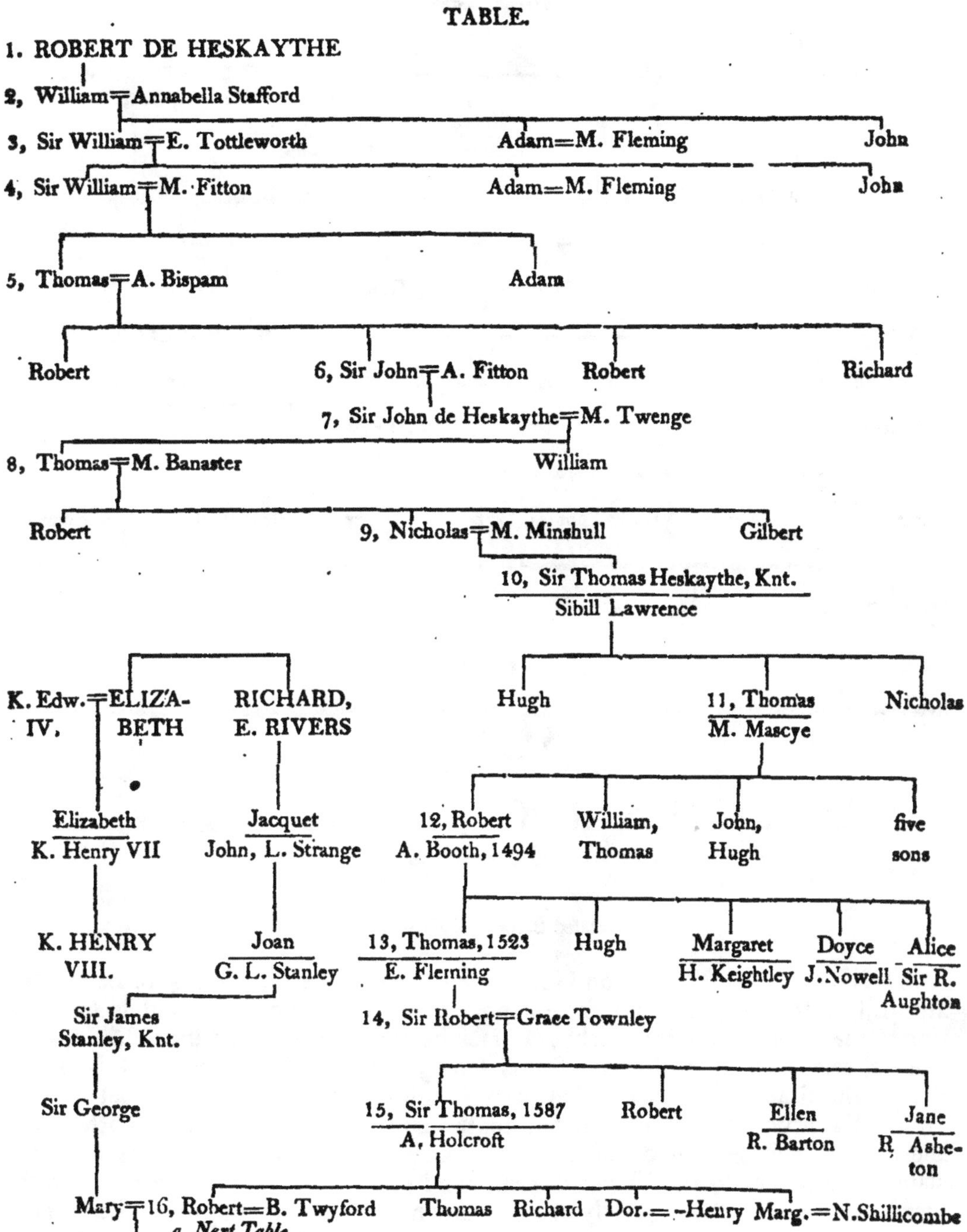
1. ROBERT DE HESKAYTHE
2, William=Annabella Stafford
3, Sir William=E. Tottleworth
Adam=M. Fleming
John
4, Sir William=M. Fitton
Adam=M. Fleming
John
5, Thomas=A. Bispam
Adam
Robert
6, Sir John=A. Fitton
Robert
Richard
7, Sir John de Heskaythe=M. Twenge
8, Thomas=M. Banaster
William
Robert
9, Nicholas=M. Minshull
Gilbert
10, Sir Thomas Heskaythe, Knt.
Sibill Lawrence
K. Edw. IV.=ELIZABETH
RICHARD, E. RIVERS
Hugh
11, Thomas
M. Mascye
Nicholas
Elizabeth
K. Henry VII
Jacquet
John, L. Strange
12, Robert
A. Booth, 1494
William, Thomas
John, Hugh
five sons
K. HENRY VIII.
Joan
G. L. Stanley
13, Thomas, 1523
E. Fleming
Hugh
Margaret
H. Keightley
Doyce
J. Nowell
Alice
Sir R. Aughton
Sir James Stanley, Knt.
14, Sir Robert=Grace Townley
Sir George
15, Sir Thomas, 1587
A. Holcroft
Robert
Ellen
R. Barton
Jane
R. Asheton
Mary=16, Robert=B. Twyford
a Next Table
Thomas
Richard
Dor.=-Henry
Marg.=N.Shillicombe

TABLE *continued.*

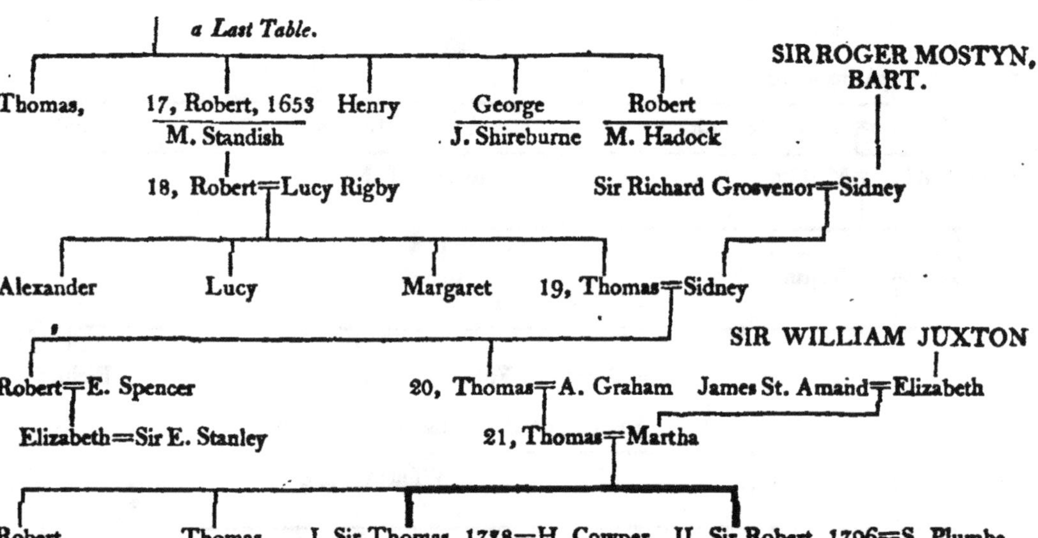

274. BAYNTUN-ROLT, of SACOMBE-PARK, Hertfordshire.

Created Baronet, July 9, 1762.

SIDNEY, in his Treatise on Government, mentions this family to be of great antiquity; that in name and ancient possessions it equals most, and is far superior to many of the nobility, whose names he enumerates; and indeed, it appears from a very curious pedigree of this family, preserved in the Royal Museum, that in the time of Henry II. they were knights of St. John of Jerusalem. Sir Henry Bayntun was knight-marshal to the king, an office of high authority in those days; whose second son, Henry, a knight of St. John of Jerusalem, was slain at Bretagne, 1201. Their descents and marriages are well preserved in this parchment, so as to be regularly brought down to Sir Henry Bayntun, Knt. temp.

Jac. I. 1616. This Sir Henry was great-grandfather to John Bayntun, of Spye-Park, Esq. who died 1717, without issue, leaving his estate to his nephew, Edward-Bayntun Rolt, second son of Edward Rolt, of Sacombe-Park, in Hertfordshire, Esq. whom he made his heir, directing him to take the name and bear the arms of Bayntun.

We find that Sir Henry Bayntun, Knt. temp. Henry IV. took part with the Earl of Northumberland, and was beheaded at Berwick. Sir Robert Bayntun, in 1471, was in arms against the king at the battle of Tewksbury, where he was made prisoner, and attainted; but his life was granted him among the very few that were spared, but by what intercession is not known.

The Bayntuns were long settled at Falston, alias Fallersdown, in Wiltshire, where they built a chapel, of which a very elegant gothic window is said to be still remaining.

Upon the death of Richard Beauchamp, Lord St. Amand, John Bayntun, Esq. who was his cousin and heir, removed to Bromham, anciently the seat of the Roches, and from them to the Beauchamps, where the family continued till the year 1652, when, at the defeat of Sir William Waller by Lord Wilmot, their house, situated near the field of battle, was burnt; they then removed to Spye-Park, and having improved and converted the lodge into a mansion-house, have made it their chief residence to this time.

2, Sir Edward, son of the said John, was in great favour with Henry VIII. He was vice-chamberlain to three of his queens, and was employed by the king to use his private friendship with Cardinal Pole (who was his cousin), to bring him to the king's views; but his endeavours had not the desired effect. He attended the king in his expedition to France, and is supposed to have died there.

3, Sir Edward, his son, succeeded him, and married Agnes, daughter of Sir Griffith Rees, or Ryce, of Cary Castle, in Pembrokeshire, and grand-daughter of Sir Rees ap Thomas, knight of the Garter, so created by Henry VII. by Catharine, daughter of Thomas Howard, second Duke of Norfolk, by whom he had several children; he was succeeded by his son,

4, Sir Henry Bayntun, who was succeeded by his eldest son,

5, Sir Edward, K. B. who married Elizabeth, daughter of Sir Henry Maynard, of Easton, in Essex, by whom he had issue,

6, —— Bayntun, K. B. his eldest son, was engaged very early in those troubles which then distracted the kingdom. He was commissioner of parliament, residing in the Scotch army, and seems to have taken a very active part in those times, and to have had the confidence of the presbyterian party. At the restoration, he was made knight of the Bath, and was also a member of the Long Parliament. He married Stuarta Thynne, eldest sister of Thomas Thynne, of Long Seat, Esq. by whom he had two sons, Henry, and Thomas, and several other children. Thomas was the father of Rachael, mother of the late Duke of Kingston.

7, Henry Bayntun was contracted, during his infancy, to Lady Sophia Osburne, daughter of the lord-treasurer Danby; but his father dying while he was on his travels, this marriage never took effect. Upon his return to England, he married Anne, eldest daughter of John, and sister and coheiress of Charles Wilmot, Earl of Rochester, (her mother was the heiress of the ancient and noble family of the Mallets, one of whom was a subscribing baron to the Magna Charta), by whom he had one son, John, and one daughter, Anne. Lady Bayntun, after the decease of the said Henry, intermarried with Francis Greville, Esq. and was mother of the late William, Lord Brooke, of Warwick Castle, father of Francis, Earl Brooke, Earl of Warwick. Anne was wife of Edward Rolt, of Sacombe Park, in the county of Hereford, Esq. aforesaid, by whom she had two sons; 1, Thomas, who died Dec. 1776; and 2, Edward, of whom hereafter.

John Bayntun, Esq. son of Henry and Anne Wilmot, was of Spye Park, and died in 1717, without issue, leaving his estate to his nephew, Edward-Bayntun Rolt, second son of Edward Rolt, of Sacombe Park, in the county of Hereford, Esq. whom he made his heir, directing him to take the name and arms of Bayntun.

I. EDWARD-BAYNTUN ROLT, Esq. second son of Edward Rolt, of Sacombe Park, in the county of Hertford aforesaid, by the aforesaid Anne, was chosen member of parliament for Chippenham in 1737, which he represented several years. In 1746, he was made groom of the bed-chamber to the late Prince of Wales; and, in 1751, he was, upon the death of Lord Baltimore, made surveyor of the duchy of Cornwall; and July 9, created a Baronet; in 1783, surveyor-general; and, in 1787, he was one of the honourable council to his Royal Highness the Prince of Wales. He married Mrs. Mary Poynter, of Herriard, in Hampshire, by whom he had issue, 1, Constantia, wife, in 1779, of Andrew Stone, Esq.; 2, Sir Andrew; 3, Elizabeth, wife, Feb. 7, 1773, of Richard Foster, Esq. Sir Edward died Jan. 1800, aged 90, and was succeeded by his son,

II. Sir ANDREW BAYNTUN-ROLT, Bart. who married, June 25, 1777, Mary-Alicia, eldest surviving daughter of the Earl of Coventry, by whom he has issue, ——, wife of the Rev. J. Starkey, of Eveleigh.

ARMS—Sable, a bend, lozengy, argent.

CREST—A griffin's head erased, sable, beaked, or, being the arms and crest of the Bayntun family.

SEAT—At Spye Park, near Colne, in the county of Wilts.

TABLE.

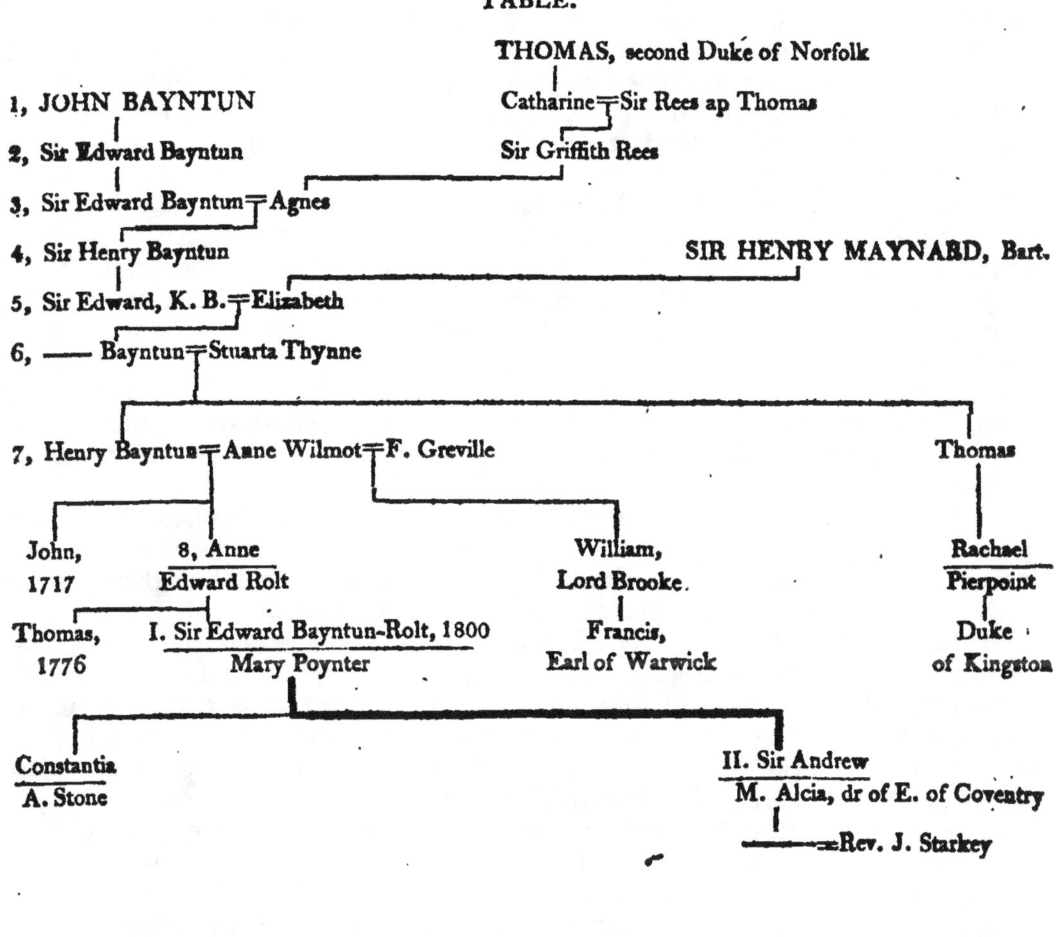

275. PAUL, of Rodborough, Gloucestershire.

Created Baronet, Sept. 3, 1762.

THE REV. ONESIPHORUS PAUL, of Warnborough, in the county of Wilts, had two sons, Nicholas, and George, who died unmarried; and one daughter Elizabeth, wife of the Rev. Thomas Prance, of Easingwood, in the county of York.

1, Nicholas Paul, the eldest son, married Elizabeth, daughter of Thomas Dean, of Woodchester, in the county of Gloucester, by whom he had two sons; 1, Dean Paul, of Stroud, in the said county, who married first, Elizabeth, daughter of John Andrews, of Stonehouse, in the same county, who died Aug. 4, 1741, without issue: he married seondly, Anne-Gastrell, daughter of John Selfe, of Cirencester, in the same county, who died Sept. 7, 1746, leaving one son; he married thirdly, Margaret, daughter of Philip Hampton, of Westbury, in the same county, who died Mar. 11, 1764, without issue.

By Anne, his second wife, he had issue, John Paul, M. D. who married Frances, youngest daughter of Robert Snow, of Hendon, in the county of Middlesex, and of London, banker, (by Valentine, daughter of George Paul, LL.D. vicar-general and king's advocate in the Commons), by whom he had issue, 1, John-Dean Paul, of London, banker; and 2, Robert, a captain in the royal navy. John-Dean married Frances-Eleanor Simpson, youngest daughter of John Simpson, of Bradley, in the bishopric of Durham, by the Right Honourable Lady Lyon, daughter of the Earl of Strathmore, by whom he hath issue, Anne-Frances, and John-Dean. Dean Paul died March 11, 1764, and, together with his three wives above-mentioned, lie buried at Woodchester.

I. ONESIPHORUS, second son of Nicholas, resided at Woodchester, where he was extensively engaged in the manufacture of the fine woollen cloths, for which that neighbourhood is distinguished, and which owe much of their present unrivalled excellence to his ingenious and spirited improvements.

In the month of August, 1750, he had the honour to receive and entertain at his house, his late Royal Highness Frederick, Prince of Wales. In 1760, he was high-sheriff of the county of Gloucester; and, on presenting an address from the said county to his present Majesty, on his accession to the throne of these realms, he received the honour of knighthood. In the second year of his present Majesty's reign, he was advanced to the dignity of a Baronet of Great Britain, by patent, bearing date Sept. 3, 1762, to him and his heirs male. He married first, Jane, daughter of Francis Blackburn, of Richmond, in the county of York, by Alice, his wife, daughter of Thomas Comber, D. D. and dean of Durham, and of Alice, daughter of William Thornton, of East Newton, in the same county, by Alice, his wife, daughter of the Right Honourable Christopher Wandesford, lord-deputy of Ireland, and sister to the Rev. Francis Blackburn, rector of Richmond, archdeacon of Cleveland, and author of the Confessional, and many other polemical works. This lady died May 26, 1748, and was buried at Woodchester, and by her he had one son and two daughters, of whom hereafter.

He married secondly, Catharine, daughter and coheiress of Francis Freeman, of Norton Male-reward, in the county of Somerset, by whom he had one son Francis, who died an infant; she died Oct. 20, 1766, without surviving issue, and was also buried at Woodchester.

He married thirdly, Sarah, daughter of John Peach, of Woodchester, and widow of John Turner, of Kingstanley, in the same county. This lady died April, 1801, and was buried at Little Ilford, in Essex.

By Jane, his first wife, he had one son, George-Onesiphorus, the present Baronet, and two daughters, Jane, wife of Thomas Pettat, of Stanley Park, in Gloucestershire, now living, and without issue; and Elizabeth, wife of George Snow, of Langbourne, in Dorsetshire, eldest son and heir of Robert Snow, of Hendon afore-mentioned; she died Jan. 7, 1772, and was buried at Woodchester, leaving one son and two daughters; 1, Robert Snow, major in the Royal Westminster regiment of Middlesex militia; 2, Jane, wife of Colonel James Clitherow, of Boston-House, in the county of Middlssex, by Anne, daughter and coheiress of Reginald Kemeye, of Bertholby, in Monmouthshire; and 3, Valentinia, who died an infant. Sir Onesiphorus died at his seat at Rodborough, in Gloucestershire, Sept. 21, 1774, aged 69, and was buried at Woodchester. He was succeeded by his only son,

II. Sir GEORGE-ONESIPHORUS PAUL, the present Baronet, who was high-sheriff for Gloucestershire in the year 1780, and is now a bachelor.

ARMS—Argent, on a fess, azure, three cross crosslets, or, in base, three ermine spots.

CREST—A leopard's head, proper, erased, per fess, gules.

MOTTO—*Pro rege et republica.*

SEAT—At Rodborough, in Gloucestershire.

TABLE.

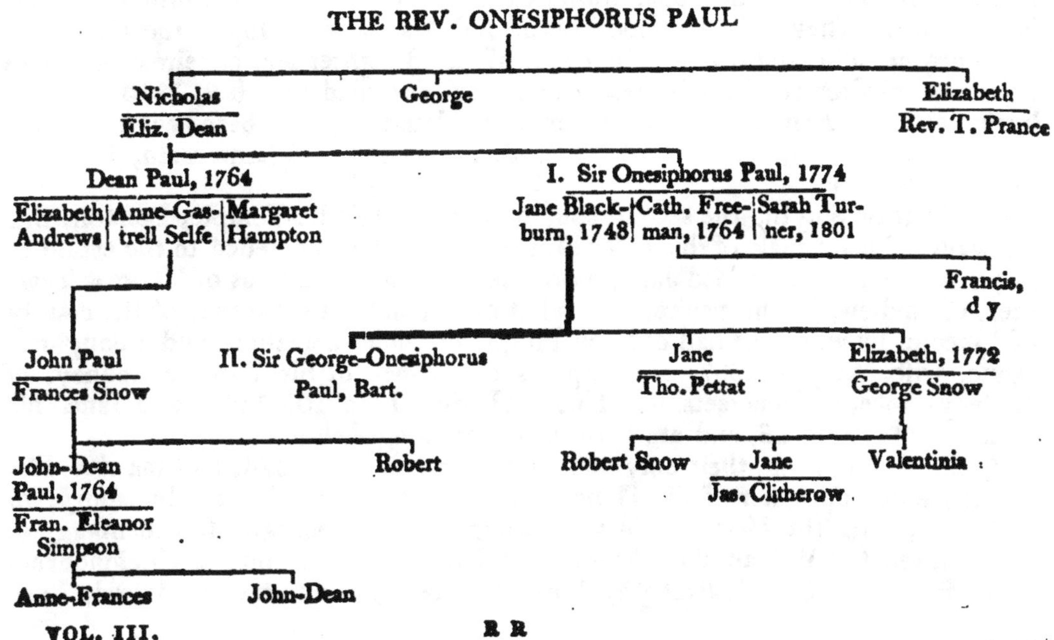

276. SMYTH, of Long Ashton, Somersetshire.

Created Baronet, Jan. 27, 1763.

THIS family was a long time seated at Ayleberton, near Lidney, in the forest of Dean, in the county of Gloucester.

1, John Smyth lived there in the year 1422, 1 Hen. VI. and had one son,

2, Robert Smyth, of the same place, living in 1440, 18 Hen. VI. and had one son,

3, John Smyth, who was living in 1449, 27 Hen. VI. whose son,

4, Matthew Smyth, married Alice, daughter of Charles Havard, of Herefordshire, by whom he had John Smyth, of whom hereafter, and ——, a daughter, wife of Thomas Phelipps, of Montague, or Montacute, in the county of Somerset, son of Richard Phelipps, of Charborough, in Dorsetshire, Esq. He died 1526, and was buried in the church of the White Friars, in the city of Bristol; Alice, his widow, died April 16, 1546, and was buried in the vault under St. Leonard's Church, in the same city.

5, John Smyth, his only son, was the first of the family who was seated at Long Ashton, which manor he purchased in 1547. He served the office of one of the sheriffs of the city of Bristol in 1532, and that of mayor in 1554. He married Joan, daughter of John Parr, Esq. and died Sept. 1, 1555, and she in 1559, and both lie buried at the upper end of the north aisle, in St. Werburg's Church, in that city. They had two sons, Hugh, and Matthew. Hugh, the elder son, was born in 1530, and married, in 1553, Maud, daughter and coheiress of Hugh Byckham, of Crowcomb, in Somersetshire, Esq. and died March 2, 1580, and was buried at Long Ashton. They had only one daughter, Elizabeth, wife, in 1573, of Edward Morgan, Esq. son of Sir William Morgan, of Lanternam, in Monmouthshire, Knt.

6, Matthew Smyth, the second son, was of the Middle-Temple, London, till, for want of heirs male of his elder brother Hugh, he succeeded to the estate at Long Ashton. He married Jane, eldest daughter and coheiress of Thomas Tewther, of Ludlow, in Shropshire, and relict of Bartholomew Skerne, of the county of Lincoln, by whom he had one son Hugh, of whom hereafter, and a daughter, Anne, wife, Aug. 2, 1587, of George, son and heir of Sir Maurice Rodney, of Rodney-Stoke, in Somersetshire, Knt. He died June 10, 1583, and Jane, his widow, 1594, aged 56, and are both buried at Long Ashton.

7, Sir Hugh Smith, their only son, was born Nov. 17, 1574, and married Elizabeth, eldest daughter of Sir Thomas Gorges, of Langford, near Salisbury, in Wiltshire, Knt. (by Helena, his wife, daughter of Wasangus Snachenberg, of Sweden, relict of William Parr, Marquis of Northampton: she was chief mourner at the funeral of Queen Elizabeth, April 28, 1603), and sister to Edward, Lord

Gorges, Baron of Dundalk, in the kingdom of Ireland, by whom he had one son Thomas, of whom hereafter, and two daughters, Mary, wife, in 1616, of Sir Thomas Smith, of Haugh, in Cheshire, Knt.; and Helena, in 1615, of Sir Francis Rogers, of Cannington, in Somersetshire, Knt; she died 1637; Sir Hugh died 1627, and was buried at Long Ashton. Dame Elizabeth, after his death, was the wife of Sir Ferdinand George, of Wrexall, in Somersetshire, Knt. who died in May, 1647; and Dame Elizabeth in 1658, and was buried at Long Ashton between her husbands.

8, Thomas Smyth, the son of Sir Hugh, was born Jan. 1609, and elected one of the representatives in parliament for the town of Bridgewater, Feb. 28, 1627; he was also chosen one of the knights of the shire for the county of Somerset, with Sir Ralph Hopton, March 30, 1640, and was, Feb. 5, 1640-1, a second time elected for the town of Bridgewater in the room of Edward Wyndham, Esq. Upon the breaking out of the civil war in 1542, he engaged himself in the royal cause, and was at Sherbourne, in Dorsetshire, with the Marquis of Hertford, and went from thence with him into Wales, where he died at the town of Cardiff, Oct. 2, 1642, and was buried at Long Ashton. He married, April 12, 1627, Florence, daughter of John, Lord Poulet, of Hinton St. George, in the county of Somerset, (by Elizabeth, his wife, daughter and coheiress of Christopher Kenn, of Kenn-Court, in the same county, Esq.) by whom he had one son Hugh, of whom hereafter, and four daughters; 1, Florence, wife, in 1653, of Sir Humphrey Hook, of King's Weston, in Gloucestershire, Knt.; 2, Mary, died unmarried, in 1660; 3, Helena, wife, in 1670, of Roger Bourne, of Gothelney, in Somersetshire, Esq.; 4, Anne, in 1670, of Sir John Knight, of Bristol, Knt. The said Florence, after the death of Thomas Smith, became the wife, in 1648, of Thomas Pigot, of Ireland, Esq. who purchased the manor of Brockley, in Somersetshire, where their descendants now reside: she died in November, 1677, and was buried at Long Ashton.

I. Hugh Smyth, only son of Thomas aforesaid, was born April 21, 1632; April 18, 1660, was created knight of the Bath; and, in the same year, was elected knight of the shire for the county of Somerset, with George Horner, Esq.; on the 16th of May, 1661, was advanced to the dignity of a Baronet of England; and, in the year 1678, was again elected knight of the shire for the same county. He married Anne (Collins says Elizabeth), second daughter of the Honourable John Ashburnham, of Ashburnham, in Sussex, Esq. groom of the bedchamber to Charles I. and II. by his first wife, Frances, daughter and heiress of William Holland, of West Burton, in the county of Sussex, Esq. by whom he had three sons; 1, Sir John Smyth, Bart. of whom hereafter; 2, Hugh, born 1662, died unmarried, and was buried at Long Ashton, Sept. 26, 1681; 3, Charles, born Oct. 1663, died unmarried at Smyrna, June, 1717: and three daughters; 1, Elizabeth, born 1655, wife of Richard Gernoen, Esq.: she died at Dublin, Dec. 26, 1717, without issue; 2, Florence, born 1657, died unmarried in 1682, at Long Ashton, and buried there; 3, Anne, born 1664, died 1665, and buried at Long Ashton. Sri Hugh died July 28, 1680, and lies buried at Long Ashton; Dame Anne, his wife, surviving him, was secondly, Oct. 10, 1681, the wife of Colonel John Ramsey, who died Oct. 10, 1689, and was buried at Long Ashton. Dame Anne died June 26, 1697, and was buried between her husbands.

II. Sir John Smyth, was born Dec. 13, 1659, was elected knight of the shire for the county of Somerset, with George Horner, Esq. March 30, 1685, and again in 1695. He married, at Henbury, in Gloucestershire, Aug. 11, 1692, Elizabeth, the eldest of the four daughters and coheiresses of Sir Samuel Astry, of Henbury aforesaid, Knt. clerk of the crown in chancery, descended from the ancient family of the Astry's, of Woodend, in Bedfordshire: she died Sept. 15, 1715, aged 46, and he, May 19, 1726, and are both buried at Long Ashton. They had three sons; 1, Sir John, of whom hereafter; 2, Hugh, born March 6, 1706, who died unmarried, Aug. 26, 1735, and was buried, the 29th following, at Long Ashton; 3, Samuel, born 1708, died at Taunton, Dec. 2, 1719, and was buried there the 4th following. Sir John had likewise five daughters; 1, Anne, coheiress to her brother, born Oct. 24, 1693, died unmarried, Dec. 21, 1760, and was buried at Henbury aforesaid; 2, Elizabeth, died unmarried, and was buried at Weston, near Bath, in Somersetshire; 3, Astrea, born Jan. 15, 1698, wife of Thomas Coster, Esq. representative in two parliaments for the city of Bristol: she died without issue, and lies buried, with her husband, in the north aisle of the cathedral church in that city; 4, Florence, the second surviving sister and coheiress to her brother Sir John, of whom hereafter; 5, Arabella, the third surviving sister and coheiress to her brother Sir John, was born March 2, 1703, wife of Edward Gore, of Flax-Bourton, in the county of Somerset, Esq. (by whom she had two sons, John Gore, of Barrow Court, in the same county, Esq.: and Edward Gore, Esq. who married Barbara, daughter and heiress of Sir George Brown, of the county of Oxon, Bart. and relict of Sir Pyers Mostyn): she died Oct. 27, 1748, aged 44, and was buried at Barrow aforesaid.

III. Sir John Smyth, the eldest son, was born July 24, 1699, and married Anne, daughter of Mr. Pym, of Oxford; she died Sept. 1733, and he, July 18, 1741, without issue, and are both buried at Long Ashton, whereby the title became extinct, and the estate descended to his three surviving sisters, Anne, Florence, and Arabella.

Florence, the fourth daughter of Sir John, and sister and coheiress of the last Sir John, was born Aug. 2, 1701, was wife, first, Feb. 15, 1727, of John Pigot, of Brockley aforesaid, Esq. who died without issue, April 30, 1730. She was, secondly, the wife of,

I. JARRIT SMYTH, of the city of Bristol, Esq. only son of John Smyth, of the same city, Esq. who was elected one of the representatives in parliament for the city of Bristol, March 17, 1756, in the room of Richard Beckford, Esq. again in 1761, and was advanced to the dignity of a Baronet of Great Britain, Jan. 27, 1763, to him and his heirs male, by Florence, his wife, who died Sept. 10, 1767, and was buried at Henbury the 17th following, by whom he had two sons; 1, John-Hugh; 2, Thomas, who married, Aug. 11, 1767, Jane, only daughter of Joseph Whitchurch, of Stapleton, in Gloucestershire, Esq. by whom he had

TABLE.

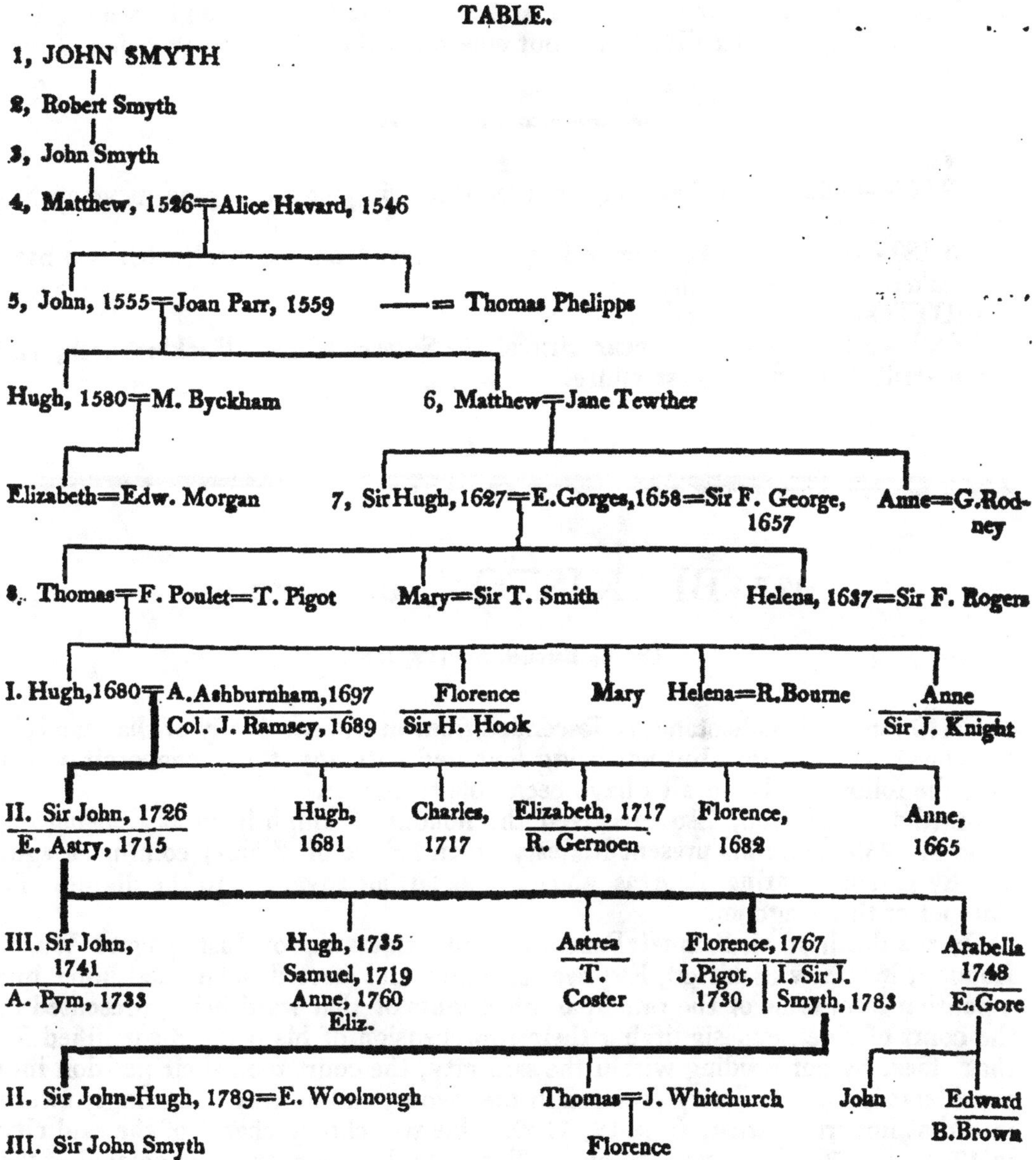
1, JOHN SMYTH
2, Robert Smyth
3, John Smyth
4, Matthew, 1526=Alice Havard, 1546
5, John, 1555=Joan Parr, 1559
——= Thomas Phelipps
Hugh, 1580=M. Byckham
6, Matthew=Jane Tewther
Elizabeth=Edw. Morgan
7, Sir Hugh, 1627=E.Gorges,1658=Sir F. George, 1657
Anne=G.Rodney
8, Thomas=F. Poulet=T. Pigot
Mary=Sir T. Smith
Helena, 1637=Sir F. Rogers
I. Hugh,1680=A.Ashburnham,1697
Col. J. Ramsey, 1689
Florence
Sir H. Hook
Mary
Helena=R.Bourne
Anne
Sir J. Knight
II. Sir John, 1726
E. Astry, 1715
Hugh, 1681
Charles, 1717
Elizabeth, 1717
R. Gernoen
Florence, 1682
Anne, 1665
III. Sir John, 1741
A. Pym, 1733
Hugh, 1735
Samuel, 1719
Anne, 1760
Eliz.
Astrea
T. Coster
Florence, 1767
J.Pigot, 1730
I. Sir J. Smyth, 1783
Arabella 1748
E.Gore
II. Sir John-Hugh, 1789=E. Woolnough
Thomas=J. Whitchurch
John
Edward
B.Brown
III. Sir John Smyth
Florence

one daughter Florence, born May 27, 1769. Sir Jarrit Smyth died Jan. 25, 1783, having almost attained his 92d year, and was succeeded by his eldest son,

II. Sir JOHN-HUGH SMYTH, Bart. who married, Sept. 1, 1757, Elizabeth, only daughter and heiress of Henry Woolnough, of Pucklechurch, in Gloucestershire, Esq. He died June 15, 1789, and was succeeded, as I am informed, by

III. Sir JOHN SMYTH, Bart. but whether son or nephew, or either, I cannot learn.

ARMS—Gules, on a cheveron, between three cinquefoils, argent, as many leopards' faces, sable.

CREST—A griffin's head erased, gules, charged on the neck with two bars, or, beaked and eared, of the last.

MOTTO—*Qui capit capitur.*

SEAT—At Long Ashton, near Bristol, in Somersetshire; Pucklechurch, and Maize-Hill, both in Gloucestershire.

277. BLAKISTON, of London.

Created Baronet, April 22, 1763.

THIS family, I understand, is descended from an ancient family of that name, in the county of Durham; but not being favoured with any thing concerning it, I give the following, being all I have been able to collect.

Matthew Blakiston, Esq. received the honour of knighthood at Kensington, June 8, 1759, upon his present Majesty (then Prince of Wales) coming of age; and by patent, bearing date as above, was farther advanced to the dignity of a Baronet of this kingdom.

On the death of Sir Samuel Pennant, Knt. alderman of Bishopsgate Ward, London, Matthew Blakiston, Esq. was proposed and elected to succeed him; but a petition from some of the principal inhabitants of that ward being presented to the court of aldermen, signifying their apprehension of his being disqualified for that office, by not residing within the said city, the court took their petition into consideration: the majority declared in his favour, and he was accordingly sworn into that important trust, June 12, 1750. He was chosen sheriff of the said city in 1753; in 1760, he served the high office of lord-mayor, and was colonel of the green regiment of the militia in the city of London.

Sir Matthew married first, ——, who died Jan. 8, 1754, by whom he had one son Matthew, who died Sept. 7, 1758, unmarried. April 8, 1760, Sir Matthew married secondly, Annabella Baillie, by whom he had one son Matthew. Sir Matthew died July 14, aged 72, and his lady, Aug. 25, 1776, became the wife of Hugh Cane, Esq. lieutenant-colonel of the fifth regiment of dragoon guards. Sir Matthew was succeeded by his only son,

II. Sir MATTHEW BLAKISTON, Bart. who, in Sept. 1782, married ——, daughter of John Rochford, Esq.

ARMS—Argent, two bars, gules, in chief, three cocks of the last.
CREST—A cock, gules.

TABLE.

278. HORTON, of CHADERTON, Lancashire.

Created Baronet, Jan. 14, 1764.

1, WILLIAM HORTON married Elizabeth, daughter of Thomas Hanson, of Tooth-hill, in the parish of Halifax, (her will was dated July 16, 1660), by whom he had three sons, William, Joshua, and Thomas; and two daughters, Sarah, wife of John Geldhill, of Bark-Island, and Elizabeth. He was succeeded by his eldest son,

William Horton, who was of Firth-House, in Bark-Island. He bought Howroyd, in Bark-Island, 15 Car. I. which he made the place of his residence: his will is dated 1655. He married Elizabeth (whose will is dated July 13, 1670), daughter of Thomas Geldhill, of Bark-Island, by whom he had two sons and three daughters; 1, Thomas, of Bark-Island Hall, born about 1651 (whose will is dated Dec. 20, 1698); he died on the 2d of January following, and was buried at Eland. He married Elverida, daughter of John Thornhill, Esq. by whom he had three daughters; 1, Elizabeth, wife of Richard Bold, of Bold, in Lancashire, Esq.; 2,

Susanna, of Richard Beaumont, of Whitley, in Yorkshire, Esq.; 3, Anne, died without issue. William, the second son, of Howroyd, died Feb. 19, 1715-16; he married Mary, fourth daughter of Sir Richard Musgrave, of Hayton-Castle, in Cumberland, Bart. by whom he had William, of Coley, in Halifax parish, who was a justice of the peace, and died in 1739-40. By Mary, his wife, daughter of —— Chester, Esq. he had one daughter Mary, living in 1766: the other son was Richard, who died S. P. The three daughters of the above William were, 1, Elizabeth, wife of William Batte, of Okewell, in Yorkshire, Esq.; 2, Sarah, of Alexander Butterworth, of Belfield, in Lancashire, Esq.; and 3, Judith, who died unmarried.

Thomas Horton, third son of the first-mentioned William Horton, was a merchant of Liverpool, and died March 30, 1660. He married Frances, eldest daughter of Thomas Throppe, of Chester, alderman and justice of the peace, but it does not appear by the pedigree that he had any issue.

2, Joshua Horton, Esq. second son of the first William, was born in 1619; he was a justice of the peace, and died of the stone, at Sowerby, April 7, 1679, and was buried there. He purchased the manor of Horton, near Bradford, in Yorkshire; and by Martha, his wife, daughter and coheiress of Thomas Binns, of Rushworth, in the parish of Bingley, Esq. who died July 23, 1694, and was buried at Sowerby, he had four sons and three daughters; 1, Joshua, died an infant; 2, Joshua, of whom hereafter; 3, Elkana, of Thornton, in Yorkshire, born Aug. 31, 1659, and died without issue at Sowerby, where he was buried, Jan. 28, 1728-9, having been a counsellor-at-law; 4, Thomas, who was a doctor of physic, born Nov. 26, 1660, died in London, March 4, 1694, and was buried in St. Thomas's Church, Southwark. He married ——, daughter of —— Watmough, of London, M. D. The daughters were, 1, Sarah, born June 22, 1654, who died Sept. 4, 1670; 2, Martha, born April 30, 1656, wife of John Gill, of Carr-House, near Rotherham, in Yorkshire, Esq.; 3, Elizabeth, died young.

3, Joshua Horton, Esq. second son of the above Joshua Horton, and grandson of the first William Horton, was born Jan. 2, 1657, and dying Dec. 15, 1708, was buried in his chapel in Oldham Church. He purchased Chaderton, which he made his residence, and which is now the seat of the present Baronet. He married, Feb. 27, 1678, Mary, daughter of Robert Gregg, of Bradley, or Harpsford, in Cheshire, by whom he had seven sons and five daughters; 1, Thomas, who died young; 2, Thomas, of whom hereafter; 3, William, baptized Oct. 12, 1686; 4, William, baptized Sept. 27, 1692; 5, Joseph, baptized March 8, 1693; 6, James, baptized April 18, 1695, who died unmarried; 7, Joshua, born Feb. 1, 1697, who died young. The daughters were, 1, Martha, wife, Nov. 30, 1697, of Richard Clayton, of Adlington, in Lancashire, Esq.; 2, Jane, of John Parr, of Liverpool, merchant; 3, Elizabeth, of William Williamson, of Liverpool, merchant; 4, Mary, baptized Feb. 4, 1690, and died without issue; and 5, Mary, baptized Aug. 13, 1696.

4, Thomas Horton, Esq. second son of Joshua, was of Chaderton, born May 4, 1685; he was governor of the Isle of Man, and justice of the peace for Lancashire. He married Anne, daughter and coheiress of Richard Mostyn, of London, merchant (a younger branch of the Mostyns, of Mostyn, in Wales, Bart. who died at Chaderton, June 17, 1725, in the 39th year of her age, and was buried at Oldham), by whom he had three sons and five daughters; the daughters were, Susanna, married to George Lloyd, of Holme, near Manchester, Esq. by whom she had Gamaliel Lloyd, of Hampstead, Esq. Sarah, Jane, Anne, and Mary; 1, Sir William, of whom hereafter; 2, Thomas, who died young, at Castletown, in the Isle of Man, June 20, 1726; 3, Joshua, of Howroyd, baptized June 1, 1720, and married first, Anne, daughter of George Clarke, Esq. governor of New York, who died without issue, May 25, 1764, and was buried at Oldham, in Lancashire; he married secondly, Oct. 20, 1765, Mary Bathier, daughter of the Rev. John Woolin, rector of Emley, in Yorkshire, and vicar of Blackbourn, in Lancashire. Thomas Horton died March 18, 1757, at Manchester, was buried at Oldham, and was succeeded in his estates by his eldest son,

I. Sir WILLIAM HORTON, Bart. created to that dignity Jan. 14, 1764, being at that time high-sheriff for the county of Lancaster, and was one of his Majesty's justices of the peace for the said county. Sir William married

TABLE.

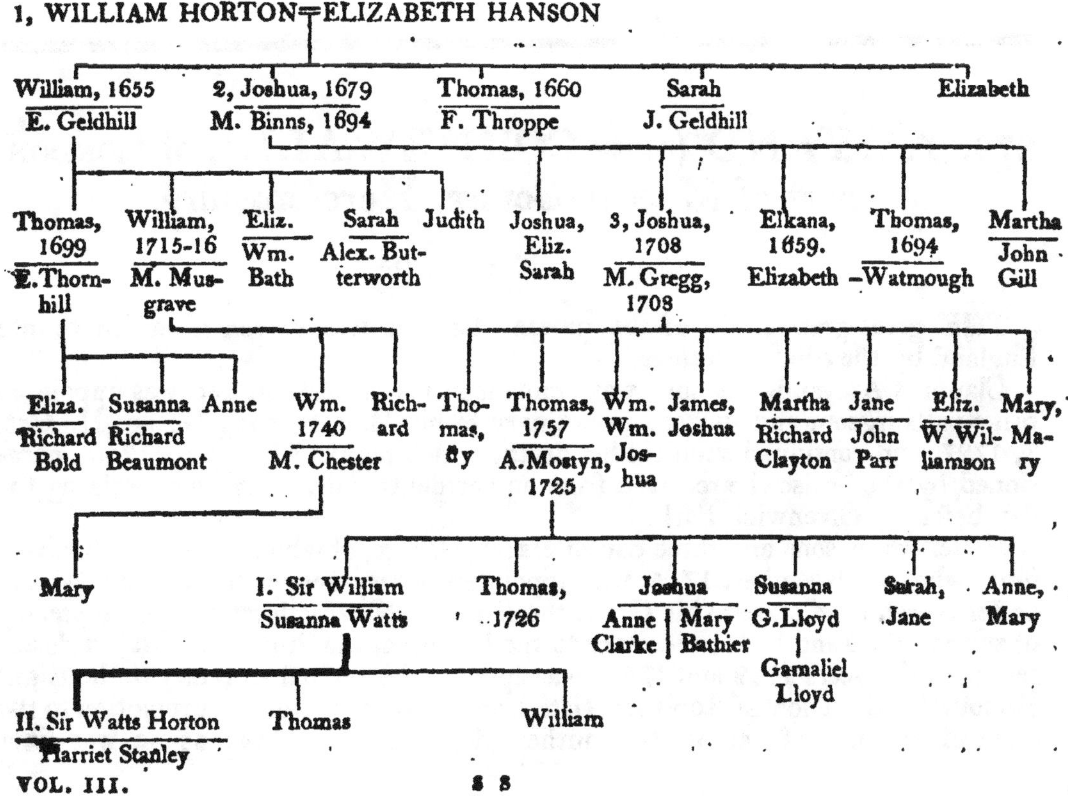

Susanna, daughter and heiress of Francis Watts, of Barnes-Hall, in Yorkshire, Esq. by whom he had three sons; 1, Sir Watts, of whom hereafter; 2, Thomas, born July 21, 1758, who married —— Stanley, eldest daughter of the late Lord Strange, and sister to the Earl of Derby; 3, William, born Oct. 21, 1767. Sir William died Feb. 25, 1774, and was succeeded by his eldest son,

II. Sir WATTS HORTON, Bart. who was born Nov. 17, 1753, and married, June 3, 1778, Harriet, sister to the Earl of Derby, by whom he has issue.

ARMS—First and fourth, gules, a lion rampant, argent, charged on the breast, with a boar's head, couped, azure, all within a bordure, engrailed, argent. Second and third, per bend, sinister, ermine and sable, a lion rampant, argent.

CREST—On a wreath, a red rose, seeded and barbed, proper, surrounded with two laurel branches, proper.

SEAT—At Chaderton, in the county of Lancaster.

The account of this family is taken from a pedigree in the Herald's College, and registered in 5th D. 14, fo. 237, certified by Ralph Bigland and Isaac Heard, Esqrs. Somerset and Lancaster heralds.

279. AMYAND (now CORNEWALL), of LONDON, now of MOCCAS-COURT, Herefordshire.

Created Baronet, Aug. 4, 1764.

THE great-grandfather of the present Baronet was driven from France into England by the edict of Nantes.

Claudius Amyand, his son, was eminent in his profession, and was appointed principal surgeon, and surgeon in ordinary to his Majesty King George II. Oct. 7, 1727, and continued such till his death, which happened July 6, 1740, occasioned by the bruises he received from an accidental fall, as he was walking the day before in Greenwich Park.

He left three sons and three daughters; 1, George, of whom hereafter; 2, Claudius, who, in December, 1745, was appointed library-keeper to his Majesty, and under secretary of state to his Grace the Duke of Newcastle, principal secretary of state in 1750 and 1751; secretary to the lords justices during his Majesty's absence, in the years 1752 and 1755; was appointed principal secretary to the Right Honourable Sir Thomas Robinson (late Lord Grantham), on his promotion to the office of secretary of state for the southern department in 1754; as he was likewise to his successor, the Right Honourable Henry Fox (afterwards Lord Holland), in Nov. 1755. He was further promoted to be one of the commissioners of the customs, in Dec. 1756; and, upon a new commission being made, Mar. 24, 1761, was named therein; and in Feb. 1765, was appointed receiver-general of the land-tax for London and Westminster. He was elected representative for Tregony, in Cornwall, in the tenth parliament, and for Sandwich, in Kent, in the eleventh parliament. He married, in Dec. 1761, Frances, daughter of the Rev. —— Payne, relict of George Compton, Earl of Northampton, and died 1774, without issue, and was buried at Langleybury, in Hertfordshire.

Thomas, the third son of Claudius, was rector of the parishes of Hambledon, in the county of Bucks, and Fanley, in the county of Oxford. He married Frances, daughter of Thomas Ryder, Esq. one of the directors of the East India Company, by whom he had one son and two daughters.

The daughters of Claudius Amyand were, 1, Anne, wife of John Porter, Esq. alderman of the city of London, and member of parliament for Evesham, in Worcestershire: she died without issue; 2, Mary, of Sir Richard Adams, Knt. one of the barons of the Court of Exchequer: she also died without issue; and 3, Judith, of the Rev. Dr. Thomas Ashton, fellow of Eton College, and rector of St. Botolph, Bishopsgate, now alive, with issue.

I. GEORGE AMYAND, Esq. the eldest son, an eminent merchant, was member in several parliaments for Barnstaple; was chosen one of the assistants of the Russia Company, in March, 1756, and a director of the East India Company in 1762; and was advanced to the dignity of a Baronet, Aug. 4, 1764. He married Maria, daughter of John Abraham Kerton, or Korton, an eminent Hamburgh merchant, by whom he had two sons; 1, Sir George, of whom hereafter; and 2, John, born Nov. 6, 1751, succeeded his father in his business as a merchant, was member of parliament for Camelford, died in 1780, and was buried at Carshalton, in Surry, in the same vault with his father and mother. Sir George had likewise two daughters; 1, Anna-Maria, wife, in 1777, of Gilbert, now Sir Gilbert Elliot, Bart. late viceroy of Corsica, and has issue; 2, Harriet, in 1777, of James Harris, Esq. now Lord Malmesbury, formerly envoy extraordinary to Berlin and Petersburgh, and ambassador to the Hague, &c. &c. and has issue. Sir George died in 1766, and his lady in 1767.

II. Sir GEORGE AMYAND, Bart. succeeded his father in title and name, and on his marriage with Catharine, daughter and heiress of Velters Cornewall*, of Moccas-Court, Herefordshire, many years member for the county, took his name and arms in 1771. Sir George was elected for the county in 1774, which he represented till 1796. By the said Catharine he has seven children; 1, Catharine-Frances, wife, March, 1796, of Samuel Peploe, Esq. son of John Peploe Birch, Esq. of Garnstone, in Herefordshire, born 1773; 2, George, born 1774;

* The family of Cornewall was formerly seated at Burford, in Shropshire, and were called Barons of Burford, afterwards at Berrington, in Herefordshire, which was sold by Charles Cornewall, late speaker of the House of Commons, to the Right Honourable Thomas Harley. One branch settled at Moccas-court, temp. Car. I. another, the present Bishop of Bristol, is settled at Diddlebury, in Shropshire.

3, Anna-Maria, born 1779; 4, Frances-Elizabeth, born 1783; 5, Charles, born 1785; 6, Harriet, born 1787; 7, Caroline, born 1789.

ARMS—Quarterly: 1st and 4th, argent, a lion rampant, gules, ducally crowned, or, within a bordure engrailed, sable, bezantée, for Cornewall; 2d and 3d, vert, a cheveron, between three garbs, or, for Amyand.

CRESTS—1st, a Cornish chough, proper; 2d, a demi-lion rampant, gules, ducally crowned, or.

MOTTO—*La vie durante.*

SEAT—At Carshalton, in the county of Surry, and Moccas-Court, in Herefordshire.

TABLE.

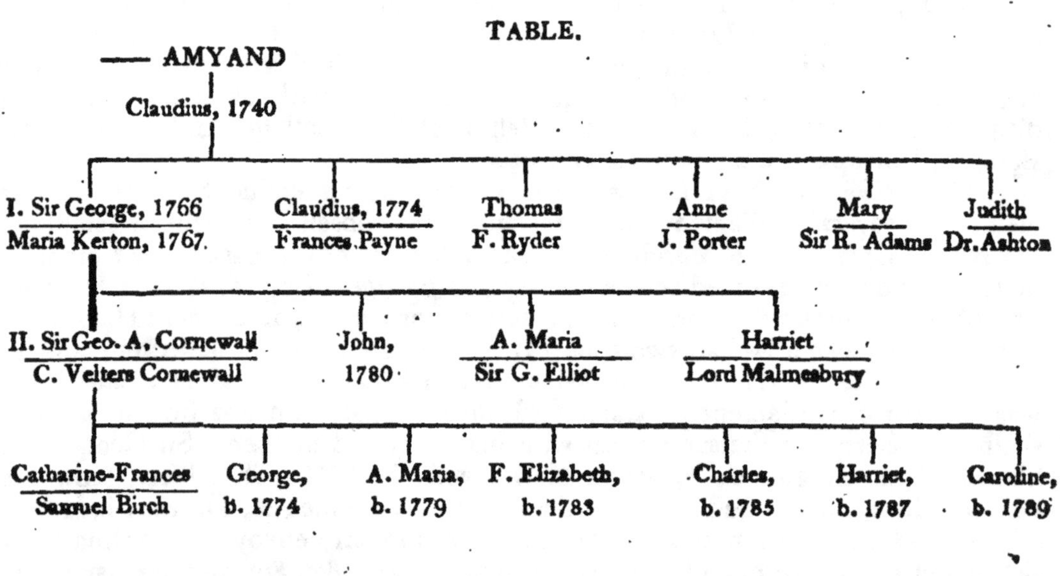

280. GORDON, of Newark-upon-Trent, Nottinghamshire.

Created Baronet, Aug. 21, 1764.

THE Gordons, of Newark-upon-Trent, in the county of Nottingham, are descended from William Gordon, of Chricklaw, youngest son of John Gordon, first Lord of Lochenvar, whose grandson was created Lord Kenmure by Charles the First.

Thomas Gordon, a cadet of that family, among many other young men of the first families in the west of Scotland, accompanied Sir Hugh Montgomery, of the family of Eglington, who being secretary for Scotland, and attending King James I. into England, was employed by that prince to levy a force in the west of Scotland, sufficient to attack the rebel Connor O'Neal, Earl of Tyrone, whom they besieged and took prisoner in Carrickfergus, and brought him over through Scotland into England.

From this Thomas, the first adventurer who settled in Ireland, descended Samuel Gordon, whose mother was Eleanor Magines, of the family of the Viscounts Evagh, of the kingdom of Ireland. He was bred up in physic, was high-sheriff for the county of Nottingham the first of George III. and married Elizabeth Bradford, niece and heiress of Sir Matthew Jenison, of Newark-upon-Trent, by whom he had one son, Sir Jenison-William, and three daughters, Catharine, Elizabeth, and Eleanor.

I. Sir SAMUEL, having first received the honour of knighthood, was, on the 21st of August, 1764, advanced to the dignity of a Baronet. He died in April, 1780, and was succeeded by his only son,

II. Sir JENISON-WILLIAM GORDON, Bart. who married, Oct. 1781, Harriet-Frances-Charlotte Finch, second daughter of the Honourable Edward-Finch Hatton, youngest son of Daniel, first Earl of Winchelsea and Nottingham, by whom he has no children.

ARMS—Quarterly: first and fourth, azure, three boar's heads erased, or, for Gordon; second and third, azure, a bend, or, between two swans, proper, for Jenison.

CREST—A demi-savage, proper, holding in his dexter hand a baton, argent, wreathed about the temples and waist.

SEAT—At Haverholm Priory, near Sleaford, Lincolnshire.

TABLE.

JOHN GORDON, L. of Lochenvar

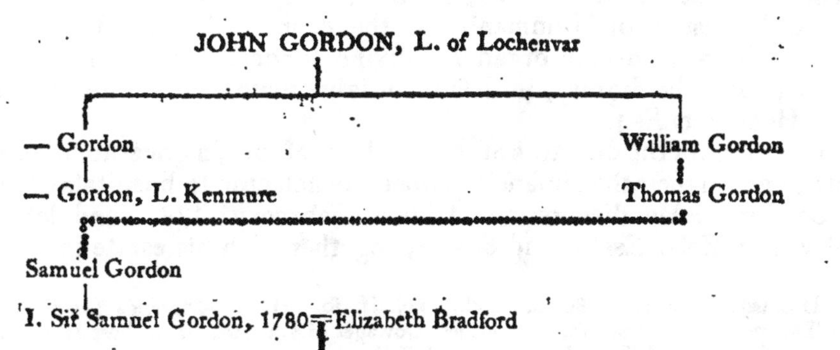

281. MAJOR, of WORLINGWORTH-HALL, Suffolk.

(With Remainder to his son-in-law, John Henniker, of Newton-Hall, Essex, Esq.)

Created Baronet, July 8, 1765.

1, WILLIAM MAJOR, descended from the family of Malgers, who came from Normandy with the Conqueror, and had many possessions in Yorkshire*, was a merchant at Bridlington, in that county.

2, John Major, his son, married Joanna, daughter of —— Peirson, by whom he had two sons, Samuel, who died at Nevis, in the West Indies, and John, of whom hereafter. This John Major died about 1690.

3, John the second son, married Elizabeth, daughter of Richard Tennant, rector of Carnaby and Boynton, in the county of York, who died 1717, and was buried at Bridlington, by whom he had one son,

I. JOHN MAJOR, late of Worlingworth-Hall and Thornham-Hall, both in the county of Suffolk, Esq. who was born at Bridlington on the 17th of May, 1698; and, on the 20th of June, 1723-4, married Elizabeth, the only daughter and heiress of Daniel Dale, of Bridlington aforesaid, merchant, who died at Thornham-Hall 1780, and was buried in Worlingworth chancel; and, in her right, succeeded to a freehold estate at Great Kelk, in that neighbourhood, now vested in their descendants, by whom he had two daughters; 1, Anne, wife of John Henniker, of Newton-Hall, in the county of Essex, Esq. of both whom hereafter; and 2, Elizabeth, wife, July 18, 1767, of Henry Brydges, Duke of Chandos, Marquis and Earl of Caernarvon, Baron Chandos, of Sudley, and Baronet, who died 1771, without issue †.

John Major was chosen an elder brother of the Trinity House of Deptford-Strond in the year 1741, and for forty years was exemplary, by his attention to the duty of that office, in promoting the safety of his own countrymen and others who navigated near our coasts. He served, in 1755, the office of high-sheriff for the county of Sussex, where he had, as his descendants have, a very considerable estate. In 1761, he was chosen representative in parliament for the borough of Scarborough, in his native county, being the first parliament held in the reign of our present most gracious sovereign. He received the honour of the freedom of that corporation in a gold box; and, in conjunction with his colleague, —— Osbaldeston, of Hummanby, in the county of York, Esq. presented their church with a handsome organ for divine service. In 1765, he was created a Baronet, and the dignity, in default of issue male, was limited to his son-in-law, John Henniker, Esq.

He was one of the directors of the South Sea House, a governor of Greenwich Hospital, and, in their then infancy, a liberal benefactor to hospitals of various natures in London. He died on the 16th of February, 1781, and left his extended realty in Suffolk, Essex, and Sussex, together with his estate in Yorkshire, to his

* Doomsday, Vol. I. fo. 86, a. tit. xli. Vol. II. fo. 321, b.—Morant's Essex, Vol. I. p. 390.

† The most noble Elizabeth, the Duchess Dowager of Chandos, is the hospitable and beneficent possessor of Thornham-Hall, in the county of Suffolk.

two daughters for life, and to their issue, which are at present enjoyed by her Grace the Duchess of Chandos, and the Hon. John-Henniker Major. Sir John Major was buried in the same vault with his deceased wife, and an handsome monument is erected over them in the chancel of Worlingworth Church. Another has also been erected to their memory in the parish church of East Grinstead, in the county of Sussex, by their grandson, the Hon. John-Henniker Major. Upon the decease of Sir John Major, the dignity of Baronet devolved, by the original patent, upon his son-in-law,

II. Sir JOHN HENNIKER, Bart.

It appears, from sundry deeds and evidence, that the family of Henniker, Heneker, or De Hanekin, has been of long continuance in Kent.

Peter de Hanekin, was lieutenant-governor of Dover Castle in 1313 *. John de Mari and Peter Hanekin, of Dover (supposed to be the same mentioned by Philipot), were sent to Great Yarmouth, to regulate the fair, 6 Edw. II. 1313 †.

Alanus de Henekin possessed the manor of Nash-Court, in the parish of Westwell, in Kent, temp. Rich. II. 1359 ‡; they afterwards, about the reign of Edward IV. wrote themselves Heneker, and resided in different parishes in the said county, where their estates lay, particularly Dover, Goodneston, Nonnington, Hythe, the Isle of Thanet, Charing, Lenham, and several others.

1, John Henneker, born in 1571, died at Lenham 1616, and buried under a monument in that church-yard, was ancestor of Charles Henniker, of Chatham, in the county of Kent: his second son,

2, John, was admitted to his freedom of Rochester by patrimony, Sept. 7, 1695, and was possessed of freehold lands in the Isle of Thanet, at Monkton, and in Rochester, of a leasehold estate, renewable for ever from the dean and chapter, and the brethren of St. Bartholomew's Hospital §; he died there, and lies buried in Chatham church-yard, where is his monument. His second son,

3, John Henniker, was baptized in Chatham, June 30, 1691, was admitted to the freedom of Rochester, Aug. 30, 1712, a Russia merchant, and the greatest importer in England of masts from Norway, Riga, and Petersburgh, for his Majesty's navy. He married Hannah, daughter of John Swanson, of London, descended from the family of that name in Yorkshire, who died in 1745: he died at Stratford-House, April 6, 1749, and was buried with his deceased wife under a monument in West Ham church-yard, Essex.

Sir JOHN HENNIKER, Bart. before-mentioned, his second son, of Strat-

* Philipot, Vill. Cantia, p. 13.

† For the maritime towns within this (the Cinque Ports) government are mentioned here. Othoma, &c. &c.

"Garionoaum, for Yarmouth, lying upon the Saxon shore, in Norfolk. And do not the barons of the ports enjoy a privilege upon the said coast, sending yearly two of their said barons, as their bailiffs, to join with them of Yarmouth, since they were incorporated in the administration of public justice during the free fishing fair, which thing they have been used to do before the town of Yarmouth was built. The fortress where the garrison appointed for the defence of this part of the Saxon shore was resident, is now called Burrough Castell, adjoining to the river of Yare (in Suffolk), as Mr. Camden has observed in the description of that place."—*Philipot*, p. 9.

‡ Rot. Esch. ejus Ann. M. 94.

§ All these estates are now in the possession of Lord Henniker.

ford-House and Newton-Hall, both in the county of Essex, Great Bealing Hall, in the county of Suffolk, and of St. Peter's, in the Isle of Thanet, in the county of Kent, was born June 15, 1724. He married, Feb. 24, 1747, Ann, eldest daughter and coheiress of Sir John Major aforesaid, who died July 18, 1792, by whom he had three sons and one daughter. He was high-sheriff for Essex in 1758; representative in parliament for the borough of Sudbury, in the county of Suffolk, in the first parliament of his present Majesty's reign, and of the town and port of Dover, in Kent, in two parliaments; he was made lieutenant and deputy warden of his Majesty's forest of Waltham in 1760, one of the deputy-lieutenants and magistrate for the county of Essex, and F. R. S.

He erected a battery, and mounted guns upon it, at Broad Stairs, Kent, in the beginning of the late war, and supplied watch clothing and a stand of arms for the defence of that part of the coast. In 1781, he succeeded his father-in-law in the dignity of Baronet; and, in 1800, he was created Lord Henniker, of Stratford-upon-Slaney, in the county of Wicklow, in the kingdom of Ireland.

John, his eldest son, born April 19, 1752, was bred at Eton school, admitted of St. John's College, Cambridge, in 1767, made master of arts by royal mandate in 1771, and a year or two after (*ad eundem*), to the same rank in the University of Oxford; he was called to the bar by the Hon. Society of Lincoln's Inn, 1777, chosen representative in parliament for the cinque port of New Romney, in the county of Kent, in 1785; he stood for the town and port of Dover, a cinque port in the same county, in 1790; took the surname and arms of Major, in compliance with the will of his maternal grandfather, Sir John Major, Bart. by royal sign-manual, Aug. 10, 1792; he was chosen for the borough of Steyning, in the county of Sussex, in 1793; rechosen, 1796; stood for Maidstone, in the county of Kent; in 1802. From June, 1798, till the 30th of April, 1802, he commanded a body of infantry, ninety in number, raised for the defence of the parish of Worlingworth (of which, jointly with the Duchess of Chandos, he is patron and lord of the manor) and of the eight adjoining parishes, Southolt, Athelington, Horham, Wilby, Brundish, Tannington, Saxtead, and Bedfield. On the return of the peace, he presented his officers and men with a silver medal, with the representation of Worlingworth church and hall, and, on the reverse, one heart surrounded by nine hands, expressive of the number of the parishes, united in a Gordian knot, with appropriate embellishments*. The colours were presented by the Honourable Mrs. Henniker Major, to the corps, in 1798, and are now placed in the parish church of Worlingworth. He is a magistrate in the counties of Essex, Suffolk, and Hants, deputy-lieutenant of the two former, and was several years one of the chairmen of the quarter-sessions of the first-mentioned, which situation he quitted from want of health. He is a fellow of the Royal Society, the Society of Antiquaries, and Society of Arts, Manufactures, and Commerce, a Proprietor of the Royal Institution, a vice-president of the Mary-le-bone Dispensary, and a governor of several hospitals in the metropolis. He was one of the original subscribers to the Association of the St. Alban's Tavern, to promote and secure internal quiet, and one of the first to set on foot voluntary contributions in 1794. He s author of Letters on Norman Tiles, and other papers read before the Society

* See the Plate.

of Antiquaries. He married Emily, daughter of Robert Jones, of Duffryn, in Glamorganshire, Esq. whose grandfather served the office of high-sheriff for that county.

2, Major, of London, merchant, born May 9, 1755, who married Mary, daughter of John Phœnix, of Rochester, in Kent, Esq. he died Feb. 2, 1789, leaving five children; 1, John-Minet, born Nov. 20, 1777, of St. John's College, Cambridge, one of his Majesty's deputy-lieutenants for the county of Essex, and magistrate for the same: he married Mary, daughter of the Rev. William Chafy, canon of Canterbury, by whom he has issue, Anne-Elizabeth, born Nov. 4, 1799, John, born Feb. 3, 1801, and Mary, born June 7, 1802; 2, Major-Jacob, born Aug. 19, 1780, a captain in the royal navy; 3, Mary-Anne, born Nov. 13, 1778, wife, Nov. 10, 1798, of Francis-William Sykes, Esq. son and heir-apparent to Sir Francis Sykes, of Baseldon, in the county of Berks, Bart. by whom she has issue, Francis, born Aug. 8, 1799, William, born Sept. 25, 1800, and Catharine, born Oct. 17, 1801; 4, Elizabeth-Dale, died an infant; 5, Elizabeth-Dale, born Nov. 4, 1783, wife, Dec. 7, 1800, of John-Simon Harcourt, of Ankerwyke-House, in the county of Bucks, Esq. representative in the last parliament for the borough of Westbury, in the county of Wilts; 6, Brydges-Jackson, died an infant.

3, Anne-Elizabeth, only daughter of Baron Henniker, was married, May 24, 1787, to Edward-Augustus, late Earl of Aldborough, of the kingdom of Ireland, who died Jan. 2, 1801, without issue. She married secondly, George Powell, of Cloveller, in the county of Limerick, in the kingdom of Ireland, Esq. second and only surviving son of Colonel Richard Powell, of the same place, and of New Garden, in the liberties of the city of Limerick; which Richard served the office of high-sheriff for that county in the year 1753, and commanded, as lieutenant-colonel, one of the regiments of militia embodied for the protection of Ireland in the rebellion of 1745. He was lineally descended from John Powell, a younger branch of the family of Judge Powell, who lies interred under a stately monument in the chancel of the cathedral of Gloucester; which John being sent into Ireland after the re-settlement of that kingdom by King James the First, was invested with the important office of surveyor-general, and was a member of the council for Munster; and having acquired property, and formed alliances with the families of Coote, Massey, Eyre, and Trench (who have all been raised to the Peerage of Ireland), settled at the castle of Cloveller, and died after the restoration of King Charles II. at an advanced age, and lies interred in the chancel of the church of Ballynard. The countess departed this life at Aldborough-House, Dublin, on the 15th of July, 1802, without issue.

4, Major-Gen. Brydges-Trecothick, was born Nov. 10, 1767, first lieutenant-colonel of the 9th dragoons, fellow of the Society of Antiquaries, member of the Royal Irish Academy, and of the Dublin Society, and one of the vice-presidents of the Western Dispensary; he offered to raise a regiment of Irish dragoons in the beginning of the late war, for general service, and commanded as a volunteer three detachments of cavalry which left Ireland for the continent, but were afterwards ordered to join the army under Lord Moira at Southampton. He was member for Kildare during the whole of the last parliament of Ireland; and married, Sept. 5, 1791, Mary, daughter of William Press, Esq. by whom he has issue, Ann, Frederick, Augustus, Aldborough-Brydges, Emily, John, and Elizabeth.

ARMS—Quarterly: 1st and 4th, azure, three pillars of the Corinthian order, fluted, or, the top of each surmounted with a ball, of the last, for Major.—Or, on a cheveron, gules, three estoils of six points, argent, between two crescents, in chief, and an escallop, in base, argent, for Henniker.

CREST—A dexter arm embowed, habited, azure, charged on the arm with a plate, cuffed, argent, holding in the hand, proper, a baton, or, for Major—An escallop shell, or, charged with an estoil, of six points, gules, for Henniker.

SEATS—At Worlingworth and Thornham-Hall, both in Suffolk.

Seats of Lord Henniker.

Stratford-House and Newton-Hall, in Essex; Great Bealing Hall, in the county of Suffolk; St. Peter's, in the Isle of Thanet, in Kent; and Stratford-upon-Slaney, in the county of Wicklow, in Ireland.

TABLE.

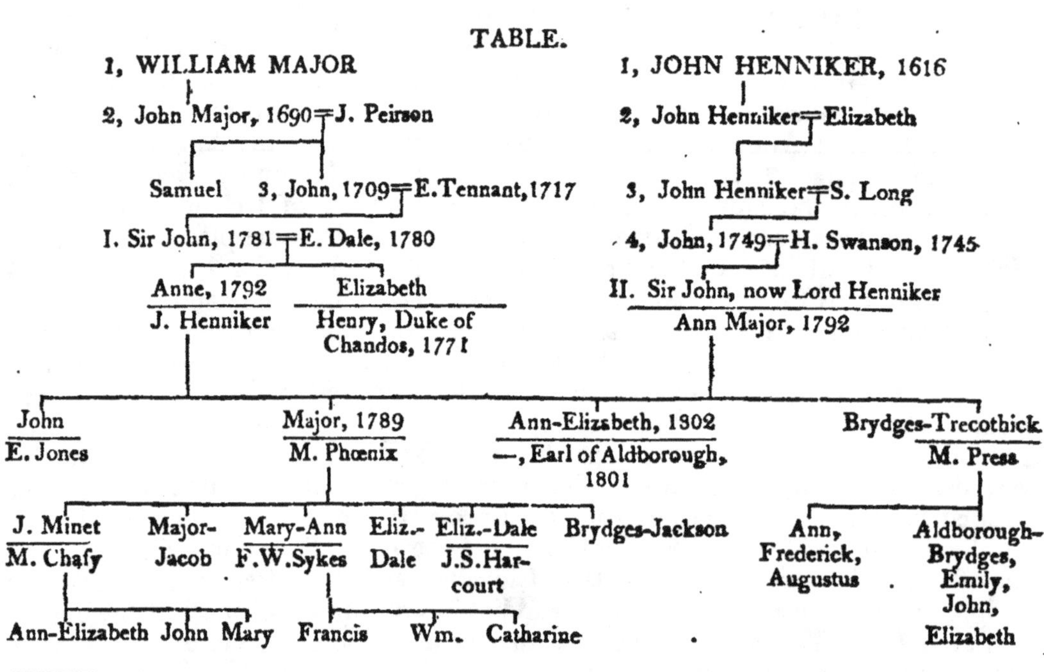

282. MAWBEY, of Botleys, Surry.

Created Baronet, June 30, 1765.

THE name of this family has been variously written, as Mawtebey, Maultby, Mauteby, Mawbie, Mawby, and Mawbey. It is descended from a family who took their name from the village of Mawtby, in the county of Norfolk, of which village they were early enfeoffed by the crown.

1, Simon de Mauteby had an interest therein in the 10th year of Richard I. when he was tenant, and Lambert Fitz-Otho petent, in a fine of sixteen acres of land. He was the father of,

2, Walter de Mauteby, who had one son,

3, Robert de Mauteby, to whom the six sons of Robert de Mauteby, his uncle, released three carucates of land in Mautby.

4, Sir Walter de Mauteby, the son of Robert, married Christian, daughter and coheiress of Sir Piers de Bassingham, sub-collector and accomptant in the 15th of King John; by whom he had two other daughters, Margaret, wife of Sir John de Flegg, and Alia, of Sir Peter de Brampton; and amongst these, Salkirk manor, in Salle, was divided, as well as other estates of the said Sir Piers de Bassingham.

This Sir Walter de Mauteby had a grant in 1248, 32 Hen. III. of free-warren in Mauteby, and he was lord thereof in the 34th and 41st years of the reign of Hen. III.

About the year 1248, Simon, the prior of Norwich, granted the manor of West Becham, in Norfolk, and all his lands there (except the advowson of the church and glebe lands) to Sir Walter de Mauteby and his heirs. Sir Walter was sued in Henry the Third's time, for imposing a new toll in Becham Fair. In 1269 (53 Henry III.) Sir Walter de Mauteby purchased Flegg Hall, in Winterton, of Sir William de Flegg, who also released to him, in the 6th year of Edward I. all his right and title in Bassingham manor, West Becham, and Matlask. Christian, his wife, brought him Mauteby's manor, in Burston. It appears, that William de Valentia, Earl of Pembroke, half-brother to King Henry III. held Matlask in capite of that king, with Saxthorp, in his 34th year, which were held of him by the said Sir Walter de Mauteby, who married Christian above-mentioned, daughter and coheiress of Sir Piers de Bassingham, by whom he had,

5, Sir Walter de Mauteby, who married Petronilla ——, by whom he had Sir Robert de Mauteby. In the 6th year of King Edward I. several messuages and lands in Salle, and in Dalling, in the county of Norfolk, were settled by fine on Sir Walter de Mauteby, and Petronilla, his wife. He was succeeded by,

6, Sir Robert de Mauteby. In the 20th of Edward I. 1292, the jury found, that neither the manor, nor any lands in Mauteby, were partable, but were to descend to Sir Robert de Mauteby, son and heir of Sir Walter; and the said Sir Robert occurs lord in 1300. In 1307, he presented Thomas de Hykeyngge to the rectory of Mautby. In 1284, Sir Robert de Mauteby had a view of frank-pledge and assize of bread and beer in his manor of West Becham. By Alice, his first wife, he had a daughter Petronilla, heiress to Roger de Somery, of one part of the manor of Brome Hall, in Norfolk, who was married to Roger, son of William de Brome: they settled, in 1302, temp. Hen. III. the manor and advowson on themselves for life, with remainder to Robert, their son. To this settlement Henry de Brome, the brother to Roger, was a party. By his second wife, Sir Robert de Mauteby had a son and successor, Sir John de Mauteby, and a daughter Sibil, wife of John Fitz-Simons, on whom he settled a moiety of the manor of West Becham, till he portioned her: he was succeeded by his son,

7, Sir John de Mauteby, who was lord of Mawtby, &c. in 1316, 9 Edw. II. and also in 1330; and in 1336, in the 10th year of Edward III. as appears by a deed of that date; he presented John de Bottesford to the church of Bassingham in 1326, of which he was lord in the 9th year of Edward II. In 1316, John Fitz-Simons, and Sibil, his wife, daughter of Sir Robert de Mauteby, released to Sir

John de Mauteby, their brother, who was then lord, their right to a moiety of West Becham manor. Sir John de Mauteby married Avelina de Grenon, of Sparham, in the county of Norfolk, with whom he had Mauteby's manor in that town. The said Avelina (called, in the 9th year of Edward II. Avelina de Mautbey) was returned lady of the said manor. He was, in the 6th year of Edward I. lord of Bassingham, West Becham, and Matlask, and was succeeded by his son,

8, Sir Robert de Mautbey, who, in 1347, 20 Edw. III. was lord of Matlask, Mawtby, Bassingham, &c. in which year he presented Thomas Feltenham to the rectory of Bassingham, and John de Batisford to the rectory of Mautbey; and the said John de Batisford dying the same year, he again presented Edmund de Mawtby to the rectory of Mawtby. He married Alianora ——: they were both living in 1355, as appears by a fine in that year. He was succeeded by his son,

9, Sir John de Mauteby, who was lord of Mawtby, Bassingham, West Becham, Matlask, Mawtby's manor, in Sparham, Mawtby's manor, in Winterton, lands in North Walsham, Worsted, Dilham, &c. held of the Abbot of St. Bennet. He presented, in 1369, Thomas de Bolours, to Bassingham church or rectory; and, on his death in 1397, Clement Hadham to the said church. In 1397, he also presented John Tydesdall to the rectory of Mawtby.

Sir John de Mawtbey, his eldest son, who died in the life-time of his father, was a feoffee for the manors of Lanwades, in Uleston, Peek Hall, in Titleshall, in Norfolk, and sealed with a plain cross; and, in the year 1374, was buried before the altar of St. Mary's, in the church of Freton St. Edmund, in Suffolk, where he lived. He left an only daughter, Alianora de Mauteby, who was married to Sir William Calthorpe, son and heir of Oliver Calthorpe, who thereupon quartered the arms of Mawtby with his own*. By the said Alianora de Mawtby, Sir William Calthorpe had a son, Sir William, father of another Sir William Calthorpe, from whom the present Earl of Egmont, of the kingdom of Ireland, is maternally descended.

Sir John de Mawteby, the father, made his last will and testament, Oct. 27 and 29, 1403, to be buried in the church of St. Peter and St. Paul, of Mauteby, in the chapel of St. Mary, by the body of Agnes, his wife, under the same marble stone on the right-hand; and appoints Robert de Martham, Geoffrey de Somerton, John de Gresham, &c. executors. He gives Robert, his son and heir, all his horses, cows, carts, corn, bees, wardrobe, and ornaments of his chapel in Mauteby manor; to John, son of the said Robert, a piece of silver, late John Mauteby's, his uncle; to Thomas, his son, another piece, &c. This Sir John died on the 30th of October, 1403, and the will was proved on the 18th of December following.

10, Sir Robert de Mawtbey succeeded the said Sir John in all his estates, his elder brother John having left behind him one daughter Eleanora, wife of Sir William Calthorpe as before-mentioned.

In 1407, the said Sir Robert de Mauteby presented John Begge to the rectory of Mawtby; and, in 1413, he enfeoffed Sir Miles Stapleton, Sir Simon Felbrigge, Sir William Argenton, &c. in the manors of Mauteby, Sparham, Bassingham,

* These arms have been variously borne by the family; sometimes azure, a cross, or; sometimes a cross, gules, fretty, or, between four eagles displayed, azure. In Upwell church are the arms of Clipsby, impaling Calthorpe, where, amongst other quarterings is, sixthly, azure, a cross formee, or, for Mawtby.

Becham, Matlask, Briston, Kirk Hall, in Salle, Flegg Hall, in Winterton, Somerton, &c.; one hundred shillings in Castre and Merkeshall, Freton manor, in Suffolk, to fulfil his will made the same year; by which he enjoins Eleanora, his wife, to pay his debts; gives twenty marks per annum, for two years, to John, his son, for his maintenance; five marks to brother John Ocle, to serve for him and his family's souls; twenty shillings per annum to Eleanor, his daughter, a nun at Shouldham; eighty pounds to the marriage of Agnes, his daughter; his wife, with the remaining profits, to keep Walter, Edward, Peter, and Thomas, his sons, till of age, and Agnes till married. All his manors, after his mother, brothers, and sisters, are provided for, to be released to John, his son, and his heirs entailed; and if Agnes dies unmarried without her portion, that to go to the repair of the south aisle of Mawtby church. Eleanora, his widow, re-married Thomas Chambers, Esq. lord of Sparham, in her right, in the year 1442, 20 Hen. VI.

Of the sons, Walter and Edward died without issue; as did Peter Mautby, Esq. the fourth son, who was buried in Sparham church, agreeably to his will, which was dated Oct. 4, 1438.

Of Thomas de Mawteby, the fifth son (the ancestor of Sir Joseph Mawbey, Bart.) more hereafter. John de Mawteby, Esq. eldest son, succeeded his father, and married Margaret Berney, daughter of John Berney, Esq. of Reedham, in the county of Norfolk, by whom he left an only daughter Margaret*, heir to the

* The said Margaret Mautby, married as aforesaid to John Paston, Esq. survived her husband; and by her will, dated Feb. 4, 1481, and proved Dec. 18, 1484, bequeaths:

"My body to be buried in the aisle of the church of Mawtby, in which aisle rest the bodies of diverse of myne ancestors. I will that my executors purvey a stone of marble to be leyde aloft upon my grave; and I will have four scotchyns set thereon, one at each corner thereof; the first, Paston and Mawteby; the second, Mawtebey and Berney, of Redeham; the third, Mauteby, and the lord of Loveyn; the fourth, Mauteby and Sir Roger Beauchamp; and in the middle of the stone a scotchyn of arms alone, and under the same "God is my Trust;" with a scripture written in the verges thereof,

"Here lyeth Margaret Paston, late wife of John Paston,
Daughter and heyre of John Mauteby, Squyr."

"Item, I will that eche pore houshold, late my tenants at Sparham, have 6s. Item, to the reparation of the church at Redeham, wher I was born, I bequethe 5 marks, and a chesible of silk, with an auble with my arms thereupon. Item, to the dean and his brethren at the chapel, a field 20s; to Edmund Paston, my son, a standing piece covered with an unicorn; to Katherine, his wife, a purpylle gurdyll, harnessed with silver and gylt; to Robert, son of the said Edmund, all my swans marken with Daweney's mark, and with the mark late Robert Cutler, clerk, and to heirs; to Anne, my daughter, wief of William Yelverton, myne green hanging in my parlour of Mauteby; to William Paston, my son, my standing cuppe, chased, parsel gylte, with a cover with my arms in the bottome, and a flate peece with a trayll upon the cover, 12 silver spoons, 2 silver salts; to John Paston, my son, a gylte cuppe; and to Margery Paston, wief of the said John, and Elizabeth, his sister, 100 marks; to Custance, barstard daughter of Sir John Paston, when she is 20 years of age; to John Calle, son of Margery, my daughter, 20l. when she cometh to age of 24; to Anne, my daughter, 10l.; to Osbern Bernet, 10 marks. John Paston, my son, Executor."

The said Margaret Mauteby, married to John Paston, Esq. was buried in the south aisle of Mawtby church. At the east end of the said church, against the south wall, lies a curious antique monument, a stone coffin, about a foot and an half deep, resting on the pavement, and about seven feet in length: on the lid of the caver (the whole being of grey marble) is the effigies of a Knight Templar, cross-legged in armour, in full proportion, his sword in a broad belt, hanging over his shoulder, in memory, as it is said, for a knight of the family of De Mawtby, and living, as the style of the monu-

great estate of the family, agreeable to the entail made thereof by her grandfather Sir Robert de Mautbey: she was the wife of John Paston, Esq. son and heir of Sir William Paston, the judge, and was greatly distinguished for her conjugal affection, piety, and prudence, as may be proved by the Paston Letters, lately published by Sir John Fenn, in which she appears an exemplary pattern for wives and mothers. By the said John Paston, Esq. she was mother of Sir John Paston, Knt. and other children, from whom was descended, in a direct male line, Sir Robert Paston, Bart. created by King Charles II. Baron Paston and Viscount Yarmouth, Aug. 19, 1673, and Earl of Yarmouth, July 30, 1679. The titles in this last family became extinct by the death of the last Earl in 1742; and many of the estates, formerly belonging to the Mautbeys, were afterwards sold in chancery to George Lord Anson, from whom they came to his nephew, the late George Adams, Esq. (who took the name of Anson) member of parliament for the city of Litchfield, and are now in his family.

Having done with this, the eldest branch of the family, we come to treat of,

11, Thomas de Mautby, Esq. fifth son of Sir Robert de Mawtby, and of Eleanora, his wife, was of Sparham, in the county of Norfolk, and was father of,

12, Walter de Mawtby, who, by Agnes Dawtree, his wife, was father of,

13, Richard Mautbey, Esq. who, by Mary, his wife, the daughter of — Baker, Esq. was father of,

14, Roger Mawtbey, Esq. of Kettering, in the county of Northampton. He married Mary Drayton, by whom he had,

15, Richard Mautbey, Esq. of the same place, who resided at South Kilworth*,

ment bespeaks, about the year 1250. In the said church was the guild of St. Peter, and the arms impaled of Mauteby and Loveyn, Mawteby and Clifton, Mauteby and Beauchamp, Mautby and Berney, also Mawtby and Marshall. The south aisle, where many of the Mawtbys were buried, and which was rebuilt by Margaret, the heiress of the family, and where she was buried, is, says Blomefield, all in ruins.

In the hall-windows of Mawtby were formerly, amongst others, the arms of Paston and Mawtby, Mawtby and Berney, Mawtby impaling Marshall, Mawtby impaling Beauchamp, and Mawtby impaling Clifton.

* *Extracts from the Register of South Kilworth, Leicestershire.*

Robertus Mawbie, baptizatus fuit Maii, A. D. 1561.
Elisabeth Mawbie, baptizata fuit 23 Aprilis, 1567.
Anna, filia Willi'mi Mawbie, bapt. 18 Sept. 1581.
Johannes, filius Willi'mi Mawbie, bapt. 10 Jan. 1583.
Willi'mus, filius Richardi Mawbie, bapt. 23 Mart. 1583.
Johannes, filius Richardi Mawbie, bapt. 29 Maii, 1586.
Richardus, filius Willi'mi Mawbie, bapt. . . . . 1588.
Elisabeth, filia Willi'mi Mawbie, bapt. 9 Feb. 1591.
Thomas, filius Willi'mi Mawbie, bapt. 22 Mart. 1594.
Richardus Mawbie, sepult. 12 Sept. 1580.
Margareta Mawbie, sepult. 3 Mart. 1597.
Willi'mus Mawbie uxorem duxit Agnetum Carei hujus parochie, 30 Jan. 1580.
Robertus Mawbie uxorem duxit Aliciam Coleman, alias Devet, 5 July, 1582.
Johannes Mawby, filius Willi'mi Mawby, bapt. 7 Sept. 1606.
Willi'mus Mawby, filius Willi'mi Mawby, bapt. 11. . . . . 1608.
Erasmus Mawby, filius Richardi Mawby, bapt. 7 Mart. 1616.

in Leicestershire, and married Margaret, daughter of — Spencer, Esq. by whom he had three sons, William, of whom hereafter, Richard, and Robert.

Elisabetha Mawby, filia Richardi Mawby, bapt. 8 Aug. 1619.
Margareta Mawby, filia Richardi Mawby, bapt. 16 Apr. 1626.
William Mawbye, the son of Thomas. . . . . 1655.
Joanna Mawbye sepulta fuit, 15 Oct. 1604.
Richardus Mawby, sepultus fuit 16 Mart. 1607.
Johannes Mawby, filius Willi'mi Mawby. . . . 1607.
Gulielmus Mawby, sepultus fuit, 19 Maii, 1621.
Agneta Mawby, sepulta fuit, 4 Nov. 1624.
Georgius Mawby, duxit uxorem Dorotheam Mawby, 10 Nov. 1622.
Richardus Mawby, sepultus fuit 9 Mart. 1662.
Elinor, wife of Thomas Mawby, buried 2 Jan. 1682.
Thomas Mawby, buried June 20, 1683.
William Mawby, buried June 25, 1688.
William Mawby, duxit uxorem Al'ce Rainer, 16th Jan. 1682-3.
William Mawby, the son of William and Al'ce, bapt. 19 May, 1684.
Thomas Mawbye, filius Gulielmi & Alicie, bapt. 22 Jan. 1685–6.
John Mawby, son of William and Al'ce, bapt. 22 Nov. 1687.
William Mawby and Elis. Ireson, married 24 April, 1707.
William, son of William and Elis. Mawby, born Jan. 2, bapt. 20 Jan. 1707-8.
Hannah, daughter of William and Elis. Mawby, born Sept. 12, bapt. priv. Sept. 22, received Oct. 10, 1709.
Alice, daughter of William and Elis. Mawby, born Nov. 30, bapt. 3 Dec. 1711.
Robert, son of Thomas and Elis. Mawby, born and bapt. Oct. 12, received 1 Dec. 1712.
Jane and Mary, daughters of William and Elis. Mawby, born and bapt. 4 Dec. 1713.
Jane and Mary, daughters of William and Elis. Mawby, buried Dec. 7, 1713.
John, son of Thomas and Elis. Mawby, born Feb. 21, bapt. March 23, 1714.
John, son of William and Elis. Mawby, born July 11, bapt. 7 Aug. 1715.
——, daughter of Thomas and Eliz. Mawby, bapt. Aug. 2, 1717.
Edward, son of William and Elis. Mawby, born Dec. 23, bapt. Jan. 1, 1718.
Elisabeth, daughter of William and Elis. Mawby, bapt. Sept. 6, 1722.
William, son of William and Martha Mawby, bapt. Dec. 4, 1732.
Alice, daughter of William and Martha Mawby, bapt. April 19, 1734.
Martha, daughter of William and Martha Mawby, bapt. July 20, 1735.
Thomas *, son of William and Martha Mawby, bapt. Jan. 7, 1736.
Elisabeth, daughter of William and Martha Mawby, bapt. 10 Nov. 1738.
Elisabeth, daughter of William and Martha Morby, bapt. Dec. 3, 1739.
Mary, daughter of William and Martha Morby, bapt. Oct. 2, 1741.
Ann, daughter of William and Martha Mawbey, bapt. May 15, 1744.
Anna, daughter of William and Martha Mawbey, bapt. Sept. 30, 1745.
John, son of William and Martha Mawbey, bapt. March 18, 1746.
John †, son of William Mawby, jun. and Martha his wife, bapt. 19 Sept. 1748.
Sarah and Jane, daughters of William Mawby, jun. and Martha his wife, bapt. May 20, 1749.
William Smith and Alice Mawbey married by banns, Sept. 26, 1736.
Edward, son of William Mawby, sen. and Elisabeth his wife, buried Oct. 25, 1737.
Elisabeth, daughter of William and Martha Mawby, buried Dec. 28, 1738.
John, son of William and Martha Mawby, buried March 21, 1746.
John Mawby, sen. buried Nov. 5, 1749.

* Now of Vauxhall, in the county of Surry. He is married, but has no child.

† Now a captain in the East India Company's troops at Bengal, whither he was sent in 1770, through the interest of Sir Joseph Mawbey, Bart.

Richard Mawtbey, the second son, married Joanna Bird, by whom he had two sons, William (father of John and William), and John, and one daughter Dorothy.

Robert, the third son, was baptized at South Kilworth, in the county of Leicester, as appears by the register of that parish, May 12, 1561, married, July 5, 1582, Alicia Coleman, by whom he had one son George, who married, Nov. 10, 1622, to his cousin Dorothy above-mentioned.

16, William, the eldest son of Richard Mautbey, Esq. by Margaret, his wife, married at South Kilworth, Jan. 30, 1580, Agnes Carey, of that parish, by whom he had three sons and two daughters, viz. Anna, John, Richard, Elizabeth, and Thomas. Their father was buried at South Kilworth, May 19, 1621.

John Mawtbey, the eldest son, baptized at South Kilworth Jan. 10, 1583, married Agnes, daughter of William Chamberlayne, of Leicester, Esq. by whom he had two sons, Roger, who died unmarried, and was buried at Leicester, and Erasmus, who apprehending the civil and religious liberties of this country to be in danger, from the arbitrary conduct of King Charles the First and his ministers, took a zealous and active part on the side of the parliament; for whose service, having, in 1643, raised a considerable number of recruits in his neighbourhood at his own expence, he conducted them to his countryman, Sir Arthur Heselrigge, Bart. with whom he was present as a volunteer at the battle fought soon after at Roundway Down, near the Devizes, in Wiltshire; where, having distinguished himself by his bravery, he was unfortunately slain, together with many other of his friends, in Sir Arthur's regiment, which had rendered itself famous for its valour, but which, in this battle, suffered very considerably. By Elizabeth, daughter of Walter Burton, Gent. of Hinckley, in the county of Leicester, he had several children, none of whom lived to be married. Their father's unfortunate death, his widow's second marriage, and the calamities brought on them by the civil war, proved extremely prejudicial to the interests of the family.

Thomas, the third son of William Mawbey, by Agnes Carey, his wife, was baptized at South Kilworth, March 22, 1594, and married Eleanor Cartwright, and by her was father of William Mawbey, born 1655, from whom the Mawbeys, still living at South Kilworth, are descended.

17, Richard, the second son of William Mawbey, by Agnes Carey, his wife, born in 1588, married Elizabeth, daughter of —— Shuckburgh, Esq. of Naseby, in the county of Northampton, by whom he had one son Erasmus, and two daughters, Elizabeth and Margaret, the first of which died unmarried, and the last without leaving issue.

Sarah, daughter of William Mawby, jun. buried Dec. 4, 1749.
Jane, daughter of William Mawbey, jun. buried Dec. 9, 1749.
Elisabeth, wife of William Mawby, sen. buried June 12, 1751.
William Mawby, jun. buried June 13, 1762.

All the births, marriages, and burials of the family of Mawbey, as above written, are faithfully extracted from the register of the parish of South Kilworth, in the county of Leicester, and diocese of Lincoln, by me, James Ancell, Minister, 12 Feb. 1763.

18, Erasmus Mawbey was baptized at South Kilworth, March 7, 1616, and, in 1694, was buried at Shenton*, in the county of Leicester. By his first wife, Mary, daughter of Robert and Mary Wright, he had seven sons, Robert, Richard, Erasmus, Thomas, John, Francis, and William. By his second wife, Eleanor Slee, of Tickenhall, in the county of Derby, he had five sons and two daughters, John, James, Mary, Isaac, Elizabeth, Joseph, and Stephen.

* *Extracts from the register of Shenton:*

Robert Maube, the son of Erasmus Maube and Mary his wife, was baptized September 1, 1643.
Richard Maube, the son of Erasmus Maube and Mary his wife, was baptized May 18, 1645.
Erasmus, the son of Erasmus Maube and Mary his wife, was baptized October 7, 1647.
Thomas, the son of Erasmus Mauby and Mary his wife, was baptized September 18, 1651.
John Mawby, the son of Erasmus Mawby and Mary his wife, was baptized October 5, 1654.
Francis, the son of Erasmus Mauby and Mary his wife, was baptized February 1, 1657.
Mary Mauby, the wife of Erasmus Mauby, was brought to bed of a boy this Tuesday morning, the last day of January, 1659, and was baptized William (*a*) the 1st day of February, 1659.
Mary Mawbe, wife of Erasmus Mawbe, and daughter of — Wright and Mary his wife, was buried January 3, 1666.
John Maube, son of Erasmus Maube and Eleanor his wife, was baptized February 18, 1669.
Margaret Maube was married February 11, 1672.
Joseph Maube, son of Erasmus Maube and Eleanor his wife, was baptized December 27, 1680.
Erasmus Mauby and Mary Fox were married by banns April 11, 1681.
Sarah Mawby, daughter of Erasmus Mawby and Mary his wife, was baptized February 12, 1681.
Katharine Mawby, the wife of Richard Mawby, was buried May 29, 1692.
Richard Mauby, the son of Richard Mauby and Mary his wife, was born June 4, and was baptized June 11, 1693.
Abraham and Isaac, the sons of Isaac Mawby and Elizabeth his wife, were baptized February 3, 1694.
Abraham and Isaac, the sons of Isaac Mawby and Elizabeth his wife, were buried February 18, 1694.
Erasmus Mawby (*b*) was buried February 20, 1694.
Erasmus, the son of Richard Mawby and Mary his wife, was born March 22, 1695, and was baptized April 14, 1695.
Thomas Brown and Eleanor Mawby, of this parish, were married October 19, 1696.
Mary, the daughter of Isaac Mawby and Elizabeth his wife, was baptized January 14, 1696.
Mary, the daughter of Richard Mawby and Mary his wife, was baptized December 27, 1698.
Mary, the wife of Erasmus Mawby, was buried February 24, 1699.
Erasmus Mawby and Sarah Parsons were married October 3, 1702.
John, the son of Richard Mawby and Mary his wife, was baptized December 28, 1703.
Erasmus Mawby was buried February 13, 1713.
Richard, the son of Richard Mawby, was buried May 9, 1717.
Richard, the son of Erasmus Mawby and Elizabeth his wife, was baptized January 22, 1719.
Elizabeth, daughter of Erasmus Mawby and Elizabeth his wife, was baptized November 5, 1722.
Erasmus Mawby and Frances Cooper were married April 7, 1724.
William, the son of Erasmus Mawby and Frances his wife, was baptized January 30, 1726.
William Mawby, son of Erasmus Mawby, was buried April 15, 1729.
Erasmus, the son of Erasmus and Frances Mawby, was baptized December 27, 1731.
Sarah Mauby, widow, was buried April 30, 1737.
Thomas Messenger and Elizabeth Mauby were married February 26, 1744.
Mary Mauby was buried April 20, 1748.
Elizabeth, the daughter of Erasmus and Mary Mawby, was baptized June 25, 1752.

(*a*) Grandfather to Sir Joseph Mawbey, Bart. He was buried at Raunston, Dec. 12, 1733.

(*b*) Erasmus Mawby, buried as above, was baptized at South Kilworth on March 7, 1616, to which the family came from Kettering, in Northamptonshire; before that, from Mautby, a village in East Flegg Hundred, in Norfolk.

Several of the above children of Erasmus Mawbey married, and left descendants, of whom it is not necessary to treat *.

19, William, the seventh son of Erasmus Mawbey, by Mary Wright, his first wife, was born Jan. 31, 1659, at Shenton, was settled at Raunston, and buried there, Dec. 12, 1733. He married Anne, daughter of Mr. John Walker, of Swannington, in the county of Leicester, by whom he had an only son,

20, John Mawbey, or Mautby, born at Raunston aforesaid, and married first, Martha, eldest daughter of Thomas Pratt, of Raunston, descended from John Pratt, Esq. colonel in the army raised by the parliament against King Charles the First, and, in 1653, one of the representatives for the county of Leicester, by whom he had four sons and four daughters, Francis, Martha, John, another John, Anne, Mary, Elizabeth, and Joseph. Their mother dying, he married secondly, Mrs. Jane Shepherd, of Raunston, widow, by whom he had no issue. He died

Erasmus (*a*), the son of Erasmus and Mary Mawby, was baptized May 7, 1754.
Frances Mauby was buried May 21, 1754.
Erasmus Mawby and Sarah Bolton were married August 20, 1755.
ROBERT COULTON, Curate of Market Bosworth (*b*).

* *Extracts from the register of Carlton Curlieu.*

This is to certify, that this is a true copy taken from the register of Carlton, in the county of Leicester, 1767, by me, J. LEDBROOKE, Curate.
Mary, the daughter of Stephen Mauby, was baptized December 7, 1718.
Mary, daughter of Stephen Mauby and Em. his wife, was buried December 1732.
Em. Mauby, the wife of Stephen Mauby, was buried March the 30th, 1741.
Elianor Mauby, the daughter of Stephen Mauby, was buried December 27, 1741.
Elizabeth Mauby was buried August 1, 1757.
Stephen Mauby was buried Jan. 3, 1765.

A true copy, taken from the Register of Sutton Cheyney, in the county of Leicester, March 10, 1767.
John (*c*), the son of Erasmus Mauby and Mary his wife, was baptized Nov. 7, 1756.
Thomas, tbe son of Erasmus Mauby and Mary his wife, was baptized August 13, 1759.
William, the son of Erasmus Mauby and Mary his wife, was baptized December 25, 1761.
Mary, the daughter of Erasmus Mauby and Mary his wife, was baptized February 24, 1764.
J. LEDBROOKE, Curate.

(*a*) This Erasmus Mawby, after having been educated at Leicester Grammar School, at the expence of Sir Joseph Mawbey, Bart. took to a sea-faring life, and became a midshipman on board the Courageux of 74 guns, commanded by Constantine, Lord Mulgrave, in which ship he was killed by a cannon-ball, in the fight between Admiral Keppel and Count D'Orvilliers, commander of the Brest squadron, on the 27th of July, 1778, after behaving with great gallantry, and while he was in the highest spirits. From his temper, activity, and general good character, it is believed he would have risen high in his profession if he had lived. Sir Joseph Mawbey, at considerable expence, placed this Erasmus Mawby's father (baptized as above, on Dec. 27, 1731), in a farm at Bagworth, where he died in 1769.

(*b*) Shenton is a chapelry dependent on Market Bosworth.

(*c*) This John Mauby was educated at Leicester Grammar-school, at the expence of Sir Joseph Mawbey, Bart. Being placed afterwards on board the Royal Admiral East India ship, he died of a fever on board that ship in the East Indies, on Jan. 1, 1779.

1754*. Of the children, Francis, Martha, the first John, and Elizabeth, died under age and unmarried. John Mawbey, Esq. the eldest surviving son, married

The following are extracts from the register of Raunston:

Ann Mouby, daughter of John and Martha Mouby, was baptized the 9th of January, 1724.
Martha, the daughter of John and Martha Mouby, was buried the 2d of July, 1729.
Joseph, the son of John and Martha Mouby, was baptized the 9th of January, 1730-1.
William Mauby was buried the 12th of December, 1733.
Martha Mauby was buried the 20th of September, 1737.
John Mauby and Jane Shepherd were married the 24th of November, 1737.
Francis, son of John and Martha Mauby, was buried the 9th of August, 1739.
Jane Mauby, the wife of John Mauby, died the 17th of April, 1747.
John Mawby and Mary Darling were married December the 27th, 1751.
Mary, the wife of John Mawby, was buried the 26th of September, 1752.
Elizabeth, daughter of John and Mary Mawby, was baptized the 26th of September, 1752, and buried the 26th of November, 1752.

* On a mural monument against the north wall of the chancel, in Raunston:

Arms—On the dexter side, or, a cross, gules, fretty, or, between four eagles displayed, azure. On the sinister, on a fess between three elephants' heads erased, argent, as many mullets of the first, for Pratt.

Mr. John Mawbey, late of this parish,
died on the 4th September, 1754, in the 62d year of his age,
descended from an ancient and genteel family,
long settled in the counties of Leicester and Northampton,
into which latter they came from the county of Norfolk,
where formerly they were owners of large possessions.
The said John Mawbey
married Martha, daughter of Mr. Thomas Pratt,
late of this parish, and by her, who died in 1737,
had the following sons and daughters:

Francis Mawbey	born	29 March, 1720,	died in August, 1739.
Martha,		2 May, 1721,	buried on 2 July, 1729.
John,		24 July, 1722,	died an infant.
John,		18 August, 1724,	now of Vauxhall, in the commission of the peace for the county of Surry.
Anne,		29 Nov. 1725,	married to Mr. John Cooper, of Burbage, in this county.
Mary,		1 August, 1726,	married to Mr. William Alcock, of this parish.
Elizabeth,		. . . .	died an infant.
Joseph,		9 Dec. 1730,	of Kennington and Botleys, in the county of Surry.

Their father, John Mawbey, above-mentioned,
was the only son of Mr. William Mawbey, of this parish,
who died in 1733, seventh son of Erasmus Mawbey, of
Shenton, in the county of Leicester, only son of Richard Mawbey,
of South Kilworth; whose elder brother John, by Agnes, daughter
of William Chamberlayne, Esq. of Leicester, was father of
Erasmus Mawbey, or Mauthy, who, in 1643, joining the regiment of
horse commanded by Sir Arthur Haselrigg, Bart. with many recruits,
raised at his own expence, was soon after killed at the battle of
Roundway-Down, near the Devizes, in Wiltshire,
valiantly fighting for the liberties of his country.
His unfortunate death, his widow's second marriage,

first, Mary, daughter of Mr. Jonathan Darling, of Raunston, and by her (who died in child-bed) he had a daughter Elizabeth, who died in two months. By his second wife, Anne, his cousin-german, daughter of Mr. William Fielding, by Anne, his wife, daughter of Mr. Thomas Pratt, he had a daughter Maria, born at Vauxhall, in the county of Surry, Sept. 28, 1756, who died of the small-pox, Dec. 12, 1764.

Anne, the eldest surviving daughter of John Mawbey by Martha Pratt, was wife of Mr. William Cooper, of Burbach, in the county of Leicester, and by him (who died in 1766) had several children, of whom three daughters are now living; the eldest, Martha, is wife of the Rev. William Cooper, of Burbach aforesaid, vicar of Chertsey, in the county of Surry, a benefice given him by Sir Joseph Mawbey, Bart.

Mary, the youngest daughter, is wife of Mr. William Alcock, of Raunston, by whom she had six children, five of whom are now living, viz. Joseph Alcock, Esq. of his Majesty's treasury; William; John, of the Temple, London; Thomas, an officer in the East India Company's troops at Bengal, in the East Indies; and Maria.

Mr. John Mawbey was possessed of a small estate in this parish, which, on his death, came to his eldest surviving son, John Mawbey, Esq. On his removal to Vauxhall, in the county of Surry, in 1755, where for many years he was an active justice of the peace, he sold the estate to his brother-in-law, Mr. William Alcock, descended from a family of that name, of Sibertoft, in the county of Northampton, whose arms are, gules, a fess between three cocks' heads, erased, argent, barbed and crested, or. Crest, on a wreath, a cock ermine, beaked, crested and wattled, or. On Mr. Alcock's death, in 1764, the estate came to, and is now the property of his eldest son, the present Joseph Alcock, Esq. of his Majesty's treasury, who is in the commission of the peace for the county of Surry, and who married, March 2, 1790, Elizabeth-Jane, sister of Richard Tayler, Esq. of Charlton House, in the county of Middlesex. John Mawbey, Esq. died without any surviving issue, June 22, 1786, at Fulbrooke, in the county of Oxford: his body was deposited in Sir Joseph Maw-

and the calamities brought on them by the Civil War,
proved greatly prejudicial to the interests of the family.
John and Richard Mawbey were the eldest sons of William
Mawbey; from Thomas, the third son, are descended the Mawbeys,
at this time of South Kilworth. The said William, with his
brothers, Richard and Robert, the last of whom was baptized at
South Kilworth (as appears by the register of that parish), on 12 May,
1561, were the sons of Richard Mawbey, Esq. by Margaret,
his wife, of South Kilworth aforesaid, born at Kettering, in the county
of Northampton, and descended of the ancient family of the Mawbeys,
or Mauthys, of the county of Norfolk.
Joseph Mawbey, Esq. of Kennington and Botleys, in the
county of Surry, sheriff, in 1757, for that county, and
afterwards member of parliament for the borough of

bey's vault, in the chancel of Chertsey church, in the county of Surry, at which time the remains of his daughter, Maria Mawbey, were placed therein, being removed from Lambeth church at the particular desire of his widow, Anne Mawbey, who enjoyed his estates in Oxfordshire and Surry. She died Sept. 11, 1796, and was also buried at Chertsey.

I. Sir JOSEPH MAWBEY, Bart. the only surviving son of Mr. John Mawbey, quitted Leicestershire at a very early age, having been educated in Surry by his uncle, Joseph Pratt, Esq. of Vauxhall, with an intention of being admitted into the church: but that uncle, who was largely engaged in the malt distillery, observing the declining state of health of another nephew, then his partner, prevailed upon him to relinquish study for business; in consequence of which, he and his brother John Mawbey, Esq. for several years carried on the malt distillery and vinegar business at Vauxhall*, which both relinquished after he was chosen knight of the shire for Surry. His uncle, at his death in 1754, left him considerable property, which was further increased on his marriage, in 1760, with Elizabeth, only surviving daughter of his cousin, Richard Pratt, Esq. of Vauxhall aforesaid; who, on the death of her brother, Joseph Pratt, Esq. in 1766, then a fellow-commoner of Trinity College, Cambridge, succeeded to all his estates.

In 1757, he served the office of sheriff for the county of Surry. At the general election in 1761, he was chosen one of the representatives for the borough of Southwark, in the twelfth parliament of Great Britain, and in March, 1768, was again elected member for the said borough. At the general election in 1774,

Southwark, dedicated this monument, in 1764,
to the memory of his parents and progenitors.

On upright stones in the church-yard:
1, Martha, daughter of Mr. Thomas Pratt, and mother to Mr. John Mawbey,
died in 1737, aged 48.
2, John Mawbey, died Sept. 4, 1754, aged 62.
3, William Alcock, died Sept. 3, 1764, aged 41.

* The works carried on by Sir Joseph Mawbey and his brother in the malt-distillery and vinegar making, were considerable enough to yield more than 600,000 l. per annum to government in duties. After the former became a member of parliament, his brother and clerks principally conducted the business. Sir Joseph lived in habits of great personal intercourse and friendship with the Right Honourable Arthur Onslow, Esq. speaker of the House of Commons, from the time of his serving the office of sheriff of Surry, till the latter's death in 1768; and he was the instrument, under providence, of saving the life of Mr. Onslow. The malt-distillery had been under prohibition from the year 1757 to 1760, on account of the high price of corn: in the latter year application was made to parliament to permit its going on again under high duties; and this begat an inquiry in the House of Commons respecting that trade, during which Sir Joseph was examined as a witness before a committee of the whole house. The speaker had retired to his own chamber, but left word with a friend to inform him when his countryman, as he called Sir Joseph, was to be examined. On his being called to the bar, the speaker quitted his chamber, and came into the gallery of the house; immediately after which, one of the turrets of the House of Commons was blown by the violence of the wind, and fell through the ceiling into the very part of the room where Mr. Onslow a minute before had been sitting. An escape so providential had its due weight on Mr. Onslow's mind, and he always afterwards attributed his escape to his curiosity in wishing to hear Sir Joseph's examination.

he was candidate to represent the county of Surry in parliament, but four other candidates having previously consolidated their respective interests against him, he was defeated at that time. Sir Francis Vincent's death making a vacancy in June, 1775, he was again a candidate to represent that county in parliament, and was chosen by a considerable majority; Sir Francis Vincent, son of the former member, and Mr. Norton, late Lord Grantley, being his opponents. In 1780, he was again knight of the shire for Surry, with Admiral Keppel, the contest lying between the latter and the Hon. Thomas Onslow; and, in 1784, was again elected for that county. He was for many years one of the chairmen of the quarter-sessions for Surry, and his life, as a magistrate and member of parliament, was active, disinterested, and independent. He was created a Baronet, by letters-patent, on July 30, 1765.

Amidst the hurry of business and public life he cultivated a love for study; and having, when a school-boy, written many poetical pieces, he afterwards, at intervals, amused himself in the same way. He was, for some years, a regular correspondent to the different Magazines, in almost all of which are many of his poetical compositions, some with his name at length, but most commonly under borrowed signatures. By his lady above-mentioned he had nine children, of which number, Catharine, Joseph, Mary, and Emily, are now living.

Catharine, the eldest, was wife, Aug. 14, 1792, of Thomas-Lynch Goleborn, Esq. of the Island of Jamaica, by whom she has had two children, one of which, a daughter, is now living*. Sir Joseph died June 16, 1798, and was succeeded by his son,

* Lady Mawbey, their mother, died at Botleys, on the 19th of August, 1790, and was buried in the family vault in Chertsey chancel on the 26th of August following. A monument to her memory is erected against the wall of the chancel, on which is the following inscription, written by Sir Joseph:

Dame Elizabeth Mawbey,
Wife of Sir Joseph Mawbey, Bart.
Of Botleys, in this parish,
After sustaining a long and painful illness,
with the greatest fortitude and resignation,
Died on the 19th day of August, 1790,
In the 46th year of her age.

"Why weep for me," the blameless woman said,
We all must die, and I am not afraid;
No good to me affords or sigh, or tear,
I've done no wrong, and therefore cannot fear;
Good works and truth shall cheer life's parting scene,
For virtue only makes the mind serene."

Yes, we must part! the conflict now is o'er,
And husband, children, friends, in vain deplore!
But ah! blest Saint! to all around impart
Thy settled goodness, thy unerring heart,
Which bade thee shine, in ev'ry state of life,
As Daughter, Maiden, Parent, Friend, and Wife;

TABLE.

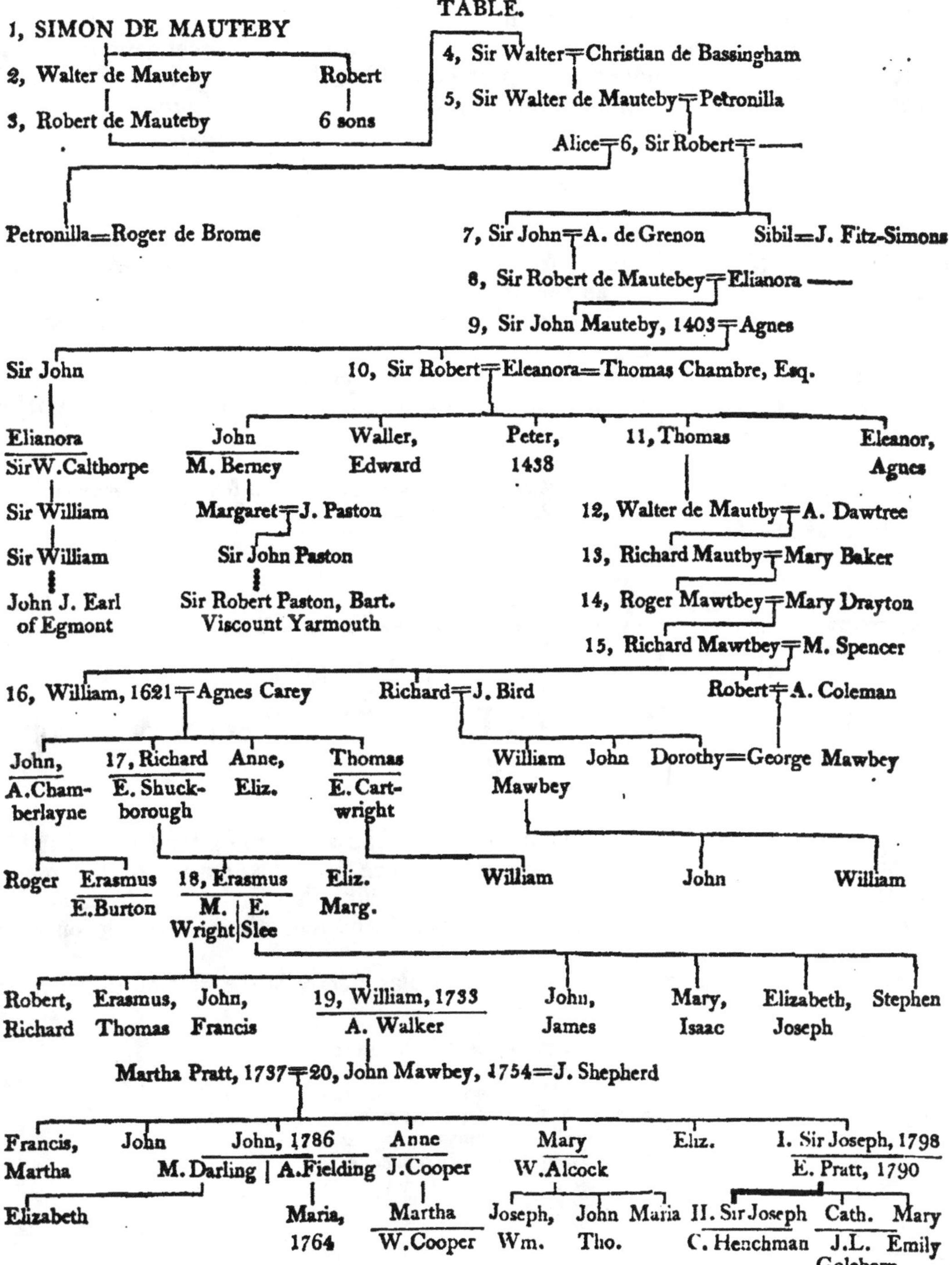
1, SIMON DE MAUTEBY
2, Walter de Mauteby
Robert
3, Robert de Mauteby
6 sons
4, Sir Walter=Christian de Bassingham
5, Sir Walter de Mauteby=Petronilla
Alice=6, Sir Robert= ——
Petronilla=Roger de Brome
7, Sir John=A. de Grenon
Sibil=J. Fitz-Simons
8, Sir Robert de Mautebey=Elianora ——
9, Sir John Mauteby, 1403=Agnes
Sir John
10, Sir Robert=Eleanora=Thomas Chambre, Esq.
Elianora
SirW.Calthorpe
John
M. Berney
Waller, Edward
Peter, 1438
11, Thomas
Eleanor, Agnes
Sir William
Margaret=J. Paston
12, Walter de Mautby=A. Dawtree
Sir William
Sir John Paston
13, Richard Mautby=Mary Baker
John J. Earl of Egmont
Sir Robert Paston, Bart. Viscount Yarmouth
14, Roger Mawtbey=Mary Drayton
15, Richard Mawtbey=M. Spencer
16, William, 1621=Agnes Carey
Richard=J. Bird
Robert=A. Coleman
John, A.Chamberlayne
17, Richard E. Shuckborough
Anne, Eliz.
Thomas E. Cartwright
William Mawbey
John
Dorothy=George Mawbey
Roger
Erasmus E.Burton
18, Erasmus M. Wright | E. Slee
Eliz. Marg.
William
John
William
Robert, Richard
Erasmus, Thomas
John, Francis
19, William, 1733 A. Walker
John, James
Mary, Isaac
Elizabeth, Joseph
Stephen
Martha Pratt, 1737=20, John Mawbey, 1754=J. Shepherd
Francis, Martha
John M. Darling
John, 1786 | A.Fielding
Anne J.Cooper
Mary W.Alcock
Eliz.
I. Sir Joseph, 1798 E. Pratt, 1790
Elizabeth
Maria, 1764
Martha W.Cooper
Joseph, Wm.
John Tho.
Maria
II. Sir Joseph C. Henchman
Cath. J.L. Goleborn
Mary Emily

II. Sir JOSEPH MAWBEY, Bart. who married, Aug. 9, 1796, Charlotte-Caroline-Maria Henchman, only daughter, by his first wife, of Thomas Henchman, Esq. of Littleton, in the county of Middlesex, a descendant from Dr. Henchman, who was concerned in protecting King Charles the Second after the battle of Worcester, by whom he was apppointed, after the Restoration, Bishop of London.

ARMS—Or, a cross, gules, fretty, or, between four eagles displayed, azure, each charged with a bezant on the breast.

CREST—On a wreath, an eagle displayed, azure, charged with a bezant on the breast.

MOTTO—*Auriga virtutum prudentia*, and *Always for Liberty*.

SEATS—At Botleys, in the parish of Chertsey, and county of Surry, and at Vauxhall, in the same county.

The foregoing account of the family of Mawtbey, or Mawbey, is derived from various accounts in the possession of the family, Blomefield's Norfolk, Maddox's History of the Exchequer, Parish Registers, English Baronetage, &c. &c.

283. KNOWLES, of Lovel Hill, near Windsor.

Created Baronet, Oct. 31, 1765.

THIS family is descended from Sir Thomas Knowles, who attended Richard I. in his wars to the Holy Land; where that prince, in consideration of the many signal marks of Sir Thomas's valour, granted him those arms which his family now bears, which are nearly the same as the Jerusalem arms, differing only in some few particulars.

I. Sir CHARLES KNOWLES, the late Baronet, was the first of this family

Bade thee be pious, feelingly to grieve
For other's wants, and silently relieve!
Bade thee, with fortitude supreme, sustain
The waste of sickness, and the rack of pain!
So shall we all obtain heav'n's blest abode,
Nor dread the presence of a righteous God.

who obtained that honour, to which he was advanced by letters-patent, bearing date Oct. 31, 1765. He served on board the Torbay, Sir Charles Wager's ship, and obtained a captain's commission, Feb. 4, 1736-7. In the year 1739, he commanded the Diamond, a forty-gun frigate, and was on the Jamaica station, under Admiral Vernon. In this ship he bombarded the castle of Lorenzo. and, at the head of a body of seamen, attacked the castle of Bocca Chica. In every stage of the memorable siege of Carthagena, he greatly distinguished himself. It was he who, in company with Captain Nathaniel Watson, took the Galicia, the last remaining ship of the Spaniards in that harbour.

In 1743, Captain Knowles commanded the Suffolk, a seventy-gun ship, at Jamaica, and was sent by Sir Chaloner Ogle, with a small squadron, having two thousand three hundred sailors and marines, and four hundred regulars on board, to attack La Guira and Porto Cavallo, on the coast of Terra Firma *. The Spaniards, expecting to be attacked, were fully prepared to receive them, so that the conflict was violent, and for a long time doubtful, but at length the ships were obliged to draw off, having received much damage, and lost many men: the Suffolk received one hundred and forty-six shot in the attack of La Guira.

In March, 1746, Captain Knowles was appointed rear-admiral of the blue, governor of Cape Breton, and commander of his Majesty's ships on that station. He afterwards commanded the fleet at Jamaica, and towards the close of the war, attacked the French at Fort Louis, in St. Domingo, which he reduced, and then went against the Spanish settlements of St. Jago de Cuba, which proved impregnable to his attacks †. He finished the naval transactions of the war, by defeating a Spanish fleet under vice-admiral Reggio, in which action, although his courage was unquestioned, yet his conduct was censured ‡.

In 1752, he was governor of Jamaica, which he resigned in 1758. He was promoted to the rank of vice-admiral of the blue, Feb. 9, 1755, made admiral thereof, Feb. 7, 1758, and promoted to be rear-admiral of the navies and seas of Great Britain, Nov. 5, 1765.

Sir Charles Knowles married first, Mary, daughter of John-Gay Alleyne, Esq. (who was created a Baronet of Great Britain, April 6, 1769), by whom he had one son, who was captain of a man of war, and perished in a storm at sea. He married secondly, Maria-Magdalena-Theresa Bouquet, born in Germany, by whom he has left one son, Charles-Henry, the present Baronet, and a daughter, Charlotte. In the latter end of 1770, our admiral was appointed chief president of the Admiralty to the Empress of Russia, and had a seat in her council. His pension was 2,250l. a-year, and 1,000l. annually, to his lady and family, with benefit of survivorship: a compliment of five hundred guineas was made for his pocket expences. He had also two aides-de-camp, at 500l. a-year each §.

On the 27th of December, he set out with his family for Petersburgh by

* Naval History, Vol. IV. P. 178.
† Ibid, Vol. IV. P. 362, 363, 364.
‡ Ibid, Vol. IV. P. 366, 370.
§ London Magazine, 1770.

the way of Calais, to take upon him that office. Having continued there some years, he revisited his native country, and died Dec. 9, 1777, at his house in Bulstrode street, in the 74th year of his age, and was succeeded by his only son,

II. Sir CHARLES-HENRY KNOWLES, Bart. who, in Dec. 1782, was appointed captain of the St. Michael, of 74 guns, which was a short time before taken from the Spaniards off Gibraltar. He is now rear-admiral of the red, and married, Sept. 10, 1800, Charlotte, daughter of Charles Johnstone, of Ludlow, Esq.

ARMS—Azure, crusuly of crosslets, a cross moline, voided, or.
CREST—An elephant, statant, argent.
MOTTO—*Semper paratus.*
SEAT—At Lovell, Berks.

TABLE.

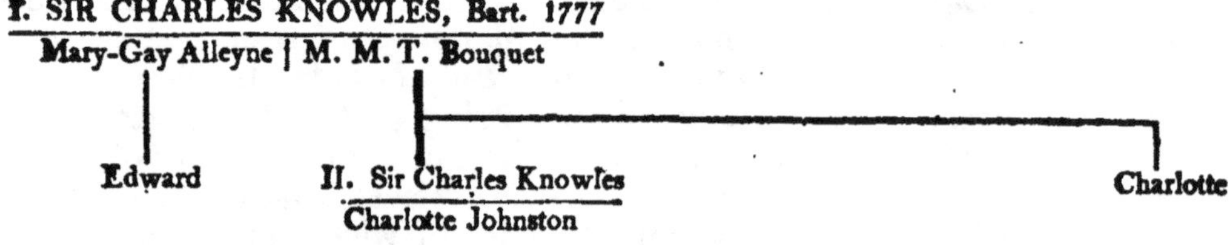

284. EAST, of Hall-Place, Berkshire.

Created Baronet, June 5, 1766.

THIS family has, for a long time, been of note in the city of London, as appears by wills and other evidences.

1, Gilbert East, of the parish of St. Botolph without Bishopsgate, Gent. was the father of,

2, William East, Esq. who was admitted of the Middle Temple, Mar. 14, 1675, and died March 4, 1726. He was buried at Witham, in Essex, in which church, on the north side of the chancel, is a very elegant monument of white and grey marble, with a long Latin inscription to the memory of him, his wife, and children. He married Elizabeth, the only daughter of Jeremy Gough, citizen of London, who was buried Nov. 22, 1748, at Witham aforesaid, by whom he had two sons and four daughters; 1, William, of whom hereafter; 2, Gilbert, was admitted of the Middle Temple, March 22, 1716. He was clerk of the assize for the northern circuit, and lord of the manor of Wenham, in Suffolk, and died unmarried. The daughters were, Mary, Anne, and Sarah, who died infants, and Martha, wife of Sir Philip Parker, of Morley Long, Bart. (brother to Catharine, mother of John Percival, Earl of Egmont, Lord Lovell and Holland, &c.) This lady died March 30, 1758, aged 60, and was buried at Erwarton, in Suffolk, leaving two daughters, Martha, wife of John-Thynne Howe, Lord Chedworth, and Elizabeth, of James Plunket, Esq.

3, William East, Esq. son and heir of the first-mentioned William, was also of the Middle Temple, and admitted into that society, Feb. 23, 1713. He was of Hall Place, in the parish of Hurley, in the county of Berks, and of Kennington, in the county of Surry. He married Anne, only daughter of Sir George Crooke, of Harefield, in the county of Middlesex, Knt. chief prothonotary of the court of common-pleas (which lady died April 1, 1762, and was buried at Witham aforesaid), by whom he had one son, Sir William, of whom hereafter, and two daughters, Anne, wife of Henry Norris, of Hempsted, in Kent, Esq. son of Sir John Norris, Knt. admiral of a squadron of his Majesty's fleet. The other daughter, Elizabeth, was wife of Sir Capel Molineux, of Castle Dillon, in the kingdom of Ireland, Bart.

I. WILLIAM EAST, Esq. son and heir of William East aforesaid, was born Feb. 27, 1737-8, and advanced to the dignity of a Baronet, June 5, 1766, to him and his heirs male. He married, June 29, 1763, at Olveston, in Gloucestershire, Hannah, the second daughter of Henry Casmajor, of Tokington, in Gloucestershire, Esq. by Elizabeth, his wife, daughter of Henry Whitehead, of Tokington, Gent. by whom he had two sons and one daughter; Gilbert, born at Hurley, April 17, 1764, and admitted of the Middle Temple, Nov. 16, 1769: he married, May 10, 1788, ——, eldest daughter of William Jolliffe, Esq; Au-

TABLE.

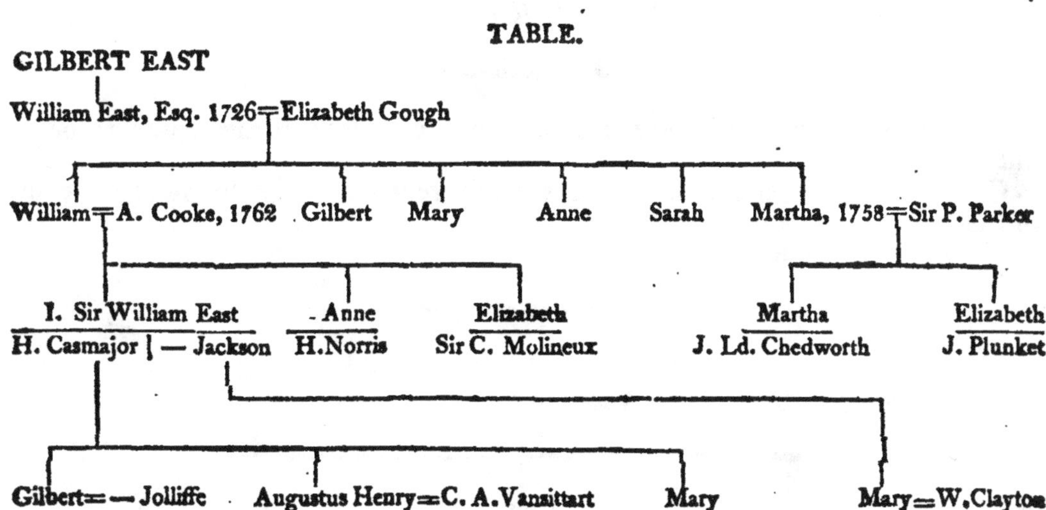

gustus-Henry, born Aug. 24, 1766, who married, Dec. 22, 1792, Caroline-Anne, eldest daughter of George Vansittart, Esq.; and Mary, born Sept. 24, 1765. Sir William East married secondly, July 28, 1768, ——, daughter of —— Jackson, by whom he had one daughter, the wife, 1785, of William Clayton, Esq. M. P. for Great Marlow.

ARMS—Sable, a cheveron between three horse's heads, erased, argent.
CREST—A horse passant, sable.
MOTTO—*J'avance.*
SEAT—At Hall Place, in Berkshire.

285. CHEERE, of Westminster.

Created Baronet, July 18, 1766.

I. HENRY CHEERE, Esq. of the parish of St. Margaret, Westminster, received the honour of knighthood at St. James's, Dec. 10, 1760, when the lord-lieutenant, deputy-lieutenants, and justices of the peace for the county of Middlesex and city and liberty of Westminster, presented a congratulatory address to his Majesty on his accession to the throne; and was farther advanced to the dignity of a Baronet by letters-patent, dated July 18, 1766.

He married Helen, daughter of Sauvignion Randall, Esq. who died Oct. 1769, by whom he had William and Charles, and other children. Sir Henry died Jan. 15, 1781, and was succeeded by his son,

II. Rev. Sir WILLIAM CHEERE, Bart.

ARMS—Quarterly: erminois and gules, over all a label of five points, throughout azure.
CREST—On a wreath, a talbot, passant, azure, collared, or, to the collar a ring of the last.
MOTTO—*Præmium virtutis honor.*

TABLE.

286. ANDREWS, of Shaw, Berks.

Created Baronet, Aug. 19, 1766.

THE family of Andrews (or rather Andrewes, for so it was spelt until the present century) here treated of, descends from a genteel stock of that name which migrated from Northamptonshire * about the beginning of the seventeenth century, to the neighbourhood of Canterbury. From thence,

1, Henry Andrewes removed to London; and, in the fatal pestilence which raged in 1665, was cut off with his whole household, except one infant,

2, Henry Andrewes, then a child in arms, alone survived, who lived to a considerable age, and having acquired some fortune by merchandize, thought it right to take out arms afresh in 1729: he died the next year †. His son,

3, Daniel, survived him but a very short time.

4, Joseph, the son of Daniel Andrews, having applied himself with uncommon diligence to the study of arithmetic, had the good fortune to be protected and encouraged by Sir Robert Walpole, by whose favour he was placed in the Pay Office, and at an uncommonly early age was appointed paymaster to the forces serving in Scotland, A. D. 1715. Some time after this, the accounts of the office being greatly confused, Mr. Andrews was recommended, young as he was, to overlook and reduce them to order. This he performed in a manner so satisfactory, that he was presented by Lord Wilmington (who could now take upon him the office of paymaster-general with security) with a bank-note of one thousand pounds, in a valuable gold box, still preserved by the family.

In 1725, Mr. Andrews married Elizabeth, the daughter of Samuel Beard, Esq. of Newcastle-under-Line, by whom he had Joseph Andrews, born 1727; and the said Elizabeth dying in child-bed, he remarried, in 1736, Elizabeth, the daughter of John Pettit, of St. Botolph, Aldgate, Esq. by whom he had James-Pettit Andrews, born 1737, and Elizabeth, who died in 1761. This James-Pettit Andrews was one of the magistrates of the Police Office in Queen-square, Westminster; he was educated by a private tutor, the Rev. Mr. Matthews, rector of Shaw, Berks, and distinguished himself for his application to literature and the polite arts. At the age of eighteen or nineteen, Mr. Andrews went into the Berkshire militia, on the first calling out of that body of men, was appointed a lieutenant, and remained in the regiment till it was disembodied. He married Anne, daughter of the Rev. —— Penrose, rector of Newbury, who died Sept. 1, 1785, and by whom

* In the grant of arms, the descent here mentioned is strongly intimated.

† It is an unpleasant circumstance, that as the whole of this branch have been Presbyterians except the present generation, it is deprived of that collateral evidence which registers of births, burials, &c. afford to those of the national church, otherwise its connection might be clearly established with a respectable family bearing the same christian names, and having five generations entered in a visitation of London, A.D. 1634. cap. 24, 324.

he had three children; 1, Sir Joseph, the present Baronet; 2, Elizabeth-Anne, wife of Charles-Henry Hunt, Esq. late of Goldicoth, in Worcestershire; 3, Charles-Gray, was a midshipman in the navy, and died Aug. 1791, aged 18. Mr. Andrews was author of several publications; amongst others, 1, Anecdotes, Ancient and Modern, with Observations, 1789, 8vo. and a Supplement to it in 1790; 2, A History of Great Britain, connected with the Chronology of Europe, 1795, 2 vols. 4to. containing Anecdotes of the Times, Lives of the Learned, with Specimens of their Works, on the Plan of the President Henault, &c. &c. (*Gent. Mag.* 1797.) Mr. Andrews retained the friendship with which he was honoured by Sir Robert Walpole until the decease of that great statesman, who, when he used to press him, as he frequently did, to serve in parliament, always received this answer. "In my line of duty at the Pay Office, I have, Sir, a plain path before me. In parliament I may disoblige my best friend and patron, by opposing, as an honest man, measures of which I may not comprehend the utility." The excuse never displeased the minister, and Mr. Andrews continued to rise in his department. He was even once named in a warrant (signed by the king *) as paymaster-general of his Majesty's forces in Great Britain. He died in April, 1753, aged 62.

I. JOSEPH ANDREWS, the son of this gentleman, went out, in 1759, as captain of a company, in almost the earliest of the militia regiments, that of Berks, to which, not long afterwards, he was appointed major. Some time after the peace of 1763, he quitted the service, as did his brother James-Pettit Andrews, who had served during the war as lieutenant to his company.

In August, 1766, Mr. Joseph Andrews was created a Baronet of Great Britain, with remainder to his above-mentioned brother, in case of male issue failing in the elder branch. In 1762, he married Elizabeth, daughter of Richard Phillips, of Tarrington, in Hertfordshire, Esq. by whom he had no issue, and died Dec. 29, 1800 †, and was succeeded by his nephew,

* Mr. Andrews held the employment only a few days. The warrant is still in possession of the family.

† The following appeared in the Gentleman's Magazine:

Dec. 29, 1800.

Died at his seat at Shaw Place, near Newbury, after a lingering and painful illness, borne with Christian fortitude, cheerfulness, and resignation, Sir Joseph Andrews, Bart. of whom it has been often remarked, no one ever spoke ill, and of whom every one, that knew his disposition, had something to say, either of his integrity, prudence, generosity, conciliatory temper, benevolence, or charity. Very happily combining his manners and the dignity of the old country gentleman, with great attention to the public institutions in London; his life and fortune were devoted to relieve the wants, and cheer the distresses of his fellow-men. Of his public spirit, the many societies in the metropolis, formed for the purposes of utility to the state, or the relief and comfort of families and individuals, bear ample testimonies. He was a vice-president of the Marine and Royal Humane Societies, of the Margate Sea-Bathing Infirmary, and of the Literary Fund. All these useful institutions were greatly indebted to his bounty and attention, and to almost every other useful establishment of public charity, he was a constant contributor. There was scarcely any one but he belonged to, and gave some of his time and attention to the management of its affairs. Of one in particular, it is said that he was offered to be made a vice-president, when several noble vice-presidents had too just cause for withdrawing their names, but Sir Joseph very resolutely and honourably declined accepting the offer. Where-ever he appeared, he claimed great respect. He said but little, but that little was always to the purpose; and while he had the command of his own temper, he maintained some influence over those whose violence of temper was to supply the place of reason; and who may think that a man's arguments are strong, because his voice is loud. A deference was paid to him by men whose only worth is their money.

II. Sir JOSEPH ANDREWS, Bart. late a lieutenant in the first regiment of foot-guards, who was born Sept. 22, 1768, and is unmarried.

ARMS—Gules, a saltire, argent, surmounted by another, azure, charged in the centre with a bezant.

CREST—Out of an eastern crown, or, a blackmoor's head, couped, having in his ear a pendant, or.

MOTTO—*Victrix fortunæ sapientia.*

SEAT—Shaw, in Berkshire.

His conversation breathed of fervent and benign philanthropy, such as the most enlightened philosophy, and the purest of religions, might with pride acknowledge. Of literary genius he was also a distinguished judge and patron. He lived in friendship with many of the most excellent persons of the age. Among these, Mr. Pye, whose erudition, taste, and genius, do honour to the laurel, cannot but deeply feel the loss of a friend so truly good, and so sincerely revered. With his brother, the late James-Pettit Andrews, Sir Joseph lived in the happiest fraternal intimacy. To the poor of his neighbourhood, on all those occasions which produce an endearing intercourse of charity and confidence, he was of all men the kindest. His loss, at the season of their annual festivity, will be severely felt by the objects of his wonted bounty.

The death of such a man is a loss to the community not easily repaired. To his relatives, his memory will be ever dear, and among his numerous friends and acquaintance, his name will be held in veneration, while there remains a regard for private worth and public virtue. Sir Joseph Andrews married, in 1762, Miss Elizabeth Phillips, a lady of family and considerable fortune in Hertfordshire; this lady survives. He was created a Baronet 1766; but having no issue, he is succeeded in title and estates by his nephew, now Sir Joseph Andrews, the only surviving son to the late amiable and well-known James-Pettit Andrews. He was interred, Jan. 7, in the chancel of Shaw Church, in a manner as private as was consistent with his rank and character, he having always expressed great dislike to the vanity of funeral pomp.

The estate and manor at Shaw was purchased, by the late Sir Joseph Andrews' father, of the representatives of Mr. Doleman's ancestor, an eminent clothier, who built it upon retiring from business on a good fortune. While in that family, it was secured in the civil war with a high bank or rampart of earth still remaining, and served the king for a temporary retreat; and, in a bow-window of the library, is still shewn a hole made by a bullet discharged at his Majesty while dressing there.

The following very elegant lines are from the pen of his friend, the Laureat:

As heaven's ambrosial gales and genial showers
Deck Nature's smiling face with vernal flowers,
So shall, lamented Andrews, o'er thy tomb,
The flowers arise of amaranthine bloom;
By those blest gales and showers matured, that blow
The sighs of virtue, and the tears of woe.

And these by his young friend J. J. S.

Though the fell tyrant, with relentless arm,
Number'd thy years as silver deck'd thy brow,
And virtue's mould, in thee, could not disarm
The uplifted dart which laid our Andrews low:
Yet, not terrific was the impending spear,
To heaven he bow'd, and dropt a joyous tear.
Long shall thy virtues, when this tottering frame,
Dust chang'd to dust, assumes its native mould,
Long shall those virtues to thy honoured name
Raise a huge hill of monumental gold,
Which shall one lesson to our minds impart,
Virtue's memorial is each grateful heart.

TABLE

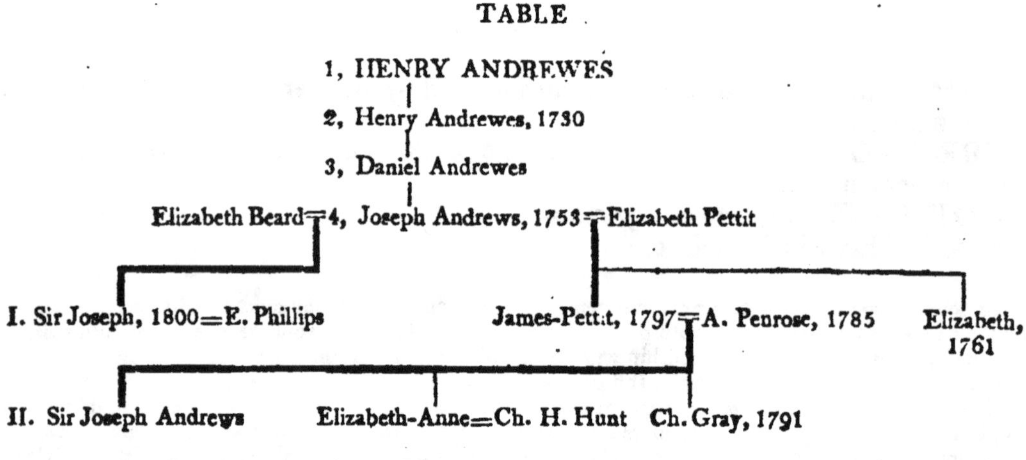

287. THOMAS, of YAPTON-PLACE, Sussex.

Created Baronet, Sept. 6, 1766.

SIR GEORGE THOMAS, who purchased Yapton-Place, in the county of Sussex, was descended of a gentleman's family originally of Monmouthshire. He was nine years governor of Pennsylvania, and thirteen years captain-general and governor in chief of the Leeward Islands, in which he several times received the approbation and thanks of their majesties King George II. and King George III. for his national services during the wars with Spain and France. When peace was restored, he returned to England, with the king's licence of absence from his government, for the benefit of his health; and was, soon after his arrival, created a Baronet by patent dated Sept. 6, 1766.

On the 18th of December following, he resigned the government of the Leeward Islands, to the general regret of the inhabitants, as well as of the British merchants concerned in the trade to them, who had publickly, and in a most distinguished manner, given the amplest testimonials of their esteem and approbation of his conduct in the administration of both governments.

Sir George married ——, daughter of —— King, by whom he had five children; 1, Lydia, wife of John White, Esq.; 2, Sir William, of whom hereafter; 3, Elizabeth, who died unmarried; 4, George, died unmarried; and 5, Margery, wife of Arthur Freeman, Esq. Sir George died Dec. 31, 1774, and was succeeded by his son,

II. Sir WILLIAM THOMAS, Bart. who married Miss Sydserfe, an heiress, by whom he had seven children; 1, Elizabeth, wife of Colonel Lyon; 2, Susan, of William Roe, Esq.; 3, Maria, of General Popham; 4, Lydia, of Alexander Adair, of Flixton-Hall, in Suffolk, Esq.; 5, Sir George, of whom hereafter; 6, Anne, wife of Stephen Popham, Esq.; and 7, Frances, of John Williams, Esq. Sir William died Dec. 28, 1777, and was succeeded by his son,

III. Sir GEORGE THOMAS, Bart, who married first, at Geneva, Mad. Sales, of Pregny la Tour; he married secondly, Miss Montague, by whom he has one son, William-Lewis-George, who married ——, daughter of —— Welch, by whom he has one daughter, Sophia.

ARMS—Argent, three lions rampant, two and one, gules, a chief, azure.
CREST—On a wreath, a demi-lion, rampant, gules.
MOTTO—*Honesty is the best Policy*.
SEAT—Yapton-Place, Sussex.

TABLE.

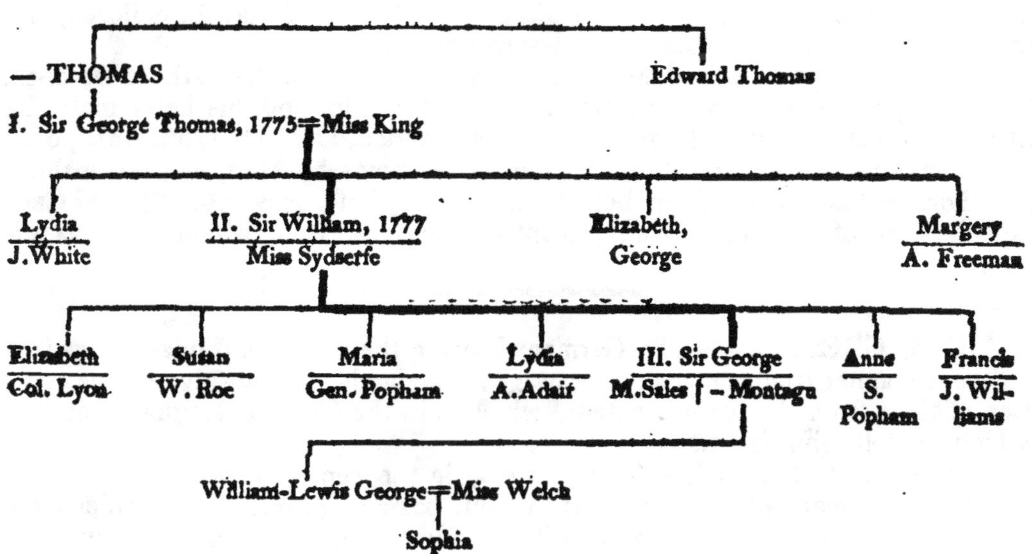

288. WOLFF, of Cams-Hall, Hampshire.

Created Baronet, Oct. 18, 1766.

1, CHARLES-GODFREY WOLFF, of St. Petersburg, Esq. descended, on the father's side, from a noble Silesian family, that had a fief under the emperors of Germany, near Breslau; but, when the religious troubles commenced in Silesia, they were forced to quit that country, and seek an asylum under the crown of Sweden, where the Lutheran religion prevailed.

When Peter the Great conquered Livonia, this Charles-Godfrey Wolff was carried, being then an infant, 1704, in captivity, into Wologoda, a town in the interior parts of the Russian empire, and, arriving at the age of maturity, settled at Moscow, where, on the 27th of January, 1739, O. S. the present Baronet was born.

I. Sir JACOB WOLFF succeeded his late uncle, Baron Jacob Wolff, in 1759 (his late Majesty's resident and consul-general), in his estates; and the Emperor of Germany, Francis the First, honoured him with the patent of a Baron, bearing date at Vienna, in July, 1761, wherein he is stiled, Jacob Van Wolff, Knt. and Baron of the Holy Roman Empire, and to all his lawful children, and their issue, males and females, in the descending line.

Sir Jacob being naturalized, settled in Hampshire, and on the 27th of October, 1766, his present Majesty was pleased to confer on him and his heirs male the title of Baronets of Great Britain. Sir Jacob married, Dec. 11, 1766, Anne, only daughter of the Right Hon. Edward Weston, of Somerby-Hall, in Lincolnshire, by whom he has one daughter, born Oct. 8, 1771, wife, Nov. 29, 1792, of Captain Parslow, of the king's own regiment of dragoons, from whom she was divorced.

ARMS, CREST, &c.—The Germans bearing their arms and quarterings in a different manner from the custom or usage in England, we shall give the description of them from the Baron's patent, which is in the German language, and of which the following is a translation:

A shield erect, divided into four quarters, in the centre of which, an escutcheon, with the arms following: vert, a wolf, passant, proper, and in chief three fleurs-de-lis, argent: the arms of Van Wolff. In the first quarter of the atchievement, or, an eagle displayed, sable, ducally crowned, gules; in the second quarter, azure, an armed arm issuing out of clouds from the sinister, grasping a sword in the attitude of striking, proper; in the third quarter, argent, a naked arm, issuing out of the clouds from the sinister, holding a palm-branch, proper; and, lastly, in the fourth quarter, or, a triangle, sable. The whole atchievement is illustrated with an imperial baron's crown, or, set with five large pearls, upon which are three open tilting helmets, azure, ducally crowned, or, lined, gules, ornamented with jewels pendant, or; the dexter mantling, green and silver, and the sinister, black and gold, intermixed: from the middle coronet, issuant, a demi-wolf, rampant, proper; on the dexter helmet, issuant, from the ducal coronet, a fleur-de-lis, argent, between two wings of a Saxon eagle displayed, tawney; and on the sinister, standing on a ducal coronet, an eagle displayed, sable, crowned as in the first quarter of arms; and lastly, for his supporters, two lions rampant, regardant, with double tails, or, tongues, gules.

MOTTO—*Dante Deo.*

SEAT—At Cams-Hall, Fareham, Hampshire.

TABLE,

—— WOLFF

Charles-Godfrey Wolff — Baron Jacob Wolff

I. Sir Jacob Wolff = Anne Weston

Capt. Parslow | Major ——

289. CHAMNEYS, of ORCHARDLEY, Somersetshire.

Created Baronet, Jan. 12, 1767.

THE tradition in Somersetshire is, that this family has been seated at Orchardley, near Frome-Selwood, in that county, from the time of the Norman conquest.

1, Sir Amian Chamneys, Knt. lived temp. Hen. II.; he had one son,

2, Sir Amian Chamneys, Knt. who married Anne, daughter of — Courtenay, Earl of Devonshire (by his wife Blanch, daughter of Lewis, King of France), by whom he had,

3, Sir John Chamneys, Knt. who married ——, daughter of Sir Richard Turberville, Knt. by whom he had one son, Sir Hugh, and one daughter Joan, wife of John de Merlaund*.

* Sir Henry de Merlaund lived temp. Edw. I. and died 12 Edw. II. leaving Henry, his son and heir, who died 30 Edw. III. and was succeeded by Henry, his son, who was a knight and celebrated warrior; he died 45 Edw. III. and his son, John, lived in the beginning of the reign of Rich. II. and was the last of this branch, leaving Joan, his wife, his heir (a).

(a) Old deeds.

4, Sir Hugh Chamneys, Knt. married Maud, daughter and heiress of Sir John Avenell, Knt. son of Sir Geffrey Avenell, Knt. by whom he had,

5, Sir John Chamneys, who married Anne, daughter of Thomas Warren, of the county of Gloucester, Gent. by whom he had two sons, Sir John, who died without issue, and Ralph, of whom hereafter; and one daughter Margaret, wife of Sir Thomas de Gournay, of Stoke, in Somersetshire, and of Gloucestershire *.

6, Ralfe Chamneys succeeded, and married Alice, daughter and heiress of — Corts, of Devonshire, Gent. by whom he had one daughter Agnes, wife of John de Flory, and one son,

7, John Chamneys, called John de Erleigh, de Orleigh, or Orcherlei, who married Beatrix, daughter of Sir John Cheverell, of Wiltshire, by whom he had one son,

8, Richard Chamneys, Esq. who married ——, daughter of —— Williamscote, of Gloucestershire, by whom he had,

9, Richard Chamneys, Esq. who married Mary, daughter of —— Stakepole, by whom he had,

10, Sir John Chamneys, Knt. who married Elizabeth, daughter of Sir Hugh Bitton, of Bitton, in Gloucestershire, by whom he had two sons, Sir Henry, of whom hereafter, and John † Chamneys, Esq. to whom the moor's head was given for a crest in the field of battle. He married Joane, daughter of Sir Humphrey Aylesworth, of Aylesworth, by whom he had two sons, 1, Thomas Chamneys, of Gutteridge, in Wiltshire, Esq. who married Alice, daughter of ——, by whom he had one son Thomas, and a daughter Joan; 2, John (the second son of John), was of Chew, in Somersetshire, and married ——, daughter of — Castelyne, by whom he had one son, Sir John Champneys, Knt. lord-mayor of London, 1534; he married Muriel, eldest daughter of John Barret, of Bell House, in Essex, Esq. and died Oct. 3, 1556, and was buried at Boxley, in Kent, where is his monument, and was succeeded by his son,

11, Sir Henry Chamneys, Knt. who married Elizabeth, daughter and heiress of Walter de Horrey: they were both living in 1463, and were buried at Frome, in Somersetshire. They had three sons, 1, Henry; 2, Richard, who died 1463, and was buried at Frome ‡; 3, Sir Thomas Chamneys, Knt. (his will dated and proved, 1505); he married Joan, daughter of William de Whatcombe, in Somersetshire, by whom he had two sons, 1, Sir Thomas Chamneys, of Orchardleigh

* Sir Thomas de Gournay possessed great estates in the eastern part of the county of Somerset, in right of his female ancestress, Eva de Gournay, sister and heiress of Maurice Berkeley, and daughter of Robert Fitzharding, by Alice, daughter and heiress of Robert Gaunt, of Folkingham, brother, and at length heir, of Gilbert de Gaunt, Earl of Lincoln, which Eva was heiress of the great houses of Fitzharding, Gournay, Gaunt, and Paganel. The grandfather of this Sir Thomas de Gournay assumed the name and arms of his grandmother, and had summons to Bristol well fitted with horse and arms. The last heir male dying without issue, the estate became vested in the duchy of Cornwall.—N.B. The Cowhill estate came by this lady, in Gloucestershire.

† Old deeds place this John higher up, as father of Thomas, who was father to Sir Henry and John, father of Sir John.

‡ His will dated 1463, proved Feb. 9, 1468.

aforesaid, K. B. he died before 1506; he married Margaret ——; 2, Richard, living at Frome, 1505: and one daughter ——, wife of John Agmondesham.

12, Henry Chamneys, of Frome-Selwood, Esq. was buried at the church of Frome, will dated July 28, 1505, proved Jan. 5, 1506. He married Jane, daughter of Gabriel Liversedge, of Vallis-House, near Frome, and heiress, by her mother, to the family of Braunch, by whom he had three sons and three daughters; 1, Henry; 2, John, of Yarnscombe, in Somersetshire, Esq. living in 1506: he married Christian, daughter of Humphrey Sydenham, of Combe-Sydenham, by whom he had Thomas, Richard, Isabella, Margaret, and Jane, the wife of H. Sydenham; and 3, Christopher, living 1506. Of the daughters, 1, Agnes, living in 1506, abbess of the monastery of Shaftesbury, received a pension of ten pounds per annum after the dissolution; 2, Elizabeth; 3, Grace, both living in 1505. Henry was succeeded by his son,

13, Henry Chamneys, of Orchardleigh, Esq.; he married Elizabeth, only daughter and heiress of — St. Maur, of Seymour's-Court, in Somersetshire: her will was dated July 5, proved July 26, 1580, and she was buried at Frome. By this lady he had six sons and two daughters; 1, John, of whom hereafter; 2, Edward; 3, Christopher; 4, George; 5, Henry; and 6, Richard, who married ——, daughter of Sir Amias Baumfield, of Hardington, Knt. These last five were all living in 1580. Joan, the eldest daughter, was wife of John Rowland, and Elizabeth, of William Cutte, Esq. Henry was buried at Frome, his will dated in 1570, and was succeeded by his eldest son,

14, John Chamneys, Esq. who was executor to his father: he married Joan, daughter of William Sydenham, and heiress to her mother, a Wyndham. He married secondly, Cecil, daughter of —, who was executrix to her husband in 1613. This John's will is dated June 18, 1607, proved Feb. 14, 1613: he had two sons, (but by which lady does not appear), John, and William, who went into Spain, and died S. P. leaving his estates to his brother,

15, John Chamneys, of Orchardley, Esq. married, 1610, Honor, daughter of Sir Francis Caldecot, Knt.: she was buried in the church of Orchardleigh, June 24, 1664, will dated May 10, 1654, proved Jan. 31, 1664-5. By this lady he had nine children; 1, John; 2, Edward, born Sept. 3, and baptized at Orchardleigh, Oct. 5, 1628, living 1654; 3, Edith, wife, Jan. 26, 1636, of Jerome Potticary, Esq.: she was buried April 2, 1636; 4, Richard, a merchant, will dated Nov. 30, 1634, proved Oct. 31, 1635, by his father; 5, William, baptized Oct. 5, 1626: he was executor to his mother's will, 1664; he married Elizabeth, daughter of ——, by whom he had five children, Anthony, born Dec. 22, 1660, Elizabeth, Richard, born Feb. 24, 1656, William, baptized Dec. 11, 1655, and John, born Jan. 18, 1657; 6, Jane, born March 8, 1628; 7, Penelope, wife, July 2, 1638, of John Greenhill, Esq.: she was buried at Orchardleigh, March 19, 1662; 8, Elizabeth, wife of Sir —— Hungerford, of Farley-Castle, Wiltshire; 9, Francis, living in 1640; 10, Honor, wife, May 30, 1649, of Henry Williams, Esq.*.

* Vide Register.

TABLE.

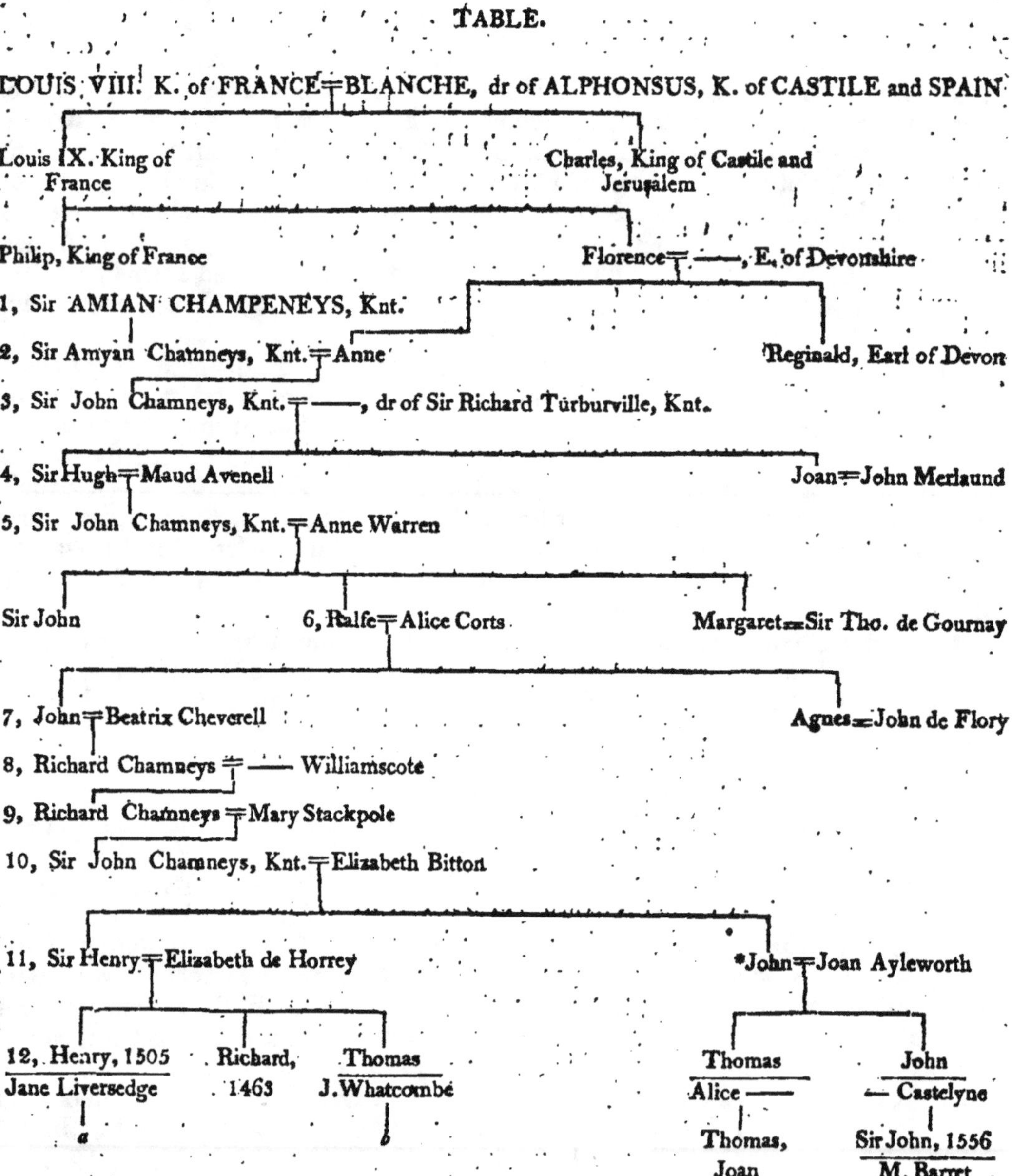

* Ancestor of the Champneys, of Kent. This John Champneys was grandfather of Sir John Champneys, lord-mayor of London in 1534.—From 1, Sir Amian, to this John, extracted from the register in Coll. Armor.

TABLE *continued.*

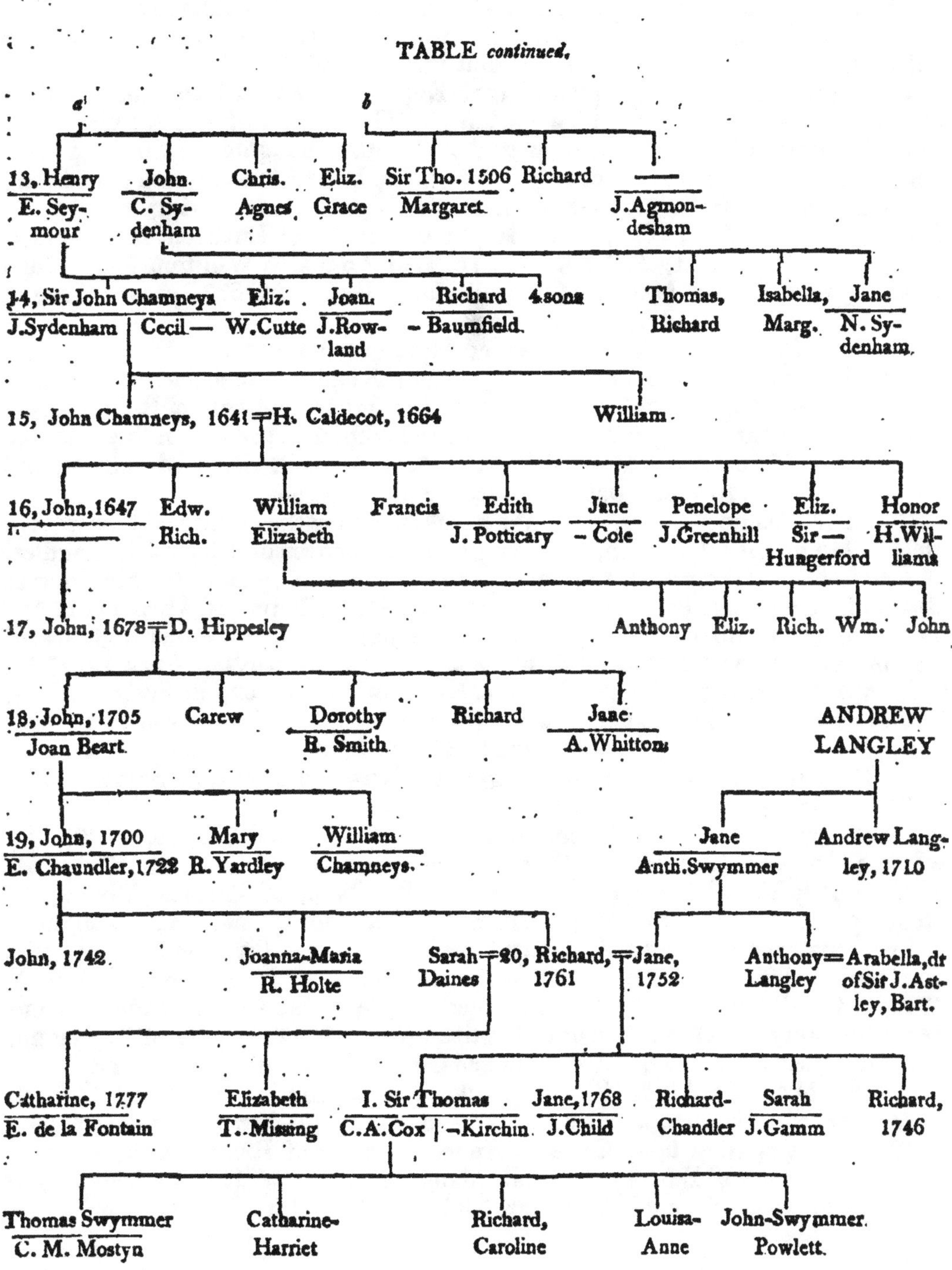

John Chamneys was buried at Orchardleigh, March 24, 1641, will dated May 7, 1640, and proved May 10, 1647, and was succeeded by his eldest son,

16, John Chamneys, of Orchardleigh, Esq. who was executor to his father's will. He was buried May 27, 1672, and was succeeded by his son,

17, John Chamneys, of Orchardleigh, Esq. who married Deborah, daughter of John Hippesley, Esq. of Stone Easton and Gameley, in Somersetshire, (and grand-daughter of Sir John Hippesley, by Dorothy, daughter of Sir John Horner, of Cloford, in the same county), by whom he had five children; 1, John; 2, Carew, mentioned in his great-grandmother's will, 1654, living in 1677; 3, Dorothy, wife, July 8, 1675, of Robert Smith, of Stony Littleton, in Somersetshire, Esq.; 4, Richard; 5, Jane, wife, 1674, of Augustus Whitton, Esq. John Chamneys was buried May 1, 1678, will dated Dec. 13, 1677, proved June 5, 1678: he was succeeded by his eldest son,

18, John Chamneys, Esq. who married Jane, only daughter of William Beart, of Wilmington, in Somersetshire, Esq. by whom he had two sons and one daughter Mary, baptized Oct. 30, 1679, executrix to her father, and wife of Robert Yardley, Esq. William, the younger son, baptized Feb. 21, 1676, was bred to the law. John Chamneys was buried April 6, 1705, will dated March 29, and proved June 11, 1705, and was succeeded by his eldest son,

19, John Chamneys, Esq. who was high-sheriff for the county of Somerset in 1695. He married Elizabeth, only daughter and heiress of Richard Chaundler, of Cam's-Hall, Hampshire (and heiress to her maternal grandfather Sir Thomas Badd, of Cam's Hall, Bart. her will dated Dec. 29, 1722, proved April 11, 1723), by whom he had three children, 1, John Chamneys, Esq. who was high-sheriff for the county of Somerset in 1695, and was buried at Orchardley, April 12, 1742; 2, Joanna-Maria, wife, 1722, of Richard Hole, of Farrington, in Somersetshire, and of Netherton, in Wiltshire, Esq. by whom she had one son, who died S. P. John Chamneys, Esq. was buried Feb. 13, 1700.

20, Richard Chamneys, Esq. the younger son, was high-sheriff for Somersetshire in 1728. He married Sarah, daughter and coheiress of Sir William Daines, of Bristol, Knt. (and sister to the Viscountess Barrington, buried Jan. 4, 1733), by whom he had two daughters, Catharine-Chandler, baptized Sept. 21, 1723, wife of Elias de la Fontain, and died 1777; and Elizabeth, of Thomas Missing, of Stebbington, in Hampshire, Esq. He married secondly, Jane, only daughter, and eventually sole heiress of Anthony-Langley Swymmer (by Jane Langley) who was buried July 13, 1752, by whom he had issue, 1, Jane, baptized Feb. 3, 1742, wife of John Child, Esq. and died 1768; 2, Richard-Chandler Chamneys, born July 13, 1743; 3, Sarah, baptized Nov. 19, 1744, wife of J. Gamm, Esq. and died 1771; 4, Richard, baptized Oct. 19, 1745, died 1646; and

I. THOMAS CHAMNEYS, Esq. who was baptized at Fareham, Oct. 9, 1745, created a Baronet, Jan. 26, 1767, and was high-sheriff for Somersetshire in 1775. He married first, Caroline-Anne, daughter of Richard Cox, of Quarley, in Hampshire, Esq. by Caroline, daughter of Sir William Codrington, of Dodington, Bart. who died at Orchardleigh in 1791. Sir Thomas married secondly, ——, daughter of Humphry Kirchin, of Stubbington, in Hants, Esq. by whom he has no issue; but by his first lady he had six children, 1, Thomas-Swymmer Chamneys, Esq. only surviving son, born May 31, 1799, high-sheriff for Somerset in 1780; he married at St. George's, Hanover-square, April 21, 1792, Charlotte-Margaret, second daughter of Sir Roger Mostyn. of Mostyn, in the county of Flint, Bart.; 2, Catharine-Harriot, born Jan. 1776, now living; 3, Richard, buried at St. George's, Hanover-square, 1770; 4, Caroline, buried at Orchardleigh, 1793; 5, Louisa-Anne, buried at Orchardleigh, June 15, 1776; John-Swymmer-Powlett, buried at Quarley, in Hampshire.

ARMS—The original armorial bearings of the family of Champnée, or Champneys, as they stand in the register of Caen, in Normandy, are, Party, per pale, or, and sable, a border engrailed and counterchanged, a lion rampant, gules.

CREST—Out of a ducal coronet, a sword erect, between two wings expanded.

SUPPORTERS—Two lions rampant, gules, crowned, murally; and by a grant of Louis the XIVth, King of France, the lions are charged, one with the arms of France, and the other of Navarre.

MOTTO—*Pro patria non timidus perire.*

SEAT—At Orchardleigh, in Somersetshire.

290. HORT, of Castle-Strange, Middlesex.

Created Baronet, Aug. 29, 1767.

1, JOHN HORT, of Marshfield, in the county of Gloucester, Esq. was the ther of,

2, Josiah Hort, archbishop of Tuam, in the kingdom of Ireland, who married Elizabeth, eldest daughter of the Hon. William Fitzmaurice, by whom he had five sons and four daughters; 1, Charles, who died without issue; 2, Josiah-George, of Hortland, in the county of Kildare, and kingdom of Ireland, married ——, daughter and coheiress of John Hawkes, Esq. both living without issue in 1771; 3, John, of whom hereafter; 4, William; and 5, Thomas. The daughters were, 1, Mary-Anne, deceased; 2, Elizabeth, wife of Sir James Caldwell, of Castle-Caldwell, in the county of Fermanagh, in the kingdom of Ireland; 3, Frances, wife of John Parker, of Barrington and Saltram, in the county of Devon, Esq.; 4, Mary, of John Cramer, of Bellaville, in the county of Meath, in the kingdom of Ireland, living in 1771. The archbishop died Dec. 14, 1751, and was buried in St. George's Chapel, in Dublin.

I. JOHN HORT, Esq. third son of the archbishop, is stiled of Castle-Strange, in the county of Middlesex. He was born in Ireland, Aug. 8, 1735, was appointed his Majesty's consul-general at the court of Portugal, and created a Baronet of the kingdom of Great Britain by letters-patent, bearing date Aug. 29, 1767, to him and his heirs male. Sir John married, Oct. 1789, ——, daughter of — Aylmer.

ARMS—Azure, a cross, or, in the first quarter, a rose, argent.

CREST—An eagle regardant, with wings expanded, proper, in his beak a chaplet, vert.

SEAT—Mulsoe, Bucks, and Hortland, in Kildare, Ireland.

TABLE.

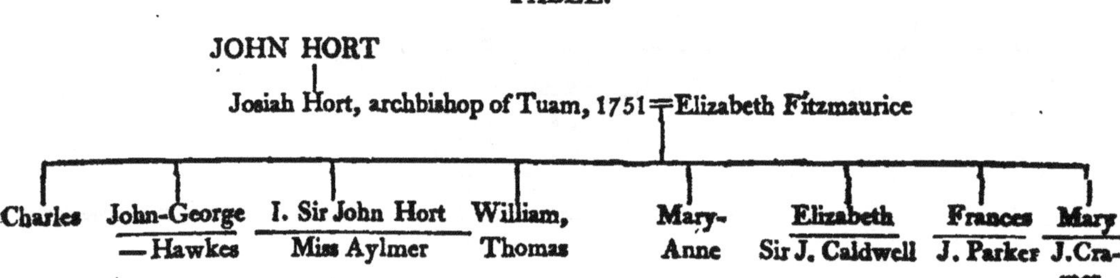

291. BURNABY, of BROUGHTON-HALL, Oxfordshire.

Created Baronet, Oct. 31, 1767.

JOHN BURNABY, of Kensington, in the county of Middlesex, Esq. married Clara, daughter of Sir Edward Wood, Knt. by whom he had six sons and three daughters; 1, John, who was many years minister to the Swiss Cantons, and secretary to the Earl of Waldegrave, ambassador extraordinary at the court of France; 2, Edward, was of Cleveland-row, St. James's, and one of the chief clerks of the treasury: he married Mary, daughter and heiress of Thomas Green, of Norlands, in the county of Middlesex, by whom he had issue, Edward-Burnaby Green, who married Miss Carteret; William-Pitt Burnaby, a lieutenant in the navy, and other children; 3, William, of whom hereafter; 4, Daniel, was rector of Hanwell, in the county of Middlesex, and fellow of St. John's College, Cambridge; 5, Robinson; and 6, Thomas, both died young.

The daughters were, 1, Clara; 2, Bathshua; and 3, Carolina, wife of Charles Waldon, son of Dr. Waldon, of Harrow-on-the-Hill, in the county of Middlesex.

I. WILLIAM BURNABY, Esq. (third son of the first-mentioned John), of Broughton-Hall, in the county of Oxford, and lord of that manor, also a captain in the navy, received the honour of knighthood at St. James's, April 9, 1754, made admiral of the red squadron of his Majesty's fleet, afterwards admiral and commander in chief at Jamaica, and in the gulf of Mexico. He assisted in settling the infant colony of Pensacola, and reinstating the logwood cutters, who had been illegally driven from thence by the Spaniards. He was high-sheriff for the county of Oxford in 1764, one of his Majesty's justiees of the peace for the said county, and created a Baronet of Great Britain by letters-patent, bearing date Oct. 31, 1767, to him and his heirs male. Sir William married first, Margaret, relict of —— Donovan, of the Island of Jamaica, Esq. by whom he had William-Chaloner and Elizabeth. Sir William married secondly, Grace, daughter of Drewry Ottley, of Bedford-row, in the parish of St. Andrew, Holborn, Esq. by whom he had Drewry, who died an infant, Edward-Augustus-Cæsar, and one daughter Georgiana-Grace. Sir William died, and was succeeded by his son,

II. Sir WILLIAM-CHALONER BURNABY, Bart. who married, June 29, 1783, Elizabeth, second daughter of Crisp Molineux, of Garboldesham, in Norfolk, Esq, by whom he had one son, now

III. Sir WILLIAM-CRISP-HOOD BURNABY, Bart.

TABLE.

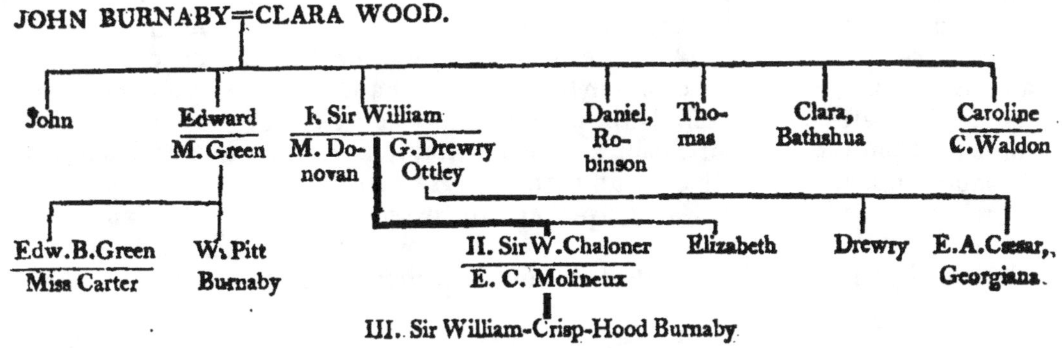

ARMS—Argent, two bars, gules; in chief, a lion passant, per pale, of the second, and vert.

CREST—Out of a naval crown, a demi-lion rampant, guardant, or, in the dexter paw, a staff, proper, thereon the flag of his own division,

MOTTO—*Pro Rege.*

SEAT—At Broughton-Hall, in Oxfordshire.

---

292. BURRARD (now NEALE), of WALHAMPTON, Hants.

Created Baronet, March 20, 1769.

1, THOMAS BURRARD, of Lymington, in the county of Hants, born 1611, married Elizabeth, daughter of Justinian Isham, by whom he had four sons and one daughter, Anne, who died unmarried; 1, Thomas; 2, John; 3, Sidney; and 4, Paul, of whom hereafter.

John, the second, but eldest surviving son, married, Jan. 9, 1666, Elizabeth, daughter and coheiress of John Button, of Buckland, in the county of Hants, Esq. by his wife, Mary Jesson, of Coventry, by whom he had two sons, John and Thomas, who both died unmarried, and five daughters; 1, Anne, died unmarried; 2, Mary, wife of Robert Knapton, Esq.; 3, Betty, of Ralph Hastings, Esq.; 4, Sarah, of Hugh Harsnet, Esq.; 5, Jane. died young.

2, Paul Burrard, of Walhampton, in the county of Hants, Esq. youngest son of Thomas Burrard, of Lymington aforesaid, married, March 20, 1678, Anne, another daughter of John Button, of Buckland, in the county of Hants aforesaid, by whom he had three sons; Paul, of whom hereafter; John and Sidney, twins, who both died young.

3, Paul Burrard, of Walhampton, in the county of Hants, Esq. the only surviving son of the above Paul, married Lucy, daughter of Sir William Colt, envoy extraordinary to the courts of Dresden, Lunenburg, Zell, and Hanover (by his wife Lucy Webb), by whom he had one daughter Mary, who died young, and five sons, 1, Sir Harry, of whom hereafter; 2, Paul, who died young; 3, William, who married first, Elizabeth, daughter and coheiress of —— De la Rose, minister from the court of Spain to Great Britain, by whom he had Lucy, and Leonora-Sophia, who both died unmarried. He married secondly, Mary Pearce, by whom he had Harriet, Harry, (perhaps the present Baronet), Mariamne, and George; 4, Paul, who died young; 5, George, who married Mary, daughter of Nathaniel Darell, of the Island of Jersey, by whom he had one daughter Anne, and two sons, Harry and Philip.

I. HARRY BURRARD, Esq. eldest son of Paul, was advanced by his present Majesty to the dignity of Baronet, by letters-patent dated March 20, 1769, granting unto the said Henry Burrard, of Walhampton, in the county of Hants, Esq. and the heirs male of his body lawfully begotten; and in default of such issue, to his brother William Burrard, of Lymington, in the said county of Hants, Esq. and the heirs male of his body lawfully begotten; and in default of such issue, then to his brother George Burrard, of the Isle of Jersey, Esq. and the heirs male of his body lawfully begotten, the dignity of a Baronet of Great Britain.

Sir Harry married first, Alicia Snape, who died without issue. He married secondly, in 1754, Mary-Frances, daughter of James Clarke, of Wharton, in the county of Hereford, Esq. by whom he had Louisa and Charles-Robert, who died young. Sir Harry died April 12, 1791, and was succeeded by (I believe) his son,

II. Sir HARRY BURRARD, Bart. who married, April 15, 1795, ———, daughter of the late Robert Neale, of Shaw House, Wilts, Esq. and has taken the name of Neale.

ARMS—Azure, a lion passant between three etoiles, argent.

CREST—On a wreath, a dexter hand and arm embowed, couped at the elbow, brandishing a sword, proper.

SEAT—At Walhampton, Hampshire.

TABLE.

1, THOMAS BURRARD = ELIZABETH ISHAM

Thomas | John | Sidney | 2, Paul Burrard = Lucy Colt | Anne

I. Sir Harry Burrard (A. Snape | M.F. Clarke) | Paul | William (E. De la Rose | M. Pearce) | Paul | George (M. Darell) | Mary, d y

Louisa | Charles-Robert | II. Sir Harry (— Neale) | Lucy, L. Sophia | Harriet, Harry | Marianne, George

293. HUME, of Wormleybury, Herts.

Created Baronet, April 4, 1769.

FROM records in the family, this appears to be a branch of the family of the Earl of Home, which settled in the county of East Lothian; a descendant of whom,

1, Alexander Home, of Kimmergham and Redhaugh, in Berwickshire, which lands he exchanged for those of Houndwood and Fernyside. He died in 1622, and was succeeded by his son,

2, Alexander Home, of Houndwood and Fernyside, in the barony of Coldingham, and parish of Ayton, in Berwickshire, who married ———, daughter of Andrew Ker, of Morrison, by — Stuart, eldest daughter of Sir Robert Stuart, of Allanbank, Bart. which family trace their lineal descent from Sir John Stuart, of Bonkill, who was great-grandfather of Robert II. King of Scotland, according to the records in the Herald's Office at Edinburgh; by whom he had five sons, 1, Andrew, of Fernyside, who married Elizabeth, second daughter of William Robertson, of Eymouth, in Berwickshire, by whom he had one daughter and heiress Elizabeth, wife, first, of William-Macfarlane Brown, of Dalgourie, eldest son of Hugh Macfarlane, of Ballanobroch, alias Keith Town, and secondly, of Robert Robertson, of Eymouth: she died without issue in 1786, by which the estate of Fernyside came to the present Sir A. Hume; 2, Alexander, who married ——, and had one son Andrew, who died without Issue; 3, Mark, who married ——, daughter and heiress of —— Quixwood, in Scotland, and died without issue; 4, James; and,

5, Robert Home, who came from Berwickshire, in Scotland, to London, called himself Hume, and died in 1732. He married Hannah, daughter of —— Curtis, of Mile-End, in Middlesex, Esq. by whom he had four sons and three daughters; 1, Alexander Hume, Esq. who married (April 5, 1733, at St. Ann's, Soho) Mary, eldest daughter of Sir Thomas Frederick, Knt. born at Fort St. George, Nov. 9, 1711, and died June 22, 1758, and was buried at Wormley, in Herts. He was member in three parliaments for the borough of Southwark, and several years an East India Director, and died Sept. 15, 1765, and was buried at Wormley: he had one daughter Mary, who died unmarried; 2, Peter, who married and had two sons, Alexander and Robert. Alexander was many years chief of the English factory at Canton, and married first, Anne, daughter of William Boughton, of Bilton-Grange, in Warwickshire, Esq. by whom he had two sons and two daughters; and secondly, Anne, daughter of — Schroëder, of Clay Hill, Enfield, in Middlesex, Esq. by whom he had two sons and three daughters: Robert was of Charles Town, South Carolina; 3, Robert, of Charles Town, South Carolina, who married Sophia, daughter of —— Wigginton, by whom he had two sons, Alexander, a captain in the East India Company's service, who died unmarried; Robert, born Dec. 4, 1724: and one daughter Susanna, born Sept. 15, 1722, wife, first, of —— Ross, and secondly, of Alexander Macleod, of Harries, in Inverness-shire, Esq. by whom she had one son Alexander, who was in the civil service of the East India Company at Madras, and took the name and arms of Hume, by royal sign manual, dated Nov. 25, 1802, pursuant to the will of his maternal uncle, Alexander Hume, Esq. and married Sophia, daughter of William Wrangham, of St. Helena, Esq. by whom he has issue: the daughters were, Sophia, wife of the Rev. Dr. William Fotheringham, of Scotland, by whom she has issue; and Elizabeth, of Robert-Bruce-Eneas Macleod, of Cadboll, in North Britain, Esq. by whom there is issue; and 4, Abraham, of whom hereafter. The daughters were, 1, Hannah, wife of William Black, of New Broad Street, London, Esq. by whom she had one daughter, born Dec. 1722, wife of William-Dixwell Grimes, of Coton House, Rugby, in Warwickshire, Esq. by whom she has one son Abraham, who married Mary, second daughter of Nathaniel Cholmendeley, of Housham and Whitby, in Yorkshire, Esq. and has issue; 2, ——, who died unmarried; 3, ——, wife of —— Dunn, Esq. by whom she had a daughter Susanna, wife of George Cuming, Esq. a director of the East India Company, by whom she had two sons, William and George, who died ———, and one daughter Mary, unmarried in 1802. Mrs. Cuming died Aug. 9, 1788.

I. ABRAHAM HUME, of Wormleybury aforesaid, Esq. youngest son, was commissary-general of the army, representative in parliament for Steyning and Tregony, was created a Baronet April 4, 1769. He married, Oct. 9, 1746, Hannah, youngest daughter of Sir Thomas Frederick, Knt. who was born Nov. 16, 1723, and died Jan. 23, 1771, and was buried at Wormley, by whom he had two sons and a daughter, 1, Abraham, of whom hereafter; and 2, Alexander, of St. Clere, in Kent, Esq. lieutenant-colonel in the Surry regiment of yeomanry, who took the name and arms of Evelyn, by royal sign manual dated July 22, 1797. He married Frances, daughter and only remaining child of William Evelyn, Esq, of St. Clere, M. P. for Hythe, in Kent. The daughter was Hannah, wife of James Hare, Esq. M. P. for Knaresborough, in Yorkshire, by whom she has one daughter Susannah. Sir Abraham died Oct. 10, 1772, aged 69, and was buried at Wormley. He was succeeded by his eldest son,

II. Sir ABRAHAM HUME, Bart. F.R.S. born in Hill street, Berkley square, Feb. 20, 1749 (O. S.) M. P. for Petersfield in 1774, and sheriff for the county of Herts the same year, now in possession of the family estate at Fernyside, in Berwickshire. He married Amelia, daughter of Dr. John Egerton, canon residentiary of St. Paul's, and Bishop of Litchfield and Coventry, by the Lady Anne-Sophia Grey, youngest daughter of Henry de Grey, Duke of Kent, married at his lordship's house in Amen Corner, St. Paul's, by Dr. Cornwallis, archbishop

TABLE.

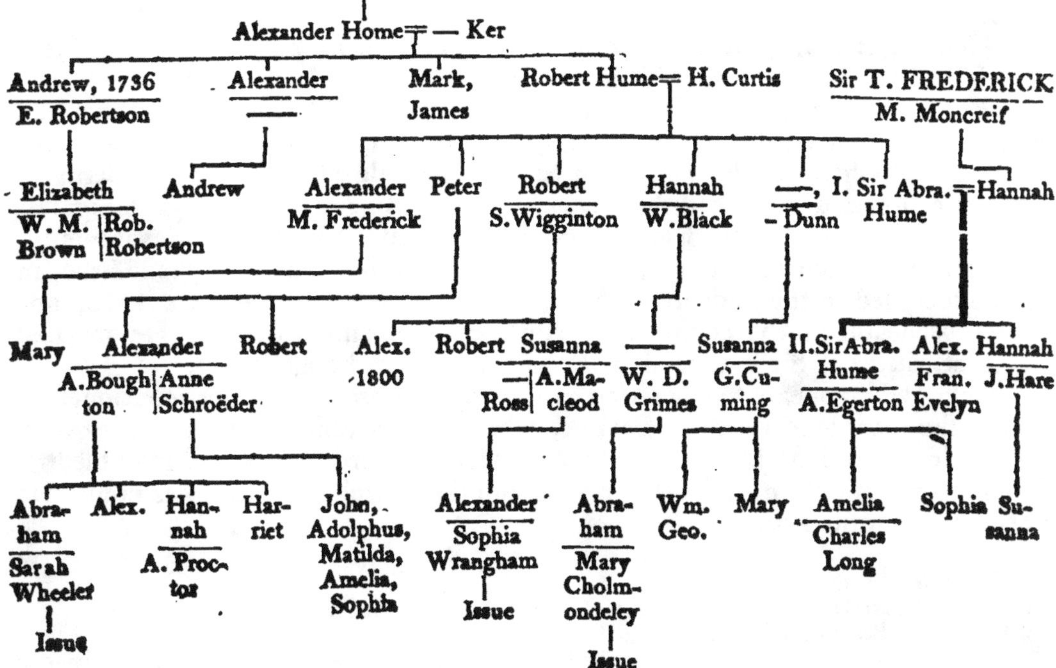

of Canterbury, the 25th of April, 1771, registered at St. Martin's Church, Ludgate Hill, by whom he has two daughters, 1, Amelia, born Jan. 29, 1772, in Hill street, baptized at St. George's, Hanover square, the late Princess Amelia being her godmother; married in Hill street, by special licence, May 28, 1793, by the Rev. Francis-Henry Egerton, prebendary of Durham, to the Right Hon. Charles Long, of Bromley Hill, in Kent, one of his Majesty's most honourable privy council, and M. P. for Wendover in 1803; 2, Sophia, born in Hill street, Berkley square, July 31, 1788, baptized at Wormley.

ARMS—Vert, a lion rampant, argent.
CREST—A lion's head erased, argent.
MOTTO—*True to the end.*
SEATS—At Wormley Bury, in Herts, and Fernyside, in Berwickshire.

294. BERNARD, of NETTLEHAM, Lincolnshire.

Created Baronet, April 5, 1769,

IS descended from Thomas Bernard, a younger son of a respectable family of this name, which was originally seated in Yorkshire, but whose chief residence was afterwards for a long period in the county of Northampton, where, and in the neighbouring counties, they have flourished in different branches for many centuries.

1, Godfrey Bernard, Armig. was living at Wanford, in Yorkshire, temp. Hen. III. The fifth in lineal descent from him was,

5, Robert Bernard, Lord of Iselham *, who married Elizabeth, daughter and heiress of Sir Nicholas Lylling, of Abington, in the county of Northampton, Knt. who was high-sheriff of that county in 1384. Their eldest son, Sir John Bernard, of Iselham aforesaid, Knt. had three daughters, his coheirs; the eldest, Margaret, was wife of Thomas Peyton, Esq. and carried the estate at Iselham into that family.

6, Thomas †, their second son, upon the death of his maternal grandfather in 1408, succeeded to the lordship of Abington; and was, in the year 1415, appointed escheator of the counties of Northampton and Rutland. He married Margaret, sister of Sir Walter Mantle, Knt. by whom he had a son,

7, John, who appears to have been of the royal household, being mentioned as such in the records of Reading, Berks ‡, where he was admitted an honorary burgess. He married Margaret, daughter of Henry, Lord Scrope, of Hambledon, Bucks, Baron of Bolton, in Yorkshire. From this match § the line was continued for three generations to,

* Camden's Brit. tit. Camb.
† They had a third son Henry, to whom his father gave lands in Guilsborough, co. Northants.
‡ " Johannes Bernard, Vectus d'ni Regis."
§ The sons were, 1, John, who continued the line; 2, Francis, whose grandson Jeremy was living at Upton St. Leonard's, in Gloucestershire, 11 Eliz. 1669, and had two sons, William and Thomas; 3, Eus-

tries, and the opposition given to the orders sent from Great Britain, made it a part of his official duty to take decisive measures for supporting the authority of government, which, however approved by ministers here, could not fail, on the spot, to weaken and gradually undermine the degree of popularity he before enjoyed. His conduct in that difficult and trying situation gave such entire satisfaction to his Majesty, that he was advanced while abroad, and without solicitation, to the said dignity of a Baronet, and was denominated of Nettleham, from an estate near Lincoln, which is still in the family, but his chief residence latterly was at Nether Winchendon and Aylesbury, in the county of Bucks.

In the year 1741, he married Amelia, daughter of Stephen Offley, of Norton-Hall, in the county of Derby, Esq. (by Mary his wife, sister to John, Lord Viscount Barrington), by whom he had six sons and four daughters; 1, Francis, who died unmarried in May, 1770; 2, Sir John, his successor; 3, Jane, wife of Charles White, Esq. of Lincoln, by whom she has a daughter Mary, and a son Charles, late of the Royal Bucks militia, with which he served in Ireland, and now of Edlington, in Lincolnshire, and has married Frances, daughter of Hezekiah Browne, Esq. in that county; 4, Thomas Bernard, Esq. of Lincoln's-Inn, barrister at law, treasurer, and a governor of the Foundling Hospital, and chancellor of the diocese of Durham, who married, the 11th of May, 1782, Margaret, daughter and coheiress of Patrick Adair, Esq.; 5, Shute, who died under age and unmarried; 6, Amelia, wife of Captain Benjamin Baker, of the fifth regiment of foot, and since of the Royal South Lincolnshire regiment of militia: she died in February, 1795, leaving three sons, Thomas, Francis, and James; 7, William, a lieutenant in the twenty-ninth regiment of foot, who was lost in the expedition to Canada in 1776: he died under age, and unmarried; 8, Frances-Elizabeth, wife of the Rev. Richard King, rector of Worthen, Salop, (second son of Henry King, of Alveston, in the county of Gloucester, Esq.), by whom she has two daughters, Amelia, wife of John Collinson, Esq. and Julia; 9, Scrope Bernard, of Nether Winchenden aforesaid, Esq. LL.D. several years one of the under secretaries of state in this kingdom, and member for Aylesbury, Bucks, in the the three last parliaments, who married, July 26, 1785, Harriet, only child of William Morland, Esq. M. P. for Taunton, in Somersetshire, by whom he has had seven children, the second of whom, Thomas, died young; and the others are William, born the 7th of July, 1786; Margaret, born the 22d of December, 1788; Francis, born the 7th of June, 1790; Thomas-Tyringham,

following (also laid before the House of Commons, and printed), adds similar expressions of approbation. "It is with great pleasure," says he, "that I have observed the manner in which you have conducted yourself during the disputes of the last year, which I cannot do without highly approving your attention and watchfulness, on the one hand to support the authority of government, and on the other, the tenderness and affection which appeared in all your letters towards the people under your government."

Sir Francis alludes, in his official correspondence, to the sacrifice which he was obliged to make to his public duty. "Such," says he, in his dispatch of the 25th of November, 1765, "I reckon my losing the general good will and good opinion of the people, not by any act of my own, but by the unavoidable obligations of my office, in a business in which I had no concern but as an executive officer.'

TABLE.

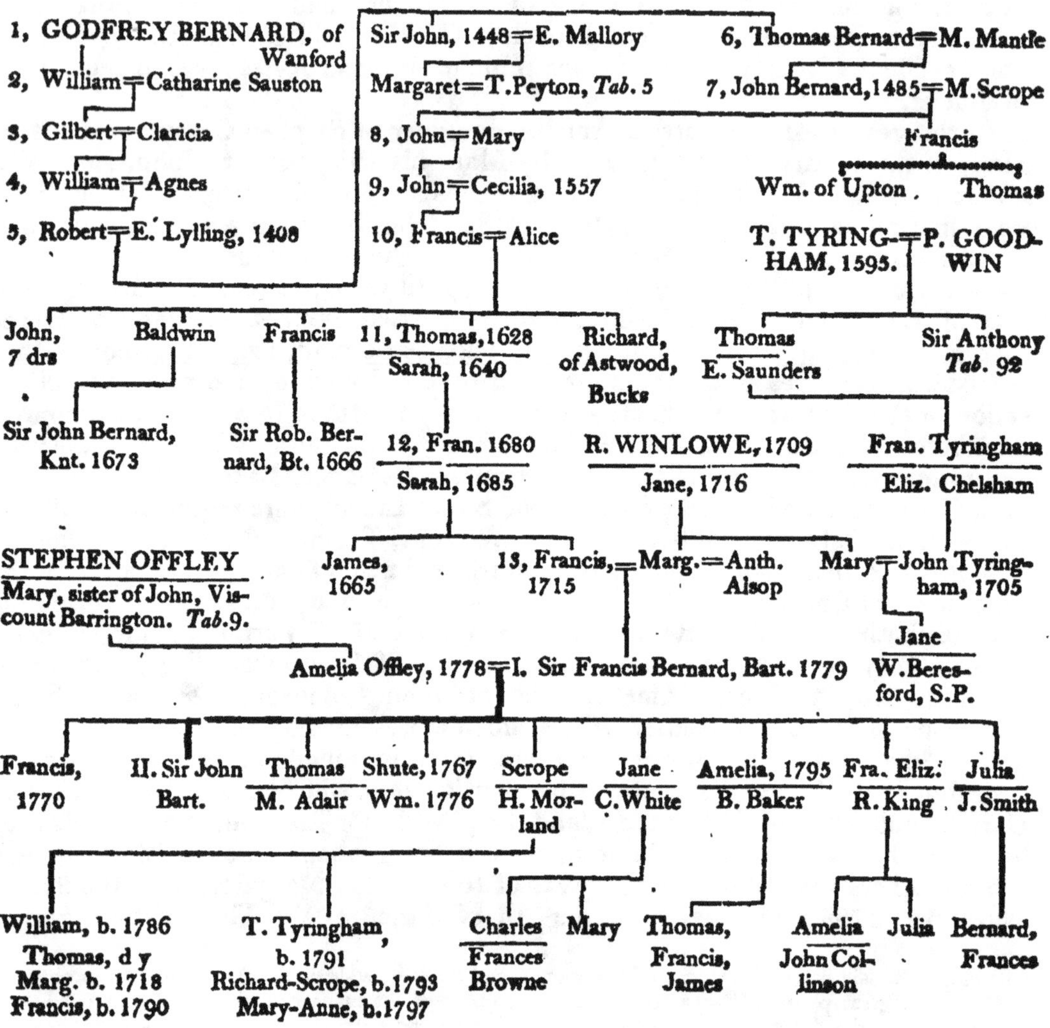
1, GODFREY BERNARD, of Wanford
2, William = Catharine Sauston
3, Gilbert = Claricia
4, William = Agnes
5, Robert = E. Lylling, 1408
Sir John, 1448 = E. Mallory
Margaret = T. Peyton, Tab. 5
8, John = Mary
9, John = Cecilia, 1557
10, Francis = Alice
6, Thomas Bernard = M. Mantle
7, John Bernard, 1485 = M. Scrope
Francis
Wm. of Upton
Thomas
T. TYRING-HAM, 1595. = P. GOODWIN
John, 7 drs
Baldwin
Francis
11, Thomas, 1628
Sarah, 1640
Richard, of Astwood, Bucks
Thomas
E. Saunders
Sir Anthony Tab. 92
Sir John Bernard, Knt. 1673
Sir Rob. Bernard, Bt. 1666
12, Fran. 1680
Sarah, 1685
R. WINLOWE, 1709
Jane, 1716
Fran. Tyringham
Eliz. Chelsham
STEPHEN OFFLEY
Mary, sister of John, Viscount Barrington. Tab. 9.
James, 1665
13, Francis, 1715 = Marg. = Anth. Alsop
Mary = John Tyringham, 1705
Jane
W. Beresford, S.P.
Amelia Offley, 1778 = I. Sir Francis Bernard, Bart. 1779
Francis, 1770
II. Sir John Bart.
Thomas
M. Adair
Shute, 1767
Wm. 1776
Scrope
H. Morland
Jane
C. White
Amelia, 1795
B. Baker
Fra. Eliz.
R. King
Julia
J. Smith
William, b. 1786
Thomas, d y
Marg. b. 1718
Francis, b. 1790
T. Tyringham, b. 1791
Richard-Scrope, b. 1793
Mary-Anne, b. 1797
Charles
Frances Browne
Mary
Thomas, Francis, James
Amelia
John Collinson
Julia
Bernard, Frances

born the 15th of September, 1791; Richard-Scrope, born the 13th of August, 1793; and Mary-Anne, born the 11th of February, 1797; 10, Julia, wife of the Rev. Joseph Smith, prebendary of Salisbury, and vicar of Melksham, in Wiltshire, by whom she has a son, Bernard, and a daughter, Frances.

Amelia Lady Bernard died on the 26th of May, 1778, and Sir Francis, the 16th of June, in the year following. He was succeeded by his eldest surviving son,

II. Sir JOHN BERNARD, the present Baronet, who is unmarried.

ARMS—Quarterly: first, a bear, rampant, sable, muzzled and collared, or; second, azure, a saltire engrailed, argent; third, argent, three lions' heads couped, gules, within a border engrailed, vert; fourth, as the first.

CREST—On a wreath, a demi-bear, as in the Arms.

MOTTO—*Bear and Forbear.*

SEATS—Nettleham, near Lincoln, and Nether Winchendon, in the county of Bucks.

295. ALLEYNE, of the Island of Barbadoes.

Created Baronet, March 20, 1769.

1, ALANUS DE BUCHENHALL, was lord of Buchenhall in the reign of Edward I. and from him the numerous branches of Allen, Allyn, Alleyn, and Alleyne, seated at Buckenhall, Brockhouse, Garrishall, Uttoxeter, and other places in the county of Stafford, derive their descent*.

2, George Alleyne, alias Allen, of Chartley, in the county of Stafford, had a son,

* The following deed is remaining in the College of Arms at London:
Henricus Allen Ballivus Fæd. Hugonis comitis Staffordiæ, &c. &c. recepi de Dno Rogero de Charleton, 9 solid. argent. Pro quarta parte unius Fæd. Fæd. et quarta parte unius Fæd. militis in Longmoro, que idem Rogerus tenet de Dno meo, &c. dat. apud Castrum Staffordiæ, anno Regni, Regis Edw. III. 47. To which is appendent, a seal, with the arms, as now borne by the family, Party per cheveron, gules, and ermine, in chief, two lions' heads erased, sable. Inscribed, *Sigillum Henrici Allen Buckenhall.*

The same coat appears to a deed executed 2 Rich. II. inscribed, Sigillum Johannis Allyn, armigeri.

By another deed, dated 16 Hen. VI. to which are witnesses, Robert Kynnerdsly, lord of Locksly, William Sandleeke, of Uttoxhather, and others, Matilda, then late the wife of John Moule, conveys to Thomas Allen, of Garrishall, all the lands and tenements in Bromshall.

Another deed, dated 5 Edw. IV. is in the following words. *Noverint universi per presentes me Thomam Allen de Garingshall attornasse et in loco meo Rad. Orchard de eadem . . . . meo filio Roberto Alleyne in villa, et campis de Bromshill.*

3, Richard Alleyne, who was seated at Grantham, in Lincolnshire, and by his second wife, ——, daughter of John Sheldon, of Beoley, in Worcestershire, had four sons; 1, Henry; 2, Thomas, father of one daughter Bridget; 3, Richard, father of George, Margaret, and Isabella; 4, George, who married Thomasine, daughter of — Ellis, of Holland, in Lincolnshire; and Elizabeth, wife of — Leverett.

Henry, the eldest son, was seated at Buckminster, in Leicestershire, and married Anne, daughter of Richard Pecke, of Wakefield, in Yorkshire, by whom he had three daughters: Joan, wife of —— Moore, of Bourne, in Lincolnshire; Joyce, of Thomas Cony, of Barton-Coyles; and Anne, of —— Kelstone: and three sons, of whom Thomas, the younger, died single. Richard, the second, was of Shillington, in Leicestershire, and by Margaret, sister of Sir Nicholas Lusher, of Putney, in Surry, was father of another Richard, who succeeded him at Shillington, and was living in 1634, having at that time, by Frances, daughter of Richard Clipson, of Manthorpe, four sons; 1, Richard; 2, Leon; 3, Anthony; and 4, Charles.

The eldest son of Henry, by Anne Pecke, was Henry, also of Buckminster, who married Bridget, daughter of Edmund, second son of Edward Busby, of Hather, in Lincolnshire, by whom he had two daughters, Elizabeth, wife of William Laurence, of Bridge, in Kent, and Anne, of Sir George Cotterel, groom-porter to King James I.; and four sons; 1, Edmund; 2, Humphrey, father of Thomas; 3, Berkeley, seated at Wilsford, in Lincolnshire, who, by Joan, daughter of Anthony Smith, of Guildford, had two sons, William and Henry, and five daughters, Mary, Anne, Bridget, Elizabeth, and Jane; and 4, George. We now return to,

4, John Alleyne, the only son of Richard, of Grantham, by his first marriage, left four sons; 1, John, who married Dorothy, daughter of —— Clerke, alderman of London, by whom he had four sons, John, George, Francis, and Richard, of whom George appears to have had one son John; 2, Francis; 3, Richard, of whom presently; and 4, William: and three daughters, Ellyn, Elizabeth, and Dorothy.

5, Richard, the third son, was of Shillington, in Lincolnshire, and married Margaret, daughter of John Wisdom, of London, merchant, by whom he had two daughters, Elizabeth and Abigail, and four sons; 1, Richard, of whom hereafter; 2, John; 3, Abel; and 4, Timothy, of Handleby, in Lincolnshire, who married Douglas, daughter of Richard Day, of Chipsted, in Surry, was, in 1634, father of one son, Timothy, and one daughter —, wife of William Moore, of Bourne, in Lincolnshire.

6, Richard Alleyne, eldest son, was D.D. and rector of Stowting, in Kent, in which neighbourhood he likewise possessed a temporal estate: he died in 1651, and was buried at Stowting, having had by his wife Christian ——, five sons; 1, John, who died 1639; 2, Thomas; 3, Richard, (sole executor of his father's will) who married Elizabeth, daughter of —— Hales; 4, Reynold; and 5, Abel, who married Frances, daughter of —— Berks, and had one daughter Christian; Anne was wife of George Laws, and Margaret, of William Culpeper.

7, Reynold Alleyne, the fourth son, was one of the first adventurers in the settlement of the Island of Barbadoes, and acquired a considerable estate there, the principal residence on which was by him named Mount Alleyne, and is now part of the possessions of Sir Reynold Alleyne, Bart. *.

He married Mary, daughter of —— Skeet (who afterwards married —— Turner, of the Three Houses in the Thickets), by whom he had two sons and a daughter, Mary, wife of ——— Rowse, of the Clift, whose descendants are still of note in the island. Of the sons, Reynold, the younger, died unmarried; but

8, Abel, the eldest, was member of council, and stiled by Oldmixon a lieutenant-general. He married Elizabeth, daughter of —— Denzy, by whom he had three sons and four daughters, of whom, Elizabeth was wife of Richard Parsons, of Mount Misery, and Lucy, of John Walter, of Busbridge, in the county of Surry, Esq.; Mary, of William Dotin, of Grenada Hill; and Arabella, of Timothy Salter, of Salter's.

Of the sons, Benjamin, the youngest, was seated at Mount Stedfast, and married Arabella, daughter of —— Pilgrim, of St. George's, but died without issue.

Reynold, the second, ancestor to the present Baronet, of whom hereafter.

Thomas Alleyne, the eldest son, succeeded his father at Mount Alleyne, was a brigadier-general, and member of the colonial assembly for St. James's. He married Judith, daughter of Sir Timothy Thornhill, of Kent, and of Barbadoes, Bart. by whom he had one daughter, Judith, wife of Littleton Meynill, of Bradley, in Derbyshire, and four sons; 1, Abel Alleyne, of Turner's Hall, Barbadoes, and of Squerrie's Court, in Kent, colonel of the Hole Town regiment, and member of the assembly for St. Andrews. He married Elizabeth, daughter and sole heiress of Sir William Booth, of Black Jacks, but died without issue; 2, Timothy Alleyne, purchased Black Jacks, and by ——, daughter of — Buttels, and relict of —— Holder, had one son Thomas, also of Black Jacks, who was member of the assembly for St. Andrews, and married Jane, daughter of —— Rollcston, (who married secondly, — Ferguson, of Sandy Lane), but died without issue; and one daughter Mary, who, by her brother's death, became sole heiress, and

* The system of arbitrary rule which, under King Charles I. and the system of open opposition to it in arms which had been carried to such excess in England, did not fail to raise among the colonists similar animosities; but the success of the republicans in Europe gave such advantage to that party in Barbadoes, as occasioned an unqualified opposition to the Lord Willoughby, the governor, against whom a deputation of several principal inhabitants, requesting assistance, was sent to England in 1650. Among these was Colonel Reynold Alleyne. Their expectation was fully answered; for, by a commission from Oliver Cromwell, a considerable military, as well as naval force, was sent to them under the command of Sir George Ascough.

The command, however, of all the troops that landed in Speight's Bay, Dec. 17, 1651, was given to the afore-mentioned Colonel Reynold Alleyne "who having (as Oldmixon, in his History of Barbadoes, says) a considerable interest in the island, was supposed to be the fittest man to lead the soldiers to gain it. The Barbadians under Lord Willoughby were posted on the shore very regularly, yet the English landed, and beat them up to their fort, which was on a sudden deserted by them after loss on both sides. On Sir George's, was that brave Barbadian, Colonel Alleyne, who was killed with a musquet shot, and much lamented, being a man of worth and honour." In consequence of this success, Lord Willoughby was forced to a capitulation of arms, which was soon followed by his embarkment for Europe.

married first, to ——— Ball, of Farmers; secondly, to —— Hooper, of Hoopers, in the Valley; and thirdly, to Jonas Maynard, of Passage; 3, Reynold, was of Mount Alleyne, and member of the assembly for St. James's. By ——, daughter and coheiress of Laurence Price, he left two daughters, his coheiresses, 1, Elizabeth, wife of John Newton, of Newtons, in Barbadoes, and of Abbots Bromley, in the county of Stafford (who dying without issue, left Mount Alleyne, and other property in Barbadoes, acquired by his marriage to Sir John-Gay Alleyne, Bart.) and 2, Judith, who died unmarried.

John Alleyne, the fourth son, was of Rock Hill, and twice married: his second wife (who, after his decease, remarried to Peter Chardon, of Boston, in New England), was Mary, daughter to his first cousin, Abel Alleyne, as shall be shewn presently, and by her he had no issue; but by his first wife, ———, daughter and coheiress of General Henry Peers, of Martin Castle, he had one daughter Judith, wife of ——— Ferguson, of Sandy Lane; and two sons, Peers, who died single, and Thomas Alleyne, who was twice married. By the second wife, who was relict of Lieutenant Alexander M'Cartney, he had no child, but by his first, Hannah, daughter of John Downs, of the Spring, he had one daughter, who died unmarried, and one son John, late of Lincoln's-Inn, barrister-at-law, who, by his wife Anne, daughter of Benjamin Roswell, of Hackney, in Middlesex, left Hannah and Anne, his daughters and coheirs.

9, Reynold Alleyne, second son of Abel and Elizabeth Denzy, seated at the Four Hills, was member of the assembly for St. Andrews, and chief judge of the Bridge Court. He married Elizabeth, daughter and coheiress of John Gay, by whom he had four daughters; 1, Elizabeth, wife of ——— Forster, of Forster's Hall; 2, Isabella, of Joseph Gibbs, of Plumb Tree; 3, Ruth, of John Holder, of Joe's River; and 4, Christian, of John Gibbs, of the Castle: and four sons, 1, John; 2, Abel; 3, Reynold; and 4, Thomas. Abel, the second son, was seated at Mount Stedfast, and married Mary, daughter of ——— Woodbridge, of Kensington, by whom he had six sons and six daughters; of the latter, Mary was the wife, first, of John Alleyne, as before-mentioned, and secondly, of Peter Chardon, of Boston; 2, Jane, wife of the Rev. Edward Winslow; 3, Benjamina-Woodbridge, unmarried; 4, Lucy, wife of John Waite; 5, Isabella, wife of —— Clarke, of Boston; and 6, Abel Dudley, wife of Henry-Evans Holder.

Of the sons, 1, Reynold, married Christian, daughter of ——— Forster, of Forster Hill (who married secondly, Jonas Maynard), but had no issue; 2, Abel; and 3, Dudley, died young; 4, Thomas, married ———, daughter of ——— Forster, of St. Philips, by whom he had two sons, Abel, living, unmarried, and John-Forster, who, by his wife Elizabeth, daughter of —— Willing, has four sons, Haynes-Gibbes, John-Gay, James-Holder, and Charles: and four daughters, Sarah, Elizabeth, Charlotte, and Margaret; 5, John, who married Elizabeth, daughter of —— Ferguson, and had one son John, and four daughters; 1, Elizabeth, wife, first, of ——— Lespinaz, governor of Demerary, and secondly, of —— Buxton; 2, Anne, wife, first, of —— Marshall, secondly, of —— Magrath; 3, Rebecca; and 4, Jane-Knowles, married at Demerary; and

6, Henry-Timothy-Peers, who, by Thomasine, daughter of John Waite, has two daughters, Susanna, and ——, wife of —— Batelli. Reynold Alleyne, third son of Reynold, by Elizabeth Gay, was seated at Jacksons, and married Elizabeth, daughter of —— Ward, of Glen Hall, by whom he had one daughter Elizabeth, wife of the Rev. John Carter, and one son Reynold, who, by Lucy, daughter of his uncle, Thomas Alleyne, had one son Thomas, and three daughters, Lucy-Dotin, Elizabeth, and Susanna.

Thomas Alleyne, fourth son of Reynold by Elizabeth Gay, was seated at Dymocks, and married first, Lucy, daughter of Wm Dotin, of Grenade Hall, by whom he had one daughter Lucy, wife, as before-mentioned, of Reynold Alleyne, and one son Abel, M. D. who, by Jane, daughter of Francis Skeet, of Mangrove, had five daughters, Christian, wife of —— White, Lucy, wife of James Handy, Judith-Susan, wife of Richard Cobham, and Jane-Abel, wife of Sir John-Gay Alleyne: and two sons, Thomas, who died without issue, and Abel, who, by Jane-Rolleston, daughter of John-Holder Alleyne, has one daughter Marian. The said Thomas Alleyne, by his second wife Susan, daughter and heiress of William Gibbs, of Black Rock (relict of —— Walker), had five sons and one daughter; 1, Susanna, wife of Thomas Carmichael. Of the sons, 1, William-Gibbes, was of Black Rock, and member of the assembly for St. Thomas's, and married, first, Mary, daughter of General John Dotin, and secondly, Elizabeth, daughter of —— Lane, but died without issue; 2, Thomas, seated at Small Hopes, and member of the assembly for St. James's. By Mary, daughter and heiress of Reynold Gibbs, of Plumb-Tree, he has had two sons, Thomas and Reynold, and three daughters, ——, wife of —— Lewis, ——, of —— Maynard, and Mary, of —— Williams; 3, John-Holder Alleyne, who married Marian, daughter of Francis Skeet, of Mangrove, by whom he had two sons, Thomas, who, by Elizabeth, daughter of —— Lynch, has issue, and William-Gibbes Alleyne, who married ——, daughter of —— Salmon, and one daughter Jane-Rolleston, wife, as above-mentioned, of Abel Alleyne; 4, Reynold; and 5, Timothy, who died unmarried. We now return to

10, John, the eldest son of Reynold and Elizabeth Gay, who inherited from his father the seat of Four Hills, received his education in England, was of Magdalen College, in the university of Oxford, and received the honorary degree of A. M. Though frequently pressed, on his return to Barbadoes, he declined taking any part in public affairs, and died at Bath in 1730, having, by Mary, daughter of William Terril, of Cabbage-Tree Hall (sole heiress of her mother, Rebecca, daughter and coheiress of Colonel Robert Spire, of Mount Stedfast, by Mary, daughter and coheiress of —— Turner, of the Three Houses in the Thickets, by his wife, daughter of —— Skeet, and relict of the before-mentioned Colonel Reynold Alleyne) who died in 1742, and was buried at St. Nicholas Church, at Guildford, in Surry, two sons and three daughters; 1, Mary, wife of Admiral Sir Charles Knowles, Bart; 2, Rebecca, wife of William, Viscount Folkestone, afterwards Earl of Radnor; and 3, Reynoldia, who died unmarried, and

TABLE.

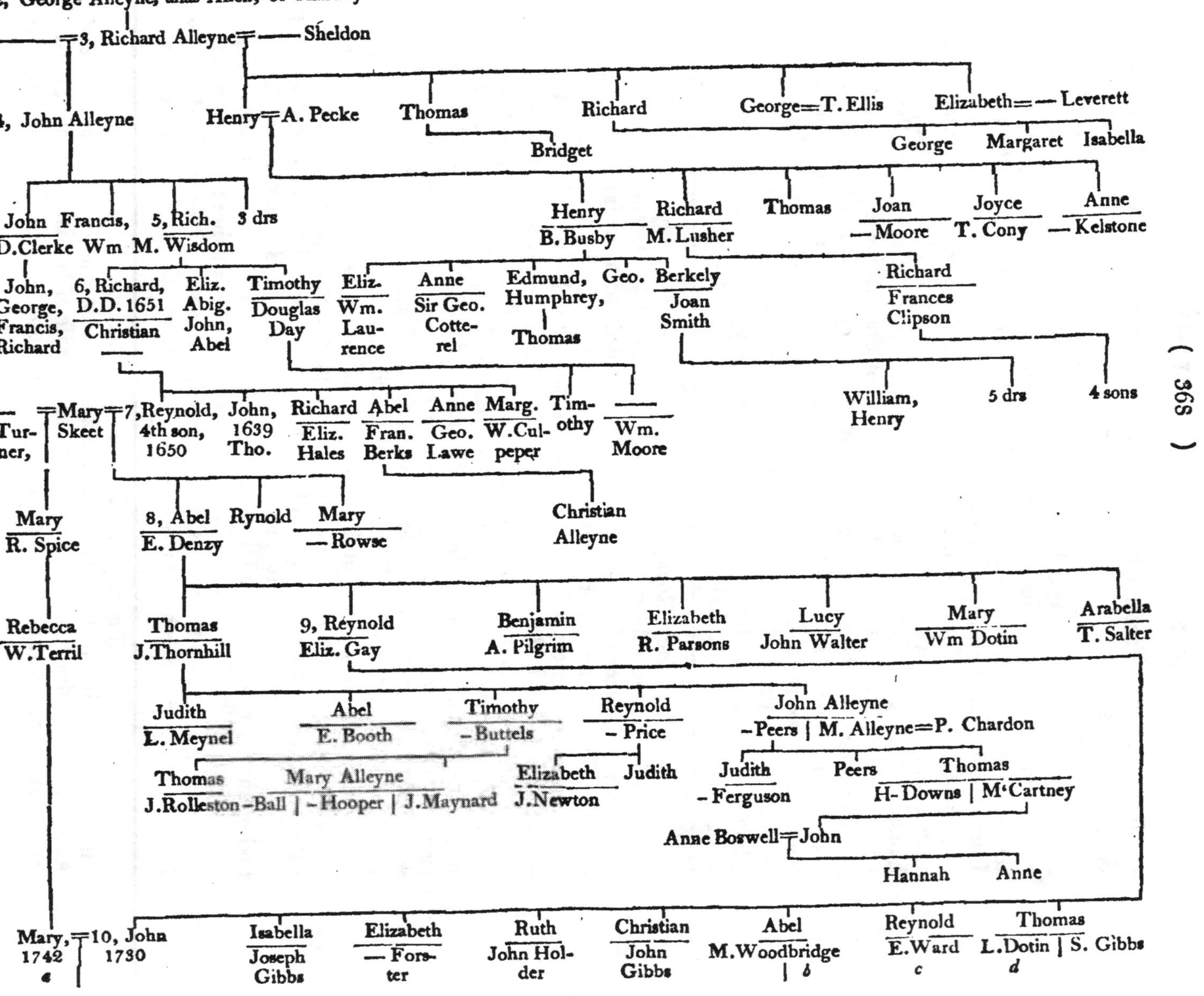
1, ALANUS DE BUCHENHALL, temp. Edw. I.
2, George Alleyne, alias Allen, of Chartley
—— =3, Richard Alleyne= —— Sheldon
4, John Alleyne
Henry=A. Pecke
Thomas
Richard
George=T. Ellis
Elizabeth=— Leverett
Bridget
George
Margaret
Isabella
John
D.Clerke
Francis, Wm
5, Rich.
M. Wisdom
3 drs
Henry
B. Busby
Richard
M. Lusher
Thomas
Joan
— Moore
Joyce
T. Cony
Anne
— Kelstone
John, George, Francis, Richard
6, Richard, D.D. 1651
Christian
Eliz. Abig. John, Abel
Timothy
Douglas Day
Eliz.
Wm. Lau-rence
Anne
Sir Geo. Cotte-rel
Edmund, Humphrey,
Thomas
Geo.
Berkely
Joan Smith
Richard
Frances Clipson
William, Henry
5 drs
4 sons
— Tur-ner,
=Mary Skeet
=7, Reynold, 4th son, 1650
John, 1639 Tho.
Richard
Eliz. Hales
Abel
Fran. Berks
Anne
Geo. Lawe
Marg.
W.Cul-peper
Tim-othy
——
Wm. Moore
Christian Alleyne
Mary
R. Spice
8, Abel
E. Denzy
Rynold
Mary
— Rowse
Rebecca
W.Terril
Thomas
J.Thornhill
9, Reynold
Eliz. Gay
Benjamin
A. Pilgrim
Elizabeth
R. Parsons
Lucy
John Walter
Mary
Wm Dotin
Arabella
T. Salter
Judith
L. Meynel
Abel
E. Booth
Timothy
— Buttels
Reynold
— Price
John Alleyne
— Peers | M. Alleyne=P. Chardon
Thomas
J.Rolleston
Mary Alleyne
— Ball | — Hooper | J.Maynard
Elizabeth
J.Newton
Judith
Judith
— Ferguson
Peers
Thomas
H- Downs | M'Cartney
Anne Boswell=John
Hannah
Anne
Mary, 1742 a
=10, John 1730
Isabella
Joseph Gibbs
Elizabeth
— Fors-ter
Ruth
John Hol-der
Christian
John Gibbs
Abel
M.Woodbridge
b
Reynold
E.Ward
c
Thomas
L.Dotin | S. Gibbs
d

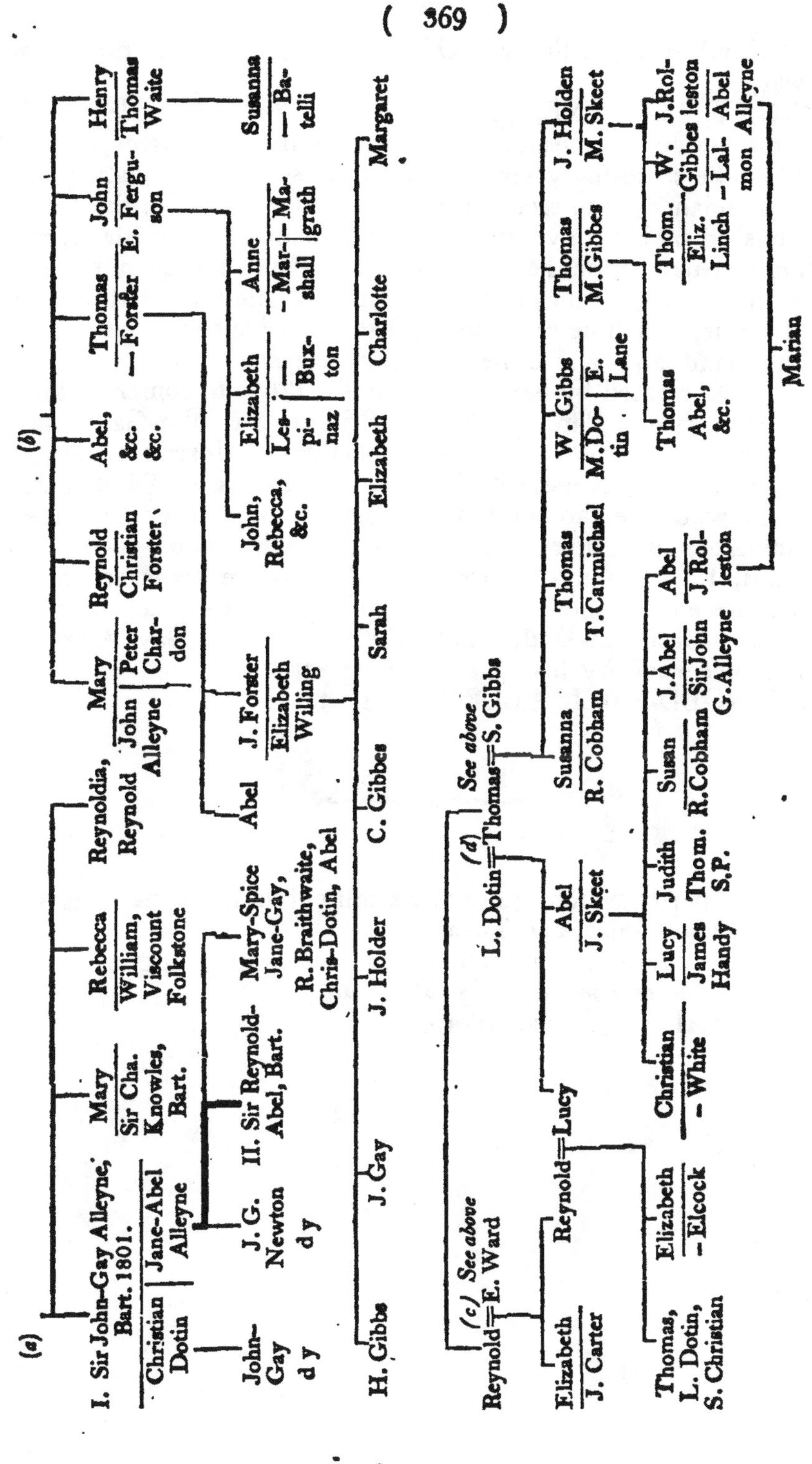
(a)
I. Sir John-Gay Alleyne, Bart. 1801.
Christian Dotin
Jane-Abel Alleyne
Mary
Sir Cha. Knowles, Bart.
Rebecca
William, Viscount Folkstone
Reynoldia,
Reynold
Mary
John Alleyne
Peter Chardon
Reynold
Christian Forster
(b)
Abel, &c. &c.
Thomas
— Forster
John
E. Ferguson
Henry
Thomas Waite
Susanna
— Batelli
John-Gay d y
J. G. Newton d y
II. Sir Reynold-Abel, Bart.
Mary-Spice Jane-Gay, R. Braithwaite, Chris-Dotin, Abel
Abel
J. Forster
Elizabeth Willing
John, Rebecca, &c.
Elizabeth
— Lespinaz
— Buxton
Anne
- Marshall
- Magrath
H. Gibbs
J. Gay
J. Holder
C. Gibbes
Sarah
Elizabeth
Charlotte
Margaret
(c) See above
Reynold=E. Ward
Elizabeth
J. Carter
Reynold=Lucy
(d)
L. Dotin=Thomas=S. Gibbs
See above
Abel
J. Skeet
Susanna
R. Cobham
Thomas
T. Carmichael
W. Gibbs
M. Dotin
E. Lane
Thomas
M. Gibbes
J. Holden
M. Skeet
Thomas, L. Dotin, S. Christian
Elizabeth
- Elcock
Christian
- White
Lucy
James Handy
Judith
Thom. S.P.
Susan
R. Cobham
J. Abel
Sir John G. Alleyne
Abel
J. Rolleston
Thomas Abel, &c.
Thom.
Eliz. Linch
W. Gibbes
- Lalmon
J. Rolleston
Abel Alleyne
Marian

was buried at Hambledon, in Surry. Of the sons, 1, Reynold, died unmarried; the second was,

I. JOHN-GAY ALLEYNE, born April 28, 1724, succeeded his father in his estate at the age of six years. Being chosen into the assembly for St. Andrews, in 1757, he so strongly recommended himself, by his distinguished and indefatigable attendance, as to secure an annual re-election. On the occasion of a pamphlet published by him in vindication of the honour of the island, respecting the expedition to Guadaloupe, he received, in his place, the unanimous thanks of the assembly; and, on a vacancy of the chair in 1767, he was, with the same unanimity, placed in it, which he constantly filled while his health permitted his residence in the island, and which he finally resigned in 1797.

His Majesty was pleased by patent, March 20, 1769, to confer on him and his heirs male the dignity of a Baronet of Great Britain. Sir John-Gay Alleyne married first, Christian, fourth daughter and coheiress of Joseph Dotin, of Black Rocks and Nicholas's, by Anne, sole daughter and heiress of Edward Jordan, of Black Rocks, by whom he had one son John-Gay, who died young. He married secondly, Jane-Abel, daughter of Abel Alleyne, who died ——, by whom he had two sons, 1, John-Gay-Newton, who died before his father, and 2, Reynold-Abel, the present Baronet; and 5 daughters, Mary-Spice, Jane-Gay, Rebecca-Brathwaite, Christian-Dotin, and Abel. Sir John-Gay Alleyne died in 1801, and was succeeded by his only surviving son,

II. Sir REYNOLD-ABEL ALLEYNE, Bart.

ARMS—Party per cheveron, gules and ermine, two lions' heads erased, or, in chief, quartering Gay, Spice, and Turner.

CREST—From a ducal coronet, an horse's head issuing, argent,

MOTTO—*Non tua te moveant, sed publica vota.*

SEAT—Mount Alleyne, in Barbadoes.

296. YOUNG, of Dominica.

Created Baronet, March 20, 1769.

1, Sir JOHN YOUNG, of Leny, Knt. temp. James I. by tradition is called a loyal cavalier: he was born 1605.

2, David Young, his son, born 1623, married the Lady Jane Grey, by whom he had one son,

3, David Young, born 1646, and married, 1679, Catharine, daughter of Sir Andrew Toshah, of Monavedt, by Catharine, his wife, daughter of Duncan Campbell, Earl of Bredalbane, by whom he had one son,

4, William Young, born Nov. 14, 1687, who was a physician of considerable eminence, and by his professional abilities and prudence, left his son a large fortune. He married, in 1720, M—— Nanton, of Antigua, by whom he had one son. He died 1741.

I. WILLIAM YOUNG, Esq. who was born 1725. He was lieutenant-governor of his Majesty's island of Dominica, and was created a Baronet of Great Britain, March 20, 1769. He married first, Sarah, daughter of Sir John Fagg, of Mystole, in Kent, Bart. who died without issue; and 2dly, in 1747, Elizabeth, (born 1729), the only child of Brook Taylor, Esq. doctor of civil law, secretary to the Royal Society, and F. R. S. by his wife Elizabeth Sawbridge, of Olantigh, in Kent; which Brook Taylor was the son of John Taylor, who was born in 1655, and purchased Bifrons, in Kent. He married, in 1682, Olivia, daughter of Sir Nicholas Tempest, of Durham, which John was the son of Nathaniel Taylor, Esq. born 1618, and was representative in parliament for the county of Bedford in 1653, clerk of the crown 1655, and in 1646, married Mary Bridges, of Goodnestone, in Kent. By the said Elizabeth Lady Young, who died July, 1801, he had one son, born 1749. Sir William died 1788, and was succeeded by his son,

II. Sir WILLIAM YOUNG, Bart. F. R. S. F. S. A. and M. P. for St. Mawes. He married, 1777, Sarah, daughter of Charles Lawrence, Esq. by his wife Mary Mihil; which Charles was the son of Thomas Lawrence (who was born 1680), a captain in the royal navy, and governor of Greenwich. He married, in 1703, M—— Soulden; which Thomas was the son of Henry, who was physician to five crowned heads, Queen Anne the last, and he was the son of Henry Lawrence, lord-president of Cromwell's council in 1653. By the said Sarah, Lady Young, who died Jan. 6, 1791, he had issue, 1, William; 2, Brook-Henry; 3, Charles; 4, Sarah; 5, Caroline: and 6, George. Sir William married secondly, April 22, 1793, Barbara, daughter of Richard Talbot, of Malahide Castle, in Ireland, Esq. by whom he has no issue.

ARMS—Or, three piles, sable, on a chief of the first, three annulets of the second.

CREST—A cubit arm erect, proper, grasping an arrow of the last.

MOTTO—*Press through.*

SEAT—Hartwell House, near Aylesbury, Bucks.

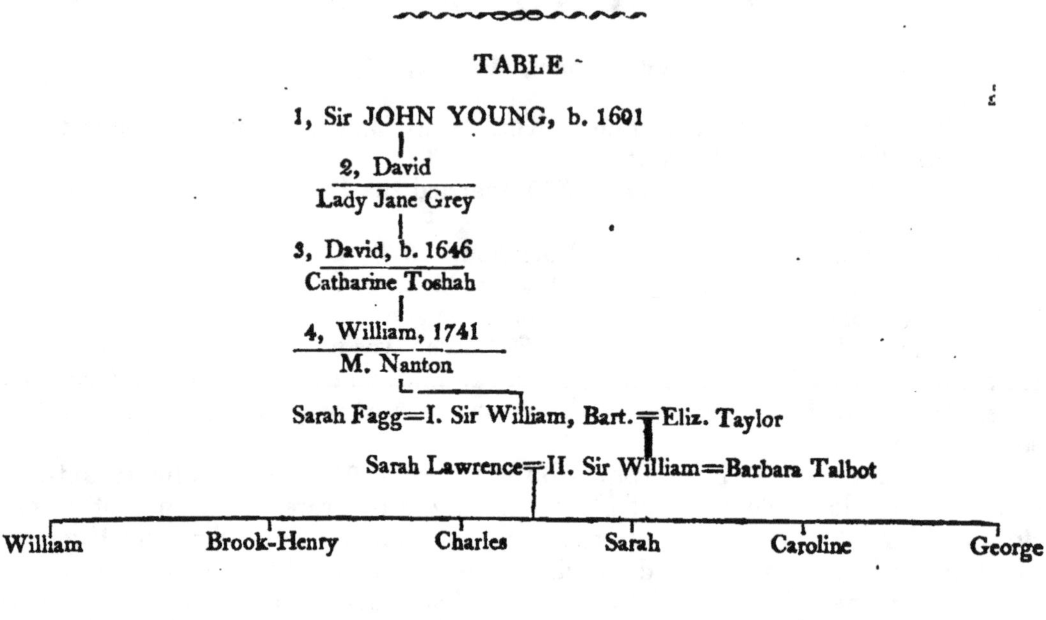

297. HARLAND, of Sproughton, Suffolk.

Created Baronet, March 19, 1771.

CAPTAIN ROBERT HARLAND, of the royal navy, married ——, daughter of —— Clyatt, by whom he had issue, 1, Frances, born 1713, wife, first, of —— Ellis, Esq. and secondly, of Sir William Gage, of Hengrave, near Bury, in Suffolk, Bart. and died without issue in 1763; 2, Edith, born 1714, wife of —— Leddeard, Esq. and died without issue; 3, Robert, of whom hereafter; 4, Anne, born 1716, died in her infancy. Mrs. Harland died in 1716, six weeks after the birth of her daughter Anne, and was buried at Highgate. On the loss of his wife, Captain Harland left Highgate, and purchased an estate at Sproughton, near Ipswich, Suffolk, where he resided till his son married, when he gave up that to him. The said Captain Robert Harland died, and was buried at Highgate.

I. ROBERT HARLAND, his only son, was brought up in the royal navy, and made captain about the year 1742. He married first, ———, daughter of —— Murlow, of Ipswich, by whom he had no issue; he married secondly, 1749, ———, daughter of Colonel Rowland Reynolds, of London, and grand-daughter and heiress of Colonel John Duncome, by whom he had issue, 1, Frances, born 1752, wife, in June, 1777, of Count Edward Dillon, and died Oct. 1777; 2, Marianne-Dorothy, born 1759, wife, Sept. 1783, of Major-General William Dalrymple, only brother of the Earl of Stair: she died Oct. 28, 1785, leaving one son, John-William-Henry, born Nov. 1784; 3, Susanna-Edith, born 1763, wife, March, 1785, of William Rowley, Esq. now Sir William Rowley, of Tendering Hall, Suffolk, Bart.; 4, Robert, of whom hereafter.

The said Captain Harland distinguished himself on various occasions during the wars of 1740 and 1755, in which the ships he commanded were engaged, so as to gain the esteem of his superiors, and acquire the reputation of an excellent intrepid officer. He was made an admiral in 1770, and a Baronet in 1771, as above-mentioned, and sailed for the East Indies, as commander in chief of his Majesty's fleet, and plenipotentiary to the Nabob of Arcot, from his Britannic Majesty, and returned to England in 1775. In 1778, he was appointed second in command in the fleet under Admiral Keppel. In 1782, he was appointed one of the lords commissioners of the admiralty, but his health declining, prevented his supporting the fatigue of business, and obliged him to request leave to resign in 1783, when he retired to his estate at Sproughton, where he died Feb. 21, 1784. He considerably increased his estates in Suffolk, by purchasing the Belstead estate, belonging to the Blois family, and an estate and manors in Wherstead, belonging to Thomas-Wenman Coke, Esq. Sir Robert died Feb. 21, 1784, and was succeeded by his son,

II. Sir ROBERT HARLAND, Bart. who was born 1765; he was a cornet in the royal regiment of dragoons, 1781, but sold out on the death of his father. He served in the West Suffolk militia till he got to the lieutenant-colonelcy. Between the years 1790 and 1794, he pulled down his residence at Sproughton, and built a handsome house on his Wherstead estate, now called Wherstead Lodge, and in May, 1801, he married Arethusa, daughter of Henry Vernon, Esq. (the elder brother of Earl Shipbrooke), late of Great Thurlow, in Suffolk, and sister of John Vernon, of Orwell Park, in the same county, Esq.

ARMS—Or, on a bend wavy, sable, three buck's heads caboshed, argent, between two sea-lions of the second.

CREST—A sea-lion, sable, supporting an anchor.

RESIDENCE—Wherstead Lodge, Suffolk.

TABLE.

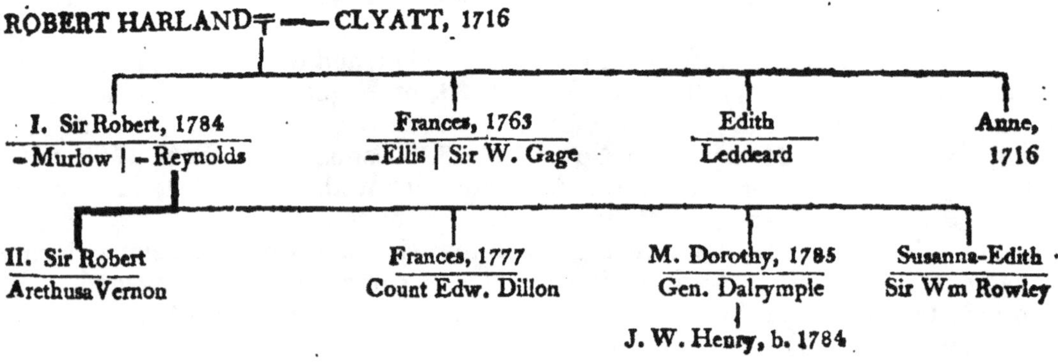

---

298. BLAKE, of LANGHAM, Suffolk.

Created Baronet, Sept. 19, 1772.

PATRICK BLAKE, great-grandfather to the present Baronet, was a younger son of the Blakes, of Cummer, in the county of Galway, in Ireland, from whence he went and settled in the Islands of Montserrat and St. Christopher's, where he married first, Mary-Anne Bohun *, by whom he had two sons, 1, Martin, who married first, Miss Trant, of Montserrat, who died soon after without issue; he married secondly, —— Liddel, by whom he had no issue; 2, Andrew Blake, married Marcella, daughter of —— French, of Ireland, by whom he had four sons; 1, Patrick, of whom hereafter; 2, Christopher; 3, Edward; 4, Arthur: and two daughters, Frances, and Marianne.

I. PATRICK BLAKE, Esq. eldest son of Andrew, was created a Baronet, Sept. 19, 1772, and married Annabella, youngest daughter of the late Sir William Bunbury, Bart. by whom he had issue, 1, Annabella, wife of Robert-Jones Adeane, of Babraham, Cambridgeshire; 2, Henrietta; 3, Frances, who died young; 4, Patrick, the present Baronet; 5, James, married Louisa, second sister of Lord

* Here lies the body of Mary-Anne Blake, alias Bohun, the wife of Patrick Blake Fitz-Peter, of Cummer, in the county of Galway, in Ireland, who departed this life the 18th day of February, 1720, in the 38th year of her age.

Here also lies the body of the above-mentioned Patrick Blake Fitz-Peter, of Cummer, in the county of Galway, in the kingdom of Ireland, late of this island, who departed this life the 7th day of March, 1744, aged 68 years.

Viscount Gage, by whom he has four sons and two daughters; 1, Louisa; 2, Henry; 3, Maria; 4, Patrick; 5, William; and 6, John. Sir Patrick Blake died, and was succeeded by his son,

II. Sir PATRICK BLAKE, Bart. who married, Aug. 12, 1789, ——, only daughter of James Phipps, of the Island of St. Christopher's, Esq.

ARMS—Argent, a fret, gules.
CREST—A leopard, passant, proper.
SEAT—At Langham, in Suffolk.

TABLE.

1, PATRICK BLAKE, 1744 = MARY-ANNE BOHUN, 1720

Martin / — Trant; 2, Andrew / M. French

I. Sir Patrick Blake / A. Bunbury; Christopher; Edward; Arthur; Frances; Marianne

II. Sir Patrick / Miss Phipps; James / L. Gage; Annabella / R. J. Adeane; Annabella, Frances

Louisa; Henry; Maria; Patrick; William; John

299. MILDMAY, of Moulsham Hall, Essex.

Created Baronet, 1611, revived 1768, again, Sept. 9, 1772.

THIS honourable family is so ancient as to have been of great consequence in the reign of King Stephen*, and it appears that one of them attended Richard I.

* Morant's History of Essex.

to the Holy Land, where, as an acknowledgement of his services, he received from that monarch an achievement and motto, which the family bear to this day.

1, Hugo Mildme, the first ancestor of whom we read, lived about the year 1147, and was succeeded by his son,

2, Robert, who was living in 1235, 19 Hen. III. and had two sons, Herbert, and,

3, Roger, who resided at Hambleton, in Lancashire, was succeeded by his son,

4, Henry Mildme, who was succeeded by his son,

5, Ralph, who had one son,

6, Henry, seated at Stonehouse*, in Gloucestershire, in 1349, who was succeeded by his son,

7, Henry, whose son,

8, Robert, was living in 1401. He was succeeded by,

9, Sir Robert, who married Matilda, the daughter and heiress of — Le Rous †, by whom he had one son,

10, Thomas, who espoused Margaret, daughter of John Cornish, of Great Waltham, Esq. and was the first of the Mildmays who had any connection with the county of Essex.

11, Walter, his son and heir, settled at Writtle, and married ——, daughter of —— Everard, of Great Waltham, by whom he had two sons, Thomas and John.

12, Thomas, the eldest son, accumulated very considerable estates in that county, and was of great consequence.

During the reign of Henry VIII. on the suppression of the religious houses, this Thomas (then Sir Thomas) was one of the auditors of the Court of Augmentations, and purchased of that monarch the manor of Moulsham *at twenty years* purchase ‡. He married Agnes, daughter of —— Reade, Esq. by whom he had four sons, each of whom became afterwards the head of a numerous family §; 1, Thomas, seated at Moulsham Hall; 2, William, at Springfield Barnes; 3, John, at Cretingham, in Suffolk; 4, Sir Walter, at Apthorpe, in Northamptonshire:

* Cart. 17. Rich. II.

† Cart. 7. Hen. VI.

‡ Six hundred and twenty-two pounds, five shillings, and eight-pence halfpenny.

§ In a few years after this period, the family of Mildmay spread almost over the whole county of Essex. In the latter end of the reign of James I. we find no less than nine considerable families of that name who had established themselves there, and were possessed of considerable estates, namely:

Sir Thomas Mildmay, Bart. of Moulsham.
Sir Henry Mildmay, Knt. of Woodham Walter.
Sir Humphry Mildmay, Knt. of Danbury.
Sir Henry Mildmay, Knt. of Wanstead.
Sir Thomas Mildmay, Knt. of Springfield Barnes.
Sir Henry Mildmay, Knt. of Graces.
Sir Walter Mildmay, Knt. of Great Baddow.
Carew-Hervey Mildmay, Esq. of Marks.
Sir Robert Mildmay, Knt. of Tarling.

and four daughters; Joanna, wife of Christopher Peyton, Esq. Thomasine, of Anthony Bencher, Esq.; the other two died unmarried.

Thomas Mildmay*, of Moulsham, married Avice, daughter of William Gernon, Esq. of London, by whom he had eight sons and seven daughters.

14, Sir Thomas, his eldest son and heir, married Frances †, only daughter of Henry Ratcliffe, Earl of Sussex, through whom afterwards the title and estate of the Fitz-Walters came into the Mildmay family. Sir Thomas died July 21, 1608, and was succeeded by his eldest son ‡,

15, Sir Thomas Mildmay, Knt. who was afterwards created a Baronet by King James I. June 29, 1611. He married first, Elizabeth, daughter of Sir John Puckering, keeper of the great seal; secondly, Anne, daughter of John Savill, Esq. but dying without issue in 1620, the title became extinct, and the estates went to his brother,

16, Sir Henry Mildmay, Knt. then seated at Woodham Ferrers, in Essex, who married Elizabeth, daughter of John Darcey, of Toleshurst-Darcey, in the same county, Esq. by whom he had three sons, 1, Robert; 2, Henry, who died unmarried; 3, Charles, married Martha, daughter and heiress of Sir Cranmer Harris, by whom he had one daughter Martha, wife of Sir Charles Tyrell, of Thornton, Bart. He died in 1654, and was succeeded by his son,

17, Robert, who married Mary, daughter and coheiress of Sir Thomas Edmonds, treasurer of the household, and many years ambassador in France, by whom he had Henry, (who died without issue), Benjamin, and Mary, the wife of Henry Mildmay, of Graces, Esq. who left five daughters, equally en-

* This Thomas was one of the auditors of the Court of Augmentations, temp. Hen. VIII. and purchased the estate and manor of Moulsham, then late belonging to the monastery of St. Peter's, Westminster, in 1539, and built a large and stately mansion-house thereon, called Moulsham Hall. He also purchased the estate and manor of Bishop's Hall, in Chelmsford, then late belonging to the Bishops of London, which, upon the surrender of Bonner, the last popish bishop, was granted to him by deed from Edward VI. dated May 8, 1549, both which grants are extant, and the estates and manors are still in the family.

He died in October, 1567, and by his will founded alms-houses in Moulsham, for the reception of six aged people, three men and three women, who should be appointed by the heir of the manor-house, leaving the sum of twenty marks, to be paid annually out of the tithes of his estate at Tarling, part to purchase an ox, to be distributed to the poor of that hamlet on Christmas-Eve, and part to be paid in money equally amongst the said six alms-people.

† The family of the Fitz-Walters possessed very extensive property in Essex in very early times (*a*). Henry I. granted them Dunmow, Edward I. Woodham, Reyndon, and Burnham, which latter possession has continued in the same line to the present period, never having suffered alienation or dismemberment, and passed with the estates of Lord Fitz-Walter to Sir W. Mildmay in 1756. They had also Shopland, Sherefield, Hallingbury, Walkern, Lexden, Bromley, Sherling, Henham, Fitz-Walters, &c.—*Dugdale.*

‡ Sir Walter, a younger son, was seated at Pishobury, in Hertfordshire, where a noble monument is erected to his memory. He married Mary, sister of Sir William Waldegrave, of Suffolk, Knt. which Sir William also married Elizabeth, sister to the said Walter, and one of the daughters of Thomas Mildmay, Sir Henry and Edward, two of his other sons, were seated at Waltham, in Essex, who, with the rest of his numerous younger children, died unmarried.

(*a*) Mon. Ang. Vol. II.

titled to the claim of the barony; 1, Mary, wife of Charles Goodwin, of Rovant, in Sussex; 2, Lucy, wife of Thomas Gardener, of Tolebury, in Essex; 3, Elizabeth, wife of Edmund Waterson, of London; and 4, Frances, wife of Christopher Fowler, of London: among the numerous descendants of which different families the title of Fitzwalter is now in abeyance.

18, Sir Henry *, the elder son of Robert, succeeded his father, but dying without issue, the property, as well as the claim to the barony, devolved on his brother,

19, Benjamin, who was summoned to parliament Feb. 10, 1669, by the title of Baron Fitz-Walter. He married Catharine, daughter of John, Lord Fairfax, of the kingdom of Ireland, son of Lord Fairfax, general of the parliament forces, by whom he had Charles and Benjamin.

20, Charles, the elder son, succeeded his father in the barony, and married Elizabeth, daughter of Charles Bertie, youngest son of Montague, Earl of Lindsey, and dying in 1728, without issue, was succeeded in the barony by his brother,

21, Benjamin, who was, in 1730, created Lord Fitz-Walter, Viscount Harwich, and married Frederica, Countess of Holderness, widow of Robert Darcy, Earl of Holderness, and one of the daughters and coheiresses of Meinhardt Schomberg, Duke of Schomberg, and marshal of France, and dying Feb. 29, 1756, without issue, this branch of the family became extinct in the male line.

We now return to

13, WILLIAM, second son of Sir Thomas Mildmay, who, in the second of Edw. VI. granted the vicarage of Great Baddow, together with the manor of Springfield-Barnes. He married Elizabeth, daughter of John Paschall, of Great Baddow, Esq. and dying 1570, was succeeded by his son,

14, Sir Thomas Mildmay, of Barnes, who married Alicia, daughter of Adam Winthorp, of Grotton, in Suffolk, Esq. by whom he had three sons; 1, William; 2, Sir Henry, of Graces †; and 3, Walter, of Portlands, in Great Baddow. Sir Thomas died 1613, and was succeeded by his eldest son,

* Sir Henry Mildmay, of this branch, laid claim to the barony of Fitzwalter, by reason of his descent from Elizabeth, sole daughter and heiress of Walter, Baron Fitzwalter, who died without issue male, 10 Hen. VI. but the troubles coming on between the king and his parliament, nothing was done. After the restoration, Henry Mildmay, Esq. grandson of the aforesaid Sir Henry, revived his claim by petition to the king, who referred it to the House of Peers; but Henry Mildmay dying soon after, his brother Benjamin pursued it; and though opposed by Robert Cheeke, Esq. who pretended himself the heir of the *whole blood*, whereas the Mildmays were of the *half blood* only, the house resolved, "That in case of dignity, the half blood was no impediment," so Benjamin was summoned to parliament 22 Car. II. as Baron Fitzwalter.—CAMDEN.

† This Sir Henry, second son to Sir Thomas, was a distinguished soldier. He is said to have acquired immortal glory (*a*), and for his services (probably in Ireland, where he was particularly active in suppressing the insurrections that prevailed about that period), had the honour of knighthood conferred on him in the field (*b*). He died 1639, and was succeeded by his eldest son Henry, who five times represented the coun-

(*a*) Ingis. Eliz. May 16, fo. 67,
(*b*) General Survey.

15, William Mildmay, who married Margaret, daughter of Sir George Hervey, constable of the Tower, by whom he had two sons; 1, Sir Thomas; 2, Carew-Hervey Mildmay *, of Marks.

16, Sir Thomas Mildmay, of Barnes, Knt. who married ——, daughter of John Ernly, of Whetham, in Wiltshire, by whom he had one son,

17, William Mildmay, of Barnes, remarkable for his bravery and loyalty to Charles I. He married Sybilla, daughter of Sir Thomas Palmer, of Wingham, in Kent, Bart. by whom he left a son,

18, William Mildmay, Esq. who became afterwards chief at Surat, in the civil service of the East India Company, and married Sarah, daughter of —— Wilcox, by whom he had one son William, and one daughter, Mary, the wife of Colonel Thomas Cockayne.

19, Sir William Mildmay was created a Baronet by his present Majesty, and to him Benjamin, Earl Fitz-Walter, devised his property, in consequence of which, he became seated at Moulsham Hall. Sir William married Anne, daughter of Humphrey Mildmay, of Shawford, Esq. one of the descendants of Carew-Hervey Mildmay, of Marks.

Sir William dying without issue in 1772, left his estates to his widow, who, at her decease in 1795, bequeathed them to the present possessor. From the second son of William Mildmay was also descended Carew-Hervey Mildmay, of Marks, who attaining the advanced age of ninety-six years, died in 1780, the last surviving male issue of the Mildmays.

From JOHN, the third son of Sir Thomas, was descended Robert Mildmay, of Tarling, in Essex. This branch is entirely extinct.

The fourth son of Sir Thomas was,

13, Sir WALTER MILDMAY, of Apethorpe, who married Mary, daughter of Sir Francis Walsingham, chief secretary of state to Q. Elizabeth, by whom he had

ty of Essex in the reigns of Charles II. and William and Mary. He married ——, the sister of Benjamin, Baron Fitzwalter, and left by her four daughters, between whose issue that title is now in abeyance.

* From Carew, in 1627, descended Francis, whose son Carew was high-sheriff for Essex in 1713. He died, leaving two sons, Carew-Hervey, of Haylegrove, in Somersetshire, and Marks, in Essex; and Humphrey, who married Letitia, sole heiress of Holiday Mildmay, Esq. of Shawford, Hampshire, by which the two branches of William and Sir Walter became united.

Carew-Hervey Mildmay, in 1634, married Dorothy, daughter of Sir Gilbert Gerrard, of Harrow-on-the-Hill, in the county of Middlesex, by whom he had

Francis-Hervey Mildmay, who married Matthew, daughter of Matthew Honeywood, of Charing, in Kent, by whom he had, 1, Carew; 2, George; 3, John; 4, Francis; 5, Walter, and several daughters: the three last sons died unmarried; George married Elizabeth, daughter of —— Banham, Esq. by whom he had Elizabeth, wife of Henry Eaton, of Raynham, in Essex, Esq.

Carew, the eldest son, was high sheriff for Essex in 1713. He married Anne, daughter of Richard Barret, alias Lennard, of Bellhouse, in Essex, Esq. by whom he had Carew and Humphrey, and one daughter Anne, wife of Thomas Saville, Esq.

Carew-Hervey Mildmay, the eldest son, married first, Dorothy, daughter and heiress of John Eastman, of Sherbourne, in Dorsetshire. He married secondly, Edeth, daughter and coheiress of Sir Edward Philips, of Montague, in Somersetshire. He was the last surviving male issue of the Mildmays, and died in 1780, aged 96.

Humphrey, the second son, married Letitia, daughter and heiress of Holiday Mildmay, of Shawford, in Hampshire, descended from Sir Walter, fourth son of Sir Thomas Mildmay aforesaid.

two sons. At the period of his marriage, he was himself chancellor of the exchequer, an office he held near twenty years in very turbulent and dangerous times. It is recorded of him *, that he was the first man who made a speech in the House of Commons of two hours; and what appears to have been thought worthy of remark, even in those days, "it was an able and an honest speech." Sir Walter was a great benefactor to Christ's College, Cambridge, where he received his education, and founded and sumptuously endowed Emanuel College. He had two sons, 1, Sir Anthony †, ambassador from Queen Elizabeth to the French court, to whom he gave his estates at Apethorpe, who married Grace, daughter of William Sheringham, Esq. and had by her an only daughter Elizabeth, wife of Francis Fane, Earl of Westmoreland ‡.

14, Sir Humphrey §, the second son of Sir Walter, inherited his estate at Danbury, in Essex, and married Mary, daughter of Henry Capel, of Hadham, in Hert-

* Parliamentary Journals.

† Here sleepeth in the Lord, with certaine hope of resurrection, Sir Anthony Mildmay, Knt. eldest sonne to Sir Walter Mildmay, Knt. chauncelor of the Exchequor, and privie counsellor to Queen Elizabeth. He was embassador from Queen Eliza. to the most Christian King of Fraunce, Henry the Fourth, anno 1596. He was to Prince and Country faithful, and serviceable in peace and warre, to friends constant, to enemies reconciliable, bountiful, and loved hospitality.

He died Sept. 11, 1617.

On the other side:

Here also lyeth Grace, Ladie Mildmay, the only wife of the said Sir Antho. Mildmay, one of the heyres of Sir Henry Sherington, Knt. of Lacock, iu the county of Wilts, who lived 50 yeares married to him, and 3 yeares a widow after him. She was most devout, unspotedly chast, mayd, wife, and widow, compassionate in heart, and charitably helpful with phisick, cloathes, nourishment, or counsels, to any in misery. She was most chearful and wise in managing estate, so as her life was a blessing to hirs, and in her death she blessed them, which happed July 27, 1620.

In front:

Thus this worthy payre having lived here worthely, dyed comfortably, belov'd of God, lamented of men, in whose memory, and to incite to the example of their vertues, Sir Francis Fane, Knt. sonne and heire to the Right Honourable Mary Nevill, Baronesse Despencer, and Mary his wife, the sole daughter and heire of the said Sir Anthony and Grace his wife, erected this Monument, anno domini, 1621.

‡ To this connection it is probable that the family of the Earl of Westmoreland owe the possession of Apethorpe. The name of Mildmay was long preserved in that family, and we find, that the Honourable Mildmay Fane, brother to the Earl of Westmoreland, and member for the county of Kent, died Sept. 11, 1715.—*Chronicle*, 1715.

§ During the troubles between Charles and his parliament, it appears that Sir Humphrey Mildmay, of Danbury, not choosing to join the prevailing party, was, by the parliament, deprived of his estate, but recovered it again, paying a composition of 1275l.

fordshire, Esq. by whom he had two sons, John, and Sir Henry, the eldest of whom espousing the cause of the king against the parliament, lost his life at the battle of Newbury, and leaving no issue, bequeathed his estates to his widow; who marrying a second husband, had by him an only daughter, —, the wife of William Fytche, Esq. whose family still continues in possession of Danbury Place.

15, Sir Henry, the other brother, appears to have been a great favourite with James I*. who not only condescended to plead his cause with Sir Leonard Holiday, whose daughter he solicited and obtained in marriage, but gave him more substantial proofs of his attachment in the grant of Wanstead, with its appurtenances, valued, a few years afterwards, at one thousand pounds per annum. The unfortunate son of James I. seems to have inherited his father's partiality towards Sir Henry Mildmay, who besides enjoying much of the private confidence of his sovereign, receiving many private obligations at his hands, was continued by him in the office of master of the jewels. Sir Henry Mildmay, nevertheless, sat as one of the judges at that tribunal which condemned to death his sovereign and benefactor. He sat the 8th, 10th, 15th, 23d, 25th, and 26th days, but did not sign the warrant for execution. He is said to have withdrawn himself in consequence of some pointed remark made by the unhappy king. Sir

* Copy of a letter from James I. to Sir Leonard Holiday. The original in possession of Sir Henry Mildmay.

JAMES, REX.

Trusty and well-beloved, we greet you well: We understand that Sir Henry Mildmay, our servant, is a suitor to your daughter, who, for his person and other external parts, may well appear to you worthy of the match with any gentlewoman of good quality. As for our opinion of him, it may be seen by this, that we have preferred him from a place of ordinary attendance about our person to a place of great charge and trust, which we never before bestowed on any man of his years; and therefore we cannot but wish him all advancement of his fortunes, and particularly in that match with your daughter; whereunto, if ye shall give your best furtherance, you shall not only give us good cause of acknowledging your respect unto us herein, but that as we have been and will be a father unto him, so we will be unto your daughter.

Given at our Court at Theobalds, fourth day, Oct. 1618.

If ye knew how far your conformity to our pleasure in this will be acceptable unto us, and profitable to yourselves, you would be willinger to perform it than we to desire it of you, for ye may be sure that however this may succeed, we will prefer him to a better place than he yet hath.

Sir Henry Mildmay seems to have borne a very active part in the proceedings of the parliament. In 1643, he was sent to receive the Dutch ambassadors at Gravesend, and to conduct them to London. In 1640, we find him delivered, as one of the English hostages, to the Scotch army, for the payment of 200,000l. for which they sold the king (*a*); and, in 1648 and 1649, he was appointed and continued one of the council of state.

By a letter from the Marquis of Worcester to Algernon Sydney, offering his services to the parliament, he begs that Lord Bradshaw, Sir Henry Mildmay, and Sydney, might be appointed commissioners to receive his particular address, and give him special orders from time to time (*b*).

These and many other instances might be adduced, to shew that Sir Henry enjoyed considerable importance in the eyes of the party he espoused. That the character of a man, whose conduct was so strongly marked with the deepest treachery and ingratitude towards the king, should be stigmatized by historians of the opposite party, is not to be wondered at: but there appear no grounds for ascribing to him not only the peculiar detestation of the royalists, but the contempt of the parliament faction. Ludlow, the only republican historian who mentions him, does not, by any means, justify this opinion.

(*a*) Whitlocke.
(*b*) Sydney's Letters.

Henry appears to have surrendered himself, with many others, on the proclamation in 1660, under the promise of life *, though subject to any subordinate punishment that might be inflicted †. He was condemned by the parliament, in 1661, to be drawn on a sledge, with a rope about his neck, to Tyburn, and thence conveyed to the Tower, to be confined for life ‡, but whether any part of this sentence was executed, I do not find. He died at Antwerp, one of the last of the Regicides, and a picture was drawn of him, after his death, now in the possession of the family. It is supposed to have been taken to shew that he died a natural death, in contradiction to an opinion that prevailed, that every one of those who sat in judgment on the king had perished by violent means. All the vast property he had accumulated was confiscated, excepting his estates at Shawford, in Hampshire, and at Newington, in Middlesex, which being the paternal estate of his wife Anne, daughter and heiress of Sir Leonard Holiday, of the city of London, and in strict settlement, were exempted from the forfeiture. Sir Henry had one son,

16, Henry Mildmay, of Shawford, whose son,

17, Holiday Mildmay, on his decease, left an only daughter,

18, Letitia, heiress in the male line of this branch. She intermarried with Humphrey, younger son of Carew Mildmay, of Marks, who was, as before related, descended from William Mildmay, of Springfield Barnes. Their issue were, Carew, and Anne, wife of Sir William Mildmay, of Moulsham, Bart. the heir of Earl Fitzwalter.

19, Carew, resided at Shawford, and married Jane, daughter of William Pescod, recorder of Winchester, and died in 1768, leaving three daughters, Jane, Anne §, and Letitia ||.

20, Jane married Sir Henry St. John, Bart. of Dogmerfield Park, Hants, (some account of whom will be given under the title of St. John), who, in the year 1793, obtained his Majesty's permission to assume the name and bear the arms of Mildmay only, in pursuance of the will of Carew-Hervey Mildmay, of Marks, Esq. whose estates descended to the eldest daughter of Carew Mildmay, of Shawford. Since that period, Sir Henry Mildmay has succeeded (in right of his wife), on the decease of the widow of Sir William in 1795, to the principal family seat and estate at Moulsham Hall: and thus the representation of the four sons of Sir Thomas Mildmay, in 1540, after the lapse of upwards of 260 years, have at length been centered in the same persons.

* Rapin.

† Ludlow, 356.

‡ Mr. Noble (a) mentions Henry Mildmay, son to Sir Henry, as one named in the commission, but it does not appear he ever sat.

§ Anne married John Clerk, Esq. of Worthing House, Hants.

|| Letitia married George William Ricketts, Esq. of Lainston House, Hampshire.

(a) Noble's Regicides.

TABLE.

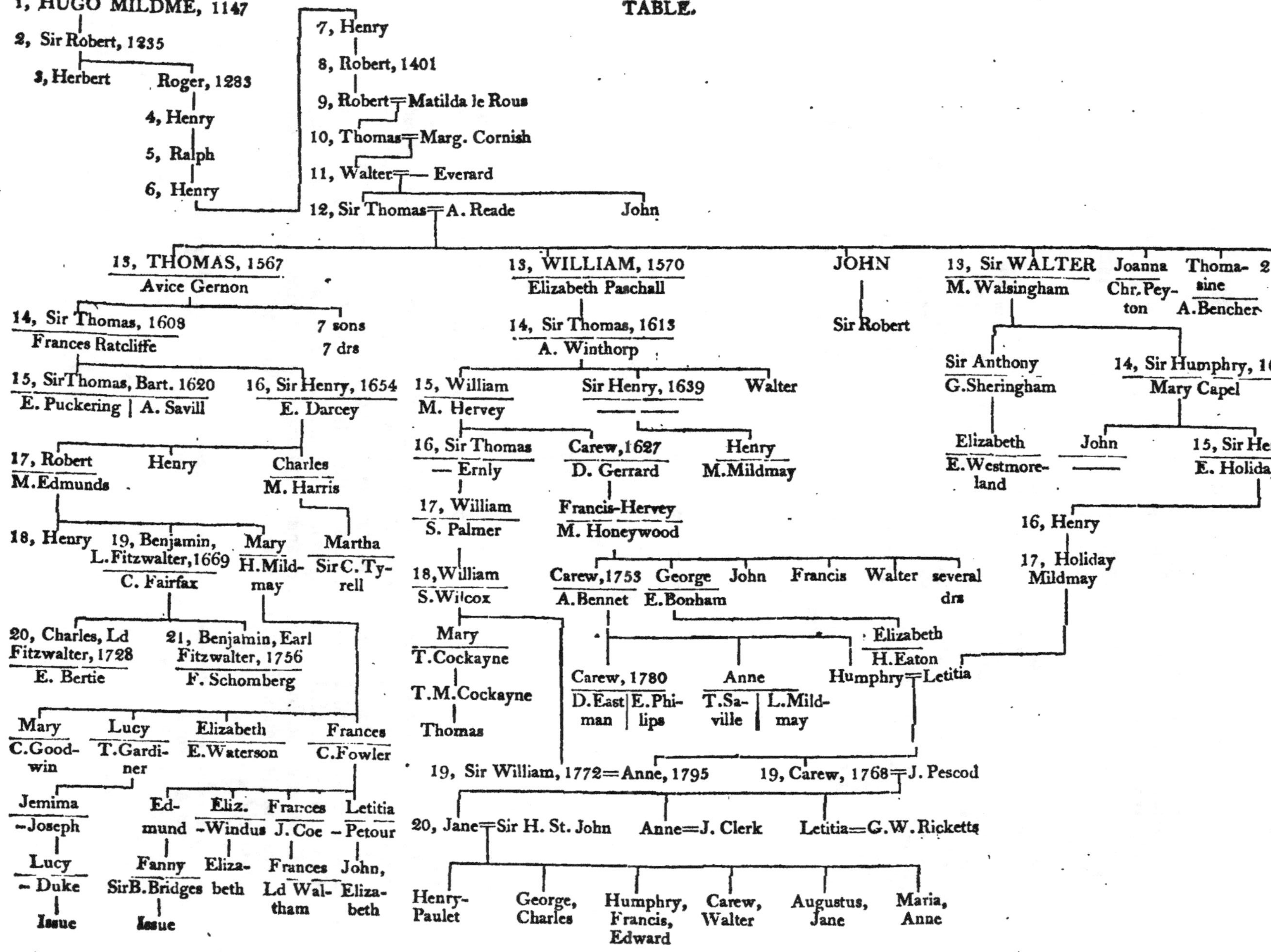
1, HUGO MILDME, 1147
2, Sir Robert, 1235
3, Herbert
Roger, 1283
4, Henry
5, Ralph
6, Henry
7, Henry
8, Robert, 1401
9, Robert=Matilda le Rous
10, Thomas=Marg. Cornish
11, Walter=— Everard
12, Sir Thomas=A. Reade
John
13, THOMAS, 1567
Avice Gernon
13, WILLIAM, 1570
Elizabeth Paschall
JOHN
13, Sir WALTER
M. Walsingham
Joanna
Chr. Peyton
Thomasine
A. Bencher
2 drs
14, Sir Thomas, 1608
Frances Ratcliffe
7 sons
7 drs
14, Sir Thomas, 1613
A. Winthorp
Sir Robert
Sir Anthony
G. Sheringham
14, Sir Humphry, 1614
Mary Capel
15, Sir Thomas, Bart. 1620
E. Puckering | A. Savill
16, Sir Henry, 1654
E. Darcey
15, William
M. Hervey
Sir Henry, 1639
Walter
Elizabeth
E. Westmoreland
John
15, Sir Henry
E. Holiday
17, Robert
M. Edmunds
Henry
Charles
M. Harris
16, Sir Thomas
— Ernly
Carew, 1627
D. Gerrard
Henry
M. Mildmay
17, William
S. Palmer
Francis-Hervey
M. Honeywood
16, Henry
18, Henry
19, Benjamin,
L. Fitzwalter, 1669
C. Fairfax
Mary
H. Mildmay
Martha
Sir C. Tyrell
18, William
S. Wilcox
Carew, 1753
A. Bennet
George
E. Bonham
John
Francis
Walter
several drs
17, Holiday Mildmay
20, Charles, Ld Fitzwalter, 1728
E. Bertie
21, Benjamin, Earl Fitzwalter, 1756
F. Schomberg
Mary
T. Cockayne
T. M. Cockayne
Thomas
Elizabeth
H. Eaton
Carew, 1780
D. Eastman | E. Philips
Anne
T. Saville | L. Mildmay
Humphry=Letitia
Mary
C. Goodwin
Lucy
T. Gardiner
Elizabeth
E. Waterson
Frances
C. Fowler
19, Sir William, 1772=Anne, 1795
19, Carew, 1768=J. Pescod
Jemima
—Joseph
Lucy
— Duke
Issue
Edmund
Fanny
Sir B. Bridges
Issue
Eliz.
—Windus
Elizabeth
Frances
J. Coe
Frances
Ld Waltham
Letitia
— Petour
John,
Elizabeth
20, Jane=Sir H. St. John
Anne=J. Clerk
Letitia=G. W. Ricketts
Henry-Paulet
George, Charles
Humphry, Francis, Edward
Carew, Walter
Augustus, Jane
Maria, Anne

ARMS—Argent, three lions rampant, azure.
CREST—On a wreath, a lion rampant, guardant, azure, armed, langued, gules.
MOTTO—*Alla ta Hara.*
SEATS—Moulsham Hall, and Marks, Essex; Dogmersfield Park, and Shawford, Hants; Hazlegrove, Somersetshire.

I find very honourable mention made in Ludlow, p. 164, of a Captain Antony Mildmay, who served in the navy under the Commonwealth. Speaking of one of those frequent actions in which the fleets, commanded by Blake and De Ruyter, were partially engaged, he says, "Captain Mildmay, of the Nonpareille, followed the Dutch fleet close, and being come up with them, commanded his small shot to be fired into that ship that made most sail, immediately after which he boarded and took her. This done, he pursued another, and in half an hour overtook her, and forced her to yield also. In one of these ships was the Dutch admiral, whom Captain Mildmay took out, with the rest of the men, and let her sink, she being so disabled, that he despaired of carrying her off.

In 1650, Captain Mildmay had a sharp fight with one frigate against three French men of war, one of which he took, having 16 guns and 4 of brass.—Whitlocke.

Who this Captain Mildmay was I cannot learn, probably the same who was member of the parliament that met in 1640 for West Loo, and to whom the order for interring Charles I. was made Feb. 6, 1648. There is a picture of him at Moulsham Hall.

St. JOHN.

THIS family is paternally descended from the Ports, lords of Basing, in Hampshire, at the time of the conquest, and maternally derive their surname from,

1, William de St. John*, who entered England with the Conqueror, whose army he attended as grand-master of the artillery, and supervisor of the waggons and carriages; for which reason, the horse's harness (or collar) was borne for his cognizance, and his name occurs in the roll of Battel Abbey. He married Olivia, daughter of Ralph de Filgiers, of Normandy, by whom he had two sons, 1, Thomas de St. John, who held lands in Oxfordshire, 13 Hen. I. and in 1112, gave † to the monks of St. Peter's, in Gloucester, his lands called Rugge, lying in Standish, and,

* Denominated from the territory of St. John, near Rouen, in the province of Normandy.
† Mon. Ang. Vol. I. p. 118.

2, John de St. John, who inherited his brother's lands in England, and principally the lordship of Stanton, in Oxfordshire, (for distinction from the other towns of the same name called Stanton St. John). This John was famous in the reign of William Rufus, being one of the twelve knights who accompanied Robert Fitz-Hamon, Earl of Gloucester, in his expedition against the Welch, and had, in reward for his services, the castle of Falmont, Faumont, or Fauman (as variously written), in the county of Glamorgan. He had two sons, 1, Roger, of whom hereafter; 2, Thomas de St. John, living 13 Hen. II.; and a daughter Avoris, who was the second wife of Bernard de St. Walery *, lord of the manor of Ambrosden, &c. in Oxfordshire.

3, Roger de St. John, the eldest son of John, married Cecily †, daughter and heiress of Robert de Haya, lord of the manor of Halnae, in Suffolk (given unto him by his kinsman Henry I.) by whom he had two sons; William ‡, mentioned among the barons and knights in the rolls, for payment of scutage for knights fees in the county of Sussex; who, between them, augmented the number of monks at Boxgrave, in that county, from three to fifteen: and one daughter,

4, Maud, was wife of Reginald *de Aurea valle*, or Orvile, by whom she had one daughter,

5, Mabil, wife of Adam de Port, a great baron, son of John, son of Henry, son of Hugh de Port, proprietor of fifty-five lordships in Hampshire, temp. William I.

6, William de St. John, son and heir of Adam de Port §, assumed the surname of his maternal grandmother ‖, writing himself, *Willielmus de Sancto Johanne, Filius & Hœres Adœ de Port.* He enjoyed the barony of Basing, and gave to the monks of Boxgrave eleven vergates of land in the town of Walborneton, and pasture for twelve oxen and as many cows, &c. He married Godechild, or Godchilda, daughter of Paganel, by whom he had four sons, 1, Robert; 2, Jeffery; 3, Adam; and 4, Thomas, who wrote himself Thomas de Port, aliter St. John, and was living in 1256.

7, Robert de St. John, lord of Basing, in 1254, obtained a charter of free

* This family derived their name from St. Walery, or Valery, in France, the port from whence Duke William set sail for his English expedition. This Bernard having incurred the king's displeasure, to make his peace, gave him his manor of Walvercote, and his right of advowson and patronage of the nunnery of Godstow, both of which he had by his wife (*a*). This Thomas was father of Roger, who, 22 Hen. II. was assessed 133l. 6s. 8d. for trespassing in the king's forests in Oxfordshire; and being dead 16 King John, Jeffery de Luci gave 300 marks for the wardship and marriage of his heir, whose name was John, who had a son John, killed at the battle of Evesham, 43 Edw. III. He was in the Holy Wars with Richard I, who, at the siege of Acre, thought of this device: he tied a leathern thong round the left leg of a certain number of his knights (one of whom was this John St. John), that they might be excited to greater courage (*b*). This, some think, the first occasion of the institution of the order of the garter.

† Mon. Ang. Vol. I. p. 594.

‡ Lib. Rub. Scac. & Col. Lib. Claudius, c. 2.

§ Mon. Ang. Vol. I. p. 594.

‖ Ibid. p. 595.

(*a*) Regist. Godstow, MSS.

(*b*) Kennet's Parl. Antiq. 147.

warren in all his demesne lands at Warnford and Chanton, in Hampshire, and others in Sussex and Berks. He had summons * to be at Chester upon Monday next after the feast of St. John Baptist, well accoutred with horse and arms, to oppose the incursions of the Welsh. In 50 Hen. III. he was governor of the castle of Porchester †, but died the next year or before ‡, for then John, his son and heir (by Agnes, daughter of William de Cantelupe), had livery of his lands, doing his homage, from whom are descended the Lords St. John, of Basing.

8, William, the brother of John §, had the castle of Faumont, in Glamorganshire, temp. Edw. I. He maried Isabel, daughter and coheiress of William Combmartin, by whom he had two sons, Henry, who died without issue, and

9, Sir John St. John, who, by Beatrix, his wife, had a son,

10, Sir John St. John, who married Elizabeth, daughter and coheiress of Sir Henry Umfreville, of Penmark, by whom he had an only son,

11, Sir John St. John, who married Isabel, daughter and coheiress of Sir John Paveley, of Panters Pury, in Northamptonshire, Knt. by whom he had,

12, Sir Oliver St. John, who married Elizabeth, daughter and heiress of Sir John Delabere, Knt. by whom he had an only son,

13, Sir John St. John, who was cousin and heir to Sir John Delabere; he was mayor of Bourdeaux from 1414 to 1421 ‖. He married Elizabeth, daughter of —— Pawlet, by whom he had one son,

14, Sir Oliver St. John, lord of Funnen, in Glamorganshire, married Margaret, daughter and heiress of Sir John Beauchamp, Knt. of Bletso, in Northamptonshire, a junior line of the Beauchamps, of Powick, branched from the Earls of Warwick, by whom he had two sons, 1, Sir John St. John, ancestor to the Lord St. John, of Bletso; and 2, Oliver, of whom hereafter: and five daughters, 1, Edith, wife of Sir Geofrey Poole, Knt.; 2, Elizabeth, of Henry, Lord Zouch, of Codnor, secondly, of John, Lord Scrope; 3, Mary, of Sir Richard Frogenhall, of Frogenhall; 4, Margaret, lady abbess of Salisbury, who died 1492; 5, Agnes, wife of David Malpas, of Cheshire.

The said Margaret Beauchamp was afterwards wife of John Beaufort, Duke of Somerset, knight of the garter, by whom she had one daughter Margaret, wife of Edmund Tudor, Earl of Richmond, by whom she had Henry VII. King of England. The said Margaret was thirdly the wife of Lionel, Lord Willes, and by him mother of John, Viscount Willes, knight of the garter, who married Cecily, second daughter of Edward IV. but died Feb. 9, 1498, leaving only one daughter Anne ¶.

15, Oliver St. John, the second son, was, as Leland writes in his Itinerary, a stout black man, and died at Fonterabia, in Spain, 1492. He married Elizabeth,

* Claus. 42 Hen. III. in dors. m. 11.
† Pal. 50 Hen. III. m. 20.
‡ Claus. 51 Hen. III. m. 17.
§ Segar's Baronage.
‖ Rymer's Fœdera, Vol. IV. part ii. p. 187, and Vol. IV. part iii. p. 197.
¶ Dugdale's Baronage, Vol. II. p. 131.

daughter of Lord Scroop, and widow of Bygod, or Bigot, who died June 12, 1503, by whom he had one son John, and three daughters; 1, Elizabeth, wife of Gerald Fitz-Gerald, eighth Earl of Kildare; 2, Eleanor, of Thomas Grey, Marquis of Dorset; 3, Margaret, lady abbess of Shafton, or Shaftesbury, in Dorsetshire.

16, John, his only son and heir, was knighted by Henry VII. having, in 1487, brought forces to the aid of the king against the Earl of Lincoln, Lambert Simnel, and their adherents, in the battle of Stoke, near Newark-upon-Trent. Margaret, Countess of Richmond, who died June 29, in the first year of her grandson Henry VIII. by her last will, dated June 6, 1508, constitutes this Sir John, who was then her chamberlain, one of her three executors, and the king, her son, supervisor, desiring him "to shew his special favour, help, and assistance, to her said executors, and to every of them. He married Joanna, daughter and heiress of Sir John Ewerby, or Iwardby*. by Catharine his wife, daughter and coheiress of Sir Hugh Armesley, of Mapledurham, in Oxfordshire, by whom he had two sons, 1, John; 2, Oliver, of Lambeth, in Surry, who married Margaret Love, of Winchelsea, in Sussex, by whom he had three sons, Sir Oliver, Nicholas, and John. This Sir John St. John died Sept. 1, 1512, and was succeeded by his son,

17, John St. John was in ward to Sir Richard Carew, of Beddington, in Surry, Knt. and married Margaret, one of his daughters, by whom he had three sons, 1, William, ancestor to the present Viscount Bolingbroke; 2, William; and 3, John.

18, William St. John, the second son, was of Farley, in Hampshire, and had one son,

19, Henry St. John, who had two sons, John, who died young, and

20, Oliver St. John, who had one son Oliver, and one daughter Christian, the wife of Ellis Mewe, of Winchester, Esq. by whom she had one son Ellis Mewe, who married Frances St. John, his cousin, of whom hereafter.

21, Oliver St. John left one daughter and heiress,

22, Frances, the wife of Ellis Mewe, Esq. her cousin aforesaid, who assumed by act of parliament, the name of St. John, in consequence of succeeding to that part of the property which belonged to this branch of the family, at Farley St. John, in Hampshire. On the death of Frances, her husband married secondly, Martha, daughter of John Goodyer, of Dogmersfield, by which marriage he acquired the present residence of the family. By his first wife he had four surviving children, 1, Paulet; 2, Ellis; 3, Goodyer; and 4, Mary, wife of John Pollen, Esq. member of parliament for Andover, and a Welch judge, who was mother of the present Sir John Pollen, Bart.

I. PAULET ST. JOHN, Esq. the eldest son, succeeded his father, and married first, ——, daughter of Sir John Rushout, Bart.; secondly, Maria, widow of Sir Haswell Tynte; and thirdly, Jane, widow of W. Pescod, recorder of Win-

* His monument is in Purley Church, Berks.

TABLE.

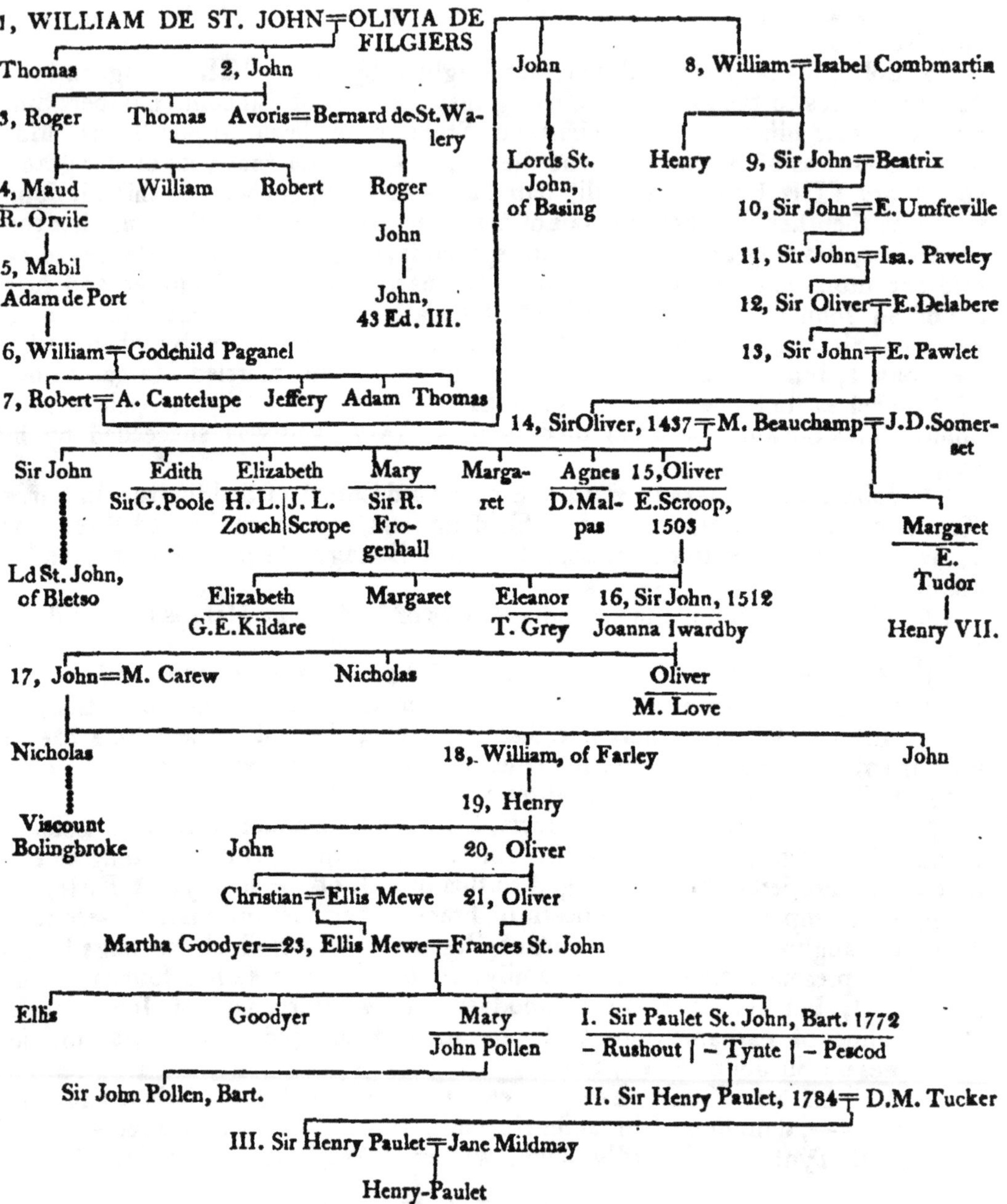
1, WILLIAM DE ST. JOHN = OLIVIA DE FILGIERS
Thomas
2, John
3, Roger
Thomas
Avoris = Bernard de St. Walery
4, Maud
R. Orvile
William
Robert
Roger
John
John, 43 Ed. III.
5, Mabil
Adam de Port
6, William = Godchild Paganel
7, Robert = A. Cantelupe
Jeffery
Adam
Thomas
John
Lords St. John, of Basing
8, William = Isabel Combmartin
Henry
9, Sir John = Beatrix
10, Sir John = E. Umfreville
11, Sir John = Isa. Paveley
12, Sir Oliver = E. Delabere
13, Sir John = E. Pawlet
14, Sir Oliver, 1437 = M. Beauchamp = J.D. Somerset
Sir John
Ld St. John, of Bletso
Edith
Sir G. Poole
Elizabeth
H. L. Zouch
J. L. Scrope
Mary
Sir R. Frogenhall
Margaret
Agnes
D. Malpas
15, Oliver
E. Scroop, 1503
Margaret
E. Tudor
Henry VII.
Elizabeth
G. E. Kildare
Margaret
Eleanor
T. Grey
16, Sir John, 1512
Joanna Iwardby
17, John = M. Carew
Nicholas
Oliver
M. Love
Nicholas
Viscount Bolingbroke
18, William, of Farley
John
19, Henry
John
20, Oliver
Christian = Ellis Mewe
21, Oliver
Martha Goodyer = 23, Ellis Mewe = Frances St. John
Ellis
Goodyer
Mary
John Pollen
Sir John Pollen, Bart.
I. Sir Paulet St. John, Bart. 1772
– Rushout | – Tynte | – Pescod
II. Sir Henry Paulet, 1784 = D.M. Tucker
III. Sir Henry Paulet = Jane Mildmay
Henry-Paulet

chester. In the year 1734, he represented the county of Hants, and soon afterwards the city of Winchester, of which place it appears he was mayor in 1772, by an inscription placed over the market-place, which was erected during the time he filled that office. He was created a Baronet in 1772, died in 1780, aged 76, and was succeeded by his eldest son by his second lady,

II. Sir HENRY-PAULET ST. JOHN, Bart. who likewise represented the county of Hants in two successive parliaments, and married Dorothea-Maria, daughter and coheiress of Abraham Tucker, Esq. of Betchwath Castle, in Surry, and dying in 1784, aged 47, was succeeded by his only son,

III. Sir HENRY-PAULET ST. JOHN, Bart. member of parliament for Winchester, who married, 1786, Jane, daughter and coheiress of Carew Mildmay, of Shawford House, in Hants, (and obtained, in 1790, his Majesty's permission to use the name and bear the arms of Mildmay only, in pursuance of the will of the late Carew-Henry Mildmay, of Haslegrove, in Somersetshire, and Marks, in Essex, Esq. whose estates devolved to the elder of the three daughters of Carew Mildmay, of Shawford), by whom he has issue.

---

300. WILMOT, of OSMASTON, Derbyshire.

Created Baronet, Sept. 19, 1772.

THIS family is a younger branch of that of Chaddesden, in the county of Derby, as will be found in the pedigree of Sir Robert Wilmot, Bart. *No.* 265.

13, Robert Wilmot, of Chaddesden, Esq. who was the common ancestor of the two families, had by Dorothy, his wife, daughter and heiress of Lawrence Shrigley, of Shrigley, in the county of Chester, four sons, of which,

14, Nicholas, the fourth son, to whom his father devised the Osmaston and other estates in Derbyshire, was born in Dec. 1611, was a student, and at length a bencher of Gray's Inn, where he took his degree of serjeant-at-law. He was honoured by the Cavendish family with particular marks of confidence and trust, relative to the restoration of King Charles II. On the 24th of May, 1661, he received a deputation from the Earl of Clare, recorder of the town and county of the town of Nottingham, to be deputy recorder thereof. The following year, the commissioners for regulating corporations in the county, attempted to remove his lordship from that recordership, but his Majesty, by his royal letter to the commissioners, bearing date the 16th of December, 1662, put an entire stop thereto. The commissioners had offered the said recordership to the said Nicholas Wilmot, which he refused, for which the Earl of Clare, in a letter bearing date the 10th of March following, returned his thanks to him in a very particular manner.

Upon the death of the Earl of Clare, the Marquis of Dorchester was elected and chosen recorder of the said town and county of the town of Nottingham; and, on the 5th day of April, 1666, the said Nicholas was appointed by his lordship deputy recorder thereof. He was knighted by Charles II. who expressed his intention of promoting him in his profession, which he declined, preferring a private life. He married Dorothy, one of the daughters of Sir John Harpur, of Calke, in the said county of Derby, Bart. by whom he had two sons, Robert and Nicholas, and three daughters, Dorothy, wife of Francis Revell, of Carnfield, in the said county of Derby, Esq.; Barbara, of Thomas Bembrigge, of Lockington, in Leicestershire, Esq.; and Elizabeth, of Nicholas Charnells, of Snareston, in the said county of Leicester, Esq.

Nicholas, the younger son, married ——, daughter and heiress of —— Chaloner, of Duffield, from whom is descended the present Edward Wilmot, of Landsdown, near Bath, in the county of Somerset, Esq.

15, Robert, the eldest son of Sir Nicholas, represented the borough of Derby in the first parliament called by King William and Queen Mary, and died in 1722, aged 82. He married Elizabeth, daughter and sole heiress of Edward Eardly, of Eardley Hall, in the county of Stafford, Esq. who was possessed of considerable estates in that county, by whom he had seven sons, 1, Robert; 2, Nicholas; 3, Edward; 4, John; 5, Charles; 6, Christopher; 7, Henry; and one daughter Anne, the wife of Robert Revell, of Carnfield aforesaid, Esq.

Nicholas, the second son, married Sarah, daughter of —— Lloyd, Esq. by whom he had one son Selden, who died unmarried, and four daughters, 1, Sarah, who died unmarried; 2, Elizabeth, wife of Lieutenant-Colonel Valentine Morris, by whom she had one son Valentine, and three daughters, Frances, who died unmarried, Sarah, wife of Henry Wilmot, of Farnborough Place, Esq. and Caroline, who died unmarried; 3, Mary, died unmarried; and 4, Margaret, wife of the Rev. Bryan Allot, of Kirk Heaton, in Yorkshire, by whom she has several children. Valentine Morris, the son, married ——, daughter of —— Mordaunt, Esq. by whom he left no issue.

John, the fourth son, married Frances, daughter of Francis Barker, Esq. by whom he had one son Robert, and three daughters, 1, Elizabeth, who died unmarried; 2, Alice, wife of John Ryder, archbishop of Tuam, and cousin-german to the late lord chief justice Ryder. His Grace left by the said Alice several sons and daughters.

Charles, the fifth son, was rector of Langley, near Derby, and married Bridget, one of the daughters of Benjamin Blundell, Esq. by whom he had one son, who died unmarried.

Christopher, the sixth son, was physician in ordinary to his Royal Highness George, Prince of Wales, afterwards George II. He married Anne, daughter of Edward Montague, of Horton, in Northamptonshire, and sister to the first Earl of Halifax, by whom he left one son, Montague Wilmot, who was colonel of a regiment of foot, and governor of Nova Scotia, where he died unmarried.

Henry, the seventh son, married Catharine, daughter of —— Dowson, Esq. by whom he left one son Henry, who, as before mentioned, married Sarah, one of the daughters of the said lieutenant-colonel Valentine Morris, and by her left one son, Henry-Valentine, the present possessor of Farnborough Place, and one daughter, Sarah Elizabeth.

16, Robert, the eldest son of the said Robert and Elizabeth, married, in 1703-4, Ursula*, one of the daughters and coheiresses of Sir Samuel Marow, of Berkswell, in Warwickshire, Bart. allied to many great and noble families, by whom he had three sons, 1, Robert; 2, John-Eardley Wilmot, of whom hereafter; and 3, Edward, who died an infant: and two daughters, Ursula, who died young; and Amabella, deceased, who was the wife of James M'Cullock, Esq. late Ulster king of arms: they left no issue.

John-Eardley Wilmot†, the second son, in 1755, who was made one of the judges of his Majesty's court of King's Bench, was knighted: he was appointed

* Lady Marow was one of the most accurate women of her time, and corresponded with Bishop Hough, who wrote her epitaph in St. James's Church, Westminster.

† He was born August 16, 1709, at Derby, and after he quitted the grammar-school there, was placed under Mr. Hunter, at Litchfield, with Johnson and Garrick, where four other contemporary judges had been educated. He was removed, in 1724, to Westminster School, under Dr. Friend, and thence to Trinity Hall, Cambridge, where he contracted such a passion for study, that he was often heard to say, his highest ambition was to become a fellow, and pass his life as that learned society. He gave a preference to the church, but his father destined him for the law, and he was called to the bar in 1732.

In 1742, he married Sarah, daughter of Thomas Rivett, of Derby, Esq. His early practice was confined to the county of Derby, but having attracted the notice of Sir Dudley Ryder, attorney-general, and lord-chancellor Hardwicke, the latter, in 1753, proposed to make him king's counsel and king's serjeant, both which he declined, from a wish to retire into the country; and, in 1754, he made his farewel speech to the Court of Exchequer. Soon after his retirement, he was summoned to succeed Sir Martin Wright as judge of the Court of King's Bench, which he accepted in 1755, though not without considerable persuasion, perhaps with regard to his family, having five children. His friend, Sir Dudley Ryder, died next year, and was succeeded by Lord Mansfield. The great seal, on the resignation of Lord Hardwicke, was put into the hands of three commissioners, of whom he was one, and appointed Mr. Melmouth, the elegant translator of Pliny and Cicero, a commissioner of bankrupts. In March, 1757, he had a most providential escape from the fall of a stack of chimnies through the roof of the court at Worcester, which killed Mr. Lawes, his first clerk, at his feet, and many others. The first object of his patronage in the church, was Mr. Shipton, of Osmaston, where he resided in the vacation, who, though he had served that church and two others for a very small stipend above thirty years, declined all preferment which might take him from his beloved flock. He died 1780, and left his savings, about two hundred pounds, to his nieces. Sir Eardley returned in a year to the King's Bench, where he had for his coadjutors, Lord Mansfield, Mr. Dennison, and Sir Michael Foster. Though the part he took was not a very conspicuous one, from his situation in the bench, and from his native modesty, his active mind was always engaged in elucidating some obscure point, in nicely weighing questions of the greatest difficulty, and contributing his share towards expediting and deciding the important suits then under discussion; and while his pervading mind suffered few crimes to escape detection and punishment, his humanity and compassion were often put to the severest trials.

The notes which he took in the course of his practice, even after he became a judge, were transcribed by his clerk, till he furnished Sir James Burrow, when he began to publish Reports in 1756. Letters passed between him and Sir Michael Foster on the act securing the independence of the judges. In 1765, a serious treaty was set on foot, for him to exchange his station for one not less honourable, but at that time less lucrative and less conspicuous, that of chief justice of Chester, then held by Mr. Morton, but the treaty was broken off. On Lord Camden's being appointed chancellor in 1766, Sir Eardley had the offer of the chief-justiceship of the Common Pleas, which his friend, Sir Joseph Yates, who was with him on the western circuit, prevailed with him to accept. In the evening of the day, Sir Eardley kissed hands on

one of the commissioners of the great seal, and, on the 17th of August, 1766, was appointed chief justice of the court of Common Pleas, and sworn of his Majesty's most honourable privy council. He married Sarah, one of the daughters of Thomas Revell, Esq. by whom he left three sons, Robert, John, and Eardley, and three daughters, Mary Marow, and Elizabeth-Mary Marow, wife of the Right Honourable Lord Eardley; and Elizabeth, of Colonel Blomefield, of the artillery. Robert died unmarried. John, of Berkswell Hall, in Warwickshire, Esq. was one of the representatives in parliament for Coventry, and a master in chancery, married to his first wife, Frances, daughter and sole heiress of —— Sainthill, Esq. and secondly, to ———, daughter of —— Haslam, Esq. by both of whom he has several children. Eardley is unmarried.

I. ROBERT, the eldest son of the said Robert and Ursula, attended his Grace the Duke of Devonshire to Ireland, upon his being made lord-lieutenant in 1737; and, on his return to England in 1739, was presented by his Grace to his Majesty, was knighted, and received letters of deputation from his Serene Highness Prince Frederick, son-in-law to his Majesty George II. to represent his person as proxy at the installation of knights of the garter at Windsor. In 17—, he was appointed by his Grace the Duke of Devonshire to be his secretary resident in Great Britain, as lord-lieutenant of Ireland, in which post he had the honour to be continued by the Earls of Chesterfield and Harrington, the late Dukes of Dorset, Devonshire, and Bedford, the late Earl of Halifax, the late Duke of Northumberland, the Lord Viscount Weymouth, the late Earls of Hertford and Bristol, and the present Marquis Townshend, successive lord-lieutenants of Ireland. In 1758, he was appointed by his Grace the Duke of Devonshire lord-chamberlain of his Majesty's household, his deputy-secretary, and upon the death of James Pelham, Esq. secretary to his Grace, was continued in that post by the Dukes of Marlborough and Portland, and to the late Marquis of Hertford till his death. He was created a Baronet of Great Britain Sept. 19, or Oct. 10, 1772. He married Eli-

being appointed chief justice, one of his sons, a youth of seventeen, attended him to his bedside. "Now," says he, "my son, I will tell you a secret worth your knowing and remembering: the elevation I have met with in life, particularly this last instance of it, has not been owing to my superior merit or abilities, but to my humility, to my not having set up myself above others, and to a uniform endeavour to pass through life void of offence to God and man."

In 1769, he presided in the memorable cause of Mr. Wilkes against Lord Halifax and others, where his conduct gave universal satisfaction, he was so entirely free from all political views. He never forgot the profession which was the first object of his choice, and for which he intended one of his sons who preferred the law. The great seal was offered Sir Eardley, on the resignation of Lord Camden in 1772, and again the same year by Lord North. His ill health now occasionally preventing his attending his court, he determined to resign without receiving any pension from the crown; but this being over-ruled by the king himself, however "surprized and disconcerted" he might be, he was under the necessity of receiving it.

He died Feb. 5, 1792, aged 82, leaving his eldest son sole executor, with directions to erect a plain marble tablet in Berkswell church, containing an account of his birth, death, dates of his appointments, and names of his children, without any other additions whatever. His person was of the middle size, his countenance commanding and dignified; his eye lively, tempered with sweetness and benignity; his knowledge extensive and profound; and, perhaps, nothing but invincible modesty prevented him from equalling the greatest of his predecessors, and fettered his abilities and learning. In private life, he excelled in all those qualities which render a man respected and beloved.

TABLE.

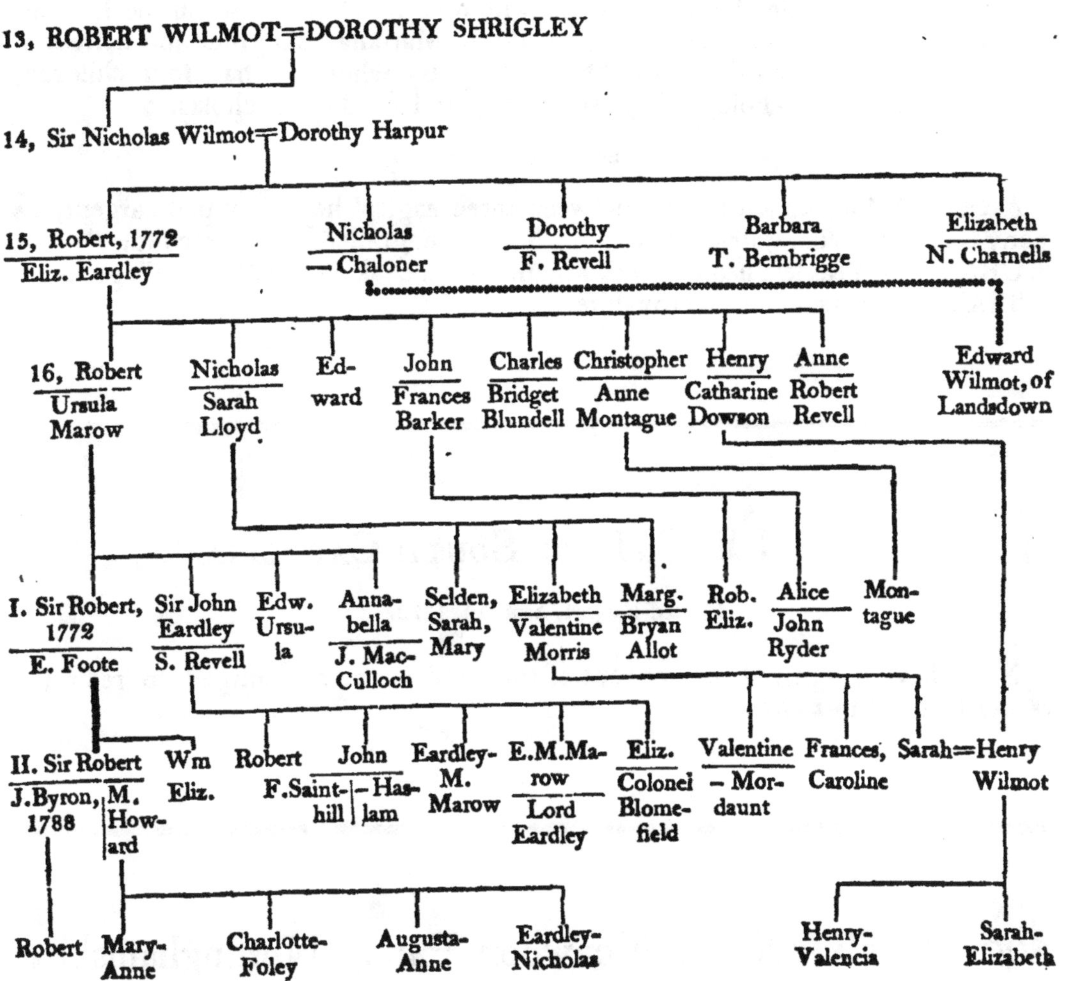
13, ROBERT WILMOT=DOROTHY SHRIGLEY
14, Sir Nicholas Wilmot=Dorothy Harpur
15, Robert, 1772
Eliz. Eardley
Nicholas
— Chaloner
Dorothy
F. Revell
Barbara
T. Bembrigge
Elizabeth
N. Charnells
16, Robert
Ursula Marow
Nicholas
Sarah Lloyd
Ed-ward
John
Frances Barker
Charles
Bridget Blundell
Christopher
Anne Montague
Henry
Catharine Dowson
Anne
Robert Revell
Edward Wilmot, of Landsdown
I. Sir Robert, 1772
E. Foote
Sir John Eardley
S. Revell
Edw. Ursu-la
Anna-bella
J. Mac-Culloch
Selden, Sarah, Mary
Elizabeth
Valentine Morris
Marg.
Bryan Allot
Rob. Eliz.
Alice
John Ryder
Mon-tague
II. Sir Robert
J. Byron, 1788
M. How-ard
Wm Eliz.
Robert
F. Saint-hill
John
— Has-lam
Eardley-M. Marow
E. M. Ma-row
Lord Eardley
Eliz.
Colonel Blome-field
Valentine
— Mor-daunt
Frances, Caroline
Sarah=Henry Wilmot
Robert
Mary-Anne
Charlotte-Foley
Augusta-Anne
Eardley-Nicholas
Henry-Valencia
Sarah-Elizabeth

zabeth, daughter of Thomas Foote, Esq.: their only surviving children are, Robert, the present Baronet, William, and one daughter Elizabeth. Sir Robert died suddenly, Nov. 14, 1772, at his country-seat at Little Ealing, in Middlesex, and was succeeded by his eldest son,

II. Sir ROBERT WILMOT, Bart. who married first, Julia, second daughter of the late Honourable Admiral Byron, who died in 1788, by whom he has one son Robert. He married secondly, in 1795, Mariana, daughter and heiress of the late Charles Howard, of Litchfield, Esq. by whom he has four children, Mary-Anne, Charles-Foley, Augusta-Anne, and Eardley-Nicholas.

ARMS—Sable, on a fesse, or, between three eagles' heads couped, argent, as many escallop shells, gules, all within a bordure engrailed, of the second.

CREST—An eagle's head erased, argent, in his beak an escallop shell, gules.

SEAT—At Osmaston, Derbyshire.

---

301. LEIGH, of South Carolina.

Created Baronet, Sept. 19, 1772.

NOT having received the account of this family, we are obliged to refer the reader to the Appendix.

---

302. SUTTON, of Norwood Park, Nottinghamshire.

Created Baronet, Sept. 25, 1772.

1, RICHARD, or ROLAND DE SUTTON, upon Trent, the first of this family, mentioned by Thoroton, in his Antiquities of Nottingham, married Alice, sister of Sir Robert de Lexington, by whom he had two sons, 1, Sir William de Sutton, who married Matildis ——, by whom he had one son Robert, who granted, confirmed, and quit-claimed to Robert, his uncle, son of Roland de Sutton, the manor of Averham, formerly Egrom, with the advowson of the church and knights fees, &c. as Sir John de Lexington held it, and also the whole land of Kelum, with the appurtenances, to be held of him and his heirs, for the service of two knight's fees, &c.*

2, Sir Robert de Sutton, the second son of Rowland, to whom his nephew gave the manor of Averham †, married first, Alice, daughter of ——, by whom he had two sons, Richard, canon of Southwell, and John, parson of Lexington. He married secondly, Isabel, daughter and coheiress of Sir Hugh Picot, by whom he had one son,

3, Sir James de Sutton, who married Agnes, daughter and heiress of Sir John Barry, of Torlaston, by whom he had two sons, Richard and Robert. Sir James died 1304.

4, Richard Sutton, his eldest son, married Alice, daughter and heiress of Sir Richard Bingham, of Bingham, the elder, Knt. and died 1339, and was succeeded by his son,

5, John Sutton, who married Alice, daughter and heiress of Henry Mustin, of Seirston, by whom he had one son, and died 1369.

6, Roland de Sutton ‡, twenty-one years of age, married Katharine, daughter of Sir Henry Hasty, Knt. by whom he had one son Henry, and died 1397.

7, Henry de Sutton, who married Margaret, daughter of Sir Hugh Hussey, of Flintham, and died 1416, and was succeeded by his son,

8, Richard Sutton, who married Katherine, daughter of —— Fitz-Williams, of Aldewack, and died 1448, and was succeeded by his son,

9, Robert Sutton, who married Elizabeth, daughter of Thomas Stanley, of Pype, by whom he had one son Henry, and died 1500.

10, Henry Sutton, who married Alice, daughter of Sir Nicholas Byron, of Coiwick, and left one son,

11, Sir Thomas, who married Katherine, daughter of Sir Thomas Basset, of Fledborough, and died 1526, leaving one son,

12, Sir Henry Sutton §, who married first, Alice, daughter of Francis Hall, of Grantham; secondly, ———, Lady Pierpoint, by whom he had no issue; thirdly, Alice, daughter of Sir Henry Harrington, Knt. relict of —— Flower, by whom he had five sons, 1, John; 2, Marc; 3, Edmund; 4, Henry; 5, Harrington: and a daughter Anne, first wife of Henry Cobham, brother of Wil-

* Ex ipso autog, pen. Rob. Dom. Lexington.

† Regist. de Ruff.

‡ It is not positively certain whether this son was by Alice or some other wife. The jury, 50 Edw. III. (a) found, that John de Sutton, of Averham, died 44 Edw. III. and left a son and heir Rowland.

§ John, son of Robert de Willoughby, Lord Eresby, and Katherine, his wife, 4 Hen. V. granted to Henry de Sutton, and others, all his lands, &c. in Averham, together with the manors of Kyrtelington, Clifton, Herdiby, and Kelham (b).

(a) Esc. 50 Edw. III. n. 60.
(b) Claus. 4 Hen. IV.

liam, Lord Cobham. By his first wife he had two sons, Edward, who married Olivia, daughter of William Cooper, of Thurgaston, but had no issue, and

13, William Sutton, his second son, who married Anne, daughter of John Rodney, of Buckwell, in Somersetshire, by whom he had Sir William, Nicholas, Edmund, John, and three daughters, Jane, Elizabeth, and Olive.

14, Sir William Sutton, of Averham, Knt. married Susan, daughter of Thomas Coney, of Basingthorpe, in Lincolnshire, by whom he had four sons, Robert, Richard, Henry, and Gervas: and four daughters, Alice, Susan, Elizabeth, and Mary.

. Robert, the eldest son, married first, Elizabeth, daughter of Sir George Manners, of Hadon, in Derbyshire, sister of John, Earl of Rutland; he married secondly, Anne, daughter of Sir Guy Palmers, and widow of Sir Thomas Browne, of Walcot, in Northamptonshire, Bart. by whom she had two daughters, Elizabeth, and Anne, widow of ——, Lord Pawlet, afterwards married to ——Stroud. He married thirdly, Mary, daughter of Sir Anthony St. Leger, warden of the king's mint, by whom only he left issue, Robert, Bridget, and Anne, born after his death, which was Oct. 13, 1668: his lady died 1669, and was buried by him at Averham. He very much increased his patrimony, and considerably assisted Charles I. with money, who created him Lord Lexington.

Richard Sutton, his brother, married ———, daughter of —— Stanhope, half sister of Philip, Earl of Chesterfield, by whom he had a son Robert, who was captain of a troop of horse, which he carried into Portugal: he died without issue male.

15, Henry, the next brother of the Lord Lexington, married Mabel, daughter of Henry Faun, by whom he had three sons, Robert, William, and Gervas.

16, Robert Sutton, the eldest son, married Katherine Sherbourne, by whom he had Robert, and Richard.

17, Robert, the eldest son, born 1671, was bred up in the diplomatic line, and was ambassador in Holland. He was appointed, immediately after the peace of Carlowitz in 1669, to succeed Lord Paget as ambassador at Constantinople, where he remained till 1717. He went back in 1718, to be ambassador mediator together with the Dutch ambassador at P——, for the peace between the Emperor, Venice, and the Turks. In 1720-1, he succeeded Lord Stair as ambassador at Paris, and was afterwards appointed ambassador to the intended congress at Cambray, which did not take place. He was made knight of the Bath, on the renewal of the order, and was of the privy-council. He was chosen into parliament, in 1720, for the county of Nottingham, and afterwards for Great Grimsby. He was governor of Bruges, in Flanders, and died in 1746*.

* On the discovery of the embezzlement in the Charitable Corporation (I think in 1721), in the first rage of the House he was expelled the House of Commons, but the proceedings in chancery afterwards cleared his character, finding the charge to lie only in the cashier, &c. Mr. Sutton having accepted the office of governor merely as a compliment, and unluckily did not attend to the business.
Vide Warburton's Note in the third Volume of his edition of Pope, 1751, p. 230.

He married (circa 1725) Judith, Countess Dowager of Sunderland, by whom he had one daughter Isabella, who died 1768, and four sons: 1, Robert; 2, Robert, who both died young; 3, John, who married Evelyn Chadwick, and died in 1772; and,

I. RICHARD SUTTON, Esq. born July 31, 1733, who was brought up at Westminster School, and Trinity College, Cambridge, and was called to the bar. He was under secretary of state from August, 1766, to September, 1772, on quitting which office he was rewarded with the Baronetage.

He was in parliament from 1768 to the last dissolution for the borough of St. Alban's, Sandwich, and Boroughbridge, successively; and was likewise lord of the treasury from 1780 or 1781, to the end of Lord Guildford's administration.

He married Susan, daughter of Philip-Champion Crespigny, of Camberwell, Esq. who died 1766, without issue. He married secondly, Anne, daughter of W. Peere Williams, of Devonshire, Esq. who died 1787, by whom he had seven children; 1, Elizabeth Evelyn, wife of the Rev. George Markham; 2, John, who married Sophia-Frances, daughter of the late Charles Chaplin, of Tathwell, in Lincolnshire, Esq. by whom he had one son, Sir Richard, the present Baronet, and one daughter, Sophia-Charlotte, who died young: he died in 1801; 3, Richard; 4, Anne-Georgiana, wife of the Rev. Robert Chaplin, son of Charles Chaplin, Esq. of T——; 5, Isabella-Frances, wife of the Rev. W. Chaplin; 6, Robert-Nassau, captain in the 58th regiment of foot; and 7, Henry, who died young. Sir Richard married thirdly, Margaret, daughter of the late John Porter, of Wandsworth, Surry, and of Catharine, daughter of Brigadier-General Sutton, who served in all Queen Anne's wars, and was governor of Bruges, in Flanders. He died in 1802, and was succeeded by his grandson,

II. Sir RICHARD SUTTON, Bart. a minor.

ARMS—Quarterly: first and fourth, argent, a canton, saliant, for Sutton; second and third, argent, a cross fleury, for Lexington.

CREST—A wolf's head erased, gules.

MOTTO—*Touts jours prest.*

SEAT—Norwood Park, Nottinghamshire.

TABLE.

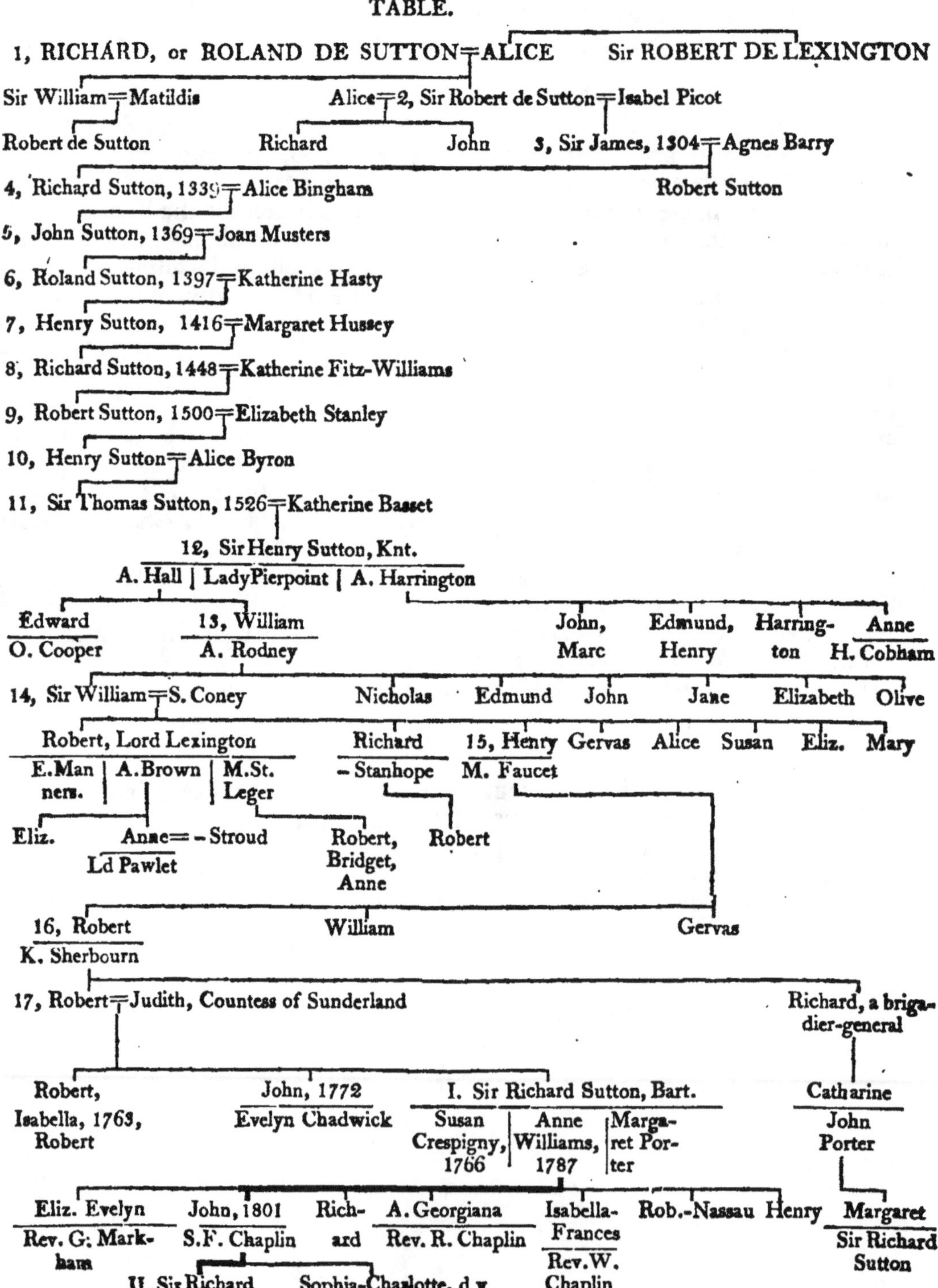
1, RICHARD, or ROLAND DE SUTTON=ALICE
Sir ROBERT DE LEXINGTON
Sir William=Matildis
Alice=2, Sir Robert de Sutton=Isabel Picot
Robert de Sutton
Richard
John
3, Sir James, 1304=Agnes Barry
4, Richard Sutton, 1339=Alice Bingham
Robert Sutton
5, John Sutton, 1369=Joan Musters
6, Roland Sutton, 1397=Katherine Hasty
7, Henry Sutton, 1416=Margaret Hussey
8, Richard Sutton, 1448=Katherine Fitz-Williams
9, Robert Sutton, 1500=Elizabeth Stanley
10, Henry Sutton=Alice Byron
11, Sir Thomas Sutton, 1526=Katherine Basset
12, Sir Henry Sutton, Knt.
A. Hall | Lady Pierpoint | A. Harrington
Edward
O. Cooper
13, William
A. Rodney
John, Marc
Edmund, Henry
Harrington
Anne
H. Cobham
14, Sir William=S. Coney
Nicholas
Edmund
John
Jane
Elizabeth
Olive
Robert, Lord Lexington
E. Manners. | A. Brown | M. St. Leger
Richard
– Stanhope
15, Henry
M. Faucet
Gervas
Alice
Susan
Eliz.
Mary
Eliz.
Anne=– Stroud
Ld Pawlet
Robert, Bridget, Anne
Robert
16, Robert
K. Sherbourn
William
Gervas
17, Robert=Judith, Countess of Sunderland
Richard, a brigadier-general
Robert, Isabella, 1763, Robert
John, 1772
Evelyn Chadwick
I. Sir Richard Sutton, Bart.
Susan Crespigny, 1766 | Anne Williams, 1787 | Margaret Porter
Catharine
John Porter
Eliz. Evelyn
Rev. G. Markham
John, 1801
S.F. Chaplin
Richard
A. Georgiana
Rev. R. Chaplin
Isabella-Frances
Rev. W. Chaplin
Rob.-Nassau
Henry
Margaret
Sir Richard Sutton
II. Sir Richard
Sophia-Charlotte, d y

303. WRIGHT, of London.

Created Baronet, Dec. 5, 1772.

FOR an account of this family, see Appendix.

---

304. PALLISER, of the Vatch, Bucks.

Created Baronet, June 25, or Aug. 6, 1778.

1, JOHN PALLISER, of Newby super Wiske, in the north-riding of Yorkshire, married Anne, daughter of Michael Meeke, of Maunby-upon-Swale, in the said county, Esq. by whom he had six children; 1, Thomas, of whom hereafter; 2, John, of Kirkby-Wyske, in Yorkshire, who married Elizabeth ——, by whom he had one son Thomas; 3, Anne, wife, first, of Richard Metcalfe, of Northallerton, in Yorkshire, who died about 1640, leaving issue; secondly, of Marmaduke Franke, of Knighton, in the said county; 4, Jane, of Thomas Pybus, of Fryergarth, in Yorkshire; 5, Elizabeth, of George Llewellyn, of Danby-upon-Wyske; 6, Mary, the eldest daughter, wife, Oct. 28, 1628, of Robert Wilson, of Thirsk, in Yorkshire, who was born June, 1603, and died March, 1681, by whom she had, amongst others, one daughter Anne, born April, 1630, died 1689: she was wife of John, eldest son and heir of John Pybus, who was born Nov. 1623, and was buried at Thirsk, 1673, by whom she had eleven children*.

* Samuel Pybus, of Thirsk, sixth son, born Sept. 1662, died Aug. 1705, buried at Thirsk, and married Anne, daughter of Bryan Taylor, of Wenthorpe, in the parish of Lockington, in Yorkshire, born 1666, died Nov. 1726, and was buried at Thirsk.

Bryan Pybus, of Dover, in Kent, second son and heir of Samuel, born Jan. 1690, died Oct. 1747, buried at Dover, and married Mary Kempster, of Harwich, in Essex, and was buried March 29, 1745, leaving one son and heir,

John Pybus, of Cheam, in Surry, and Greenhill Grove, in the county of Herts, born November 22, 1727, died June 22, 1789, and buried at Cheam. He married Martha, youngest daughter and coheiress of Charles Small, of Lewisham, in Kent, born July, 1734, and living 1799, by whom he had eight children; 1, John, born Nov. 9, 1754, married Anne, daughter of Richard Cooper, born April 24, 1763, died June 7, 1798, by whom he has two children, Martha, born April 29, 1789, and John, born Feb. 12, 1792; 2, Catharine, died young: 3, Anne, born Nov. 1756, widow of Brigadier-General Sir Robert Fletcher, Knt. who died Feb. 16, 1794; 4, Martha, born April 16, 1758, wife first, of Major Arthur Lysaght; secondly, of John Briggs, and died July 30, 1781, leaving three sons; 5, Margaret Clive, died young; 6, Elizabeth, died young; 7, Charles-Small Pybus, one of the lords commissioners of his Majesty's Treasury, and member of parliament for Dover, born Nov. 3, 1766, unmarried, 1799; 8, Catharine-Amelia, born Jan. 20, 1776, unmarried, 1799.

2, Thomas Palliser, eldest son of John, aged 59, in Aug. 1665, married Joan, daughter of Richard Franklin, of Blubber Houses, in Yorkshire, by whom he had three sons; 1, John; 2, William, bishop of Cloyne 1692, archbishop of Cashel 1694, died 1726; 3, George.

3, John Palliser, eldest son, was aged twenty-six years in Aug. 1665, and married Ursula, third daughter of Sir Hugh Bethell, of Ellerton, in Yorkshire, Knt. by whom he had five children; 1, Thomas Palliser, of Porto Bello, in the county of Wexford, in Ireland, a colonel in the army, aged three years in August, 1665, lived to the age of 105: he married ——, daughter and heiress of Colonel Wogan, of Rath Coffee, in the county of Meath, in Ireland, by whom he had five children; 1, Juliana-Hyde, who died about 1783, the wife of Captain John Orseur †, by whom she had Mary, wife of George-Robinson Walter, of whom hereafter; 2, Thomas, who died without issue; 3, William, who married ——, daughter of ——— Savage, by whom he had Philip Palliser, of Barnyforth, county of Wexford, in Ireland, and had one daughter living 1774; 3, Walter, of Dublin, post-master, who had a son Richard, a counsellor at law in Dublin, who died unmarried 1774; 4, John, died nnmarried.

Hugh Palliser, the second son of John and Ursula, of whom hereafter; 3, John, aged two years in August, 1665; 4, Frances; 5, Walter, of North Deighton, in the county of York, married Elizabeth, daughter of ——— Sterne, of the county of York, who was buried at Washingbrough, near Lincoln, by whom he had two children alive, and the Rev. Walter Palliser, impropriator of Laneham, rector of Stokenham, and vicar of Great Drayton and Askham, in Nottinghamshire, died June, 1778, and was buried in the chancel at Laneham. Alice was the wife of Robert Cooper, and died before 1778, and was buried at Laneham aforesaid, leaving a son, Robert-Palliser Cooper, Esq. an admiral in the royal navy, living a widower and without issue in 1799; and a daughter Elizabeth, wife of William Clarke, and living 1799.

4, Hugh Palliser, the second son, of North Deighton, in the parish of Kirk Deighton, in Yorkshire, Esq. a captain in the army, baptized at Newby Wiske, Sept. 7, 1671, married Mary, eldest daughter of Humphry Robinson, of Thicket Priory, in the parish of Cottingworth, in Yorkshire, Esq. by whom he had one

† William Orseur, Esq. lord of the manor of Plumland, in Cumberland, married Anne, eldest daughter of Robert Lamplugh, of Dovenby, by whom he had

William Orseur, lord of the manor of Plumland, Esq. who married Mabel, daughter of William Osmotherley, of Langrigge, by whom he had

William Orseur, Esq. his eldest son, who married Bridget, daughter of John Milsgrave, of Plumpton, and died April 5, 1660.

William Orseur, Esq. their son, lord of the manor of Plumbland, living April, 1665, aged 47. He married Elizabeth, daughter of Sir Charles Howard, of Croglin Hall, in Cumberland, Knt. (by Dorothy, his wife, daughter of Sir Henry Widdrington, of Widdrington, in Northumberland, which Sir Charles was the son of William, Lord Howard, of Naworth Castle, son of Thomas Howard, Duke of Norfolk, attainted and beheaded in 1572), by whom he had several sons.

John Orseur, of the county of Wexford, in Ireland, Esq. the fifth son, was captain of horse, and died about the year 1753. He married Juliana Palliser, as in the text, by whom he had Mary, his second daughter and coheiress, born at Dublin, and wife, 1765, of George-Robinson Walters above-mentioned.

son, Sir Hugh Palliser, Bart. of whom hereafter, and three daughters; 1, Rebecca, of whom hereafter; 2, Alice, wife, first, of John Clough, of the city of York, Esq. and died without issue; and 3, Ursula, widow of John Fletcher, Esq. a captain of horse, and died in Nov. 1796, aged 74, leaving one daughter Rebecca, wife of Carr Ibbetson, of Cocken, in the county of Durham, Esq. living without issue in 1799.

I. HUGH PALLISER, of the Vatch, in the county of Buckingham, Esq. admiral of the white, governor of Greenwich Hospital, sometime one of the lords commissioners of the Admiralty, and representative in parliament for Huntingdon, born at North Deighton aforesaid, created a Baronet of Great Britain to him and his heirs male, and in default thereof to his nephew, George-Robinson Walters, Esq. and his heirs male, and died unmarried March 19, 1796, aged about 74, and was buried at Chalfont St. Giles, Buckinghamshire.

Rebecca (his sister above-mentioned) died before 1789, she was wife of William Walters, Esq. a major in the army, who died Feb. 28, 1789, aged 83, buried at Lyme-Regis, in Dorsetshire, by whom she had one son, George-Robinson Walters, and two daughters, Mary, wife of the Rev. John Hinde, of Rippon, in Yorkshire, living 1799; and Ursula, wife, first, of William Easterfield, of Croydon, in Surry, who died about 1777, by whom she had issue: she was secondly, wife of William Smith, of London, living 1799, by whom she had issue: she was buried at Kennington about 1790.

George-Robinson Walters, the only son, was a captain in the royal navy, born at Gibraltar, 1765, married Mary, second daughter and coheiress of John Orfeur, of the county of Wexford, in Ireland, Esq. living in 1801, by whom he had two sons and two daughters, Hugh-Palliser Walters, the present Baronet; William, a lieutenant in the army, died at St. Vincent's, April 23, 1798, unmarried; Catharine, born at Ross, Feb. 13, 1773 (twin with William), and died young; Juliana, died an infant.

II. Sir HUGH-PALLISER WALTERS, of Barnyforth, in the county of Wexford, in the kingdom of Ireland, and of Lee, in Kent, Bart. born at Ross, in the county of Wexford aforesaid, Oct. 27, 1768, and succeeded to the title of Baronet in virtue of the limitation, in the patent of creation, to Sir Hugh Palliser, Bart. above-mentioned, in 1796. By royal sign manual, bearing date Dec. 13, 1798, he and his issue were authorized to take the surname and arms of PALLISER only. He married Mary, youngest daughter and coheiress of John Gates, of Dedham, in the county of Essex, Esq. married at Queen-square chapel, Bath, Jan. 18, 1790, by whom he has issue Hugh Palliser, born at Greenwich May 8, 1796, and Mary-Anne-Rachel, born March 16, 1798.

ARMS—Per pale, sable and argent, three lions rampant, counterchanged.

CREST—Out of a ducal coronet, gules, a demi-eagle, with wings elevated, or.—Granted to Sir Hugh Palliser, of Deptford, in Kent, Oct. 8, 1773.

SEAT—At Lee, in Kent.

ARMS OF WALTERS—Azure, a griffin segreant, argent, armed and beaked, or, a bordure invecked, ermine.

CREST—Out of a mural crown, or, a cubit arm in armour, erect in the hand, proper, a forked pennon, gules, charged with eight bezants, the staff and spear head, or.

ARMS OF PYBUS—Paly of six, or and gules, a bend, vaire.

CREST—A demi-lion rampant, gules, ducally crowned, or, and gorged with a collar, vaire.

TABLE.

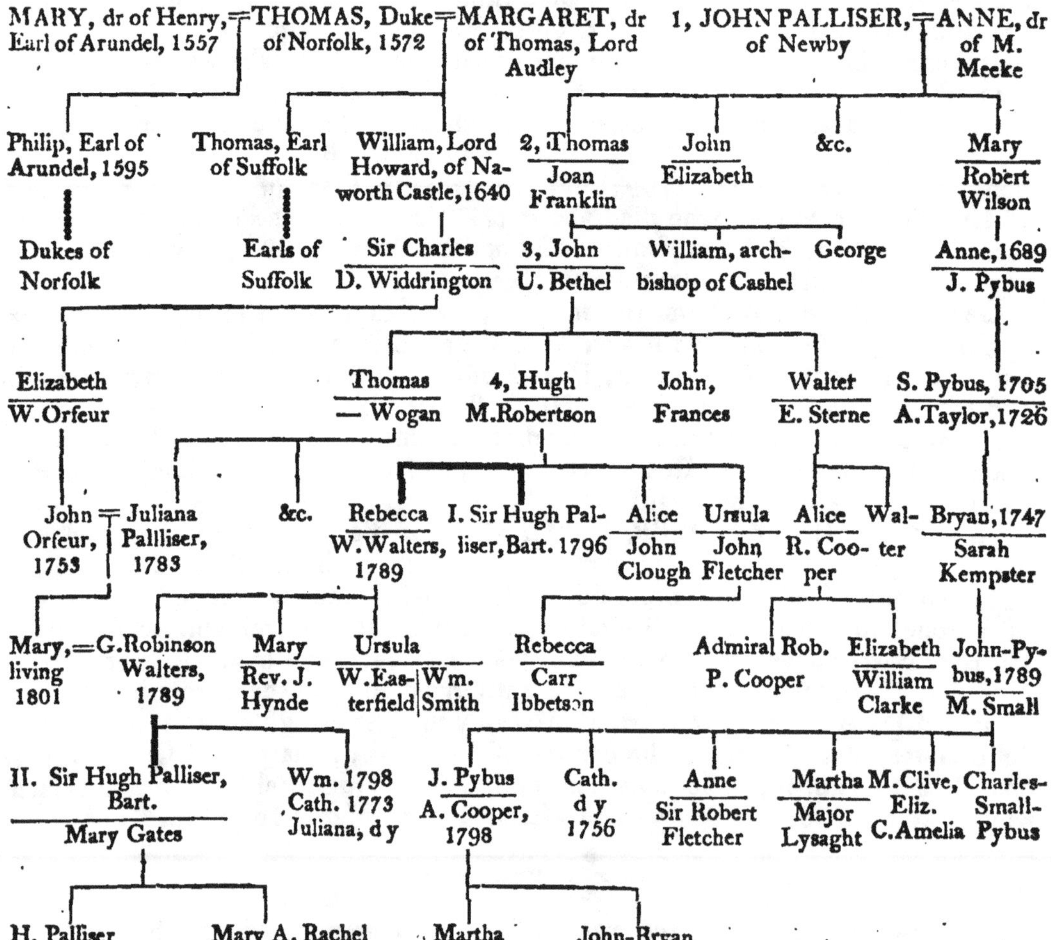

305. HUGHES, of East Bergholt, Suffolk.

Created Baronet, July 17, 1773.

BY a very elegant emblazoned pedigree drawn up in 1622, by Jacob Chaloner, of London, Gent. it, appears that the family of Hughes is descended, first, from Gwaith Voed Mawr, Prince of Cardigan, by Morveth, daughter and heiress of Ynyr, King of Gwent; secondly, from Llewellyn with the Golden Chain, of Yalle, by Eva, daughter of Blethen ap Knyvyn, Prince of Powis; thirdly, from Conan, son of Jago ap Idwell, Prince of Wales, by Ranulphe, daughter of Alfryd, King of Dublin; fourthly, from Elinstan, a natural son of Gwaith Voed, Prince of Cardigan; fifthly, from Howell Dda, King of South Wales; sixthly, from Lluddock, eldest son of Tudor Trevor, by Anghared, daughter of Jago ap Idwall, King of Wales; seventhly, from Rees, son of Tudor, King of South Wales, by Gwenlian, daughter of Jestyn ap Gwrant, Prince of Glamorganshire; eighthly, from Kynan, third son of Gwaith Voed, by Eva, sister of Jestyn ap Gwrant, Prince of Glamorganshire. As it would swell my work too much to follow the whole pedigree, I shall content myself with tracing the present Baronet from,

1, Howell the Good, King of All Wales, who died in 946, married Janne, daughter of Cader, Earl of Cornwall.

2, Owen, his eldest son, married Anghared, daughter and heiress of Llewellyn ap Mervyn, ap Roderick the Great.

3, Meredith, his son, had a daughter,

4, Anghared, the wife of Knyvyn, son of Gwerstan, King of Powis, son of Gwaith Voed, Prince of Cardigan, by Morveth, daughter and heiress of Ynyr, King of Gwent.

5, Bletyn, their son, Prince of Powis, was the father of,

6, Cadwgan, who married Gwenlian, daughter of Gruff ap Conan, Prince of North Wales.

7, Madock, their son, had one daughter,

8, Margaret, the wife of Keiline, second son of Eunythe, Lord of Clinton, by whom she had one son,

9, Ithell, who married Eva, daughter of Owen Brogentyn, by whom he had one son,

10, Llewellyn, of Diffryncloyd, who married Sibell, daughter of Llewellyn ap Movyddyn, ap Sandiff, by whom he had one son,

11, Madock, of Diffryncloyd, who married Gwenlian, daughter of Jerworth ap Madock, ap Kirrde slaidd, by whom he had one son,

12, Ithell, of Diffryncloyd, surnamed the Red, who married Molly, daughter of Jerworth ap David, ap Cowryd, by whom he had,

13, Howell, of Diffryncloyd, who married Gwenhayver, daughter of Howell ap Madock, of Llanlidan, by whom he had,

14, Gruffeth, of Diffryncloyd, who married Morveth, daughter of Llewellyn ap Jevan Crach, by whom he had,

15, Alayne, of Diffryncloyd, who left one son,

16, Jenkyn, who left one son,

17, John, of Diffryncloyd, who married Gwenhwyan, daughter and heiress of Jenkin ap Llewellyn Vychan, ap Yollen, son of Jevaffe ap Madock, ap Grono, who married Jannet, daughter of Henry Lacy, Earl of Lincoln, by whom he had one son,

18, Hughe, who married Anne, daughter and heiress of Bellyn ap Towna, ap Jevan, of Ruthland, by whom he had one son,

19, Thomas HUGHES, of Diffryncloyd, in Denbighshire, who married Katherine, daughter of Matthew ap Gruffith, ap Robert, by whom he had one son,

20, Sir Thomas Hughes, of the city of Wells, in Somersetshire, Knt. living in 1622, who married first, Hester, daughter of William Jonnes, doctor of the civil law; he married secondly, Frances, daughter of Nicholas Mytine, of Norfolk, by whom he had issue, 1, Thomas, of whom hereafter; 2, James; 3, Jane; 4, Elizabeth; and 5, Katherine, wife of Thomas Cooke, of ———, in Hampshire.

21, Thomas Hughes, of Tichfield, in Hampshire, married Eleanor, daughter of —— Wattes, of Limehouse, in Middlesex, by whom he had five sons and two daughters, Mary and Elizabeth; 1, George, who married Jane Veazey; 2, Thomas, who married Elizabeth Roach, by whom he had two sons and two daughters, Robert, Mary, Elizabeth, wife of Manly Callis, of Deptford, and Thomas, who died without issue. Robert, the elder son, married Lydia, daughter of Captain Gunman, by whom he had two daughters, Catharine, wife of John Sayer, of Berkshire, Esq. and Alice, of James Calder, of Scotland, Esq.; 3, Henry, of whom hereafter; 4, Kenrick, married Jane Wise; and 5, Richard.

22, Henry Hughes, the third son, married Mary Wise, sister to his brother Kenrick's wife, by whom he had two sons, Henry and Richard; Henry married Elizabeth, daughter of William Young, of Dover, by whom he had one daughter. Alice, wife of the Rev. Mr. Monney, of Dover, in Kent.

23, Richard Hughes, of Deptford, Esq. second son, a naval officer, married Mary, daughter of Isaac Loader, Esq. by whom he had two sons, Richard, of whom hereafter; 2, Robert Hughes, Esq. an admiral, who married Sarah, daughter of Alexander Collingwood, of ——, in Northumberland, Esq. by whom he had one son, and a daughter Mary, wife of Henry Osborn, of Bedfordshire, Esq. and Catharine.

I. RICHARD HUGHES, Esq. the elder son, had attained the rank of captain in 1729, and after serving for many years with great respectability in that capacity, he was appointed to the honourable and lucrative station of commissioner of the dock-yard at Portsmouth. When the present king first visited that grand naval arsenal, his Majesty resided, and was entertained with a magnificence suitable to so high a rank, at his house, and was so well pleased with the conduct and behaviour of this officer, that he created him a Baronet, July 7, 1773. Sir Richard married Joanne, daughter of William Collyer, of ——, Esq. captain in the royal navy, by whom he had two sons, Sir Richard, of whom hereafter, and the Rev. Robert Hughes, of Plymouth Dock, Devonshire, and rector of Trimley St. Mary, Suffolk, who married Grace, daughter of Thomas Mangles, of ——, Devonshire, Esq. by whom he had two sons, Richard and Robert, both clergymen. He married secondly, ——, by whom he had two daughters, Mary, wife, first, of Thomas Collingwood, Esq. of Unthank, in Northumberland, captain in the royal navy; secondly, of Lieutenant-Colonel Heywood, gentleman of the bedchamber to his Royal Highness the Duke of Gloucester. Sarah died unmarried.

Sir Richard enjoyed a long life, and died a commissioner of the navy, at the age of seventy-one, in 1780 *, and was succeeded by his son,

II. Sir RICHARD HUGHES, Bart. was born at Deptford, in Kent, where part of his patrimonial fortune is situated, in 1729. He was bred at the academy at Portsmouth; and, besides the usual attainments while there, translated the Spectators into French, a language of which, early in life, he acquired a complete mastery, and has occasionally recourse to at the present day, with all the facility and elegance of a well-bred native.

Young Hughes, while yet a boy, went to sea with his father, in the capacity of

* Sacred
to the Memory
of Sir Richard Hughes, Bart.
one of the principal Officers and Commissioners
of His Majesty's Navy,
who died
September XXIII,
Aged LXXI.
In the year of our Lord MDCCLXXX.
In his private station
he was truly amiable;
In his professional character
justly respectable.
In him his family regret
an affectionate Relation,
Society an useful Member,
Religion a real Ornament.
May the approbation he acquired
from all orders and degrees of men,
for his upright life and pleasing manners,
and the honour he received
from his Sovereign,
for his good and faithful services,
Be the prelude only
of applauses from Angels,
and acceptance from the King of Kings!

midshipman, and during the war of 1741, was made an officer by Admiral Matthews, then serving in the Mediterranean*; but so young was he at that period, that he was under the necessity of actually wearing a wig, in order to acquire a more manly appearance.

He continued on the same station during the remainder of that war, and was raised to the rank of post captain in 1754 or 1755, after which he successively commanded the Fox and Thames frigates. While on board one of these, he was employed on a secret mission of great importance, which he accomplished to the entire satisfaction of the Board of Admiralty: this was a survey of the river Garonne, which he completed as high as Bourdeaux.

Nor were his services overlooked; for, on the breaking out of the next war, Captain Hughes was appointed to the command of the York, a sixty-gun ship, with which he assisted at the siege of Pondicherry, under Sir George Pocock.

Having injured his health by his exertions in a climate unfavourable to English constitutions, no sooner was the place taken, than the admiral, in consideration of his services, sent him home with the welcome dispatches, containing an account of the surrender of that important fortress, on which occasion he was most graciously received, and obtained a handsome gratification.

During the interval of peace, Captain Hughes had the Worcester, a sixty-four gun ship, then stationed at Plymouth; and, on the breaking out of the colonial war, he was appointed to the Centaur, a seventy-four. On quitting the command of this vessel, he was nominated lieutenant-governor of Nova Scotia, and commissioner of the dock-yard at Halifax. While there, he was of the most essential advantage to government; for, not choosing to consider his situation as a mere sinecure, he rendered an important service to his native country, by causing the woods to be inspected and surveyed; he also obtained masts, spars, and other naval stores, for our dock yards, on the most advantageous terms. Indeed, so meritorious was his conduct considered at home, that on his return to England he was honoured with a private audience of the king, and received his Majesty's thanks.

Captain Hughes continued in America until he was promoted to the rank of rear-admiral of the blue, in 1780. His first service in that capacity was as port-admiral at Deal, where he only remained a few months. After this, he hoisted his flag on board the Princess Amelia. During the memorable expedition for the relief of Gibraltar, under the late Lord Howe, admiral Sir Richard Hughes was second in command of the rear division of the fleet; and immediately subsequent to the partial action of the 20th of October, 1782, off the coast of Spain, which ended in the retreat of the enemy, he was detached with eight sail of the line to the West Indies, to join admiral Pigot, who then commanded on that station.

During his passage, when about fifty leagues to the eastward of Barbadoes, Admiral Hughes had the good fortune to fall in with a squadron of the enemy,

* He was appointed a lieutenant about the year 1744-5.

in consequence of which one of the vessels under his command captured the Solitaire, a French sixty-four gun ship, and retook the Speedy packet*.

On the conclusion of the American war, Sir Richard was left in the command of the Leeward Island station; in consequence of which, the task devolved upon him of ceding such islands to the French as had been taken from them during the war, a service for which he was admirably qualified, in consequence of his elegant manners, his noble demeanour, and that critical knowledge of their language, to which we have already alluded.

After remaining three years in the West Indies, he was appointed to the command at Halifax, where he remained during the same term, and became a vice-admiral in 1791 †.

He has risen by seniority to the rank of admiral of the white ‡, but has never been employed; he has, however, frequently tendered his services, and is ready and as able, at this moment, to serve his country, as ever he was at any former period of his life.

He married, about 1760, Jane, daughter of William Sloane, of South Stoneham, Hampshire, nephew of Sir Hans Sloane, by whom he had two sons and two daughters, Richard Hughes, Esq. captain in the navy; John-Thomas Hughes, Esq. professor of the civil law in the Island of Jamaica; Louisa died unmarried; Rose-Mary, wife of John Brome, Esq. major in the army, nearly related to the Earl of Villamont.

ARMS---Azure, a lion rampant, or.
CREST---On a wreath, a lion couchant, or.
SEAT---At East Bergholt Lodge, in Suffolk.

* The Ruby, of sixty-four guns, commanded by Captain, afterwards Sir John Collins, was the ship that came up with and engaged the Solitaire; and, after an action of forty-one minutes, the enemy lost her mizen mast, and was compelled to strike. In consequence of the Admiralty letters recording the transaction, the commander of the Ruby received the honour of knighthood.

† The family of this veteran officer has, in some measure, been *devoted* to the naval profession, he himself having served no fewer than fifty-six years, and his father and grandfather one hundred and four, in all one hundred and sixty, a period of time unequalled perhaps by any other family in the kingdom. In addition to this, it is not to be forgotten, that he has bred his eldest son to the sea, and that he is now master and commander.

Along with Sir Richard's professional abilities, he unites a taste for the *belles lettres*, seldom acquired by those who have dedicated their lives to the sea service; and, among other European languages, is particularly conversant in the Italian. He also possesses considerable talents for poetry (*a*), in which he has been imitated by his two sons, and the productions of his muse have been gay and serious, satirical and plaintive; in the last of these, an address to his youngest daughter, now no more, does great credit to him, both as a poet and a father.

Among other celebrated men who have served under admiral Hughes, the names of Lord Nelson and Sir Sidney Smith ought not to be forgotten. The "hero of the Nile" commanded the Boreas, during four years, on the Leeward Island station, while Sir Richard's flag was flying there; and when the inhabitants of Ipswich wished to testify their joy for the memorable victory at Aboukir, he and admiral Reeves were, with becoming propriety, delegated to wait on Lady Nelson, and do the honours of the day.

‡ His commission is dated Feb. 14, 1799, and he stands next in the list to Samuel, Viscount Hood.

(*a*) John Hughes, author of the Ode on the Peace of Ryswick, 1697, the Siege of Damascus, and also of several papers in the Spectator, Tatler, and Guardian, was of the same family as Sir Richard Hughes.

TABLE.

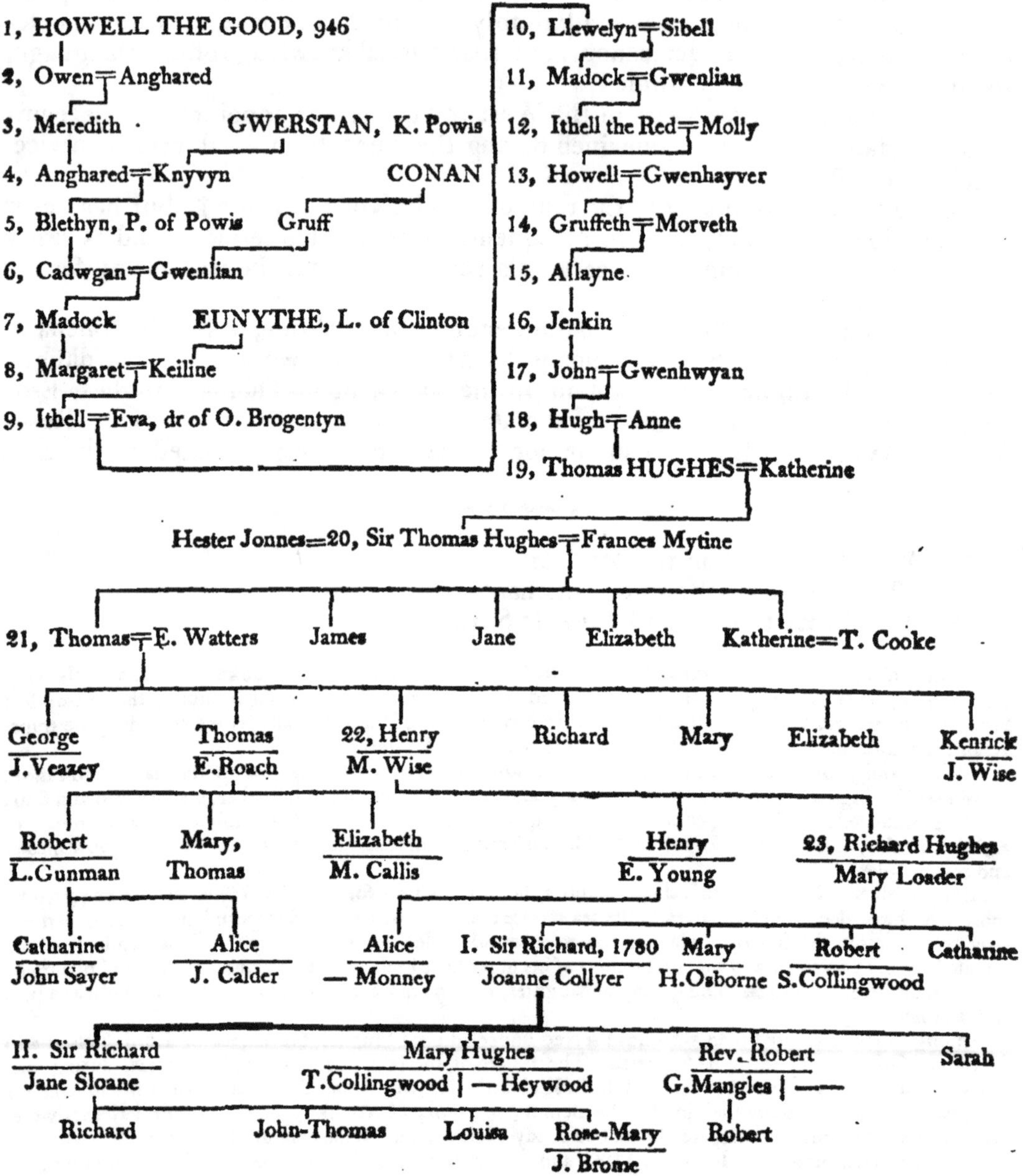
1, HOWELL THE GOOD, 946
2, Owen=Anghared
3, Meredith
GWERSTAN, K. Powis
4, Anghared=Knyvyn
CONAN
5, Blethyn, P. of Powis
Gruff
6, Cadwgan=Gwenlian
7, Madock
EUNYTHE, L. of Clinton
8, Margaret=Keiline
9, Ithell=Eva, dr of O. Brogentyn
10, Llewelyn=Sibell
11, Madock=Gwenlian
12, Ithell the Red=Molly
13, Howell=Gwenhayver
14, Gruffeth=Morveth
15, Allayne
16, Jenkin
17, John=Gwenhwyan
18, Hugh=Anne
19, Thomas HUGHES=Katherine
Hester Jonnes=20, Sir Thomas Hughes=Frances Mytine
21, Thomas=E. Watters
James
Jane
Elizabeth
Katherine=T. Cooke
George
J. Veazey
Thomas
E. Roach
22, Henry
M. Wise
Richard
Mary
Elizabeth
Kenrick
J. Wise
Robert
L. Gunman
Mary,
Thomas
Elizabeth
M. Callis
Henry
E. Young
23, Richard Hughes
Mary Loader
Catharine
John Sayer
Alice
J. Calder
Alice
— Monney
I. Sir Richard, 1780
Joanne Collyer
Mary
H. Osborne
Robert
S. Collingwood
Catharine
II. Sir Richard
Jane Sloane
Mary Hughes
T. Collingwood | — Heywood
Rev. Robert
G. Mangles | —
Sarah
Richard
John-Thomas
Louisa
Rose-Mary
J. Brome
Robert

306. CLAYTON, of ADLINGTON, Lancashire.

Created Baronet, May 3, 1774.

1, ROBERT DE CLAYTON, a man of valour, and skilled in arms, who came into England with William the Conqueror, was born at Caudevec, in Normandy, and for his laudable services had the manor of Clayton, in Lancashire, given him. He had three sons, John, William, and Robert, and two daughters, Mary and Alice. John de Clayton went with William II. into Northumberland, in 1090, against Malcolm, King of Scotland, who had invaded England, and was slain in battle near Penrith, in Cumberland.

2, William de Clayton, second son of Robert, married Dame Mary Hyde, of Yorkshire, by whom he had two sons, Robert, and William, who made a vow never to marry. He had a motto he was wont to repeat:

"*Tu ne cede malis; sed contra audentior ito.*"

He served King Stephen in a great many troubles, particularly when Ranulph, Earl of Chester, and some others, in the absence of Stephen, took possession of London. A very terrible battle was fought on Candlemas-Day, where "*God wot, William de Clayton lost his life in* 1141."

3, Robert de Clayton succeeded his father in 1130, and married Margaret Osbaldeston, of Osbaldeston, near Ribblechester, by whom he had two daughters and one son.

4, William de Clayton, who married Elizabeth Farrington, of a *good stock and lineage*, by whom he had three sons, Richard, Thomas, and Robert, and two daughters, Margaret and Elizabeth: he died in 1152, and was buried at Leyland.

Richard, the eldest son, became a priest, and *indeed he was a man of God, given to prayer and much alms:* he died at Poictou. Thomas, the second son, died without issue.

5, Robert de Clayton, the third son, married, in 1151, Elizabeth Parker, by whom he had seven children; 1, William; 2, Robert; 3, John; 4, Thomas; 5, Mary; 6, Sarah; and 7, Elizabeth.

William, Robert, and Thomas, went with King John, in 1200, into Normandy, and also to Angiers, and several other places. William and Robert both died abroad, but Thomas returned.

6, John, the third son, in 1204, married Cicely, daughter of John Peel, of Peel, by whom he had two sons, William, and Thomas, and died in 1209. William died in the seventh year of his age, 1213.

7, Thomas de Clayton, the second son, married Ruth, daughter of John de

Latham, by whom he had three sons, John, Robert, and William, and three daughters, Anne, Mary, and Elizabeth.

8, John de Clayton married, 1263, Ruth de Latham, and had two sons, Thomas and Ralph, and two daughters, Elizabeth and Margaret, and died at Clayton in 1280.

9, Ralph de Clayton left three sons, John, Giles, Nicholas, and two daughters, Elizabeth and Jane.

10, John de Clayton married, in 1307, Mary, daughter of Hugh de Langtown, by whom he had three sons, John, Richard, Robert, and two daughters, Margaret and Elizabeth. This John went with Henry of Lancaster, Earl of Derby, into France, in the reign of Edw. III. 1347.

11, John de Clayton, the eldest son, when but twenty-three years old, 1356, went with John of Gaunt to assist the King of Navarre against the French, and accompanied King Edward in most of his troubles. He left four sons, 1, John; 2, William, who, on going into Spain in 1386, 9 Rich. II. had letters of protection for a year*; 3, Ralph; 4, Robert: and two daughters, Margaret and Sarah: he died in 1399.

12, John de Clayton married, in 1390, Dame Mary Fereby, by whom he had three sons, Thomas, Robert, and William: and two daughters, Jane and Helen. He went, in 1393, with the Dukes of Lancaster and Gloucester, into France, to treat of peace, and died in 1440.

13, Thomas de Clayton, his eldest son, married Dorothy Thelwell, of Thelwell, in Cheshire, with whom he received that village as a marriage portion †. He had two sons, John, born 1419, and William, 1420, died without issue, 1471: and three daughters, Mary, born 1421; Dorothy, 1423; Jane, 1424. He died 1426.

14, John de Clayton, eldest son, married, 1440, Mary Mainwaring, of Cheshire, by whom he had two sons, Thomas, born 1441, William, 1442, and two daughters, Mary, born 1443, and Dorothy, 1444: she died in childbed 1445, and he married secondly, Jane Clifton, of Clifton, by whom he had two sons, Robert, born 1448, and Richard, 1449, and one daughter Elizabeth, born 1450.

Thomas de Clayton was disinherited for disobeying his father and mother; he married and had four sons, William, born 1463, John, 1464, Robert, 1465, Thomas, 1470.

Robert, the elder son by the second wife, died at Paris without issue, in 1471.

15, Richard, the younger son, married Elizabeth, daughter of Sir Peers Leigh, a man of *courage and valour*, son of Sir Peers Leigh, who was at the battle of Cressy, and had Lyme, in Cheshire, given him for his services. He was also

* Rymer's Fœdera.

† This estate continued in the family till about 1561, when it was sold by John Clayton to Richard Brooker, of Norton, Esq.—*See Leicester's Hist. Antiq.* Part IV. 373.

with Richard II. when he was taken at Chester, and beheaded by Henry IV. Richard dying without issue, was succeeded by

16, William, son of Thomas Clayton, who married Mary Atherton, of Atherton, by whom he had four sons, Thomas, born 1485, William, 1487, Richard, 1488, Giles, 1489, and a daughter Margaret, born 1490, and died at Chester 1493. His sons all dying without issue, he was succeeded by,

17, Robert Clayton, third son of Thomas who was disinherited, succeeded to the estates in Lancashire; he was born 1497, and married Jane Farrington, by whom he had four sons, Thomas, born 1498, John, 1499, Edward, 1505, Richard, 1506, and three daughters, Sarah, born 1500, Susanna, 1502, and Catharine, 1503. He died 1510, and was buried at Leyland.

18, Thomas Clayton, in 1569, married Anne Jackson, of Bocking, in Essex, by whom he had two sons, Robert, and William, of whom hereafter; and dying 1580, was buried at Leyland.

19, Robert Clayton was of St. John's College, Cambridge, and married and left one son John, born 1596, and dying 1599, was succeeded by his son,

20, John Clayton, who married Joanna, daughter of Sir Robert Pye, by whom he had Richard, Dorothy, and Elizabeth*. He died December 20, 1623, aged 29.

21, Richard Clayton married —— Farrington, of Worden, but dying without issue by a fall from his horse, the family estates of Clayton and Crooke went, by virtue of the settlement, to Dorothy, his eldest sister, who was the wife of George Leicester, of Toft, in Cheshire, Esq. †

22, William Clayton, second son of Thomas Clayton and Anne Jackson, married, in 1582, Elizabeth, daughter of Nicholas Rigby, Esq. of Harrock, in Lancashire, by whom he had five sons, Thomas, born 1585, William, 1587, John, 1588, Ralph, 1589, Richard, 1592, and three daughters, Elizabeth, born 1594, Lettice, 1595, and Anne, 1596.

23, Thomas Clayton, eldest son, had the estates of Fulwood, in Lancashire, settled upon him and his issue. He married Anne, daughter of Robert Blondell, of Ince, by whom he had issue, Robert, Thomas, born 1630, and Anne.

24, Robert Clayton, of Fulwood, the eldest son, married Eleanor, daughter of John Atherton, of Busie, Esq. by whom he had four sons, Thomas, William, John, and Richard, and four daughters, Anne, Margaret, Elizabeth, and Mary.

25, Thomas Clayton, the eldest son, had one son,

26, Robert Clayton, who was brought up at Westminster school, and was under the private tuition of Zachary Pierce, then a king's scholar, and afterwards Bishop of Rochester. From thence he was removed to Trinity College, Dublin, where he became fellow. Not satisfied with having received a scholastic education, he made the tour of Italy and France. In 1723, he married Catharine, daughter of Nehemiah, lord chief baron Donellan; in 1729, he was doctor of

* This John settled Crooke and Clayton on his son Richard and his issue male, in 1628, and, for want of issue male, on his eldest daughter Dorothy.

† See Leicester's Hist. Antiq. Part IV. 381.

divinity, and was advanced to the see of Killala in Jan. 1729-30, and in 1735, was translated to the see of York, on the death of Dr. Peter Brown, and to the see of Clogher in 1745 *. It is apparent from his writings, that he was a man of a great capacity, of a vigorous imagination, and of extensive learning. The accuracy of his judgment does not seem to have been equal to his other qualities. From the liveliness of his fancy, he was sometimes carried, perhaps too boldly, into the regions of conjecture; but these occasional faults were amply compensated for, by the liberal views of things, the general good sense, and the variety of useful information with which his works abound. He left several works in manuscript, which are now (1784) in the possession of his executor, Dr. Bernard, Dean of Derry.

He was member of the Royal Society, and of the Society of Antiquaries. He maintained a regular correspondence with several gentleman of eminent literature in this country, and among the rest, with the learned printer, Mr. Bowyer, to whom he made a present of the copyright of all his works published in England. His Lancashire estate he bequeathed to his nearest male heir, Richard Clayton, Esq. chief justice of the common pleas in Ireland; but the greatest share of his fortune is inherited by Dr. Bernard, who married his niece, and of whom we need not say, that he is a gentleman whose respectable character is well known in the world †.

27, Thomas Clayton, the brother of the bishop, married Anne, another daughter of John Atherton, Esq. by whom he had five sons; 1, Thomas; 2, John; 3, Richard; 4, Thomas, of whom hereafter; 5, Robert: and seven daughters; 1, Anne, wife of John Williamson, of Liverpool; 2, Eleanor, of Nicholas Rigby, of Harrock, Esq.; 3, Sarah, of Daniel Sephton, of Skelmesdale, Esq.; 4, Ruth; 5, Margaret; 6, Mary; and 7, Catharine. This Thomas purchased the lordships and estates of Hillington, and settled at Adlington, where he died in the 92d year of his age, and was buried at Standish. His lady died before him in 1695, and was buried at Standish.

28, Thomas, the eldest son of Thomas Clayton and Anne Atherton, married, in 1697, Martha, daughter of Joshua Horton, of Chaderton, by whom he had five sons; 1, Thomas; 2, William; 3, Richard; 4, Edward; 5, John: and four daughters; 1, Mary; 2, Anne; 3, Sarah; and 4, Betty. He died at Adlington, in the 61st year of his age, and was buried at Standish, 1728; his wife died in 1723, and was also buried at Standish.

Thomas, his eldest son, died at Brazen Nose College, Oxford, in the 19th year of his age, 1717.

William, the second son, died at Adlington, June, 1735, unmarried, and was buried at Standish.

Richard, the third son, was brought up to the bar, and became lord chief jus-

* Lord Primate Boulter's Letters, Vol. I. p. 340. Vol. II. p. 134.

† Biographia Britannica.

TABLE.

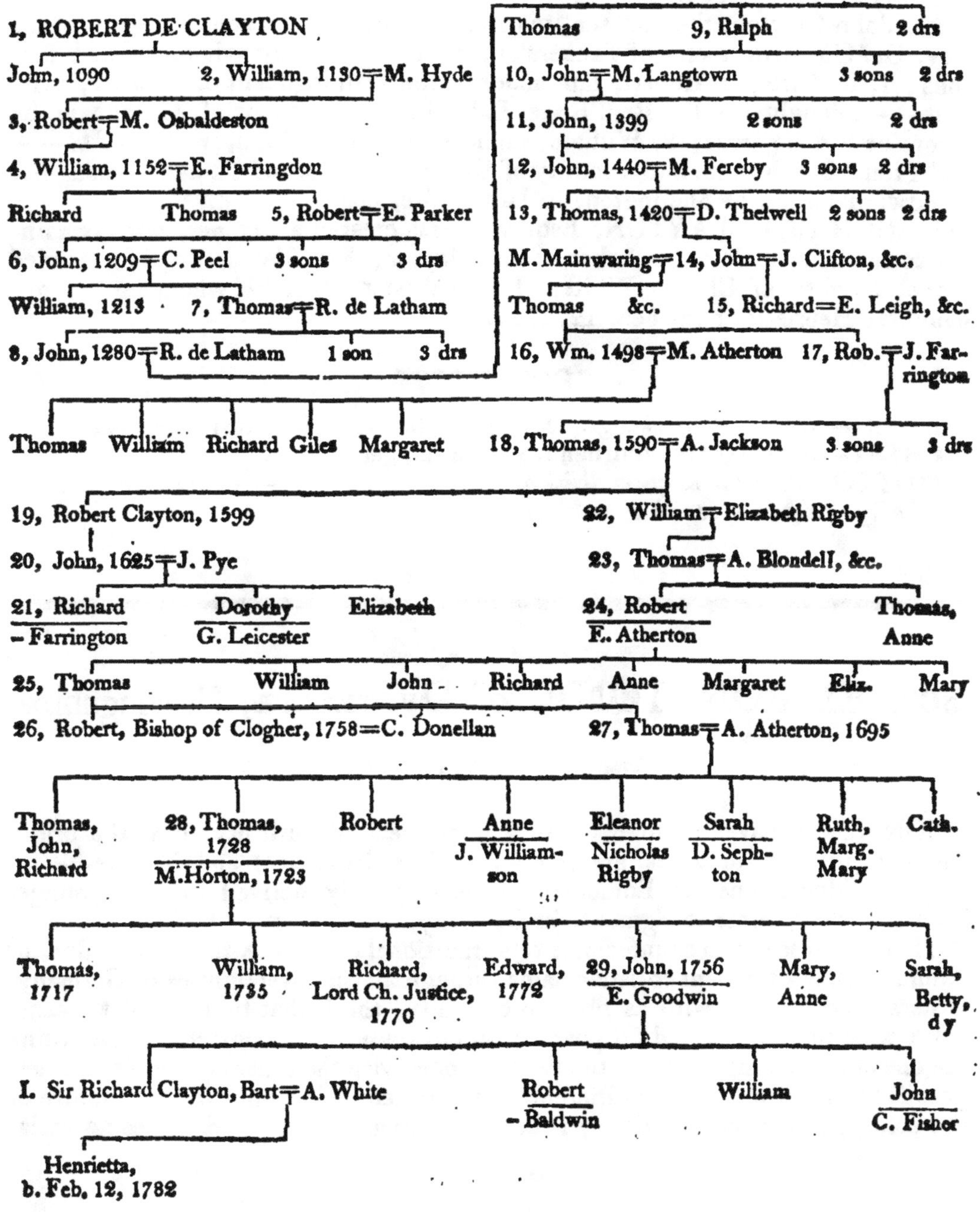
1, ROBERT DE CLAYTON
John, 1090
2, William, 1130=M. Hyde
3, Robert=M. Osbaldeston
4, William, 1152=E. Farringdon
Richard
Thomas
5, Robert=E. Parker
6, John, 1209=C. Peel
3 sons
3 drs
William, 1213
7, Thomas=R. de Latham
8, John, 1280=R. de Latham
1 son
3 drs
Thomas
9, Ralph
2 drs
10, John=M. Langtown
3 sons
2 drs
11, John, 1399
2 sons
2 drs
12, John, 1440=M. Fereby
3 sons
2 drs
13, Thomas, 1420=D. Thelwell
2 sons
2 drs
M. Mainwaring=14, John=J. Clifton, &c.
Thomas
&c.
15, Richard=E. Leigh, &c.
16, Wm. 1498=M. Atherton
17, Rob.=J. Farrington
Thomas
William
Richard
Giles
Margaret
18, Thomas, 1590=A. Jackson
3 sons
3 drs
19, Robert Clayton, 1599
22, William=Elizabeth Rigby
20, John, 1625=J. Pye
23, Thomas=A. Blondell, &c.
21, Richard
Farrington
Dorothy
G. Leicester
Elizabeth
24, Robert
F. Atherton
Thomas,
Anne
25, Thomas
William
John
Richard
Anne
Margaret
Eliz.
Mary
26, Robert, Bishop of Clogher, 1758=C. Donellan
27, Thomas=A. Atherton, 1695
Thomas,
John,
Richard
28, Thomas,
1728
M. Horton, 1723
Robert
Anne
J. Williamson
Eleanor
Nicholas Rigby
Sarah
D. Sephton
Ruth,
Marg.
Mary
Cath.
Thomas,
1717
William,
1735
Richard,
Lord Ch. Justice,
1770
Edward,
1772
29, John, 1756
E. Goodwin
Mary,
Anne
Sarah,
Betty,
d y
I. Sir Richard Clayton, Bart=A. White
Robert
Baldwin
William
John
C. Fisher
Henrietta,
b. Feb. 12, 1782

tice of the common pleas in Ireland, which office he resigned in 1770, and died a few months afterwards at Adlington, July 8, 1770, aged 68.

Edward, the fourth son, was major of the 9th regiment of dragoons, and died in 1772, at Adlington, unmarried.

29, John Clayton, the fifth son, married Elizabeth, the second daughter of the Rev. Dr. Goodwin, rector of Tankersley, in Yorkshire, by whom he had four sons; 1, Richard; 2, Robert, late major of the 17th regiment of infantry, married ——, daughter of the Rev. Roger Baldwin, M. D. rector of Aldingham, by whom he had no issue; 3, William, unmarried; and 4, John, rector of C—— and Frome St. Quintin, in the county of Dorset, who married Catharine, daughter of Edward Fisher, of Sherington, in Lancashire, Esq.

I. RICHARD CLAYTON, Esq. who was created a Baronet, with remainder to the heirs male of his father, John Clayton, Esq. deceased. He married Anne, daughter of Charles White, of Manchester, Esq. by whom he has one daughter Henrietta, born Feb. 12, 1782.

ARMS—Argent, a cross engrailed, sable, between four torteaux, gules.
CREST—A dexter arm and hand, with a dagger.
MOTTO—*Probitatem quam divitias.*
SEAT—At Adlington, Lancashire.

---

307. EDMONSTONE, of DUNTREATH, Stirlingshire.

Created Baronet, May 3, 1774.

SOME who have inquired, with a good deal of curiosity, into the origin and antiquity of surnames, are of opinion that the ancient and honourable family of Edmonstone, or Edmonstones, is originally derived from a younger branch of the Counts of Egmont, in Germany.

That which seems to countenance this traditional descent is, that Edmundus, or Admundus, is a frequent christian name through all the sovereignties of Germany. Others, and perhaps with as great probability, think that they are of the same stock with the Seatons and Oliphants; and to support this conjecture, they think the one and the same arms * of the Edmonstones with the other two noble families, goes far to confirm this, the difference among them being only in the tincture or the colour, which the heralds say is but an accidental thing, and makes no varia-

* Three crescents.

tion in the coat armorial; for it is a maxim among heralds, that coats of arms are a more sure mark and evidence of descent in blood and sameness of kindred than surnames, which are but the invention of later times.

However, it is well known that there were no distinguishing appellatives, but what were personal, known in England before the conquest, nor in Scotland before King Malcolm Canmore, or his son King David, who succeeded his father; for in that reign it is evident, from unquestionable vouchers, that many surnames began to be taken up for distinction's sake, so did this surname of Edmonstone then first take its beginning.

Sir James Dalrymple, in his Historical Collections relating to the Scots History, observes, that, in the time of King David, there appears a gentleman of rank who is a witness in the charters granted by that prince, and got from him lands in Lundonia, which included the three Locheans, the Slype of Edinburgh, the conglabularies of Haddington and Lithgow, which from thence, according to a custom which then prevailed, he called Admonston, and after Edmonstone, after his own name.

The same Admundus, which Sir James conjectures so reasonably to have been the common ancestor of this family, is a witness to the charter by King David, *Waltero de Ridle de terris de Ridle, &c.**

John Edmondston, Knt. temp. David II. for the merit of his services to that prince, had grants and charters of lands under the great seal, *Dilecto & fideli suo Johanni Edmonston, militi*; this was *sibi et heredibus suis*, and bears date at Aberdeen, Nov. 5, 1362, and also of the office of coroner for the county of Edinburgh in fee, as appears by the charter, still extant, in the registers of the great seal, in the public archives at Edinburgh. He had another charter under the great seal, *Dilecto & fideli suo Johanni de Edmonston, milite, terras Baroniæ de Boyne, in vicecomitatu de Banff*. This charter, which is also in the rolls of King David, bears date March 7, 1369.

1, Sir John Edmondston married Isabella, widow of James, Earl of Douglas, killed at the battle of Hexham, and daughter of Robert II. King of Scotland †.

During this reign, Sir John was chosen one of the commissioners for prolonging the peace with England. He was again named ambassador for the same purpose, treaty dated April 2, 1408, and named again the following year.

Sir John designs himself of that Ilk, together with Davy, his son and heir apparent, parties to an indenture of the one part, and Patrick, count palatine of Strathern, with the consent of Euphane, his wife, on the other, relating to a charter of confirmation they had procured from the Regent, the Duke of Albany, to

* Sir James Dalrymple's Appendix.

† Charter under the great seal from Robert II. granting to Sir John de Edmondston and Isabella, Countess of Douglas, *filiæ nostræ carissimæ*, and their heirs, the barony of Ednam, in the county of Roxburgh. Fresh grants of the barony of Boyne, and of Tilly-Allan, in the county of Clackmannan; probably also at this time, a grant of the barony of Culloden, in the county of Inverness. Fresh grants and charters of Ednam from Robert III. to Sir John and Isabella, Countess of Douglas, *Sorori nostræ*. Dated at Edinburgh April 25, 1392, in the third year of his reign.

Sir John and his son, of the barony of Tilly Allan. Dated at Perth, March 7, 1410.

Sir John Edmondston, by his wife, had two sons, and one daughter; 1, Sir David, of that Ilk, his son and successor; 2, Sir William, of Culloden, the direct ancestor of the house of Duntreath; and 3, Mary, married to Sir Andrew Ker, of Fernyhurst, ancestor of the families of the Duke of Roxburgh, Marquis of Lothian, and Lord Jedburgh.

2, Sir David Edmondston. In several charters, the Regent, Duke of Albany, designs him, *nepos noster*, the Countess of Douglas being his sister, so described in a charter granted by the Regent to his son John, Earl of Buchan, dated 1416. Sir David died 1426, and was succeeded by his son,

3, Sir James, of that Ilk, who was knighted at the baptism of the twin born sons of James I. Prince Alexander and Prince James, in 1430.

Under that designation, a witness to a charter granted to William, Lord Creighton, in 1440: it was an investiture of part of his estate, upon his own resignation in 1458.

He married Janet, daughter of Sir Alexander Napier, of Marchieston, justice-general of Scotland in the reign of James II. and dying without male issue, left two daughters, his coheirs; 1, Elizabeth, wife of Sir Patrick Bl—, younger son of Robert ———, of that Ilk, in Berwickshire, and nephew to Dr. Robert Bl———, first archbishop of Glasgow: with this marriage the barony of Tilly Allan went away; and 2, Margaret, wife of Sir Walter Ogilvie, of Findlater and Deskford, who got thereby the barony of Boyn. Both these families, in consequence of these marriages, quarter the arms of Edmondston with their own.

2, Sir William, of Culloden, the first of the family of Duntreath, was the second son of Sir John, by the Lady Isabella, Countess Dowager of Douglas and Mar, eldest daughter of King Robert II. by Queen Euphane, his second wife, daughter of Hugh, Earl of Ross. He was knighted by King James I. and married Mary, Countess Dowager of Angus, daughter to Robert III. King of Scotland, and his first cousin: she had been married first, in 1397, to Sir George Douglas, Earl of Angus, and had two sons, ancestors of the Duke of Douglas; secondly, in 1404, to James Kennedy, son and heir of Sir Gilbert Kennedy, ancestor of the Earls of Cassilis; thirdly, to Sir William Graham, of Kincardin, ancestor of the Dukes of Montrose; and, being yet *but a young woman*, fourthly, to Sir William Edmondstone, of Culloden. But being within the degrees of affinity prohibited by the canons, a dispensation from Rome was obtained by means of the Pope's legate, who was then in Scotland.

Sir William had one son William, and one daughter ———, the wife of Sir Adam Cunningham, of Caprington, in Airshire, whose son, Sir Adam, married a daughter of —— Crawford, of Kilbirny, ancestor of the Viscount Garnock. His daughter was wife of Sir William Stuart, of Garlies, ancestor of the Earls of Galloway.

Grant from Isabel, Duchess of Albany, Countess of Lenox, who had a conjoint enfeoffment with the duke her husband, to Sir William and his wife Mary,

Countess of Angus, of the earldom of Lenox in fee; but this succession was defeated by the attainder of Murdoch, Duke of Albany, and Duncan, Earl of Lenox, father to the Duchess.

Upon the death of the Duchess, the crown got into possession of the earldom of Lenox, which was granted for life to the Duchess' natural grandchild, the Lord Evandale, by Lord James Stuart, her son; but the earldom of Duntreath was particularly excepted by King James II. by a charter, under the great seal, to William Edmondston de Culloden, and Mary, Countess of Angus, his wife, *avitæ nostræ carissimæ*, and William, their son and heir apparent, and their heirs. Sir William died in 1460, leaving his son and heir,

3, William, of Culloden and Duntreath, so designed in a service on a precept of the chancery in 1461; and was named, by King James III. one of ths lords of the session. He died next year.

This William added to his arms the tressure, as a mark of royal descent, as now borne by the family, as also the supporters. A seal of his, so emblazoned, appendent to a resignation into the hands of James III. by William Graham, of Garvoch, a younger son of the Lords Graham, and the Countess of Angus, his wife; and because the resigner has not a seal of his own, he says, *Accommodavi sigillum fatris carissimi mei Willielmi Edmondston de Duntreath.* They were brothers by the same mother*.

He married, in 1473, his near relation, and a near branch of the royal family, Matilda Stuart, grand-daughter of the Duke and Duchess of Albany, and daughter of their son, Lord James Stuart. She was sister to Sir Andrew Stuart, of Strathaven, afterwards Lord Evandale, and chancellor to James II. to Walter Stuart, ancestor to the Earls of Murray, and to the Lords of Ochiltree and Evandale †, by whom he had, 1, Archibald, his successor; 2, James, who married ——, daughter and heiress of Cunningham, of Polmaize, in Stirlingshire, and stiled of Polmaize: she died S. P. and he married secondly, Elizabeth, daughter of Murray, of Touchadam, in Stirlingshire, with whom he had a joint enfeoffment under the great seal of the lands of Buchguhaderick; 3, James, provost of the collegiate church of Kiskheugh; 4, John, who married ——, daughter of Sir John Stuart, of Blackhall, &c.; 5, George; 6, William, deputy-master of the household to James IV.: and two daughters, 1, Matilda, wife of Laurence, Lord Oliphant; 2, Mary, of William, grandson and heir of Sir Humphrey Cunningham, of Glengarnock, in Airshire.

This William purchased, 1484, of Henry Wardlaw, the lands of Cambuswallace, in the stewartry of Menteith, and sheriffdom of Perth. This William died 1468 ‡, and was succeeded by his eldest son,

* This deed, with the seal appendant, was produced to Sir James Erskine, of Cambo, Bart. Lord Lyon king at arms, who being satisfied that the seal, so emblazoned, had been always borne by the family, he confirmed the bearings, and granted an extract, as usual in such cases.

† This appears by a precept of seisin granted by him, Nov. 6, 1456, directed to his bailiff, for giving seisin of the lands of Dungoyich, in the barony of Duntreath, to Matilda, his wife. In the deed, described as William, son and heir apparent of Sir William de Duntreath.

‡ Qu. Some mistake in this part of the pedigree, as this William is stated as dying at three different times.

4, Archibald, who was knighted by King James III. He was cousin-german to the Lord Evandale, at that time the king's chancellor*, and married Janet, daughter of Sir James Shaw, of Sanchy, Knt. comptroller of Scotland in the reign of James III. and sister to Robert, Abbot of Paisley, afterwards Bishop of Murray, and neice to George Abbot, of Paisley, treasurer of Scotland in the reign of James IV. by whom he had two sons, 1, William, of whom hereafter; 2, James, a witness, 1506, to a charter of alienation by his elder brother of the lands of Culloden to Alexander Strachan, of Scots-town, confirmed and ratified by a charter under the great seal. This James was the ancestor of that branch of the family denominated of Ballenton: he married Agnes, daughter of James Ridheugh, of Tilychaddill, comptroller of Scotland under James IV. Several Edmonstones, in the stewartry of Menteith, are descended from this branch.

Sir Archibald had likewise several daughters, nobly married, viz.

1, Janet, second wife of William, Lord Graham, the first Earl of Montrose, by whom she had several daughters: the first, Margaret, was contracted to the Master of Lenox, but the marriage never took place. She afterwards married Sir John Somerville, a branch of Lord Somerville's family. Sir John Somerville, his son, had a son, Sir James, and several daughters, one married to Walter, the first Lord Blantyre, another married to John Skeen, registrar of Scotland in King James the Sixth's time; a third married Adam Whitefoord, of that ilk; a fourth to James Dunlop, of that ilk. William, Earl of Montrose, by his countess Janet Edmonstone, had a second daughter, Nicholas, wife of John Murray, of Abercairn; the third daughter, Agnes, was wife of Humphrey Colquhoun, son and heir of Sir John Colquhoun, of Luss.

2, Christian, second daughter of Sir Archibald, was wife of John, Master of Ross, stiled there John Ross, of Melvil, grandson and heir apparent of John, the first Lord Ross, of Hawkhead and Melville, and had issue Ninian, Lord Ross, his father's successor, who, by Janet, his wife, daughter of Matthew, Earl of Lenox, had issue Robert, who, by Agnes, daughter of John Moncrief, of that ilk, left only one daughter Jean, wife of John, Lord Fleming, and had issue. James Ross, the Lord Ross's second son, succeeded his father in the honour, whom whom is descended William, Lord Ross, now extinct. James, Lord Ross, had by his wife, daughter of Robert, Lord Semple, Robert and William, both Lords Ross, and three daughters; 1, Jane, wife, first, of Sir James Sandilands, ancestor of the Lord Torpichen; secondly, to Henry Stuart, of Craigie-hall; 2, Elizabeth, wife of Allan Lockhart, of Cleghorn; and 3, Dorothy, of James Cunningham, of Aikel.

3, Elizabeth, was wife of John, Master of Eglintoun, son and heir of Hugh, Lord Montgomery, first Earl of Eglintoun; he died before his father in 1520, but left issue two sons and a daughter, Archibald, Master of Eglintoun, his grandfather's successor, and died unmarried; Hugh, the second Earl of Eglin-

* Precept out of chancery, directed to Alexander Cunningham, of Polmaize, sheriff of Stirlingshire, for investing Archibald of Duntreath as heir to his father.

toun; and Christian, wife of Sir William Douglas, of Drumlanrig, ancestor to the Duke of Queensbury.

4, Margaret, was wife of George Buchanan, grandson and heir apparent to Walter Buchanan, of that ilk, and had a son John, married to a daughter of William Livington, and had a son who succeeded his grandfather Sir George. She had likewise a daughter Margaret, wife of George Stirling, of Glorat, constable and governor of Dunbarton Castle, and ancestor of Sir James Stirling, of Glorat, Bart.

5, Barbara, wife of Sir James Mushel, of Benbank, in Perthshire, a family now extinct, but from the younger sons of this family are descended many families in Perthshire; and from daughters are sprung, among others, the Lord Burleigh, the Lord Cranston, the Dons, of Newton, &c. &c.

Archibald died 1502, and was succeeded by his son,

5, William, who was appointed stewart of Menteith, and captain principal and constable of the castle of Down, in the county of Perth, by James IV. before 1509; knighted by King James, 1507; described in several deeds, as Miles; alienated the lands of Culloden to Alexander Strachan, of Scots-town, *ut ante*, July 30, 1506, ratified by a charter under the great seal; and married, first, Sibylla, daughter of Sir William Bailie, of Lamington, in the county of Lanerk, by whom he had, 1, Sir William, his son and successor; 2, Archibald Edmonstone, of Spital-town, who married Agnes, daughter of Nicol Cornuall, of Bonhard, from whom is descended that branch of the family in Stirlingshire; 3, James, the first of the branch of the Edmonstones of Newton and Cambuswallace, in the stewartry of Menteith and shire of Perth. Other branches of Edmonstones settled in the stewartry of Menteith are descended from this family; and 4, Robert, proprietor of Cambuswallace, in Menteith.

Sir William had also the following daughters; 1, Marian, wife of John Campbell, of Glenorchie, ancestor of the Earls of Breadalbane, by whom he had two daughters, who were coheiresses to part of his estate; Margaret, the eldest, was wife of Edward Riddoch, of Talliechadill and Culliebragan, in Perth; and Christian was wife of George Hume, of Argathie, a brother of the house of Polwarth; 2, Mary, of Robert Hamilton, of Inchenachen, in Linlithgowshire; 3, Margaret, of —— Stewart, of Craigarnell; and 4, Elizabeth, of John Logan, of Balvie, in the county of Dumbarton, hereditary bailiff of the earldom of Lenox.

Sir William married secondly, Sibylla Carmichael, daughter of Carmichael, of that ilk, in the county of Lanerk, from whom the Earls of Hyndford are descended*. Sir William was succeeded by his son, May 6, 1516.

6, William, described as the eldest son of Sir William, slain at Flodden, in a precept out of chancery. Being much in favour wiih John, Duke of Albany, the regent, during the minority of James V. he, together with his brother Archibald, were appointed, in 1516, joint keepers of the castle of Down, and stewart of the

* A charter under the great seal to Sir William, and Sibylla Carmichael, his wife, of the lands of Carrbuswallace on his own resignation, Aug. 15, 1515, barely a full month before he was slain at the battle of Flodden Field.

stewartry of Menteith and Strathgartney, which office he held eighteen years, till it was conferred, by an heritable grant, on Sir James Stuart, brother of the Lords Evandale and Methven, which last was married to the queen mother.

William Edmonstone was much irritated at being deprived of an office that had been so long in his family, but he suppressed his resentment for a time; but, upon the death of the king, the Earl of Arran succeeding to the regency, and having confirmed the above grant to Sir James Stuart, the anger of the house of Duntreath broke out, and the laird and his two brothers, Archibald and James, happening to encounter Sir James Stuart in the high street of Dumblain, a scuffle ensued, in which Sir James was killed, Whitsunday, 1543.

A remission for this offence was afterwards granted to William and his brother by the Duke of Chatellerault, and Earl of Arran, the governor, under the great seal, Sept. 4, 1547.

James, the brother of William, had a grant of the lands of Bidnoch, in the stewartry of Menteith, in 1558; and also a grant of the lands of Balloch from the Earl of Lennox, confirmed by a charter under the great seal, in 1566.

Sir William married first*, Agnes Stuart, daughter of Matthew, the second Earl of Lennox: she was aunt to Matthew, Earl of Lennox, grandfather and regent to James VI. and first monarch of Great Britain. Her mother, the Countess of Lennox, was daughter to James, the first Lord Harrington, by the Lady Mary, his wife, daughter to James II. King of Scotland. After the death of the Lady Agnes Stuart, he married secondly, Margaret, daughter of Sir James Campbell, of Lanners, a son of the house of Glenorchie, and ancestor of the Earls of Loudon. Her mother was Agnes, the daughter of John Moncrief, of that ilk, in Perthshire, by whom he had a numerous issue; 1, Sir James, and several daughters, 1, Margery, wife of Mungo Graham, of Rattern, a younger son of William, the second Earl of Montrose, and ancestor of the Grahams of Merehill, in Perthshire; 2, Sibella, wife of John Stuart, son and heir of Matthew Stuart, of Barscute, in Renfrewshire, lineally sprung from Robert Stuart, a younger son of Alexander Stuart, of Darnley, ancestor of the Earls and Dukes of Lennox in the reign of Robert III. Thomas, a descendant, in 1670, sold his estate at Baiscute, and went over to Ireland, where he died; 3, Anabell, wife of John, son and heir of George Stirling, of Glorat, in Stirlingshire, who defended the castle of Dumbarton, during the minority of Queen Mary, against Matthew Earl of Lennox. He was afterwards constable and governor of the castle, and was the ancestor of Sir James Stirling, of Glorat, Bart.; 4, Marian, wife, first, of David, son and heir of Robert Semple, of Nobleston, in Dumbartonshire. From the heir of that marriage descended the Grahams, of Gartmore; she was secondly, the wife of Robert Deniston, of Colgrain, in the same county, from whom that family are descended; and thirdly, she married John Shaw, of Bargaran, in Renfrewshire; 5, Elizabeth, wife of John, son and heir of Walter Stirling, of Balagan, brother to the laird of Glorat; and 6, Janet, wife, in 1544, of Luke, brother to Stirling, of Keir. Sir William was succeeded by his son,

7, Sir James Edmonstone, constituted, in 1578, justice deputy under the Earl of Argyll, the justice-general. In 1584, he was named one of the assessors

* See Addenda I.

to the justiciary, for the trial of William, Earl of Gowrie, for the treasonable attempt of detaining the king at the Earl's own house at Ruthven, near Perth, who was condemned and suffered for high-treason.

Sir James was soon after knighted, and was accused, together with Malcolm Douglas, of Mawis, and John Cunningham, of ——, by one Robert Hamilton, of ——, of a design to seize upon the king, and to convey him to some place of security till they should advertise the banished lord who had been outlawed for the treason for which the Earl of Gowrie suffered. It was believed that it was little more than a loose discourse; however, Sir James and the rest were made prisoners, and were indicted of high treason. Upon reading the indictment, Sir James confessed such discourse had passed, and threw himself on the king's mercy; however, the rest were found guilty of having held this discourse, which was deemed treasonable, and were executed. It seems Sir James was pardoned, but he retired from court, and resided at Duntreath, which he enlarged.

A new investiture of the estate at Duntreath, confirmed by a charter under the great seal by James VI. March 28, 1568, with the consent of James, Earl of Murray, his tutor, and the regent. The fee is provided in succession to James, son of William Edmonstone, of Duntreath, the heirs male of his body, remainder to Archibald Edmonstone, of Spitaltown, remainder to James Edmonstone, of Ballinton, remainder to James Edmonstone, of Newton, and the heirs male of their bodies, remainder to the heir male whomsoever.

Sir James married first, Hellen, daughter of Sir James Stirling, of Keir, by Jean, his wife, daughter of Dr. William Chisholm, Bishop of Dumblain, by a daughter of the family of Montrose. One of her sisters married John Napier, of Marchiston, ancestor of the Lord Napier; another, to Sir William Murray, of Polmaize; another, to Sir John Houston, of that ilk; and another, to Sir George Munshel, of Burnbank. By this lady, Sir James had, 1, William, his heir; 2, John; and three daughters, viz. 1, Mary, wife of John Cunningham, of Cunningham Head, Airshire, and had issue, Sir William Cunningham, a Baronet, in 1627; Alexander; Barbara, wife of James Fullarton, of that ilk; Jean, wife to her cousin James Edmonstone; Elizabeth, wife of Sir George Cunningham, who resided in Sweden; and after his death, to Walter Sandilands, of Hilderston, second son of James, the second Lord Torpichen.

Mary, the wife of Cunningham, of Cunningham Head, married secondly, Sir William Graham, of Brackoe, younger son of John, the third Earl of Montrose. By him she had a son, Sir William, who, by Mary, his wife, daughter of Sir Dignel Campbell, of Auchinbeck, had a son, Sir William, who was long the heir male and tutor of the family of Montrose, and next in succession to the Marquis of Montrose. He died S. P.

2, Margery, wife of Claud Hamilton, son and heir of Claud Hamilton, of Cockney, in Dumbartonshire: the heir of this family went to Ireland.

3, Hellen, wife of John Lennox, of Bransogle, in the county of Lennox, and had issue; descended from Donald Lennox, son of Duncan, Earl of Lennox.

Sir James married secondly, Margaret, daughter of Sir John Colquhoun, of Luss. Her mother was Agnes, daughter of Robert, Lord Boyd. Sir James enters into this marriage with the consent of his eldest son William, by whom he had, 1, Robert, who was provided to certain lands, which, on his death without issue, reverted to the family; 2, Elizabeth, wife of James Edmonstone, of Balasen and Broick; 3, Margaret; 4, Agnes; and 5, Jean. Sir James was succeeded by his eldest son,

8, William, who married Isabel, daughter of John Halden, of Gleneagles, in Perth (her mother was Isabel, daughter of Sir David Hume, of Wedderburn, in Berwickshire), by whom he bad, 1, Archibald, his successor; 2, James, who married Jean, daughter of John Cunningham, of Cunningham Head; 3, John, married Elizabeth, daughter and sole heiress to James Emmerton, of Bolvan, and got by her also the lands of Balybantro, in the north of Ireland; 4, Robert; and 5, Andrew, who both died S. P. Sir James had also several daughters, viz.

1, Hellen, wife of John Dolloway, of Balie Hill, in the county of Antrim, in Ireland, and had issue, Archibald, Alexander, and Hellen, wife of Andrew Clements, a merchant. Mrs. Dolloway married secondly, Colonel James Wallace, of Achavo and Dundonald, who was defeated, at the head of the disaffected people of the south-west, by the king's forces, upon the Pentland Hills, in 1666. Wallace was attainted by a sentence of the court of justiciary, but was never apprehended, and escaping to Ireland, married Mrs. Dolloway.

2, Jean, wife of Sir Robert Adair, of Kilhill, in Wigtownshire, by whom she had, William, Alexander, Robert, Isabel, wife of Robert Macdowal, of Logan, in the county of Wigton, Anne was wife of Mr. Kennedy, a minister, and Jean was wife of Mr. Patrick Adair. William * was succeeded, June 18, 1633, by his eldest son,

9, Archibald, a strong presbyterian, was chosen member for the county of Stirling in the parliament that met at Edinburgh, and was opened with great solemnity by King Charles I. in person. He opposed strongly the court in their attempt to get the king to name the apparel of the churchmen, apprehending it might be the means of introducing the surplice, to bring the church of Scotland in nearer conformity to that of England, which was then much dreaded. He also joined with the Earl of Rothes, the Lords Loudon, Balmerino, Lindsey, and Bulleigh, in opposing every measure which he deemed an incroachment on the constitution, in the face of the king, who marked the vote of every member which went against himself or his prerogative.

He married Jean, daughter of Archibald Hamilton, of Halcraig, in Lanerkshire. He was one of the sons of Hans Hamilton, the first Protestant vicar and exerter, as he is called at Dunlop, at the time of the reformation of religion, and was lineally descended from Sir David Hamilton, of Cadgrow, ancestor of the Duke of Hamilton and Earl of Abercorn. This vicar of Dunlop was father of Sir James Hamilton, afterwards created Viscount Claneboy, and his son Earl of Cranbrassil, in Ireland.

* This William was the first of the family who settled in Ireland. See Note at the end of this account

Jean Edmonstone's mother was Rachel, daughter of Walter Carmichael, of Park and Hyndford, and sister to James, the first Lord Carmichael, and ancestor of the Earl of Hyndford. After her husband's death, she was, secondly, the wife of Sir William Mure, of Rowellan, by whom she had a daughter, wife first, of William Railston, of that ilk, in Renfrew, and secondly, of John Boyle, of Kilburn, grandfather to the Earl of Glasgow.

Archibald Edmonstone, of Duntreath, had issue by his wife Jean Hamilton, 1, William, who was deaf and dumb, and did not succeed to the estate; he had great vivacity and quickness of imagination, cheerful, with a strong memory, and handsome in his person. He lived to a great age, and died several years after the Revolution.

10, Archibald succeeded his father in his estate. There were also two daughters, 1, Helen, wife of Thomas Mure, of Monkridden, in Airshire, and had issue; and 2, Isabel, who died unmarried.

Archibald married Anna-Helena, daughter of Colonel Walter Scot, of Hartwoodburn, relict of Sir William Adair, of Kilhill, and had issue by her, 1, Archibald; 2, Walter; 3, William, who all died young; 4, Archibald, who succeeded his father; and five daughters.

1, Elizabeth, wife of James Montgomery, of Rosemond, a near branch of the Montgomerys, Earl of Mount-Alexander, whose first ancestor, Sir Hugh, of Braidstone, was lineally descended from a younger brother of the Montgomerys, now Earls of Eglintoun, in the days of James III. She had two sons by Mr. Montgomery, 1, William, who became heir to the estate of Mount-Alexander, and title of Lord of Ards, but dying before the late Earl, and without issue male, all the titles of that family became extinct; and 2, Hugh: also three daughters, Anne-Hellen, Elizabeth, and Martha.

2, Jean; 3, Margaret; 4, Isabel, who all died young; 5, Anne-Ellen, wife of a relation of her own, Alexander Dolloway, of Belliehill, member of parliament for the borough of Carrickfergus, and had issue Robert and Archibald. Archibald was succeeded by his only surviving son,

11, Archibald, who married first, Anne Erskine, daughter of David, Lord Cardross, by Dame Catharine Stuart, his wife, one of the daughters and coheiresses of Sir James Stuart, of Strathbrench and Kirkhill, in the county of Linlithgow, and by her he had one daughter Catharine, wife of —— Kennedy, of ———, Esq. in Ireland, and by him has one daughter.

He married secondly, Anne, daughter of the Honourable John Campbell, of Mammore, second son of Archibald, Earl of Argyll, and brother to Archibald the first Duke of Argyll, by ———, daughter of John, Lord Elphinstone, who married the daughter of Charles, Earl of Lauderdale. Upon the death of the last heir male of the first duke without issue male, the title of Duke of Argyll descended upon John, son of the above John Campbell, of Mammore, and brother to Anne, the wife of Archibald Edmonstone, of Duntreath. By her he had issue, 1, Archibald, now Sir Archibald Edmonstone, of Duntreath, created a Baronet of Great Britain, May 3, 1774; 2, Campbell, lieutenant-governor of Dumbarton-Castle, deceased. He married ——, daughter of —— Alexander, Esq. merchant, in Glasgow, and had issue four sons, all deceased, and six daughters now living; 3, Charles, a major in the army, who was likewise married, but died without issue: and two daughters.

Archibald Edmonstone died, and was succeeded by his eldest son and heir,

I. Sir ARCHIBALD EDMONSTONE, who was born at Silver Banks, in Dumbartonshire, Old Michaelmas Day, Oct. 10. 1717, was thirty-five years in parliament. He married first, Susanna-Mary, only daughter of Roger Harenc, Esq. and sister of Benjamin Harenc, of Foots-cray Place, in Kent, Esq. by whom he has had five sons and three daughters; 1, Archibald, a lieutenant in the first regiment of foot-guards, who died July, 1780; 2, William-Archibald, now in the East Indies; 3, Charles, one of the six clerks in chancery, who married Emma, fifth daughter of Richard-Wilbraham Bootle, of Lathom House, in Lancashire, Esq. by whom (who died Nov. 1797) he has issue a son Archibald, and a daughter Mary-Emma; 4, George, in holy orders; 5, Neil-Benjamin, now in the East Indies; 6, Susanna-Margaret, wife of James Trecothick, of Addington-Place, in Surry, Esq. and has issue two sons, Barlow and James, and four daughters, Susanna, Anne, Louisa, and Charlotte; 7, Anne-Mary, wife of Henry Read, of Crowrodin, in Wiltshire, Esq. a major-general in the army: she died in 1791, leaving issue two daughters, Mary-Anne and Louisa; 8, Sarah, who died young.

Sir Archibald married secondly, Hester, daughter of Sir Gilbert Heathcote, of Normanton, in Rutlandshire, Bart. who died in the year 1796, without issue.

ARMS—Or, three crescents, gules, within a double tressure, flowred and counterflowred.

CREST—Out of a ducal coronet a swan's head and neck, proper.

SUPPORTERS—Two lions rampant, gules.

MOTTO—*Virtus auget honorem.*

SEAT—At Duntreath, Stirlingshire.

I. See P. 420. No. This William Edmonstone was appointed one of Queen Mary's privy council in 1565; the Earl of Lennox, his relation, being father to Henry, Lord Darnley, who was married to the Queen; and having the management of the Queen's affairs, was knighted soon after, and appears to have been in a sederent of the council, dated July 22, 1565. He was also present at another meeting of the council, July 29, 1565, in which he is designed as Willielmus Edmonstone, de Duntreath, miles.

N. B. * P. 422. William, the son of Sir James Edmonstone, raised, by wadsett, a very considerable sum of money upon the estate of Duntreath, which had been much impoverished by his father, from the then Lord Kilsyth, with which he went to Ireland, and purchased very large estates in the counties of Antrim and Down; but much the greater part of these was afterwards sold by his son, in order to redeem the Scotch estate; some part of which, however, was irrecoverably lost. Afterwards, the residence of the family was partly at Redhall, in the county of Antrim, in Ireland, and partly at Duntreath, till, in the year 178–, the present Sir Archibald Edmonstone sold the remainder of the estate in Ireland, and bought the estate formerly the property of the Visc. Kilsyth, in Stirlingshire, who was attainted in the year 1715, part of which originally appertained to the barony of Duntreath, and was aliened by William Edmonstone, of Duntreath, as above-mentioned.

Cadets of the Family of Edmonstone.

Edmonstones, of Broick and Ballybantro, in Ireland, sprung from James, the second son of William Edmonstone, of Duntreath, who married Isabel, daughter of John Halden, of Gleneagles.

Edmonstones, of Newton and Down, descended from James, a younger son of Sir William Edmonstone, of Duntreath, who married Sibylla, daughter of Sir William Baillie, of Lammington.

ROBERT II. KING OF SCOTLAND, 1390
Elizabeth Muir | Euphane Ross

TABLE.

Robert III. King of Scots, 1406
Arabella Drummond, 1401

Isabella, Countess Dowager of Douglas and Mar
James, Earl of Douglas | 1, Sir John Edmondston

Mary, Countess Dowager of Angus, 1452
George, E. of Angus, 1402 | Sir James Kennedy | Sir Wm Graham | Sir William Edmonston, 1460

2, Sir David, 1436 — 2, Sir William, 1460; Mary, dr of Rob. III — Mary; Sir A. Ker 1460

3, Sir James
J. Napier

Elizabeth; Sir P. Bl- — Margaret; Sir W. Ogilvie

3, Sir William
Matilda Stuart

Sir A. Cunningham

4, Archibald, 1502; Janet Shaw — James; – Cunningham | E. Murray — James, Geo. — John; – Stuart — Wm — Matilda; Ld Oliphant — Mary; W. Cunningham

5, William, 1516; Sibylla Bailie | Sibylla Carmichael — James; Agnes Ridheugh — Janet; William, Earl of Montrose — Christian; John Ross — Elizabeth; John Eglintoun — Margaret; George Buchanan — Barbara; Sir James Mushel

6, Sir William, 1578; A. Stuart | N. Campbell — Archibald; A. Cornhall — James, Robert — Marian; J. Campbell — Mary; R. Hamilton — Margaret; – Stewart — Elizabeth; J. Logan

7, Sir James; H. Stirling | M. Colquhoun — Margery; M. Graham — Sibella; J. Stuart — Anabell; J. Stirling — Marian; D. Semple | R. Deniston | John Shaw — Elizabeth; J. Stirling — Janet; L. Stirling

8, William, 1633; I. Halden — John — Mary; J. Cunningham — Margery; C. Hamilton — Helen; J. Lennox — Robert — Margaret — Elizabeth; J. Edmonstone — Agnes, Jean

9, Archibald; J. Hamilton — James; J. Cunningham — John; E. Emmerton — Robert, Andrew — Helen; J. Dolloway — Jane; Sir R. Adair

William — 10, Archibald = A. H. Scot — Helen = Thomas Mure — Isabel

Archibald, — Walter — William — 11, Archibald; A. Erskine | A. Campbell — Elizabeth; J. Montgomery — Jean, Margaret, Isabel — A. Helen; A. Dolloway

Catharine; – Kennedy — I. Sir Archibald; S. Harenc | H. Heathcote — Campbell = – Alexander; 4 sons, d y, and 3 drs — Charles = —

Archibald — William-Archibald — Charles; Emma Bootle — George — Neil-Benjamin — Susanna; J. Trecothick — Anne-Mary; H. Read — Sarah, d y

Archibald — Mary-Emma — Barlow, James — Susanna, Anne — Louisa, Charlotte — Mary-Anne — Louisa

Archibald Edmonstone, of Duntreath, Knt. married Anabella, daughter of James IV. King of Scotland, who married Margaret, daughter of Henry VII. King of England.

The above is extracted from a copy of a paper found by the present Sir Archibald Edmonstone, with the manuscript of the family, but it does not appear to be there vouched as authentic.

---

308. HANMER, of HANMER, Flintshire.

Created Baronet, May 3, 1774.

CAMDEN makes honourable mention of this family *, which has had its residence in the parish which bears the same name from a very early period.

In the reign of Edward the First,

1, Sir John de Hanmer, Knt. †, assumed the surname of Hanmer ‡. Like other large proprietors on the borders, he was a supporter of the English interest; and, early in the reign of the same king, was appointed constable of Caernarvon Castle.

He married Hawis, daughter and heiress of Enion ap Gwillim, ap Griffith ap Gwin-win-win, Lord of Upper Powis, and descended from Bledwyn ap Kynwin, Prince of all Wales. By this lady he had three sons, Owen, surnamed Goch, David, and Philip. Owen succeeded his father, 2 Edw. II. and dying without issue, divided his estste between his brothers David and Philip.

2, Philip Hanmer became at length sole heir to the whole estate of his father. He married Agnes, daughter and heiress of David ap Rired ap Rees Says, and had issue by her two sons, David and Jenkin: also two daughters, Margaret, the wife of Morgan Goch, ap Griffith ap Jerworth voel, and Myrawwy, the wife of Gruff ap Howel de Overton.

3, Sir David Hanmer, Knt. succeeded his father. He was appointed one of the justices of the court of King's Bench on the 26th of February, 1383, and in 1387, 10 Rich. II. had the honour of knighthood conferred on him. He married Agnes, daughter of Llewelin ddu ap Griffith ap Jerworth voel, and had issue two sons, Griffith Hanmer, of Hanmer, Esq. who, by Gwerville, daughter of Tudor ap Grono, of Anglesey, had only a daughter, the wife of John Puleston, of Emral, Esq. and Jenkin Hanmer, and one daughter named Margaret, the

* "Nor remains any thing to be mentioned, except Hanmere, seated by a lake or mere, whence that ancient and honourable family that dwells there took the name of Hanmer."—*Camden's Brit. Flintshire.*

† The older genealogists trace the descent of this person from Meredith, Lord of Rhi whi rieth and Coed Talog, brother of Griffith, Prince of North Wales, as does also a printed book of pedigrees by Reynolds.

‡ Vide Mr. Camden's Latin Letter to Mr. Hanmer, Harl. M.S. 7017.—The general assumption of the surname, which took place about this period, shews the advances society had then made in population and improvement.

wife of the celebrated Owen Glendowr, Lord of Glendowrdvy, by whom she had several children *.

4, Jenkin Hanmer, of Hanmer, Esq. afterwards Sir Jenkin Hanmer, Knt. succeeded his father, and became the common ancestor of several branches of this family, amongst which his estate was divided. By his first wife Margaret, daughter and heiress of David ap Blethyn Vychan, of Okenholt, descended from Edwyn, Lord of Tegangle, otherwise Englefield, he had his son Griffith, from whom the Hanmers, of Hanmer Hall, descended. By his second wife Eve, daughter and heiress of David ap Grono ap Jerworth, of Llai, he had three sons; 1, John Hanmer, of Haghlton and Llai, in the county of Flint (whose grand-daughter and heiress was the wife of Sir Roger Puleston, of Emral); 2, Edward Hanmer, of Fenneshall, in the parish of Hanmer, from whom the present Baronet is lineally descended; and 3, Richard Hanmer, of Bettisfield. Sir Jenkin Hanmer was a zealous supporter of his brother-in-law Glendowr, and was slain at the battle of Shrewsbury on the 22d of July, 1403, "valiantly fighting against the usurper Bolingbroke †." On a failure of issue in the Bettisfield branch of the family, the Hanmers, of Hanmer Hall, became possessed of the greater part of Bettisfield: the elder branch of Hanmer Hall flourished through many generations, till it ceased in male descent on the death of the late Sir Thomas Hanmer ‡. It produced several distinguished characters on whom we could enlarge, did our limits allow it: five of the nine descendants of Griffith we find returned to parliament for the county of Flint. Sir John Hanmer, Knt. the sixth in descent from Griffith, was created a Baronet on the 8th July, 1620, 18 Jac. I. The late Sir Thomas Hanmer was the fourth and last Baronet of the house: he was chosen knight of the shire for Flintshire, and afterwards for the county of Suffolk. At an early age, he was much engaged in public affairs, and in the house of commons such was the opinion entertained of his talents and integrity, that his influence was sensibly felt there. He was a strenuous supporter of the Hanoverian succession, and the celebrated representation of the state of the nation, which was presented to Queen Anne by the lower house of parliament, was written by him; and, in the twelfth year of her reign, being then only in the thirty-fourth year of his age, he was chosen speaker of the house of commons §. From a literary leisure towards the close of his life, sprang the edition of Shakspeare; and if Pope's hostility be not forgotten, it should also be remembered, that this hostility was excited by the acrimonious jealousy, not of himself, but of Warburton, whose dupe (on this

* The Bard sung her praises in the following lines:

A Gwraig orau ore gwragedd!	His wife the best of wives!
Gwynn y Myd, oi Gwin ai midd	Happy am I in her wine and metheglin.
Merch eglur, Llin Marchawglyw,	Eminent woman, of a knightly family,
Urdol, hael, o ricol ryw,	Honourable, beneficent, noble,
ai blant a ddenant bob ddan,	Her children come in pairs,
Mythod tig o bennacthan.	Beautiful nests of chieftains.

† Pennant's Wales, I. 220.

‡ Its matrimonial alliances are (chronologically) with the Dutton family, Kynaston, of Hardwick, Brereton, of Malpas, Salter, of Oswestry, Salisbury, of Lleweney, Talbot, Earl of Shrewsbury, Mostyn, of Mostyn, Trevor, of Trevallyn, Baker, of Whittingham, Hervey, of Ickworth, North, of Mildenhall, and Bennet, Earl of Arlington.

§ In addition to other authorities referring to this period, see Dr. Swift's Diary, in Vol. 19 of his works, pages 136 and 266, &c. and the History of the Four last Years of Queen Anne, in Vol. 18.

occasion at least) he was. A later editor*, and celebrated critic, in discussing the relative merit of his predecessors, speaks thus of Sir Thomas and his work: that "he was eminently qualified by nature for such studies; that he had what is the first requisite to emendatory criticism; that intuition, by which the poet's intention is immediately discovered, and that dexterity of intellect which dispatches its work by the easiest means. He had undoubtedly read much; his acquaintance with customs, opinions, and traditions, seems to have been large, and he is often learned without shew. He seldom passes what he does not understand, without an attempt to find or to make a meaning, and sometimes hastily makes what a little more attention would have found. He is solicitous to reduce to grammar what he could not be sure that his author intended to be grammatical." Sir Thomas married first, Isabella, daughter and heiress of Henry Bennet, Earl of Arlington, widow and relict of Henry, Duke of Grafton; and she dying in the year 1723, he afterwards married Elizabeth, daughter and heiress of Thomas Folkes, of Barton, in the county of Suffolk, Esq. Sir Thomas died in the year 1747, without issue by either of his wives, and was buried in the family vault in the south aisle of Hanmer church, where a marble monument is erected to his memory †. He was distinguished for

* Dr. Johnson's Preface to his Shakspeare, Page 47, edition the second.

† The epitaph inscribed thereon is as follows:

Honorabilis admodum Thoˢ. Hanmer, Barᵗ.
W. Hanmer, arm. è Peregrinâ H. North,
de Mildenhall, in com. Suffolciæ, Baronetti,
Sorore et hærede.
Filius
Johannis Hanmer, de Hanmer, Bar.
Hæres Patruelis
Antiquo gentis suæ et titulo et Patrimonio successit
Duas uxores sortitus est
Alteram Isabellam honore à Patre derivato de
Arlington, comitissam
deeinde celcissimi Principis ducis de Grafton viduam
dotariam
Alteram Elizabeth Thomæ Folkes de Barton in
com. Suff. arm.
Filiam et hæredem.
Inter humatitis studia feliciter enutritus
Omnes liberatium artium disciplinas avidè arripuit:
Quas morum suavitate haud leviter ornavit.
Post quam excessit ex ephebis,
Continuo inter populares suos famâ eminens,
Et comitatûs sui legatus ad parliamentum missus,
ad ardua regni negotia per annos prope triginta
se accinxit;
Cumq. apud illos amplissimorum virorum ordines
Solerit nihil temere effutire
Sed probè perpensa diserte expromere
Orator gravis et pressus
Non minus integritatis quam eloquentiæ laude
commendatus;
Æque omnium utcunq; inter se alisqui,
dissidentium
Aures atque animos attraxit,
Annoq. demum MDCCXIII. regnante Annâ,
Felicissimæ florentissimæ-q, memoriæ reginâ
ad prolocutoris Cathedram
Communi senatûs universi voce designatus est
Quod munus
Cum nullo tempore non difficile
tum illo certe negotiis
et variis et lubricis et implicatis difficilimum
cum dignitate sustinuit,
Honores alios et omnia quæ sibi in lucram
cederent munera.
Sedulo detractavit,
Ut rei totus inserviret publicæ
Justi rectiq. tenax
et fide in patriam incorruptâ notus
Ubi omnibus quæ virum civemq. bonum
decent officiis satisfecisset
Paulatim se a publicis conciliis in otium
recipiens
Inter literarum amœnitates
inter ante actæ haud insuaves recordationes
inter amicorum convictus et emplexus
Honorifice consenuit,
Et bonis omnibus, quibus charissimus
vixit
Desideratissimus obiit.

Hic. juxta aneres avi, suos condi voluit
es curavit Gul. Bunbury, Bars. Nepos
et Hæres.

the gentlemanly refinement of his manners, as well as for the more intrinsic merit of a well cultivated mind. Sir Thomas bequeathed his Suffolk estates * to Sir William Bunbury, of Stoke and Stanney, in the county of Chester, Bart. his nephew and heir at law, whereby that family acquired its Suffolk property; but, in the history of his family, it ought not to be forgotten that Sir Thomas Hanmer was the first proposer of a measure that has restored to unity the family estate, enjoyed as a divided inheritance by the different branches of the family from the death of Sir Jenkin Hanmer, and now united and preserved (with its principle of duration strengthened) to its male representative; for, in the year 1733, by a settlement then made by him and his kinsman, Thomas Hanmer, of Fenneshall, Esq. the uses of the Flintshire estates of both branches of the family, were limited to the same male heir, and by its operation the estate of the present Baronet (with the exception of the Haghlton and Llai estate) is nearly identified with that of his ancestor Sir Jenkin Hanmer, in the time of Henry the Fourth. We now return to,

5, Edward Hanmer, who succeeded to the lordship of Finnes. He married Margaret, daughter of Maurice ap Jevan Gythyn, by whom he had two sons, Griffith and Philip.

6, Griffith Hanmer succeeded his father, and married Margaret, daughter of Meredith Lloyd, of Lloyd and Maen, Esq. and had issue by her six sons and four daughters; 1, Jenkin, his eldest son and heir; 2, Lawrence; 3, Edward; 4, William; 5, David; and 6, Matthew; and Elizabeth-Rose, Margaret, and Blanche. Griffith died in 1501, and was succeeded by his son,

7, Jenkin Hanmer. He married Margaret, daughter of Thomas Dymock, of Willington, Esq. and had issue, William, and four daughters; Ellen, the wife of John Hanmer, son of Sir Thomas Hanmer, of Hanmer Hall; Maud, the wife of Edward Lloyd ap David, of Powis; Margaret, of Henry Parry, of Basingwork, Esq.; and Catharine, of James Pickering, of Titchmarch, in the county of Northampton, Esq.

8, William Hanmer, of Fennes-Hall, Esq. married Ellen, daughter of Sir Thomas Hanmer, of Hanmer Hall, Knt. by Jane, daughter of Sir Randle Brereton, and had issue by her William, his eldest son and heir, and five younger sons, namely, Thomas, Humphrey, Griffith, Christopher, and Henry; and five daughters, 1, Ellen, the wife of Edward Winstanley; 2, Maud, of P. Davis, of Anglesey, Esq.; 3, Margaret, of Randle Brereton, of Kiddington, in the county of Chester, Esq.; 4, Eleanor, of John Griffith, and afterwards of Philip Oldfield, of Oldfield, in the county of Chester, Esq.; and 5, Catharine. William Hanmer died in the year 1570. The entry in the register, which records his burial, is accompanied by the following testimony of his merits: "William Hanmer, of Fennes Hall, Esq. justice of the peace, a right worshipful gentleman, the succour of his country, and the comfort of the poor." He was succeeded by his son,

* Barton he acquired by his marriage with Miss Folkes; the Mildenhall estate he inherited from his mother, the sister and heiress of Sir Henry North, Bart.

9, William Hanmer, who married Margaret, daughter and heiress of David Kynaston, of Crickett, in the county of Salop, Esq. and had issue three sons, William, Thomas, and John, and four daughters, 1, Mary, the wife of William Davis, of Willington, Esq.; 2, Jane, of Thomas Rode, of Rode; 3, Maud; and 4, Ellen. He died in 1589, and was succeeded by his eldest son,

10, Sir William Hanmer, who had the honour of knighthood conferred on him on the 23d of July, 1603, at Whitehall, by King James the First. He married Eleanor, daughter of Edward Dymock, of Willington, Esq. and had issue William, who, in 1621, died without issue, Thomas, and Humphrey, and one daughter Catharine. Sir William Hanmer died in 1621.

11, Thomas Hanmer succeeded to the estate of his father, and married Catharine, daughter of Thomas Puleston, of Emral, in the county of Flint, Esq. He died in the year 1625, and was succeeded by his son,

12, William Hanmer, who married first, Eleanor, daughter of Peter Warburton, of Warburton and Arley, in the county of Chester, Esq.: she died in the year 1649, and he married secondly, Mary, daughter and coheiress of Ralph Sneyd, of Keil, in the county of Stafford, Esq. During the great rebellion, he was an active royalist*, for which he afterwards smarted severely under the hands of the sequestrators; he was at length permitted to compound for his estate, upon paying the sum of 1370*l*. He died in the year 1669, and left issue by his first wife an only son, Thomas, and one daughter named Catharine.

13, Thomas Hanmer succeeded his father: he married Jane, daughter of Sir Job Charlton, of Ludford, in the county of Hereford, Bart. (son of Sir Job Charlton, the speaker of the House of Commons). He died in the year 1701, leaving issue two sons, William, and Job, hereafter mentioned, and one daughter Dorothy, wife of James Cornwall, of Berrington, in the county of Hereford, Esq. by whom she had Jacob Cornwall, Esq. the father of Charles Wolfran Cornwall, the late speaker of the House of Commons, and several other children †. He was succeeded by his eldest son, William Hanmer, of Fennes-hall, Esq. who married Esther, daughter of John Jennens, of Birmingham, in the county of Warwick, and also of Gopsal, in the county of Leicester, Esq. by whom he had three sons, Thomas, William, and Humphrey, and three daughters, Phælicia, the wife of Staunton Degge Clerk; Susanna ‡, of Reginald Pindar Lygon, of

* As was also his contemporary kinsman, Sir Thomas Hanmer, of Hanmer Hall, whose services in the royal cause recommended him to King Charles II. who, among other marks of royal favour, bestowed upon him an extensive grant of coal mine, which the family still possesses.

† One daughter, Emma, was the wife of Thomas Vernon, of Hanbury Hall, in the county of Worcester, Esq. whose daughter and heiress married the Honourable Mr. Cecil, afterwards Marquis of Exeter.

‡ The late William Jennens, of Acton Place, in the county of Suffolk, Esq. was first cousin to this Susanna. He was the only son of Robert Jennens, who was the younger son of John Jennens beforementioned, the great Warwickshire iron-master. His mother, whose maiden name was Guidart, was maid of honour to Queen Mary, and he had the honour of a royal sponsor in the person of King William. He died in the month of June, 1798, in the 97th year of his age. At the time of his death he was in possession of real estates to the amount of about 8,000*l*. per annum, and a personal estate of rather more than 800,000*l*. The old bureaus and drawers of his two houses at Acton and in Gros-

Maddersfield, in the county of Worcester, Esq. by whom she had one son, the present William Lygon, Esq. and a daughter, the wife of the Honourable Mr. John Yorke, and Mary, who died unmarried. William Hanmer, the father, died in the year 1724, and was succeeded by his eldest son Thomas Hanmer, who married Lady Catharine Percival, daughter of John, the first Earl of Egmont. He sat in parliament for the borough of Castle Rising, in the county of Norfolk, and dying without issue, was succeeded by his brother William Hanmer, who, in the year 1747, on the death of Sir Thomas Hanmer, by virtue of the settlement of 1733, became possessed also of the Hanmer Hall and Bettisfield estates. He married his cousin, Elizabeth Jennens, sister and heiress of the late Charles Jennens, of Gopsal, Esq. and had by her one daughter, Esther, the wife of Asheton Curzon, of Hagley, in the county of Stafford, Esq. afterwards Lord Viscount Curzon, by whom she had one son, the late Penn Asheton Curzon, Esq. and two daughters, Esther, the wife of Sir George-Smith Bromley, Bart. and Mary, the wife of Lord Viscount Stawell. William died without male issue, and was succeeded by his brother Humphrey Hanmer, Esq. He married Catharine Quartermain, an Irish lady, and dying in the year 1773, without issue, the estate, by virtue of the same settlement, descended to the issue of the before-mentioned,

14, Job Hanmer, Esq. one of the benchers of the Honourable Society of Lincoln's Inn. He married Susanna, the daughter and heiress of Thomas Walden, of Sympson-Place, in the county of Bucks, Esq. by whom he had issue one son, the late Sir Walden Hanmer, and two daughters, Cassandra, who died young, and Susanna, the wife of Ralph Leycester, of White Place, in the county of Berks, clerk*. Mr. Hanmer died in the year 1738.

I. WALDEN HANMER, Esq. the only son and heir of Job, and in descent the fifteenth from Sir John de Hanmer. He had all the advantages (the parent the credit) of a well regulated education: Eton School, and Baliol College, Oxon, formed part of its course. He became a student of Lincoln's Inn, where he was

venor Square, produced about 24,000*l*. When sinking under the feebleness of age, and when wealth was no longer another name for power, it was his good fortune to be attended by servants who appear to have been the faithful guardians of his person and also of his property; those, who by law are appointed to do the honours of the intestate, will, without doubt, perform that part of their duty which consists in making a suitable provision for those whose long and faithful services claim it. About a twelvemonth before his decease, Mr. Jennens instructed a person to prepare his will, and a will was accordingly prepared: it was found amongst his papers, with the usual seal affixed to it, but no signature. The history of this instrument, as far as it respects the great mass of Mr. Jennens' fortune, excites some curiosity, but we spare our observations: beyond this it merely directs the payment of several (comparatively) small legacies, some to acknowledge the claims of friendship and kindred, others to hospitals and servants. Let it suffice to say, the party at whose desire it was drawn up, notwithstanding impaired sight, was able (*having found his spectacles*) to read it, and therefore he did not choose to proceed further in its execution. The Right Honourable Dowager Lady Andover (descended from another daughter of John Jennens), and the above-mentioned William Lygon, Esq. have obtained administration of his immensely large personal estate; and the Honourable Mr. Curzon, the infant son of the late Penn Asheton Curzon, Esq. succeeded to his real estate as heir at law: the two last claim their respective rights through branches of the family we are treating of; we notice, in their proper places, their connections with it.

* His father was a younger brother of Mr. Leycester, of Toft, in the county of Chester.

called to the bar about the year 1745*. At an early period of his practice, he retired from his profession, when there was a fair expectation of his making no inconsiderable figure in it: with qualities to render him useful in society, his life was not without exertion. On retiring from the bar, he took upon himself the duties of the magistrate in the several counties with which he was connected; in that capacity he was cool, vigilant, and discriminative; and the same sense of honour that influenced his private life, accompanied the discharge of the humble, though useful duties of the country magistrate. He sat for two parliaments as burgess for the borough of Sudbury, in the county of Suffolk. Upon the death of Humphrey, his cousin-german, he succeeded to the family estate; and, upon the 3d day of May, 1774, was, by his present Majesty, created a Baronet of Great Britain. He married Anne, the youngest daughter and one of the coheiresses of Henry-Vere Graham, of Holbrook Hall, in the county of Suffolk, Esq. †, and had by her five sons; 1, Thomas, the present Baronet; 2, Job Hanmer, of Holbrook Hall, Esq. the *hæres factus* of his mother's estate. He married Maria, daughter of John Syer, of Lavenham, in the county of Suffolk, Esq. and has issue two sons and one daughter; 3, the Rev. Graham Hanmer, A. M. rector of St. Bartholomew Exchange, in the city of London, and of Sympson, in the county of Bucks, and vicar of Hanmer. He married Elizabeth, daughter of John Child, of Waldingfield parva, in the county of Suffolk, clerk, and has issue three sons and four daughters; 4, Edward Hanmer, barrister-at-law, of Stockgrove, in the county of Bucks. He married Arabella, daughter of Thomas Pennant, of Downing, in the county of Flint, Esq.; and 5, Walden-Henry Hanmer, one of the six clerks in the court of chancery: and one daughter, Anne-Eleanora Hanmer, the wife of the Reverend George Turnor, second son of Edmond Turnor, of Panton-House, in the county of Lincoln, Esq. and has issue one daughter. Lady Hanmer died in the year 1778, and Sir Walden in 1783, in the 66th year of his age‡. He was succeeded by his eldest son and heir,

II. Sir THOMAS HANMER, the present Baronet. He married Margaret, eldest daughter and coheiress of George Kenyon, of Peel, in the county of Lancaster, Esq. cousin-german to the Right Honourable Lloyd, Lord Kenyon, the late lord chief justice of the Court of King's Bench, and has issue by her, Thomas, born in the year 1781, Job-Walden, in 1782, John, in 1784, George-Edward, in 1786, Henry, in 1789, and William, in 1792: and one daughter Margaret, in 1785, married, in 1803, to the present Lord Kenyon.

* He served the office of treasurer in 1774, and, at the time of his death, was the senior bencher of the society.

† She had two sisters, Catharine, the wife of Langhorn Warren, of Great Bromley, in the county of Essex, clerk, by whom he had several children; and Eleanor, the wife of Sir William Bunbury before-mentioned, by whom she had the present Sir Charles Bunbury, and several other children. Mr. Graham's possession of Holbrook Hall was in right of his wife Catharine, the eldest daughter, and ultimately the heiress of Samuel Warner, of that place, Esq.

‡ They were buried in the chancel of the church at Sympson, where a handsome marble monument is erected to their memory.

TABLE.

GWYN-WIN-WIN, Lord of Upper Powis

Griffith

Gwillim

Enion

1, Sir John de Hanmer, Knt.=Hawis
temp. Edw. I.

Owen, O. S. P. — David, O. S. P. — 2, Philip=Agnes ap David ap Rired ap Rees Says

3, Sir David Hanmer=Agnes ap Llewellyn — Jenkin Hanmer — Margaret — Myranwy

Margaret, dr of David, of Blethen Vychan=4, Sir Jenkin Hanmer, Knt.=Eve, dr of David ap Grono ap Jerworth — Margaret=Owen Glendowr

Hanmers, of Hanmer Hall — J. Hanmer, of Haghlton and Llai — 5, Edward Hanmer, of Fennes Hall, Esq.=Maurice ap Jevan — R. Hanmer, of Bettisfield

6, Griffith Hanmer, ob. 1501=Margaret ap Meredith Lloyd — Philip

7, Jenkin=Margaret Dymock — Laurence, Edward, William — David, Matthew — Elizabeth, Rose — Margaret, Blanch

8, William, ob. 1570=Ellen Hanmer, of Hanmer Hall — Ellen — Margaret — Catharine

9, William, ob. 1589=Marg. Kynaston — Thomas, Humphry, Griffith — Christopher, Henry — Ellen, Maud, Margaret — Eleanor, Catharine

10, Sir William, ob. 1621=Eleanor Dymock — Thomas, John — Mary, Jane — Maud, Ellen

William Hanmer, O. S. P. — 11, Thomas, ob. 1625=Cath. Puleston — Humphrey — Catharine

Mary Sneyd=12, William=Eleanor Warburton

13, Thomas, 1701=Jane Charlton — Catharine

(a) *Next page.*

TABLE *continued.*

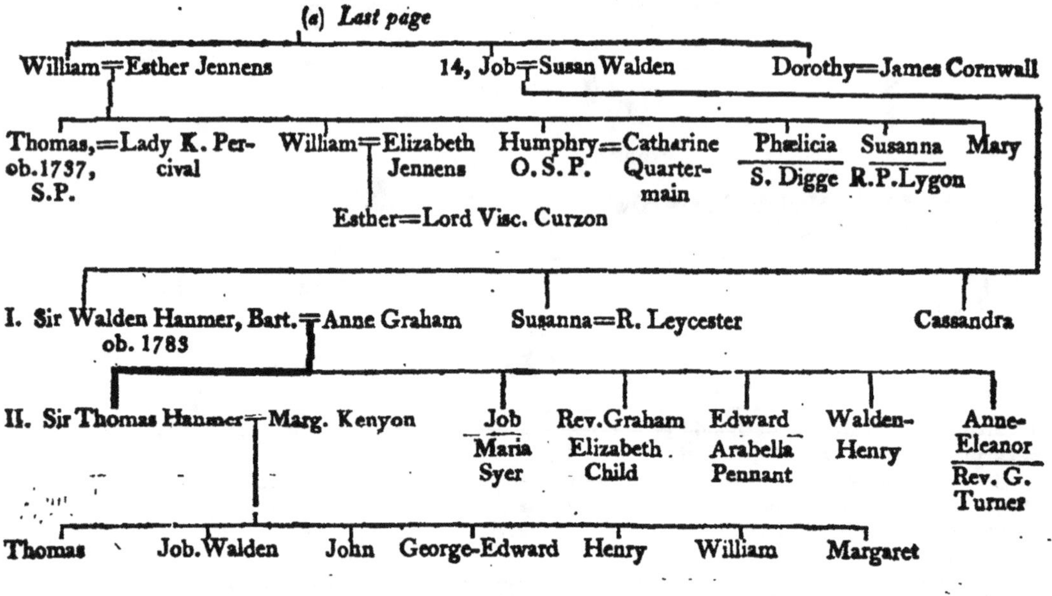

ARMS—Argent, two lions, passant guardant, azure, armed and langued, gules.

CREST—On a cap of dignity, azure, turned up ermine, a lion guardant, sejant, argent.

MOTTO—*Gard l'honneur.*

SEATS—Bettisfield Park and Hanmer Hall, Flintshire, and Sympson Place, Bucks.

---

309. LEMON, of CARCLEW, Cornwall.

Created Baronet, May 3, 1774.

1, WILLIAM LEMON, of Carclew, in Cornwall, Esq. well known in that county for his extensive mining and commercial concerns, who served the office of high-sheriff for that county, was the grandfather of the present Baronet. He married Isabella Vibert, of a family formerly of some note in the west of Cornwall, but I believe at present extinct. His son,

2, William Lemon, Esq. married Anne, daughter of John Willyams, of Carnanton, in the county of Cornwall, Esq. (by Anne, only daughter of John Oliver, of Falmouth, Esq.) by whom he had two sons and two daughters, 1, Sir William; 2, ——, a daughter, who died young; 3, Anne, wife of John Buller, of Morval, in the county of Cornwall, Esq.; 4, John, formerly a lieutenant-colonel in the horse-guards, at present colonel of the Cornwall and Devon miners. He was formerly in parliament for West Loo and Saltash, but in the last and present for Truro.

I. WILLIAM LEMON, Esq. born in 1748, was created a Baronet of Great Britain, May 3, 1774. He served in parliament for Penrhyn, from Dec. 1769 to 1774; and, at the general election in 1774, he was returned for the county of Cornwall, which he has represented ever since. He married Jane, eldest daughter of James Buller, of Morval, in Cornwall, Esq. and of Jane, his wife, daughter of Allen, first Earl Bathurst, by whom he had, 1, Anne, wife, Sept. 6, 1796, of Sir John Davie, of Creedy, Bart. by whom she has four children, John and William, twins, born March 8, 1798, Anne-Jane, born in London, June 19, 1800, and Frances-Juliana, born 1802; 2, Maria; 3, William, born 1774, died March, 1799; 4, Louisa, married, in 1802, to Colonel Dyke, of the Guards, third son of Sir John Dyke, of Lullingston Castle, Kent; 5, Harriet; 6, John, born 1779, died young; 7, Emma; 8, Frances; 9, Isabella-Jane; 10, Charles, born 1784; 11, Tryphena-Octavia, died young; and 12, Caroline-Matilda.

ARMS—Argent, on a cheveron, between three mullets, gules, an eagle displayed, or.

CREST—On a wreath of the colours, a lion passant, gules, the body charged with three mullets in fess, or.

SEAT—Carclew, in Cornwall.

TABLE.

JOHN OLIVER

WILLIAM LEMON=ISABELLA VIBERT   JOHN WILLYAMS=ANNE

William Lemon=Anne Willyams

I. Sir William=Jane Buller   Anne=John Buller   John

William, b. 1774, d. 1799 | John, b. 1779, d y | Charles, born 1784 | Anne = Sir J. Davie | Maria | Louisa = Colonel Dyke | Harriet, Emma, Frances | I. Jane, T. Octavia, d y | Caroline-Matilda

John   William   Anne-Jane   Frances-Juliana

310. BLAKE, of Twisel Castle, in the northern district of the County Palatine of Durham.

Created Baronet, May 3, 1774.

THIS family is of British extraction, and traditionally descended from Ap Lake, whose name appears as one of the Knights of King Arthur's Round Table.

Succeeding generations seem to have paid little attention to the orthography of the name, so variously do we find it written. In the first instance, by dropping the initial letter, it was rendered P'Lake, and then, by compression, Plake, one entire word, both of which alike producing a sound and utterance uncouth and inharmonious, it was corrupted into Blague, to the confusion of all etymological explanation, had it so continued; but chance or design applied a remedy, by substituting Blaake, and ultimately Blake, which latter reading took place many centuries back, and has continued invariably the same from that period to the present day.

In the reign of Henry the Second, and in the chivalry of those times, one of this family, an high-spirited adventurous youth, among others of the like temperament, from whom many of the most considerable Irish families date their origin, quitting his native soil, volunteered his services, and followed the fortunes of that celebrated chieftain Richard de Clare, Earl of Pembroke, surnamed Strongbow, whom he accompanied in his memorably successful expedition to Ireland, and from which country he never returned; but after various military exploits and public services, seated himself, in honourable and well-earned repose, at Menlaw, in the county of Galway, where he built himself a castle, and where his posterity in a right line have continued to flourish ever since: and whose collateral descendants branching off at various periods, established in the same county the respective families of Ardfry, Mulloughmore, and Drum. The advancements of this family are as follows:

In the year 1622, Walter Blake, of Menlaw Castle, Esq. was created a Baronet.

In the year 1772, Patrick Blake, of Langham, in the county of Suffolk, Esq. of Irish extraction, and proprietor of large West India property, was created a Baronet by patent dated Sept. 19.

In the year 1800, Joseph-Henry Blake, Esq. afterwards Lord Wallscourt, son of the present representative of the Ardfry family, in consideration of the zeal and loyalty displayed by him during the late rebellion, was raised to the peerage of Ireland by patent.

Such was the rise and growth of the Blakes of Ireland; and, as the accidental meeting of old friends after long separation, has always been deemed a circumstance of peculiar delight, so, in like manner, but in a much greater degree, was the satisfaction which attended the revival of a long-lost intercourse between two families, originally one and the same, but for ages kept separate, that took place by the marriage of Robert Blake, Esq. a native of Ireland, lineally descended from the first of the name in that kingdom, with Sarah, third daughter of Sir Francis Blake, of Ford Castle, in the county of Northumberland, Knt. by which marriage he was not only possessed of the castle and appurtenant lands of Twisel, but also became the happy instrument of bringing the English and Irish Blakes, after an interval of many centuries, again into compact; in consequence of which, a patent of arms was granted by his present Majesty to the late Sir Francis, son of that marriage, whereby, to illustrate and uphold in perpetual remembrance that singularly fortunate family occurrence.

Sir Francis Blake, of Ford Castle, father of Sarah, the wife of Robert abovementioned, was lineally descended from the original English stock of that name, anciently seated at Calne*, in the county of Wilts, afterwards of Easton Town, alias Essington, in the county of Hants. He married Elizabeth, daughter and coheiress of William Carr, of Ford Castle aforesaid, Esq. and by that marriage became proprietor of the said castle and appurtenant lands of Ford. He served in two parliaments for the borough of Berwick-upon-Tweed, and would probably have retained his seat for life; but aspiring to the representation of the county of Northumberland, he gave offence to his old constituents, and in the double pursuit failed in both. He was knighted by King William, of whom he was a most zealous supporter, and in whose confidence he stood high. He was much about the king's person, though in no office under him, and on all occasions was received and entertained by him as a friend. Higher honours than had been conferred were in his offer, but having no male issue, and having already secured by his loyal attachment, and other good qualities, the esteem of his sovereign; finding, besides, that respect, the tribute paid to his merit, spontaneously flowing, every where attended him, and that no titles in the predicament in which he stood, without other inducement to accept than the mere gratification of personal vanity, could add to his consequence, but, subject to such construction, might probably lessen him in the opinion of the world, he judiciously declined them.

Francis, the father of Sir Francis last above-named, was anciently of the Fine Office, and at that time an inhabitant of the village of Highgate, where he died, and lies buried. He was a man distinguished, through the course of a very long life, by many excellent qualities, and, among others, by superior intellect, by spotless integrity, by an indefatigable attention to business, by an unwearied delight in doing good, and, to crown the whole, by piety the most sincere and exemplary.

Sir Richard Blake, of Clerkenwell, in the county of Middlesex, Knt. to whose memory a monument is erected in the Savoy Chapel, with an inscription, relating

* In the chancel of the parish church is a fair monument in memory of Roger, son and heir of Robert Blake, of Calne aforesaid, Esq.

principally to his genealogical descent, was younger brother to Francis, of Highgate.

But of all the eminent men of this family, or indeed of any other family or clime, Admiral Blake, so renowned in our annals, stands most prominently forward. The *amor patriæ*, so rarely felt, so little heard of in these degenerate times, was his ruling passion, his whole soul was absorbed in it: compared with that consideration, every other earthly concern was to him but as chaff. Neither self-interest, nor family advantages, nor even his own advancement, otherwise than feeling, as doubtless he must have felt, that the energies which he possessed would enable him effectually to serve the state;—none of these, nor any thing of the kind by which the generality of men are swayed, were ever allowed for an instant to draw off his thoughts from his darling object. With that in view, toil was to him divertisement, perils were pastime, danger was delight, life had no charms, death had no terrors, when any way standing in competition with the good of his country. The whole tenour of his conduct, and every incident of his life, confirms this report. For instance: no sooner was the voice of his country heard in distress, than losing sight of all those comforts that attach to a private independent station, to the full enjoyment of which the patrimony to which he had succeeded was abundantly ample; no sooner, I say, did the plaints of his country reach his ear, than regardless of self, he hastened to her relief, and performed in her service such exploits, gave such specimens of noble daring, such proofs of dauntless courage, of stedfast resolve, contempt of danger, and presence of mind in all extremities, as faith itself could not have credited, had there remained one particle of doubt respecting the authenticity of the facts that have been handed down to us. Next in evidence follow these particulars: His declaration on the death of the king, which he deemed disgraceful to the nation—his exhortation to his officers, when Cromwell usurped the government—the removal of his own brother from a lucrative place of trust of his own appointment, for incapacity to serve the public—and lastly, his unexampled magnanimity in pouring into the public coffers the pecuniary fruits of all his victories, without the reserve of a doit to himself, for he did not die five hundred pounds richer than when he started in life,—those and various other traits which might be adduced, must necessarily bring home to the conviction of the most incredulous what has here been averred, that *his soul was absorbed in the love of his country*. He died on his own element, Aug. 17, 1657, and in the 59th year of his age, *unmarried*, which some may lament; but all must acknowlege, he did not stand in need of issue either to perpetuate his name, or record his renown, neither of which will be forgotten till time shall be no more. His funeral obsequies, and the honours that were paid to his remains, did credit to his employer, and to the nation at large, but the removal of his body afterwards was of a contrary description: he fought for his country, and his country's gratitude was impeached by that impotent attempt to debase his memory.

Robert above-mentioned, of Twisel Castle, had issue by Sarah, his said wife, three daughters, 1, Eleanor, wife of Alexander Collingwood, of Unthank, in the county of Northumberland, and had issue; 2, Anne, wife of William Stowe, of the town of Berwick-upon-Tweed, and had issue; 3, Elizabeth, wife of Stanwix Nevinson, of Newby Stones, in the county of Westmoreland, Esq. and had no issue: and one son Francis, who married Isabel *, second daughter and coheiress of Samuel Ayton, of West Herrington, in the county palatine of Durham, Esq. by whom he had issue, 1, Robert, a youth of extraordinary promise and expectation, but prematurely cut off in the twenty-first year of his age, Jan. 25, 1754. His remains were deposited in the south cloister of Westminster Abbey, where a monument is in preparation to be erected to his memory; and 2, Sarah, wife of Christopher Reed, of Chipchase Castle, in the county of Northumberland, Esq. and had issue, 3, Isabella, who died unmarried; 4, Francis; 5, William; 6, Eleanor; and 7, Anne; the three last died infants.

I. FRANCIS, the present Baronet, married Elizabeth, only surviving daughter of Alexander Douglas, Esq. †, late chief of the English settlement at Bussorah, in Persia, by Elizabeth, his wife, a native of that country, by whom he had issue, 1, Elizabeth; 2, Francis, colonel of the late north fencible regiment of infantry, to the command of which he was appointed by designment of his father in the application he made to government, in which station he acquitted himself, like many beside, much to his credit, both as a soldier and a gentleman, but otherwise like very few, greatly to the detriment of his private fortune; 3, Robert-Dudley, colonel in the army; 4, Isabella; 5, Sarah; 6, William; and 7, Eleanor-Ann. Sarah died an infant; all the others are living, and unmarried.

Sir Francis Blake, late of Twisel Castle, father of the present Baronet, inheriting the spirit and patriotism of his ancestors, took a very active part in support of government during the rebellion which broke out in the year 1745. But literature was his great delight, to which he was unremittingly addicted through life, devoting his time and attention principally to mathematics and philosophy, on which subjects he left behind him in the hands of the public many valuable specimens of his skill and knowledge. He died March 30, 1780, aged 72, and his remains were deposited in the parish church of Haughton-le-Spring, beside those of his dear wife, agreeable to his own request, where a monument is in forwardness to be erected to his memory.

ARMS—Argent, a cheveron between three garbs, sable, in a canton azure, a fret d'or.

CREST—A martlet argent, charged in the breast with a fret, gules.

SEATS—Twisel Castle, Durham, and Fowberry Tower, Northumberland.

* To whose memory a monument is erected in the parish church of Houghton-le-Spring, in the county palatine of Durham.

† Alexander, the father of the present Lady Blake, of the ancient family of Douglas, of Edrington Castle, in the shire of Berwick, North Britain, died on his passage home, leaving two daughters, Elizabeth and Sarah (the latter died an infant), coheiresses of his fortune under the guardianship of George Dudley, Esq. late of Hart-street, Bloomsbury-square, many years a director of the East India Company, and chairman of that company.

In grateful remembrance of whose parental care of his ward, in memory of his most exemplary discharge of the trust reposed in him, and in testimony of the high estimation in which his honoured name is held, the baptismal name of Dudley, in addition to Robert, was given by his parents to their second son.

TABLE.

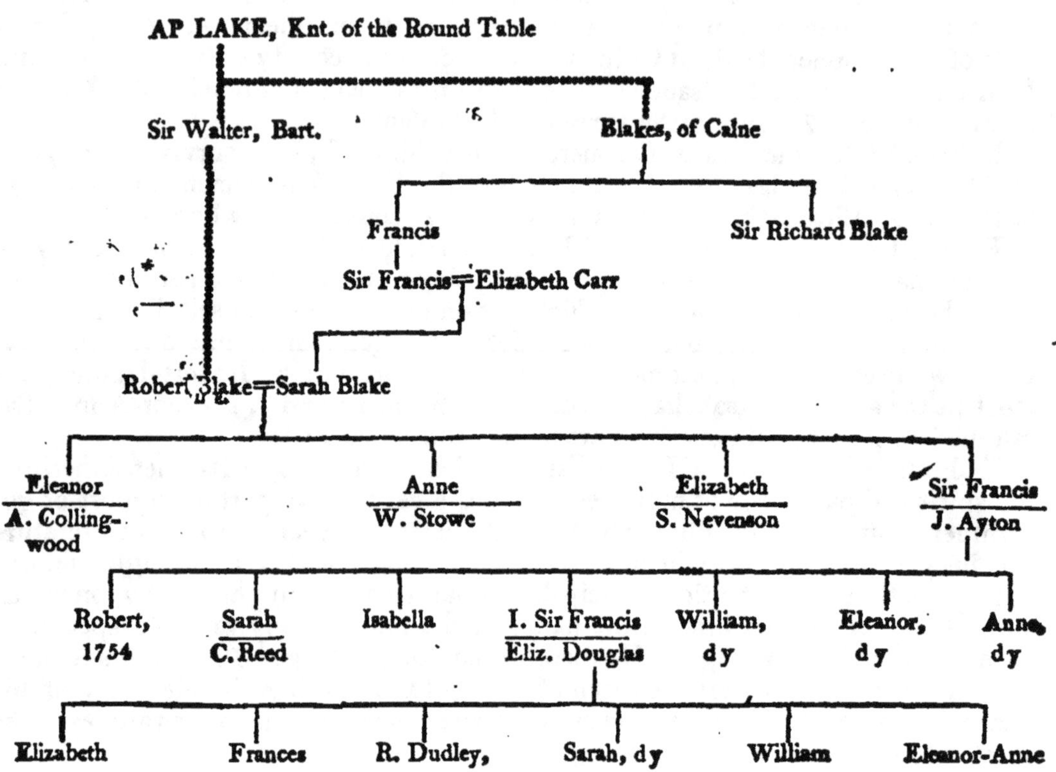
AP LAKE, Knt. of the Round Table
Sir Walter, Bart.
Blakes, of Calne
Francis
Sir Richard Blake
Sir Francis=Elizabeth Carr
Robert Blake=Sarah Blake
Eleanor
A. Colling-wood
Anne
W. Stowe
Elizabeth
S. Nevenson
Sir Francis
J. Ayton
Robert, 1754
Sarah
C. Reed
Isabella
I. Sir Francis
Eliz. Douglas
William, dy
Eleanor, dy
Anne, dy
Elizabeth
Frances
R. Dudley,
Sarah, dy
William
Eleanor-Anne

311. FOLKES, of HILLINGTON, Norfolk.

Created Baronet, May 3, 1774.

1, MARTIN FOLKES, Esq. was a barrister-at-law, and afterwards attorney-general in the reign of Queen Anne. He had a son,

2, Martin Folkes, Esq. whose son,

3, Martin Folkes, Esq. of Rushbrook, in Suffolk, barrister-at-law, married Dorothy, second daughter and coheiress of Sir William Hovell, of Hillington, Knt. (and became possessed of one-third part of the Hovell estate *), by whom he had three sons and one daughter; 1, Martin, who married —— and

* The family of Hovell is of great antiquity. Richard Hovell held of Baldwin, abbot of Bury, in the time of the Conqueror, a lordship at Wigvereston, in Suffolk; and five freemen held lands under the said Richard.

Sir John Hovell, of Wratting Parva, in Suffolk, was living in 1370.

William Hovell, of Rishangles, in Suffolk, died 1433, and by Beatrix, his wife, daughter of Sir John Thorp, of Ashwell-Thorp, was father of Richard Hovell, who married Frances, daughter of Arthur Hopton, Esq. of Westwood, in Suffolk, widow of Sir Thomas Nevile, and left William, his son and heir, of Ashfield, in Suffolk, who died July 7, 1534. By Elizabeth, his wife, daughter of Rowland Harsike, of Lopham, Esq. he was father of William Hovell, of Ashfield, who married Anne, daughter of Thomas Gaway, of Harleston, Esq. and Ann Basingborn, his wife, by whom he had a son William, of Stratfield Hall, in Hadleigh, Suffolk, who married Anne, daughter of Richard Turner, of Norton.

The church is a single pile; that, and the chancel, are covered with tile, and has a square tower with one bell.

On the north wall of the chancel is a mural monument, with the effigies of a gentleman in his gown, and his wife, on their knees, thus inscribed:

> The monument of Richard Hovell, of Hillington, in the countie of Norfolk, Esq. being of the age of 77 years and upwards, finished his course the 30th of November, 1611, in peace with God, in charity with all men, and now resteth here with expectation of the resurrection, in assurance of eternal glorification. Margery Hovel, wife of the aforesaid Richard Hovell, Esq. deceased, and one of the daughters and heyres of John Ford, of Frating, in the countie of Essex, Esq. who having lyved vertuously and comfortably with her said husband 44 years, did beare unto him 4 sonnes and 9 daughters, whereof there are yet 12 alive to her great comfort, being all grown to the perfect state of men and women.

On the summit is the shield of Hovell, sable, a crescent, or, impaling Ford, argent, a wolf salient, sable.

On another mural monument are the effigies of a man in armour, and his wife, kneeling at a desk, with the arms of Hovell and Ford quarterly, impaling, or, on a bend, vert, three bucks heads caboshed, argent, Fernley.

At the north-east corner of the chancel is an altar tomb of marble, and iron rails before it, with the arms of Folkes: vert, a flower de lys, and Hovell, in an escutcheon of pretence; the crest, an arm erect, holding a spear.

> Here lyes the body of Martin Folkes, late of Hillington, in the county of Norfolk, Esq. who was born the 28th day of August, 1640, and died the 17th day of February, 1705.

had one son Martin, who died young, and two daughters; Dorothy, wife of William Rishton, Esq. who left a son, Martin-Folkes-William, who married Mary, daughter of Stephen Allen, Esq. of King's Lynn, in Norfolk, and two daughters; Lucretia, wife, first, of —— Phippen, Esq. by whom she had no issue; and secondly, of Chaffin Edgell, Esq. by whom she has several children; Dorothy, wife, first, of Samuel Jesse, and secondly, of —— Church, Esq. but has no issue by either; Lucretia, second daughter of Martin Folkes, was wife of Sir Wm. Bettenson, Bart.; 2, William, of whom hereafter; and 3, Henry, who married ——, daughter of ——, by whom he had one son Henry, who died S. P. and one daughter Lucretia-Elizabeth, wife of Griffith Phillips, Esq. by whom she had two sons and two daughters, John-George, who married and has issue, Herbert, who died S. P. Dorothy, wife of Francis Plowden, Esq. barrister-at-law, by whom she has issue; and Elizabeth, wife of —— Harris, Esq. by whom she has issue.

The daughter of Martin Folkes and Dorothy Hovell was, Elizabeth, wife of Thomas Payne, Esq. by whom she has two daughters; 1, Elizabeth, wife of Henry Vernon, of Thurlow, in Suffolk, Esq.; and 2, Etheldreda, of Sir John Cust, Bart. speaker of the House of Commons, by whom she had one son Brownlow, many years member of parliament for Grantham, in Lincolnshire, and since created a peer, by the title of Lord Brownlow, of Belton, in Lincolnshire. He married first, Jocosa-Catharine, daughter of Sir Thomas Drury, Bart. of Overston, in Northamptonshire, by whom he had a daughter, who died young. He married

On a grave stone:

Lillius Hovell, filius Guli. Hovell, militis, et uxoris ejus, Etheldredae, obt. 3 die Maij. Ao. Domi. 1664, ætatis suæ die 24to.

Thomas, the second son of Sir Will. Hovell, knight, and Dame Etheldreda, his wife, born the last day of Febr. 1667, and died the 14th day of October, 1668.

Hic jacet corpus Gulielmi Hovell, militis, qui obt. 4 die Martii 1669, ætatis suæ 33; and the arms of Hovell.

William Posthumus, the younger son of Sir William Hovell, Knight, and Dame Etheldreda, his wife, born the 8th day of August, 1670, and dyed the 12th day of April, 1671.

Maria, conjux Johis. Novell, rectoris hujus ecclesiæ, obt. Nov. 28, 1706.

Richard Hovell, Esq. son to Sir Richard Hovell, of Hillington, died Oct. 23, 1715, aged 70.

To this church belonged two rectors, each having a mediety: the one was called the patronage of Ralph Cynezy, the other that of John Blome, each valued at eight marks, and paid peter-pence, 6d. the one was in the patronage of that lordship, which Berner held at the conquest; the other is that which was held by Eudo, son of Spiruwin.

Sir William Hovell, by his Lady Etheldreda Lilly, had three daughters, his coheiresses, Clementina, Dorothy, and Etheldreda. Clementina was wife, first, of Charles Stuart, Esq. father of Sir Simeon Stuart, Bart.; and secondly, of Sir T. Montgomery; by the latter she had a son Captain Montgomery, who died S. P. and a daughter ———, wife of —— Colclough, Esq. by whom she had a daughter Louisa-Maria-Elizabeth, wife, first, of the Rev. Mr. Merrick, and secondly, of Sir James Johnstone, Bart. who dying without issue, left her moiety of the Hovell estate to Sir Martin-Browne Folkes. Dorothy, the second daughter, being wife of Martin Folkes, Esq. grandfather of Sir Martin-Browne, brought another moiety into this family; and Sir Martin's father purchasing from the Wake family, who had married the other coheiress Etheldreda, Sir Martin is now in possession of the whole estate.

secondly, Frances, daughter of Sir Henry Banks, of Wimbledon, in Surry, Bart. by whom he has a large family. Sir John Cust had also two daughters; 1, Anne, wife of Jacob Reynardson, of Holywell, in Lincolnshire, Esq. by whom she has four daughters; and 2, Elizabeth, of Simon Yorke, Esq. of Erthiggin, in Denbighshire, and has several children.

4, William Folkes, Esq. second son of Martin Folkes, married first, Ursula, daughter of Samuel Taylor, Esq. of King's Lynn, in the county of Norfolk, by whom he had four daughters; 1, Ursula, wife of John Macbride, Esq. an admiral in the British navy, by whom he has Mary-Anne and John-David; 2, Dorothy, wife of Edmund Rolfe, of Heacham, in the county of Norfolk, by whom he has two children, Dorothy-Mary and Edmund; 3, Mary, wife of John Balchen West, Esq. of Woodcock Lodge, in the county of Herts, by whom he has seven children; Thomas, a captain in the army, Henry, a captain in the navy, Maria, Gilbert-Hervey, Edward, Fanny, and Martin-John; 4, Elizabeth, wife of Maximilian Western, Esq. of Cokethorpe, in the county of Norfolk, by whom he has three children, Elizabeth, Maximilian, and Frances. He married secondly, Mary, the only daughter of Sir William Browne, of King's Lynn, in the county of Norfolk, Knt. M. D. by whom he had one son,

I. Sir MARTIN-BROWNE FOLKES, who was created a Baronet May 3, 1774, and married (Dec. 28, 1775) Fanny, daughter and coheiress of Sir John Turner, of Warham, in the county of Norfolk, Bart. by whom he had; 1, Martin-William-Browne, who died S. P. 1798, aged about twenty years; 2, Fanny-Mary; 3, Anna-Martina; 4, William; 5, Henry; 6, Caroline, which three last died young; 7, William-John-Henry; and 8, Lucretia-Georgiana.

ARMS—Quarterly: 1st and 4th, per pale, vert and gules, a fleur-de-lis, argent; 2d and 3d, gules, a cheveron, between three lion's gambs erased and erect, all within a border, argent, on a chief of the last, an eagle displayed, sable.

CREST—A dexter arm embowed, habited per pale vert and gules, cuffed ermine, holding in the hand, proper, a spear, of the last.

MOTTO—*Qui sera sera—Principiis obsta.*

SEAT—At Hillington, Norfolk.

It is somewhat remarkable, that the property divided between the three daughters of Sir William Hovell should now all again centre in the present Baronet.

TABLE.

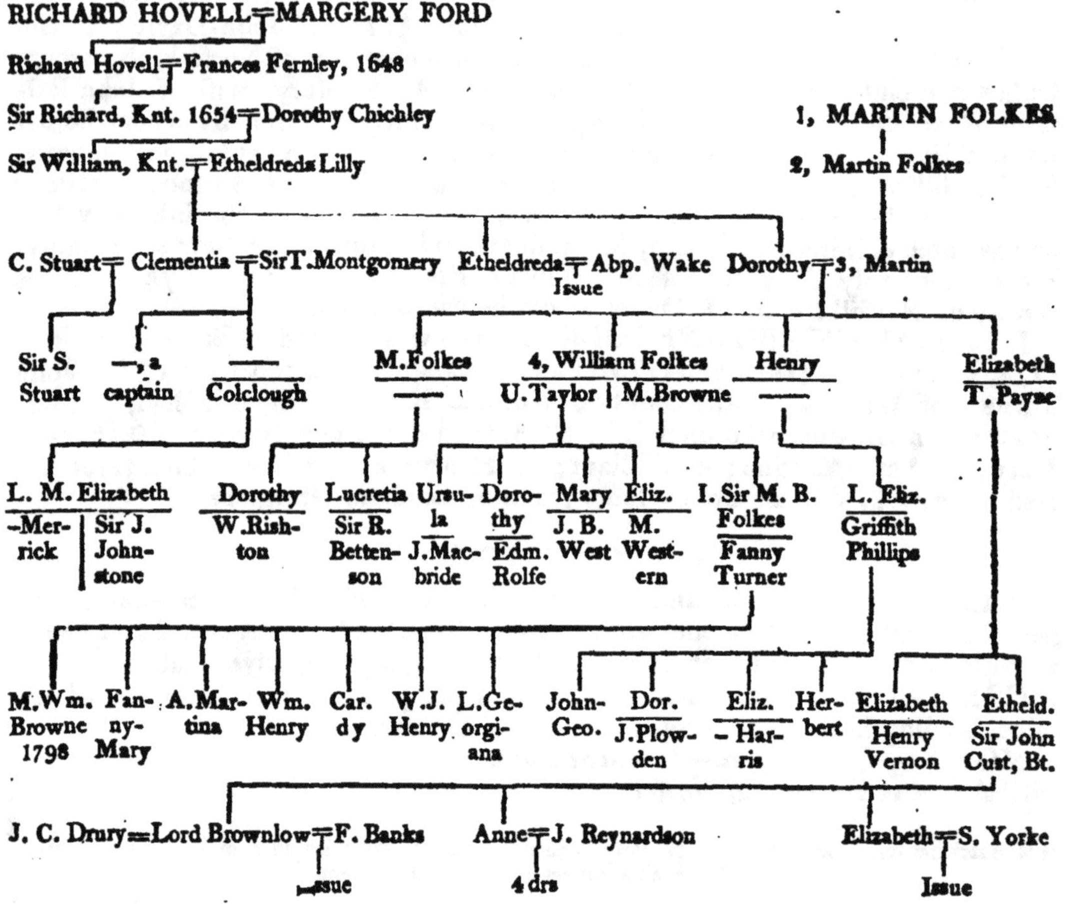
RICHARD HOVELL=MARGERY FORD
Richard Hovell=Frances Fernley, 1648
Sir Richard, Knt. 1654=Dorothy Chichley
Sir William, Knt.=Etheldreda Lilly
1, MARTIN FOLKES
2, Martin Folkes
C. Stuart= Clementia =Sir T. Montgomery
Etheldreda=Abp. Wake
Issue
Dorothy=3, Martin
Sir S. Stuart
—, a captain
— Colclough
M. Folkes
—
4, William Folkes
U. Taylor | M. Browne
Henry
—
Elizabeth
T. Payne
L. M. Elizabeth
-Merrick
Sir J. Johnstone
Dorothy
W. Rishton
Lucretia
Sir R. Bettenson
Ursula
J. Macbride
Dorothy
Edm. Rolfe
Mary
J. B. West
Eliz.
M. Western
I. Sir M. B. Folkes
Fanny Turner
L. Eliz.
Griffith Phillips
M. Wm. Browne 1798
Fanny-Mary
A. Martina
Wm. Henry
Card y
W. J. Henry
L. Georgiana
John-Geo.
Dor.
J. Plowden
Eliz.
- Harris
Herbert
Elizabeth
Henry Vernon
Etheld.
Sir John Cust, Bt.
J. C. Drury=Lord Brownlow=F. Banks
Issue
Anne=J. Reynardson
4 drs
Elizabeth=S. Yorke
Issue

312. GIBBES, of SPRING HEAD, in the Island of Barbadoes.

Created Baronet, May 30, 1774.

IT has been a constant tradition in this family, that its ancestor was among the attendants or followers of William the Conqueror into England. The presumption of its original settlement in Britany or Normandy, is confirmed by the evidence of different French authors. According to Morerj (Dict. tom. 3, p. 986), Robert de Guibe, son of Adonet de Guibe, a gentleman of Britany, was appointed to the bishopric of Treguen in 1483; translated to that of Rennes in 1502, and thence to the archiepiscopal see of Nantes in 1506. Louis XII. sent him as ambassador to Rome, where he was raised to the cardinalate by Pope Julius II. and died in 1513. The transition of the spelling of the surname from *Guibe* to *Gib*, *Gibe*, and *Gibbe*, may be accounted for by the difference between the English and the French pronunciation; and, in its subsequent mutation to *Gibbs* and *Gibbes* (the several variations appearing among the records of the Herald's College), it shared the same fate with the surnames of all the most ancient families of the kingdom.

An ancient paper, long in the possession of the family of Jenking Gibbes, sometime resident at Folkstone, in the county of Kent, confirms the opinion of the antiquity of this family. It states, "that George Gibbes, one of his ancestors, went into Gloucestershire, and married the daughter and heiress of — Purland, of Purland, Esq. bearing, for their coat-armour, *argent, on a bend, sable, three martlets of the first, between six mullets of the second.* But, upon the application of William Gibbes (great-grandson of the above Jenking Gibbes, who was descended from the family of Gibbes, of Devonshire) to the College of Arms, in the year 1574, Robert Cook, alias Clarencieux king of arms, did, on the first day of February, in that year, grant and confirm to the said William Gibbes the arms which had descended to him from his ancestors, viz. *quarterly*, in the first, for GIBBES, *silver, three Danish axes, sable:* in the second, for CHAMPNI, *two fusells, gules.* And inasmuch as there was no Crest or cognizance to the said arms, as commonly to such ancient arms there belongeth none, the said Clarencieux king of arms, did assign, give, and grant to these his ancient arms, the Crest hereafter following, viz. *Upon the helmet, a wreath, silver and sable, thereon an armed arm, sable, purfled gold, holding a battle axe, mantled, doubled, silver.*"

Various branches of this family were settled in the counties of Devon, Somerset, Warwick, and Kent.

In Sir William Pole's Collections towards the History of Devonshire, he observes, that John Gibbe was possessed of the lands of Fenton, in that county, in the year 1377. His grandson John, who married ——, the daughter of William May, wrote his name Gibbes. Their son Thomas, who married Anne, the daughter of Sir William Courtney, of Powderham, in Devonshire, Knt. reassumed the former spelling of Gibbe. But William, the only son and heir of Thomas, subscribed himself Gibbes. These instances are adduced in support of the opinion, that the several branches of this family, although dispersed over different parts of the kingdom, are undoubtedly descended from a family which existed in Britany or Normandy before the conquest of England.

That branch which was established in the county of Kent, was invariably designated Gibbes, from Jenking Gibbes above-named, down to Robert Gibbes, who first settled in Barbadoes, and went from thence as governor of South Carolina. He was the son of Stephen Gibbes, of Edmondstone Court, in Kent.

The branch of Sir Henry Gibbes, of Honington, in Warwickshire, spelt the name like the family established in Kent, as appears by Dugdale's Antiquities of the former county.

Among the descendants of a branch long seated at Bedminster, near Bristol, was James-Alban Gibbes, son of William Gibbes, of that city: he was appointed lecturer on rhetorick at Rome, by Pope Alexander VII. in the School of Sapientia. Leopold, Emperor of Germany, made him his poet laureat in 1667; and, at the same time, decorated him with a gold chain and medal, as a mark of his esteem for his great piety and learning; which Dr. Gibbes, in the year 1670, transmitted to the University of Oxford, with a request that it might be preserved among its archives. He died in 1677, aged 66 years, and was buried at Rome, in the church of Saint Maria Rotunda*.

These branches of the family are here mentioned thus particularly, because we find some of their descendants among the first and most considerable persons who effected the settlement of the island of Barbadoes. The first adventurers to that colony made so favourable a report of its beauty, fertility, and healthfulness, that many persons of ancient and loyal families in this kingdom, who were dissatisfied with the times, were encouraged to retire there with the hope of enjoying ease and liberty in the acquirement of a fortune. Among the earliest settlers of that description was the first Philip Gibbes, the lineal ancestor of the present Baronet. We find also, that Thomas Gibbes, a collateral of this family, was appointed a member of the first council holden at Barbadoes; and, that John

* As a further testimony of the consideration in which he was held by the learned of that city, his bust was placed in, and now fills, one of the niches in the Pantheon there, bearing the following inscription:

D. O. M.
Jacobus Albanus Gibbesius,
Doctor Oxoniensis,
Poeta Laureatus Cæsarius,
Pontificis Eloquentiæ Professor
Emeritus,
Obiit VI. Kal. Julii, M.DCLXXVII.
M. P.

Gibbes, of another branch of it, was at the head of the council board there in the year 1697. Such was the consideration, and such the character, of the persons by whom Barbadoes was so rapidly settled, and such was their merit, that King Charles the Second created twelve gentlemen of that island Baronets of Great Britain.

The ancestors of the present Baronet were possessed of a considerable estate in Bedminster, and in the city of Bristol.

1, William Gibbes, of the parish of Bedminster, and of the said city, by his will, dated March 17, 1602 (which is in the Bishop's Office at Bristol, not registered, but filed, and appears to be all of the testator's hand-writing), states, that his father had lands in Redcliffe-street, Bristol, and was buried at St. Thomas's, near that city. William Gibbes had three wives, by whom he had issue, three sons, Philip, Henry, and George, and five daughters.

Philip Gibbes, the eldest son and heir, was admitted to his freedom of the city of Bristol by patrimony, Oct. 5, 1586. He had, by his father's will above referred to, the fee simple of certain parts of his estates in the said city, which had sometime belonged to his grandfather. He married, had issue, and dying in 1626, was interred at St. Thomas's, near Bristol. His will, dated Dec. 3, 1626, was proved in Bristol, and also in the Prerogative Court of Canterbury. George Gibbes, the third son of William, was also of Bristol, and married and had issue; he died Feb. 19, 1650, aged 78, and was buried at St. Mary, Redcliffe.

2, Henry Gibbes, of the said city of Bristol, Esq. second son of William Gibbes aforesaid, was executor to the will of his father, 1603. He married Anne, daughter of Thomas Packer*, of Cheltenham, in the county of Gloucester, Esq. who died before her husband, and was buried in St. James's Church, Bristol. The will of Henry Gibbes, Esq. bears date Nov. 11, 1634, the codicil April 7, 1635, and was proved June 9, 1636, by his son Henry, hereafter mentioned. He had issue by Anne, his said wife, three sons and three daughters, viz. 1, William Gibbes, who died about 1634, having married and left issue; 2, Henry Gibbes, of the city of Bristol, Esq. executor to his father's will in 1636, married twice, and left issue. His will, dated Nov. 16, 1666, was proved Oct. 12, 1667; 3, Philip Gibbes, of whom hereafter. Of the daughters of Henry and Anne Gibbes abovementioned, Elizabeth was wife of Thomas Lloyd, of Bristol, Gent. was living in 1634, and had issue; Margaret, of —— Bird, Gent. and was living in 1666; and ———, of Walter Stevens, Gent. and died before her husband, leaving issue.

3, Philip Gibbes, of the parish of St. James, in the island of Barbadoes, Esq. third son of Henry and Anne Gibbes aforesaid, was the first of this family who set-

* Thomas Packer was the son of another Thomas Packer, and grandson of Thomas Packer, both also of Cheltenham. His grandmother (wife of the last-named Thomas) was Margaret, daughter of John Kiblewhite, of Fawley, in the county of Berks. Her sister Mary married William White, of Reading, and was the mother of Sir Thomas White, Knt. founder of St. John's College, Oxford. By this connexion, the family of the present Baronet are entitled to the benefits accruing to the founder's kin of that college.

tled in that colony about the year 1635. He died in 1648, bequeathing his estates in the said island to his son and heir,

4, Philip Gibbes, of Barbadoes aforesaid, Esq. who died in July, 1697, having made his will on the 1st of November, 1695. He married twice. By his first wife he had three daughters, 1, Anne, wife of Captain William White; 2, Elizabeth, of ——— Dawson, Esq.; and 3, Margaret, first the wife of Sir John Yeamans, Bart. and secondly, of William Foster, Esq. Philip Gibbes had issue by his second wife, Willoughby, daughter of —— Yeamans, Esq. and widow of —— Smith, Esq. (who survived him, and was his executrix in 1697), three sons, 1, Philip; 2, Yeamans; and 3, John: and four daughters, 1, Sarah, wife of John Herbert; 2, Willoughby, of John Musgrave; 3, Mary, of John Pyke, all of South Carolina, Esqrs; and 4, Margaret, the wife of Jacob English, of Barbadoes, Esq. John, one of the two younger sons, was dead before 1697.

5, Philip Gibbes, of the island of Barbadoes aforesaid, Esq. eldest son and heir of Philip and Willoughby Gibbes, was born in 1687, and died Oct. 6, 1726, leaving issue by Elizabeth, his wife, daughter and heiress of Samuel Irish, Esq. (by Elizabeth, his wife), three sons, Philip, Samuel, and John; and three daughters, Elizabeth, wife of William Howard, Esq.; Anne, of Lieutenant-Colonel —— Neblett; and Sarah, of —— Brandford, Esq.

6, Philip Gibbes, of the island of Barbadoes, Esq. eldest son and heir of the said Philip and Elizabeth Gibbes, held several of the most considerable situations in it. He was born Feb. 1710-11, and died in Dec. 1763, having had issue by Elizabeth, his wife, daughter of John Harris, Esq. Philip, the present Baronet, Reynold, William, and William, who died infants, and a daughter Mary.

I. Sir PHILIP GIBBES, Bart. of Spring Head, in the island of Barbadoes, eldest and only surviving son and heir of Philip Gibbes, Esq. and Elizabeth his wife, was born on the 7th of March, 1730-31. He was advanced to the dignity of a Baronet of Great Britain, by patent dated May 30, 1774, to him and the heirs male of his body. He married Agnes, daughter and heiress of Samuel Osborne, of the island of Barbadoes, Esq. Feb. 1, 1753*, who is now living, and by whom he hath two sons and two daughters. Philip Gibbes, Esq. his eldest son and heir apparent, and the sixth Philip in regular succession, is a member of the council of Barbadoes, and is unmarried; Samuel-Osborne Gibbes, Esq. second son of Sir Philip and Dame Agnes Gibbes, also living and unmarried. Of the daughters, Elizabeth, the eldest, married, Dec. 29, 1797, at St. Marylebone, in the county of Middlesex, to the Right Honourable Charles Abbott, now speaker of the house of commons, and one of his Majesty's most honourable privy-council; and Agnes, the youngest, now living and unmarried.

ARMS—Per fess, argent, and ermine, three battle-axes, sable.

CREST—An arm embowed in armour, garnished, or, and charged with a cross, couped, gules, in the hand, proper, a battle axe, as in the Arms.

MOTTO—*Tenax propositi.*

SEAT—Spring Head, in the Island of Barbadoes.

* Arms of Osborne, Quarterly, azure and erminois, a cross, argent.

TABLE.

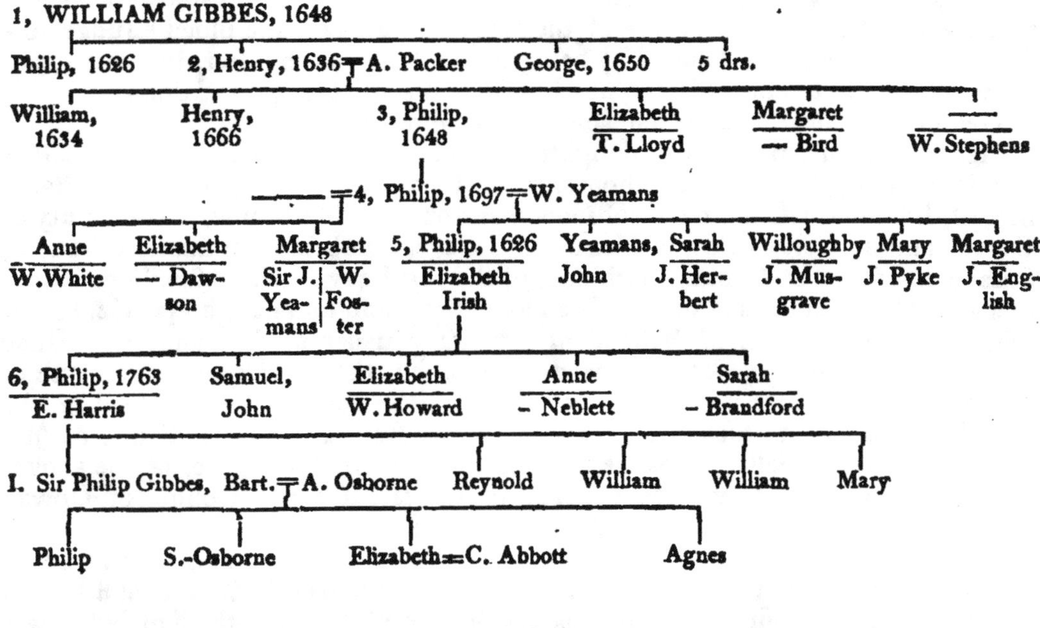

313. SMITH, of SYDLING, Dorsetshire.

Created Baronet, May 3, 1774.

THIS family is descended from Sir George Smith, who was high sheriff of the county of Devon, and of the city of Exeter, in the reign of Queen Elizabeth, (as mentioned in Isaac's History of Exeter) to whose memory there is a mural monument erected in that cathedral. His family held considerable possessions both in that county, and in Somersetshire, where they have resided. His daughter was wife of the famous General Monk, the restorer of monarchy, who for his services, was afterwards created by Charles II. Duke of Albemarle, Knight of the Garter, &c.

Sir George Smith, Knt. son of the above Sir George, represented the city of Exeter in parliament; but dissipating his large fortune, and selling several manors in Devonshire, as appears by Sir William Pole's History of that County, some of the descendants entered into merchandize, and others settled abroad.

—— Smith, grandson of the last-mentioned Sir George, was consul-general at Cadiz, in Spain.

George Smith, great grandfather of the present Baronet, held estates in Somersetshire, and had nearly been one of the many sacrifices of the bloody Judge Jefferies, (in the reign of James II.) being particularly sought after, but was lucky enough by flight to effect his escape: he left two sons, George and John.

George, the eldest, had several sons, one of whom was

Henry, who married Mary, daughter of John Hill, Esq. by whom he had a very large family, three only of whom survived them, viz. 1, John, the present Baronet; 2, Edmund, LL. D. rector of Goodmanstone and Melcombe, in the county of Dorset, and formerly fellow of Magdalen College, Cambridge, unmarried; and 3, Susannah, widow of Captain Bechinoe, of the royal navy, whose family consisted of a son, Henry, supposed to have been lost at sea, and four daughters, viz. Mary, married to William, Lord Bellenden, hereditary usher of Scotland, now Duke and Earl of Roxburgh, &c. by the death of John, the late Duke, on the 19th of March, 1804, without issue male, and whose titles and estates devolved on the said Lord Bellenden; Susannah, married to the Rev. Thomas Williams, A. M.; Elizabeth, and Arabella, unmarried. Elizabeth, another daughter of the above-named Henry and Mary, was married to the late George Gould, of Upway House, Dorsetshire, Esq. and died without issue.

I. JOHN SMITH, Esq. was educated at Harrow school, and the university of Cambridge, where he took his degree of A. M.; he is also F. R. A. S. and LL. D. He succeeded, as heir at law to his cousin, Sir William Smith, Knt. who was sheriff of the county of Dorset in 1738, one of the sheriffs of London in 1744, and elected alderman of that city in 1746. He died in 1752, and was buried in a vault, under the church of Sydling, with his lady and daughter, who died before him. Sir John married first, Elizabeth, daughter and heiress of Robert Curtis, of Wilsthorpe, Lincolnshire, Esq. by whom he had four sons and five daughters, who died in their early infancy, and one son, and two daughters, who survived her, viz. John-Wyldbore (so named from his maternal great uncle Matthew Wyldbore, Esq. representative for the city of Peterborough, who dying a bachelor, left his large possessions to this family), Elizabeth and Amelia, unmarried. John-Wyldbore Smith was born May 19, 1770, and married May 13, 1797, Elizabeth-Anna, daughter of the Rev. James Marriott, LL. D. of Horsmonden, in Kent, by his wife Catherine, the grand-daughter and last surviving representative of Sir John Bosworth, chamberlain of the city of London, receiver-general for the county of Middlesex, which offices he gained by a contest, memorable for being the most severe ever known in that city.

The issue of John-Wyldbore and Elizabeth-Anna Smith are, John-James, born April 10, 1800; William-Marriott, born Aug. 31, 1801; Ann-Elizabeth, born May 11, 1803.

The late Lady Smith died Feb. 13, 1796, at their house in Grosvenor-street, London, and was buried in the family vault at Sydling, where an elegant monument has been erected to her memory. Sir John married secondly, Jan. 1, 1800, Anna-Eleanora (daughter of the late Thomas Morland, of Court Lodge, in Kent, Esq.) by whom he had a daughter still born.

ARMS—Sable, a fess cottized, between three martlets, or.
CREST—A greyhound sejant, collared, or.
MOTTO—*Semper fidelis.*
SEAT—Sydling St. Nicholas, Dorsetshire.

TABLE.

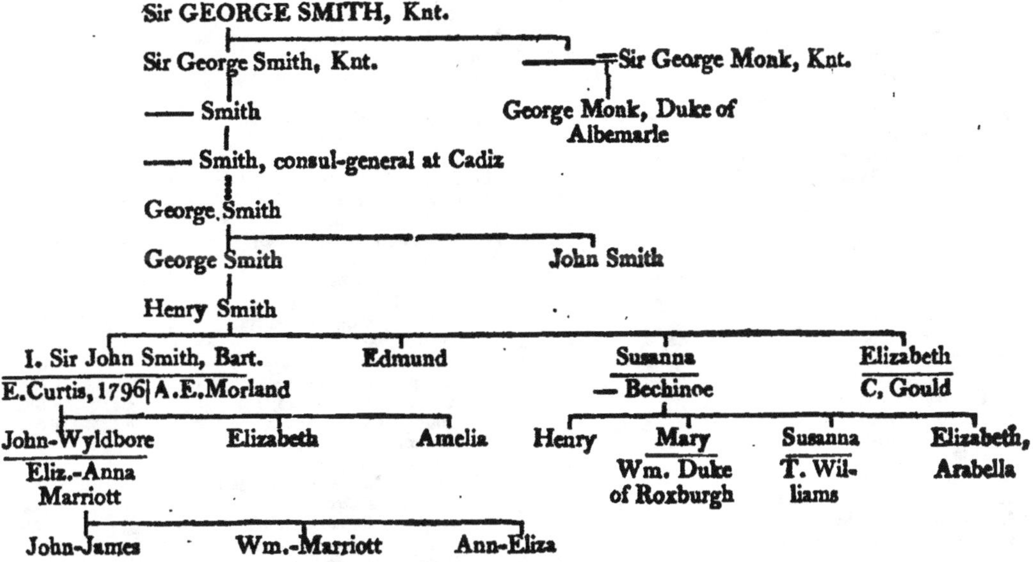

END OF VOL. III.

CONTENTS OF VOL. III.

[To the Binder.—These four pages are intended as a cancel to Vol. III.]

Presented to this Work by
Sir George Shuckburgh Evelyn Bar.t

Mutlow Sc. Rufsell Co.t

Presented to this work by the
Hon.ble John Henniker Major.

Drawn, & Engrav'd. by F. Adolpho. 19. Castle St. Leicester Sq.re

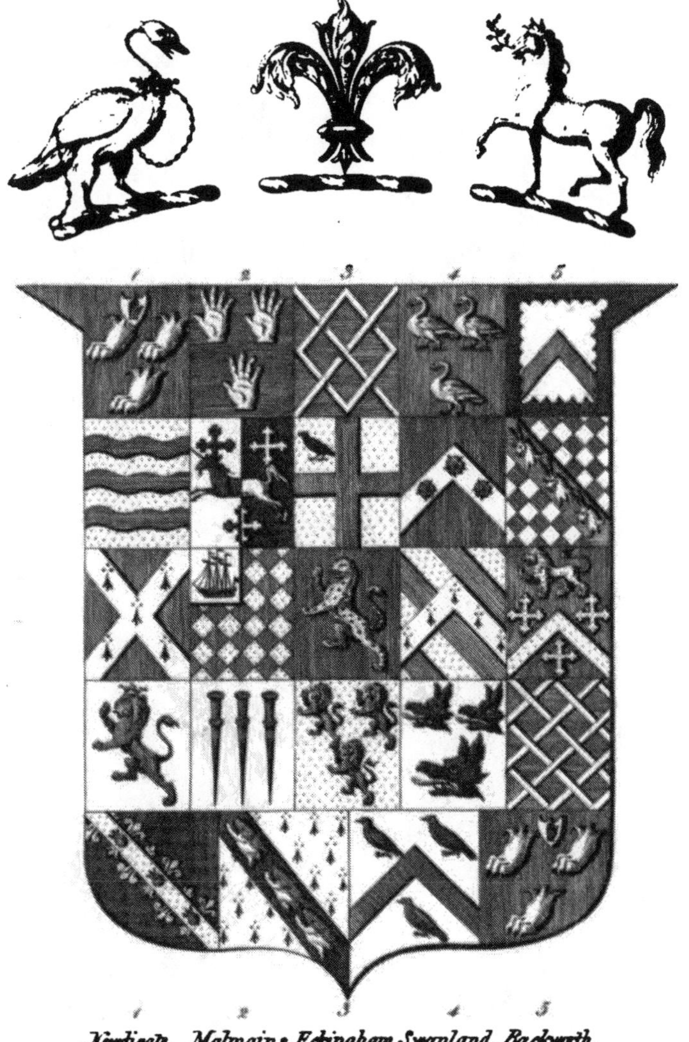

1	2	3	4	5
Newdigate.	Malmains.	Eckingham.	Swanland.	Backworth.
Samford.	De Leyre.	Rokesley.	Knolles.	Young.
Nevill of Raby.	Nevill Admiral.	Bulmer.	Inglebert.	Mablethorpe.
Hilton.	Burden.	Cresacre.	Cradock.	Cave.
Bromflett.	Genell.	Cliffe.	Newdigate.	

Presented to this work by
Sir Roger Newdigate. Bar.t

W.I.White. Sc. 14 New Street Square.

Presented to this work by
Sir Willm Smijth. Bart.

Adelphe. & Castle Street Leicester Sq.

* 96 omitted Pl. 5.

Plate XI.

193 Standish

194 Dyke

195 Cotton

196 Newdigate

197 Poole of Poole

198 Oxenden

199 Dyer

200 Beckwith

201 Parkyns

202 Bunbury

203 Parker of London

204 Davers

205 Richards

206 Dashwood

207 Child

208 Blois

209 Lawson of Isel

210 Williams Wynne

211 Molesworth

212 Ramsden

Adelphi sc.! 396. Oxford . St.

225 Dashwood King
Omitted see Plate XVII.

Adelpho Sc.

233 Warrender
234 D'Aeth
235 Milner
236 Elton
237 Bridges
238 Blunt of London
239 Codrington
240 Frederick
241 Vandeput
242 Mitchell
243 Hill
244 Clayton of Marden
245 Brown of Westminster
246 Heathcote of London
247 Heathcote of Hursley
248 Page Turner
249 Payne
250 Armytage
251 Hulse
252 Beauchamp Proctor

Adolpho. sc

F. Adolphus sc.

Pl. 13.

Adolpho sc.

Pl. XVI.

Adolpho Sc.